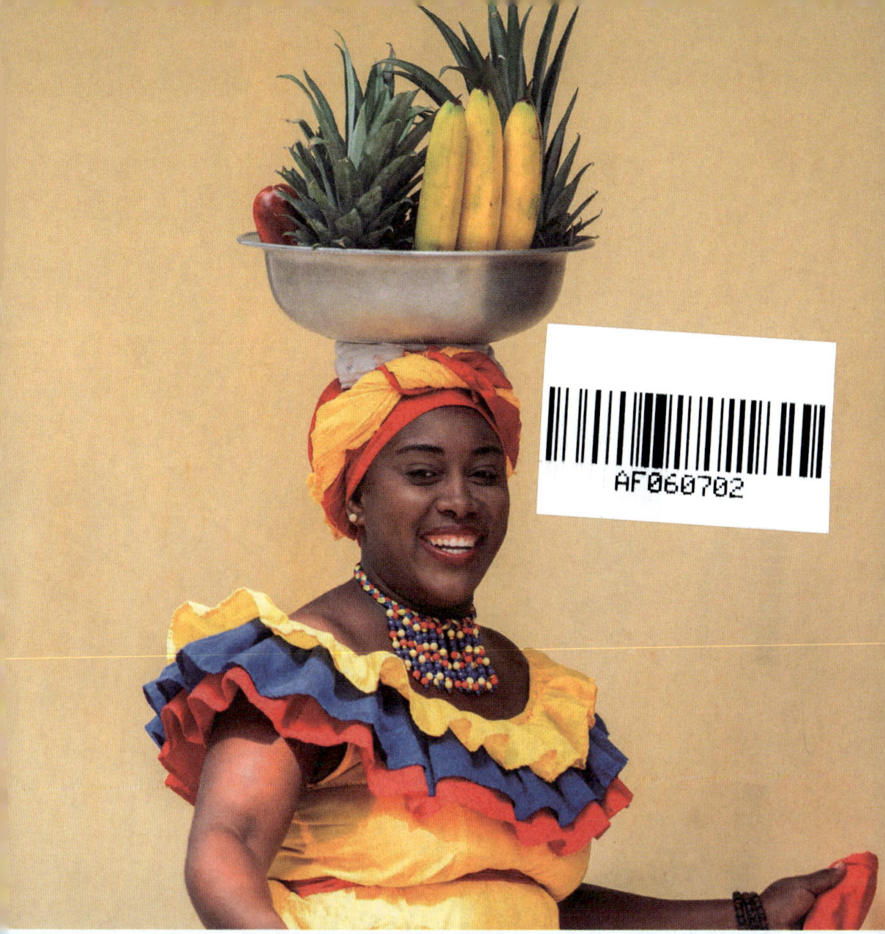

THE ROUGH GUIDE TO
COLOMBIA

Written and researched by
Daniel Jacobs, Robert Savage and Stephen Keeling

Contents

INTRODUCTION   4

Where to go	5	Things not to miss	12
When to go	10	Itineraries	20
Author picks	11	Sustainable travel	22

BASICS   24

Getting there	25	Sports and outdoor activities	36
Visas and entry requirements	27	Health	38
Getting around	28	Crime and personal safety	42
Accommodation	31	Culture and etiquette	45
Food and drink	32	Shopping	46
Festivals	35	Travel essentials	47

THE GUIDE   54

1 Bogotá	55	5 Medellín and the Zona Cafetera	205
2 North of Bogotá	85	6 Cali and the southwest	251
3 The Caribbean coast	125	7 The Pacific coast	299
4 San Andrés and Providencia	185	8 Los Llanos and the Amazon	319

CONTEXTS   336

History	337	Religion in Colombia	366
Natural Colombia	355	Books	370
The music of Colombia	360	Spanish	373

SMALL PRINT AND INDEX   378

COLOURFUL CARTAGENA

Introduction to
Colombia

From tropical Caribbean beaches to jagged Andean peaks, pristine Amazon rainforests to ancient jungle ruins, Colombia boasts a treasure trove of landscapes, along with languid colonial towns and dynamic, modern cities. The vibrant cultural mix ranges from Indigenous Andean culture to the legacy of Gabriel García Márquez, the literary giant who left his stamp on elegant Cartagena and enigmatic Mompox; activity wise, you can salsa the night away in Cali or get your thrills mountain biking and whitewater rafting in San Gil. Despite a long history of domestic conflict, Colombia is home to some of Latin America's most welcoming people, with Bogotá and Medellín offering culinary, art and live music scenes to rival Buenos Aires or Mexico City. In just ten years the country has been transformed from narco-state to a nation on the rise, with a stable democracy, booming economy and burgeoning tourist industry.

Problems remain of course, but despite the stereotypes Colombia is far safer today than many other Latin American countries. While foreign visitors are rarely, if ever, affected by drug-related or political violence, in many parts of Colombia you can still feel as if you are visiting uncharted territory, with mainstream tourist infrastructure only slowly being developed and tour buses a very unusual sight – for now.

The only country in South America to border both the Pacific and the Caribbean, the diverse ecosystems and regions of Colombia are surprisingly distinct, with the cultural divide between the central Andean cities and the Caribbean coast especially acute. Indeed, Colombia has always had a reputation for beauty, and it was likened to paradise by the first Spanish Conquistadors in the sixteenth century. Things started to go wrong after independence was declared in 1810, with Simón Bolívar's "Gran Colombia" (which included modern-day Venezuela and Ecuador) falling apart in 1830 and civil wars raging between Conservatives and Liberals on-and-off until relatively recently. The rise of the cocaine industry in the 1970s and 1980s (mostly due to massive US demand) led to increased violence, while Communist-inspired guerrilla groups like FARC championed rural opposition to the central government. Today most of the 1980s cocaine kingpins are dead or in jail and a peace deal was finally secured with FARC – it's a challenging but hopeful period for Colombia, and an incredibly fascinating and rewarding time to visit.

Where to go

Cosmopolitan **Bogotá** is, like most capitals, a busy and traffic-snarled commercial centre, with a vibrant cultural scene, excellent museums and lively nightlife, rapidly developing into one of South America's most enticing cities, though it needs time to work its charms – set high in the wet and cool Andes, don't expect a tropical paradise. As you head north from Bogotá through the mountains to **Bucaramanga**, picturesque colonial towns like **Barichara**, **Pamplona** and **Villa de Leyva** give way to warmer, river-fed bastions of adventure tourism such as **San Gil**.

Most visitors make time – and rightfully so – to head further north to the **Caribbean** for the sun and sand. Just a stone's throw from the beach, the walled city of **Cartagena** is the biggest Spanish colonial port in South America

> **FACT FILE**
> - Colombia's 49 million people enjoy the world's 29th largest **GDP** (fourth largest in Latin America).
> - Colombia has a large **Indigenous population**, with over one hundred distinct groups and just under two million people (many living in reserves or *resguardos*): the biggest populations live in La Guajira, Cauca and Nariño *departamentos*, while the Amazon region contains the most groups.
> - Colombians enjoy **booze**, with *aguardiente* (an anise-flavoured spirit) the most popular (especially in the Andes) and rum more prevalent along the Caribbean coast. Bizarrely, Scotch whisky, in the form of "Old Parr" (no longer sold in the UK), is also widely drunk.
> - Gabriel García Márquez (1927–2014) is Colombia's only **Nobel Prize** winner – he won for literature in 1982.
> - Arrested in Venezuela in 2012, Daniel "El Loco" Barrera was the last of Colombia's major drug barons to face justice. The legacy of "cocaine king", **Pablo Escobar**, lives on at his vast former estate near Medellín, populated with hippos descended from those he kept as pets.
> - Colombian *telenovelas* (**soap operas**) have been incredibly successful, including *Betty la fea* (remade as *Ugly Betty* in the US) and 1990's juggernaut *Café, con aroma de mujer* ("Coffee, with the scent of a woman").
> - Colombia has won a total of just 34 **Olympic medals** since 1932 (including five golds – two in weightlifting, two in cycling and one for women's triple jump).

and one of its most artfully restored, a gorgeous melange of narrow streets, blossom-smothered haciendas and Baroque churches. To the south lie the sun-drenched islands of the **Rosario and San Bernardo chains**, as well as low-key **Tolú**, while **Capurganá** and **Sapzurro** offer pristine sands and snorkelling as well as a less-travelled route into Panama. East of Cartagena, the major city of **Barranquilla** is best known for its mind-blowing **carnival** but is rapidly recapturing its title of cultural capital; while historic **Santa Marta** and the fishing village of **Taganga** are near **Parque Natural Nacional Tayrona**, whose untouched jungles and picturesque beaches are unrivalled. Santa Marta also makes a great base for the five-day trek to the isolated archeological ruins of **La**

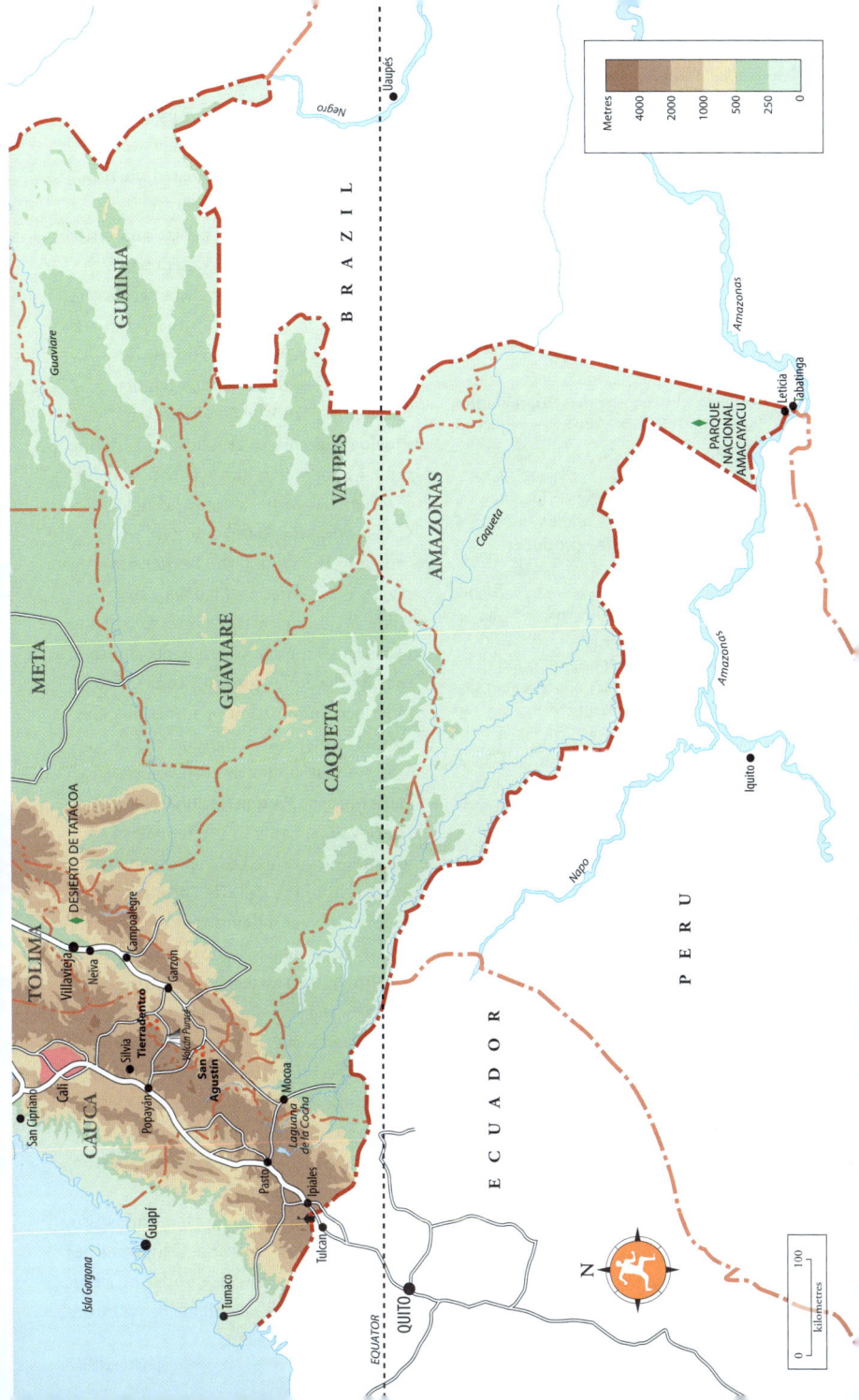

COLOMBIAN COFFEE

Is Colombian coffee really that good? Well, sort of. Most commercially sold coffee is a blend of *arabica* and *robusta*, but Colombia only produces the superior **arabica** bean and the version grown here, thanks to a combination of Andean soils and climate, is arguably the world's finest. The National Federation of Coffee Growers of Colombia were also way ahead of their time when they began marketing the drink in the late 1950s, based on a campaign featuring the moustachiod "**Juan Valdez**", a fictional coffee farmer, along with his trusty mule "Conchita". Today Colombia's answer to Starbucks can be found across South America and as far afield as Kuwait, while the nation remains the world's **fourth-largest coffee producer**, supplying 6 percent of the market. However, the version you are served in the country itself is often not the best. Part of the problem is technical – high-quality **espresso machinery** makes good coffee, and few cafés beyond Colombian big cities possess such equipment and many of the choicest beans are reserved for the export market. Your best bet is to stay on a coffee **finca** (farm) or a small homestay in the countryside, where the beans are so good and the locals so discriminating, your brew (served *café tinto*, black, of course) is likely to be sensational.

Ciudad Perdida, the "Lost City", and **Aracataca**, the birthplace of Gabriel García Márquez. The thinly populated province of **La Guajira** is an arid, desert region inhabited by the **Wayuu** people and pitted with giant dunes; while **Valledupar** is the home of *vallenato* music and offers access to the mountain villages of the Wintukuas and Kankuamo peoples. Almost un-Colombian in their feel, the remote Caribbean islands of **San Andrés** and **Providencia** both offer scintillating diving, crystal-clear waters and – particularly in Providencia's case – a unique, English, Creole-speaking **Raizal** culture.

West of the capital, the **Tierra Paisa** region is anchored by **Medellín**, an Andean city on the rise, home to enticing restaurants, museums and parks. South of the city the coffee-growing **Zona Cafetera** offers accommodation in authentic *fincas* (**coffee farms**) and sensational trekking. You can soak up the awe-inspiring glaciers of the **Parque Nacional Natural Los Nevados**, bathe in the **Termales San Vicente** (hot springs) or view the bizarre wax palms of the **Valle de Cocora**.

The southwest is dominated by **Cali**, another up-and-coming city best known for being the Colombian home of **salsa**, while **Popayán** boasts an incredibly unspoiled colonial centre as well as alluring side-trips including hot springs and Andean condors. Well worth the effort to get to, the mysterious stone statues of **San Agustín** and the remote pre-Hispanic tombs of **Tierradentro** are some of South America's most enchanting treasures. Heading on to Ecuador you pass through amicable **Pasto** and the **Santuario de Las Lajas** near the border, but it's worth considering a diversion to Colombia's **Pacific coast**, a very remote area almost impossible to access overland. **Whale-watching** is a major attraction here, as are its undeveloped sandy beaches, Afro-Colombian culture and rainforests – some of the wettest on earth.

To the southeast, Colombia's stake of the **Amazon** dips below the Equator and is also inaccessible by road. Centred on the easy-going frontier town of **Leticia**, it may not be as well known as Peru's or Brazil's Amazon region but it's a lot friendlier, offering a host of jungle experiences and a more adventurous gateway into the neighbouring countries.

When to go

Colombian climates vary wildly. Most of the country may lie just north of the equator, but that doesn't mean you should leave your cold-weather gear at home. Bogotá sits in damp, **tropical highlands** and can get chilly at night – heavy jackets and scarves are the norm year-round. Thanks to its moderate altitude and mild climate, **Medellín** in contrast is known as the "city of eternal spring", though it also rains here quite a lot (May and October). Visit the **Caribbean coast** – including Cartagena – however, and you'll be sweltering at any time (the Pacific coast is just as hot, but wetter, while La Guajira is baking but dry). Colombia's proximity to the equator does keep regional temperatures stable throughout the year, at around 24°C along the coast and 7–17°C as you move higher inland. However, rainfall varies with the seasons. In the **Andean region** there are two dry and two wet seasons per year, the driest months being from December to March and July to August. In low-lying areas, especially **southern Colombia**, rainfall is more constant but showers never last very long. The **Amazon climate** is uniformly wet the entire year. Bear in mind that the most intense tourist seasons, with the highest prices, are from December to February and Semana Santa (Easter Week), the week before Easter, with July and August another increasingly busy holiday period.

AVERAGE TEMPERATURES AND RAINFALL

	Jan	Feb	Mar	Apr	May	Jun	Jul	Aug	Sep	Oct	Nov	Dec
BOGOTÁ												
max/min °C	18/6	18/7	19/8	18/8	18/8	17/8	17/8	17/7	18/7	18/8	18/8	18/7
max/min °F	64/43	64/45	66/46	64/46	64/46	63/46	63/46	63/45	64/45	64/46	64/46	64/45
rainfall (mm)	40	50	80	110	100	60	40	40	50	140	110	60
CARTAGENA												
max/min °C	29/23	29/24	30/25	30/25	30/26	30/26	30/26	30/26	30/25	30/25	30/25	30/24
max/min °F	84/73	84/75	86/77	86/77	86/79	86/79	86/79	86/79	86/77	86/77	86/77	86/75
rainfall (mm)	00	00	00	20	90	100	80	110	130	220	130	30
CALI												
max/min °C	28/19	29/19	29/19	28/19	28/19	28/19	29/19	29/18	28/18	28/18	27/18	28/19
max/min °F	82/66	84/66	84/66	82/66	82/66	82/66	84/64	84/64	82/64	82/64	81/64	82/66
rainfall (mm)	50	60	100	140	110	60	30	50	60	120	110	70
MEDELLÍN												
max/min °C	26/17	26/18	26/18	26/18	26/18	26/18	26/17	26/17	26/17	25/17	25/17	25/17
max/min °F	79/63	79/64	79/64	79/64	79/64	79/64	79/63	79/63	79/63	77/63	77/63	77/63
rainfall (mm)	50	60	100	180	190	130	110	130	150	200	140	80
BUENAVENTURA												
max/min °C	28/23	28/23	27/23	28/24	28/23	27/23	28/24	27/23	27/23	27/23	27/23	27/23
max/min °F	82/73	82/73	81/73	82/75	82/73	81/73	82/75	81/73	81/73	81/73	81/73	81/73
rainfall (mm)	54	45	39	63	99	105	84	108	111	153	183	114

Author picks

Scaling the heights of its awe-inspiring national parks, enduring sweltering jungle heat and traversing some of Latin America's most isolated roads, our hard-travelling authors have visited every corner of this diverse country – from the Afro-Caribbean villages of Providencia to the rainforests of the Amazon. Here are their personal favourites:

Best microbrews Colombia has joined the craft beer revolution, with Bogotá Beer Company (see page 80), Nevada Cervecería in Minca (see page 169) and 3 Cordilleras (see page 222) in Medellín the leaders of a growing list.

Sunday Gospel Raizal Baptist churches on Providencia and San Andrés (see page 198) come alive on Sunday mornings with lung-busting, soulful Gospel choirs that match anything in Harlem.

Beaches to skip the crowds Playa Taroa (see page 180) in La Guajira is mesmerizing, Bahía Manzanillo (see page 201) on Providencia Island is a tranquil oasis, and gorgeous beaches on the Pacific coast like Playa Juan de Dios (see page 312) are often deserted.

Graffiti art Colombian street art is at its most exuberant in Bogotá, where there's even a graffiti tour (see page 74); the murals in Cartagena's Getsemaní are just as creative (see page 133).

Football – Colombia-style Colombian football (soccer) is on the rise, and watching a live match is a thrilling experience; try Atlético Nacional in Medellín (see page 224) or Millonarios in Bogotá (see page 83).

Live that García Márquez fantasy Visit swelteringly hot Mompox (see page 149), a real-life Macondo trapped in a nineteenth-century time warp.

Salsa hotspots Learn the moves at *Swing Latino* (see page 257) in Cali before getting down at *Chango* (see page 263); in Barranquilla it's always a party at *La Troja* (see page 159).

Best market Cartagena's Mercado Bazurto is a crazy, messy adventure with some of the tastiest street food in the country (see page 136).

> Our author recommendations don't end here. We've flagged up our favourite places – a perfectly sited hotel, an atmospheric café, a special restaurant – throughout the Guide, highlighted with the ★ symbol.

MERCADO BAZURTO, CARTAGENA
STREET ART IN BOGOTÁ

20
things not to miss

It's not possible to see everything that Colombia has to offer in one trip – and we don't suggest you try. What follows is a selective and subjective taste of the country's highlights: gorgeous colonial cities, spectacular mountains, magnificent beaches, exuberant celebrations and stunning natural phenomena. All entries have a page reference to take you straight into the Guide, where you can find out more.

1 PROVIDENCIA
See page 199
Gorgeous jungle-smothered Caribbean island, with diving off the world's third largest barrier reef, idyllic beaches and a distinctive Raizal culture.

2 MUSEO DEL ORO, BOGOTÁ
See page 66
Colombia's ancient civilizations were masters of gold art; see intricate jewellery and the golden raft of the Muisca people.

3 THE STATUES OF SAN AGUSTÍN
See page 283
Captivating archeological site in the hills, best known for its giant stone heads, carved hundreds of years ago by a lost civilization.

4 THE COLONIAL CHURCHES OF POPAYÁN
See page 270
The colonial capital of the southwest has retained its all-white, elegant character with handsome churches and mansions close to volcanoes, hot springs and Indigenous markets.

5 PARQUE NACIONAL NATURAL LOS NEVADOS
See page 234
Tantalizing combination of snow-capped volcanoes, craggy glaciers, churning rivers and wild plains of *páramo*.

6 MEDELLÍN
See page 206
Cable cars traverse the slopes of this fashionable Andean city, home to illuminating museums, enticing restaurants and legendary artist Fernando Botero.

7 MOMPOX
See page 149
Enjoy the languid lifestyle at this isolated colonial enclave, where rocking chairs and street parties occupy the cobbled streets late into the night.

8 COFFEE FARMS
See page 241
Colombian coffee is the world's best, and staying on a traditional hacienda will immerse you in the sights and heavenly aromas of the trade

9 AMAZON JUNGLE EXCURSIONS
See page 324
Colombia's Amazon region is still largely untamed wilderness, with Leticia the best base for forays into the rainforest.

10 ADVENTURE SPORTS IN SAN GIL
See page 108
The adventure sport hub for whitewater rafting, mountain biking, caving, rappelling and trekking.

11 TREKKING TO CIUDAD PERDIDA
See page 174
The five-day trek to the "Lost City" of the Tayrona is one of South America's great adventures, featuring cool forest streams, Indigenous villages and jungle-strewn ruins.

12 VILLA DE LEYVA
See page 95
Beautifully preserved colonial village in the Andes, with low-slung adobe houses, fine restaurants and a string of picturesque waterfalls nearby.

13 PARQUE NACIONAL NATURAL TAYRONA
See page 171
Wonderfully preserved slice of Caribbean coast, with the jungles and white-sand beaches backed by lofty peaks.

14 ZIPAQUIRÁ SALT CATHEDRAL
See page 89
Bizarre but jaw-dropping sight, with vast halls, crosses and altars carved out of an old salt mine.

15 SALSA IN CALI
See page 257
The capital of salsa is all about clubs, shows and dance classes, with beats and rhythms sure to get you moving.

16

17

16 WHALE-WATCHING
See page 312
Colombia's lush Pacific coast is one of the world's best places to see humpbacks and their new-born calves.

17 JOHNNY CAY
See page 194
Just off San Andrés, this perfect desert island has a distinctive Afro-Caribbean feel.

18 THE TOMBS OF TIERRADENTRO
See page 279
Mystifying underground tombs high in the Andes, surrounded by Nasa communities and spectacular waterfalls.

19 MUSEO BOTERO, BOGOTÁ
See page 62
Essential homage to one of the greatest contemporary artists in South America, featuring plenty of his signature plump ladies.

20 CARTAGENA'S OLD TOWN
See page 126
Latin America's colonial jewel, a city of Baroque churches, elegant mansions, shady plazas and those giant Spanish walls.

Itineraries

The following itineraries span the entire length of this incredibly diverse country, from the historic cities of the Caribbean coast, to the mighty Andes and rainforests of the Amazon.

CLASSIC COLOMBIA

This three-week tour gives a taster of Colombia's landscapes and cities.

❶ **Bogotá** Colombia's capital is home to the Gold Museum, craft beers, the Museo Botero and just to the north, the mind-blowing salt cathedral. See page 56

❷ **San Agustín** Travel south to Colombia's most enchanting and mysterious pre-Hispanic ruins, featuring giant carved heads. See page 283

❸ **Popayán** Soak up the refined colonial streetscapes before hiking the Puracé volcano, or exploring the tombs of Tierradentro. See page 270

❹ **Zona Cafetera** Head north into the Andes and the main coffee zone around Salento, visiting nature reserves near Manizales and the glaciers of Los Nevados. See page 230

❺ **Medellín** Take in the sights, cable cars and Botero sculptures of Colombia's up-and-coming second city. See page 206

❻ **Santa Marta/Taganga** Cut across to the oldest city in Colombia and the backpacker village of Taganga, for the cheapest diving in the Caribbean. See page 159

❼ **Tayrona/Ciudad Perdida** Lounge on the pristine beaches of Tayrona or tackle the five-day jungle trek to the "Lost City". See page 171

❽ **San Gil** On the way back to Bogotá stop off at Colombia's adventure sport capital for whitewater rafting, hiking and biking. See page 106

OFF THE BEATEN TRACK

You'll need at least four weeks to tackle Colombia's wilder adventures. This route starts in Bogotá and requires several domestic flights.

❶ **The Amazon** From Bogotá, fly deep into the Amazon at the port of Leticia for excursions into the rainforest. See page 324

❷ **Parque Nacional Natural Los Nevados** Back in the Andes, hike the volcanoes and glaciers of Colombia's most spectacular national park. See page 234

❸ **Whale-watching** The Pacific coast and the Bahía Málaga are visited by hundreds of humpbacks (July and November). See page 312

❹ **Nuquí** Take a boat ride up the coast to languid Afro-Colombian villages, hot springs and isolated Emberá communities. See page 307

Create your own itinerary with Rough Guides. Whether you're after adventure or a family-friendly holiday, we have a trip for you, with all the activities you enjoy doing and the sights you want to see. All our trips are devised by local experts who get the most out of the destination. Visit **www.roughguides.com/trips** to chat with one of our travel agents.

❺ Capurganá Fly via Medellín to the series of tiny villages and white-sand beaches along the Panama border. See page 147

❻ Providencia Travel overland to Cartagena for the flight to San Andrés and on to Providencia, Colombia's Caribbean paradise and dive centre. See page 199

❼ La Guajira Fly back to the mainland to explore the remote Wayuu villages and spectacular beaches of this isolated desert region. See page 177

ARTS AND ARCHITECTURE

The land of García Márquez has a rich history of arts and architecture. This route could be completed in two to three weeks by bus between Cartagena and Nariño.

❶ Cartagena Soak up the colonial atmosphere and stroll the walls of Colombia's most alluring city. See page 126

❷ Aracataca The sleepy birthplace of Márquez is a short drive south of Santa Marta, home to a thoughtful museum. See page 169

❸ Valledupar The base for trips to the Wintukua and Kankuamo homelands of the Sierra Nevada. See page 181

❹ Mompox Head south to Colombia's most atmospheric and time-warped colonial town, a real-life Macondo. See page 149

❺ Barichara Travel into the Andes to this picturesque village of whitewashed adobe homes and Spanish chapels. See page 110

❻ Villa de Leyva A short drive south lies this equally charming Spanish Andean village, founded high in the central ranges. See page 95

❼ Museo Botero Venture into Bogotá to visit this sensational homage to Colombia's best-known artist. See page 62

Sustainable travel

Colombia has become an unexpected international role model for sustainable travel in recent years. However, this success and the progress to date is fragile.

Years of conflict within Colombia left a near-devastating environmental legacy behind. Unchecked, warring factions extracted minerals like mercury from the earth with no regard for the toxic fallout, in addition to committing deforestation on a scale never seen before. Worse still was the illicit growing of crops to feed troops, which stripped the soil of its fertility for years to come. With peace, however, came a chance for the tide to be turned and in partnership with the United Nations, Gustavo Petro, Colombia's recently installed president, is working to stem the tide.

COLOMBIA'S CHALLENGES AND OPPORTUNITIES

In 2022, history was made when Colombia elected as President its first ever left-wing candidate, Gustavo Petro. Petro, however, inherited a nationwide ecological emergency after his predecessor, Iván Duque, oversaw the deforestation of 1.7 million acres during the preceding four-year term. Petro also inherited a dire water toxin and pathogen pollution problem – the result of decades of unregulated mercury extraction, compounded by gold mining with minimal environmental oversight. The water crisis has also been further worsened by deliberate crude oil spills from warring guerrilla squads.

With little to no time to waste, the new administration got to work and Rodrigo Botero was appointed the director of the Foundation for Conservation and Sustainable Development. Boiling the problem down to its root cause, the money and greed of cattle ranching and land grabbing, Botero introduced bills to monitor and regulate Colombia's cattle and dairy supply chain. Progress is slow, but it is being supported by many of the restaurateurs and resorts across Columbia, and its tourism sector, with farm-to-table credentials being placed front and centre.

SUPPORT THE ORANGE ECONOMY

The Colombian government has renewed support for the Orange Economy initiative, providing funds and logistical help to tour operators and resorts that invest in the sustainability of the environments that they help others to explore. Travellers can, in turn, support these efforts by shortlisting the attractions currently working in this space. Before creating your itinerary, be sure to check if the attraction is part of the Orange Economy initiative or whether they are in the process of applying.

PRIORITISE SIGHTSEEING AT NATURAL RESERVES AND ECO-CONSERVATIONS

Colombia has a wealth of reserves, conservation areas and eco-parks, all working to champion, sustain and showcase eco-tourism. Supporting these attractions by prioritizing them on your sightseeing itinerary is a great way to lend your support. A great option close to Salento and west of Bogotá is the **Kasaguadua Natural**

COCORA VALLEY, JUST OUTSIDE OF SALENTO

SUSTAINABLE TRAVEL

RIPE COFFEE CHERRIES

Reserve (w kasaguaduanaturalre-serve.org). Spanning 12 hectares of rainforest, the reserve has two private owners (one Colombian and one British) who offer guests walking tours through the forest, with insightful commentaries about the conservation and sustainability work underway.

Beyond Manizales and the rainforest canopy, the Parque Nacional Natural Los Nevadosis is an important ecological attraction (w parquesnacionales.gov.co). Here, the park rangers help to protect some of the last surviving snow-capped peaks in the tropics. Home to a variety of at-risk ecosystems, the indigenous animals include mountain tapirs, spectacled bears, and for the lucky few who catch a glimpse, the majestic Andean condor. A short drive west of Cali the **Ecoparque Río Pance** (w crpcali.com) is another poster child for positive change. Free to visit (donations are welcome), the park is a fiercely protected reserve that follows the river along a four-kilometre-long trail. Lined with trees and bamboo groves, this is an essential natural habitat for birds and butterflies.

PARTNER WITH PICOTORO ECOTURISMO

Beyond Cali and indeed across Columbia, the Picotoro Ecoturismo organisation (w picoloro.co) offer a variety of tours, transport and accommodation bundles, that only involve operators with a commitment to sustainability and the conservation of natural resources. They also provide training opportunities and hiking tips for explorations at altitude, which in turn help to employ Indigenous guides, fuelling local economies in the process.

GREEN ACCOMMODATION OPTIONS

Before you pick your final accommodation options, check online, or call ahead to see if they are certified as sustainable by Colombia's Ministry of Trade, Industry, and Tourism. You'll often find this information on a hotel's website listed under an eco-friendly policy section or similar — with links to other local organisations and attractions, also certified as sustainable.

OTHER WAYS TO HELP

Making small changes to your daily sightseeing routine is another great way to make a cumulative change and reduce your carbon footprint as you explore Colombia. Buying food, for example, from markets supplied by local producers helps to shorten supply chains with the added benefit of extra fresh eats. Other easy-to-adopt daily changes include bringing your own reusable water bottle to fill up at hotels and attractions and saving your recyclable materials until you come across the appropriate recycling bins in the country's larger towns and cities.

CHIVA BUS

Basics

- **25** Getting there
- **27** Visas and entry requirements
- **28** Getting around
- **31** Accommodation
- **32** Food and drink
- **35** Festivals
- **36** Sports and outdoor activities
- **38** Health
- **42** Crime and personal safety
- **45** Culture and etiquette
- **46** Shopping
- **47** Travel essentials

Getting there

Most visitors to Colombia arrive by air. Fares do not tend to vary too much from one time of the year to another, although from South Africa they do rise slightly in winter (July and August). Colombia also has land borders with five other countries, although you can only access most of the country directly by land from Venezuela and Ecuador. It's also possible to arrive by boat from Panama, and of course you can fly in directly from pretty much any major South American city, as well as from Panama and Mexico.

Flights from the UK and Ireland

The only **direct flight** from the UK or Ireland to Colombia is the service from London Heathrow to Bogotá (4 weekly; 11hr 10min) with Avianca (Wavianca.com). Generally, it will work out cheaper to fly with a European airline such as Iberia (Wiberia.com), Air Europa (Waireuropa.com), Lufthansa (Wlufthansa.com) or Air France (Wairfrance.com), changing planes in Madrid, Frankfurt or Paris, or with a North American airline such as Air Canada (Waircanada.com), Delta (Wdelta.com) or American Airlines (Waa.com), changing in Toronto or a US airport. From the UK, you can expect the cheapest round trip fares with an online firm such as Expedia (Wexpedia.co.uk) or Ebookers (Webookers.com), and to pay slightly more if you fly in July or August. From Ireland, you likely pay more. Also be aware that the cheapest flights from Ireland, and from British cities other than London, may require two changes of plane en route.

Flights from the US and Canada

There are **direct flights** to Bogotá from New York (5hr 45min), Miami (3hr 40min), Orlando (4hr), Atlanta (4hr 50min), Dallas (5hr 20min), Houston (5hr), Los Angeles (7hr 15min) and Toronto (5hr 55min). New York and Miami also have direct flights to Cartagena and Medellín, and Miami even has one to Cali (3hr 55min). The main **operators** are Avianca (Wavianca.com), Delta (Wdelta.com) and American Airlines (Waa.com), plus Air Canada (Waircanada.com) out of Toronto and LATAM (Wlatam.com) from Miami. Fort Lauderdale is also well connected, with direct flights to Bogotá (3hr 40min), Cartagena (2hr 55min) and Medellín (3hr 30min), mostly run by Jet Blue (Wjetblue.com) and Spirit (Wspirit.com). Cartagena, Medellín and Cali are also served from Miami. From elsewhere in North America, you'll need to change planes in New York, Toronto, Atlanta, Texas or Florida, or else fly via Mexico with Aeromexico (Waeromexico.com) or via Panama with Copa (Wcopaair.com).

You can book round trip tickets from most US cities to Bogotá with online firms such as Expedia (Wexpedia.com) or Orbitz (Worbitz.com). The **cheapest deals** are often via Fort Lauderdale with Jet Blue or Spirit. In Canada, the cheapest fares are from Toronto. Expect to pay slightly more when flying from Montreal and Vancouver.

Flights from Australia, New Zealand and South Africa

From **Australia** and **New Zealand** the most direct route to Colombia would in principle be via Chile, and indeed LAIAM (Wlatam.com) do fly from Sydney and Auckland to Santiago and from Santiago to Bogotá. Unfortunately, the two flights don't really connect up on current timetables, so in practice, unless you stop over in Santiago (or spend a long time in its airport), you'd need to change planes again in Lima. It may be feasible to fly via Chile with just one change using a combination of Qantas (Wqantas.com.au) and LATAM or Avianca (Wavianca.com), but your cheapest option will in any case probably be with an American carrier such as Delta (Wdelta.com), United (Wunited.com) or American Airlines (Waa.com), changing planes once or possibly twice in the United States.

From **South Africa**, your most direct route will be via São Paulo using a combination of SAA (Wflysaa.com) with either LATAM or Avianca, but you may well

---

A BETTER KIND OF TRAVEL

At Rough Guides we are passionately committed to travel. We believe it helps us understand the world we live in and the people we share it with – and of course tourism is vital to many developing economies. But the scale of modern tourism has also damaged some places irreparably, and climate change is accelerated by most forms of transport, especially flying. We encourage all our authors to consider the carbon footprint of the journeys they make in the course of researching our guides.

pay less to fly via Europe with Lufthansa (W lufthansa.com) or Air France (W airfrance.com). A round trip from Johannesburg to Bogotá is generally cheapest when booked through an online agency.

AGENTS AND OPERATORS

Journey Latin America UK W journeylatinamerica.co.uk. Top UK Latin America specialists, offering flights and packages in Colombia.
North South Travel UK W northsouthtravel.co.uk. Friendly, competitive travel agency, offering discounted fares worldwide. Profits are used to support projects in the developing world, especially the promotion of sustainable tourism.
RedTag Canada W redtag.ca. Canadian youth and student travel firm.
See Colombia Travel UK W seecolombia.travel. Packages and tailor-made tours.
Soliman Travel UK W solimantravel.com. UK-based South America specialists, with flights and a large range of packages.
South America Travel W southamerica.travel. US-based South America specialists.
Trailfinders UK W trailfinders.com, Ireland W trailfinders.ie. One of the best-informed and most efficient agents for independent travellers in Britain and Ireland.
USIT Ireland W usit.ie. Ireland's main youth and student travel specialists.

By land, sea or riverboat from neighbouring countries

Frequent international bus services connect Colombia with **Venezuela** and **Ecuador**, but there can be security issues with both borders, so be sure to check the situation in advance (see page 52). Boats on the Amazon from **Brazil** or **Peru** serve Leticia (see page 329) – although you'd have to fly from there to anywhere else in Colombia – and it's possible to get to Colombia by sea from **Panama** and sometimes from Ecuador.

Note that if entering by land, you must use an **authorized border crossing**. If you are planning to cross the border somewhere unusual, make sure it's a legal crossing point; entering the country at an unauthorized crossing point is a criminal offence.

From Venezuela

There are four border crossing points from Venezuela to Colombia, of which two (at Arauca and Puerto Carreño) are not considered safe for tourists at all. Of the other two crossings, the most popular is from **San Cristóbal to Cúcuta** (see page 123), on the main route from Caracas to Bogotá, but for the Caribbean coast, the crossing at **Paraguachón** (between Maracaibo and Maicao) is more useful (see page 179). Even here, you will need to check up on the latest information and consider whether it is wise to travel in Venezuela – Western governments are currently advising against casual travel there, and in particular near the border. In addition, the Venezuelan government has a habit of suddenly closing the border, and at present it is open to pedestrians only, with no direct transport across it, although that may change.

From Panama

There is **no safe land route** from Panama into Colombia, due to the presence of drug traffickers and paramilitaries, not to mention the threat of kidnapping in the Darién Gap. If not pressed for time, you may be able to find a boat from Jaqué to Solano (see page 304), or a combination of boats via the San Blas archipelago, taking four to five days. Operators include Blue Sailing (W bluesailing.net) and Colombia Panama Sailing (W colombiapanamasailing.com); *Casa Viena* in Cartagena posts current information on its website at W casaviena.com/sanblasisland.

From Ecuador

From Ecuador, the only sure land-crossing is at **Rumichaca Bridge** on the Pan-American Highway (see page 297). Even here, bandit activity makes it inadvisable to travel at night, so be sure to reach Pasto (the first Colombian town with accommodation) while it's still light. There are direct buses from Lima and Quito to Bogotá, run by firms such as Cruz del Sur (W cruzdelsur.com.pe) and Rutas de América (W rutasenbus.com), but the journey can be long and gruelling (three days from Lima to Bogotá), so it's better to do the route in stages than in one go. There is another, less-used land-crossing at **San Miguel**, between Mocoa (see page 292) and the Ecuadorian town of Lago Agrio, but this route can be unsafe depending on the security situation, so do not attempt to use it without seeking current local advice first.

From Brazil and Peru

Although both Brazil and Peru have long land borders with Colombia, the only place where you can actually cross is at **Leticia** in the southeast corner of the country (see page 329), which you can access by boat from Iquitos in Peru, or by land from Tabatinga in Brazil (which can in turn be accessed by riverboat from Manaus). The trouble with this route is that you cannot travel on from Leticia to the rest of Colombia by land, so you'll either have to fly, or take a very long detour via Ecuador, which would take a good three to four weeks. From most of Peru, the obvious land route into Colombia is via Ecuador (see above).

Visas and entry requirements

Citizens of the UK, Ireland, the USA, Canada, Australia, New Zealand and the EU do not need a visa to visit Colombia as a tourist for up to ninety days, but South Africans do. Full details of which nationalities do need a visa can be found on the Colombian foreign ministry's website at W cancilleria.gov.co/tramites_servicios/ visa/requisitos. To enter Colombia, you need a passport still valid for at least six months, and in principle an onward ticket, which you may possibly be asked to show. Entering from another South American country, especially by land, you may also be asked to show a yellow fever vaccination certificate (see page 40).

Upon arrival, all visitors receive an **entry stamp** in their passports, usually for sixty days. You can request up to ninety days, and at airports you'll probably get it, although it's less likely if you are entering by land. Double-check the stamp straightaway for errors. To avoid bureaucratic problems, make sure you get an entry stamp if coming in overland and that you get a departure stamp upon exiting.

A **visa extension** of up to ninety days, called a *Prórroga de Permanencia*, can be obtained for a fee at offices of Migración Colombia (W migracioncolombia. gov.co). Offices are listed on their website under "Entidad": Quiénes Somos: Regionales. The fee has to be paid at a bank. You'll need two passport photos with a white background, photocopies of your passport (ID page) and entry stamp, as well as the original, and an onward ticket.

If you are a Colombian citizen (for example, if you were born in Colombia or if either of your parents is Colombian), regardless of any other nationality you may hold, you are required to enter and leave the country on a Colombian passport, and it is not unknown for people with dual nationality to be prevented from leaving until they get one.

Airport **exit tax** should be included in your air ticket. If you've been in Colombia for less than sixty days, you may possibly even be able to get it refunded (ask when you check in, but note that it may require a printout of the breakdown of your ticket fees).

Customs allowances

You are allowed to bring in duty-free two bottles of wine or spirits, plus up to 200 cigarettes or 250 grams of tobacco or 50 cigars, and perfume for personal use. Electronic equipment for your own use is fine, but brand-new electronic goods may be queried if there's any suspicion they are not for personal use. Any cash or financial instruments worth more than US$10,000 must be declared. When leaving, aside from the obvious check for drugs, you may be asked to show proof of purchase for any emeralds, gold or platinum you have obtained in the country.

COLOMBIAN EMBASSIES AND CONSULATES ABROAD

A directory of Colombian embassies and consulates worldwide can be found at W cancilleria.gov.co under "Embajadas y Consulados en el Exterior".

Australia Level 2, 40 Macquarie St, Barton, Canberra, ACT 2600 (W australia.embajada.gov.co); Suite 2, Level 12, 100 Walker St, North Sydney, NSW 2060 (W sydney.consulado.gov.co); plus consulates in Melbourne and Perth.

Brazil SES, Av das Nações, Lote 10, Quadra 803, Brasília DF, CEP 70444-900 (W brasil.embajada.gov.co); Rua Tenente Negrão 140, 7th floor, Itaim Bibi, São Paulo SP, CEP 04530-030 (W saopaulo. consulado.gov.co); Rua 20 No. 651a, Barrio Parque 10, Conjunto Castelo Branco, Manaus, Amazonas (W manaos.consulado.gov.co); Rua General Sampaio 623, Tabatinga, Amazonas, CEP 69640-000 (W tabatinga.consulado.gov.co); plus consulates in Curutiba, Fortaleza, Recife and São Gabriel da Cachoeira.

Canada 360 Albert St, Suite 1002, Ottawa, ON K1R 7X7 (W canada. embajada.gov.co); plus consulates in Toronto, Montréal, Vancouver and Calgary.

Ecuador Av 12 de Octubre 24–528 at Luis Cordero, Edificio World Trade Center, Tower B, 14th floor, Quito EC170143 (W ecuador. embajada.gov.co); plus consulates in Esmeraldas, Guayaquil, Nueva Loja, Santo Domingo and Tulcán.

Ireland 48 Carriglea, Killenard, Co Laois (E colombianconsulate@ eircom.net).

New Zealand Level 16, 191 Queen St, Auckland, 1010 (W auckland.consulado.gov.co).

Panama Punta Pacífica, Edificio Oceanía, Torre 2000, 17th floor, office 17c, Panama City (W panama.embajada.gov.co); Edificio Colón Plaza 2000, suite 61, Primer Alto, Colón (W colon.consulado. gov.co); Sector 2, main street, opposite Infoplaza and diagonally opposite the Catholic Church, Jaqué (W jaque.consulado.gov.co); plus consulates in David and Puerto Obaldia.

Peru Av Víctor Andrés Belaúnde 340, office 602, San Isidro, Lima (W peru.embajada.gov.co); Calle Moore 249, Iquitos (W iquitos. consulado.gov.co).

South Africa 177 Dyer Rd, Hillcrest Office Park, Woodpecker Place, 2nd Floor, Pretoria 0083 (W sudafrica.embajada.gov.co); 18 Birkenhead Rd, Bloubergrant Table View, Cape Town 7441 (T 021 556 6669).

UK 3 Hans Crescent, London SW1X 0LN (W reinounido.embajada. gov.co).

USA 1724 Massachusetts Ave NW, Washington, DC 20036 (W estadosunidos.embajada.gov.co); plus consulates in Atlanta,

Boston, Chicago, Houston, LA, Miami, Newark, New York, Orlando and San Franciso.

Venezuela Segunda Av de Campo Alegre, con Av Francisco de Miranda Torre Credival, 11th floor, Caracas (W venezuela.embajada.gov.co); C 11 No. 8–5 (between cras 18 & 19), Barrio Obrero, Parroquia Pedro María Morantes, San Cristóbal (W sancristobal.consulado.gov.co); plus consulates in Barinas, Barquisimeto, El Amparo, Machiques, Maracaibo, Mérida, Puerto Ayacucho, Puerto La Cruz, Puerto Ordaz, San Antonio del Táchira, San Carlos de Zulia, San Fernando de Atabapo and Valencia.

Getting around

Colombia's generally reliable and numerous buses are your best bet for intercity travel, though increased competition between domestic airlines means that air travel is often only slightly more expensive than the bus, and is of course a lot faster. For some destinations – the islands of San Andrés and Providencia, obviously, but also Leticia in the Amazon – flying is the only feasible way of getting there from the rest of the country, while some places on the Pacific coast are accessible only by boat.

By bus

Buses are the main form of long-distance public transport in Colombia, and every Colombian city has a bus station (*terminal de transportes*) for intercity arrivals and departures. On many routes there will be a choice of options varying in speed, comfort and price, so it's a good idea in big bus stations to shop around at different companies' kiosks. Some companies sell their first batch of seats at low prices, putting them up as they run out of places. Generally, the larger, long-distance buses have reclining seats, toilets and videos (usually American films dubbed into Spanish), and the air conditioning can be fierce, so bring warm clothing or you may end up shivering.

Fares are very reasonable for the 1000km journey between Bogotá and Cartagena, while the fare from Bogotá to Cali, which is about half as long, is even more affordable. Prices may vary depending on the level of comfort, and sometimes on whether you book while the cheapest tickets are still available.

Intercity buses may stop at military checkpoints (*requisas*), sometimes at night. These are usually brief stops, but it's possible that you'll be asked to show ID, so you should have it on you. Especially on short routes, the bus may turn out to be minibus (*buseta*) or shared taxi (*colectivo*, which may in fact be a minibus anyway), and where you have the choice, this may be cheaper and/or faster than a full-sized bus. You'll have less legroom on a minibus, but you'll usually escape the video and super-cold a/c. Especially if you board a bus with no advertised fare, it may be worth checking the fare with fellow passengers before the ticket collector gets to you, just to be sure you aren't overcharged (although that would be unusual in Colombia). *Colectivos* only leave when they have enough passengers, so you may want to hold off paying your fare and stowing your luggage until you can see that it really is nearly full and ready to depart.

For a note on **safety** on buses, see page 75.

MAIN INTERCITY BUS COMPANIES

Berlinas W berlinasdelfonce.com
Bolívariano W bolivariano.com.co
Coomotor W coomotor.com.co
Copetran W copetran.com.co
Expreso Brasilia W expresobrasilia.com
Expreso Palmira W expresopalmira.com.co
Flota Magdalena W flotamagdalena.com
Transipiales W transipialesvirtual.com

By plane

Flying between cities can save an awful lot of time, and fares are generally quite low. There are more than half a dozen domestic airlines in Colombia. The main national carriers, **Avianca** (W avianca.com), **Copa** (W copaair.com) and to a lesser extent **LATAM** (W latam.com), cover the important routes out of Bogotá, and differ little in terms of fares or service. Avianca and Copa offer some routes between regional cities. Copa have now transferred some of their routes to a no-frills airline called Wingo (W wingo.com). The no-frills budget airlines **EasyFly** (W easyfly.com.co) offers a slightly wider choice of inter-regional routes than the main carriers. Small, remote and out-of-the-way places are served by the state-owned airline **SATENA** (W satena.com), which was set up with exactly that purpose in mind.

The very cheapest "promo" (promotional) fares are available sporadically and you would normally need to book at least a couple of months ahead to get them, but booking in advance doesn't necessarily guarantee a low fare. Even if you book well ahead, you'll still be lucky to get a "promo" fare for the date you want, although you stand more chance if you are flexible about your dates. The next fare up is "econo" (economical), and this can still vary depending on demand and availability, and will have conditions such as penalties for cancelling or changing your dates. Prices of available tickets may go up as you approach the date of the flight, but they occasionally fall in last-minute deals. It may also be cheaper to buy your ticket via a local travel agent than online or direct from the airline. Demand is highest during holiday periods, particularly Semana Santa (the week leading up to Easter), when it's a good idea to book well in advance. Other peak times are around Christmas, and in the main holiday period, which is from mid-June till the end of August. A useful website to compare air fares is W lostiquetesmasbaratos.com.

If you're lucky enough to get a promotional fare, or book with a no-fills airline out of season, you can sometimes bag a bargain. On the other hand, if all the "econo" tickets are gone, you'll have to pay the full "flex" economy fare, although this does allow you to change your dates or cancel without charge.

By train

Colombia's rail network is now used almost exclusively for freight. The only passenger train service left in the country is a weekend-only tourist train: the **Tren Túristico de la Sabana** from Bogotá to Zipaquirá (see page 73). For a more unusual rail transport experience, residents of San Cipriano, a roadless village in the jungle west of Cali, have created their own system of rustic, motorbike-powered trolleys along the railway line connecting the village with Córdoba on the Cali–Buenaventura highway.

By car

Driving in Colombia can be expensive. Car rental rates are high and highway tolls are also quite steep. Security has vastly improved, and road conditions are mostly good, but there are still high rates of car theft, while the Amazon region and a lot of the Llanos and the Pacific coast cannot be reached by road from elsewhere in the country.

You can drive on a licence from home if you are in Colombia for less than a month, but you'll still need an international licence if you want to rent a car. You must have your licence and ID (passport, in other words) on you when driving, as well as the papers for the car. The minimum age for driving is eighteen.

All cars must be locally insured. Short-term car insurance (SOAT) is sold by Previsora Seguros (W previsora.gov.co), whose offices are listed on their website under "Sedes y Puntos de Venta".

Car rental

To rent a car, you'll need your passport, a credit or debit card and an international driving licence. The major international car rental franchises such as Budget (W budget.com.co) and Avis (W avis.com.co) operate in Colombia, along with local operators such as Milano (W milanocar.com), or the South American firm Localiza (W localiza.com), whose rates tend to be cheaper, per week for the smallest car with unlimited mileage.

When picking up a rented car, always give it a thorough check and make sure the tyres are in good nick, with a working spare on board. You probably won't be allowed to leave the car at a city other than the one where you picked it up.

Security

You'll come across a lot of police and army **checkpoints** on the road, where they'll want to check your

ROAD DISTANCES (KM)

	Bogotá	Bucaramanga	Cali	Cartagena	Cúcuta	Manizales	Medellín	Popayán	Santa Marta	Tunja
Bogotá	x	439	484	1178	649	299	552	633	1139	147
Bucaramanga	439	x	932	917	210	738	1543	1072	700	292
Cali	484	923	x	1088	1133	275	462	149	1305	361
Cartagena	1178	917	1088	x	1050	879	626	1237	217	1554
Cúcuta	649	210	1133	1050	x	984	1201	1282	833	502
Manizales	299	738	275	879	984	x	253	424	1096	446
Medellín	552	1543	462	626	1201	253	x	611	843	699
Popayán	633	1072	149	1237	1282	424	611	x	1454	780
Santa Marta	1139	700	1305	217	833	1096	843	1454	x	992
Tunja	147	292	361	1554	502	446	699	780	992	x

ID and maybe see what you have on board. Police and soldiers are generally friendly to motorists, and are unlikely to put the bite on, like their counterparts in some other Latin American countries. They are however concerned with security, and they may be inclined to give foreign drivers a more thorough check than Colombians. In such situations, always be patient, polite and friendly. Should you need the highway police, call (from a mobile phone) ☎767.

Rates of car crime in Colombia are high, with break-ins and car theft common. When parking in cities, try to make sure that your car is guarded. You can do this by leaving it in a car park, or by parking in a street with a guardian, whom you should tip. Most hotels will have safe parking facilities.

If you have an accident the police will want to view the scene exactly as it was at the time; you must not move your vehicle until they arrive, even if it is in an inconvenient position. To do so may be deemed an admission of guilt and liability.

Petrol

Petrol (*gasolina*) is sold by the US gallon (3.8 litres, or about a fifth smaller than a British gallon), with ordinary petrol (*corriente*) working out to be the cheapest option, high-octane (*extra*) being slightly more and diesel (*Aceite Combustible para Motores*, or *ACPM*) coming in somewhere in between. The price is often slightly less at night, and prices drop by about a quarter south of Popayán (around Pasto) and towards the Venezuelan border (around Cúcuta).

ADDRESSES

Getting around Colombian cities is facilitated by a foolproof arithmetic numbering system, derived from the original Spanish grid layout. The street titles indicate their direction: calles (abbreviated C – as in this Guide – or Cl) run east–west, with numbers getting higher as you go north, while carreras (abbreviated Cra – the style followed in this Guide – Kra or K) run north–south, with numbers getting higher as you go west. Addresses tell you not only the street but also the exact block. For example, the address Cra 73 No.12–20 can be found on Carrera 73, at number 20 in the block above Calle 12. Generally speaking, therefore, the address alone should tell you almost exactly where a house or building is located. As in the US, the first floor of a building is the ground floor.

Roads and traffic

Traffic circulates on the right, and the normal **speed limit** is 80km/h (49mph) in open country, dropping to 60km/h (37mph) in built-up areas, and 30km/h (18mph on residential streets. **Seat belts** are compulsory in car front-seats, as are crash helmets on motorbikes. Colombian drivers can be aggressive (especially trucks and buses), and also quite reckless, ignoring speed limits, red lights and traffic regulations, failing to indicate, and overtaking on both sides. Mopeds and motorbikes weave in and out of traffic, often appearing unexpectedly in your blind spot. On the other hand, drivers can be very courteous about things like allowing cars out of side streets. Everyone uses their horn a lot, but it tends to be a quick pip rather than a blaring honk, and it's mostly just to remind other motorists that the driver is there.

Roads are generally well maintained, but large potholes are not unknown, not all roads are surfaced, and the rainy season can play havoc with road conditions, causing landslides and mudslides as well as widespread flooding. It's always safest to drive in daylight.

Beware of speed humps, which are not well indicated, and may not be obvious until it is too late to slow down. Indeed, signposting in general is sparser than it might be. Note also that in some cities (currently Armenia, Barranquilla, Bogotá, Bucaramanga, Cali, Cartagena, Cúcuta, Medellín, Pereira and Santa Marta) there is a "*pico y placa*" system, under which vehicles whose registration ends in specific digits are banned from driving on certain days in order to reduce congestion and pollution. This is enforced with traffic cameras, and driving on the wrong day can land you a hefty fine; for further details, see Ⓦeltiempo.com/servicios/pico_placa.

Highways have toll booths at frequent intervals, and although you'll have to pay at each one (the price varies with the type of vehicle), these can easily mount up if you're driving any substantial distance. It's a good idea to keep a stack of C$5000 and C$10,000 bills to pay your tolls with.

Taxis

Given high crime rates in parts of some Colombian cities, you'll often want to take a **cab** rather than wander around town late at night, and certainly, when arriving in a city with all of your baggage, cash and ID on you, be sure to take a cab straight to your hotel. Taxis in most cities are inexpensive and metered, but in most towns on the Caribbean coast you'll probably have to agree a price with the driver, which means you should know in advance what the going rate is if you don't want to be overcharged. It's also a good idea to carry small bills or you may well find that the driver doesn't have change (although, strictly speaking, it's then their responsibility to go and find some). **Tips** are not necessarily expected, but are appreciated.

Particularly in Bogotá, but even in Medellín and Cali, robbery of passengers by cab drivers – though rare – is not unknown. To prevent this, it is best, especially at night, to call for a cab or pick one up from a taxi rank rather than hailing one, and if you have a mobile phone handy to do it, photograph the registration and send it to yourself before getting in. Alternatively, if you have a smartphone that works locally, Easy Taxi (weasytaxi.com) covers most Colombian cities; Uber is illegal but operates nonetheless.

By bicycle

For all its steep mountain roads and reckless drivers, Colombia is a country where people love to **cycle**. Bicycle shops and cycle repair shops are very common, and in many cities – Bogotá in particular – there are good cycle-path networks, and on Sundays many roads become car-free to make special Sunday cycle routes called *ciclovías*. Bicycle rental is widespread, and some hostels rent out bikes.

Other transport

Something between a bus and an oversized pick-up, the usually brightly decorated **chiva** is still in use on rural routes, often with people aboard the luggage rack on top as well as inside the vehicle. In the coffee-growing areas in particular, a common mode of transport is the hardy **Willys jeep**, with two rows of seats in the covered interior and more passengers clinging to the back. These tend to be inexpensive, but the ride can be bumpy and you are squeezed in with mounds of luggage. Some towns have **tuk-tuks** (auto-rickshaws) or motorbike taxis, known as **mototaxis**.

Accommodation

With the return of stability to Colombia, tourists and business travellers are coming back, and new hotels are opening to cater for them. In terms of tourism, the biggest growth so far has been among backpackers, leading to a surge in cheap hostels. At the top end of the market, many hotels are more business- than tourist-oriented, but new hotels are opening up all the time to cater for tourists both foreign and Colombian, and "boutique hotels" are springing up all over the place. Also, of course, rooms in private homes and small bed and breakfast places can be booked online.

Hotels, motels, fincas and posadas

Top-end **hotels** in the major cities tend to cater mostly for business travellers, while those in coastal resorts are used mainly by well-heeled Colombians, but there's a high level of professionalism, and most four- and five-star hotels employ English-speaking staff. Bogotá and Medellín in particular are well stocked with five-star business hotels, while Cartagena has the best choice of luxury tourist accommodation (with some of the highest rates in Colombia). Room rates are usually cheaper if booked online, particularly through discount agents such as Expedia or Orbitz.

Mid-range options – hotels, *posadas* or *hospedajes* (guesthouses) – can be thin on the ground and in some places you may have to downscale a little. Where they do exist, however, guesthouses can be a real bargain for a double room with private bathroom. Increasingly, small boutique hotels are opening up, often in charming old buildings with lots of character, but you still won't find them everywhere. In the coffee-growing region, you can stay on an old *finca* (see page 241).

Cheap hotels can be found in the more run-down parts of city centres, often around transport terminals.

ACCOMMODATION PRICE CODES

The hotel prices quoted in this book are for the least expensive room for two people in high season, not including breakfast – but do allow for the fluctuations outlined above. Other options are usually available, including rooms with two beds, single rooms, dormitory accommodation in hostels and so on. The following key has been outlined based on these criteria. It has been applied throughout the guide to all accommodation listings and all prices are in Colombian Peso.

$	$200,000 or lower
$$	$200,000–$400,000
$$$	$400,000–$600,000
$$$$	$600,000 and over

They might, however, not be located in the safest part of town. As for **motels**, note that the term as used in Colombia does not so much mean a place for drivers overnighting on the road as a venue for illicit sexual liaisons, with rooms often rented by the hour. This doesn't mean that you can't stay at them, but be aware that they may not be strictly respectable, nor very quiet.

Also worth noting is that expensive hotels in particular may add 16 percent **VAT** to your bill. In principle, non-resident foreigners taking "tourist packages" (room plus breakfast, for example) are exempt from this, and you should usually be able to persuade your hotel to drop the charge on that basis. Some hotels also add an insurance charge *seguro hotelero*, which is supposed to be optional, so if you haven't opted to pay it (and this may be worth bringing up when you check in), they should not be charging you for it.

In resorts and places popular with visitors, rates will be highest in the Christmas and New Year period, Semana Santa (Holy Week) and *puentes* (long weekends, when Monday is a public holiday). Prices in resort hotels may also go up at weekends and in July and August. In big cities, on the other hand, business hotels in particular may offer weekend discounts.

Breakfast is often included in room rates in mid-range and upmarket Colombian hotels and we note in the hotel listings when this is the case.

Hostels

With the huge rise of backpacker tourism in Colombia, cheap **hostels** are prolific. Most offer a choice of dormitory accommodation or private rooms. Some are more spacious than others, and facilities typically include wi-fi, use of a kitchen, a laundry service, and sometimes bicycle rental, a library or book exchange, even a film library on occasion. Many offer local tours or excursions. **Breakfast** is often thrown in, but it won't amount to very much – if you want a serious breakfast, you'll probably need to find it elsewhere. The other thing to note about hostels is that some are party hostels catering for a young, up-for-it crowd, while others are more sedate and may frown on rowdy behaviour, so choose accordingly. A number of websites offer online booking, or you can book through the hostel's own website – it's wise to check both as the price may differ.

Hostelling International (HI), the official worldwide youth hostel federation, has seven hostels in Colombia, with dorm accommodation, and often with private rooms, too. HI hostels can be booked online at Ⓦ hihostels.com. Some may offer discounts for HI members.

HOSTEL-BOOKING WEBSITES

Colombian Hostels Ⓦ colombianhostels.com.co
Hostel World Ⓦ hostelworld.com/hostels/Colombia

Camping

Camping is an option in some rural areas and national parks, particularly Parque Nacional Tayrona on the Caribbean coast and Parque Nacional Cocuy in the highlands, but elsewhere campsites are uncommon. Some hostels in rural areas allow camping in their grounds. If you hike to the Ciudad Perdida (see page 174) you'll get to sleep in hammocks with mosquito nets. If you intend to camp on private land, always get permission from the landowner first, and make sure it is safe to camp.

If you're driving a **campervan**, and not using a campsite, be sure to park somewhere safe. Sometimes police or army personnel may allow you to park near their checkpoints.

Food and drink

Colombian food is hearty and filling rather than spicy or exotic (although they do spice it up a bit more on the coast). Expect to eat a fair bit of stodge – be it rice, potatoes, plantain or cassava (or all of those) – usually accompanied by meat or fish, some beans or lentils, and occasionally the odd vegetable, all well-cooked but nothing too fancy.

Breakfast

Big hotels should lay on a **breakfast** buffet where you can choose from numerous different dishes. Cheap hostels on the other hand usually offer a smaller breakfast of toast and coffee, with maybe an egg if you're lucky. In restaurants, a Colombian breakfast typically consists of *huevos pericos* (scrambled eggs

---

> ### ACCOMMODATION ALTERNATIVES
>
> Useful websites that provide alternatives to standard hotel and hostel accommodation.
> **Airbnb** Ⓦ airbnb.com
> **Booking.com** Ⓦ booking.com
> **Vacation Rentals by Owner** Ⓦ vrbo.com

with onion and tomatoes), accompanied by a bread roll or an *arepa* (cornmeal patty). You may also get *caldo* (broth), usually *de costilla* (made from beef ribs). Other breakfast dishes include *calentado*, originally made from reheated leftovers of the previous day's supper, and consisting of refried rice and beans, with meat, egg and a sausage (called a *chorizo*, but not like the Spanish sausage of the same name). A quick working breakfast might consist of a *tamale* (stuffed cornmeal cake) with coffee or hot chocolate. In Bogotá, the most traditional breakfast is hot chocolate with bread and cheese.

Lunch and dinner

Lunch (*almuerzo*) is a full-on meal consisting of soup, a main course and usually a dessert. It's also a good time to fill up if you're on a budget, because many places offer a low-priced set lunch called a *comida corriente* or *menú executivo*, where you pay a fixed price for two or three courses, generally with a choice of options for the main. Alternatively, you might opt for just a *plato del día* ("dish of the day"), which will be a single, large, bargain-priced combo dish. And should you want it spicy, most restaurants will have some *ají*, a hot salsa made with tomatoes, coriander (cilantro) and chilli, which you can spoon on as gingerly or as copiously as you like.

Colombian **soups** can easily be a meal in themselves. Examples include *mondongo*, a soup of tripe and vegetables, or *cazuela*, which is a thick soup, usually of fish and seafood, similar to a chowder. *Ajiaco* is somewhere between a soup and a stew, made with chicken, potatoes, corn and a South American herb called *guasca* (sometimes known in English as "gallant soldier" or "potato weed"), and usually garnished with avocado.

Expect a **main course** of fish and rice or meat and rice. Antioquia (the region around Medellín) is the best place to get a *bandeja paisa*, which is a big plate of beans and rice with a fried egg, a sausage and often other additions such as *patacones* (fried squashed plantain), *arepas* (cornmeal patties) or *chicharrón* (crispy fried pork belly), but it's available nationwide and you can often get it cheaply at market stalls.

Desserts include rice pudding or various other milk-based puds, often topped with *arequipe* (caramelized condensed milk, like Argentina's *dolce de leche*). Another popular dessert is *bocadillo de guayaba*, a solid guava jelly commonly served with a light white cheese (*quejata* or *queso fresco*) – note that *bocadillo* ("mouthful") in Colombia is referring to this dish, not a sandwich as it does in some other Spanish-speaking countries.

Having stuffed yourself at lunchtime, you won't want quite such a heavy **dinner** and you'll find that Colombian restaurants tend to close quite early. Places that are open late may sell pizza, or cheese *arepas*.

Local specialities

With such geographical diversity, you can expect a fair bit of variation in the **local cuisine**, depending on the climate, cultural influences and what's available locally. On the **coast**, of course, you'll find a lot of fish and seafood, and even, if you're lucky – and especially on the islands of San Andrés and Providencia – lobster or crawfish. In the **Caribbean** region particularly, they'll eat it with *arroz con coco*, slightly sweet rice cooked with coconut milk.

In **Cali and the south**, guinea pig, known as *cuy* or *curí*, sometimes crops up on the menu. Also typical of the Valle de Cauca region around Cali is *sanchocho*, a meat soup with potato, plantain or cassava (or all three), and *pan de bono*, a kind of bread roll made from corn and cassava flour with cheese and egg. **Tolima**, the region between Bogota and Cali, is famous for its *lechona*, stuffed suckling pig, as well as *viudo de pescado* ("fish widower"), a soup made from local river fish with green plantains and cassava, typically accompanied by *hogao* (a tomato and onion sauce).

In the **Llanos** and **Amazon** regions, the food more resembles that of other South American countries such as Brazil, with a big emphasis on barbecued meat, but also a lot of delicious Amazon river fish. And for something exotic, don't miss out on the *hormigas culonas* (fried giant ants), found particularly in the **Santander** region (see page 110).

Street food

Snacks are available on street corners nationwide. **Tamales** are cornmeal cakes stuffed, usually with meat, and steamed in a corn husk or a banana leaf. They vary widely across the country, and every region has its own local version. The most famous are those from Tolima (*tamales tolimenses*), which are stuffed with chicken, pork, rice and peas. **Empanadas** (pasties) are another popular snack, stuffed with meat, cheese or a rice-based filling; in Colombia they are invariably deep-fried. **Arepas** (cornmeal bread patties) are often sold at street stalls too, especially around breakfast time, usually topped with butter and sometimes stuffed with cheese.

You'll always find **sweets** within easy reach. Rather than white sugar, Colombian sweets tend to be based on *panela*, a form of semi-refined cane sugar,

EATING PRICE CODES

The restaurant prices quoted in this book are for a two-course meal for one including a glass of wine or similar. The following key has been applied throughout the guide based on these criteria and all prices are in Colombian Peso.

$	$50,000 or under
$$	$50,000–$150,000
$$$	$150,000–$300,000
$$$$	$300,000 and over

similar to jaggery, which is sold in bricks or tablets in any grocery; if you want to buy it for your own use, bear in mind that you'll need a hammer or a big stone to break it up. Popular sweets include *cocadas* (coconut macaroons), *merenguitos* (mini-meringues) and *roscones* (sweet bread rings with a guava jelly filling). *Obleas* are wafers which you can have with a choice of sweet toppings, covered with another *oblea* to make a sandwich. Even stickier confections such as *brevas con arequipe* (figs stuffed with caramelized condensed milk) are often available on the street.

Vegetarian food

Colombians tend to like their meat, and **vegetarianism** is not very traditional, but as everywhere else, it's growing. In any city you'll find a decent spread of vegetarian dishes in most eating places, and often a selection of vegetarian restaurants, although it may be harder if you're vegan. Certainly, you'll be eating a lot of **rice and beans**, and if you eat cheese, a lot of **cheese arepas**. Crepes & Waffles (W crepesywaffles.com), a chain of restaurants serving, as their name suggests, **crêpes and waffles** with a range of sweet and savoury toppings, always has a good variety of veg options. If you want to tell people you're vegetarian, the Spanish is "*soy vegetariana*" if you're female, or "*soy vegetariano*" if you're male; for a vegan, it's "*soy vegana*"/"*soy vegano*". You may need to impress this on people in small-town Colombia or else you may find, having asked for a dish without meat, for example, that you get given one with chicken. If you want to be really sure, you could say, "*No como* (I don't eat) *ni carne* (either meat), *ni pollo* (nor chicken), *ni pescado* (nor fish), *ni huevos* (nor eggs), *ni productos lacteos* (nor dairy products)."

Fruit

Of the more familiar **tropical fruits**, bananas come in all shapes and sizes. A banana in Colombia is *banano*, or less commonly *banana*, while *plátano* is a plantain. A *limón* is a lime (a lemon, not commonly seen, is *limón real*). Colombian pawpaws (*papaya* in Spanish, of course) are big and full of flavour, as are mangoes (equally easy in Spanish: *mango*), and watermelons (*sandía*), not to mention pineapples (*piña*). Passion fruits have different names depending on the type: *maracuyás* are big and yellow with thick skin and are the most flavoursome, but *grenadillas* are easier to peel and less messy to eat; *gulupas* are small, purple and often quite tart, while *curubas* ("banana passion fruit" in English) are green and elongated.

Colombian fruits you may know from other tropical countries (or even from home) include soursops (*guanábana*), custard apples (*chirimoya*), starfruits (*carambola*), guavas (*guayava*, often used to make syrups and jellies), Cape gooseberries (*uchuva*) and guineps (*mamoncillo*, sometimes called "Spanish limes"). Names you may know from other Spanish-speaking countries can be confusing however: in Colombia, a *higo* ("fig") is not an ordinary fig but a "Barbary fig" or prickly pear, while an actual fig is called a *breva*. A *nispero* is not a loquat but a sapodilla or chicu. Its larger cousin, the sapote or chupa-chupa fruit (*zapote*) makes a good milkshake and some people freeze its pulp to eat as a dessert. The tree tomato (*tomate de árbol*), more correctly called a tamarillo in English, is not very sweet if you just eat it straight, but it's commonly made into a refreshing juice.

And then there are fruits you rarely see elsewhere. The dragon fruit (*pitaya*) is so strange-looking that it used to feature as an alien fruit in *Star Trek*. The easiest way to eat it is to halve or quarter it down the middle with a sharp knife. A *lulo* looks like a persimmon but is actually more closely related to a tomato, with quite an acidic flavour; it's most popular as a juice. The round, maroon-skinned *corozo* is the fruit of the coyure palm tree, and not unlike a cranberry in tartness; again, the best way to consume it is as a juice. Likewise the *borojo*, a forest fruit rich in minerals which is reputed to be an aphrodisiac.

Drinks

Colombia has a huge variety of fresh **fruit juices** and **milkshakes**. A *salpicón* is a medley of juices diluted with carbonated water. *Champús* is an altogether different fruit drink, thickened with corn and spiced with cinnamon and cloves. Fizzy soda pops include local brand Postobón, and there's also Malta, a malty soda reminiscent of sweet stout. On the coast, don't miss *limonada de coco*, a zingy real lemonade made with lime and coconut.

Hot drinks

Colombian **coffee** (*café*) is of course world-famous. Time was, Colombia used to export all its best coffee, but now you can get a decent brew in most places. The Colombian chain *Juan Valdez* (wjuanvaldezcafe.com), with branches all over the place, looks like *Starbucks* or *Costa*, but its coffee is much better. Good espresso is increasingly available in other establishments as well, although the majority of Colombians still drink more dilute black coffee (*tinto*) and – whisper this shocking truth quietly – a lot of people still drink instant.

Colombian hot **chocolate** is made by dissolving cocoa bars in hot water with a little milk, and is often spiced with cinnamon or even vanilla. Cooked up in a metal jug called a *chocolatera* and frothed up with a wooden paddle-stick called a *molinillo*, it is often taken for breakfast instead of tea or coffee.

Coca leaf tea (*té de coca*) is a favourite with tourists, and also widely drunk among Indigenous communities. Don't expect a cocaine-like hit from it: it's more akin in its effects to a nice cup of tea (which you needn't expect to find in Colombia, unless you happen to like a teabag dunked in lukewarm water). If you prefer to avoid the stimulant effects of coffee, chocolate or coca leaf, you could try *flor de jamaica* (Jamaican sorrel, a variety of hibiscus), which makes a tart and refreshing bright-red infusion. *Agua panela* is just hot water with *panela* dissolved in it, and sometimes a squeeze of lime.

Alcohol

Like most countries, Colombia has a range of industrially produced **beers** (*cerveza*), which are drinkable enough but generally light on flavour. Almost all are brewed by the Bavaria brewery, whose brands include Aguila (light), Poker (slightly more flavoursome) and Club Colombia (slightly pricier, and available in light and dark varieties). In addition, Colombia has a growing number of **craft beer** producers. In the capital, the Bogotá Beer Company (BBC; wbogotabeercompany.com) has branches throughout town, and serves a variety of beers, including English-style ales, many of which are available in bottles around the country. Also in Bogotá, the *Palos de Moguer* chain serves its own craft beer, and Medellín has two craft breweries, Tres Cordilleras and Apóstol. Many microbrewery beers are unavailable outside the *departamento* where they're made, and some, to be frank, are valiant efforts rather than great beers.

Don't expect much in the way of decent **wine** (*vino*), although you may get some imported from Chile or Argentina. A small amount is now being produced locally, too, particularly in the Boyacá region north of Bogotá. More interestingly, **chicha** is an Indigenous drink made from corn or sometimes cassava; in some areas this is traditionally chewed in the mouth before fermentation. At one time *chicha* was illegal, but you can now buy it in bars dedicated specifically to it. It's a bit of an acquired taste, and novices may prefer a fruit-flavoured version.

Colombia's **spirit** of choice is **aguardiente**, a firewater distilled from sugar cane and usually flavoured with aniseed; most foreigners go for the *sin azúcar* version, which has no added sugar. On the Caribbean coast in particular, people prefer **rum** (*ron*), which is generally pretty decent; Ron Viejo de Caldas, Ron Medellín or Dictador are good brands, and all offer bog-standard or aged versions. The other spirit popular in Colombia is a brand of Scotch **whisky** called Old Parr.

Festivals

Colombia has local festivals by the dozen, and there's always one going on somewhere. Wherever it is, there'll be parades, pageants, colourful local costumes, food and, of course, lots of music and dancing. Depending on the region, the celebrations will incorporate Spanish, Indigenous or African elements, and most probably all three. There will also probably be a religious element since many of these festivals celebrate the local patron saint's day. Others may celebrate the harvest of the most important local produce, especially coffee, and big cities may have cultural festivals dedicated to things like film, poetry or music.

Certain festivals are celebrated nationwide, but Mardi Gras (*Carnaval*), when Catholics traditionally let their hair down for the last time before the six solemn weeks of Lent, is strangely not among them: the only places that really go to town for Mardi Gras are Baranquilla and Mompox, although Tumaco on the Pacific coast has a Fire Carnival at the same time (see page 317). Other cities, such as Pasto and Bogotá, have "carnivals" at other times of the year.

Semana Santa (Holy Week) is the last week of Lent leading up to Easter, which, from a religious perspective, is the most important festival of the whole year. The date for Easter varies, and the dates of several other religious celebrations vary with it – Mardi Gras, for example, is always forty days before Easter. Semana Santa begins with Palm Sunday, a week before Easter Sunday, celebrating Jesus' arrival in Jerusalem, leading up to Good Friday, the day of his crucifixion, and Easter Sunday, the day of his resurrection. Most people take time off work for Holy Week, and try to spend it with their families. The most colourful celebrations, featuring processions, pilgrimages and special church services, are held in Mompox and Popayán, and there are also special celebrations in Ipiales, Pamplona, Pasto and Tunja.

The other big annual festival period, of course, is **Christmas** and the **New Year**. Christmas celebrations begin on December 7, known as *El Día de las Velitas* (Candle Day), when the festive decorations go up, and candles are lit to celebrate the immaculate conception of the Virgin Mary on the next day, which is a public holiday. From December 16, religious people celebrate the Novena, or nine days of prayer in the lead-up to Christmas, the last being Christmas Eve, which is nowadays when presents are usually given, and it is the evening dinner on Christmas Eve rather than the midday meal on Christmas Day which for Colombians is the big family get-together. New Year celebrations are as wild and hedonistic as anywhere else in the world, and the Christmas period ends with Twelfth Night (Epiphany), known in the Spanish-speaking world as *El Día de los Reyes Magos* (or just *Reyes*), when the three kings arrived bearing gold, myrrh and frankincense; at one time this was when presents were exchanged, but that has now shifted to Christmas Eve.

A FESTIVAL CALENDAR

JAN & FEB
Carnaval de Blancos y Negros Pasto, **Jan 2–7**. See page 295.
Riosucio Carnival Riosucio, **week of Jan 6, odd-numbered years**. See page 234.
Feria de Manizales Manizales, **first week in Jan**. See page 234.
Festival Internacional de Música Cartagena, **early Jan**. See page 139.
Fiestas de Nuestra Señora de La Candelaria Cartagena, **Jan 24 to Feb 2**.
Hay Festival Cartagena, **late Jan/early Feb**. See page 139.
Festival Internacional de Cine Cartagena, **late Feb**. See page 139.
Barranquilla Carnival Barranquilla, **Feb or early March**. See page 158.
Fire Carnival Tumaco, **Feb or early March**. See page 317.

MARCH–MAY
Francisco el Hombre Riohacha, **March**. See page 179.
Holy Week (Semana Santa) Nationwide, **March or April**; especially Tunja, Mompox and Popayán. See pages 95, 155 and 276.
Festival Iberoamericano de Teatro Bogotá, **March or April, even-numbered years**. See page 83.
Vallenato Festival Valledupar, **late April or early May**. See page 183.
Festival de la Cultura Wayuu Uribía, **late May (sometimes held in Aug)**. See page 179.

JULY–AUG
Rock al Parque Bogotá, **early July**. See page 83.
Colombiamoda Medellín, **late July**. See page 224.
Fiestas del Mar Santa Marta **late July**. See page 166.
Feria de las Flores Medellín, **late July and early Aug**. See page 224.
Festival Internacional de la Cultura Tunja, **Aug**. See page 95.
Festival Música del Pacífico Cali, **Aug**. See page 264.
Bogotá Carnival Bogotá, **5–6 Aug**. See page 83.
Guabina and Tiple Festival Vélez **first or second weekend of Aug**. See page 100.
Festival de las Cometas Villa de Leyva, **mid-Aug**. See page 100.

SEPT
Festival de Teatro Manizales, **Sept**. See page 234.
Festival Mundial de Salsa Cali, **Sept**. See page 257.
Congreso Gastronómico de Popayán Popayán, **mid-Sept**. See page 276.
Jazz al Parque Bogotá, **mid-Sept**. See page 83.
Festival de Jazz Mompox, **late Sept**. See page 155.

OCT–DEC
Yipao Parade Armenia, **mid-Oct**. See page 243.
Día de Brujitas (Hallowe'en) Santa Marta, **Oct 31**. See page 166.
Independence of Cartagena Cartagena, **Nov 11**. See page 139.
Golden Pirarucú Music Festival Leticia, **late Nov/early Dec**. See page 332.
Festival de Luces Villa de Leyva, **7–9 Dec**. See page 100.
Aguinaldo Boyacense Tunja, **16–22 Dec**. See page 95.
Feria de Cali Cali, **25–30 Dec**. See page 264.

Sports and outdoor activities

Adrenaline junkies have a treat in store in Colombia. From almost every vantage point there's a snow-capped peak to climb, an untamed river to ride or some sunken coral reef to explore.

Favourite activities include hiking and trekking, sometimes with a bit of climbing thrown in, and scuba diving or at the very least snorkelling around the coral reefs of the country's limpid, tropical seas. If that doesn't float your boat (or even if it does), there are rivers gushing with whitewater rapids for a bit of rafting or kayaking, and the Caribbean coast also offers opportunities to windsurf and to kitesurf, as does Lago Calima in the southwest.

Aside from that, the country has a passion for cycling, which its mountainous terrain has done nothing to dispel. For paragliding, suitable locations lie within easy reach of Bogotá, Medellín and Cali, and it's also possible to go caving or abseil down waterfalls, notably in the region of San Gil (see page 106), which has become the country's top destination for outdoor sports.

If your tastes run to watching sport rather than playing it, Colombian football (soccer) has recently made a big splash on the world stage, and you could do worse than watch a match in the country itself. Check out, too, *tejo*, a game played in bars nationwide.

Hiking and trekking

With the country's huge range of landscapes and terrains, from highland to lowland and desert to jungle, **hiking** in Colombia is second to none. There are demanding week-long adventures in the mountains, and spectacular jungle treks, but if you just fancy a nice walk amid beautiful scenery, you could enjoy plenty of shorter but no less attractive rambles around Salento in the country's coffee-producing region. Many of the best hikes and treks will be within Colombia's national parks, and accommodation on long treks may be limited to camping.

The most popular **jungle trek** is the four- to six-day jungle trail to the spectacular ruins of Ciudad Perdida (see page 174), but jungle trekking is also available in the Amazon region around Leticia (see page 324). If spectacular desert landscapes take your fancy, try the Tatacoa Desert north of Neiva (see page 289) and the arid wilderness of La Guajira (see page 177); the capital, Bogotá, is a handy base for hikes in the nearby *páramo* terrain of high moorland verging on tundra, an ecosystem almost unique to Colombia (see page 74). With peaks as impressive as any in the Andes, Colombia offers mountain treks among the snow-capped peaks of the Sierra Nevada del Cocuy (see page 103) or the volcanoes of Los Nevados (see page 234). Gentler walks can be found among the lush, scenic hills of the coffee-growing region around Salento (see page 243) and the Cocora Valley (see page 247), or the archeological site at Tierradentro (see page 279).

Snorkelling and scuba diving

Colombia's waters are a good (and cheap) place to learn to **scuba dive**. The country's 3000km of coastline borders both the Caribbean and the

> **TOP 5 NATIONAL PARKS**
> **El Cocuy** See page 103
> **Los Nevados** See page 234
> **Puracé** See page 277
> **Serranía de la Macarena** See page 322
> **Tayrona** See page 171

Pacific, with enough islands, cays and coral reefs to keep any diver happy. Particularly on the Caribbean coast, around Santa Marta and Cartagena, and on the islands of San Andrés and Providencia – home to the world's third-largest barrier reef – operators offer four- or five-day PADI certification courses (expect expect to pay slightly less in Taganga, which is currently the cheapest place to do it). Be sure to enquire about the reputation of dive operators before signing up, check their PADI or NAUI accreditation and the instructor-to-student ratio, and ask for recommendations from other divers. Snorkelling is also particularly good on the islands. The Pacific coast offers more challenging **diving** opportunities, around the Isla Malpelo and Isla Gorgona, but these take some getting to, and are not for beginners.

Rafting and kayaking

If shooting down whitewater rapids on an inflatable raft or in a kayak gets your pulse racing, then you've come to the right place. Colombia has **rapids** from grade one through to grade six, so whether you're a beginner or a veteran, there'll be a river to suit you. The country's adrenaline sports capital is San Gil (see page 108), close by the Suárez, Fonce and Chicamocha rivers, all of which offer superb rafting opportunities. The Río Negro near Bogotá (see page 74) and the Río Magdalena near San Agustín (see page 287) also offer rafting and kayaking.

Football

Just as it is in most South American countries, **football** (*fútbol*, meaning soccer) is Colombia's most popular spectator sport. The game was introduced in 1903

> **TOP 5 BEACHES**
> **Isla Múcura** See page 145
> **Johnny Cay** See page 194
> **La Barra** See page 312
> **Playa Cristal** See page 172
> **Playa Juan de Dios** See page 312

COLOMBIA AND THE WORLD CUP

Colombia's first appearance in the World Cup was in 1962, but the country didn't achieve footballing fame until the 1990s, when it wasn't entirely for the right reasons. Unfortunately, this was the era of the cocaine cartels, already responsible for murdering a number of officials for failing to ensure wins on cartel-placed bets. Colombia qualified for the World Cup in 1990, going out at the group stage, but entered the 1994 tournament with much optimism after beating Argentina five–nil to qualify. Alas, a defeat in the opening match was followed by a humiliating loss to the United States involving an own goal by **Andrés Escobar**. After receiving death threats, Escobar was infamously shot down in Medellín a week later. Despite this, Colombia qualified in 1998, going out in the group stage yet again. They didn't reappear until 2014 – when they produced their best performance ever, impressing the world as they topped their group and made it through to the quarter finals, with playmaker **James Rodríguez** winning the Golden Boot as the tournament's leading goal-scorer – and then qualified again in 2018.

by British workers on the Barranquilla railway, and Barranquilla FC was founded in 1909 as the nation's first football club.

Colombia made the quarter finals of the World Cup in 2014 (see page 38) and elsewhere on the international stage, Colombian clubs have twice won the Copa Libertadores, South America's equivalent of the Champions League; Medellín's Atlético Nacional nabbed it in 1989, and Once Caldas from Manizales were the surprise underdog champions in 2004.

The league football season in Colombia has two halves: *apertura* (Jan–May) and *finalización* (July–Dec), and the country's knockout cup competition, the Copa Colombia, is an annual tournament. The top clubs are from Bogotá (Santa Fe and Millonarios) and Medellín (DIM and Atlético Nacional), and local derbies between these clubs are guaranteed to be colourful and exciting affairs, although they are also the top matches for violence between the fans, and the hardest to get tickets for. For most other matches you don't need to buy tickets in advance: just turn up at the ground and buy on the gate; if buying from touts, be aware that their tickets may be forgeries, and if so, will be rejected by entry machines on the gate.

Tejo

Colombia's own native sport is **tejo**, which is largely associated with drinking – in much the same way that darts is in Britain. The *tejo* itself is a hefty (0.75kg) iron puck, which is thrown some 20m towards a target embedded in an approximately metre-square box of clay, not flat but tilted up towards the players. In the middle is the bullseye (*balazo*), with four little packets of gunpowder (*mecha*) placed around it. The game works on a system of points – hitting the bullseye gets six points, exploding one of the *mechas* bags three, and getting closer to the bullseye than any other player nets one point.

Supposedly, *tejo* is pre-Hispanic and was originally played with gold discs rather than iron pucks, but this popular belief doesn't seem to be backed up by much in the way of actual evidence. What is certain is that you'll find *tejo* bars nationwide, and they're a lot of fun and an extremely good way to meet people. Normally it's free to play and you just pay for your drinks, but in some *tejo* courts they aren't keen on tourists turning up to play when serious games are on, so it's a good idea to ask in advance.

Bullfighting

Bullfighting, though in decline, retains a strong following in Colombia, despite opposition from animal lovers, which included an unsuccessful 2013 attempt by Bogotá's mayor to close down the local bullring. The main season is December to February, and Colombian bullfights attract matadors from as far afield as Spain, as well as local talent. Other bloodsports, such as cockfighting, are still popular informally in rural areas.

Health

Colombia is a tropical country, where germs breed fast, but it's also a country where hygiene is generally good, and most travellers who come here catch nothing more serious than a dose of the runs, if that. Defend yourself against mosquitoes, which can spread not just malaria but also dengue, zika, chikungunya and yellow fever, and make sure you're covered by a

comprehensive health insurance policy (see page 48).

There are no compulsory **vaccinations** required to enter Colombia from North America, the British Isles, Australasia or South Africa, but you should have a yellow fever vaccination certificate if entering from a neighbouring country – you may be asked to show it, especially if crossing by land, and some countries may require you to have one if arriving from Colombia. It is in any case a good idea to have a yellow fever jab, to make sure you are up-to-date with protection against tetanus and diphtheria, and to get vaccinated against Hepatitis A and typhoid, and it's worth visiting your doctor at least four weeks before you leave to check that you've had all the shots you need. It's also wise, especially if you're going to be away for a few weeks, to get a dental check-up before you leave home.

Tap **water** is chlorinated and safe to drink in big cities, slightly less so in small towns and rural areas. If in doubt, ask local residents. Bagged and bottled water is in any case widely available. If you're going far off the beaten track, you may want to take water purification tablets, or just boil your water for a few minutes before drinking it.

Diarrhoea and dysentery

Diarrhoea may just be due to your body being unfamiliar with local bacteria, but if accompanied by cramps and vomiting, it could be food poisoning of some sort. Either way, it will probably pass of its own accord in 24 to 48 hours without treatment. In the meantime, replace lost fluids by drinking plenty of water. For severe diarrhoea, and whenever young children have it, add oral rehydration salts, available at any pharmacy under the brand name Sueroral. If you can't get this, dissolve half a teaspoon of salt and three of sugar in a litre of water.

To avoid diarrhoea, make sure all food you eat is freshly cooked, keep an eye out for cleanliness on street stalls, avoid food that has been left out to breed germs, and always peel or at least wash fruit before eating it. Salads are healthy, but slightly risky, although they should be OK in clean establishments. Shellfish is also a potential risk for food poisoning, so be extra careful when eating them, especially in ceviche (raw seafood cocktail in lime juice) – only eat it if it's super-fresh.

If you do go down with the runs, avoid greasy food, heavy spices, caffeine and most fruit and dairy products; some say bananas, pawpaws or coconut water can help, while plain yogurt or a broth made from yeast extract (such as Marmite or Vegemite) can be easily absorbed by your body when you have diarrhoea. Drugs like Lomotil or Imodium plug you up – and thus undermine the body's efforts to rid itself of infection – but they can be a temporary stop-gap if you have to travel. If symptoms persist for more than three days, or if you have a fever, seek medical advice. In particular, if your diarrhoea contains blood or mucus, the cause may be dysentery or giardia. With a fever, it could be caused by bacillic dysentery, and may clear up without treatment, but similar symptoms without fever may indicate amoebic dysentery, which is more serious, and can damage your gut if untreated. The usual cure is a course of metronidazole (Flagyl), an antibiotic that may itself make you feel ill, and should not be taken with

---

YAGÉ (AYAHUASCA)

Yagé (ayahuasca), taken during shamanic ceremonies, is a blend of two ingredients: one contains the main psychoactive chemicals, while the other (the ayahuasca or *yagé* vine itself) activates them by suppressing the body's production of an enzyme called mono amine oxidase (MAO), which would otherwise break them down. But MAO protects your body from certain substances, which can become dangerously toxic in its absence. The most important of these is alcohol, which you should never take within 24 and preferably 48 hours of imbibing ayahuasca. Medicines such as anti-depressants, anti-histamines and many cold treatments can also be dangerous in combination with ayahuasca. And while some ayahuasca ceremonies are indeed conducted responsibly by genuine Indigenous shamans (regular events with large congregations are always best), there are a lot of cowboys about, and going off with such people can be dangerous. Take this seriously: in 2014 **British teenager Henry Miller died** after taking part in a ceremony of dubious authenticity near Mocoa, his body dumped by the roadside. If you do decide to take part in a shamanic ceremony, treat the process with respect – fasting may be required – and prepare for a mind-altering experience (as well as some nausea and vomiting if you don't fast beforehand).

alcohol. Similar symptoms, plus rotten-egg belches and farts, indicate giardia, for which the treatment is again metronidazole. If you suspect you may have any of these, seek medical help.

Malaria, dengue, zika and chikungunya

Malaria, caused by a parasite that lives in the saliva of female *Anopheles* mosquitoes, is endemic in some parts of Colombia. Areas above 1700m (such as the capital) are malaria-free, as are most places in the Andes such as Medellín and Cali. On the Caribbean coast, the cities of Cartagena, Barranquilla and Santa Marta are malaria-free, but surrounding areas have some degree of risk. San Andrés and Providencia are malaria-free. Really risky areas for malaria are the Pacific coast and the Amazon. For more information on malaria in Colombia, check the Centers for Disease Control and Prevention website at ⓦcdc.gov/travel/destinations/traveler/none/colombia, or the Fit for Travel website at ⓦfitfortravel.nhs.uk (click on "Destinations", then "Colombia", then "Malaria map").

If you are travelling to any part of the country where there may be malaria, you should definitely be taking **malaria prevention pills**, which you take with or after food, not on an empty stomach. The drug usually recommended for Colombia is mefloquine (Lariam), taken weekly from a week before arrival until four weeks after your return – don't forget to keep taking the pills after you get back, as malaria can linger in your body and may not become apparent for some weeks, and not finishing a course can create resistant strains. Mefloquine is quite a heavy-duty drug, which can have unpleasant side effects, and it is not recommended for everybody, so always get medical advice before taking it. Alternatives include proguanil (Atovaquone, Malarone, Paludrine), taken daily from two days before arrival until a week after returning home, or the antibiotic doxycycline, taken daily from two days before arrival until four weeks after return; again with these, always get medical advice before starting a course.

Malaria is not infectious, but can be dangerous and sometimes even fatal if not treated quickly, so you should seek medical help immediately if you experience fever, shivering and headaches. If you are somewhere really remote, where there is no doctor, and need a stop-gap treatment, and if you have not already been using it as a preventative, take 500mg of mefloquine every eight hours until you can get to a doctor.

The most important thing, obviously, is to avoid mosquito bites altogether. Though active from dusk till dawn, female *Anopheles* mosquitoes prefer to bite in the evening. Wear long sleeves, skirts or trousers, avoid dark colours, which attract mosquitoes, and put repellent on all exposed skin, especially feet and ankles, which are their favourite targets. Health departments recommend carrying brands with fifty percent **DEET**, or icaridin or PMD; you can buy these online or from travel clinics at home. Otherwise, Colombian brand Bye-Bye has 28 percent DEET plus citronella oil, but depending on where you are it is not always easy to find (branches of Farmasanitas should stock it). Another Colombian brand, Nopikex, with 23.8 percent DEET, is widely available and also comes in a kids' version with just 10 percent DEET. In mosquito-infested areas you should also sleep under a net if you can – one that hangs from a single point is best (you can usually find a way to tie a string across your room to hang it from).

Another illness spread by mosquito bites is **dengue fever**, whose symptoms are similar to those of malaria, plus a headache and aching bones. Dengue-carrying mosquitoes are particularly prevalent in urban areas and on the Caribbean coast during the rainy season, and they fly during the day, so wear insect repellent even in the daytime if mosquitoes are around. There is no drug to prevent dengue, so guarding against mosquito bites is your sole defence. The only treatment is complete rest, with drugs to assuage the fever – and take note that a second infection can be fatal. Also now present in Colombia, especially on the Caribbean coast is **chikungunya**, similar to dengue and characterized by fever, joint pain and muscle pain. Like dengue it is spread by day-biting *Aedes* mosquitoes, and like dengue, it does not respond to any known treatment, so you just have to wait for it to pass, which is usually a matter of days, but can take weeks. **Zika virus**, which can cause severe disabilities in your baby if you get it when pregnant, is also present in Colombia; again, it is spread by *Aedes* mosquitoes and the only current defence is to avoid getting bitten. Anywhere below 2000m is a risk zone.

Yellow fever

Yellow fever is another mosquito-borne viral disease, which is endemic anywhere under 2300m (so Bogotá is free of it, but not many other places are). Yellow fever can be fatal, but luckily it is rare, even in places where it is endemic. Low-lying jungle areas have the highest degree of risk.

The easiest way to protect yourself is to get a yellow fever vaccination. This was formerly considered to be valid for ten years, but is now reckoned to give life-long protection to most people. When you get your vaccination, be sure to get a certificate and carry it with you. In some countries you cannot enter without it, and Colombian immigration may well demand it if you are coming from a neighbouring country, especially by land; likewise, neighbouring countries may require it if you are arriving from Colombia, as may one or two other countries worldwide, including Australia and South Africa. If you have already had the shot but lost your certificate, or if your certificate is over ten years old (and therefore invalid), you may be able to get an exemption certificate instead of having to have the injection again. Even with the vaccination, however, your first line of defence is to guard against mosquito bites by wearing long sleeves, applying high-DEET or PMD repellent and sleeping under a net.

Symptoms of yellow fever include headache, fever, abdominal pain and vomiting, and though victims may appear to recover, without medical help they may suffer from bleeding, shock and kidney and liver failure. While you're waiting for help, it is important to keep the fever as low as possible and prevent dehydration.

Other bites and stings

Particularly in jungle areas, it's best to leave all creepy-crawlies alone and never handle them; things like ants, caterpillars and bees can give nasty stings and bites, sometimes leaving you with a day or two's fever as well. Some spider bites can even be lethal.

Colombia is home to nearly 300 species of **snake**, of which a substantial number are venomous, including over thirty species of brightly banded coral snake (*serpiente de coral*), as well as pit vipers (*víbora* or *taya equis*) and even rattlesnakes (*cascabel*). Generally, they're more afraid of you than you are of them, and they'll avoid you if you make enough noise and don't go around sticking your hand under rocks or into crevices. But many of the most venomous snakes are tiny, easily able to snuggle inside a shoe or a rucksack pocket, so always shake out hammocks and clothes, keep rucksack pockets tightly closed and take special care when it rains, as snakes, scorpions and other nasty beasties quite sensibly head for shelter in huts. If you do get bitten, remember what the snake looked like (kill it if you can do so without receiving more bites), try not to move the affected part (tourniquets are not recommended due to dangerous risk of gangrene – if you do use one, it's vital to relieve it for at least ninety seconds every fifteen minutes), and seek immediate medical help: antivenins are available in most hospitals. Sucking out the poison only works in movies, and trying to suck it out can actually make things worse.

The most venomous Colombian **scorpion** is a species called *Centruroides exilicauda*, related to the Arizona bark scorpion; its sting is extremely painful but should not be life-threatening except perhaps to small children and elderly people. Nonetheless, seek medical help immediately if stung.

Even without the aid of hostile beasties, cuts and wounds can easily get infected in tropical heat and humidity. Always clean cuts or bites with alcohol, iodine, Dettol or purified water, dry them with a clean tissue or towel, and cover them with a plaster to keep them clean, even if you would not bother to do so at home.

Altitude and heat problems

Two other common causes of health problems in Colombia are altitude and the sun. The solution in both cases is to take it easy. **Altitude sickness** (soroche) may affect travellers at altitudes over 2500m, including those flying directly to Bogotá (2640m), where you may find any activity strenuous for the first couple of days, and the thin air is made worse by the high level of air pollution. Take time to acclimatize before continuing your journey, drink plenty of water and avoid alcohol. Weakness and fatigue are common side effects so get plenty of rest within the first few days of arriving. If going to higher altitudes (mountain climbing, for example), you may develop symptoms of **Acute Mountain Sickness** (AMS), such as breathlessness, headaches, dizziness, nausea and appetite loss. More extreme cases may include vomiting, disorientation, loss of balance and coughing up of pink frothy phlegm, all of which are danger signs and can be fatal if left unheeded. A slow descent should bring immediate recovery.

Tolerance to the **sun** similarly takes a while to build up. To avoid burns, use a strong sunscreen and apply regularly. If you're walking during the day make sure you wear a hat or keep to the shade. Be sure to avoid dehydration by drinking enough (water or fruit juice rather than beer or coffee), and don't exert yourself for long periods of time in the hot sun. Be aware that overheating can cause heatstroke, which is potentially fatal. Signs are a very high body temperature without a feeling of fever, accompanied by headaches, disorientation and even irrational behaviour. Lowering body temperature (a tepid shower, for example) is the first step in treatment.

Less serious is **prickly heat**, an itchy rash that is in fact an infection of the sweat ducts caused by excessive perspiration that doesn't dry off. A cool shower, zinc oxide powder and loose cotton clothes can help.

Rabies

Rabies exists in Colombia, and the rabies vaccine is advised for anyone who will be more than 24 hours away from medical help, for example if going trekking in remote areas. Best advice is to give dogs a wide berth, and not to play with animals at all, no matter how cuddly they may look. A bite, a scratch or even a lick from an infected animal could spread the disease – as can **vampire bats**, which really do exist in Colombia, although they tend to attack livestock rather than people. These mini-Draculas are mainly to be found in the Llanos and Amazon regions, where you should never sleep uncovered for that reason. Bat bites are distinctive because bat saliva contains an anticoagulant, so wounds will continue to bleed for some time after the attack. Rabies can be fatal, so if you are bitten, assume the worst and get medical help as quickly as possible. While waiting, wash any such wound immediately but gently with soap or detergent and apply alcohol, iodine or an antiseptic if possible. If you decide to get the vaccination, you'll need three shots spread over a four-week period prior to travel.

Getting medical help

For minor medical problems, head for a **pharmacy** (*farmacia*). Pharmacists are knowledgeable and helpful, and many speak some English. Many pharmacies also have a delivery service. For more serious complaints you can get a list of English-speaking **doctors** from your government's nearest consulate. Big hotels and tourist offices may also be able to recommend medical services. Private **hospitals** in big towns are up to international standards, but treatment can be expensive – make sure you are covered by medical insurance (see p.47), and be aware that even then you may still need to pony up some cash before they'll treat you. Smaller towns and villages are far less likely to have anything in the way of medical facilities.

Medical tourism is a growing movement in Colombia, as people come for treatments and procedures which would cost a lot more at home. Typically, this is for cosmetic surgery. The US embassy in Bogotá warns that it regularly hears of American citizens dying or suffering complications from this kind of surgery in Colombia, and advises extreme caution. At the very least, always do some background research into the credentials of any practitioner you are thinking of consulting in Colombia, make sure you will have fast access to emergency care if complications arise, and check that such care will be covered by your insurance.

Crime and personal safety

Everyone knows Colombia's dangerous, right? Well actually, no. With peace deals between the government and guerrillas, and the shift of the main cocaine gangs to Mexico, most of Colombia is now safer than many other Latin American countries.

Guerrillas and bandits

The majority of **guerrilla** or paramilitary activity is now confined to rural areas near the borders with Panama and Venezuela, but plain old bandits may also operate anywhere that government control is patchy. For this reason, it's imperative that you keep your ear to the ground and avoid any areas that remain dangerous. The travel advisories put out by Western governments (see page 52) list areas to avoid, and you should stay out of them, not least because your travel insurance won't be valid. **Areas to be avoided** currently include: remote areas of the department of Chocó, plus northern Antioquia, southern Córdoba, and southern Bolívar; rural areas bordering Venezuela in Norte de Santander and the Llanos, and much of the Llanos *departamentos* of Meta, Caqueta, Vichada, Guaviare and Gainia (although these are now gradually opening up following the government's peace deal with FARC), some rural areas of Nariño and Putumayo (the *departamentos* bordering Ecuador); and one or two rural parts of western Cauca and the southwest of Valle de Cauca, including the Parque Nacional Natural Munchique.

Time was, all bus journeys were at risk of hold-ups and the danger of kidnapping for ransom was so great that any Colombian who could afford to would fly between cities rather than take the bus. Nowadays that danger has greatly diminished, and bus journeys between the main cities are safe, even at night. Buses do still get held up from time to time, however, and overnight bus travel **south of Popayán** is still best avoided.

Street crime

Street robbery is mostly of the snatch-and-grab variety, but it's also possible you'll be held up, often by jittery kids who may be armed. If somebody does rob you, don't resist: hand over what you've got with no fuss – it's only money, and not worth getting shot or knifed for. Don't carry large amounts of cash with you on the street, nor credit, debit or ATM cards (as some robbers may hold you until you've emptied your account with them), but do carry enough to pay off anyone who robs you. Be aware that robbers often work in pairs, with one to distract you while the other (possibly motorbike-borne) makes the snatch. Shoulder bags, handbags, wallets, phones and passports are all tempting targets. Always carry a **photocopy of your passport** with you (the main page and the page with your entry stamp), but unless travelling out of town, leave the original somewhere safe; most hotels have locker facilities. A **padlock** may be handy: in some cheap hotels you can secure your room with it, and hostels may have lockers for your valuables.

When using an ATM, be aware of who's around. Robbers may watch people at ATMs, calling an accomplice to tip them off that a mark is approaching. Avoid street ATMs if possible in favour of those in malls or inside banks or supermarkets. The other hotspots for robberies are bus terminals and airports – never leave your baggage unattended, and beware of deliberate distractions when you've put it down. Holiday periods in particular, when transport terminals are heaving, are top times for thieves.

It's always better to take a taxi at night in Colombian cities than to wander back to your hotel on foot, especially if you've been drinking. However, robberies involving taxi drivers are not unknown: in what's known as the *viaje de millionario* ("millionaire's ride"), the driver takes the victim to a remote place where armed accomplices rob them. In Bogotá and other big cities, it's therefore better to call a cab or take one from a taxi rank than just hail one. If you do get a cab on the street, make sure the doors can be opened from the inside, never get a cab with anyone in it other than the driver, and don't allow the driver to pick up any other passengers. You could also text someone the cab's registration number, just in case, making sure the driver sees you do it.

Con tricks tend to involve well-dressed, well-spoken Colombians approaching a foreigner on the street to befriend them for no apparent reason, or claiming to be police. They may even have fake police ID. Typically they have some spiel about wanting to check whether your money is counterfeit, or needing to check your immigration status. They may even be joined by an accomplice who will also claim to be police. In fact, undercover police are not authorized to stop and check tourists for currency, ID or immigration status, and no plain-clothes police officer should ever approach you in the street about such things. In any such case, you can insist on going to the nearest police station (this works best if you actually know where it is). Alternatively, if you can speak enough Spanish, pull out your phone and call the police to check. Another tactic is to walk away from them into view of a CCTV camera belonging to a nearby shop or business premises, which your fake cop will obviously be anxious to avoid.

THE ART OF NOT GIVING PAPAYA

One thing you don't want to do in Colombia is to **dar papaya** – "give pawpaw" or, less literally, "be asking for it". What it means is not to draw attention to yourself. If you wander down the street with your wallet sticking out of your back pocket, or flash your cash in a bar, or go off to buy cocaine with some guy you just met on the street, you are *dando papaya* and likely to be taken advantage of.

Avoid street moneychangers: there is no black market currency rate in Colombia so anyone offering you an enhanced rate of exchange is setting you up for a con or a robbery. Ditto for anyone offering emeralds at amazing prices. Counterfeit notes are common, and it's always worth checking the watermark and metal strip are there (you can even buy counterfeit-detector pens). Someone spraying dirt on your shoes or clothes may be distracting you for a robbery – be on your guard immediately if this happens, especially if the person then turns round and offers to help you clean it up.

Finally, much though you may fancy an aimless stroll around town, many cities have areas of high crime that outsiders avoid, and which you don't want to wander into unawares. Know therefore where you're going, be aware of which parts of town are unsafe, and don't wander aimlessly into neighbourhoods you don't know.

Spiking

A drug called **burundanga** (scopolamine) – extracted from the *Brugmansia* or devil's trumpet tree, which is widely grown for its beautiful flowers – is sometimes used to incapacitate victims to rob or rape them.

Burundanga is tasteless and odourless and can be added to drinks or cigarettes, its precise **effects** vary depending on the dose and the person, but it leaves the victim insensible, and it appears to make them completely suggestible – some accounts tell of victims being taken to an ATM and told to withdraw money, and complying. The drug also leaves you with memory loss, and overdose can be fatal. The solution: never accept drinks, sweets, chewing gum or cigarettes from strangers or new friends, especially if you are on your own, and never leave drinks unattended in a bar. If you start to feel dizzy or disorientated for no apparent reason, especially if accompanied by sudden dryness of the mouth, try to alert people around you. Drunken male tourists going off with groups of attractive young Colombian women are frequent victims, and prostitutes in particular have been known to spike their punters.

Police and army

Colombian **police** have a mixed reputation for corruption, but Policía Nacional officers are generally conscientious and extremely helpful to tourists, and special tourist police exist in some cities and resorts. Police do not usually put the bite on foreigners. Police and army personnel at **road checkpoints** really are concerned with security, and you should always be polite, patient and respectful to them. They may ask for ID, which it is illegal not to carry. In town, you can carry a photocopy of the main page and entry stamp in your passport; on intercity journeys, have your actual passport about your person to show if necessary. In particular, soldiers at checkpoints on the road between Popayán and Ipiales, close to the Venezuelan border and all along the coast may well ask for ID, and may take you off the bus and fine you or even arrest you if you don't have it.

If you get robbed, you'll need to go to the local police station and report the crime. The police will take down your report of the crime (called a *denuncia*) and give you a copy, which you'll need for insurance and other purposes (as ID, for example, if your passport has been stolen). The report should list every item you have lost, and you should check that it is absolutely accurate before you sign it.

Drugs

Cocaine, heroin and marijuana are all **illegal**, and even though you cannot actually be prosecuted for possessing a personal amount (this is not fixed, but it used to be up to a gram of cocaine or twenty of marijuana), you'll still get trouble if caught with any. Dealers often set up their punters for extortion by corrupt police, and honest police may search you if they think you have some. **Airports** are full of sniffer dogs and X-ray machines, passengers are thoroughly checked, and attempting to export any illegal drug is a trafficking offence carrying a penalty of at least five years in jail. Importing undeclared money (which dogs can also sniff) is likewise a criminal offence if it exceeds US$10,000. **Prisons** in Colombia are not pleasant, and even after release you may be prohibited from leaving the country while on parole. All in all, it's really not worth the risk.

Aside from the law, there is an ethical reason not to buy illegal drugs: money from their sales fuels criminal gangs and paramilitary groups, and deforestation from coca, opium and even marijuana plantations is a growing problem. Add to that the massive environmental damage caused by cocaine laboratories spilling chemicals such as sulphuric acid and kerosene onto the countryside and into rivers, let alone the herbicides sprayed on plantation areas by law enforcement agencies, and it's clear that buying cocaine in particular is not only bad for you but it's also bad for the local people, the economy and the environment.

Cocaine in Colombia will be stronger than at home but could possibly be cut with things such as levamisole, a veterinary de-worming drug with potentially nasty side effects. Even nastier is **basuco**, a paste of semi-refined cocaine, full of solvents and other unpleasant chemicals from the refining process, which has become a ghetto drug in much of Latin America; smoked rather than snorted, it's as addictive as crack, and even more harmful to the body.

On the other hand, the **coca leaf** from which the drug is derived, in its natural form, is neither harmful nor illegal (although it is a controlled drug in most Western countries). Used by pretty much all of Colombia's Indigenous peoples since time immemorial, it is grown for this kind of traditional use in small patches, and taken with a little bit of alkaline ash to stimulate salivation. Rather than really chewing it as such, people take a quid of it, put a dab of ash on, crush it into a ball (*bola*), and push it into the side of their mouths, letting it gradually dissolve over some hours, with just a little chew every so often to help it along. Its effects are subtle, but it heightens alertness, suppresses appetite and keeps you going at work in high altitudes, creating a mildly pleasant numb feeling in the back of your throat. It is also commonly drunk as a tea.

In these days of skunk-type crossbreeds, the **marijuana** of Colombia can be less potent than that of British Columbia, or even Britain, but it's still strong and widely available, even if classic Colombian varieties such as Santa Marta's famous *punta roja* ("red spot") are less renowned than they once were.

Opium is also produced in Colombia, but appears on the street only as heroin. Some tourists try the psychedelic jungle brew **ayahuasca** (*yagé*), which is legal, but does have certain potential hazards (see page 39).

Culture and etiquette

Colombians are generally formal and courteous, and it's a good idea to follow suit. Colombia is also a deeply religious country and it's wise to avoid open disrespect of religion.

Colombian Spanish is quite formal. It's normal to address people as *señor* or *señora*, and to use the polite third-person form of "you" (*usted*), although that is changing.

Men shake hands when they meet; women exchange a peck on the right cheek. Men and women do not normally exchange kisses unless they know each other, so it's safest to stick to a handshake unless the other party offers a kiss. Colombians appreciate a firm handshake and a friendly smile. Sincerity in expression, often expressed via good eye contact, is valued more highly than the typical Western stream of pleases and thank-yous. When you meet someone for the first time, the thing to say is *"Mucho gusto"* (basically, "A pleasure to meet you").

As elsewhere in South America, used toilet paper is never flushed, but put into a bin next to the toilet. This is to avoid blocked drains, but it takes some getting used to. It's also a good idea to carry some with you, as not all public toilets supply it.

Sex and gender issues

Although in some ways quite progressive (around a third of politicians and diplomats are female, for example, which puts most Western countries in the shade), Colombia can be very old-fashioned when it comes to relations between the sexes. A lot of this takes the form of chivalry; men tend to open doors for women, let them go first in queues and give up seats on public transport.

Women travellers

Women travelling in Colombia, especially if young, can expect a certain amount of cat-calling from men in the street. The best thing to do is to ignore it. Be aware also that accepting a drink from a man, or even chatting to him, may be construed as a come-on for sex. You'll probably get less hassle if you dress modestly, and of course a wedding ring helps (even wearing a cross round your neck can make people think you're chaste), but isn't foolproof.

On a more practical level, contraceptives and tampons may be hard to find outside of the main cities, so it's a good idea to have some with you.

Male travellers

Male tourists should conversely be aware that chatting to women may be interpreted as hitting on them, not only by the woman in question, but also by her jealous, macho boyfriend. In a nightclub, couples dance together and properly; dancing freestyle on your own is unusual.

LGBTQ+ travellers

Since same-gender sex was legalized in 1981, Colombia has become one of Latin America's most gay-friendly countries. Same-sex marriage became legal in 2013, and most large cities – Bogotá in particular – have a thriving gay scene. Gay characters also now feature regularly in Colombia's kitschy TV soap operas, and the age of consent has been fixed at 14 regardless of sex or gender. Unfortunately, that is not to say that homophobia has disappeared completely: lesbians, gay men, and in particular trans sex workers still get attacked with sickening regularity, extreme right-wing groups put sexual minorities in with street children, sex workers and vagrants as targets for "social cleansing", no laws ban discrimination in housing or employment, and same-sex couples still don't feel safe enough to kiss or hold hands in public. Small-town Colombia in particular remains very conservative in its attitudes towards homosexuality.

You'll find LGBTQ+ scenes in Bogotá, Medellín, Cali and Cartagena. In Bogotá, gay bars and nightspots are concentrated in Chapinero. Some hotels are now starting to declare themselves as gay-friendly, and with tourism of all varieties on the rise, businesses would of course be foolish to miss out on the tourist 'pink peso'.

ONLINE LGBTQ+ INFORMATION

Colombia Diversa ⓦ colombiadiversa.org. The country's main LGBTQ+ rights organization.
EgoCity Magazine ⓦ egocitymgz.com. Online gay mag, with LGBTQ+ news, and listings for Bogotá and Medellín, in Spanish.
International Gay & Lesbian Human Rights Commission ⓦ outrightinternational.org. International LGBTQ+ rights organization with information on Colombia.

Tipping

In **restaurants**, a 10–15 percent **tip** (*propina*) is the norm. Some establishments will ask you if you'd like a tip to be included when you ask for the bill (this is called a *propina voluntaria*), while some add it on automatically, but not all pass it on to the staff, so you may want to opt out of the service charge and give your tip directly to the waiter or waitress, or just give them a bit extra anyway, with a "gracias" to let them know it's because you appreciate their service. In cheap diners, you're not expected to tip, but nobody will object if you do. In a café or bar, you can just round up the bill to the nearest thousand pesos.

In **hotels**, porters, doormen and bellhops get a tip of C$2000–5000. Chambermaids might get around the same for each day you stay, but you should give it to them directly rather than leave it in the room, as many hotels prohibit chambermaids from picking up any money from a room, even if it's clearly a tip.

Taxi drivers don't expect a tip but always appreciate one. For short taxi trips, you can round up the fare to the next thousand pesos. The guys loading baggage into the boot at airports expect a small tip of C$1000 or so. Hairdressers typically get a ten percent tip, as do tour guides.

Shopping

Crafts in Colombia may not be quite the snip they are in Peru, Bolivia or Ecuador, but they can be better quality and you'll certainly run across plenty of things you'll want to buy. Haggling is not widespread, but prices are to a certain extent negotiable in markets and other informal shopping locales.

Clothing and textiles

The Colombian garment par excellence is a shortish woollen poncho called a **ruana**. You'll see people of both sexes wearing these all over the place, in styles traditional and modern. The most traditional variety comes from Boyacá, where it's handmade by Indigenous families. Antioquian *ruanas* are simpler and more sombre in colour, while the striking red- or pink-edged blue *ruanas* worn by the Guambiano people of Cauca can be found, among other places, at the market in Silvia (see page 276).

Another super-Colombian piece of apparel is the **sombrero vueltiao**, Colombia's national hat, made from a local grass fibre called *caña flecha* (arrow cane, also known as wild cane or *caña brava*). The hat originates with the Zenú people of Córdoba and can be bought in Valledupar (see page 181), but today you'll find it sold nationwide.

Molas are colourful reverse-appliqué cloth panels, originally made to decorate the front and back of blouses worn by Guna women of the Colombia/Panama border region. Nowadays they are very popular tourist souvenirs, sold as wall hangings. In principle, the most authentic *molas* are ones which Guna women have worn as clothes and then sold off when the original garment gets worn out.

Hammocks are very popular, made of cotton and usually multicoloured. The most interesting is the *chinchorro*, made by the *Wayuu* people of La Guajira, which has a more open weave and is traditionally made in natural colours of brown, cream and grey. The Wayuu also make woven bags called **susus**, which are sold along the beachfront in Riohacha.

Musical instruments

The twelve-string Colombian guitar known as a **tiple** might appeal to serious musicians, but it's hardly a casual souvenir. Along with the six-string **bandola**, these are most associated with the town of Chiquinquirá in Boyacá.

Woodwork

In Pasto, woodwork is laquered with layers of a resin (*barniz*) extracted from the seeds of the mopa-mopa tree. Nowadays the seeds are crushed by machine, but at one time people had to chew them up to extract the resin, which is then coloured and stretched into thin sheets, cut into shape and applied to the wood. Chiquinquirá in Boyacá produces **tagua**, the "vegetable ivory" made from the seed of a palm tree (called an ivory palm) which grows in the forest.

Coffee and cigarettes

Colombian **coffee** is world famous and you'll surely be wanting to take some home if you visit a coffee farm. Even if not, it's worth popping into a supermarket for some before you leave. Also, if you haven't graduated onto e-cigs, you may want to know that Colombia's Pielroja **cigarettes** contain unfiltered tobacco with no artificial flavouring. Note that they are not sold at airport duty-free shops.

Emeralds and gold

Colombia is the best country in the world to buy **emeralds**, and the easiest in which to get ripped off buying them. The main emerald market is around Avenida Jiménez in Bogotá (see page 82). The most expensive emeralds, with a prized dark green colour, retail for as much as US$10,000 per carat, or more. Lighter-coloured ones go for around US$200 per carat. You can also buy non-gem-quality emeralds quite cheaply. Bogotá is a particularly good spot for buying emeralds as most of them are mined nearby.

More than a few people come looking for emeralds as an investment. This might be possible – *if* you can tell whether a gem is high or low quality, *if* you can tell whether it's real or fake, *if* you can tell whether or not it's been heat-treated to disguise its flaws, *if* you can look at a stone through a magnifying glass and tell how much it's worth, and *if* you have connections at home to sell emeralds at a good price as well as reliable connections in Colombia to buy them from: if all those things are true, then you can turn a profit (although legally, of course, you have to pay duty on them). On the other hand, if you know nothing about gemstones, then steer well clear. Sharks abound, and in these waters an amateur will be eaten for lunch.

Gold can be a good buy in Colombia – Mompox (see page 154) in particular is known for its fine gold and silver filigree work. For gold, as for emeralds, you may be required when leaving the country to show proof that you bought it legally.

Travel essentials

Accessible travel

Colombia is making some progress on **accessibility**, but it's slow. Meanwhile, ordinary Colombians are generally helpful and understanding of disability, especially as many people have serious disabilities due to injuries sustained from landmines or in the country's dark years of trouble and civil war.

A 2013 Disability Act bans discrimination and obliges local authorities to consider citizens with disabilities in their development plans, while TV stations have to provide subtitles or signing for people with impaired hearing, although of course it's Colombian signing and the subtitles are in Spanish. Aside from that, Colombia is hard going if you have restricted mobility, and especially if you're in a chair. Sidewalks are narrow and bumpy, and you'll rarely find ramps at intersections, while cafés, restaurants and hostels with wheelchair access are thin on the ground. And you'll be very lucky to find any information signs in Braille. This is just starting to change. Increasingly, public buildings have ramps (most hospitals, for example), and new ones must do by law, but it will be a fair while before all public buildings are properly accessible.

Few small hotels or hostels are wheelchair accessible, and if you use a chair, you may well have to resort to upmarket hotels, a number of which now have specially adapted rooms. LateRooms.com (W laterooms.com) allows you to screen its hotels for accessibility – when you get the list of hotels in Colombia or a specific town, check "Adapted for people with reduced mobility" under "Facilities" in the left-hand bar. Some restaurants are now taking steps to improve access, but they remain a minority. Ordinary buses are not very accessible and you may well need help boarding and disembarking. New city transport systems are properly accessible however, including Medellín's Metro system and Bogotá's Trans-Milenio buses. Bogotá now has a bar run by and for deaf people (see page 81).

Because the return of tourism to Colombia is so new, many operators specializing in accessible travel do not as yet cover the country. The company Evaneos has information about the progress to date and a number of up to date, online resources to help with planning a trip (W evaneos.com/colombia). The national organization for blind people is the Instituto Nacional Para Ciegos (W inci.gov.co), and for deaf people it's the Federación Nacional de Sordos de Colombia (W fenascol.org.co).

Costs

If you stay only in hostel dorms, eat cheap breakfasts, stick to cheap lunchtime set menus, use only public transport in cities, and don't travel around too much between them, you can get by on C$150,000 (£20/US$30/€23) a day, although C$250,000 (£38/US$52/€43) would give you more waggle room. Double that and you could stay in a modest hotel, eat a reasonably priced but decent meal every day and travel around town by taxi rather than by bus or on foot. If, on the other hand, you want to stay in a good hotel, eat well, fly when you have a long distance to cover, and buy any souvenirs you've a mind to, then you'd need to be budgeting for something more like C$900,000 (£125/US$175/€150) a day. All in all, expect to be paying less than you'd pay in Europe or North America, slightly less than in Brazil, but slightly more than you'd be paying in, say, Ecuador or Peru.

Electricity

The supply is 110v 60Hz. Sockets have two flat pins, as in North America. Adaptors that will take European or Brazilian (two round pin) plugs are easy to find, but adaptors that take British, Irish and Australasian plugs are less easy to come by, and best brought from home, although they do exist in Colombia: branches of the stationery chain Panamericana (W panamericana.com.co) often stock them; otherwise, the area around the junction of Calle 14 and Carrera 13 in Bogotá is a good place to look. Appliances designed for a 220v or 240v supply may need a transformer.

Insurance

It's frankly reckless to travel without insurance cover. Home insurance policies occasionally cover your possessions when overseas, and some private medical schemes include cover when abroad. Bank and credit cards often have certain levels of medical or other insurance included and you may automatically get travel insurance if you use a major credit card to pay for your trip. Otherwise, you should contact a specialist travel insurance company. A typical travel insurance policy usually provides cover for the loss of baggage, tickets and – up to a certain limit – cash or cheques, as well as cancellation or curtailment of your journey. Most of them exclude so-called dangerous sports unless an extra premium is paid: in Colombia this could include mountaineering, scuba diving, caving and even whitewater rafting. For medical coverage, check whether benefits will be paid as treatment proceeds or only after returning home, and whether there is a 24-hour medical emergency number. When securing baggage cover, make sure that the per-article limit – typically under £700/US$1000 – will cover your most valuable possessions. If you need to make a claim, you should keep receipts for medicines and medical treatment, and in the event you have anything stolen, you must obtain an official crime report (*denuncia*) from the police (see page 44).

Internet

Wi-fi zones aren't exactly thick on the ground but are gradually becoming more widespread and most hotels and hostels have wi-fi, usually free to guests. An increasing number of bars and restaurants now have wi-fi, and occasionally shopping malls and even city squares may have it, as may some long-distance buses. Internet cafés can be found even in small towns, usually charging around C$1500/hr, and often offering cheap international phone calls as well, plus computer services such as scanning and printing.

Laundry

Most hotels and even hostels provide a pricey laundry service (always check the cost in advance). If you're staying for a while, it may be best to come to a private arrangement with one of the cleaning staff, giving better rates for both of you. Laundries (*lavandería*) and dry cleaners (*tintorería*) are not hard to come by, especially in big cities, but coin-operated machine laundromats are unusual. Normally you leave your washing, they do a service wash, and you pick it up later. Some places charge by the item (*por prenda*), others by weight (*por kilo*) – by weight is invariably cheaper. Prices are typically around C$5000 per kg. Cheapest of all is to wash it yourself, although you'll need a place to dry it, and some hotels specifically prohibit doing laundry in your room.

Living in Colombia

There are three main ways to stay in Colombia for longer than your tourist visa: you can teach, study, or volunteer for an NGO project.

The obvious thing to **teach** is English, and for that you will certainly need a TEFL or TESOL qualification. Pay is not great, but you may be able to supplement it with private classes. Your school will have to organize a work visa for you, and you will need to get a foreigners' ID card (*Cédula de Extranjería*).

The obvious thing to **study** is Spanish. A number of universities and language schools run courses, particularly in Bogotá and Cartagena. Nueva Lengua (wnuevalengua.com) offers a variety of general and specialist courses in Bogotá, Cartagena and Medellín. Contact details for schools offering Spanish courses are given in the Directory sections in this Guide for Bogotá (see page 83), San Gill (see page 110), and Medellín (see page 224).

Volunteering is another possibility, and a number of NGOs based in Western countries or in Colombia itself (see below) are recruiting volunteers for a number of projects, often to do with helping communities

---

ROUGH GUIDES TRAVEL INSURANCE

Looking for travel insurance? Rough Guides partners with top providers worldwide to offer you the best coverage. Policies are available to residents of anywhere in the world, with a range of options whether you are looking for single-trip, multi-country or long-stay insurance. There's coverage for a wide range of adventure sports, 24-hour emergency assistance, high levels of medical and evacuation cover and a stream of travel safety information. Even better, wroughguides.com users can take advantage of these policies online 24/7, from anywhere in the world – even if you're already travelling. To make the most of your travels and ensure a smoother experience, it's always good to be prepared for when things don't go according to plan. For more information go to wroughguides.com/bookings/insurance.

recover from the damage done during the periods of trouble and civil war.

STUDY, WORK AND VOLUNTEER PROGRAMMES

AFS Intercultural Programs W afs.org. Intercultural exchange organization with programmes in more than fifty countries, including Colombia (W afs.org.co).
Globalteer W globalteer.org. Volunteer group running a children's care home in Medellín, taking paying volunteers.
Goals for Peace W golesporlapaz.org. Project run in association with the *Kasa Guane* hostel in Bucaramanga which takes volunteers for short or long periods (see page 115).
Healing Colombia W healingcolombia.org. Takes volunteers in projects to help underprivileged and disabled kids.
United Planet W unitedplanet.org. Places volunteers in a variety of Colombian projects.

Maps

A number of firms produce **maps** of Colombia that are available in travel bookshops abroad. Nelles Verlag, for example, produces a two-sided **road map** of Colombia and Ecuador on a scale of 1:2,500,000, with insets for, among others, Bogotá, Medellín and Cartagena, while Freytag-Berndt do one of Colombia, also double-sided, at 1:1,000,000, and the International Travel Maps *Colombia* map is on 1:1,400,000 with insets for Bogotá, Medellín and Cartagena. For practical purposes, however, the best road maps are produced by ITMB and Reise Know-How, both on a scale of 1:1,400,000, clearly laid out, and printed on waterproof, tear-proof plastic instead of paper.

In Colombia itself, the Instituto Geográfico Agustín Codazzi (IGAC; W igac.gov.co) publishes maps of most cities and *departamentos*, and also a *Guía de Rutas*. Available at any good bookshop, this is basically a **road atlas** of Colombia, although based on routes between specific cities rather than being divided into two-page rectangles of territory like a conventional road atlas. IGAC also has a number of maps on its website.

Media

For all its instability and upheavals, Colombia has a strong and robust tradition of **press freedom**, and as befits a country with 94-percent literacy, a wide range of newspapers and magazines, almost all in Spanish. Note however, that although the press is in principle free, and papers express a wide range of views, press owners tend to be closely tied to political interests – indeed, some are active politicians. But this is not limited to Colombia and is the case in many countries.

Colombian **newspapers** tend to be regional rather than national. The paper with the biggest circulation is Bogotá's *El Tiempo* (W eltiempo.com), which has been going since 1911 and is generally regarded as being in the centre politically. Also from Bogotá, and even older than *El Tiempo*, is *El Espectador* (W elespectador.com), founded in 1887, which prides itself in being politically independent. Both *El Tiempo* and *El Espectador* are available nationwide.

Foreign newspapers are not so easy to come by, but there are a couple of local English-language publications. The main English-language journal is Bogotá's *The City Paper* (W thecitypaperbogota.com), published monthly.

Colombia's main **talk-radio** station is Caracol Radio (W caracol.com.co), which broadcasts in Spanish, obviously. The BBC World Service (W bbc.co.uk/worldserviceradio) and the Voice of America (W voanews.com) do not broadcast in English to South America, so the only way to listen to them is online.

The five national **television** channels are supplemented by a number of local stations. Caracol TV and RCN TV are the main commercial networks, specializing in soap operas (*telenovelas*). The main state-owned channel is *Señal Colombia*, which puts out a selection of cultural programming. Any reasonably sized hotel will have satellite TV with CNN, the BBC and other international English-language broadcasters.

Money

Colombia's **currency** is the **peso**, originally divided into 100 centavos, although you won't see any centavos nowadays. Coins are for 50, 100, 200, 500 and 1000 pesos, and notes for 1000, 2000, 5000, 10,000, 20,000 and 50,000 pesos. Changing large banknotes can be problematic outside the big cities, so it's a good idea to keep cash in smallish denominations if possible. Like most Latin American currencies, Colombian pesos use the dollar sign ($), sometimes given as C$, Col$ or COP to distinguish it from the US dollar and other non-Colombian monetary units. We denote it as C$ throughout the Guide.

Cash and plastic

ATMs are plentiful, with at least one even in the smallest of towns. Some have quite a low single-withdrawal limit, and many only allow as little as C$300,000 (£60/US$75), which can make withdrawals expensive if your bank levies a transaction charge. Other banks allow more: Bancolombia machines allow up to C$600,000, for example, and some Citibank machines will dispense up to C$1,000,000. You can also change cash in a bank, but it can be time-consuming. Where they exist, independent **moneychangers** (*casas de cambio*) offer better rates, have more flexible hours and provide a faster service than banks. There is no black market for foreign currency in Colombia and anybody offering to change cash on the street is almost certainly trying to work a scam on you.

Opening hours and public holidays

Business hours are Monday to Friday from 8am until 6pm. Many businesses also often open on Saturdays until mid-afternoon. Shops typically open the same hours but stay open all day on Saturdays. Outside of Bogotá, many businesses close at noon for a two- or three-hour siesta. Commercial hours in cities in warmer areas such as Cali may start and end earlier. Banks open around 9am to 4pm; *casas de cambio* stay open later.

Most **public holidays** in Colombia are Roman Catholic religious celebrations, some of which are moveable, which is to say that when they occur depends on the date of Easter. Holy Week, the week running up to Easter Sunday, called Semana Santa in Spanish, is a popular holiday period, which many people take off work and try to be with their families. Easter Monday is not a public holiday, but the Thursday and Friday of Holy Week (Maundy Thursday and Good Friday) are. Otherwise Mondays are favoured for public holidays. Thus the Feast of Ascension, Corpus Christi and Sacred Heart Day are held, respectively, six, nine and ten weeks after Easter Monday. Many other celebrations, if they do not actually fall on a Monday, are celebrated as public holidays on the Monday immediately following, making a long weekend known as a *puente*.

Phones

Public **phone offices** (*telecentros*), with cabins to make domestic or international calls, are common throughout Colombia, but prices vary a lot, so it may be worth shopping around. Most internet cafés also have telephone facilities, and kiosks selling top-up minutes for mobile phones will also usually let you make calls. With the proliferation of free wi-fi, Skype is often now the most economical way to call.

If you have a phone that will work in Colombia, it's cheap and easy to buy a **SIM card** from one of the country's mobile phone service providers, Tigo (Wtigo.com.co), Movistar (Wmovistar.co) and Claro (Wclaro.com.co). Claro generally has the best coverage. Note however that dual band phones from Britain or Australasia will not work in Colombia, even with a local SIM card. A GSM-enabled phone from North America should work, as will any quadri-band phone and most tri-band phones. Cheap local handsets are in any case widely available. Note, however, that it will usually cost you less to call from a public phone office or a street stall than from your own mobile handset. Indeed, street sellers adver-

PUBLIC HOLIDAYS

Jan 1 New Year's Day (Año Nuevo)
Jan 6* Epiphany/Twelfth Night (Día de los Reyes Magos)
March 19* St Joseph's Day (Father's Day)
March or April Maundy Thursday (Jueves Santo)
March or April Good Friday (Viernes Santo)
May 1 Labour Day (Día del Trabajo)
May Ascension (Ascensión del Señor)
May or June Corpus Christi
May or June Sacred Heart (Sagrado Corazón)
June 29* Saint Peter and Saint Paul (San Pedro y San Pablo)
July 20 Independence Day (Declaración de la Independencia)
Aug 7 Battle of Boyacá
Aug 15* Assumption of the Virgin Mary (Asunción de la Virgen)
Oct 12* Columbus Day (Día de la Raza)
Nov 1* All Saints' Day (Día de Todos los Santos)
Nov 11* Independence of Cartagena
Dec 8 Immaculate Conception (Inmaculada Concepción)
Dec 25 Christmas Day (Navidad)
* If the day itself is not a Monday, the public holiday is on the Monday following

USEFUL TELEPHONE NUMBERS

EMERGENCIES AND INFORMATION
General emergency ☎123
Ambulance ☎125
Red Cross ☎132
Police ☎112
Highway Police ☎127
Fire ☎119
Directory enquiries ☎113
International operator ☎159

INTERNATIONAL CALLS
Omit the initial zero from the area code when dialling the UK, Ireland, Australia, New Zealand or South Africa.

	From Colombia	To Colombia
Australia	☎00 + carrier code + 61	☎0011 57
Ireland	☎00 + carrier code + 353	☎00 57
New Zealand	☎00 + carrier code + 64	☎00 57
South Africa	☎00 + carrier code + 27	☎09 57
UK	☎00 + carrier code + 44	☎00 57
US and Canada	☎00 + carrier code + 1	☎011 57

tising "*minutos*" (phone minutes) are invariably the cheapest way to make most calls, and certainly to any Colombian mobile phone.

When calling from abroad, the international country code for Colombia is 57. To call a Colombian landline from abroad, dial the international access code (00 from the UK, for example), followed by the single-digit Colombian area code (1 for Bogotá, for example) and the seven-digit landline number. To call a Colombian mobile, dial the access code, followed by 57, and then the ten-digit cellphone number, which will start with a 3.

To call abroad from Colombia, you start by dialling 00. If you are happy to use the main national phone company, Telecom, you then just dial your country code (44 to the UK, for example) and the number (in some cases omitting any initial zeros in the area code). If you want to use a different firm (which may be cheaper), you need to add their carrier code after the 00 (5 for UNE, 7 for ETB, 9 for Movistar, 414 for Tigo). Similarly, to make a long-distance call within Colombia, you dial 0, then the carrier code if desired, then the single-digit area code (1 for Bogotá, etc) and the seven-digit landline number. To call a landline from a mobile, dial 03, then the single-digit area code, and then the seven-digit landline number. To call a mobile from a landline, dial 03 and then the ten-digit mobile number. Remember to check your call rates and any additional charges before making international calls.

Post

You can send a letter abroad from almost anywhere in the country, using the 4-72 **post offices** (generally Mon–Fri 8am–noon & 2–5pm, Sat 8am–noon). Note that street post boxes have now disappeared from Colombia, so to mail a letter you have to take it to the nearest 4-72 office or to their local agent. A postcard costs less than a letter – C$4000 to most parts of the world – but not all offices seem aware of this. Letters take around ten days to the USA, two to four weeks to the rest of the world. Packages are best sent via private firms such as Deprisa (W deprisa.com), or with FedEx (W fedex.com/co) or DHL (W dhl.com.co).

Time

Colombia is on GMT–5 year-round, with **no seasonal change** for daylight saving.

Tourist information

Colombia's **tourist office** (W colombia.travel/en) operates information offices (Puntos de Información Turística, or PiTs), marked with a distinctive red "i" sign, in almost every town, although their staff don't always speak English. You'll find the contact details for PiTs listed individually in the relevant chapters of this Guide, and you can find their locations nationwide at W pitscolombia.com.co. Although guerrilla insurgen-

TOP 5 CHILDREN'S ATTRACTIONS

Acualago water park See page 117
Fossil museum See page 97
Parque Explora See page 217
Parque Nacional del Café See page 242
Parque Nacional del Chicamocha See page 113

cies, cocaine trade turf wars and potential instability are all calming down, it is still a good idea before heading out to check the travel advisory web pages maintained by Western governments.

ONLINE INFORMATION

Central Intelligence Agency Ⓦ cia.gov/the-world-factbook/countries/colombia/summaries The CIA's spooky stats on Colombia.
Colombia Reports Ⓦ colombiareports.com. Latest news, sports, culture and travel in English.
Colombia SA Ⓦ colombia-sa.com. Geographic, topographic and cultural information.
Colombia Travel Ⓦ colombia.travel/en. Colombia's official tourist information site.
Expat Chronicles Ⓦ expat-chronicles.com/category/colombia. Excellent Colombia tales in this American expat's blog.
Parques Nacionales Naturales de Colombia
Ⓦ parquesnacionales.gov.co. Portal to Colombia's national parks.

GOVERNMENT TRAVEL ADVISORIES

Australian Department of Foreign Affairs
Ⓦ smartraveller.gov.au
British Foreign & Commonwealth Office Ⓦ gov.uk/foreign-travel-advice/colombia
Canadian Department of Foreign Affairs Ⓦ travel.gc.ca/destinations/colombia
Irish Department of Foreign Affairs Ⓦ dfa.ie/travel/travel-advice
US State Department Ⓦ travel.state.gov

Travelling with children

Colombians normally travel *en famille*, and hotels usually make allowances for this. Most large and even medium-sized hotels will have facilities for **children**, including playgrounds and paddling pools, although a crèche will be less common. You can usually have a child's bed placed in a double room for not very much extra.

On long-distance buses, children pay the full fare, but on *busetas* and *colectivos* you can usually take a small child on your lap without payment. Some restaurants offer child portions or even children's set meals, and some may even have a highchair available. Baby milk and disposable nappies (diapers) are widely available in supermarkets and pharmacies. It's OK to breast-feed a child in public in Colombia, although wealthier Colombian women don't do it.

Be aware that health risks such as sunburn or diarrhoea, a minor inconvenience perhaps to an adult, can be dangerous to a small child. Don't forget to tell them about rabies and warn them not to play with animals. It's a good idea to travel with a few sachets of rehydration salts (see page 39) in case of diarrhoea.

Bogotá

- 58 La Candelaria
- 65 City centre
- 69 La Macarena
- 70 North Bogotá

VIEW OF BOGOTÁ

Bogotá

Colombia's capital is a city that divides opinion. Its detractors cite poverty, gridlocked traffic and crime, as well as depressingly regular rain, and with over eight million tightly packed inhabitants and some decidedly drab neighbourhoods, Bogotá rarely elicits love at first sight. Given a day or two, however, most people do fall for this cosmopolitan city with its colonial architecture, numerous restaurants and raucous nightlife. In any case, love it or hate it, odds are you'll have to pass through it at some stage during your travels in Colombia.

Bogotá is bounded on its western side by the Río Bogotá, and to its east by the **Cerro de Monserrate**, a mountain ridge topped by a church that can be seen from pretty much anywhere in town, making it a very useful landmark. Thus constricted (although seeping out beyond its traditional boundary on the west side), the city's expansion has largely been to the north and south. The southern end of town consists of down-at-heel *barrios* largely inhabited by people who've come in from the countryside seeking work. To the north by contrast, Bogotá has swallowed up former satellite towns that have now become pleasant uptown neighbourhoods such as **Chapinero** – fresh and hilly, full of trendy cafés, and home to the city's epicentre of gourmet dining, the "**Zona G**". At the far northern end of town, **Usaquén**, formerly a village and indigenous reserve, is now a posh suburb with a popular Sunday market. The city's oldest neighbourhood, **La Candelaria**, lies at what was once the junction of two rivers, the Río San Agustín (which now runs under Calle 7), and the Río San Francisco, which still flows through the centre of town to this day, in a channel down Avenida Jiménez. La Candelaria is home to some of South America's most impressive colonial buildings, and is the neighbourhood where most tourists – and certainly most backpackers – choose to stay. The downtown **city centre**, though more modern than La Candelaria, gives the impression of having gone slightly to seed, and is nowadays to a large extent upstaged as a commercial and business district by smarter uptown neighbourhoods such as the **Zona Rosa**. The city's nightlife zone, Zona Rosa positively heaves with clubs and restaurants, which only really comes to life after nightfall. All over town, one thing you'll notice is the vibrant and colourful graffiti and street art, a result of the city's liberal attitude to graffiti, which has made it a mecca for street artists from around the world.

Situated on the Sabana de Bogotá, Colombia's highest plateau and 2600m up in the Andes, Bogotá can be cold and wet year-round. March to May and September to November are the wettest periods, while late December through January is the sunniest time of year.

Brief history

Bogotá started life as Bacatá, seat of the Zipa, supreme chief of the **Muisca** people's southern confederation (see page 99). After defeating the Muiscas in battle in 1538, the Spanish Conquistador **Gonzalo Jiménez de Quesada** founded today's city, calling it Santa Fe de Bogotá, or just **Santa Fe**. In 1550, it was made capital of New Granada, and – with its name trimmed to just plain Bogotá – it remained the capital of Gran Colombia after independence in 1819, when its population was around 30,000.

In 1884, Bogotá got a **tram** system, which really helped draw it together. The trams ran until 1948, by which time the city had around half a million residents. That year saw the assassination of the massively popular Liberal Party leader **Jorge Eliécer Gaitán**, sparking off a huge riot called the **Bogotazo** (see page 67), which left over six hundred dead and destroyed half the city centre.

CAPITOLIO NACIONAL DE COLOMBIA

Highlights

❶ **Plaza de Bolívar** Explore Bogotá's history via its cathedral, law courts and a couple of palaces – or have your photo taken with a llama. See page 59

❷ **Museo Botero** Marvel at the biggest and best collection of works by Colombia's favourite artist, all for free. See page 62

❸ **Museo del Oro (Gold Museum)** Stuffed to the rafters with gold, gold and more gold from pre-Hispanic Colombia – no wonder the Spanish thought it was El Dorado. See page 66

❹ **Cerro de Monserrate** Take the funicular or a cable car, or just climb up the stairs to this popular pilgrimage site for a fantastic bird's-eye view over the whole city. See page 68

❺ **Cementerio Central** Wander this fascinating cemetery where most of Colombia's presidents lie buried, as well as British and Irish troops who fell fighting for Bolívar. See page 70

❻ **Dine out in La Macarena** This bohemian inner-city neighbourhood has become Bogotá's favourite place to eat out, full of new and innovative restaurants serving cuisine from Colombia, South America and the world. See page 79

❼ **Zona Rosa nightlife** The epicentre of Bogotá's evening entertainment is chock-full of bars, clubs, cafés and restaurants, and throbs to the beat of everything from house or hip-hop to rock or salsa. See page 80

HIGHLIGHTS ARE MARKED ON THE MAPS ON PAGES 60, 66 AND 72

In the second half of the twentieth century, industrialization and civil war prompted a mass **influx** of peasant farmers from rural areas into slums on the southern approach to the city – in marked contrast to the affluent neighbourhoods in the northern part of town. The result is a vibrant city of some eight million people, but with huge disparities of wealth.

La Candelaria

The city's oldest and prettiest neighbourhood, **La Candelaria**, is full of colourfully painted colonial residences, with an increasing number of cheap hostels, bars and restaurants. It stretches from Calle 7 to the south to Avenida Jiménez de Quesada (Calle 13) to the north, bounded by Carrera 10 to the west and the mountains to the east. This is by far the most interesting part of town, where you'll find the lion's share of Bogotá's sights, including museums, old churches and historical buildings. Unfortunately, it's not crime-free, although a strong daytime police presence helps matters; in daylight, take elementary precautions, and at night stick to well-peopled streets.

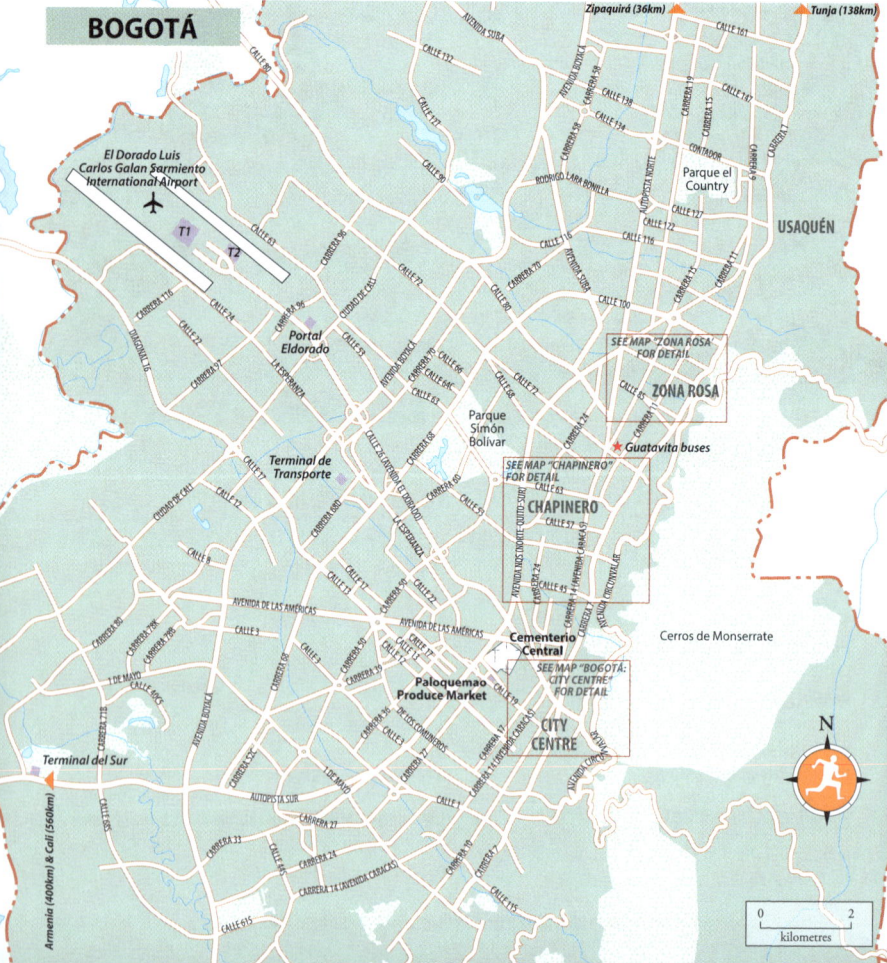

STAYING SAFE

These days Bogotá is no more dangerous than any other South American city, but there are still **areas of high crime** and neighbourhoods controlled by drug gangs. The first rule therefore is not to go wandering aimlessly into areas you don't know. Even the city centre, at night, can be quite dubious – you should stick to well-peopled streets and avoid back alleys. La Candelaria, the main tourist area, can also be dodgy after dark, and has several crime-ridden neighbourhoods around it, so you should stick to streets with a lot of people and avoid wandering around alone. The **Parque de los Periodistas**, the large square between La Candelaria and the centre, is particularly worth avoiding at night. Macarena is generally OK, but **La Perseverancia**, immediately to its north, is not safe, even in daylight. **Tunnels and underpasses** are of course mugging hotspots, especially when there aren't many people about. It's also a good idea to avoid taking **busetas** after dark, although the TransMilenio is well policed and usually safe enough, give or take the odd pickpocket. If in doubt, **call a cab** – and do, yes, call one if possible (see page 75) rather than hailing one on the street. Looking like a gringo doesn't help matters of course, so if you can **dress to pass as Colombian**, so much the better. And obviously, you never want to be carrying any more cash or valuables on you than necessary, which includes credit and debit cards.

Plaza de Bolívar

The heart of La Candelaria is the **Plaza de Bolívar**, awhirl with street vendors, llamas and pigeons (which you can buy corn to feed) and surrounded by monumental buildings spanning more than four centuries, many covered with political graffiti. In the evenings, street-food carts appear.

The 1846 **statue** of Simón Bolívar in the middle of the square is by the Neoclassical Italian sculptor Pietro Tenerani, best known for sculpting papal busts in the Vatican. It's the city's oldest outdoor sculpture, and is particularly popular with the pigeons. The French-style 1907 **Palacio Liévano** on the square's west side houses the mayor's offices. On the south side, where the Spanish viceroy's palace once stood, the **Capitolio Nacional**, with its imposing, colonnaded stone facade, is the seat of Colombia's legislature; designed by the Caribbean-born Danish architect Thomas Reed, its first stone was laid in 1848 (you can see it on the bottom right-hand corner of the supporting wall) but thanks to assorted political upheavals, the building wasn't actually finished until 1926. In the southeast corner of the square, the unassuming **Casa de los Comuneros** is seventeenth century; the exact date of construction is unknown, but the Spanish-born chronicler Juan Flórez de Ocáriz was living in it by 1674.

Palacio de Justicia

C 12 No. 7–65 (Plaza de Bolívar) • Not open for casual visits • Free • Ⓜ San Victorino

The mausoleum-like **Palacio de Justicia**, housing Colombia's Supreme Court, presides over Plaza Bolívar from its north side. The original 1921 building was burnt down by protestors in the 1948 **Bogotazo** (see page 67). In 1985, its successor was occupied by **M-19 guerrillas**, who took 300 hostages including 44 judges. When the army stormed the building three hours later, they took the ground floor but the guerrillas held the upper floors and about a third of their hostages. The army flushed them out the next day, leaving dead a dozen judges and five top M-19 commanders as well as nearly a hundred soldiers and civilians. The ensuing fire burned for two days. Controversy still rages over exactly who was killed, who by, and whether other bodies were illegally dumped in the same grave. It seems that the cocaine cartels had paid M-19 to attack the building, destroy court records, and kill judges favouring extradition of drug barons to the US; whatever the truth, the deaths of the M-19 leaders was probably instrumental in bringing the group to the negotiating table and ending its armed struggle, so perhaps the hundred victims didn't die in vain.

BOGOTÁ LA CANDELARIA

ACCOMMODATION		EATING				SHOPPING	
Alegria's Hostel	13	Hotel de la Ópera	10	Crepes & Waffles	4	La Puerta Falsa	8	Emerald Market	3
Anandamayi Hostel	12	Karuss Hostel	8	Enchiladas	12	Quinua y Amaranto	11	Emerald Trade Center	2
Aragon	5	Muisca	11	La Hamburgueseria	10	ReverdeSer	1	Éxito	5
Casa Deco	6	Onde Pepe Hostel	2	Hibiscus Restaurant	5	Rosita	7	Librería Lerner	1
Casa Galeria	7	The Orchids	9	Kutral	2	Sant Just	3	Only	4
Cranky Croc	3	Prisma Hostel	1	Paella	9	Trattoria Nuraghe	6	Pasaje Rivas	6
Hostal Sue	4								

The **new building** dates from 1999. Above its entrance are engraved the optimistic words of Francisco de Paula Santander (see page 122), one of the country's founding fathers: "Colombians: arms have given you independence; laws will give you freedom."

Cathedral

Cra 7 No. 10–80 (Plaza de Bolívar) • Free • ☏ 1 341 11954 • Ⓜ San Victorino

The **Cathedral** or, to give it its full title, **Catedral Primada de Colombia** (Primary Cathedral of Colombia), on the east side of Plaza Bolívar, stands on the spot where the city's founder, Gonzalo Jiménez de Quesada is supposed to have celebrated Bogotá's first ever Mass in 1538, in a makeshift chapel with mud walls and a grass roof. Work on a permanent church began in 1553, but the roof fell in just before completion. Undeterred, the pope promoted the church to cathedral status anyway, and a new building was finally installed in 1590, only to be levelled by an earthquake in 1785 – the Chapel of the Virgin of Perpetual Help, left (north) of the main altar, is one of the few original sections remaining. Today's building was begun in 1805 under **Fray Domingo Petrés**, a Capuchin friar and New Granada's foremost architect. The imposing **facade** is his doing, although the tastefully restrained cream and gold **interior** dates from after his death. The cathedral's impressive **organ** was installed in 1890.

Like many large Catholic churches, the cathedral has a number of smaller chapels on each side, dedicated to various saints. These are generally closed off by railings, so that you can see into them but not go in. The most interesting chapel is to the right (south) of the main altar, which is dedicated to Bogotá's patron, St Elizabeth of Hungary. In the middle of it is **Gonzalo Jiménez de Quesada's tomb**; the recumbent marble figure of Quesada lying on top of it is not sixteenth-century, but was sculpted by the Colombian artist Luis Alberto Acuña when Quesada's remains were moved here from the Cementerio Central (see page 70) in 1938. On the chapel's left (east) side, a bust of independence leader **Antonio Nariño** (see page 96) marks the spot where his earthly remains are interred, and an urn holds those of Bolívar's foreign and finance minister **Pedro Gual**.

The chapel next door to St Elizabeth's, dedicated to St James the Apostle, is the burial place of Bogotá's seventeenth-century Baroque painter **Gregorio Vázquez de Arce**, whose depiction of St James reappearing on horseback to help the Christian Spaniards in a ninth-century battle against the Moors forms the chapel's centrepiece. To its right, Vázquez was not responsible for the rather gruesome portrayal of the decapitation of St Catherine of Alexandria, which is by his contemporary, Gregorio Guiral, but the *Adoration of the Magi* on the chapel's left-hand wall is indeed by Vázquez, and marks the spot where he lies.

Capilla del Sagrario
Cra 7 No. 10–40 (Plaza de Bolívar) • Free • Ⓜ San Victorino

The **Capilla del Sagrario** (Sacristy Chapel), on the east side of Plaza Bolívar, is strictly speaking part of the Catedral Primada; there's a connecting door but it's kept closed, and really the Capilla is a separate building, and not even next-door. It's also older, having been commissioned in 1660 by a devout Spanish sergeant-major, **Gabriel Gómez de Sandoval**, who had already bought up the houses that previously stood here. Finished in 1700, it is adorned throughout with wonderful paintings by Gregorio Vázquez de Arce, originally fifty in number, although only 36 survive. They mostly depict scenes from the Bible, although the characters in them look and dress more like people of Vázquez's day. The elegantly proportioned **facade** is considered the finest in New Granada Baroque, though is not entirely original: having weathered a number of earthquakes, it was realigned stone by stone in 1953.

Casa del Florero
C 11 No. 6–94 (Plaza de Bolívar) • Guided tours available in Spanish • Ⓦ bit.ly/florero • Ⓜ San Victorino

In the northeast corner of Plaza Bolívar, the **Casa del Florero** ("House of the Vase"), with its green veranda, was the scene of momentous events on **20 July 1810**. With Spain under Napoleonic occupation, South America was up in arms, but Bogotá remained under Spanish control, and its *Criollos* (locally born colonials), to their chagrin, were still subject to official discrimination. To demonstrate the extent of Spanish arrogance, a group of them came to this house to ask its proprietor, the Spanish merchant Joaquín Gonzalez Llorente, to borrow a vase for a dinner honouring the royal commissioner Antonio Villavicencio, a *Criollo* sympathizer. When Llorente predictably refused, they seized the vase and broke it. They and their supporters then started a fight in the street outside, calling on the people of Bogotá to rise up against colonialism, which they duly did, forcing the viceroy to agree to local rule. For this *Grito de Independencia* ("cry of independence"), July 20 has been celebrated as Independence Day ever since.

Today the Casa del Florero houses a **Museo de la Independencia** (Independence Museum), explaining the events of that fateful day. And pride of place, naturally, goes to the very vase that started it all.

Casa de Nariño

Cra 8 No. 7–26 • 45min guided visits by appointment; to book click on "Casa de Nariño", top right, then "Solicitar Visita", top right again, and scroll down for the link to the online *formulario de registro* which you need to fill in – you'll need your passport number • Free but ID required • W petro.presidencia.gov.co • M San Victorino

A couple of blocks south of Plaza de Bolívar, the heavily fortified presidential palace and compound, **Casa de Nariño**, done in the style of Versailles, is where Colombia's president lives and works. To join a guided tour in English or Spanish, book online (see page 74); when you come, turn up fifteen minutes early and bring your passport, but don't bring bags, phones or cameras, as you can't take them in or deposit them anywhere. It's also possible to watch the ceremonial **changing of the guard** three times a week (Wed, Fri & Sun at 4pm) – best viewed from the east side of the palace.

Museo Botero

C 11 No. 4–41 • Free • Free guided tours (Spanish and English); charge for audio guides from museum shop with deposit of ID • W banrepcultural.org/bogota/museo-botero • M Las Aguas

Three blocks southeast of Plaza Bolívar, in a fine colonial mansion surrounding a lush courtyard, the **Museo Botero** contains one of Latin America's largest collections of modern and Impressionist art, donated in 2000 by Colombia's most celebrated artist, **Fernando Botero** (see page 213), to the chagrin of some in his home town, Medellín, who wanted the museum there. They're right to be jealous: this is an absolutely wonderful collection, and not to be missed by anyone with even a passing interest in modern art.

Works by Botero

The museum has 123 paintings and sculptures by Botero himself. You're greeted at the door by a giant hand, and there's a study of how to paint hands among the pictures in **Room 4**, which also has portraits by Botero of the painters Cézanne and Courbet (not from life, as they lived before Botero's time). **Room 5** has a plumped-up version of a character from a famous picture by the seventeenth-century Spanish painter Diego Velázquez, no relation to Eliseo Velásquez, whose 1950s guerrilla group are portrayed at the end of the room taking a rest in the forest.

Some of the museum's best works are in **Room 6**, including a picture of Botero in his studio painting a plump, pink, naked model, another of a man and a woman in the bathroom, a cherubic Mona Lisa and a still life of bananas – fat ones, obviously.

Upstairs, the small paintings in **Room 9** include a depiction of the 1988 massacre of Mejor Esquino, when 27 peasant farmers were murdered by a paramilitary group in rural Córdoba, for reasons unknown. Next door in **Room 10**, a very well-fed Death (and surely only Botero could make a skeleton look podgy) has traded in his scythe for a guitar. The paintings in **Room 11** include an ill-shaven cat-burglar making his getaway across the rooftops, and in the next space, Popoyán being shaken by its devastating 1983 earthquake. **Room 12** is devoted to sculptures, including a representation of the ancient Greek tale of Leda and the Swan, plus the biblical characters Adam and Eve, who can also be seen enjoying a postcoital apple downstairs in Room 3.

Works by other artists

Botero also gave the museum a huge collection of works by other artists, including almost everyone who was anyone in Impressionist and modern art. **Room 7**, on the upper floor, has a macabre study of a child by Francis Bacon, and a colourful view of

London's Mornington Crescent by Frank Auerbach. Downstairs, **Room 1** is devoted to Impressionists and post-Impressionists, among them Toulouse-Lautrec, Renoir, Pissarro, and a rather grey winter scene of Amsterdam by Monet. **Room 2** moves on into Cubism and Surrealism, with works by Picasso, Miró, de Chirico, Delvaux, Max Ernst, Braque and Chagall. **Room 3** has a couple of works by Botero (including an erotically charged drawing of Adam and Eve), but also drawings and studies by people like Lucian Freud, Henry Moore, Klimt, Dégas and Matisse. A trio of Picassos includes a *Guernica*-esque study of a goat's skull in black, brown and grey.

Casa de Moneda

C 11 No. 4–93 • Free • W banrepcultural.org/bogota/casa-de-moneda • M Las Aguas

Next door to the Museo Botero, the stone-built **Casa de Moneda**, formerly the Mint, illustrates the history of money in Colombia from pre-Columbian barter systems to the design and production of modern banknotes and coins. Ramps lead to the **Colección de Arte**, featuring a permanent exhibition of works owned by the Banco de la República. The predominant focus here is on contemporary Colombian artists, but the pieces on display range from seventeenth-century religious art through to modern canvases by twentieth-century painters.

Museo de Arte del Banco de la República

C 11 No. 4–21 • Free • W banrepcultural.org/bogota/museo-de-arte • M Las Aguas

On the same block as the Casa de Moneda and Museo Botero, the **Museo de Arte del Banco de la República** is a modern, airy building by local architect Enrique Triana Uribe, dating from 2004, that houses free, temporary exhibitions of edgy art and photography. Installations and exhibitions change regularly, but there's always something interesting to see.

Museo Militar

C 10 No. 4–92 • Free, but ID required • T 1 315 0111 • M Las Aguas

Run by the military, three blocks southeast of Plaza Bolívar, the **Museo Militar** showcases weaponry through the ages, jaunty military uniforms, model battleships, anti-aircraft guns and other articles relating to the art of war. There's a room dedicated to the history of the army, one for the navy, one for the air force, and one dedicated to the 1950–53 Korean War, in which Colombian troops fought alongside those of the US, Britain, Canada, Australia and New Zealand. The cannons, machine guns, rifles and pistols in the arms room will certainly interest gun enthusiasts.

Palacio de San Carlos

C 10 No. 5–51 • Closed to the public • M San Victorino

The **Palacio de San Carlos**, two blocks southeast of Plaza Bolívar on Calle 10, and home to the Foreign Affairs Ministry, was built from local stone and timber in the 1580s, since when it has withstood multiple earthquakes and served as a Jesuit seminary, printing press, library, barracks and, not least, presidential palace.

The grand but rather plain **facade** is set back from the road, but to its right, the first window that isn't set back was used by **Simón Bolívar** to escape when a group of would-be assassins turned up while he was in the bath. Luckily, his mistress, **Manuelita Sáenz**, managed to tip him off, then went out to greet the conspirators and kept them talking while he made his soapy getaway. For her cool-headed courage she is still remembered as the Liberator's liberator. A **plaque** under the window itself invites you in Latin: "Halt your pace briefly, observer, if you're free to, and marvel at the escape route by which the father and saviour of the country, Simón Bolívar, liberated himself on that evil September night of the year 1828".

The ornate *fin-de-siècle* building directly opposite the Palacio de San Carlos is the 1892 **Teatro Colón** (weneldelia.gov.co), Bogotá's poshest theatre.

Museo de Trajes Regionales

C 10 No. 6–18 • Charge (free last Fri of the month) • T 1 341 0403, W uamerica.edu.co/museodetrajes

Manuelita's own house, one block west of Palacio de San Carlos, is now a **Museo de Trajes Regionales** (Regional Costumes Museum), exhibiting clothes and textiles from around the country, past and present, including replicas of some of Manuelita's dresses.

Museo Colonial

Cra 6 No. 9–77 • Charge, free on Sun (ticket includes Museo Iglesia de Santa Clara; see page 65) • W www.museocolonial.gov.co • M San Victorino

Just around the corner from the Palacio de San Carlos and a block southeast of Plaza Bolívar, the **Museo Colonial**, once a Jesuit university, has installed exhibits on life in New Granada, turning it from a Colonial Art Museum into just a Colonial Museum, but it's still the art that makes it worthwhile. Some of the **religious sculptures** that once adorned sixteenth-, seventeenth- and eighteenth-century churches are quite exquisite, but the best items of all are works by New Granada's top artist, **Gregorio Vázquez de Arce**, whose studio is re-created in one of the rooms, although it looks rather too much like somebody's tidied it up for him. On top of that, the museum has 76 of Vázquez's paintings and even more of his drawings, all in a lovely old house built in 1604.

Museo Arqueológico (MUSA)

Cra 6 No. 7–43 • Charge • W museoarqueologicomusa.com • M San Victorino

A block east of the Casa de Nariño, three blocks south of Plaza Bolívar, the **Museo Arqueológico** (Archeological Museum, commonly abbreviated as MUSA) is housed in the former home of Spanish viceroy, the **Marqués de San Jorge**. Quite the palatial mansion, it was built in the late eighteenth century and was in place by 1784 when its original owner, Field Marshal Agustín Londoño sold it to the future *marqués*, then just plain old Jorge Miguel Lozano de Peralta. The king promoted him to the peerage three years later.

The **collection** consists of pieces – mostly ceramic, but also some textiles – from all over the country, largely pre-Hispanic. There are some lovely little statues, lots of cups, bowls and vases, and explanations in English as well as Spanish. However, although the exhibits are interesting and well laid out, the building itself is a lot more impressive than anything in it.

Museo Histórico de la Policía Nacional

C 9 No. 9–27 • Free • W policia.gov.co/historia/museo • M San Victorino

In the former police HQ, two blocks west of Plaza Bolívar, the **Museo Histórico de la Policía Nacional** (Police History Museum) can be a worthwhile visit depending on your guide: you have to take a tour in English or Spanish given by conscripts doing their national service in the police (and may have to wait a few minutes while they locate an English-speaker). If you get the full tour, you'll be shown old police vehicles, uniforms (Colombia's are modelled on those of the Mounties) and a whole floor of confiscated **weapons** and riot gear. Pride of place goes to the basement exhibition on **Pablo Escobar**, featuring his cousin's gold-trimmed Harley, his own satellite phone and favourite guns, a dummy of his bullet-riddled corpse, a tile from the roof on which he

CHURCHES OF LA CANDELARIA AND THE CITY CENTRE

In addition to its Cathedral, La Candelaria and the adjoining part of the downtown area are teeming with some of the best-preserved colonial-era churches and convents in Latin America:
Museo Iglesia de Santa Clara Cra 8 No. 8–91 (charge, free on Sun; ticket includes Museo Colonial; ⓦmuseocolonial.gov.co). Overlooking Casa de Nariño (see page 62), the austere, early seventeenth-century exterior, formerly part of a convent, contrasts sharply with its opulent gold-plated interior, beautiful ceiling and wonderful collection of paintings.
Iglesia de San Agustín C 7 No. 6–25 (free). This charming little stone church, built in 1668 and well worth popping into for its wonderful starry decor and fine paintings, was at the centre of the 1862 Battle of San Agustín between troops loyal to presidential rivals Mariano Ospina and Tomás Cipriano.
Iglesia de San Francisco Cra 7 No. 15–25, at Av Jiménez (free). Built at the beginning of the seventeenth century, San Francisco is appropriately noted for its particularly splendid 1623 golden retablo (grand altarpiece).
Iglesia de la Concepción C 10 No. 9–50 (free). The soaring vault in this modest 1595 church is a fine example of the Moorish-influenced Mudéjar style popular in the sixteenth century.
Iglesia de San Ignacio C 10 No. 6–35 (free). The largest and most impressive of the colonial-era churches is the domed San Ignacio founded in 1610 as the first Jesuit church in New Grenada.
Iglesia de Veracruz C 16 No. 7–19 (free; ⓦplaveracruz.arquibogota.org.co). Originally dating from 1546, but severely damaged by an 1827 earthquake and rebuilt in the 1960s, this church is the last resting place of some eighty independence fighters shot by the Spanish in 1816.

was shot, plus his desk, with more secret hiding places than you can shake an Uzi at. There's also a great view across the city from the roof.

Plazoleta del Chorro de Quevado
C 13, at Cra 2 • Ⓜ Las Aguas

Seven blocks east of Plaza Bolívar is La Candelaria's most charming little square and the centre of its nightlife, **Plazoleta del Chorro de Quevado**. Even in the daytime, it's a pretty little place, but of an evening it really comes alive, and the area around it is particularly popular with students.

Before the Spanish turned up, this was the centre of the Muisca settlement. After the Spanish conquest, Bogotá's first church was built here, and in the nineteenth century a fountain was installed. Both were destroyed in the 1890s, but in 1969 a replacement fountain and a replica church were built in an attempt to restore the square to its previous state. Authentic it may not be, but the streets leading off it are lined with convivial little bars and restaurants. In particular, **Callejón del Embudo**, the narrow, cobbled stretch of Carrera 2 leading north under the arch with a statue of a juggling monocyclist on top, is a great spot to find bars serving *chicha* (see page 35).

City centre

Downtown Bogotá is the city's **commercial centre**. It's dominated by rather ugly office buildings: much of the centre was destroyed in the 1948 Bogotazo riots, and such of its grand old buildings as survived were mostly demolished in the 1970s to be replaced with the concrete blocks that stand today. Nonetheless, there remain a scattering of historical buildings, and some interesting museums.

The downtown area's main thoroughfare is **Carrera 7**, a largely pedestrianized shopping street that's been a road since pre-Hispanic times. Between calles 22 and 23, the impressive facade of the **Teatro Municipal**, built in 1938, should wow fans of Art Deco, who will also appreciate the **Personería de Bogotá** building just down the street at No. 21–34, and the **Biblioteca Nacional** on Calle 24, where the nation's collection of books and manuscripts resides.

Parque de Santander

Cra 6–7, at C 15–16 • Ⓜ Museo del Oro or Ⓜ Las Aguas

The heart of the downtown area is the **Parque de Santander**, an open square rather than a park as such, named after Bolivarian general and Colombian president Francisco de Paula Santander (see page 122), whose statue stands in the middle of it.

Museo del Oro (Gold Museum)

Cra 6 No. 15–82 • Charge, free on Sun; audioguide charge • Free guided tours in English • ⓦ banrepcultural.org/bogota/museo-del-oro • Ⓜ Museo del Oro or Ⓜ Las Aguas

If you like your bling, you'll love the **Museo del Oro (Gold Museum)** on the east side of Parque de Santander, which holds the world's biggest collection of gold ornaments, some 55,000 pieces strong. The collection itself occupies the middle two floors, with the ground floor used for temporary exhibitions and the top floor given over to an "exploratorium" of Colombia's indigenous cultures.

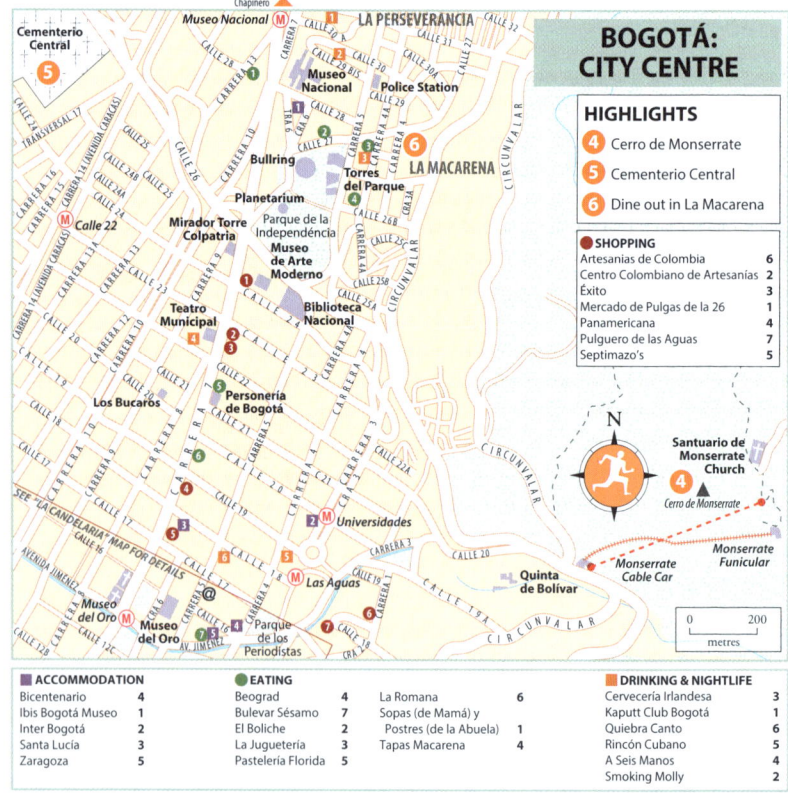

> ### GAITÁN'S ASSASSINATION AND THE BOGOTAZO
>
> Just a block south of the Parque de Santander, Carrera 7 No. 14–35 was the location, until its demolition in the 1970s, of the Agustín Nieto Building, where the Caudillo del Pueblo ("People's leader") **Jorge Eliécer Gaitán** worked, and outside which he was gunned down on April 9, 1948 as he left to go for lunch. A wall covered in commemorative plaques now marks the spot. His murderer, **Juan Roa Sierra**, then sought refuge in the Droguería Granada, a drugstore attached to a hotel on the corner of Calle 15, where the **Banco de la República** now stands. When the shopkeeper asked him why he'd done it, he replied, "Oh señor, powerful things that I can't tell." And when the shopkeeper pressed him further, saying, "Tell me who told you to do it, because in moments you're going to be lynched by the people," all that Roa would answer was "I can't." Moments later, he was indeed lynched and silenced forever. Still incensed – for of course they knew that Roa had been acting on orders – the crowd went on to burn down half the city centre in **riots** that lasted into the night. The repercussions of the assassination are still being played out today. Meanwhile, when the Agustín Nieto Building was eventually pulled down, its front door was rescued, and can now be seen at Gaitán's former home in Chapinero (see page 71).

The permanent collection starts on the second floor with a display on **metallurgy**, and the differences and similarities between gold, silver, copper and platinum. Then there are examples of gold ornaments from some of the country's early cultures, including the recurring symbolism of animals such as jaguars, birds and bats, and human/animal hybrids representing shamans taking on animal form to travel to the spirit world. Some of the commonest gold items, aside from jewellery, are **containers for lime ash** to be added to coca leaf when chewing it. The prong used to extract and dab on the ash is often topped with elaborate figures.

On the third floor, the section on **cosmology and symbolism** contains the museum's top exhibits, including an exquisite mask-like representation of a human face from Tierradentro, and the piece that started the whole collection: a gold container for lime ash in the form of a gourd whose sensuous curves elegantly evoke the human female form. There's also a set of the full gold finery worn by a chieftain or a shaman on ceremonial occasions. And although pre-Hispanic Colombians didn't snort cocaine, they did blow psychedelic *yopo* snuff up each other's noses for shamanic purposes: such gold trays and snuffing tubes are also on display. In what they call the Sala de la Ofrenda ("offering room") is the museum's other top treasure, a filigree **gold model of a raft** made from reeds, with one large and several small human figures aboard, almost certainly representing the inauguration ritual of the Zipa (Muisca ruler) on the Laguna de Guatavita (see page 91). Finally, you get shut into a darkened circular room where, to the sound of water and shamanic chanting, the lights gradually come on to reveal hundreds of gold ornaments surrounding you, and still more in the glass floor beneath you.

Museo de la Esmeralda (Emerald Museum)

Edificio Avianca, C 16 No. 6–66 (23rd floor); sign in on the ground floor • Charge • Ⓦ museodelaesmeralda.com.co • Ⓜ Museo del Oro or Ⓜ Las Aguas

On the north side of Parque de Santander, way up on the 23rd floor of the Avianca Building, the **Museo de la Esmeralda (Emerald Museum)** explores everything from geology to the cutting process. The visit consists of a guided tour, in Spanish, starting with a video show, before you enter through an "emerald tunnel" featuring mock-ups and explanations of the different types of emerald mines in Colombia. Of course, there are lots of emeralds on show (and some of them are very lovely), and at the end – you may be forgiven for thinking that this is the whole point of it – there's an opportunity

> **EMERALDS**
>
> Emeralds are deep green in colour, a lot softer than diamonds, rubies or sapphires, and almost always have **inclusions** – tiny air pockets or minute fragments of extraneous solids within the stone, which can make them rather fragile. For the same reason, there are microscopic fissures all over the surface of a stone, and cut emeralds are therefore usually treated with **oil**, which fills the crevices and smooths out the refraction, making the stone clearer; this does however mean that stones need to be re-oiled every ten years or so. Unoiled emeralds are uncommon and expensive.
>
> Emeralds are found in several countries, but **Colombia** is the biggest producer and its stones are considered the best, typically selling, for example, at three times more than those of the world's second-largest producer, Zambia. **Quality** is measured by colour (dark is best), clarity and of course size. Colombia's emeralds are mostly mined in the *departamento* of Boyacá, north of Bogotá, with the top stones coming from Boyacá's famous mines at Muzo and Chivor.

to buy some green, sparkly gems at rather inflated prices. On your way out, check the excellent views over the city from the museum foyer.

Quinta de Bolívar

C 20 No. 2–91 Este • Charge, free on Sun; audioguide charge • Guided tours in Spanish and English • ⓦ quintadebolivar.gov.co • Ⓜ Las Aguas

On the eastern edge of the city centre, at the foot of the Cerro de Monserrate, is the **Quinta de Bolívar**, a spacious colonial mansion with beautiful gardens (kept in their original form) where Simón Bolívar lived sporadically between 1820 and 1830. The informative museum retells the story of Bolívar's final, desperate days in power before being banished by his political rivals, with a collection that includes a plethora of Bolívar paraphernalia including his military medals, billiard table and a bedpan which he may have used. The sword, however, is a replica: the original (which may in any case not have belonged to Bolívar) was stolen in 1974 in the debut act of guerrilla group M-19. When they handed in their arsenal in 1991, it was quickly shuttled into the vaults of the Banco República.

Cerro de Monserrate

Cerro de Monserrate • **Santuario;** Free • ⓦ santuariomonserrate.org • **Funicular railway**; charge • **Cable car**; charge • **Footpath**; Free • ⓦ cerromonserrate.com • Ⓜ Las Aguas

Perched high above the city centre is one of Bogotá's most recognizable landmarks, the **Cerro de Monserrate**. This rocky outcrop is crowned by the **Santuario de Monserrate** church, which offers spectacular views back down on the seemingly endless urban sprawl that is Bogotá. To reach it, you have the choice of a **funicular railway** (mainly mornings) and a **cable car** (*teleférico*, mainly afternoons). Alternatively, when it's open, it's a ninety-minute trek up the 1500-step stone **footpath** that begins at the base of the hill and leads to the summit 600m above.

Be aware that there are reports of **robberies** both on the way up the hill and also on the walk between the Quinta de Bolívar (see page 68) and the cable car and funicular stations. The safest (and cheapest) time to go is Sunday, when you'll be accompanied by thousands of pilgrims hoping for miracles from the church's dark-skinned Christ.

Museo de Arte Moderno (MamBo)

C 24 No. 6–00 • Charge • ⓦ mambogota.com • Ⓜ San Diego

On Calle 24 at Carrera 6, Bogotá's **Museo de Arte Moderno** (Modern Art Museum, commonly abbreviated as **MamBo**) has the largest collection of contemporary

Colombian art in the country, running the gamut from photography and painting to sculpture and graffiti. Frequently changing **exhibits** tend to focus on works by Latin American and in particular Colombian artists, but it also has works by Picasso, Magritte, Francis Bacon, Andy Warhol, Salvador Dalí and Joan Miró, as well as Colombia's "big five": Fernando Botero, Alejandro Obregón, Enrique Grau, Edgar Negret and Eduardo Ramírez Villamizar. The **building** itself is a pretty cool example of modern architecture by French-born Bogotano architect Rogelio Salmona.

Mirador Torre Colpatria
Cra 7 No. 24–89 • Charge • ☎ 1 745 6300 • Ⓜ San Diego

Panoramic 360-degree views can be had from the **Mirador Torre Colpatria**, atop Colombia's tallest skyscraper (162m), built in 1979. Views of the city are great, if not a patch on those from the Cerro de Monserrate, though you may sometimes have to queue to get in. What's arguably much more of an attraction is the pretty **light show** on the tower after dark – especially at Christmas time – which can be seen for free from almost anywhere in town.

La Macarena

North of Calle 26 is one of Bogotá's most appealing *barrios*, the villagey, bohemian district of **La Macarena**, known popularly as "Zona M" or even just "El Barrio Bohemio". Most of the houses in this hilly neighbourhood date from the 1950s and 1960s, when the area became built-up, but even before that, the cops at the **police station** on Carerra 5 (opposite Calle 29 Bis) became famous for supporting their protesting fellow citizens in the **Bogotazo** (see page 67), when a young Fidel Castro was apparently among those who came here to collect arms.

On the neighbourhood's west side, the **Parque de la Independencia**, a vital piece of urban greenery, is home to Bogotá's **planetarium**, and to the Moorish-style **bullring** where bullfights take place in January and February. Cuddling up to the bullring, Rogelio Salmona's curved 1960s brick tower blocks, the **Torres del Parque**, are a prominent landmark.

Nowadays, La Macarena is super-hip and trendy, full of bars and restaurants, not to mention a profusion of art galleries. It's especially buzzing on a Friday night, when the bars are full of students from the **University of Cundinamarca** on Calle 28. As always with such places, gentrification now threatens its vitality, but for the time being at least, this is one of Bogotá's most congenial neighbourhoods, and well worth checking out.

Museo Nacional
Cra 7 No. 28–66 • Ⓦ museonacional.gov.co • Ⓜ Museo Nacional

In the very northwest of La Macarena, on Calle 28, Colombia's **Museo Nacional** (National Museum) is located in what was once a prison. The late nineteenth-century **building**, in the shape of a cross (so the guards in the middle could see every wing), was designed by the architect Thomas Reed. The three floors are arranged in chronological order, from the ground up. Unfortunately, the explanations are in Spanish only; there are information cards in English for a few areas, but they're patchy and out of date.

Lower floors
The museum's **ground floor** is dedicated to Colombia's pre-Hispanic peoples. There are lots of pots and figurines, but the main attractions are in the small rooms around the large iron meteorite in the centre: a thirteenth-century tomb from Nariño, a collection of gold and emerald jewellery, and a gaggle of 1500-year-old mummies from the Sierra Nevada del Cocuy.

The **middle floor** covers the colonial period, with morbid seventeenth-century religious images in Room 9 depicting the sufferings of Jesus, and most poignantly, African ritual objects made by first-generation slaves as a prayer aid to end their own suffering. Room 11 is mostly dedicated to paintings of battles and heroes of the independence struggle.

Top floor

Art lovers should make a beeline for the museum's top floor, where the paintings include some of **Fernando Botero**'s largest canvasses in the centre space, and some that you'd never guess were by Botero – among them a picture of a child in the style of Francis Bacon (but fat), and (in Room 17) some actually quite slender residents of the San Bernadino islands collecting coconuts, one of Botero's very early works.

Room 15 is full of portraits of long-dead politicians, and in **Room 16**, the first cell on the left displays the axes used to murder Liberal civil war leader Rafael Uribe Uribe in 1914 (see page 213). The second cell on the right has some dark and faintly disturbing paintings by **Enrique Grau**, including a depiction of Nona (one of the Fates in Greco-Roman mythology) knitting the thread of life, another of two wild dogs with an animal skull, and one of a wretched-looking street girl described as a "young Communist". Room 16's **sculptures** include a rather ghostly-looking smoothed-out marble head of Jesus by Gustavo Arcila Uribe entitled *Sermon del Monte* (Sermon on the Mount).

Room 17 has a couple of examples of the hauntingly colourful work of **Alejandro Obregón**: *Mascaras* (Masks) and *Cosas de la Luna* (Things from the Moon). Far more gruesome is **Ignacio Gómez Jaramillo**'s *Martirio de Galán* (Martyrdom of Galán), depicting the dismembered corpse of José Antonio Galán, who led the *comunero* revolt (see page 341). Galan was sentenced to death by the Spanish in 1782, after which his body was cut up and distributed around the villages that had taken part in the rising as a warning to any other would-be insurgents.

North Bogotá

North of La Macarena, the neighbourhoods get a whole lot more exclusive, with bigger houses, chic fashions and classy shopping. **Sights** as such are much thinner on the ground than they are in La Candelaria or the city centre, but the northern *barrios* are leafier, quieter and a lot more laidback. The communities up here were originally separate towns. Some were absorbed into Bogotá in the late nineteenth century with the coming of **trams**, pulled at first by mules, until they were electrified after 1910. Even then, the northernmost communities such as **Usaquén** remained separate towns until 1954, when Bogotá was hived off from the *departamento* of Cundinamarca and made into a Distrito Capital, effectively its own *departamento*, incorporating Usaquén and other suburbs.

Cementerio Central

Cra 20 No. 24–80 • Free • ☎ 1 269 3141 • Ⓜ Calle 26

Just northwest of La Macarena, in the *barrio* of Los Mártires, Bogotá's main cemetery, the **Cementerio Central**, opened in 1836, after Simón Bolívar's government banned further churchyard burials. Full of fascinating tombs, monuments, statues and grand mausoleums, it's a place you can wander for hours, enjoying the company of the dead.

Inmates of the cemetery include most of Colombia's former **presidents**, from Francisco de Paula Santander onwards, along with **poets** such as José Asunción Silva and León de Greiff; Oreste Síndici, the composer of Colombia's national anthem; and **Leo Kopp**, who founded the Bavaria brewery. In front of Kopp's mausoleum, a golden statue of him is said to grant miracles to those who whisper their requests in his ear – and there's often a queue of people waiting to do just that.

On the south side of the Cementerio Central, and actually slightly older, is a **British Cemetery**. Here rest fallen members of the British Legion – volunteers from Britain and Ireland, largely veterans of the Napoleonic Wars, who came over to help Bolívar's forces fight for independence from Spain.

Chapinero

The leafy residential neighbourhood of **Chapinero** starts at Calle 39 and officially stretches all the way to Calle 100, although Chapinero proper (Chapinero Alto) really only extends up to around Calle 65. Its main artery is Carrera 7. Chapinero grew up as a satellite town in the early nineteenth century, when the artisans who had their workshops here included the *chapineros* – makers of a cork-soled goatskin shoe called a *chapín* – from whom the *barrio* takes its name. In 1884, the arrival of tram lines joined it to the city, and today it is best known as the centre of Bogotá's **gay** scene, especially since it elected lesbian activist Blanca Durán to be its mayor from 2008 to 2012. One of the city's top dining areas, the **Zona G** (that's "G" for gourmet), borders it to the north, between calles 65 and 72.

Casa Museo Jorge Eliécer Gaitán

C 42 No. 15–52 • Free • Free guided tours in Spanish offered hourly • W patrimoniocultural.bogota.unal.edu.co • M Calle 45

A white suburban **villa** on Calle 42, at the southern end of Chapinero, was from 1933 to 1948 home to **Jorge Eliécer Gaitán**, a former Bogotá mayor whose 1948 murder sparked off the Bogotazo riots (see page 67). Although he was a career politician, Gaitán

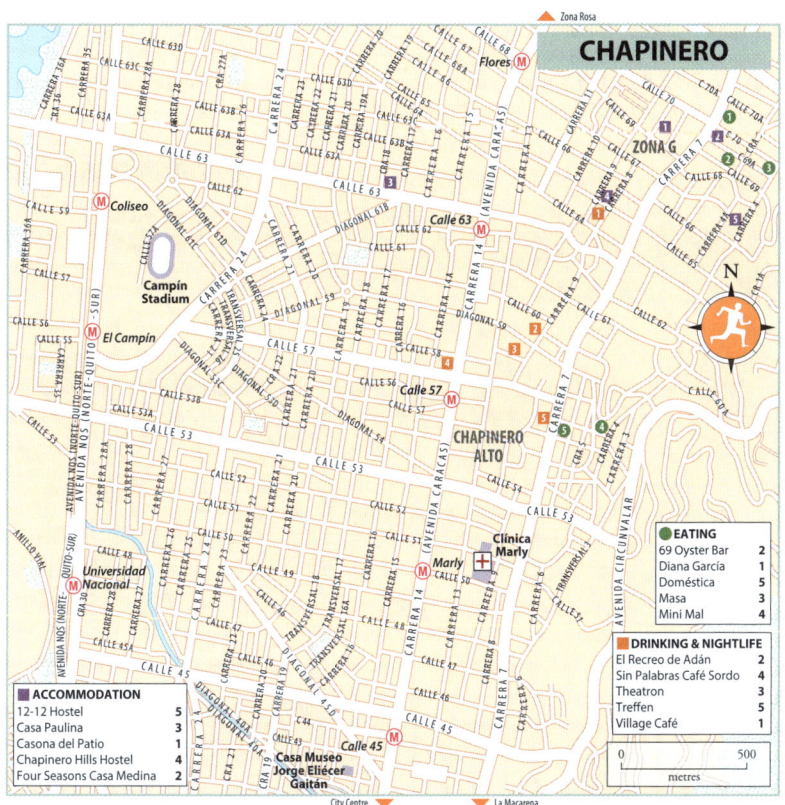

seemed to genuinely care about ordinary people, and he worked hard for social justice. As the Liberal Party's presidential candidate, he was widely expected to win the 1950 election and then bring in radical social reforms. His murder convinced many that the establishment would never allow change via the ballot box, a conclusion that boosted popular support for armed revolutionary groups and led to decades of bitter civil war.

As a museum, his home is all rather intimate – visitors get to see his **living room** and **study**, as if he were still living there, as well as the suit he was wearing when he was gunned down, the gun that did it, and even the door of the Agustín Nieto Building, out of which he had just emerged when shot – it was rescued and brought here when the building was demolished in the 1970s (see page 67). In the **garden** you can see a 1948 tramcar.

Zona Rosa

Ⓜ Héroes

At the northern end of Chapinero, between calles 79 and 85, the **Zona Rosa** ("pink zone" – the name in Spanish signifies glitzy rather than gay) is an upscale commercial neighbourhood of nightclubs, boutiques and shopping malls. Its epicentre is the **Zona T**, a pedestrianized zone around Calle 83 and Carerra 12A, which is an excellent starting point for a stroll around the Zona Rosa, be it by day or by night.

Parque 93

Ⓦ parque93.com • Ⓜ Virrey

North of the Zona Rosa, and even more exclusive, the neighbourhood of **Chicó** is commonly referred to as **Parque 93**, as it is centred on a small park of the same name between calles 93A and 93B. As well as being a well-heeled residential area, this is also a business district, with a refined nightlife, and the sort of cafés and restaurants where

■ ACCOMMODATION		● EATING		■ DRINKING & NIGHTLIFE		● SHOPPING	
93 Luxury Suites	1	Arrogante Restaurante Bogotá	2	Bogotá Beer		Jhonny Cay	8	Artesanias de
BOG Hotel	5	Central Cevicheria	4	Company	2	La Hamburguesería	3	Colombia	2
Cité	3	Cooking Taichi	1	El Coq	5	Once Once	4	Centro Comercial
Click-Clack	2	Di Lucca	3	El Recreo de Adán	1	La Villa	6	Andino	3
Virrey Park	4	Wok	5	Frites Artois	7			El Balay	1

> **THE TREN TURÍSTICO**
>
> The **Tren Turístico de la Sabana** (w turistren.com.co) to Usaquén and Zipaquirá is a treat for rail enthusiasts rather than a practical mode of transport. It leaves Bogotá's Estación de la Sabana (C 13 No. 18–24) on Sat, Sun and public holidays at 8.30am, calling at Usaquén and Zipaquirá before turning round and coming back (with a 2hr layover at Cajicá), getting into Bogotá at 5.30pm. Check online for the latest round trip fee. Occasionally, it's pulled by a steam locomotive.

a Bogotano executive might take a foreign client to clinch a vital business deal. The *parque* itself is a well-manicured rectangle of green, a city block in size – just about big enough for the neighbourhood's *habituées* to walk their poodles of a morning.

Museo del Chicó
C 7 No. 93–01 • Charge • w museodelchico.com • m Virrey

Four blocks east of Parque 93, forming a rather larger park, are the grounds of an eighteenth-century colonial hacienda, now open to the public as the **Museo del Chicó**. Like the building itself, a fine example of a colonial mansion of the time, the interiors have been restored to their original state, with paintings, furniture and chinaware of the era. Unless you have a specific interest in colonial architecture and interiors, it isn't really worth the haul up from La Candelaria or the city centre just to see it, but it's certainly worth popping in if you're uptown.

Usaquén
TransMilenio feeder service M82/K86, with a stop at Calle 116, links Usaquén via Cra 7 to Museo Nacional (where you can change onto TransMilenio trunk services) and the airport

East of Carrera 7 between calles 112 and 121, **Usaquén** was originally a Muisca settlement. With the arrival of the Spanish, the residents managed to come to an arrangement with them, allowing Usaquén to remain an indigenous reserve, and by the time the colonial authorities ended this in 1779, the population had become pretty mixed anyway. Usaquén remained a town in its own right until absorbed by the capital in 1954, and still seems a place apart from Bogotá's hurly-burly.

What most visitors – including those on the Tren Turístico (see page 73) – come to Usaquén for is its Sunday **flea market** (*mercado de las pulgas*), where you'll find handicrafts galore but hopefully no actual fleas (see page 82). The main square, **Plaza de Usaquén**, would do any small town proud; with its trees and greenery, it's almost a little park, and indeed sometimes goes by the name "Parque de Usaquén". The church on its east side, the **Iglesia de Santa Bárbara**, graced by a stone portico and whitewashed tower, was built in 1665.

ARRIVAL AND DEPARTURE BOGOTÁ

BY PLANE
El Dorado International Airport El Dorado Airport (w eldorado.aero) is 14km northwest of the city centre. There are two terminals, 500m apart (buses connect them if you don't want to walk). Terminal 1 is for all international and many domestic flights. Terminal 2, also called "Puente Aereo" is for the remaining domestic flights, mostly to the south and west of the country. You'll find banks and ATMs at both. Left luggage in Terminal 1 is at the far end of the arrivals section, by gate 1.

By taxi to the city centre The easiest and safest way into town is by taxi. A cab takes about 40min to the city centre, depending on traffic. Agree the price with the driver when you get in, or insist on the meter. Use only authorized taxis, which stop outside arrivals. The lads who load your baggage into the back expect a tip but will understand if you have no change.

By TransMilenio to/from the city centre TransMilenio bus #1 runs from Universidades in the city centre (free interchange with Las Aguas) to Portal Eldorado, where you change onto the K86 for the last 2km to the airport (or pick up the K86 itself at Museo Nacional or on Cra 7 in Chapinero). The journey should take around 45min. From the airport (outside gates

1 and 8 at Terminal 1 and across C 26 from Terminal 2), take M86 to Portal Eldorado and then #1 to Universidades. You can buy and recharge TransMilenio cards inside gate 5 at Terminal 1. It's not a great idea to use the TransMilenio too late in the evening if carrying all your baggage and worldly wealth (remember that you still have to get from the station to your hotel). The service in any case stops at 11pm (10pm on Sun).

By bus to/from the city centre If you really have no more baggage than you can squeeze onto your lap, you can take a *buseta* into town (1hr) across the way from gate 9 of the arrivals section of Terminal 1 or across C 26 from Terminal 2. Those showing the destination "Centro" or "Germania" run along C 19 to Cra 4, where you can also pick them up going the other way (destination: "Aeropuerto"). It is not advisable to take *busetas* after dark, and they dry up around 9pm anyway.

BY BUS

Terminal de Transporte All major inter-city bus services arrive and depart at the large, modern Terminal de Transporte (Diagonal 23 No. 69–60; ⓦterminaldetransporte.gov.co), located 8km northwest of the centre in Ciudad Salitre. It's divided into five colour-coded *módulos* (units), four for departures and one for arrivals. All arrivals roll up at *módulo* 5 (purple), which has a tourist information desk. For departures, *módulo* 1 (yellow) serves destinations south of the capital; *módulo* 2 (blue) serves places east and west; *modulo* 3 (red) serves places north of the city, and also handles international departures; *módulo* 4 (green) is for *colectivos*. Taxis are available here and can connect you to the city centre. Buses from the terminal do not serve the city centre, and the nearest TransMilenio stop, ⓂEl Tiempo (served by route #1 to Universidades), is ten blocks away. Services to the south, including Armenia and Cali, stop at the Terminal del Sur, west of the centre on the Autopista Sur, linked to TransMilenio stop ⓂPortal del Sur, 700m to its east, by local buses; it can save time to pick up your bus here, but at peak periods buses may already be full when they arrive, which means you won't get a place.

Destinations Armenia (4–6 hourly; 7hr); Barranquilla (15 daily; 18hr); Bucaramanga (3–4 hourly; 10hr); Cali (4–5 hourly; 10hr); Cartagena (19 daily; 22hr); Cúcuta (10–12 daily; 15hr); La Plata (for Tierradentro) (7 daily; 9hr); Lima, Peru (3 weekly; 72hr); Manizales (24 daily; 8hr); Medellín (5–6 hourly; 9–10hr); Pasto (8 daily; 22hr); Pereira (2–4 hourly; 9hr); Popayán (6 daily; 12hr); Quito, Ecuador (3 weekly; 28hr); San Agustín (7 daily; 12hr); San Gil (3–4 hourly; 7hr 30min); Santa Marta (11 daily, mostly overnight; 18hr); Tunja (3–4 hourly; 3hr).

Portal del Norte TransMilenio station Buses leave from here for Zipaquirá, Suesca and Guatavita, with one-stop TransMilenio transit to the nearby Terminal del Norte, the best place to pick up buses for Tunja. Buses also run to Guatavita from Cra 13, at C 72.

Destinations Guatavita (every 15min; 1hr 30min); Suesca (every 15min; 1hr); Tunja (3–4 hourly; 2hr 30min); Zipaquirá (every 5–10min; 1hr).

INFORMATION

Tourist information The local tourist office (ⓦbogota.gov.co/mi-ciudad/turismo) has its most central PiT (Punto de Información Turística) in the Casa de los Comuneros, at Cra 8 No. 9–85 in the southwest corner of Plaza de Bolívar. There are others at the airport (both terminals), bus terminal and in the Parque de Independencia on Cra 7, at C 26. They are very helpful, give out a free city map, and can handle most queries in English.

Listings The monthly free English-language *The City Paper* (ⓦthecitypaperbogota.com) has news and local information.

TOURS

Andes Ecotours Cra 3 No. 12B–89 ⓦandesecotours.com. Offers 8hr hikes in the Parque Nacional Natural Sumapaz south of town or the Parque Nacional Natural Chingaza east of town, with their unique, tundra-like *páramo* ecosystem.

Bogotá Bike Tours Cra 3 No. 12–72, La Candelaria ⓦbogotabiketours.com. Their 4hr city bicycle tour starts from their office at 10.30am and 1.30pm daily (arrive 30min early to choose your bike) and take you to parts of the city that other tours don't reach.

Bogotá Craft Beer Cra 3 No. 12c–90 ☎5 482 3113. Showcasing that there's more to Colombian beer than your run of the mill offerings from big brands like Aguila, the Bogotá Craft Beer tour offers a carefully curated insight into Bogotá's craft beer scene.

Bogotá Graffiti Tour ⓦbogotagraffiti.com. This excellent 3hr walking tour takes in some of Bogotá's considerable collection of street art (no set fee but a donation is suggested); reserve ahead.

Impulse ☎1 753 4887 ⓦimpulsetravel.co. Offers group or tailor-made tours including a 5hr coffee tour or rafting on the Río Negro.

GETTING AROUND

BY TRANSMILENIO

The **TransMilenio** (ⓦtransmilenio.gov.co) is a "Bus Rapid Transit" or BRT system, which means that it's an ersatz metro system using buses that run in their own dedicated lanes, with stations rather than stops. There are trunk and feeder lines with express and all-stops services, and interchange stations

where the lines meet, often requiring a change of platform. A real metro system is currently under construction, with the first section due to open in 2028.
Opening times Runs roughly 5am–midnight Mon–Sat, 6am–11pm Sun, and during rush hours it can get extremely crowded. Unfortunately, the most useful city-centre station, Museo del Oro, is open at peak times only.
Routes Quite complicated, and the colours on the map are not like metro lines, as any given route will run over several of them. Most routes have a letter and a number. The letter tells you the final destination (so one route has different letters in each direction), and a single-digit number denotes a *servicio corriente*, which runs all day every day and stops at all stations. B5, for example, serves all stops from Portal Norte in the north to Portal del Sur in the south; in the other direction, it's G5. Routes with double-digit numbers serve limited stops and may run limited hours. A few crucial "trunk routes" have numbers only. If you have internet access, you can plan a route using the app CityMapper, but if you haven't pre-planned, each station should somewhere have route maps posted up for all the buses that stop there, and the platforms should have signs indicating which buses stop at them and when they run. Staff are very helpful if you're lost, but aren't likely to speak English.
Fares To use the system, you have to buy a pre-paid card which you load up with credit, but you may be able to ask somebody with a card to let you through on theirs in exchange for cash (this is quite common practice).

BY BUS AND BUSETA
There are lots of privately operated buses around town, mostly minibuses (*buestas*), but you probably won't use them much. They're a bit of a crush, and they don't necessarily have bus stops as such but stop anywhere in the street. There isn't much point worrying about their arcane numbering systems – the important thing is where they're going, which is indicated on the front; the trick is to spot your destination in time to hail the bus. The TransMilenio also has some hybrid buses that run on ordinary roads as well as in the special TransMilenio lanes, and these do have bus stops, which other buses will also use.
Safety It is not a good idea to use buses after dark, and the later it gets the more this is true. They dry up around 10pm anyway.

BY TAXI
Taxis are the safest way to get about, especially after dark, when even for short distances it's best to order a cab. A good third of the taxis on Bogotá's roads are unlicensed, and unlicensed cabbies have been known to rob or assault passengers, so try to phone, rather than hail a taxi.
Taxi companies Reliable firms include TaxExpress (☎ 1 411 1111) and Taxis Ya (☎ 1 333 3333) near the centre, Taxis Libres (☎ 1 211 1111) uptown. Bogotá is also covered by Cabify (w cabify.com/es) and, not entirely legally, by Uber.
Fares All cabs have meters and you should insist they use them.

BY CAR
Driving in Bogotá can be quite stressful. Traffic is often frozen for hours in a frustrating gridlock, and when it does get going, drivers and motorcyclists weave in and out on both sides, turn or change lanes without indicating, and can drive quite aggressively. Right of way at junctions is not always clearly defined, and often just depends on who pushes in front first.
Pico y placa Bogotá has a *pico y placa* scheme, under which vehicles with odd numbers on their plates are banned from driving in most of the city during weekday rush hours (6–8.30am & 3–7.30pm) on odd-numbered dates, and cars with even numbers on even-numbered dates (which is a bit tough on odd-numbered plate holders, who face restrictions on slightly more days of the year). The city council's website (w bogota.gov.co) has a link for *pico y placa* details which doesn't always work, but you can find clear information (in Spanish) at w mundonets.com/pico-y-placa-bogota.
Car rental Avis, Cra 19 No. 122–79, suite 59 ☎ 1 629 1722, and at the airport ☎ 1 745 6613; Budget, C 26 No. 96–66 ☎ 1 745 4811 and at the airport ☎ 321 427 7730; Localiza, Cra 58 No. 127–59, suite 240 ☎ 1 745 7813, and at the airport ☎ 317 667 4788.

BY BICYCLE
Despite the mountains surrounding it, Bogotá itself is largely pretty flat, and it's become the most bicycle-friendly city in South America, with an extensive network of cycle routes, although not all of them are on dedicated cycle lanes. There's a map of them online at w bikemap.net/en/l/3688685. Every Sunday morning (7am–2pm), many of Bogotá's main roads close to traffic in a civic attempt to get people cycling, known as Ciclovía. There's a blog in English on cycling in Bogotá at w mikesbogotabikeblog.blogspot.com.

USEFUL TRANSMILENIO ROUTES
Remember that route numbers with letters are for one direction only.
B74 Universidades (or sometimes Las Aguas) (for La Candelaria) – Calle 57 (for Chapinero) – Héroes (for Zona Rosa) – Portal Norte
J72 Portal Norte –Héroes – Calle 57 – Las Aguas or Universidades
#1 Universidades (free interchange with Las Aguas) – El Tiempo – Portal Eldorado (connected by K86/M86 to the airport)

ACCOMMODATION

La Candelaria is home to most of Bogotá's backpacker hostels, and it's where the action is so far as sights are concerned; it also has a couple of good upmarket hotels. Accommodation in the **city centre** is sparser, but it does have at least one real gem of a place and a few good modern hotels. If, on the other hand, you prefer somewhere safer and less "street", then you're better off **uptown**, although you are then further from the main sights. At upmarket places, you'd be unlucky to have to pay the full rack rate that we quote, especially at weekends or if you book online. As an alternative to hotels, Oasis (⊚oasiscollections.com) offer **apartments** with hotel services such as cleaning and linen changing.

LA CANDELARIA

Alegria's Hostel C 9 No. 2–13 ☎1 442 2384; Ⓜ Las Aguas; map p.60. Friendly, charming and very cosy, this laidback little hostel at the top end of La Candelaria has four- and ten-bed dorms, and private rooms (shared bathroom), wi-fi, a kitchen, two patios and barbecue. On the downside, it's a bit of climb from town (but good exercise), and when it's full – being small – it's pretty damn full. Breakfast included. $

Anandamayi Hostel C 9 No. 2–81 ☎1 341 7208; Ⓜ Las Aguas; map p.60. A cut above your average hostel, set in a restored colonial house around three flower-filled, hammock-strung courtyards frequented by hummingbirds. Rustic dorms and private rooms come with lockers, and shared bathrooms have spacious stone showers. At night, guests gather around the woodfire stove in the communal kitchen, where there's coffee, coca tea and *agua de jamaica*. Small breakfast included. $

Aragon Cra 3 No. 12C–13 ☎1 342 5239; Ⓜ Las Aguas; map p.60. OK, it's rather drab, the mattresses aren't the most comfortable, and it looks like nothing here's changed since it was built in the 1930s, but if you want a private room that's cheaper than a hostel (especially if you're alone), this isn't a bad choice at all: it's clean, with wi-fi throughout (though bathrooms are shared), the rooms are warm and largish, and you could even say it has a kind of period charm. $

★ **Casa Deco** C 12f No. 2–6 ⊚hotelcasadeco.com; Ⓜ Las Aguas; map p.60. This well-run hotel in a smashing Art Deco building is elegantly modern inside with cool, spacious rooms, wooden floors and service with a smile. If there are any quibbles, it's that the location is not the quietest, nor the soundproofing the best, but even that gives you a real feel of being right in the heart of Bogotá, in a hotel that's not run-of-the-mill deluxe but somewhere a bit special. Breakfast included. $

Casa Galeria Cra 2 No. 12B–92 ⊚casagaleria.co; Ⓜ Las Aguas; map p.60. A homely little hostel-style hotel (not a hostel as such; it doesn't have dorms), right in among the *chicha* bars and head shops of Callejón del Embudo. It has great breakfasts, its own coffee shop and two brightly painted courtyards to hang out in – all in all, small but sweet, and although the rooms can get cold, they provide hot water bottles. Breakfast included. $$

★ **Cranky Croc** C 12D No. 3–46 ⊚crankycroc.com; Ⓜ Las Aguas; map p.60. A super-friendly, Australian-owned hostel with sparklingly clean dorms and rooms, well thought out to ensure you have everything you need: very comfy bedding, plenty of power points, free wi-fi and computer terminals, a kitchen with coffee on tap, a restaurant, a smoking terrace, and more than enough bathroom facilities so you'll never have to wait (you can tell the owner's been a backpacker himself). $

Hostal Sue Cra 3 No. 12C–18 ☎1 341 2647; Ⓜ Las Aguas; map p.60. This well-maintained hostel (pronounced "Suey" rather than "Soo") has a party vibe and just about everything a backpacker could want: neat dorms, on-site bar, bean-bag-stacked TV lounge, kitchen, free coffee, laundry service, ping-pong table and regular pub crawls. Breakfast included. $

Hotel de la Ópera C 10 No. 5–72, ⊚hotelopera.com.co; Ⓜ Las Aguas; map p.60. Sumptuous five-star with lashings of history located next door to the Teatro Colón and opposite the Palacio de San Carlos. You get a choice of colonial or Art Deco wings, the first of which once housed Spanish settlers and later Simón Bolívar's private guard. The hotel has a spa with a swimming pool, and the quietest rooms are at the top; insist on one with a window facing outward. Breakfast included. $$

Karuss Hostel Cra 3 No. 12F–28 ☎1 875 5998; Ⓜ Las Aguas; map p.60. A beautifully kept budget option in a lovely old house with a heritage feel that combines some of the comforts of a boutique hotel with backpacker-friendly facilities. Breakfast is included, and very good. On the downside, the walls are rather thin, and sound carries. $

Muisca C 10 No. 0–25 ⊚hotelmuisca.com; Ⓜ Las Aguas; map p.60. Up at the top of Candelaria, with a panoramic terrace, this little boutique hotel (just fourteen rooms) has a pre-Hispanic Muisca theme, offering ceremonies with "ancestral experiences" and ritual healing. It's a lovely old building but the rooms are rather small and some of them are quite dark (ask for one with an outside window). It's also not a great area to wander around alone after nightfall, when you should take a cab to get back here. Breakfast included. $$

Onde Pepe Hostel C 12C bis No. 2–94 ☎1 572 2314; Ⓜ Las Aguas; map p.60. Very clean and well-located little hostel with a variety of rooms: quiet, respectable and family friendly. Breakfast included. $

The Orchids Cra 5 No. 10–55 ⊚theorchidshotel.com; Ⓜ Las Aguas; map p.60. A beautiful little boutique hotel done out in a curiously harmonious blend of modern, classic and kitsch that somehow works brilliantly, with chandeliers, old-fashioned couches and even the odd chaise longue. There's a choice of deluxe rooms (which are indeed deluxe) or suites (which are indeed sweet), staff are punctilious to a fault, and they even throw in a free walking tour of the *barrio*. Breakfast included. $\overline{\underline{\$\$\$}}$

Prisma Hostel Cra 4 No. 11–88 wpaxer.com; wLas Aguas; map p.60. Formerly Swiss- but now Canadian-run, the *Martinik* retains its reputation for being one of the cleanest, best-kept and best-value hostels in town, but those with an aversion to street sounds should opt for a room upstairs or at the back. Breakfast included. $\overline{\underline{\$}}$

CITY CENTRE

Bicentenario Cra 4 No. 16–03 wbhhoteles.com; wLas Aguas; map p.66. Cool, modern rooms in light-on-the-eye grey, cream and beige, of which rooms #1–7 on each floor have fantastic panoramic views over the *Parque de los Periodistas* and Monserrate. The location couldn't be more central and you should be able to get a lower rate if you book online. Breakfast included. $\overline{\underline{\$\$}}$

Ibis Bogotá Museo Transversal 6 No. 27–85 wibis.com; wMuseo Nacional; map p.66. Clean, modern, safe and – yes, OK – a bit bland, the *Ibis* is a reliable if unexciting mid-market chain hotel, usually offering sizeable weekend discounts. Handy for the Museo Nacional, and just a short (if steep) climb away from La Macarena's cosmopolitan dining. Note that the price includes VAT, which they say you can claim back at the airport. $\overline{\underline{\$}}$

Inter Bogotá Cra 3 No. 20–17 winterbogotahotel.com; wUniversidades; map p.66. The public areas in this quirky little hotel are a bit like a rather random art gallery. Rooms are small and the service can sometimes be sporadic, but the staff are generally obliging and there's a restaurant, car park and sauna. It's worth asking for a room with a window facing outward rather than into the light well; rooms at the front have Monserrate views but those at the back are quieter and some have balconies. $\overline{\underline{\$\$}}$

★ **Santa Lucía** C 18 No. 6–27 whotelsantalucia.com.co; wLas Aguas; map p.66. A stone's throw from the Gold Museum, this lovely little boutique hotel in a beautifully restored colonial mansion – formerly owned by Simón Bolívar and for a time home to his mistress Manuelita Sáenz – is a real diamond in the rough, the rough being the not-very-salubrious streets around it (budget eating aplenty, posh dining nil, but of course you can eat in). Aside from that, the location's very handy, and the hotel itself is perfect, with a spa, gym, bar and restaurant, personalized service, and great breakfasts on a bright, covered patio. Breakfast included. $\overline{\underline{\$}}$

Zaragoza C 13 (Av Jiménez) No. 4–56 ☎ 1 284 5411; wLas Aguas; map p.66. A modest but friendly little place with a central location and a nice Art Deco facade. All rooms have bathrooms with hot water, some have small balconies overlooking Av Jimenez, and some even have embellishments that less modest establishments would spin up as period features. $\overline{\underline{\$}}$

CHAPINERO AND ZONA G

12-12 Hostel C 67 No. 4–16 ☎ 1 874 4231; wFlores; map p.71. Snazzy modern decor; lovely staff; good hot showers; super-comfy beds which you can curtain off, each with its own light; big kitchen and dining table; safe, quiet neighbourhood with good eating nearby: what's not to like? $\overline{\underline{\$}}$

★ **Casa Paulina** C 63 No. 17–18 wedificiopaulina.es.tl; wCalle 63; map p.71. A few blocks west of Chapinero proper, this is one of the few good budget options uptown; and it's as sweet as pie: quiet, clean and friendly, with free coffee on tap and a lovely, homely feel. $\overline{\underline{\$\$}}$

Casona del Patio Cra 8 No. 69–24 ☎ 1 212 8805; wFlores; map p.71. It looks like a suburban house on a quiet residential street, but this bright, friendly little mid-range hotel is very handy for the Zona G's dining options, and the peaceful location is a definite plus (rooms facing the street are actually quieter than those facing the little garden in the middle). Rooms are spotless but on the small side, and you may or may not appreciate the firm mattresses. Breakfast included. $\overline{\underline{\$\$}}$

Chapinero Hills Hostel C 65 No. 8–31 ☎ 1 311 8089; wCalle 63; map p.71. This friendly, low-priced hostel on the edge of Zona G is very handy for eating and nightlife. Bunks and rooms are comfortable, a good breakfast is thrown in, and while the hostel's a 15min walk from the main TransMilenio route, regular buses along Cra 7 connect it to La Candelaria and the airport. $\overline{\underline{\$}}$

Four Seasons Casa Medina Cra 7 No. 69A–22 wfourseasons.com/bogotacm; wFlores; map p.71. There's a classic feel to this efficiently-run hotel with carved wooden doors and sober furnishings, although it's to a certain extent phoney (the building dates from 1945, not 1845). Formerly independent, it's now been taken over by the Four Seasons chain, but retains its warm, relaxing atmosphere, and the staff are super-helpful. Rates drop substantially at weekends and off-season. $\overline{\underline{\$\$\$\$}}$

ZONA ROSA AND PARQUE 93

93 Luxury Suites Cra 13A No. 93–51 w93luxurysuites.com; wVirrey; map p.72. The name is in no way misleading: it's off Calle 93, it's all suites, and they really are luxury, with good-size bedrooms and living rooms, plus TVs, equipped kitchenettes (including a washing machine), bathroom and an extra toilet. All the electrical stuff is controlled with a tablet, which is admittedly a bit of a pain if all you want to do is pull the blinds down, but it's super-modern and very plush, and more like taking a luxury apartment than a hotel room. Breakfast included, and there are discounts if you stay more than four days. $\overline{\underline{\$\$\$}}$

BOG Hotel Cra 11 No. 86–74 wboghotel.com; wCalle 85; map p.72. A smart, modern hotel with big scenic windows (so it's worth taking a room on a high floor). There's a good restaurant, with big buffet breakfasts, and a rooftop bar and pool, as well as a spa and small gym. Prices vary by the day, but tend to be less at weekends than midweek. $$$

Cité Cra 15 No. 88–10 w citehotel.com; m Virrey; map p.72. A good deluxe hotel next to a little strip park (that is, a long, thin park with a stream running through it), with a good, heated rooftop pool – great if the weather is hot, but bear in mind that it usually isn't. The rooms are bright and spacious but the beds don't have much give, and it's worth asking for a room overlooking the park rather than the street. Breakfast included. $$

Click-Clack Cra 11 No. 93–77 w clickclackhotel.com; m Virrey; map p.72. Located in the Chicó *barrio*, a block east of Parque 93, this is one self-consciously sleek hotel: "We like to see ourselves," they say, "as a factory of experiences," and it's true that it's a bit up itself, and a bit pricey, but it really is rather stylish and the staff are friendly and cool in all the right ways. Beds are queen-size, and though it does lack some luxury facilities such as a pool and gym, the hotel is full of modern design ideas, aimed at a well-heeled but young clientele, and rather more interesting than the usual five-star options. Breakfast included. $$$$

Virrey Park Cra 15 No. 87–94 w hotelvirreypark.com; m Virrey; map p.72. This hotel is located next to the strip park from which it takes its name, which means you can get a room with a view of the park – it's certainly worth asking for one which doesn't overlook the street. The rooms aren't huge but they're good value and the Zona T (heart of the Zona Rosa) is just a short walk away. Breakfast included. $$

EATING

Expect to find posh restaurants **uptown** (Chapinero, Zona Rosa, Parque 93), less expensive eating in **La Candelaria** and the **city centre**, and small, innovative, bistro-type places in **La Macarena**. In all of these neighbourhoods, **vegetarians** are well catered for, with veg options on the menu in most places bar the most basic (or those specifically specializing in grilled meats). The prime area for **budget eating** is around the junction of Cra 5 with C 18 in the city centre, where, come lunchtime, you'll find no shortage of diners offering *comidas corridas*. Another good area for cheap eats is Pasaje Hernández, on C 12A at Cra 8. Filling Colombian **breakfasts** of *caldo* and *huevos pericos* are often available in local markets such as the one on Cra 2 at C 12C in La Candelaria. For espresso-based **coffees**, *Juan Valdez* (w juanvaldezcafe.com) have branches all over the place.

LA CANDELARIA

Crepes & Waffles C 13 (Av Jiménez) No. 4–55 w crepesywaffles.com.co; m Museo del Oro or m Las Aguas; map p.60. A hugely popular chain restaurant that fulfils every savoury or sweet craving with a monster menu of crêpes and waffles, plus excellent ice cream, not to mention a big range of salads including a serve-yourself salad bar. There are over 50 more outlets across town, detailed on their website. $

Enchiladas C 10 No. 2–12 t 1 649 2112; m Las Aguas; map p.60. Tuck into enchiladas, burritos and other Mexican staples at this colourful spot decorated with black-and-white film stills and Mexican paraphernalia. The home-made salsas have a real kick to them and they even do a decent *pollo en mole poblano* (chicken in chocolate and chilli sauce; don't knock it until you've tried it). $

La Hamburguesería C 11 No. 2–78 w lahamburgueseria.com; m Las Aguas; map p.60. This great little chain offers a huge variety of burgers (with chilli, with blue cheese, with tahini and *tabbouleh*…), including a plain old quarter-pounder (and even then, you have a choice of buns, sauces and relishes, and they ask how well done you want it), or there is a veg-burger option, plus side-dishes, starters and desserts. Eleven other locations around town are detailed on their website; the Zona Rosa branch doubles up as a live music venue (see page 81). $

Hibiscus Restaurant C 12D bis No. 2–21 w hibiscus-restaurante.negocio.site; m Las Aguas; map p.60. A spot-on little place for a low-priced breakfast, lunch or dinner: nothing fancy but filling, staple dishes, well cooked, with set menus. $

Kutral C 17 No. 2–60 w kutral.wix.com/kutral; m Las Aguas; map p.60. The chef here's from Argentina, so don't bother with the rabbit food: go straight for the quarter-kilo baby beef or the striploin with garlic mushrooms, with a bottle of full-bodied Argentine red to wash it down. $$

Paella C 11 No. 5–13 t 1 566 7083; m Las Aguas; map p.60. This lovely Spanish restaurant does what it says on the tin, with a choice of three paellas (Valencian, seafood-only, or the house paella with seafood and Spanish chorizo). It also has a range of other fine Spanish dishes, as well as Spanish and South American wines – or, if you prefer it, sangría – and a real Castilian ambience. $

La Puerta Falsa C 11 No. 6–50 t 1 286 5091; m San Victorino; map p.60. Founded in 1816, this is the oldest, best and possibly smallest place to get a chocolate *completo*, consisting of a mug of hot chocolate, bread and butter, an *almojábana* (cheesy cornflour roll) and a wedge of Colombian cheese. It's a traditional breakfast, but you may prefer it at teatime. And if you still have room, this is also the spot for Bogotá's best (though far from cheapest) *tamales*. $

★ **Quinua y Amaranto** C 11 No. 2–95 w quinuay amaranto.com; m Las Aguas; map p.60. A tiny place with an open kitchen and delicious vegetarian set lunches, largely organic. Dishes change daily, but include things like black bean soup, mushroom risotto, salads and guacamole. They also sell wholewheat *empanadas*, bread, eggs and coffee. $

ReverdeSer C 17 No. 2–46 t 1 284 0820; m Las Aguas; map p.60. Wholemeal, organic vegetarian restaurant, for those who take their healthy eating seriously, and it's pretty tasty too. A veg-burger in a wholemeal bun is a popular choice, or there's a set menu available, and they sell wholemeal breads and cakes to take away. $

Rosita C 12B bis No. 1A–26 ☎ 1 283 6737; Ⓜ Las Aguas; map p.60. Aimed unashamedly at students and backpackers, this is one of the few La Candelaria restaurants open late seven days a week. The food is well priced and not at all bad, especially if you stick to Colombian dishes (such as *ajiaco santandereño*), or pasta (such as spag bol). Any of the three floors gives you a view over the comings and goings on Plazoleta del Chorro de Quevado, and the top floor has live music in the evenings. On the downside, service can be rather slow. $$

Sant Just C 16A No. 2–73 Ⓦ instagram.com/santjust bogota; Ⓜ Las Aguas; map p.60. We can't tell you what's on the menu at this innovative little French-style café-restaurant, because they change it every day depending on what fresh ingredients are available and what they feel like cooking, but we can tell you that it's going to be absolutely delicious, and very reasonably priced indeed. $$

Trattoria Nuraghe C 12B No. 6–58 (upstairs) Ⓦ nuraghe bogota.wixsite.com/trattorianuraghe; Ⓜ Museo de Oro; map p.60. Some of the very best pasta in town, including proper, Italian-style *fettuccine alla carbonara*, or *penne acciughe e gamberetti* (with anchovies and prawns in a creamy sauce), all made with pukka ingredients including real Italian cheeses. Choosing between the dessert options is a dilemma of Solomonic proportions, but the chocolate cake is sublime. $$

CITY CENTRE

Bulevar Sésamo C 13 (Av Jiménez) No. 4–64 ☎ 1 341 3983; Ⓜ Museo del Oro or Ⓜ Las Aguas; map p.66. This bright, busy vegetarian canteen serves a great-value *menú ejecutivo* (noon–4pm, but get there early as they sometimes run out), including soup, main course, salad selection and fruit, and otherwise has healthy veg-burgers and other vegetarian snacks. $

Pastelería Florida Cra 7 No. 21–46 ☎ 1 393 7874; Ⓦ Universidades; map p.66. A real Bogotá institution, going since 1936. The ground floor is a superb patisserie and elegant coffee lounge, just the place for a coffee and a pastry when you're downtown, although service can be slow. If you need a full meal, pop upstairs to the no-less-elegant *Salón Republicano*, where you can tuck into a house lasagne or a filet mignon steak. $$

La Romana Cra 7 No. 19–48 Ⓦ laromana.co; Ⓜ Universidades; map p.66. Great pasta, with a choice of 26 different pastas, long (including spaghetti), short (including penne) or filled (including two types of ravioli), accompanied by a choice of 24 different sauces. The service could be better, but the pasta's great, and they do good bread and breakfasts too. $$

Sopas (de Mamá) y Postres (de la Abuela) Suites 2–41, Edificio Bavaria, Cra 13 No. 27–98 Ⓦ sopasy postres-mrg.com; Ⓜ Museo Nacional; map p.66. The original branch of this popular restaurant has unfortunately closed but you can still lunch on soups like *mamá* used to make (such as plantain soup with meat and potatoes) and desserts like grandma used to make (such as figs with *arequipe*) at this and thirteen more branches around town, and they also deliver. $

LA MACARENA

Beograd C 26B No. 4A–16 ☎ 1 283 4866; Ⓜ Museo Nacional; map p.66. The proprietor of this great little Serbian restaurant is immensely proud of her country's cuisine and she's determined that you'll love it too, even if you can't pronounce it. Among the excellent dishes on offer, *Gulaš serbio* is Serbian goulash – not the same as the Hungarian variety – while *pijani zec* is rabbit in white wine sauce. So what's the Serbian for "yum!"? $$

El Boliche C 27 No. 5–66 Ⓦ restauranteelboliche.com; Ⓜ Museo Nacional; map p.66. An unpretentious little place that offers two things – pasta and *milanesa* (breaded meat). Both come in several varieties, both are cooked to perfection, and you can opt for one or the other, but your best bet is to go for half and half, either pasta with *milanesa*, or half a plate of pasta with one sauce and half with another. Lunchtimes are often very busy; evenings quieter. They also have a branch in Candelaria at C 12B No. 2–97. $

La Juguetería C 27 No. 4A–03 Ⓦ restaurantelajugueteria. com.co; Ⓜ Museo Nacional; map p.66. A very stylish and fun restaurant with a toyshop theme, toys on the walls, a pinball machine, and even one table inside a big cup, although it has to be said that the decor takes precedence over the cuisine, which is decent but not outstanding. The dishes, inevitably, have silly names: barbecue ribs, for example, are "Miss Piggy" and fish of the day is "Capitán Haddock". At weekends you'll need to book. $$

Tapas Macarena Cra 4A No. 26B–01 ☎ 1 310 2277; Ⓜ Museo Nacional; map p.66. This isn't the only place in La Macarena where you can *tapear*, and it certainly isn't the cheapest, but it's the best. A list of what's available is chalked up daily, including the likes of sautéed octopus or beef satay, and there are good wines and local or imported beers to wash it down. It's only a little place so it's a good idea to book. $$$

CHAPINERO AND ZONA G

69 Oyster Bar C 69A No. 5–59 ☎ 1 249 0426; Ⓜ Flores; map p.71. It started off as just an oyster bar, but this is now one of Bogotá's top spots for super-fresh seafood, whether served raw or cooked just to tenderness. Of course you can still start off with oysters (starting at the half dozen), or have mussels (plated in half a kilo portions) served in a choice of five different ways. $$

Diana García Cra 7 No. 70–94 Ⓦ restaurantedianagarcia.

co; ⓂFlores; map p.71. It may look like a café from the outside, and it's open mornings for an excellent breakfast, but this is also Bogotá's foremost *costeño* restaurant (for cuisine from the Caribbean coast), as evidenced by their superb *posta negra* (pot-roast beef in black sauce) or *róbalo caribeña* (sea bass in white wine sauce), not to mention the friendly and informal service. They also have a branch in Usaquén at C 116 No. 7–15. $$

Doméstica C 57 No. 56–35 ☎1 467 2409; ⓂCalle 57; map p.71. A laidback, airy little Chapinero café, where they serve up a range of gourmet *empanadas* including the *andino*, filled with chicken and corn, or the *persé*, stuffed with rocket (arugula), black olives, tomato and ricotta. $

Masa C 70 No. 4–63 ☎1 255 4138, ⓦsomosmasa.com; ⓂFlores or Calle 57; map p.71. The Bogotá outlet of a well liked chain, this is the most indulgent place in town to enjoy comfort foods and baked goods. With elegant decor and well-presented dishes, it serves up some of the tastiest frittatas around, followed by some wonderfully flavoured acai bowls, with oodles of desserts on offer to boot. $$

Mini Mal Transversal 4 bis No. 57–52 ⓦwww.mini-mal.org; ⓂCalle 57; map p.71. Interesting and innovative Colombian regional dishes, with starters like squid *chicharrón*, main dishes such as *arawak karib* (sea bass encrusted with cassava flour in a guava, feijoia and dill sauce) and desserts made with exotic fruits. $$

ZONA ROSA AND PARQUE 93

Arrogante Restaurante Bogotá C 82 No. 9–11 ⓦbogota.arrogante.world; ⓂHéroes; map p.72. If you're looking for a posh Italian feed, this could be the place: it's comfortable and well-appointed, and the food is classic cuisine, well-cooked and well-served, from an extensive menu. $$

★ Central Cevichería Cra 13 No. 85–14 ⓦtakami.co/central-cevicheria; ⓂHéroes; map p.72. No prizes for guessing what's top of the menu here: ceviche, with a choice of fish, prawn, octopus, or a mixture of everything, and when you've decided which of those you want, there's a choice of twelve different dressings, some spicy, some not. Any way you want it though, it's going to give your taste buds a big, fresh zing. $$

Cooking Taichi Cra 14 No. 93–14 ☎1 256 9600; ⓂVirrey; map p.72. The finest Chinese in town, where you can start with a wonton soup before you sink your teeth into some Cantonese-style roast duck or Szechuan-style fried duck. $$

Di Lucca Cra 13 No. 85–33 ⓦdiluccarestaurante.com; ⓂHéroes; map p.72. Munch on wood-fired pizzas (pizza margherita), home-made pasta (*linguine alle vongole*) and expertly cooked risotto (vegetarian) at this smart Italian restaurant. $$

Wok Cra 13 No. 82–74 ⓦwok.com.co; ⓂHéroes; map p.72. One of ten branches around town of this chain of pan-Asian restaurants with cool, modern decor and a menu clearly constructed by someone who knows Asian food. Choose from heaped noodle salads, Thai curries, sushi, tempura and much more. The fish is responsibly sourced, and the lemonade is delicious. Spice fans should ask for extra chilli. $$ Mon–Sat noon–10.30pm, Sun noon–9pm.

USAQUÉN

Bicono Usaquen Cra 6A No. 117–35 ☎1 479 0684. A trendy fast food joint within painfully hip polished concrete surrounds. Expect a Colombian spin on all the classics here, with everything from fried chicken sandwiches to heavily spiced mac and cheese. $

Madison Burger Club C 119 No. 5–80 ☎1 214 2153. Top-notch hamburgers with a range of delicious choices including *iberica* (with Spanish chorizo), *americana* (with crispy bacon and cheddar) or Madison (with pulled pork and pepper jack cheese). They also have veg-burgers and excellent draught beer. $$

DRINKING AND NIGHTLIFE

Bogotá is well furnished with drinking holes, some a bit rough around the edges, others quite refined. Most bars serve only the Bavaria brewing company's proprietary brands (Club Colombia, Aguila and Poker), but a few serve "craft" beers too. A lot of bars also have music and dancing, whether that's salsa, rock, reggae or electronic dance music. Most also serve food. Local papers *El Tiempo* (ⓦeltiempo.com/cultura/entretenimiento) and *El Espectador* (ⓦelespectador.com/entretenimiento) carry entertainment **listings** on Fridays.

BARS

Bogotá Beer Company C 85 No. 13–06, Zona Rosa; ⓂHéroes; map p.72; C 12D No. 4–02, La Candelaria ⓂLas Aguas; map p.60; ☎1 742 9292. The British-influenced "BBC" brew their own range of fine ales and lagers, and serve them in 0.57-litre UK pints, with footie on the telly when there's a big match. The Zona Rosa branch was the original in what's now a chain, but the La Candelaria branch is more like a proper local.

Cervecería Irlandesa Cra 4A No. 26D–15, Macarena ⓦcerveceriairlandesa.com; ⓂMuseo Nacional; map p.66. This isn't just the usual international-style "Irish" pub: for a start, they brew their own Irish-style beers, including a stout and a red ale, as well as an IPA, hand-pulled from the barrel and very good. There's decent food and free popcorn too, and it's particularly popular on Friday and Saturday nights.

Frites Artois C 82 No. 12–09, Zona Rosa ⓦstellaartois.co/frites-artois; ⓂHéroes; map p.72. Lauded as the world's first purely Stella Artois beer bar and restaurant, Frites Artois is an always jubilant spot with nightly specials.

Jhonny Cay Cra 13 No. 82–17, Zona Rosa ⓦjhonnycaybar.com; ⓂHéroes; map p.72. Reggae, soca and calypso bar where there are live bands on Fri and Sat, a laidback crowd, and a range of exotic cocktails and mocktails.

Quiebra Canto Cra 5 No. 17–76, Centro ☎ 1 243 1630, Ⓦ quiebracanto.com; Ⓜ Las Aguas; map p.66. This ever-popular salsa bar has been going for over thirty years. The music is tip-top, and it's much favoured by musicians and intellectuals. Anyone dances with anyone and the vibe is super-friendly.

Rincón Cubano Cra 4 No. 18–50 (2nd floor), Centro ☎ 1 283 1593; Ⓜ Las Aguas; map p.66. With excellent music and some pretty sharp dancing on the floor, this hugely popular Cuban-style downtown salsa bar can get quite packed out on a weekend.

A Seis Manos C 22 No. 8–60, Centro Ⓦ aseismanos.com.co; Ⓜ Calle 22; map p.66. Cool, spacious, French-run bar: minimalist decor, food, patio, meetings, film shows, bands and events; hip as hell, nuff said.

Sin Palabras Café Sordo Cra 7 No. 57–47, Chapinero ☎ 310 551 4473; Ⓜ Calle 57; map p.71. The name means, "Wordless Deaf Café", and it's run by deaf people for deaf people, but for anyone else as well. The staff are all deaf, and they use Colombian signing, but if you don't know that, you can write your order down, or point to it on the menu, and they have little signs with questions like "¿Qué quieres?" ("What do you want?") and "¿Necesitas algo más?" ("Do you need anything else?"). There are games like Jenga or dominoes, and music videos (normal volume) with big screens, subtitles and a pulsing dance floor to feel the beats.

Smoking Molly C 29 bis No. 5–74, Macarena Ⓦ smokingmolly.com.co; Ⓜ Museo Nacional; map p.66. This is a rock and blues bar with live music and decent burgers (it's also open for lunch); sometimes they put on stand-up comedy during the week, so check what's on first (under "Eventos" on their website).

Treffen Cra 7 No. 56–17, Chapinero ☎ 1 377 7935; Ⓜ Calle 57; map p.71. A colourful subterranean bar where the cutely kitsch decor is based on a theme of toys and board games, with spaces for all kinds of amusements, including karaoke, and even an area dedicated to the 1970s.

CLUBS

Andrés Carne de Res Hogar Encendido, C 3 No. 11A–56, Chía Ⓦ andrescarnederes.com. 25km north of town, this huge restaurant, with eleven dining areas and a 62-page menu, doubles up as an extremely popular nightclub with two dancefloors, a permanent party atmosphere, and walls and ceilings decked out with love hearts and knick-knacks (which they make themselves, and which you can buy). The easiest way to get here is on an excursion offered by pretty much all of Bogotá's hostels, usually for a fixed fee before drinks (which aren't cheap).

El Coq C 84 bis No. 14–02, Zona Rosa ☎ 1 611 2496; Ⓜ Héroes; map p.72. Behind the discreet red, white and green door (no sign, just a cockerel logo high above the door and to the right), this trendy little club looks like someone's living room, complete with armchairs and sofas (and OK, yes, a tree), or, when they pull back the ceiling, someone's cosy little back yard. The music is indie to techno, the atmosphere intimate, the crowd chic.

La Hamburguesería C 85 No. 12–49, Zona Rosa ☎ 1 610 2001, Ⓦ lahamburgueseria.com; Ⓜ Héroes; map p.72. Yes, a burger bar, and part of a city-wide chain (see page 78), but also a live music venue, and a good one. This is where a lot of local bands launch their new releases, and it's an important venue so far as Bogotano rock is concerned. Entry for concerts is usually free on Fridays. Music Fri & Sat from 9pm.

Once Once C 84 bis No. 13–86, Zona Rosa ☎ 300 757

LGBTQ+ BOGOTÁ

Chapinero is the centre of LGBTQ+ life in Bogotá, and particularly Calle 59 between Carrera 7 and Avenida Caracas (Carrera 14). You'll find Bogotá listings at Ⓦ egocitymgz.com.

LGBTQ+ BARS AND CLUBS

Kaputt Club Bogotá Cll 72a 10, Av. Caracas Ⓦ kaputtclub.com; map p.66. This weekend-only club spans eight large event spaces, with industrial chic decor and every style of music imaginable. The custom neon lighting throughout makes this spot photo worthy to boot.

El Recreo de Adán Cra 12A No. 79–45, Zona Rosa ☎ 1 248 6362; Ⓜ Héroes; map p.71. A bright, friendly and easy-going café-bar where a lot of LGBTQ+ people meet up at the start of a night out, or just for a drink or a coffee, a snack or a meal, or even a game of Scrabble. Also has a branch in Chapinero at Cra 9 No. 59–85.

Theatron C 58 No.10–18, Chapinero Ⓦ theatron.co; Ⓜ Calle 57; map p.71. Huge LGBTQ+ disco with ten different spaces, including one exclusively for women, a capacity of some 8000 people, and a choice of sounds ranging from Latin to electronica to retro to crossover. The cover charge typically includes a barra libre with unlimited Colombian spirits till 2am.

Village Café Cra 8 No. 64–29, Chapinero Ⓦ facebook.com/VillageBogota; Ⓜ Calle 63; map p.71. Bogotá's first LGBTQ+ café, and a good place to kick off a night out, find out what's going on, or just to have a coffee or a cocktail while taking in a bit of music (indie, house, retro).

3785; ⓜHéroes; map p.72. No caps or trainers allowed in this refined Zona Rosa nightspot billed as "an exclusive bar where you can synchronize with the universe". There's electronic music, a decent lightshow, and a terrace café out front for chilling out and having a chat.
La Villa Cra 14A No. 83–56, Zona Rosa ☎ 313 236 4413; ⓜHéroes; map p.72. Unashamedly aimed at foreigners – but at foreigners who want to meet locals – this club with modern-rustic decor and upbeat music holds "Gringo Tuesdays" weekly (starting with a conversation session to practice your Spanish and/or help Colombians practice their English).

SHOPPING

MARKETS

Emerald Market Cra 6 between C 12C and Av Jiménez, by Plazoleta Rosario, La Candelaria; ⓜMuseo del Oro; map p.60. Every day during the week, emerald dealers gather here to do business, right out in the street, pulling gemstones out of paper wraps, examining them with eyeglasses and haggling over the price. It may look like some shady black-market operation, but many of the emerald dealers are legit, trading outside to take advantage of direct sunlight. You definitely wouldn't want to buy gems here yourself unless you really know your stuff (see page 46), but it's fascinating to watch.

Mercado de Pulgas Usaquén; ⓜPepe Sierra. There are three parts to this "flea market", but none of them are flea markets in the usual sense. On C 116 Bis between Cra 6 and Cra 7, there's a (daily) market selling low-priced arts and crafts, hippy-type jewellery, incense and suchlike. On Cra 6A between C 119 and C 119B, you'll find home-made cakes and jams, toys, bags and purses, and cosmetics made with things that more commonly go into food. Finally, in a car park on Cra 5 opposite C 119B, there's a slightly more upmarket section, selling posher crafts and jewellery, clothes and fancy toiletries, with some food stalls too. Bric-a-brac is notable by its absence in all three sections.

Mercado de Pulgas de la 26 Cra 7, at C 24 and around, Centro; ⓜCalle 26; map p.66. Bogotá's biggest and most interesting flea market. There's plenty of junk and bric-a-brac of course, bargains of all sorts, books and records, things that are more like proper antiques, food, crafts and jewellery. Even if you don't buy anything, it's a worthwhile downtown Sunday stroll.

Paloquemao C 19 No. 25–02; ⓜPaloquemao. The city's main produce market, a massive circular complex whose main section is a maze of fruit and veg stalls piled high with huge quantities of fresh produce, while other areas sell eggs and dairy products, or meat or fish. There's a particularly large and colourful section for flowers.

Pulguero de las Aguas Cra 3 No. 17–10, La Candelaria/Centro; ⓜLas Aguas; map p.66. Informal flea market in a car park and neighbouring stretch of Cra 3. Bric-a-brac, handicrafts and general junk – nothing massively exciting, but a fun browse, and local if you're in La Candelaria.

CRAFTS

Artesanías de Colombia Cra 2 No. 18A–58 (Plazuela de las Aguas), La Candelaria ☎ 1 284 3095, ⓜLas Aguas, map p.66; C 86A No. 13A–10, Zona Rosa ☎ 1 691 7149, ⓜHéroes; map p.72. High-quality, fairtrade crafts from an organization dedicated to using original materials and maintaining Colombia's craft traditions. They've got everything from hammocks to Werregue spiral basketwork coasters. Entry to the Las Aguas shop is via a beautiful seventeenth-century cloister that was originally part of the neighbouring Nuestra Señora de las Aguas church.

El Balay Cra 15 No. 75–75, Zona Rosa ☎ 1 217 0762; ⓜCalle 76; map p.72. A good choice of handicrafts from around Colombia, especially good on clothing including *ruana* ponchos and *vueltiao* hats, moccasins made with raw cowhide, and shoes with *mola* (reverse-appliqué) uppers, not to mention blankets, shawls, carvings and basketware. Well worth a browse.

Centro Colombiano de Artesanías Cra 7 No. 22–66, Centro ☎ 1 336 4709; ⓜCalle 22; map p.66. A little mall of shops selling typical tourist souvenirs, including bags, leatherware, "I ♥ Colombia" mugs, T-shirts, even emeralds (non-gem-quality ones are good value).

Pasaje Rivas Cra 10 No. 10–54, La Candelaria; ⓜSan Victorino; map p.60. Lots of crafts at good prices in this L-shaped passageway full of handicraft shops that's been going since 1893. There's basketware, kitchenware, pottery, furniture and more.

CLOTHES, ACCESSORIES AND COSMETICS

Centro Comercial Andino Cra 11 No. 82–71, Zona Rosa ⓦcentroandino.com.co; ⓜHéroes; map p.72. Bogotá's favourite shopping mall is not really a place you'd come to buy anything you can't get at home – it's full of stores selling the usual designer brands at the usual international prices – but it's a favourite hangout of well-heeled Bogotanos, with a food court and a cinema.

Emerald Trade Center C 13 (Av Jiménez) No. #5–43, Centro; ⓜMuseo del Oro; map p.60. A mall of shops selling emeralds, and a good place to come if you're no expert but looking for somewhere reliable to buy a stone or an item of emerald jewellery.

Only Cra 7 No. 12A–36 & No. 21–37, La Candelaria ⓦalmacenesonly.com; ⓜMuseo del Oro; map p.60. Pile 'em high, flog 'em cheap clothes-store chain (with other branches around town), handy if you need basic clothing supplies such as socks or underwear, or a towel.

BOGOTÁ FESTIVALS

Around Easter in every even-numbered year, the **Festival Iberoamericano de Teatro** (facebook.com/FITBogota) is a two-week festival of theatre and performance, including dance, music, circus and puppet shows. In early July, Parque Simón Bolívar is the venue for **Rock al Parque** (rockalparque.gov.co), a three-day festival of – as you may have guessed – rock in the park; the same park has a **carnival** on August 5 or 6 to celebrate the anniversary of the city's foundation. In mid-September, there's a weekend of jazz at **Jazz al Parque** (jazzalparque.gov.co), whose main venue is Usaquén's Parque el Country. Late October sees the **Festival de Cine de Bogotá** (Bogotá Film Festival; bogocine.com), featuring films from South America and around the world, mostly in Spanish of course, with (unusually for a film festival) almost none in English. And in November, **Salsa al Parque** (salsaalparque.gov.co) is a weekend of free salsa bands in Parque Simón Bolívar.

MUSIC AND BOOKS

Librería Lerner C 13 (Av Jiménez) 4–35, La Candelaria librerialerner.com.co; Museo del Oro or Las Aguas; map p.60. A large, central bookshop with a small but good selection of English-language books in the basement. There's also a branch uptown at Cra 11 No. 85–52.

Panamericana Cra 7 No. 18–48, Centro panamericana.com.co; Las Aguas; map p.66. Sells books, magazines, a few maps and some simple electronic goods.

Septimazo's Cra 7 No. 17–52 (upstairs), Centro; Museo del Oro; map p.66. A very informal market selling CDs, DVDs and Blu-rays.

SUPERMARKETS

Éxito Cra 7 No. 11–30 (off Plaza de Bolívar), La Candelaria San Victorino, map p.60; Cra 7 No. 22–36, Centro (Las Nieves), Las Nieves, map p.66; exito.com. The two most central branches of Colombia's biggest supermarket chain, with others across town.

DIRECTORY

Banks and exchange A number of moneychangers can be found around the junction of Av Jiménez with Cra 6 in the city centre; rates vary so ask around before choosing. There are concentrations of banks with ATMs on Cra 7 immediately north of Parque de Santander and at C 16–C 17 and C 19–C 20.

Embassies and consulates Australia, Edificio Tierra Firme, Cra 9 No. 115–06/30, suite 2002, Campo Alegre ☎ 1 657 0800; Brazil, C 93 No. 14–20 (8th floor), Chicó ☎ 1 635 1694; Canada, C 7 No. 114–33 (14th floor), Campo Alegre ☎ 1 657 9800; Ecuador, C 89 No. 13–07, Chicó ☎ 1 212 6512; Ireland (honorary consul), Av Americas 56–41, San Rafael ☎ 1 432 0695; New Zealand, covered by embassy in Chile ☎ +56 2 261 63000; Panama, C 92 No. 7A–40, Chicó ☎ 1 257 5067; Peru, C 80A No. 6–50, Los Rosales ☎ 1 746 2360; South Africa (honorary consulate, no published address) ☎ 1 214 0397; UK, Cra 9 No. 76–49 (8th floor), Bellavista ☎ 1 326 8300; USA, Cra 45 No. 24B–27, Quinta Paredes ☎ 1 275 2000; Venezuela, Cra 11 No. 87–51 (5th floor), Zona Rosa ☎ 1 644 5555.

Football Bogotá's two clubs, Santa Fe and Millonarios, share the Campín stadium at Cra 30 with C 57 (El Campín). Except for *clásicos*, you can generally just roll up on match days and buy tickets on the gate.

Health Decent private clinics include: Clínica de Marly, C 50 No. 9–67, Chapinero ☎ 1 343 6600, marly.com.co; Clínica del Country, Cra 16 No. 82–57, El Retiro ☎ 1 530 0470, clinicadelcountry.com. There's a 24hr doctors' call-out service: ADOM Salud Domiciliaria (☎ 1 256 3930, adomsaluddomiciliaria.com).

Internet Loads of places, including: MDC Taiwan, C 12B No. 5–19, La Candelaria; Euronet, Cra 5 No. 16–90, Centro; Típicos Muzo de Colombia, C 13 (Av Jiménez) No. 4–76, Centro.

Laundry Lavandería La Candelaria, C 12D No. 3–75, La Candelaria; Lavandería Megarápido, Cra 3 No. 12C–23, La Candelaria (also has a great clothes repair service).

Police Policía de Turismo, C 28 No. 13A–24 ☎ 1 337 4413 or ☎ 1 243 1175.

Post office Cra 8, at C 12, La Candelaria. Típicos Muzo de Colombia, C 13 (Av Jiménez) No. 4–76, Centro.

Spanish courses PEPE (Programas de Español para Extranjeros; ☎ 316 463 5724, ✉ colombia.pepe@gmail.com) offer private classes at all levels. Spanish World Institute, Cra 4A No. 56–56, Chapinero (spanishworldinstitute.com) offers a week's classes (15hr) for a charge and registration fee. Other options include International House, C 10 No. 4–09, La Candelaria (ihbogota.com), or Nueva Lengua, C 69 No. 11A–09, Zona G (nuevalengua.com).

Tejo bars *Los Bucaros*, C 20 No. 8–74 – the bar and the neighbourhood are a bit rough and ready, fine during the day, but not after dark.

Visa extensions Migración Colombia, C 26 No. 59–51 (Edificio Argos), Torre 3, 4th floor, Centro Administrativo Nacional; CAN.

North of Bogotá

- 86 Zipaquirá
- 90 Suesca
- 91 Laguna de Guatavita
- 91 Tunja
- 95 Villa de Leyva and around
- 103 Parque Nacional Natural el Cocuy
- 105 Guadalupe
- 106 San Gil and around
- 113 Bucaramanga and around
- 118 Pamplona
- 121 Cúcuta and around

BARICHARA

North of Bogotá

North of Bogotá, the Eastern Cordillera stretches up towards – and indeed along – the Venezuelan border. These mountainous highlands played a pivotal role in forging Colombia's national identity, for this is the region that was so crucial to Simón Bolívar's forces in the struggle for independence, and the homeland of Bolívar's great ally and rival Francisco de Paula Santander. Even before that, it was the heartland of the *comunero* revolt of the 1780s. It's a rugged and very beautiful region, with national parks such as the Parque Nacional el Cocuy, with its glacial lakes and snow-capped peaks, and the Parque Nacional del Chicamocha, where you can gape in awe at the scenic Río Chicamocha canyon.

Divided between the *departamentos* of Cundinamarca, Boyacá, Santander and Norte de Santander, this is Colombia's geographical heart. On the southern edge of the region, in Cundinamarca, the *departamento* immediately surrounding Bogotá, attractions such as the salt cathedral at **Zipaquirá**, the rock-climbing centre of **Suesca** and the Muiscas' sacred lake, the **Laguna de Guatavita**, can all be visited on day-trips from the capital. Further afield, in Boyacá, the *departamento*'s capital of **Tunja**, one of Colombia's oldest cities, is famous for its sixteenth-century churches and frescoes, while an hour further northwest is one of Colombia's best-preserved colonial towns, **Villa de Leyva**.

Further north, the two *departamentos* of Santander and Norte de Santander straddle the Eastern Cordillera, getting noticeably nippier as you rise towards the border between them. The *departamento* of Santander is dominated by its capital, the lively, modern – and warm – city of **Bucaramanga**, but the big draw from a tourist point of view is the adventure-sports centre of **San Gil**. Over the *cordillera*'s watershed, Norte de Santander's exhilarating capital of **Pamplona** is the last mountain town before you head inexorably down towards the coastal plain of Venezuela.

Zipaquirá

Once the country's most important city, **ZIPAQUIRÁ**, 48km north of Bogotá, grew rich on its salt mines and is today best known for its fabulous **subterranean salt cathedral**, which draws tourists from far and wide. It's an easy and very popular day-trip from Bogotá, but you could equally stay the night here. Either way it's best to visit during the week, since half of Bogotá descends on the cathedral at the weekend. There's information (in Spanish) on the town's attractions at Wzipaquira-cundinamarca.blogspot.com.

Brief history

The land on which Zipaquirá now stands was once a seabed. As the mountains rose, the sea became an inland salt lake and eventually dried up, leaving huge deposits of **salt**. When the Spanish arrived, the Muiscas were mining this by open-cast methods, making it into loaves, which they used as a medium of exchange. This method of mining continued into the colonial period until, in 1801, the German explorer Alexander von Humboldt suggested digging shafts and tunnelling for the salt. Kilometre after kilometre of tunnels were subsequently excavated on multiple levels, but nowadays more sophisticated methods are used, pumping in water to dissolve the salt and then extracting it – to this day the mines here produce half of all the salt consumed in Colombia.

VILLA DE LEYVA

Highlights

❶ **Zipaquirá salt cathedral** The world's only underground cathedral is both impressive and eerie, hewn out of solid salt in a mine that's been in use since pre-Hispanic times. See page 89

❷ **Villa de Leyva** Walk the cobbled streets of this beautifully preserved sixteenth-century town surrounded by spectacular mountains, or use it as a base to explore the nearby attractions. See page 95

❸ **Parque Nacional Natural el Cocuy** A trekkers' paradise, full of snowy peaks, high-altitude lakes and dramatic scenery. See page 103

❹ **Adventure sports near San Gil** Colombia's adrenaline capital has a whole menu of thrills and spills on offer, from speeding down the rapids to soaring the thermals. See page 108

❺ **Barichara** With a name that means "place of relaxation", this gorgeous and rather refined old town, full of whitewashed *pisé* houses, has a calm and unstressed pace of life. See page 110

❻ **Bucaramanga** This exciting, modern city full of young people is known for its *parques* (green city squares) as well as its excellent nightlife. See page 113

❼ **Pamplona** Up in the mountains, the cool, clean air in this easy-going colonial city is a refreshing change after the heat of lower-altitude places in both directions. See page 118

HIGHLIGHTS ARE MARKED ON THE MAP ON PAGE 88

Town centre

The **town centre** may not have any compelling attractions, but it's a *simpático*, quite charming, little place and worth more than a passing glance. It's centred on two large squares, a block apart. The **Parque Principal** (Cra 7–8, C 4–5) is dominated on its north side by a church faced in stone on its bottom storeys, and in rather crumbling brickwork above that. Work on the church (which is actually Zipaquirá's real cathedral) started in 1805, as a plaque above the left-hand entrance states, but it wasn't finished until 1916.

HIGHLIGHTS

1. Zipaquirá salt cathedral
2. Villa de Leyva
3. Parque Nacional Natural el Cocuy
4. Adventure sports in San Gil
5. Barichara
6. Bucaramanga
7. Pamplona

NORTH OF BOGOTÁ

On the east side of the *parque*, the *Belle Epoque*-style town hall wouldn't look out of place in provincial France. A block east of the Parque Principal, the **Plaza de la Independencia** (Cra 5–6, C 4–5) is where you'll find the town's main concentration of bars and cafés.

Salt cathedral

Southern end of Cra 6 (500m south of the town centre or 1km south of the bus terminal) • guided tours; charge • ⓦ catedraldesal.gov.co • 20min on foot or take a taxi from the bus station

Zipaquirá's famous **salt cathedral** was inaugurated in 1995, to great fanfare, having replaced an earlier underground cathedral that closed because of potential collapse. The cathedral lies completely below ground, topped by a hill that the Muiscas were already mining for salt before the Spanish arrived. The rock into which the cathedral was hewn is 85 percent salt, and glistens in places with crystals of iron pyrites ("fool's gold"). Entry is by **guided tour** only, in English or Spanish, but once inside, you're free to wander about on your own.

The first part of the tour covers the **Via Crucis**, fourteen chapels – the Stations of the Cross – built into the solid salt. Each a different combination of colours, they glow like marble in the soft light. From the last chapel you proceed to the **dome**. It may seem somewhat throwaway having a dome in an underground passage for no apparent reason, but a true cathedral apparently has to have one. The actual **nave** does not have a dome, but it does have the world's largest subterranean cross, a beautiful rock-salt ceiling with the natural black and white swirls of salt veins in it, and a large marble medallion in the floor reproducing Michelangelo's *Creation of Adam* from Rome's Sistine Chapel.

Having oohed and aahed at the cathedral itself, stop at the inevitable souvenir shop, where you can see a **water mirror** (a rock-salt ceiling reflected in a shallow pool – more impressive than it sounds), and a rather tacky eight-minute sound and light show. More worthwhile is the fifteen-minute **3D film** (with English subtitles), which explains the history of the salt mines.

Ruta minero

When you buy your entry ticket for the salt cathedral, you can also pay to add some optional extras. By far the best is the **ruta minero**, which involves spending thirty minutes pretending to be a miner. This also gives you access to the vast network of tunnels at this, the third and most recent level of mines in the complex, of which the cathedral takes up less than a tenth. You are advised, however, not to wander off on your own, in case you get lost.

Museo Arqueológico

Cra 1 No. 6–21 • Charge • ⓦ zipaquiraturistica.com

By the entrance to the salt museum site, the small **Museo Arqueológico** houses more than a thousand mostly ceramic artefacts from all over pre-Hispanic Colombia. Those made by the local Muisca people are a lot less interesting than the pottery belonging to the Tumacos of the southwest, many of which feature large erect phalluses, while figurines made by the Guanes in what is now the *departamento* of Santander show how they deliberately deformed their craniums to look, as they saw it, more elegant.

ARRIVAL AND DEPARTURE   **ZIPAQUIRÁ**

By bus To get to Zipaquirá from Bogotá, take the TransMilenio to the Portal del Norte station at the end of the B line (B74 from Las Aguas), and go through the turnstile to the other side of the platform, where there are frequent buses to Zipaquirá ("Zipa"). In Zipaquirá, the terminal is on Cra 7 between Nos. 10–17 and 10–43, about 500m north of the Parque Principal. For Suesca and Tunja, get a bus to Biceño and change there.

Destinations Biceño (every 15min; 30min); Bogotá (every 5–10min; 1hr).

By train The Tren Turístico de la Sabana (ⓦ turistren.com.co) departs from Bogotá's Estación de la Sabana (C 13 No.

18–24) on Sat, Sun and public holidays only, at 8.30am, arriving at Zipaquirá's station (Cra 11A at C 4) at 11.30am. It leaves just ninety minutes later, and stops at Cajicá for more than two hours, getting back into Bogotá at 5.30pm. It's possible to add on a visit to the salt cathedral on a round trip, rejoining the train at Cajicá.

ACCOMMODATION

Cacique Real Cra 6 No. 2–36 w hotelcaciquereal.com. The old wing in this lovely little hotel, dating from the 1820s, provides bags of period charm. Rooms are old-fashioned in style with modern creature comforts. The new wing has larger, brighter and less charming rooms. Either way, it's the best hotel in town. Breakfast included. $\overline{\underline{\$}}$

Hotel Colonial C 3 No. 6–57 t 1 852 2690. In the old wing, which is indeed colonial, rooms lead off the inner patio, now covered with a transparent plastic roof. There's also a new wing with less quaint but brighter rooms, one of which (for an extra fee) is much bigger and has a jacuzzi. $\overline{\overline{\$}}$

EATING

Brasas del Llano C 1 No. 8–75 t 311 226 2921. The best in a row of Llanero restaurants (look for the life-size plastic cow), where the meat is proudly displayed being barbecued on large skewers out front, and served up (veal or pork with all the trimmings) in a covered yard decorated with everything from old petrol pumps to a mock-up of a British phone box. $\overline{\underline{\$}}$

Don Facundo Cra 5 No. 4–21 t 314 236 5995. There are cheap Colombian breakfasts and *almuerzos corridas* on offer at this unpretentious diner on the Plaza de la Independencia, though the house speciality is *sobrebarriga* (flank steak). $\overline{\underline{\$}}$

Sucursal Paisa Cra 8 No. 3–32 t 1 852 7209. As its name tells you, this is a Paisa restaurant, nothing fancy but neat and pleasant, where you can fill up on well-cooked Antioquian dishes such as *bandeja paisa* or *mondongo*. $\overline{\underline{\$}}$

Suesca

Some 65km north of Bogotá, the small town of **SUESCA** is one of Colombia's top **rock-climbing** destinations. Other adventure sports are available, from abseiling to paintballing, but it is the sandstone cliffs on the town's doorstep that steal the show, offering traditional and sport rock-climbing with more than six hundred routes including multi-pitch.

The gateway for the rocks is **Vereda Cacicazgo**, 500m short of town, where you'll find the hostels and adventure sports companies. From there it's a pleasant walk along the rail track to the rocks themselves.

ARRIVAL AND DEPARTURE   SUESCA

By bus To get to Suesca from Bogotá, take the TransMilenio to the Portal del Norte station at the end of the B line (B74 from Las Aguas), walk to the northern end of the platform and go through the turnstiles to the other side, where there are buses to Suesca (every 15min; 1hr). You'll probably want to get off at Vereda Cacicazgo rather than in the town centre.

ACTIVITIES

Explora Share w explore-share.com/trip/rock-climbing-suesca. This local firm organizes guides and rock climbing itineraries around Suesca, with a pick up point in the town centre.

ACCOMMODATION

Hostal Caminos De Suesca Vereda Cacicazgo, La Playa-Suesca w caminosdesuesca.wixsite.com/hostal. A charming little place, extremely homely, with outdoor dining out back. Breakfast is simple, but you can use the kitchen to cook your own. $\overline{\underline{\$}}$

Hostal Torre Alta Vereda Cacicazgo, 500m off the main road t 311 513 9310. In a peaceful, rural location, and not easy to find (coming along the main road from Suesca, turn left just after the railway, then right after 300m, just after a bridge over a ditch; follow the path round, and then straight ahead where it narrows), this modern building has fresh dorms, en-suite rooms, a kitchen and an oven. Breakfast included. $\overline{\underline{\$}}$

EATING

Doña María Vereda Cacicazgo, on the main road (Cra 4) No. 103 t 321 995 7333. A great little restaurant on the main drag, handy for breakfast, and lunch (*almuerzo corriente*, with friendly staff and tasty food. $\overline{\underline{\$}}$

El Nómada Vereda Cacicazgo, on the main road (Cra 4) No. 105 w elnomadahostel.com. This hostel and adventure activities agency (it also offers yoga) has a good café where you can get sandwiches to take with you to the rocks, or sit in for savoury crêpes (the "hippy warrior" with pulled beef, *refritos*, mozzarella-style cheese and sour cream is popular), plus cold BBC beer. $

Laguna de Guatavita

Parque Natural Laguna de Guatavita • entry by guided tour only (2–3hr) • Charge

The Spanish believed the region around Bogotá had a secret source of gold. They called it El Dorado, and it became their unholy grail. At **Laguna de Guatavita**, a small lake 75km north of Bogotá, they thought they'd found it.

The lake was sacred to the Muiscas, and legend has it that the Muisca ruler Zipa (see page 99), on his inauguration, would be smeared all over with honey and covered in gold dust before riding out into the lake on a reed raft and diving in to offer the gold to the lake's resident goddess, and as a symbol of fertilization. When he emerged from the water, drums would sound and offerings of gold and emeralds would be thrown into the lake. The discovery of a gold model of the raft (now in Bogotá's Museo del Oro; see page 66) lent credence to the myth and attempts over the years to drain the lake have yielded a few trinkets, which it seems were thrown in as offerings, although on nothing like the scale that the gold-obsessed Conquistadors were hoping for.

The lake is in a crater that was previously thought to have been created by a meteorite strike; scientists now think it resulted from the collapse of a salt bed. It is part of a private park, and to visit you have to take a **guided tour** from the entrance, which involves a 7km hike. Note that this is uphill and that you are at an altitude of 3100m, somewhat higher than Bogotá, so it can be cold, and climbing will be more strenuous.

ARRIVAL AND DEPARTURE LAGUNA DE GUATAVITA

By bus In Bogotá, direct buses for Guatavita leave from Cra 13 at the corner of C 72 and from Portal del Norte TransMilenio station at the end of the B line (B74 from Las Aguas or Universidades, depending in the day time; roughly every 15min; 1hr 30min). To get from there to the park entrance at weekends, you can take a *colectivo* from the main square, but during the week you may have to find a taxi or even walk (the turn-off for the lake, halfway between Guatavita and the town of Sesquilé, is accessible by bus). To travel between Guatavita and Suesca, take a bus to the Guatavita turn-off on the main road at Sesquilé, and another from there.

ACCOMMODATION

La Juanita Finca Verde Represa de Tominé ☏ 310 213 5794. An old farmhouse with *pisé* walls, run on permaculture principles as a tiny "eco hotel", with just one double room and a four-bed dorm, but offering various services, including transport to the lake. Most guests take full board. Advance reservation only. $$

Tunja

To many tourists, Boyacá's capital, **TUNJA**, is just a place to change buses on the way to Villa de Leyva, and certainly, if all you're doing is arriving and leaving via the bus depot, it looks a pretty grimy, nondescript place. But get off the bus and wander into town and it's a different story entirely: not only is Tunja's centre compact and attractive, but it's also home to some of the best-preserved **colonial homes and churches** in the country. Unfortunately, the churches open only for Mass, so to see them, you either have to creep in during the service and be discreet, or arrange a visit with the tourist office.

Brief history

According to legend, there were continual wars between the various **Muisca tribes** living in the Boyacá region, until the chiefs decided to choose a supreme ruler, called the **Zaque** (the local equivalent to Bogotá's Zipa), who would have authority over all of them. The first Zaque was called **Hunzahua**, and so his capital was named **Hunza** after him.

In 1537, a Spanish expeditionary force under **Gonzalo Jiménez de Quesada**, in search of gold, conquered Hunza. After disposing of the Zaque and taking as much gold as they could find, the Spanish then, in 1539, declared the foundation of a new city in Hunza's place, called **Tunja**, which became one of the biggest in New Granada.

Social discontent in the late eighteenth century saw Tunja at the heart of the **Revolt of the Comuneros** (see page 341), and the revolutionaries – whose revolt was largely fed by resentment against the state tobacco monopoly, many local farmers being small-scale tobacco producers – were cheered by the townspeople when they arrived on 17 May, 1781 to sack the city's tobacco warehouses. The insurrection ended with agreements, which the authorities reneged on, a fact no doubt remembered when Tunja rose up against Spain in 1811 and declared independence as the **Republic of Tunja**. Spanish forces regained the city in 1816, but three years later, Simón Bolívar marched in to take over, and at the **Battle of Boyacá**, just out of town (see page 94), secured a famous victory that settled the independence question once and for all.

Plaza de Bolívar

Cra 9–10, at C 19–20

The city's main square, **Plaza de Bolívar** is a large open space dominated by an imposing equestrian statue of El Libertador, who had his most famous victory just down the road (see page 94), and of Tunja declared, "This city is heroic", as a plaque on the statue's plinth testifies.

The square is surrounded on three sides by impressive old buildings. On its east side stands the **cathedral**, the oldest church in Colombia, which dates back to 1574, although it has been altered somewhat since, most particularly in 1910 when the Neoclassical gable and the dome on the bell tower were added.

Opposite the cathedral, the **Casa de la Cultura**, with its long wooden veranda, is an original building from 1546. Simón Bolívar slept here the night before the Battle of Boyacá.

Casa del Fundador

Cra 9 No. 19–56 • Free • ☎ 8 742 3272

A few doors from the cathedral, the **Casa del Fundador** is the 1540 home of Gonzalo Suárez Rendón, who founded the Spanish city of Tunja on the ruins of Muisca Hunza. The **tourist office** on the ground floor issues tickets and provides a guide (there's usually one who can speak some English) to show you around the upstairs.

The first room you come to is the **reception hall**, where a false ceiling fell away in 1865 to reveal an amazing set of **frescoes** of animals and fruit trees painted on the real ceiling behind it. The frescoes are slightly later than those in the Casa de Don Juan de Vargas (see page 93) – the rhino, for example, is copied from the one there.

ACCOMMODATION		EATING			
Alicante	3	El Atrio	4	Protamales	2
Casa Real	5	Empanadas Tipicas del Valle	5	Son y Sabor	6
Dux	4	Macedonia	1	**DRINKING**	
Hunza	2	El Maizal	3	Pussini	1
Posada de San Agustín	1	Popeyes's	7		

Next is the **master bedroom**, whose ceiling frescoes of hunting scenes are evidently by a different hand than those in the reception hall, although they also show animals (such as giraffes), which the artist can only have known from pictures. Beyond the bedroom, the **oratory** was used, in what must have been a very religious household, specifically for praying. It leads through to the **women's quarters**, where women (who didn't leave the house without a male relative as chaperone) practised crafts such as spinning, safely ensconced away from prying eyes. The last room, the dining room, has a series of painted panels in blue and orange.

Casa de Don Juan de Vargas

C 20 No. 8–52 • last entry 30min before closing • Charge • 8 742 6611

Like the Casa del Fundador (see page 92), the **Casa de Don Juan de Vargas**, around the corner, has ceiling frescoes that were hidden for many years behind a false ceiling. The house belonged to the king's secretary, who commissioned it in 1585. The frescoes must have been painted soon after. Brighter and more vibrant than those in the Casa del Fundador, they are also more Spanish and less South American in style. They begin in **Don Juan's office** with the shield of Huelva (Don Juan's home city in Spain), and two pictures of Hercules flanked by a lion and a tiger, representing Spain's power.

The most impressive frescoes are in the **main hall**, where the centre of the ceiling is given over to monograms representing the Holy Family in a pious tribute, although a comparison with modern-day street tags is hard to resist. Nor is this ceiling wholly Christian, for on one side we find the Roman god Jupiter with goddesses Minerva to his left and Diana to his right. On the other side, Don Juan's coat of arms has elephants to its right, and over on the left, a rhinoceros, which is clearly based on an engraving by the German artist Albrecht Dürer, and was itself copied in the Casa del Fundador.

Beyond the main hall, the **bedroom** no longer has its bed, but it does still have its original washbasin. The **dining room** has its tables and chairs, and the **kitchen** has its fireplace, although the oven is a reconstruction. As in the Casa del Fundador, you're given a little tour (20–30min) and these things are explained to you in Spanish, or in rudimentary English.

Iglesia de Santo Domingo

Cra 11 No. 19–55 • Free • 8 742 4725

The most richly decorated of Tunja's colonial churches, and the one you should really try to see if you can, is the **Iglesia de Santo Domingo**, a block west of Plaza de Bolívar. Most particularly, the **Capilla del Rosario**, to the left as you enter, is a riot of gold-encrusted royal red. It's surrounded with eighteen panels in relief depicting the life of Jesus, and behind its altar is a statue of the Virgin of the Rosary (one of the many manifestations of the Virgin Mary), and a kitschy altar decorated with plates and mirrors in a style reminiscent more of India than of South America.

Iglesia y Convento de Santa Clara la Real

Cra 7 No. 19–58 • Free • 310 666 9946

Two blocks east of Plaza de Bolívar, the 1571 **Convento de Santa Clara la Real** was the first convent in New Granada. Its chapel, the **Iglesia de Santa Clara la Real**, is full of religious paintings, largely from the seventeenth and eighteenth centuries, but its original decor combines Indigenous and Catholic imagery in a nifty bit of syncretism. The sun on the ceiling, for example, will have reminded all the locals of Sue, the Muiscas' sun god and chief deity, with an implied message that the Christian God is one and the same.

Puente de Boyacá

Km 110, Crta Bogotá–Tunja • Local bus from the main terminal (every 15min; 20min) or any Tunja–Bogotá bus with space

About 16km south of Tunja on the main road back to Bogotá is a reconstructed colonial-era bridge, **Puente de Boyacá**. It may not look very important now, but back in the day it was a strategic river crossing on the main road to Bogotá. It was victory here at the **Battle of Boyacá** in 1819 (see page 94), which cleared the way for Simón Bolívar and his freedom fighters to march triumphantly on Bogotá, and guaranteed their victory in the struggle for independence.

ARRIVAL AND INFORMATION TUNJA

By bus The bus terminal (☎ 8 744 4404) is at Cra 7 No. 16–40, on Av Oriental five blocks southeast of Plaza de Bolívar. Especially at night, buses may just drop you outside. A new and far less conveniently situated terminal is under construction but it is not clear when it will be completed. Heading to Bogotá, all buses from Tunja will drop you at Terminal del Norte (see page 74) on request.
Destinations Bogotá (every 10–12min; 3hr); Bucaramanga (every 30min; 7hr); Cartagena (4 daily; 22hr); Chiquinquirá (every 15min; 2hr); Medellín (1 daily; 10hr); Pamplona (5 daily; 10hr); San Gil (every 30min; 4hr 30min); Villa de Leyva (about every 15min; 45min).
Tourist information The friendly and helpful tourist office is at the entrance to the Casa del Fundador on Plaza de Bolívar at Cra 9 No. 19–56 (Tues–Sun 9am–11.30am & 2–4.30pm; ☎ 8 742 3272).

ACCOMMODATION

Alicante Cra 8 No. 19–15 ☎ 310 852 1636; map p.92. A cool, modern little hotel, very clean, with a sunny covered patio. All rooms have bathrooms, but windows look inwards only. $

Casa Real C 19 No. 7–65 ☎ 8 743 1764; map p.92. A good-value, friendly and atmospheric place in a colonial building between the bus station and Plaza de Bolívar. The rooms are large, all with private bathrooms, but some of the beds are a bit hard. $

Dux C 19 No. 10–78 ☎ 8 742 5736, ⓦ hotelduxtunja.com.co; map p.92. This creaky old hotel in a colonial building just off the main square is friendly and respectable, and has a certain charm. The *Calle Real*, a few doors down, is slightly less creaky and very slightly pricier. $$

Hunza C 21A No. 10–66 ☎ 8 742 4111; map p.92. The city's top hotel, modern, standard and business-oriented with a steam room and an indoor pool – if you value comfort over character, this is the place. Continental

---

THE BATTLE OF BOYACÁ

By mid-1819, **Simón Bolívar's armies** had triumphed in Venezuela, but most of New Granada, including the capital, Bogotá, remained in Spanish hands. Incredibly, and in the face of huge obstacles and lethal terrain (and with terrible casualties on the way), Bolívar led his army straight across the Eastern Cordillera to Boyacá. Because Bogotá had only a small force of defenders, a Spanish army were on their way from the coast to shore it up, but Bolívar's forces intercepted them at the Battle of Vargas Swamp, near Paipa, and forced them to retreat. He followed up this success by taking the city of Tunja, where supplies meant for the loyalists also fell into his hands.

The Spanish now regrouped and headed for **Boyacá bridge**, which Bolívar needed to cross in order to march on Bogotá. His forces consisted of the men who had come over the mountains with him, and included a legion of British and Irish troops – largely veterans of the Napoleonic Wars, whose presence had already proved crucial – plus men he had recruited locally. Although they slightly outnumbered the 2940 loyalist troops, only the British and Irish were actually professional soldiers.

The two armies engaged on **7 August, 1819** when the Spanish sent an advance force to hold the bridge. Bolívar sent a force under Francisco de Paula Santander (see page 122) to cut them off from their rearguard, which he then engaged with the bulk of his troops. The battle lasted around two hours, at the end of which the loyalists were routed, and some 1600 of them were captured, including the leader of the loyalist forces in New Granada, Colonel José María Barreiro. When the viceroy and his government in Bogotá heard the news, they fled. Bolívar entered the capital three days later, unopposed.

breakfast included. Discounts often available. $\overline{\$\$}$
★ **Posada de San Agustín** C 23 No. ⓦposadadesan agustin.co; map p.92. Cosy rooms in a beautiful old family house on a lovely little square with an old church. Most but not all have a terrace, so be sure to ask for one. Breakfast included. $\overline{\$\$}$

EATING

El Atrio Cra 9 No. 19–48 (on Plaza Bolívar) ☏ 8 553 9126; map p.92. This is a little café by the cathedral with a pleasantly old-fashioned tearoom kind of feel. Aside from coffee, they serve fruit salad (you may want to ask them to hold the cheese), or strawberries and frothy cream. $\overline{\$}$

Empanadas Típicas del Valle C 19A (Pasaje Vargas) No. 10–87; map p.92. A little hole in the wall that serves only *empanadas*, of which it offers a fair variety, some filled just with meat, others with cheese and veg, and even sweet ones with cheese and guava jelly. $\overline{\$}$

Macedonia C 23 No. 9–16 ☏ 8 205 3758; map p.92. A deservedly popular restaurant where the menu is short but sweet, the prices reasonable, and the specialities mostly fish-based – garlic trout, for example, or a seafood *cazuela*. The dish of the day is always good. $\overline{\$\$}$

El Maizal C 9 No. 20–30 ☏ 8 743 3079; map p.92. This atmospheric restaurant in an old house serves up straight forward but tasty meals, with lots of locally-caught fish, fried yucca, plantains and mondongo soup. $\overline{\$}$

Popeyes's C 19 No. 8–38 ☏ 320 397 2914; map p.92. A cheerful *asadero* – cheekily named with a nod to the US-based fried chicken chain – behind the cathedral. Chickens are roasted over charcoal and served by the quarter. You can also opt for a *tabla mixta* (two meats, fries and salad). It's open after most other places have closed. $\overline{\$}$

Protamales Cra 9 No. 22–80; map p.92. The better of two competing places next door to each other, and a good spot for a cheap Colombian breakfast. As their name suggests, they also have *tamales*. $\overline{\$}$

Son y Sabor C 19A (Pasaje Vargas) No. 10–71 ☏ 8 740 2970; map p.92. The best of a slew of places in this little passage off Plaza de Bolívar, all offering moderately priced breakfasts and lunches. Here you can get your teeth into a grilled trout or roast rabbit, or just get the *comida corriente*. $\overline{\$}$

DRINKING

Pussini Cra 10 No. 19–53 ⓦpussini-cafe-bar.negocio. site; map p.92. A café during the day, this cosy little place gradually becomes a bar as the evening wears on until nighttime finds it the most happening place on the square. Typically, you'd get a table, order a bottle of rum or *aguardiente*, and share it till it's finished, but they also do cocktails, mocktails and even beer.

DIRECTORY

Festivals Tunja holds one of the most colourful Semana Santa (Holy Week) celebrations in the country, with costumes and processions. The Festival Internacional de la Cultura (ⓦ fic. boyaca.gov.co), held in Aug, celebrates the arts in general, but in particular music, theatre and dance, with artists from around the world, and performances in Plaza de Bolívar as well as smaller events around town. Shortly before Christmas, on 16–22 Dec, Tunja hosts the Aguinaldo Boyacense, a largely religious celebration, with parades, costumes and fireworks.
Internet Centrocopias, Cra 9 No. 19–94, on Plaza de Bolívar; Internet, C 11 No. 19–8, upstairs.
Police Cra 4 No. 29–62 (☏ 8 740 5510).

Villa de Leyva and around

Tucked against the foot of spectacular mountains, 40km west of Tunja, scenic **VILLA DE LEYVA**, with its cobbled streets and whitewashed houses is must-see showcase of **colonial architecture**. It certainly looks and feels immaculately preserved, right down to hand-painted tiles prohibiting horseback riding and car traffic along the main plaza. Founded in 1572, the town is named after the then president of the *audiencia* (ruling council) of New Granada, Andrés Díaz Venero de Leiva, and the untroubled ambience and mild, dry climate make it a perfect place to relax. The narrow streets throng with day-trippers from Bogotá on weekends, but the rest of the time, this lovely place reverts to its former tranquil, timeless self, and as you sit in the 400-year-old plaza sipping beer or sangría, you'll be able to appreciate why many describe it as Colombia's prettiest town. No less attractive is the **surrounding countryside** where, aside from the natural beauty of the location, there are ancient archeological remains, even more ancient fossils, waterfalls and a winery to seek out, be it on foot, on horseback, by bicycle, by taxi or on quad bike. On Saturday mornings, a lively **market**, mostly featuring fruit, veg and clothing, is held in the Plaza de Mercado.

Plaza Mayor

Villa de Leyva's impressive **Plaza Mayor** is the largest in Colombia, all 14,000 square metres of it, paved with large cobblestones and surrounded by attractive colonial facades. Many have porticos and verandas, although most of the buildings behind them have been reconstructed. The stone **well** in the middle of the square was the townspeople's main source of water until the twentieth century. Dominating the plaza on its southeast side is the huge stone portal of the seventeenth-century **Iglesia de Nuestra Señora del Rosario** (Cra 9 No. 12–58), rebuilt after an 1845 earthquake but still containing many of its original artworks.

Casa Museo Luis Alberto Acuña

Cra 10 No. 12–83 • Charge • ☎ 8 732 0422

The **Casa Museo Luis Alberto Acuña** occupies a lovely old house on the northwest side of the Plaza Mayor. It houses the most comprehensive collection of sculptures and other artwork by influential, avant-garde twentieth-century artist Luis Alberto Acuña, who lived here for the last fifteen years of his life (he died in 1994), and most of the works on show date from that period. The large, colourful murals in the courtyard, depicting Muisca mythological figures, betray the strong influence of Mexican muralists such as Frida Kahlo's husband Diego Rivera. It was Acuña himself who set up the museum to house not only his own works of art but also his collection of antiques, which are also on display.

Museo del Carmen

C 14 No. 10–53 • Charge

On the Plazuela del Carmen, facing the imposing Monasterio de las Carmelitas and its attached church, is the **Museo del Carmen**, justifiably famous for its collection of religious art. In it, you'll find large numbers of wooden icons from the Church's early years of proselytizing in the New World, as well as altarpieces and paintings that date back to the sixteenth century, displayed in six rooms adjoining a pretty patio.

Casa de Antonio Ricaurte

C 15 No. 8–19 • Free

On the corner of Calle 15 and Carrera 8, on Plaza Ricuarte, the **Casa de Antonio Ricaurte** was the birthplace of Antonio Ricaurte, a national hero who fought for Bolívar. Since 1970, it's been run as a museum by the Colombian air force. Ricaurte died in the Battle of San Mateo in 1814, when royalists had gained control of the Bolivarians' main ammunition store. Realizing that this would win them the battle, Ricaurte shut himself up in it with a barrel of gunpowder and lit it, blowing up the ammunition depot, the royalist troops, and of course himself. The museum contains some of Ricaurte's personal objects and documents (labelled in Spanish only), plus modern military paraphernalia. There is also a beautiful garden, which is reason enough to visit.

Casa Museo de Antonio Nariño

Cra 9 No. 10–25 • Free • ☎ 8 732 0342

The **Casa Museo de Antonio Nariño** was home, in his later years, to independence hero Antonio Nariño. Captured by the Spanish after translating and distributing the

French revolutionary work *Declaration of the Rights of Man*, Nariño escaped twice and came home to set up the Army of the South, fighting the Spanish in Popayán, only to be captured again. The museum contains a few of his personal effects, but is of more interest as a beautiful colonial house, with furniture and objects of the period including a couple of early nineteenth-century revolvers. It also has a pleasant garden at the back.

Casa Terracota

Via Sachica • Charge • w casaterracota.com

Two kilometres west of town, **Casa Terracota** is a house made out of local clay – 400 tonnes of it – by architect Octavio Mendoza. More than just a little Gaudí-esque, the house eschews conventional shapes, straight lines and right angles, and most of the furniture is built in. The floor is tiled, and a lot of broken glazed tiles are made into mosaics to give colourful touches, especially in the bathroom. There are also some nice bits of ironwork, most notably a giant spider hanging from a windowed dome in the middle. The idea of the house was to be a sustainable form of architecture for the region, but the time needed to build like this made that idea impractical, so it remains one of a kind.

Museo del Fósil

Km 4, Ruta de Santa Sofía • Charge • T 312 580 1158

The star of the **Museo del Fósil**, 4km west of town along the road to Santa Sofía, is the fossil of a 120-million-year-old baby kronosaurus, a prehistoric marine reptile. The arid desert highlands surrounding Villa de Leyva attract trekkers, but 120 million years ago the huge flood plain would have been better suited to scuba diving. The ocean waters have since retreated, leaving the country's largest repository of marine fossils. The kronosaurus is the most complete example of its species so far discovered and was found here by a local resident in 1977.

Centro de Investigaciones Paleontológicas

Km 4, Ruta de Santa Sofía • Museum charge, excavation site charge • 321 978 9546 • cipaleo.com

Across the road from the Museo del Fósil, the **Centro de Investigaciones Paleontológicas** is a scientific research centre that maintains a small museum and a mock-up of a paleontological excavation site. A guide will show you around the **museum**, whose array of fine fossils includes not only run-of-the-mill ammonites and trilobites, but also ancient marine turtles, ichthyosaurs (marine reptiles that looked like dolphins, but with much sharper teeth), plesiosaurs (with big flippers and long necks) and the only sabre-tooth-tiger fang so far unearthed in Colombia.

At the mock-up **excavation site** next to the centre, play at being a paleontologist and see how fossils are detected and unearthed. Children will love it, but in wet weather it can get pretty muddy.

Estación Astronómica Muisca

Vereda Monquirá, 6km northwest of town • guided tours; charge • 8 770 3132

A kilometre off the Ruta de Santa Sofía, 2km from the Museo del Fósil, the **Estación Astronómica Muisca** is Colombia's answer to Stonehenge. It's an archeological site containing a Muisca **solar observatory** that dates back to early centuries AD. The observatory takes the form of 115-odd stone columns arranged in rows. From the length and direction of their shadows, the Muiscas were able to determine the time of year and thus work out when to start planting their crops.

In addition to the small stone columns of the observatory, there are thirty much larger **megaliths**, which are plainly phallic in form and were found strewn about the site. Most of them have been hauled upright, but there's a school of thought that says they would have been upside-down, penetrating the earth to symbolize its fertilization. When the Spanish Conquistadors found the phallic columns, they were apparently so horrified at this pagan sexuality that they called the site "el Infiernito"(the little hell), a name still used today.

Visitors are taken round on a **guided tour** by a local archeologist. The explanations given are very informative but in Spanish only.

ARRIVAL AND DEPARTURE — VILLA DE LEYVA

By bus The bus station is three blocks southwest of the Plaza Mayor, towards the road to Tunja. The fastest and most comfortable buses to Bogotá are the two daily services run by Libertadores. There are no direct buses to San Gil – it's possible to travel via Arcabuco, but you'll have more frequent and more reliable connections if you go back to Tunja and change there instead. For Zipaquirá, take a Bogotá-bound bus to Briceño and change.

Destinations Bogotá (15 daily; 4hr); Chiquinqirá (roughly hourly; 1hr 30min); Ráquira (4 daily; 45min); Tunja (about every 15min 5.45am–7.30pm; 45min).

INFORMATION AND TOURS

Tourist information The tourist office is at Cra 9 No. 13–04 (8 732 0232). There's also an office at the bus station.
Colombian Highlands Hostel Renacer (see page 99), colombianhighlands.com. An array of local excursions, including hiking, abseiling and horseriding, with a ten percent discount for hostel guests. It's also a major tour operator on a national level, in particular offering tours to the Llanos and Amazon regions in areas that are otherwise hard to access.

GETTING AROUND

You can cycle, travel by horseback (this can be arranged with tour companies in town) or even walk to some sites, though the winding roads can be dangerous for unwary pedestrians.

By taxi You can rent a taxi for the day to drive you from site to site around the city (negotiate your rate).
By bicycle Bikes can be rented at *Zona de Camping El Paraíso* (see page 99; 312 559 8067).

ACCOMMODATION

Casa de Las Aguas Cra 10 No. 10–81 8 732 0711, casadelasaguas.com.co; map p.97. A well put together hotel, run by retired architects who have put their heart and soul into the renovations here. The two cabins

THE MUISCA PEOPLE

The **Muiscas** were the people living in most of Cundinamarca, Boyacá and southern Santander when the Spanish arrived. Their language was related to those of today's U'wa and Páez peoples. Although it isn't entirely clear when their culture first arose, it's thought to have been at some time between about 500 BC and 800 AD.

By the time of the Spanish invasion, the Muiscas were organized into tribal confederations, of which the two biggest had their capitals at Bacata (Bogotá), where the ruler was called the Zipa, and at Hunza (Tunja), whose ruler was the Zaque. The Muiscas' main deity was the sun god **Sue** (pronounced "soo-ay"), and like many ancient peoples, they had a good knowledge of **astronomy**, which they used to determine the times for planting and harvesting crops. They also mined and traded precious minerals such as gold, emeralds and salt, and they drank *chicha*, an alcoholic beverage made from fermented corn.

After defeating them in battle, the Spanish destroyed the Muiscas' political structures and forcibly converted the people to Christianity, creating **reservations** where they were kept as forced labour. Following independence, most of the reservations were dissolved and such Muiscas as remained gradually merged into the general population. From the end of the 1980s however, people of Muisca descent began taking steps to **revive** their ancient culture, and today a few thousand people can still identify themselves as Muisca, although their language is no longer spoken.

---

available are both equally lovely and worth the price. $$$
★ **Hostel Renacer** Cra 10 No. 21–Finca Renacer (up path by No. 21–26) w renacerhostel.com; map p.97. Owned by Oscar Gilède, the English-speaking biologist behind Colombian Highlands (see page 98), *Hostel Renacer* is a haven surrounded by trees and mountain views. Hammocks, free wi-fi and hot drinks, a fridge full of beer and heaps of information, plus rooms with huge windows and comfortable beds, make it popular with backpackers, and you can also camp. The location, about 1km uphill from the centre, is a bit of a pain, but they'll refund your taxi fare from the bus station. Camping/person with own tent or campervan, dorms and doubles available. $
Hostería del Molino la Mesopotamia Cra 8 No. 15A–265 ☎ 8 578 6405; map p.97. An old watermill, dating from 1568, with its own spring in lovely and extensive grounds. The rooms are very rustic, which has its charms, but also its downside (creepy-crawlies can get in, for example), and most aren't reached by the wi-fi. Breakfast included. $$

Plaza Mayor Cra 10 No. 12–31 w hotelplazamayorvilladeleyva.com; map p.97. Faced throughout with brick, this hotel on the Plaza Mayor isn't five star but is certainly decent enough, with a ten-percent discount any day but Sat and a nice roof terrace overlooking the square. On the downside, standard rooms, though cool with tiled floors, mostly have only internal windows, making them a little dark; upstairs rooms get more light, have fireplaces, and cost a bit more. Breakfast included. $$
Posada de San Antonio Cra 8 No. 11–80 w hotellaposadadesanantonio.com; map p.97. High beds, high ceilings and attractive rooms in this beautiful old house on a pretty square (overlooked by the balcony rooms). Facilities include a jacuzzi and steam room. Breakfast included. $$$
Zona de Camping El Paraiso C 11 at Cra 10 ☎ 311 550 7687; map p.97. One of several campsites around town offering low-priced, no-frills camping on a large patch of grass surrounded by a wall. Basic toilet/shower block (cold water only). Great mountain views. Wi-fi in reception area only. $

EATING

The food scene is very diverse; there are **gourmet food courts** at Casona La Guaca (Cra 9 between C 13 & C 14) and Casa Quintero (Cra 9, at C 12).
Carnes y Olivas Cra 10 No. 11–55 ☎ 8 732 1368; map p.97. A good place for meat, if not for olives. The menu includes dishes such as *lengua en salsa de uchuvas* (tongue in Cape gooseberry sauce) or *sobrebarriga* (flank steak). Alternatively, go for the good-value, three-course *menú del día* (with meat or trout). $$
Casa Blanca C 13 No. 7–02 w facebook.com/CasaBlancaRestauranteVilladeLeyva; map p.97. Refined, posh eating, with tablecloths, where specialities include *bagre criollo* (catfish with tomatoes and onions) or chicken *ajiaco*. Food is well presented, served by waiters dressed in claret-coloured aprons. $
Casa San Pedro C 12 No. 10–96 w casasanpedro.com.co; map p.97. A smashing little restaurant a block west of the main square, serving wonderful pasta, and in particular the house speciality, *pasta a la rueda de parmesano*, fettuccine slapped straight from the pan into a wheel of parmesan

> ### VÉLEZ'S GUABINA AND TIPLE FESTIVAL
>
> Every year, on the first or second weekend in August, the town of **Vélez** – 89km northwest of Tunja, and 17km off the junction of highway 62 with the 45A Bogotá–Bucaramanga road at Barbosa – hosts a festival of **guabina**, a local genre of dance and music, and **tiple**, the Colombian guitar, of which the best are made in Chiquinquirá.
>
> Held every year since 1940, the festival is a three-day celebration of local folk music and tradition, where the streets throng with people in local **costume** to the lively sound of popular guitar music. The festival centres on the cathedral in the main square, and ends with a procession of flowers. Local **foods** available include the *piquete veleño*, a huge plate of meats and starchy veg, Vélez's answer to Antioquia's *bandeja paisa*, and – since the town is just across the *departamento* line in Santander – Santanderino specialities such as roast goat, as well as the renowned *bocadillo veleño* (Vélez-style guava jelly).

cheese, and scraped around before being transferred onto your plate. $\overline{\underline{\$\$}}$
Chez Remy Local 10, C 10 No. 6–67 ● 322 398 9084; map p.97. A French restaurant with loads of decadent options that will delight anyone seeking a break from heavier fare. There are light bites galore (tartine provençale), soups, vegetables in cheese and mustard sauce, plus all the French classics. $\overline{\underline{\$\$}}$
Emell's Bakery-Pastelería Artesanal Cra 10 No. 11–85 ● 8 416 3710; map p.97. Come here if you want to skip the main course and get straight onto the dessert. There are cakes and tarts, as promised (Colombian *torta negra* – black cake), rice pud, rum custard, coffee and all sorts of after-dinner treats. $\overline{\underline{\$}}$
La Waffleria de la Villa La Casona de Arroyo, Cra 9 No. 14–14 ● facebook.com/lawaffleriadelavilla; map p.97. A cute little café dishing up all the crêpes and waffles your heart may desire. Crêpes come savoury (chicken and spinach in bechamel sauce), or sweet (strawberry, banana and chocolate). The waffles are all sweet, and include strawberries and cream or apple, peach, cinnamon and maple syrup. $\overline{\underline{\$}}$
Zarina Casa Quintero, Cra 9 No. 11–75 ● 8 765 9615; map p.97. International fusion dishes with a strong Middle Eastern and Thai influence. Try *kibbeh* with *tahina*, a big selection of *meze*, or a huge veg platter. $\overline{\underline{\$}}$

DRINKING

La Cava de Don Fernando Cra 10 No. 12–05 ● 8 254 7418; map p.97. Across the Plaza Mayor from the church, this is Leyva's top rock bar. There are always rock videos playing, and the beer and spirits are reliably good, with Colombian craft brews and quality whiskies and tequilas.
Dorkneipe Cra 9 No. 12–88 ● 310 875 4698; map p.97. The most popular bar on Plaza Mayor, the town's nightlife hub. You can get the usual beers, or be more discerning and go for BBC craft beers or imported German lagers.

DIRECTORY

Banks and exchange There are several banks with ATMs on the main square and around town; Bancolombia, Cra 9 No. 11–25, is currently the only bank in town that will change cash dollars.
Festivals Villa de Leyva's most important annual event is the Festival de Luces (Festival of Lights), a fireworks extravaganza on December 7-9 that gathers the best of the region's pyrotechnicians to celebrate the Día de las Velitas (see page 36). During Semana Santa (the week leading up to Easter), an acoustic music festival, the Encuentra de Música Antigua, is held in the town's churches ● facebook. com/pg/MusicAntiguaVdeL, while the popular Festival de las Cometas (Kite Festival), held in the Plaza Mayor over a weekend in early to mid-Aug, sees the country's finest kite-flyers compete in a variety of categories as spectators shout encouragement.
Internet Café Internet la Casona, C 13 No. 8–03; Vill@ Digital, Cra 9 no. 11–52.
Laundry Lavandería Milan, C 10 No. 8–27.
Police Cra 10 No. 11–10 (● 8 732 0236).
Tejo Hostal Renacer (see page 99) offers mini-tejo, which is a beginner-friendly version of the game.

Santuario de Iguaque

Entrance around 15km north of Villa de Leyva • Charge (bring ID) • ● naturariguaquesp.weebly.com; visits should be booked at least a day in advance (a week ahead for weekends or holiday periods) at ● iguaque@parquesnacionales.gov.co, but guides, equipment and lodging should be booked through Comunitaria Natuar Iguaque (● 312 585 9892, ● naturariguaque@yahoo.es)

The large nature reserve of **Santuario de Iguaque** can be visited as a day-trip from Villa de Leyva. Along with excellent hiking it has eight lakes, the most famous of which, **Laguna de Iguaque**, was believed by the Muiscas to be the birthplace of humanity. At an altitude between 3550m and 3700m, it can be pretty cold and wet, so come equipped; the best time to vist is in January and February, or July and August. Note that you must arrive at the entrance by 10am unless you have booked an overnight stay.

ARRIVAL AND DEPARTURE   SANTUARIO DE IGUAQUE

By bus To get to the reserve by 10am, you need to take a bus bound for Arcabuco at 6am or 7am and ask to be dropped off at Casa de Piedra (aka Los Naranjos) at Km 12; from there it's a 3km walk to the visitor centre. You'll need to return to Casa de Piedra by 4pm for the last bus back to Villa de Leyva.

ACCOMMODATION AND EATING

Centro de visitantes 3.5km from Laguna de Iguaque ☎ 312 585 9942, @ naturariguaque@yahoo.es. Visitor centre offering simple but neat and clean shared accommodation, a camping area and food. Note that you must reserve accommodation in advance by email. Camping areas and dorms available. $\overline{\$}$

Ráquira

Tiny **RÁQUIRA**, 25km southwest of Villa de Leyva, is famous countrywide for its pottery – even the name means "City of Pots". Besides perusing the many pottery workshops, you can check the craft shops around the main square for hammocks, jewellery, woodcarvings and ponchos. Sunday is market day and a particularly good time to visit. There isn't much else to see in Ráquira, but it's an easy day-trip from Villa de Leyva or even Tunja. The **Parque Principal** is quite pretty, decorated with pottery statues, including one of local musician Jorge Velosa, who had a band called Los Carrangueros de Ráquira, and started a whole musical genre called *carranga*. There's also a fountain in the form of a boy urinating, to rival the more famous one in Brussels.

ARRIVAL AND DEPARTURE   RÁQUIRA

By bus and colectivo For Villa de Leyva, buses depart outside the bus company office on the main square at *La Chicharra* café (Cra 4 No. 2–11). For Chiquinquirá, there are frequent *colectivos*: pick them up just over the bridge from the main square at C 2 with Cra 5; they leave when they have five or more passengers. Buses to Bogotá leave from the same place. To get to Ráquira from Tunja, take a bus for Chiquinquirá and get off at Tres Esquinas, the junction near Tinjacá, 4km from Ráquira; there's usually a taxi or a car waiting at the petrol station at the junction to take you into Ráquira as a *colectivo*, but failing that, a minibus *colectivo* from Chiquinquirá shouldn't be long in coming, or you can walk. From Ráquira to Tres Esquinas, *colectivos* are sometimes available from the corner of Cra 3, at C 3 on the Parque Principal (failing that, take a Chiquinquirá-bound *colectivo*, or a taxi).
Destinations Bogotá (2 daily; 5hr); Chiquinquirá (about every 15min, depending on demand; 1hr); Tunja (from Tres Esquinas, about every 15min; 1hr 30min); Villa de Leyva (4 daily; 45min).
By taxi Ráquira can be reached from Villa de Leyva by taxi.

ACOMMODATION AND EATING

Sausage fans may want to stop off on the way between Leyva and Ráquira at **Sutamarchán**, the *longaniza* capital of Colombia, where you'll see *longaniza* sausages by the yard hanging by the roadside to buy or stop and eat.
Casa Nemqueteba Cra 3 No. 3–10 ☎ 8 735 7083. On the corner of the Parque Principal, this restaurant in a nice old building has an open, airy space downstairs and a more classic room upstairs, serving dishes such as grilled trout or *jiambre*. $\overline{\$}$

Hotel Suaya C 4 at Cra 3 ☎ 8 249 0295. A sweet little hotel on the main shopping street where the rooms are all done out in jolly pastel colours, all en suite, most with balconies, but no wi-fi. $\overline{\$}$
Restaurante La Terraza Cra 3 No. 4–08 ☎ 315 358 3749. Cool, modern restaurant serving traditional Boyacan and Colombian dishes. Get stuck into a *cocido boyacanse* (Boyacá-style stew) or a hearty *ajiaco*. $\overline{\$}$

SHOPPING

Todo Ráquira Cra 3 no. 3A–05 ⓦ todoraquira.com. If you're after pottery, this is the place. The front looks like all the other souvenir shops in town, but it has a large range of crockery and cookware at very good, fixed and displayed prices. The back (on C 4) is a big warehouse full of local pottery, mostly unglazed, with anything from flowerpots to piggy banks. Branches in Bogotá and Medellín.

Chiquinquirá

A major religious pilgrimage site, where thousands flock to see the image of the Virgin of the Rosary in the local basilica, **CHIQUINQUIRÁ** is also known for its fine guitars, the country's best. Some 47km west of Villa de Leyva, it's a friendly and laidback little town, with two main squares: **Plaza de Bolívar** (Cra 11–12, C 17–18), where the basilica is located, along with a bunch of restaurants, cafés and souvenir or craft shops; and **Parque de Florez** (Cra 8–9, C 16–17), which is dominated by banks and hotels. East of the centre, on Carrera 7 at Calle 22, the old **train station** is now a cultural centre, but it still has an original steam train standing at the platform.

Basilica de Nuestra Señora del Rosario
Plaza de Bolívar • Free • w virgendechiquinquira.com

At the western corner of Plaza de Bolívar stands the **Basilica de Nuestra Señora del Rosario**, with a handsome facade in light yellow sandstone. Every year, on 9 July (the Virgin's feast day) and 26 December, thousands of pilgrims stream to the church to see a painting of the Virgin Mary in her incarnation as the Virgin of the Rosary, flanked by St Antony of Padua and St Andrew the Apostle.

The picture holds pride of place in a grandiose *retablo* behind the main altar. It was painted in Tunja in 1560–62 by Alonso de Narváez, on a rather flimsy cotton canvas, using colours that incorporated local vegetable dyes. The Dominican friars housed it in one of their chapels, which unfortunately had a leaky roof, and when the picture became damaged, they took it down and dumped it in a disused oratory in Chiquinquirá, where it deteriorated further. A devout Spanish woman by the name of María Ramos refurbished the oratory and used the painting as an object of veneration until, on December 26, 1586, it was suddenly and miraculously restored to its original, pristine state. Word spread, and people started coming to see it. Soon more miracles were being reported. The site became a church and when it fell into disrepair, the Dominicans had the current building erected to replace it. It was consecrated in 1823, when, having become an incarnation of the Virgin in her own right, the Virgin of Chiquinquirá was made the patron saint of Colombia.

ARRIVAL AND DEPARTURE   CHIQUINQUIRÁ

By bus and colectivo The bus terminal is 600m southwest of town on Cra 9 at C 4, but buses to Villa de Leyva can be picked up near the centre on Cra 7 (they often wait under the footbridge at C 17), as can buses to Tunja and Bogotá, and *colectivos* to Ráquira (about every 15min, depending on demand).

Destinations Bogotá (about every 15min; 4hr); Tunja (about every 15min; 2hr); Villa de Leyva (approximately hourly; 1hr).

ACCOMMODATION

Real Muisca C 16 No. 9–22 w hotelrealmuisca.webnode.com.co. A friendly little hotel off the Parque de Florez, with immaculate if rather small and slightly chintzy rooms. Breakfast available but not included. $$

Sarabita C 16 No. 8–12 t 8 726 2079. There's a whiff of wood polish about this hotel on the Parque de Florez, which has an old-fashioned and somewhat slightly shabby charm about it, and was evidently once quite grand, in a modest kind of way. Breakfast available but not included. $$

EATING

Cafisterra C 17 No. 11–35 t 320 899 1888. You can get breakfasts, juices and *tamales* at this restaurant on Plaza Bolívar, set lunches, plus dishes such as *churrasco* or *cazuela*. $

Donatello C 18 No. 9–80 t 312 417 7563. This busy little *restaurante popular*, its walls decorated with interesting old photos of Chiquinquirá, offers a solid Colombian breakfast, a lunchtime set menu, a selection of cheap combos, and dishes such as baked *bagre* (catfish) or *churrasco*. $$

SHOPPING

Casa Norato Cra 11 No. 17–102 (on Plaza de Bolívar) ☎ 312 440 1884. If you've come to Chiquinquirá to pick up a guitar, this is the place: they make their own, in a variety of types and qualities, and are happy to tell you all about them (if you can speak Spanish) and let you try before you buy.

Fabrica de Articulos de Tagua C 18 No. 11–74 (on Plaza de Bolívar) ☎ 313 333 6961. The name of the shop ("Factory of *Tagua* Items") is pretty self-explanatory, and they do an attractive range of animals and other carvings made in their own workshops from *tagua* ("vegetable ivory"; see page 46).

Parque Nacional Natural el Cocuy

Park offices: C 5 No. 4–22, El Cocuy (☎ 8 789 0359); Transversal 4, No. 6–60, Güicán (☎ 8 789 7280) • Entry to protected areas; charge (discount for under-25s), plus compulsory rescue insurance; charge per day (or show proof of adequate travel insurance coverage) • W parquesnacionales.gov.co

Rising to a high point of 5330m above sea level, and taking in 32 glacial lakes and 22 snow-capped peaks, **PARQUE NACIONAL NATURAL EL COCUY** contains many natural splendours with little sight of other people. However, access to the best parts of the park has been curtailed: in particular, the popular six-day trek around the east side of the park's main peaks has been closed to the public following objections from local U'wa residents about it crossing their reserve, and you are not allowed to reach the snowline at any point in the park due to concerns about possible contamination of drinking water sources. The result is that only three **trails** on the western side of the park are now open to visitors.

The starting points for any visit are the towns of **El Cocuy** and **Güicán**, where you can obtain entry permits from the park offices and buy your obligatory rescue insurance (you may be exempt from this if you can show that your travel insurance already covers it). You'll also need to contract a local **guide**: you'll pay a set fee per group per day for a qualified guide, or for a locally registered *interprete local*. Guides can be engaged from the Asociación de Guías de Gûican y Cocuy (Aseguicoc; see page 104). You should register at the park office the day before you set off. You'll want to spend a day in El Cocuy or Güicán adjusting to the altitude in any case; there are local hikes you can do from each.

El Cocuy is the more convenient of the two starting points for the **Lagunillas Pulpito** and **Laguna Grande** trails, Güicán for the **Ritacuba** trail. As well as taking time to adjust to the altitude, be prepared for cold and wet climatic conditions. It gets bitterly cold at night in particular, so pack warm clothes, and ideally, waterproofs and a four-season sleeping bag (you can rent sleeping bags from tour companies, but they may not be as warm as you need). It's also wise to bring UV-protective goggles and factor 50+ sunscreen. Pack as light as possible, however, as you'll be carrying your own gear. By far the best **weather** is from December to February, when the park is at its busiest.

In the way of **wildlife**, you may be lucky enough to spot a condor. You should at any rate see some bright orange cocks-of-the-rocks (tunkis), and you'll certainly see plenty of frailejones, a type of flower with succulent leaves and a fat trunk that looks a bit like a yucca tree, but is in fact a relative of the sunflower.

The Lagunillas Pulpito trail

The most popular of the three permitted hiking trails is the **Lagunillas Pulpito trail**, the base for which is *Cabañas Sisuma* (☎311 255 1034; charge per person), at 4000m altitude, near Laguna Pintada. It's a good idea to spend a day here acclimatizing to the altitude before embarking on the hike. It is in any case a four-hour walk from the main drop-off point at Alto de la Cueva to the cabañas. From *Cabañas Sisuma*, the trail leads east to a place called Hotelito, and then northeast towards el Pulpito del Diablo (the Devil's Pulpit), a column of rock that sits dramatically in the middle of a glacier. The hike (up to just short of the snowline) is 12km each way, and you should be able to get there and back in around ten to twelve hours.

The Laguna Grande trail

The base for the **Laguna Grande trail** (Sendero Laguna Grande de la Sierra) is *Hacienda la Esperanza* (☏ 314 221 2473; charge per person including breakfast), a homely old *finca* near the village of La Capilla. From *Hacienda la Esperanza*, the trail leads southeast towards a cave called Cueva de los Hombres, then east towards a lake called Laguna Grande de la Sierra, and around the north of that to the edge of the Pico Cóncavo glacier. This hike is 9.6km long and takes nine to ten hours for the round trip.

The Ritacuba trail

For the **Ritacuba trail**, which is in the park's northern sector, Güicán is the most convenient starting point. From here, you can hike in five hours or so to *Kabañas Kanwara* (☏ 311 231 6004; charge per person and by advance reservation only), where it's best to stop and acclimatize. From *Cabañas Kanwara* the trail runs for 5km towards Ritacuba Blanco, the Eastern Cordillera's highest peak (5330m), stopping just short of the snowline. In fact, thanks to global warming, that snowline is receding at an alarming rate: in the 1950s it was at 4500m, but by 2012 it was up to 4900m, and some estimates reckon all the glaciers in El Cocuy will be gone completely in the next two or three decades.

ARRIVAL AND DEPARTURE   PARQUE NACIONAL NATURAL EL COCUY

By bus There are six daily buses to El Cocuy and Güicán from Bogotá (14hr) and Tunja (11hr) – two in the morning and four overnight. Going back, the first departure is at 3am from Güicán, 4am from El Cocuy, with two buses later in the morning and three overnight. Note that it can get pretty cold on the overnight buses – be sure to take enough warm clothing or blankets. There is no direct transport between Cocuy and Bucaramanga, but you can avoid going all the way down to Tunja by travelling via Capitanejo, although the road from there to Bucaramanga isn't great (it takes about 11hr), and you may have to find a connection in Málaga.

Destinations from Güicán via El Cocuy Bogotá (6 daily; 14hr); Tunja (6 daily; 11hr); Capitanejo (3 daily; 3hr 30min).

To the park From Güicán or El Cocuy it takes 5hr to hike to the park entrance. Renting a vehicle to take you up there is an option and the cost can be divided by up to six people. Milk trucks (*lecheros*) no longer take passengers.

GUIDES AND TOURS

Asociación de Guías de Gûican y Cocuy (Asegecoc) ✉ aseguicoc@gmail.com; in El Cocuy c/o Wilson Torres ☏ 311 255 1034); in Güicán c/o Alejandro López ☏ 314 252 8977.

Colombia Trek ⓦ colombiatrek.com. This agency, run by bilingual climber Rodrigo Arias, can organize a trip if you don't want to do it independently.

ACCOMMODATION

Most visitors use **El Cocuy** as a base for the Lagunillas Pulpito and Laguna Grande trains, **Güicán** for the Ritacuba Trail.

Brisas del Nevado Cra 5 No. 4–59, Güicán ⓦ brisasdel nevado.com. The best hotel in town, with private baths in most rooms and a restaurant serving delicious takes on local specialities. $$

Hotel Casa Muñoz Cra 5 No. 7–26, El Cocuy ⓦ hotel casamunoz.com. Modern, not terribly memorable hotel on the main square, with functional, clean rooms around a flower-filled courtyard and reliable hot showers. $

Hotel el Edén Transversal 2 No. 9–58, Güicán ☏ 311 808 8334. Family-run guest-house popular with travellers, with assorted wildlife in the garden and (mostly) en-suite rooms filled with the smell of pine. It's a 10min walk from the main square: take Cra 4, bear right where it forks, turn right at the basketball court, then first right and second left. $$

La Posada del Molino Cra 3 No. 7–51, El Cocuy elcocuycasamuseo.blogspot.com. An allegedly haunted colonial mansion featuring a handful of en-suite rooms with some period furniture and unusual bathrooms. $$

Guadalupe

Some 140km kilometres north of Tunja, and 74km southwest of San Gil, the charming town of **GUADALUPE** has only recently become popular as a tourist destination, not only with foreigners, but also with weekenders from Bogotá and Medellín, joining the Bucaramanga cognoscenti who've been coming for a while. Consequently it can get full at weekends, but tends to be quiet during the week, which is the best time to come. Guadalupe's main draw is its **gachas** – natural rock-pool "jacuzzis" in a nearby river, one of several local natural attractions – but the town itself is also a pretty little place.

Guadalupe centres on a **Parque Principal**, dominated by the **Santuario de Nuestra Señora de Guadalupe**, a very handsome church that looks colonial but in fact only dates from 1967, when it replaced an earlier wooden structure. Although the church is now dedicated to Mexico's Virgin of Guadalupe, she's only been the town's patron saint since it was reconstructed. The town has always been called Guadalupe, but its patron saint was previously Our Lady of Moguer, a Spanish incarnation of the Virgin, whose image was superseded by that of her Mexican self after the Basilica in Mexico donated her image to the reconstructed church. The humble **Capilla de San Martin**, across the square, really does date from the eighteenth century, but it's rarely open, and pretty plain inside.

La Gloria and La Salitre

1km southeast of town

La Gloria is a local beauty spot where a waterfall feeds a natural swimming pool. Like Las Gachas (see page 105), it can get quite crowded at weekends, but during the week it has few visitors, and you may even have it to yourself. To find it, head down Calle 4 to the Terpel gas station, and follow the road round to the left; La Gloria is signposted (left) after 800m. Nearby at **La Salitre** (a short walk across pasture fields) the action of eddies in formerly acidic waters has carved holes into a limestone riverbed, as at Las Gachas, but the hollows are smaller here, and yellow rather than red in colour.

Las Gachas

3km south of town

Guadalupe's number one attraction is the **Quebrada de las Gachas**, a shallow river running over red rocks, where the swirling action of its once-acidic waters has carved natural "jacuzzis" into the limestone riverbed. The name *gachas* is a Guane word meaning "cooking pots", but the water is always cool, and a pleasure to bathe in, especially on a hot day. You can even slide into them along the riverbed. Come during the week if you can, when there are usually very few people around; they can get quite crowded at weekends.

To **reach the Gachas** (around 1hr), head down Calle 4 for 500m or so to the Terpel gas station, then straight ahead down a paved path, the route of the old Camino Real, which gives way after another 500m to the original rock-paved road. Follow this for a couple of kilometres through lush countryside (the local cattle are well fed, their meat as a result very good), until you reach a small stream; cross that, and the Quebrada de las Gachas is 200m further. Follow it upstream to find a pool of your choice (the first two are quite deep, and difficult to climb out of, so avoid them). The best footwear for covering this section is socks alone; you'll get better traction on the sometimes slippery rocks than you would in sandals or barefoot.

The Cueva de los Pericos circuit

A 7hr hike (or 5hr excursion with 4WD) northeast of town takes in three natural beauty spots. The large **Cueva de los Pericos** ("cave of the parakeets") is so called because it was once home to a large number of parakeets. Sadly, like much of the local fauna (armadillos were also once common in the countryside around Guadalupe), they have been hunted to near extinction locally over the last thirty years. Just a few hundred metres north of the cave, **Casacada de la Llanera** is an impressive local waterfall, while 500m northwest of that is **Piedra del Sapo** ("toad rock"), which lives up to its name, being a rock that looks like a toad, and has a *mirador* with great views over the countryside. You can get information on how to follow this route, either on foot or with 4WD, from José Navarro at his hostel (see page 106). There's a **map** of the route at ⓦbit.ly/pericosroute.

ARRIVAL AND DEPARTURE — GUADALUPE

By bus and colectivo There are direct buses to Guadalupe from Bogotá (1 daily; 8hr) and Bucaramanga (1 daily; 5hr 30min) but most people travel to Oiba, on the Bogotá–Bucaramanga road between Tunja and San Gil, from where *colectivos* (7 daily; 45min) ply the road to Guadalupe. The last *colectivo* for Guadalupe leaves Oiba at 7pm. The operator, Cootrasarauta, has an office on the main square at C 6 No. 3–70 (next door to *Hostel José Navarro*).

ACCOMMODATION

Hostel José Navarro C 6 No. 3–70 ☎311 835 1573. Most accommodation in town is in small *hospedajes*, but this is the place to come first; the eponymous owner is not only Guadalupe's number-one tourist guide, but can also fix you up with accommodation in homes and *hospedajes* across town. José's hostel itself is small but comfortable, with two good doubles and a dorm, shared bathroom facilities and no hot water. $

Hotel Colonial Cra 5 No. 6–01 ☎313 394 4335. The best hotel in Guadalupe, nothing fancy, with plain but respectable rooms. The best, brighter, options have external windows. They offer coffee in the morning but no breakfast. The town's only souvenir shop is next door. $$

EATING AND DRINKING

There's only one **bar** as such in town, usually closed, but people drink beer in cafés and shops. A couple of places sell the local brew, *guarapo*, which is made from *panela* and fruit, can be a bit rough and ready, but is cheaper than beer and certainly worth a try.

Bonanza Cra 3 No. 4–90 ☎310 219 3359. Good, solid, local grub. The speciality is *churrasco*, made from the very cattle you see grazing the pastures around town, and very good it is too. The restaurant also sells locally produced coffee, which, grown in the shade rather than in direct sunlight, has a lower yield but a finer flavour than the coffee of the Zona Cafetera. $$

La Esquina del Buen Sabor Cra 5 No. 5–65 ☎7 407 4877. The best restaurant in town and a good spot for breakfast or lunch. Their *almuerzos* are especially good, and there's usually a choice of fish, chicken or local beef. $

San Gil and around

Colombia's adventure sports hotspot, **SAN GIL** is one of the biggest backpacker draws in the country. The town itself is small, friendly and easy to get around (give or take the odd steep hill), but what brings in the visitors is the opportunity it affords to take part in high-adrenaline sports such as whitewater rafting, paragliding and other exciting outdoor activities in the surrounding countryside. San Gil is also an excellent base for day-trips to the colonial town of **Barichara** and the **Parque Nacional del Chicamocha**.

In the way of sights, on the other hand, San Gil itself doesn't really have very much. The tree-shaded main square, **Parque la Libertad** gets quite animated after sundown, when people come to hang out in the cool of the evening. The **cathedral**, in the northwest corner, is worth a second glance. It was built in the late eighteenth century, in rich, tawny sandstone from Barichara, and its *retablo*, in white with gold and red trimming, is quite magnificent.

Parque el Gallineral

Cra 11 (Malecón), opposite C 6 • Charge (extra with swimming pool access) • ☎7 723 7342

San Gil's main attractions lie outside town, but if you want a quiet moment in between adventures, make your way to the large riverside **Parque el Gallineral**,

extending over four hectares, its trees atmospherically festooned with tendrils of "old man's beard" moss, giving it quite a magical feel. There's a swimming pool and a good restaurant, and the entrance fee gets you a wristband that means you can go in and out of the park all day. To get here, head down to the river and turn left along the Malecón to its end.

Pozo Azul and Pescaderito

Pozo Azul Km 2 San Gil–Aratoca road • Free • **Pescaderito** C 10, Curiti • Free • Take a local bus to Curiti, from where you can take a *mototaxi* or a 40min walk

Pozo Azul is a swimming spot just a twenty-minute walk out of town (follow the main road, Carrera 11, east from town; where it forks, bear left towards Aratoca and it's just ahead on your left). There are a series of small **waterfalls** here and a natural **pool** to swim in. Further afield, **Pescaderito**, 15km northeast of San Gil, near the town of Curiti, offers a series of five pools with small cascades.

ARRIVAL AND INFORMATION   SAN GIL

By bus The main terminal (w terminalsangil.gov.co) is 1km west of town on the south side of the river on Av Santander (Cra 12). Local buses to the Parque la Libertad leave from outside the terminal. Taxis also run from here and into town. Buses (*colectivos* really) to nearby destinations use *El Terminalito* on the corner of C 17, at Cra 10.

Destinations from the main terminal Bogotá (every 15–20min; 7hr 30min) via Tunja (4hr 30min); Bucaramanga (every 30min; 2hr 30min); Cúcuta (12 daily; 8hr 30min).

Destinations from El Terminalito Barachara (every 30min; 45min); Charalá (every 30min; 30min).

Tourist information Punto de Información Turística, Cra 11 (Malecón) near end of C 7.

ACCOMMODATION

Centro Real C 10 No. 10–41 w facebook.com/hotel.centroreal; map p.107. The best of a handful of small, cheap hotels on this block, where your cheerful little cubbyhole has windows onto an inner covered patio (pricier a/c rooms have exterior windows), plus bathroom and TV; not large, but cosy. $$

★ **Macondo Hostel** Cra 8 No. 10–35 w macondohostel.com; map p.107. The Australian owner is a mine of information about the town and it's an excellent place to organize your outdoor adventures, with lots of backpacker-friendly creature comforts to boot – jacuzzi anyone? $

Puerto Bahía C 6 No. 9–112 w hotelpuertobahiasangil.com; map p.107. Near Parque el Gallineral, this unassuming little hotel has bright, modern rooms and a

small pool and gym, and is about as deluxe as you're going to get in town. The price rockets between Christmas and 15 Jan plus during *puentes* and Semana Santa. $\overline{\$\$}$
Sam's VIP Hostel Cra 10 No. 12–33 ❼ 7 249 7400; map p.107. On the main square, with a terrace overlooking the square and a small rooftop pool, not to mention two kitchens and an easy-going vibe. A small breakfast is thrown in. Dorms $\overline{\$}$, doubles $\overline{\$\$}$
Santander Alemán Terrace View Cra 10 No. 15–07 ❼ 7 247 2741; map p.107. A slightly sedate, family-friendly hostel near the *terminalito* (local bus station), modern, fresh and clean, where each four-bed dorm and private room has its own bathroom. And there's a terrace with a view over the rooftops, as promised. Reductions for longer stays. $\overline{\$}$

EATING

For **breakfast** head for the market on Cra 11 between C 13 and C 14, where the food stalls at the back offer steaming *caldos*, freshly scrambled eggs, coffee and juice. $\overline{\$}$
Coffee House C10 No. 8–44 ❼ 322 429 0323; map p.107. A good place for a range of set breakfasts, or coffee at any time, and they also do *quesadillas*, burritos and other substantial snacks, including several vegetarian options. $\overline{\$}$
★ **Doña Eustaquia** C 3 No. 5–39, Valle de San José

ADVENTURE SPORTS AROUND SAN GIL

Adrenaline junkies are spoilt for choice by the array of **adventure sports** on offer in San Gil. Many of them involve speeding down rapids in a variety of craft from kayaks to hydroboards, but there are also caves to spelunk, thermals to soar and waterfalls to abseil. You can book all sports via hostels such as *Macondo*, *Sam's* and *Santander Alemán*, and you should pay the same as you would if you book direct. The staff at *Macondo* are particularly helpful and knowledgeable. Adventure sports are potentially dangerous, people do get hurt, and you are strongly advised to use a well-established, reliable operator with full insurance, medical facilities and back-up, which you can be sure of by booking through *Macondo* or going direct to the operators.

MOUNTAIN BIKING

One of the best, easiest and most popular activities is an all-day bike trip, all downhill, through spectacular scenery and taking in the little-visited Yariguíes national park across the canyon. **Colombian Bike Junkies** runs a tour most days if they can find a minimum group of four (charge per person).

WHITEWATER RAFTING AND KAYAKING

There are two main whitewater rafting routes: a hair-raising day-trip down the Grade IV/V (depending on the season) Río Suarez is popular. Alternatively, ditch the boat and do it on a metre-long foam riverboard, in what is variously known as river-boarding or hydrospeeding. For all of these, the leading operator is **Colombia Rafting Expediciones**. A more sedate half-day on the Río Fonce (Grade II/III) is offered by **Aventura Total**. Colombia Rafting Expediciones also offers one-day and three-day kayaking courses.

PARAGLIDING

There are two popular paragliding trips: a short, fifteen-minute flight over pretty countryside at Curiti, and a longer, 25–35-minute flight, 1km up over the Chicamocha canyon. You'll need sunscreen, proper shoes or trainers (not sandals or flip-flops) and a warm top. The leading operator is **Nativox**.

ABSEILING

Known locally as rappelling or *torrentismo*, this involves a climb down the 60m Cascadas de Juan Curi waterfall, followed by a dip in the pool at the bottom. The falls are at 25km out of town on the way to Charalá, reached by bus from the Terminalito (take the Charalá bus and ask for *las casacadas*), or by taxi (your hostel may be able to organize a shared one), or by bicycle. Before you set out, you'll need to arrange guides and equipment, which can be rented from **Páramo Santander Extremo**. You'll get very wet so it's a good idea to bring a dry set of clothes, a swimsuit and closed shoes (not flip-flops).

(off the Charalá road, 15km south of San Gil) w bit.ly/eustaquia; map p.107. The most famous *chorizo* sausages in Santander, and deservedly so. They breed their own pigs, make their own sausages, grill them over a wood fire and serve them in a *guarapo* sauce accompanied by steamed cassava. You can get a bus to Valle de San José from San Gil (every 30min from the Terminalito), or take a detour on your way back from abseiling at the Cascadas de Juan Curí. $\overline{\underline{\$\$}}$
Donde Betty Cra 9 No. 11–96 ☏ 7 724 0771; map p.107. A café in the day, a bar by night, but a convivial meeting place either way, handily located on the northeast corner of the main square. As well as coffee and beer, they do natural juices and superb scrambled eggs – try the *huevos rancheros* (with tomato, chorizo and coriander) or the *huevos israelies* (with onions and spinach). $\overline{\underline{\$}}$
Gringo Mike's C 12 No. 8–35 w gringomikes.net; map p.107. Large, tasty and filling California-style burgers, with veg versions available for slightly less. They even make their buns. $\overline{\underline{\$}}$
El Maná C 10 No. 9–49 ☏ 300 460 6269; map p.107. Ask local people for advice on restaurants and you'll probably be directed here: *El Maná* is extremely popular for its dependable and great value set meals, which come with a choice of dishes such as grilled trout and *carne asado* (grilled meat). $\overline{\underline{\$}}$
Sevilla Cra 9 No. 10–25 ☏ 7 723 6673; map p.107. A

CAVING

There are two popular caving trips around San Gil and both last about 90min. **Gua-iti** offers a visit to the stalactite-encrusted Cueva Vaca, providing head-torches, helmets and other equipment. **Páramo Santander Extremo** offers a waist-deep wade through the bat-infested Cueva del Indio, which is easier but slightly less exciting.

BUNGEE JUMPING AND ZIP LINING

Colombia Bungee Jumping offers a 70m jump, just out of town at Km 2 on the Charalá road. You can just turn up, but it's better to book or at least call to check that they are running that day (depending on weather conditions, jumps may be suspended). **Peñon Guane** has a 500m zip line with great views, straight across a canyon; they're based at Peñon Guane, 2km out of town on the Barichara road, accessible on the Barichara bus or by taxi.

CANYONING

This involves hiking/scrambling along the foot of a canyon, and is usually taken in a package with zip lining and abseiling thrown in. The more exciting (and strenuous) option is offered by **Ecolombia Experience** from Peñon Guane, and includes two zip lines, two rappels, a scrambling hike through a canyon and a visit to natural rock pools. Slightly less testing is the 225m zip line, two rappels and a canyon hike and rock pool visit offered at Pinchote (3km southwest of San Gil) by **San Gil Extremo**.

ADVENTURE SPORTS OPERATORS

Aventura Total C 7 No. 10–27 w aventuratotal.com.co. Rafting on Rio Fonce, generally gentler adventure activities.
Colombian Bike Junkies w colombianbikejunkies.com. Mountain-biking tours. No San Gil office, but can be booked through hostels.
Colombia Bungee Jumping Km 2, San Gil–Charalá road w bungee.co. Bungee jumping.
Colombia Rafting Expediciones Cra 10 No. 7–83 w colombiarafting.com. The leading operator for rafting, kayaking and other whitewater sports.
Ecolombia Experience Peñon Guane, Km 2, San Gil–Baruchara road w sangildeportesextremos.com. Canyoning at Peñon Guane.
Gua-iti C 9 No. 13–10, Curiti (12km northeast of San Gil) ☏ 312 421 7948. Caving at Cueva Vaca.
Páramo Santander Extremo Via Principal, Entrada al Municipio, Páramo (19km south of San Gil) w paramosantanderextremo.com. The leading operator for abseiling and caving; also paragliding and paintballing.
Peñon Guane Peñon Guane, Km 2, San Gil–Baruchara road ☏ 317 331 4945. Zip lining.
Rios Expediciones Cra 12 (Charalá road) No. 7–70, Barrio La Playa w rioexpediciones.com. Whitewater rafting.
San Gil Extremo Centro Comercial El Puente (the shopping mall across the river at the bottom of C12) w sangilextremo.com.co. Canyoning at Pinchote.

EDIBLE ANTS IN SANTANDER

Fried *hormigas culonas*, or **fat-bottomed ants**, are a delicacy of the Santander *departamento*. Regarded as an aphrodisiac, they have been eaten since pre-Hispanic times. The ant, a species of leafcutter, is harvested during the rainy season when the queens and drones emerge from their nests to mate and start new colonies. Only the queens are harvested, soaked in brine and then roasted or fried. Unfortunately, because the queens are so vital to the continuation of the species, the practice of eating them is now threatening their numbers, and in some places, people have even started farming the ants so as to conserve their wild population.

The ant season is in March and April when the first rains start, and that's when stalls set up around town, and most particularly on the corner of Carrera 11 with Calle 10. Even out of season, this is the place where you can always buy ants, either at *Cafetería la Once*, Cra 11 No. 10–04, or a couple of doors along in the coffee warehouse at Cra 11 No. 10–16.

---

fruit shop out front, juice bar at the back, where you can get *jugos* made with water, or with milk for a little extra. They also do fruit salads (you may want to ask them to hold the cheese) and breakfasts.

DRINKING AND NIGHTLIFE

La Habana C 8 No. 10–23 • 300 407 5138; map p.107. The town's liveliest bar, with sport on the TV early on and music later, sometimes with dancing.

La Isla Av Santander Km 1; map p.107. West of town on the south side of the river, 300m past the bus terminal, La Isla is a gas station surrounded by restaurants and, downstairs, three music bars: *El Rodeo*, which plays traditional Colombian rhythms; *Caña Brava*, which is a karaoke bar; and *Big Shot*, where a younger crowd dance to reggaeton and more electronic-type beats.

DIRECTORY

Health There's a public hospital (Hospital Regional de San Gil, Cra 5 No. 9–102 • hregionalsangil.gov.co) and a private clinic (Clínica Santa Cruz de la Loma, Av Santander No. 24A–28 • 7 724 2100). Both are adequate for minor problems, but for anything serious, get yourself to the Hospital Regional Manuela Beltrán in Socorro, 23km southwest of San Gil (Cra 16 No. 9–53, Socorro • hospitalmanuela beltran.gov.co). All reputable sports firms have insurance cover for any injuries.

Internet Terena la Novena, Cra 9 No. 10–55, 2nd floor; a nameless shop on Parque La Libertad at C 12 No. 9–23.

Police The tourist police have a kiosk on the Malecón opposite C 7 (• 350 304 5600).

Spanish course Connect 4, Cra 8 No. 12–19 (• connect4.edu.co) offers four fun and handy one-day courses, teaching absolute beginners how to meet and greet, make bookings or talk about specific things in Spanish.

Tejo Comité Municipal de Tejo, C 18 No. 24–62 • 7 724 4053. They take their *tejo* quite seriously here, and don't like beginners turning up to play on match nights, so the best way to come is with *Macondo* hostel, who bring a group on Tues nights at 8pm.

Barichara

Just 21km northwest of San Gil, the beautiful colonial town of **BARICHARA** is one of the best preserved in the country. Its streets lined with original houses in whitewashed *pisé* and the golden local sandstone – known as "Barichara stone"– upmarket Barichara rather looks down its nose at the region's more popular colonial towns of Villa de Leyva (see page 95) and Girón (see page 117).

Barichara boasts some pretty little colonial churches, and there's an easy downhill hike to the village of **Guane**, where you can get a bus back. At the northern end of town, Calle 1 offers impressive views across the valley of the River Suárez, with a *mirador* (viewing platform) opposite the junction with Carrera 9. Tuk-tuks in the main square offer a 1hr 15min tour of the town.

Catedral de la Inmaculada Concepción

Cra 7 at C 5, Parque Principal • Free

Presiding over Barichara's Parque Principal from its northwest corner, the **Catedral de** la Inmaculada Concepción is an imposing eighteenth-century edifice wrought from beautiful local sandstone. The golden yellow of its facade – which turns a gorgeous russet colour at sunset – is broken only by the white marble figure of the Virgin Mary and Holy Spirit (represented as a bird at her feet) directly above the main door.

Casa de la Cultura
C 5 No. 6–29 • Charge • 7 726 7002

In the southwest corner of the main square, Barichara's **Casa de la Cultura** is essentially a nice old colonial house that's open to the public. True, it displays a rather random and cursory selection of fossils, old typewriters and Guane pottery, and there'll be someone to show you around, but none of this would be really worth bothering with if it weren't for the opportunity to wander round the patio and admire the colonial architecture.

Escuela Taller de Barichara
Cra 5 No. 4–26 • Free • 7 726 7577

A block south of the main square, the **Escuela Taller de Barichara** is a school for traditional crafts. Around the patio garden of the fine old house are workshops where students learn pottery, candle making and furniture making, and anyone can stop by and watch. There's another branch just round the corner on Calle 4, where they learn bookbinding and weaving. The products made are on sale in the lobby of the main school, and you're welcome to buy, but there's no pressure. The patio has a café where you can stop for a caffeine fix.

Capilla de Santa Bárbara
Cra 11, at C 6 • Free

The prettiest of Barichara's small churches, the **Capilla de Santa Bárbara** is directly aligned with Calle 6, making a picturesque backdrop when looking up the street, and giving a view straight down it from the front door. The church is not open for regular Mass, but is popular for weddings and is sometimes used for art exhibitions. The building dates from the eighteenth century, but by the end of the twentieth it was in such a ruinous state that it had to be reconstructed. The facade (which looks especially nice when floodlit at night) is original and you can see an Indigenous influence, particularly in the doorposts flanking the main entrance and the little face carved above it.

Should you be lucky enough to find the church open, pop inside to admire the austere interior and the beautifully painted wooden *retablo*. The backward-sloping floor is a little bit strange but at least the congregation had no trouble sitting back in their seats.

Capilla de Jesús Resucitado
Cra 7, at C 3 • Free

At the western end of Carrera 7, the **Capilla de Jesús Resucitado**, built in 1797, has rather a plain exterior, made with local stone, and rather a plain interior too, its dark wooden *retablo* giving it quite a sombre feel. Indeed, this is far from inappropriate given that the church is next to the town **cemetery** and is largely used for funerals. The cemetery itself is worth a look, its tombs made largely of local stone. The grandest are at the back.

The Camino Real
Trail C 1, opposite the end of Cra 10 and C 4 • **Museum** Guane • Charge

Starting from the junction of Calle 4 and Carrera 10 with Calle 1, the **Camino Real** is a 9km stone-paved trail, very popular with hikers and downhill all the way, passing through a cactus-filled valley with great mountain views. The trail goes back to pre-Hispanic times, when it was used by the Indigenous Guane people. It ends up at the tiny village of **Guane**, from where there are twelve daily buses back to Barichara and San Gil, the last at 5pm (but check at the bus company's office in Barichara, in case the times have changed). While waiting for the bus in Guane, you could eat in one of the local restaurants or check out the village's small paleontology and archeology **museum**.

ARRIVAL AND INFORMATION   BARICHARA

By bus Buses to San Gil (every 30min; 45min) leave from the bus company's office in the main square at Cra 6 No. 5–74.

Tourist information The tourist office on Cra 5, at C 9 doubles as a souvenir shop and gives out free maps.

ACCOMMODATION

Casa de Hercilia C 3 No. 5–33 ☏ 7 641 1841; map p.111. A light and airy guesthouse that oozes tranquillity, with hammocks, beanbags and leafy pot plants liberally scattered throughout. It also has a well-equipped communal kitchen. Thick walls may sometimes impede the wi-fi signal. $$

★ **Casa Oniri** C 6 No. 7–55 ⓦ casaoniri.com; map p.111. A super-cool designer boutique hotel (just eight rooms) in a mid-nineteenth-century house, stunningly beautiful with the hint of a Moroccan *riad*. Everything is white and minimalist, with a central patio courtyard with a shallow pool (for admiring, not swimming in), and a roof terrace offering views over town – the latter is a wonderful location for a romantic meal, which they can rustle up, no problem. Breakfast included. $$$$

Color de Hormiga/Casa de Hormiga reserve Cra 7 No. 7–78 ☏ 7 726 7156; map p.111. The proprietor of this hostel used to run a restaurant specializing in ants (*hormigas culonas*). In addition to the hostel itself, in a quiet street just two blocks off the main square, they also have a reserve 1km east of town, where you can stay among birds and butterflies, leafcutter ants and even porcupines, armadillos and opossums, with accommodation in an old *finca*. Hostel dorms $, hostel doubles $$, finca doubles $$$

Hotel Misión Santa Bárbara C 5 No. 9–08 ⓦ hotelmisionsantabarbara.com; map p.111. A group of old colonial houses turned into a great hotel, where every room is different but most are spacious and all are well appointed. There's a good pool, too. Breakfast included. $$$

Tinto Hostel Cra 4 No. 5–39 ☏ 7 726 7725; map p.111. This hostel has quite a rustic feel, with wooden fittings and tiled floors. There's a lush garden, good views, hammocks and even a small pool. $

EATING

El Balcón de mi Pueblo C 7 No. 5–62 ☏ 318 280 2980; map p.111. A good place to sample *Santanderino* cuisine. There are daily set meals, or go for a *bandeja típica*, with a mix of local specialities including goat and dried meat. $

La Brasa Misifu Cra 6 No. 6–31 ☏ 7 726 7321; map p.111. This *Santanderino* restaurant is the best place in town to try the local speciality, *cabrito con pepitoria* – roast goat served with a mash made from its blood and offal, which may not sound very appetizing, but is actually quite delicious, somewhere between haggis and black pudding. $$

El Cabrito al la Brasa C 6 No. 5–03 ☏ 7 421 9600; map p.111. A good-value small restaurant where they have a great value set menu and good breakfasts. They also serve *chicha* (a traditional alcoholic corn brew). $

Panadería Central C 6, at Cra 6, no. 5–82; map p.111. This bright bakery on the main square doubles as a café, with espresso-based coffees, plus juices and cakes – churros stuffed with *arequipe*, even. $

Shambalá Cra 7 No. 6–18 ☏ 319 615 5603; map p.111. Not strictly speaking a veggie restaurant, as it has a few non-veg dishes, but it's all natural food, with a strong Asian influence, and most of the options are vegetarian. They offer Mediterranean-style veg noodles or Thai-style veg noodles. Space is limited, so you may have to squeeze in. $$

Parque Nacional del Chicamocha

Km 54 Via Bucaramanga–San Gil • Charge • w parquenacionaldelchicamocha.com

Parque Nacional del Chicamocha, between San Gil and Bucaramanga (39km and 54km respectively), was created to display the rugged natural beauty of the **Chicamocha Canyon**. In fact the park takes in only a small part of the canyon, but it does offer a selection of different activities; this tends to make it feel less like what you'd normally think of as a national park and more like a theme park.

The canyon is 227km long and up to 2km deep. The best way to get sweeping views of it is to take the **cable car** (*teleférico*), which is 6.3km long, running down into the canyon and over to the other side. Be aware that there may be a long queue, and you may have to wait for as much as an hour to get on. You can alternatively watch the scenery whizz by at much higher speed – although without actually crossing the canyon – by hurtling along a **zip line** (*cable vuelo*), of which there are three: one long, one shorter but higher, and one for children. There is also a series of scenic plazas and a 360° lookout point (*mirador*) for nice views.

If all you want is to admire the natural beauty of the canyon, on the other hand, you don't actually need to enter the park at all: there's a **restaurant** at the gate where you can stop for a snack or a meal with a view, and you can then just take a walk outside the park and enjoy the scenery for free.

ARRIVAL AND DEPARTURE   PARQUE NACIONAL DEL CHICAMOCHA

By bus Any bus between San Gil and Bucaramanga can drop you at the entrance, which is about an hour from San Gil and 1hr 30min from Bucaramanga.

ACTIVITIES

At the park entrance you can book **zip lining**, **ice skating**, **paragliding** and the **cliff swing**, but for the paragliding it would be advisable to book ahead (☎ 7 724 3839 or ☎ 313 857 1363) and for the cliff swing it is usually better to go with a firm such as Nativox or Páramo Santander Extremo from San Gil or Colombia Paragliding from Bucaramanga (see pages 108 and 115).

Bucaramanga and around

With well over half a million inhabitants, **BUCARAMANGA** is Colombia's ninth-largest city, but with very low rates of crime and unemployment, it has managed to escape many of the problems that beset other Colombian conurbations. Dotted with lots of green spaces – well over a hundred of them – Bucaramanga prides itself on being Colombia's most beautiful city. The centre may be low on specific attractions, but it makes a great jumping-off point for visits to nearby **Girón**, it's a convenient stopover for anyone travelling between Bogotá and the Caribbean coast (or Venezuela), and the surrounding mountains make for superb paragliding. At 950m above sea level, Bucaramanga is hot all year round, but rarely unbearably so. Its wettest months are April and October.

Brief history

Bucaramanga was founded in 1622, but played second fiddle to neighbouring Girón for the first two centuries of its life. In the 1860s and 1870s, its population was swollen by an influx of German immigrant adventurers, not without local opposition. In 1886 Bucaramanga was made **capital** of the Santander *departamento*, and has never looked back. Although the decisive battle of the Thousand Days' War was fought at Palonegro, near where Bucaramanga's airport now stands, the city itself was largely unaffected by the war, remaining quite prosperous amid the chaos. But its biggest growth spurt was in the second half of the twentieth century, which saw it all but swallow up neighbouring towns such as Floridablanca and Girón.

Parque García Rovira

Cra 10–11, at C 35–37

Although Bucaramanga's main square is the Parque de Santander, its administrative centre is the **Parque García Rovira**, nine blocks west, where the mayor's office and the *departamento* government face each other on the north and south sides. Rather more attractive than either is the nineteenth-century **Iglesia de San Laureano**, in yellow and white, on the east side of the square, and, in the square's northwest corner, the oldest church in Bucaramanga, the simple, whitewashed **Capilla de los Dolores**, which dates from 1750 and opens only for special events (often on Saturdays, for weddings). The statue in the middle of the square is of local boy **Custodio García Rovira**, who was elected president of the short-lived independent United Provinces of New Granada (see page 343), but was captured and executed by the Spanish when they regained control in 1816.

Casa de Bolívar and around

C 37 No. 12–15 • Charge • 7 630 4258

Simón Bolívar spent a grand total of seventy days in 1828 living in Bucaramanga, enough for the locals to dub the beautiful late eighteenth-century house where he stayed **Casa de Bolívar**. Just two blocks east of the Parque García Rovira, it now contains a small historical museum, with a miscellaneous collection of exhibits labelled in Spanish only. There are assorted **relics** of the independence struggle and the Thousand Days' War, including bullets, guns, shells and bayonets, some of the pots and pans Bolívar used when staying here, and portaits of Bolívar and of his aide-de-camp, Daniel Florence O'Leary, who was from Cork in Ireland. The most

ACCOMMODATION		EATING				DRINKING & NIGHTLIFE		SHOPPING	
Balmoral	3	Battuto	9	Locoyote	2	La Birrería 1516	5	San Francisco	
Chicamocha	2	Bobby & Friends	8	Masai Gourmet	4	BPM	1	Leather Market	1
Kasa Guane		La Carreta	6	Mercagán	5	Calison	3		
Bucaramanga (KGB)	1	Eskarola Restaurante		El Viejo Chiflas	1	La Esquinita	2		
Principe	4	Gourmet	3			El Guitarrón	4		
Tryp Bucaramanga	5	El Gran Balcón	7						

> ## ACTIVITIES IN BUCARAMANGA
>
> Although it is no San Gil when it comes to adventure sports (see page 108), Bucaramanga is a good base for **paragliding** and **rock climbing**, and offers opportunities for voluntary work in the local community.
>
> ### PARAGLIDING
>
> Local firm **Colombia Paragliding** (w colombiaparagliding.com) offers flights at eight different flying sites including the Chicamocha Canyon. At their main site, Las Aguilas, they have their own hostel, where you can stay while enjoying flights in the morning and again in the afternoon. They also offer a ten-day paragliding course including accommodation.
>
> ### ROCK CLIMBING
>
> The **rock wall** at La Mojarra, an hour by bus from Bucaramanga (changing at Piedecuesta) and 5km before the town of Los Santos, has two hostels especially for rock-climbers – *Refugio de la Roca* (w refugiolarocacolombia.com) and *Juan Palitos* (t 300 223 9349) – both of which rent out equipment. There are also two **indoor climbing walls** in town: Boulder House at Cra 36 No. 51–79 (t 317 335 1171), and Espacio Vertical at C 35 No. 32–93 (t 316 868 7706).
>
> ### VOLUNTEERING
>
> *Kasa Guane* hostel (see page 116) is closely involved with an initiative called **Goals for Peace** (w golesporlapaz.org), which runs sporting and craftwork activities for children in one of the poorest parts of town, as well as English classes, and can take volunteers for as short or as long as you like.

interesting exhibits, however, are artefacts of the Guane people who were living in the region at the time of the Spanish conquest. Aside from numerous ceramics and textiles, there are three **mummies**, including one of a child, and a cabinet of the **skulls** of Guane aristocrats, who used head vices to deform them in a manner they apparently considered beautiful.

Across the street from the Casa de Bolívar, in a nineteenth-century house, the **Casa de la Cultura** (C 37 No. 12–46; free) houses free art exhibitions.

Museo de Arte Moderno

C 37 No. 26–16 • Free • w museodeartemodernodebucaramanga.com

Located just off Carrera 27, the **Museo de Arte Moderno de Bucaramanga (MAMB)** puts on temporary exhibitions of work by local and nationwide artists. It also displays a constantly changing selection from its permanent collection of modern painting and sculpture, which includes work by Andy Warhol and local artist Guillermo Espinosa.

ARRIVAL AND DEPARTURE — BUCARAMANGA

By plane Palonegro airport is 25km west of Bucaramanga, with taxis available here. There is also a *colectivo* service between the airport and C 35 No. 20–23, just off the Parque de Santander in the city centre (t 7 642 5250), as well as *colectivos* from the airport to other parts of town (buy a ticket from the desk in arrivals); the same firm also offers an "expreso" service (much the same as a taxi), bookable by phone or at their office or airport desk.

Destinations Bogotá (12–15 daily; 1hr 5min); Cartagena (1 daily; 1hr 20min); Cúcuta (1–4 daily; 45min); Medellín (1–4 daily; 55min); Panama City (4 weekly; 1hr 30min).

By bus The Terminal de Transportes (w terminalbucaramanga.com) is 4km south of town, halfway to Girón. Taxis to the city centre are available, or there are buses; returning to the airport you can pick up buses in town on Cra 15 or Cra 33.

Destinations Barranquilla (22 daily; 11hr); Bogotá (every 20–30min; 10hr); Cartagena (20 daily; 12hr); Cúcuta (every 20–30min; 5hr); Medellín (18 daily; 8hr); Pamplona (every 20–30min; 3hr; plus *colectivos*); San Gil (every 15–30min; 2hr 30min); Santa Marta (10 daily; 10hr); Tunja (every 20min–1hr; 7hr).

By colectivo For San Gil, rather than go to the bus terminal, it's faster to pick buses up at a junction called Papi Quiero Piña, south of town in Floridablanca, accessed by bus from Cra 33 towards Piedecuesta (but check on boarding that the bus will pass Papi Quiero Piña). For Cúcuta, *colectivos* leave from the Parque del Agua, Diagonal 32 No. 30A–51.

GETTING AROUND

Bucaramanga is compact enough to explore on foot, but there are a number of options.

By bus You're unlikely to use buses except to visit satellite towns such as Girón, Floridablanca or Piedequesta.

By Metrolinea Bucaramanga has a BRT system, Metrolinea (wmetrolinea.gov.co), which is like Bogotá's TransMilenio.

ACCOMMODATION

Balmoral Cra 21 No. 34–75 wfacebook.com/hotel balmoralbucaramanga; map p.114. A good-value city-centre hotel done out in modern style with jolly orange and white decor. The rooms are compact but fully equipped, with private bathroom, a/c and minibar. $$

Chicamocha C 34 No. 31–24 whotelchicamocha.com; map p.114. This extremely well-run five-star may not have the plushest rooms of any deluxe hotel worldwide, but they've got everything you need, including 24hr room service, a fully equipped gym and spa, with Turkish bath and sauna, two bars, three restaurants and a large pool. Buffet breakfast included. $$$

★ **Kasa Guane Bucaramanga (KGB)** C 11 No. 26–50 ☏ 7 274 2199; map p.114. Friendly hostel in the university area, north of the centre, handy for student hangouts – and with its own terrace bar, and a restaurant that makes a decent stab at Middle Eastern veg grub. This is the best place to stay if you want to find out about activities such as paragliding or rock climbing, and the owners also run a volunteering project (see page 115). Breakfast included. Dorms $, doubles $$

Principe Cra 17 No. 37–69 ☏ 7 656 3844; map p.114. This little mid-range hotel has been going since 1938, although it's been well modernized. You have the choice of a fan (but only twin beds) or, for very little more, a/c (twin or double), and it has its own restaurant. Breakfast included. $$

Tryp Bucaramanga Cra 38 No. 48–66 wwyndham hotels.com; map p.114. A very cool, modern deluxe hotel where all the beds are at least queen-size, the staff aim to please, and facilities include a restaurant, bar and gym, although no pool. It's worth asking for a room on the top floor with a city view. Small discount at weekends. Buffet breakfast included. $$$

EATING

Battuto C 55 No. 36–17 wbattuto.cluvi.co; map p.114. The best Italian food in town, with an open kitchen. Lots of classic pasta dishes, for sure, but they recommend a simple option like *tagliatelle cacio e pepe* (with pecorino romano cheese and pepper) to properly taste the hand-made pasta itself. If that hasn't plugged the gap, check out the ossobuco, or just go straight on to a dessert like the pannacotta in limoncello sauce. $$

Bobby & Friends Cra. 31 No. 52A–31 wfacebook.com/ bobbysKoreanfood; map p.114. Something different for a change: good Korean food including a copious *sam gyoob sal* (Korean barbecue cooked right there at the table). $

La Carreta Cra 27 No. 42–27 ☏ 7 643 6680; map p.114. Set up in 1957 by former Argentina and Atlético Bucaramanga midfielder Roberto Pablo Janiot, this excellent Argentine restaurant will prepare a perfect chorizo steak (sirloin strip, the favourite Argentine cut), done to whatever turn you desire. There isn't much for vegetarians, but non-carnivores can go for a fish option such as salmon steak in mustard sauce. $$$

Eskarola Restaurante Gourmet Cra 29 No. 40–54 ☏ 7 634 0509; map p.114. This popular fish restaurant serves a range of succulent dishes made with anything from trout or salmon to sea bass or bocachico, but the house speciality is *mojarra* (tilapia) stuffed with prawns in a rich seafood sauce – absolutely delicious. $$

El Gran Balcón Cra 14 No. 37–85 ☏ 7 642 3104; map p.114. Despite the name, this homely restaurant doesn't actually have a balcony, but it does have a choice of lunchtime set menus: a plain old *ejecutivo* or, for not much more, a healthier version with less salt, less sugar and brown rice instead of white. $

Locoyote Cra 34 No. 35–18 ☏ 7 813 3931; map p.114. A fast food restaurant made from a few transport containers, a VW campervan and some oil-barrel couches, plus open-air (but covered) seating, upstairs or downstairs. With decent burgers, fries, ribs and beers, it isn't exactly haute cuisine, but it's cool and fun, with a good vibe. $

Masai Gourmet C 43 No. 35–49 ☏ 320 400 6459; map p.114. This restaurant is a top spot for those who like a meat heavy menu. Top of the billing is roast goat, be it in the classic form of *cabro al horno* (with all the trimmings), or the less classic form of a goatburger. You can get pork or beef here too. $$

Mercagán Cra 33 at C 42 wmercaganparrilla.com; map p.114. A top-whack steak house where you can choose your cut, its size and how you like it done. Their best cut is *lomo fino* (filet mignon), but they'll slice it out thin unless you ask for it *en bloque* (unsliced), which you should do, especially if you don't want it too well done in the middle. Other branches around town are listed on the website. $$$$

El Viejo Chiflas Cra 33 No. 34–10 ⓦ elviejochiflas restaurante.inf.travel; map p.114. *Comida típica* including *cabro en salsa* (goat in sauce) or a big mixed grill for two. It's open 24hr from Thurs to Sun, so very handy after a late night out. $$

DRINKING AND NIGHTLIFE

La Birrería 1516 Cra 36 No. 43–46 ⓣ 7 669 0656; map p.114. A cool bar, literally, as it's open on two sides, usually has football on the TV (including English Premier League matches regularly, Scottish Premiership matches on occasion), Bogotá Beer Company and imported Belgian beers, and bar food including ribs, steaks and burgers.

BPM Cra 27 No. 10–21 ⓣ 318 210 0116; map p.114. An upstairs music bar near the university and popular with students, with mostly indie-rock-type sounds, and often with local bands playing live, especially at weekends. They also have jam sessions and open-deck nights.

Calison C 33 No. 31–35 ⓣ 7 634 8927; map p.114. This salsa club has been a favourite since it opened in 1993. There's no entry fee, you just pay for drinks, and the music is solid salsa, much of it from the collection of vinyl and CDs they keep behind the mixing desk.

La Esquinita C 22 No. 25–55 ⓦ facebook.com/la esquinitabucaramanga; map p.114. Great retro decor, including old Mexican movie stills, and a collection of records to match, at this salsa and Latino classics club which has been going since 1964 and tends to attract a slightly older crowd than your average Bucaramanga disco.

El Guitarrón Cra 33 No. 37–34 ⓣ 317 253 9756; map p.114. Not what you really expect in Colombia: a mariachi bar – one of a slew on this strip, in fact – with live mariachis in full costume performing nightly from 10pm.

SHOPPING

San Francisco Leather Market Cra 22 C 19–C 24; map p.114. An area of leather shops rather than a clearly defined market as such, this is the place to look for shoes, sandals, belts, bags, wallets, purses and anything made of leather. Good quality at good prices.

DIRECTORY

Consulates Brazil, Cra 19 No. 35–02, 2nd floor, suite 209 (ⓣ 7 634 4000); Venezuela, Cra 37 No. 52–75 (ⓣ 7 643 6621).

Festivals The Ferias Bonitas, held on 13–23 Sept, are ten days of parades, music and performance, mostly held in the city's numerous *parques*.

Internet Plenty of small places, including Graficopias, C 34 No. 20–01 and Fido.net, Cra 20 No. 34–14.

Laundry Express Wash, C 36 No. 33–38.
Health Clinica Chicamocha, C 40 No. 27A–22 (ⓦ clinica chicamocha.com).
Police Policía de Turismo, Parque de los Niños, C 30 at Cra 27 (ⓣ 7 634 5507).
Swimming pools Acualago, in nearby Floridablanca (C 29 No. 10–13; ⓣ 318 345 1501) is a huge water park with fairground-style rides for kids and for grown-ups (charge).

Girón

Just 7km from Bucaramanga across the Antonia Santos double bridge, **GIRÓN** – full name San Juan de Girón – is a charming colonial town of one-storey whitewashed houses with black doors and window shutters, giving it a rather sober monochrome look. The streets are cobbled and the stream, which runs along Calle 29, is crossed by a series of pretty bridges. The **Parque Principal**, with its tree-shaded benches, is overlooked by a white church, built in 1646 but reconstituted to its present form in 1833 and promoted to the status of **Basílica Menor** in 1998. More tranquil than the Parque Principal is the smaller **Plazuela de las Nieves**, bounded by Carreras 27 and 28, and by Calles 28 and 28A, with a beautiful little stone chapel, the mid-eighteenth-century **Capilla de Nuestra Señora de las Nieves**, which opens only for Mass.

ARRIVAL AND INFORMATION　　　　　　　　　　　　　　　　　　　　　　　　GIRÓN

By bus You can catch buses for Girón on Cra 33 in Bucaramanga. For the return journey, pick them up on C 27 in Girón.

Tourist information The tourist office is at C 30 No. 26–64.

ACCOMMODATION

Girón Chill Out Cra 25 No. 32–06 w gironchillout.com. A quiet little boutique hotel in a typical old Girón house just a block off the main square, with an in-house restaurant. It's worth paying a bit more for a large, split-level room. Breakfast included. $$

Las Nieves C 30 No. 25–71 t 7 646 8968. Cheaper rooms with ceiling fan and rather better ones with a/c; in all of them the windows open only onto the central patio, which has its own canaries and doubles as a restaurant (see page 118). Rooms on the top floor are best. Breakfast included. $$

EATING

La Casona C 28 No. 28–09 (on Plazuela de las Nieves) w lacasona-restaurante.com. The best restaurant in town, serving meals in a lovely little courtyard with tinkling fountains. Top regional dishes include *cabro con pepitoria* (goat with a side of black pudding made from its blood and offal) and *sobrebarriga criolla al horno* (roast flank steak). $$

Heladería las Nieves C 27 No. 28A–12 (on Plazuela de las Nieves) t 316 746 6729. Interesting home-made popsicles in flavours such as milk and *bocadillo*, soursop, carrot or *salpicón* (fruit salad). They also sell a delicious gloopy form of *chicha* made from *corozo* (coyure palm fruit) and *panela* (unrefined sugar). When the shop itself is closed, you can try round the corner at C 29 No. 26–87. $

Las Nieves C 30 No. 25–71 t 7 646 8968. The central patio of this hotel on the main square (see page 118) is also a restaurant serving breakfast and filling but unexciting lunchtime set menus. It's also quite an elegant spot in which to take coffee. $$

Pamplona

At 2200m, with an agreeably cool climate, sitting in a valley in the Eastern Cordillera and surrounded by green mountain scenery, **PAMPLONA** has a laidback pace and a bevy of small museums. It was founded by the Spanish in 1549, and soon became a centre for learning and religious institutions. In 1644 and 1875, the city was devastated by earthquakes but neither destroyed as many of its lovely old houses

as the building boom of the 1990s. Still, there's enough of the old town left to appreciate, and while it can't boast the nightlife of Bogotá or Bucaramanga, the large student population keeps it lively.

Parque Agueda

Simón Bolívar gave Pamplona the title "patriotic city" for its staunch support of the independence movement, but Pamplona doesn't have a Plaza de Bolívar. Instead, its main square – complete with **cathedral** on its south side – is called **Parque Agueda Gallardo**. It is named after a 60-year old Pamplonese woman who in 1810 snatched the baton of authority from the governor of New Granada and broke it in a gesture of support for Bogotá's *Grito de Independencia* (see page 61), upon which the townspeople arrested and imprisoned the hapless governor.

Plazuela Almeyda

Four blocks south of Parque Agueda, grassy **Plazuela Almeyda** is the centre of Pamplona's nightlife scene, such as it is. A large white **obelisk** commemorates the pro-independence guerrilla force set up in 1817 by two local brothers, Ambrosio and Vicente Almeyda, to harry the loyalist Spanish army in the region. Also in the Plazuela Almeyda, a **monument** commemorates the daring prison break-out on 22 July, 1819, led by Pamplonese revolutionaries José María Mantilla and José María Villamizar, who went on to reorganize the local resistance forces in support of Bolívar. The prison they broke out from stood in the Parque Agueda Gallardo, to the left of the cathedral.

Museo de Arte Moderno Ramírez Villamizar

C 5 No. 5–75 • Charge • ☎ 7 226 7648

On the north side of the Parque Agueda Gallardo, the **Museo de Arte Moderno Ramírez Villamizar** showcases the work of twentieth-century local artist Eduardo Ramírez Villamizar, mostly consisting of abstract geometric **sculptures** in metal and wood. The building dates from 1549, and on the stairs, an anonymous seventeenth-century **fresco** of St Christopher is partly preserved. The last room upstairs displays some of Ramírez Villamizar's **paintings**, which are older than his sculptures and include a 1945 self-portrait. The other paintings are abstract, but less so than the sculptures. Ramírez Villamizar's ashes repose in an urn in the main patio.

Museo Casa Colonial

C 6 No. 2–56 • Free • ☎ 7 568 2043

Three blocks west of the Parque Agueda Gallardo, the **Museo Casa Colonial** is a rather miscellaneous collection sparsely labelled in Spanish. Really, it's a museum of local interest rather than for tourists, but it's free, and it does have a few interesting bits and pieces to its name. Pride of place goes to the **skull** of independence supporter Juan Esteban Ramírez, still hanging in the metal cage in which the Spanish authorities displayed it as a deterrent to others after his execution.

Museo Arquidiocesano de Arte Religioso

Cra 5 No. 4–53 • Charge • ☎ 7 568 2816

You'll need to get your skates on to vist the **Museo Arquidiocesano de Arte Religioso**, one block north of the Parque Agueda Gallardo, as it's only open for a couple of two-hour windows a day. It's worth making the effort, though, as it's the most substantial of the city's museums. The **ground floor** is dedicated to painting and sculpture, with a lot of statues of saints, some very well executed, as well as paintings on religious themes including pictures of the Four Evangelists (the gospel authors, Matthew, Mark, Luke and John) by New Granada's leading artist, Gregorio Vázquez de Arce, and other equally fine works, largely anonymous. The **second floor** has an impressive display of liturgical props, beautifully wrought in silver and gold, while the **third floor** displays ecclesiastical robes, and more interestingly, houses the eclectic collection of objects bequeathed by the museum's founder, father Enrique Rochereau.

Casa Anzoátegui
Cra 6 No. 7–48 • Charge • 311 825 0596

Two blocks south of the Parque Agueda Gallardo, **Casa Anzoátegui** is named after independence hero José Antonio Anzoátegui, who died here in 1819, having survived the Battle of Boyacá and been promoted to general by Bolívar, only to be struck down by sudden illness a few months later at the age of 30. The house belonged to the Vargas de la Rosas family, who were strong supporters of the independence movement and often accommodated its leaders; Simón Bolívar stayed here on occasion. The exhibition itself has replicas of Anzoátegui's sword and uniform, plus actual weapons from the independence struggle (although they weren't his), but the explanations are in Spanish only.

Museo de Fotografía Antigua de Toto
Cra 7 No. 2–44 • Charge

Pamplona's quirkiest and most engaging museum, the **Museo de Fotografía Antigua de Toto**, three blocks northeast of the Parque Agueda Gallardo, is a ramshackle collection of old photographs, originally gathered in 1960 to celebrate the 150th anniversary of the *Grito de Independencia*. The eponymous Toto, a local artist, left them on display, and his sons have continued to do so. There are some from almost every decade of the twentieth century, and a few from the nineteenth, not all in very good condition, it has to be said, although the local university has long since digitalized them for posterity. The most interesting images are of places in town such as the cathedral, which you can see in the 1880s, just after it was shaken up by the 1875 earthquake, and then again in 1901, after it had been restored, and in the 1950s, with its bell tower replaced. Also on display are works of art by Toto and his son Emiliano, and a model of Pamplona as it was in 1985.

Iglesia del Humilladero
C 2 No. 6–83 • Free • bit.ly/humilladero

The **Iglesia del Humilladero**, at the top end of Carrera 7, was originally just a little hermitage, but was rebuilt as a church in 1613. The building, whitewashed inside and out, is quite austere in its simplicity, but it boasts a beautifully realistic sculpture of Christ on the Cross, probably executed in Spain in the early seventeenth century, and located behind the altar. To its left and right are images of the two thieves who were crucified with Jesus, sculpted by the Spanish artist Juan Bautista Guzmán in 1595. It was most likely Guzmán who created the main image too.

Behind the church is the town **cemetery**, which is also worth a visit. Here the deceased are not buried in the ground but stacked in walls of graves, four high, each with a window bearing the name and often a picture of the person buried within.

ARRIVAL AND INFORMATION · PAMPLONA

By bus and colectivo The bus terminal is 600m east of Parque Agueda Gallardo, just beyond the junction of C 4 with C 9. It's an easy walk into town; otherwise, a taxi is an option. For Cúcuta and Bucaramanga, in addition to buses, there are also *colectivos*, which leave when full and are faster. **Destinations** Bogotá (every 20min–hourly; 13hr); Bucaramanga (every 30min; 3hr); Cúcuta (every 40min; 2hr); Tunja (5 daily; 10hr).

Tourist information PiT (Punto de Información Turística) in the town hall, C 5 No. 6–19.

ACCOMMODATION

1549 Hostal C 8B No. 5–84 ⓦ1549hostal.com; map p.118. Despite the name, this isn't a hostel but a boutique-ish hotel with a bar, on a quiet street. Rooms are stylish and very comfortable, some with fireplaces, and there's a bar and restaurant. Breakfast included. $\overline{\$}$

El Álamo C 5 No. 6–68 ☎7 568 2137; map p.118. A good-value budget hotel, with clean, simple rooms and en-suite bathrooms. Ask for a room on the fourth floor, where there are good views on both sides. $\overline{\$}$

Cariongo Cra 5, at C 9 (Plazuela Almeyda) ☎568 1515, ⓦhotelcariongo.com; map p.118. It may look like a utility building from the outside, but this is the closest you'll get to a deluxe hotel in town, with lush gardens. The best, quietest and most modern rooms are at the end of the gardens, away from the main building; ask for *la parte atrás* when you book (the price is the same). Breakfast included. $\overline{\$\$\$}$

Imperial Cra 5 No. 5–32 ☎7 568 2571; map p.118. It's worth paying a bit more at this hotel on Parque Agueda Gallardo to get a bigger, brighter special room with a view over the square – those on the fourth floor are best. All have bathrooms and 24hr hot water. $\overline{\$\$}$

★ **Solar** C 5 No. 8–10 ☎7 568 2010; map p.118. In an old house dating from 1776, this place is an utter bargain, especially if you take one of the huge upstairs rooms complete with bathroom and kitchen, and even more so if you bag the split-level room no. 6. The downstairs rooms are slightly less of a bargain, and they adjoin the restaurant, so they aren't always quiet, but they're still a pretty good deal. Breakfast included. $\overline{\$\$}$

EATING

La Casona C 6 No. 7–58 ☎7 568 3555; map p.118. Neighbour and rival to *Delicias del Mar*, a bit more modern and a bit more chic. Here you can feast on a fisherman's platter (mixed seafood *gratinée*), or a *paella valenciana* (with seafood, pork and chorizo). $\overline{\$\$\$}$

Cositas Ricas C 6 No. 6–65 ☎7 568 4831; map p.118. A decent little restaurant for a moderately priced feed on the likes of *churrasco* (barbecued beef) or sea bass or trout, or a seafood *cazuela*. $\overline{\$\$}$

Delicias del Mar C 6 No. 7–60 ☎7 568 4558; map p.118. Popular seafood restaurant where the *cazuela* is popular or you can go for a *róbalo a la marinera* (sea bass with prawns in a seafood sauce). $\overline{\$\$}$

Piero's Pizza Cra 5 No. 8B–67 ⓦpizzapieros.com; map p.118. Run by an expat Italian but catering to local tastes, this pizzeria offers classics such as a plain old Napolitana (*margherita*), or very non-Italian choices such as the Hawaiian. Or opt for pasta such as the cannelloni or ravioli (choice of meat or spinach-and-cheese filling). They also have a café next door and a takeaway counter selling pizza by the slice.

Solar C 5 No. 8–10 ☎7 568 2010; map p.118. You get a posh weekday *comida corrida* in the eighteenth-century courtyard here, or you can opt for treats such as rib-eye steak or sea bass *meunière*. $\overline{\$\$}$

DIRECTORY

Festivals Pamplona puts on a particularly good Semana Santa (Holy Week, the run-up to Easter), with processions bearing images of saints and of the Virgin. Coinciding with it is a festival of sacred choral music. There's a smaller procession to the Iglesia del Humilladero in mid-Sept every year.

Internet Ciber Net, Pasaje Ortún Velásquez (off Parque Agueda Gallardo to the left of the cathedral) No. 6–19; Cyber Stiver, C 5 No. 7–60.

Cúcuta and around

The busy border town of **CÚCUTA** is the last stop before Venezuela, and basks in hot tropical sunshine. The capital of the Norte de Santander *departamento*, Cúcuta was the scene of an important battle in 1813, which kicked off Simón Bolívar's campaign to liberate Venezuela from Spanish rule. The satellite town of **Villa del Rosario** was the birthplace of Francisco de Paula Santander (see page 122), and the location of the Congress of Cúcuta of 30 August 1821, which ratified the independence and union of Venezuela and New Granada as Gran Colombia, with Bolívar as its president and Santander as its vice-president. There isn't much else to see in Cúcuta, which was largely destroyed by an earthquake in 1875, but aside from the heat – and an unpleasantly dodgy bus station – it's a reasonable place to spend the night on your way to or from Venezuela. Note that carreras in Cúcuta are called **avenidas**, and start at zero rather than one (as indeed do calles). The **main square** is not Plaza de Bolívar, but Parque de Santander, with a statue to match.

Villa del Rosario

Km 6, Autopista Internacional • Bus showing both "Villa del Rosario" and "San Antonio" from Cúcuta terminal or Diagonal Santander at C 8 or at Ventura Plaza mall (ask for "Zona Histórica de Villa del Rosario")

The site of the 1821 Congress of Cúcuta is conserved as a **Parque Gran Colombiano** (or "Parque Histórico") on the east side of the town of **Villa del Rosario**, on the road to the Venezuelan border. The congress took place in a church, the **Templo del Congreso**. Unfortunately, this was largely destroyed in the 1875 earthquake, and little of it above waist height remains. The dome of the church was reconstructed, however, and stands as a monument to the historic event, with a statue of Bolívar placed directly beneath it.

Immediately to the north of the site is the **Casa de Santander**, where Bolívar's ally and then rival, Francisco de Paula Santander was born in 1792. Guides are on hand to show you around (in Spanish), and you can see some of Santander's swords and spurs, and visit his office, which is preserved much as it was when he was alive. In the garden, you can see the well and the huge oven in which bread was baked daily for the household and all their workers, the Santanders being major landowners and employers.

ARRIVAL AND DEPARTURE   CÚCUTA

By plane Cúcuta's Camilo Daza airport (w cuc.aerooriente.com.co) is 5km north of town. Taxis will run you from here to the centre of town or there are buses (in town, pick them up on Av 3). The only direct destination currently is Bogotá (9–12 daily; 1hr 5min).

By bus and colectivo Buses and *colectivos* use Cúcuta's

FRANCISCO DE PAULA SANTANDER

Colombia's fourth president, **Francisco José de Paula Santander y Omaña**, was born to an upper-class family in Villa del Rosario in 1792. Following the *Grito de Independencia* in 1810 (see page 61), he joined the pro-independence forces, retreating, when the Spanish regained control, into the Llanos region on the Venezuelan border, where he joined up with Bolívar's forces, and served as one of El Libertador's most able generals during the key battles of the independence campaign.

In 1821, at the **Congress of Cúcuta**, Santander was chosen as Bolívar's vice-president in Gran Colombia, and actually took control of the country's day-to-day administration while Bolívar was away liberating Ecuador and Peru. Gradually however, **political differences** between the two men emerged. Santander was a great believer in the rule of law – indeed, he became known as El Hombre de las Leyes ("the man of laws") – and balked at Bolívar's pragmatism in bending the law to suit prevailing circumstances. In particular, Santander opposed any reform of the constitution before the ten-year period in which no changes were supposed to be made to it. When he and his supporters blocked reform, Bolívar declared himself dictator and abolished the post of vice-president.

Shortly after this, an attempt was made to **assassinate Bolívar**. Santander was blamed, and he may have been involved – historians still debate this – but Bolívar pardoned and exiled him. He returned after Bolívar's death in 1832 to take up the post of president.

Francisco de Paula Santander died of tuberculosis in 1840 at the age of 47, but the ideological differences between him and Bolívar outlasted them both. By the end of the 1840s, the opposing factions had coalesced into two political parties, of which the Liberals regard Santander as their ideological forefather, while the Conservatives see themselves as continuing the legacy of Bolívar. Meanwhile, in his home *departamento*, El Hombre de las Leyes, as a native son, is revered even more than El Libertador.

TO AND FROM VENEZUELA

When crossing the border between **Cúcuta** in Colombia and **San Antonio del Táchira** in Venezuela, you must complete border formalities on both sides: get an exit stamp from the country you are leaving and an entry stamp for the country you are entering. Make sure you stop at both border posts to do this. If you don't, you may be turned back, you may be fined, and you may have problems if you ever come back to either country. The border is open daily 6am–7pm (at the time of writing), but the Venezuelans sometimes close it for days at a time. To get to the border town of San Antonio del Táchira, take a local bus from the terminal or along Diagonal Santander (for example at C 8 or at Ventura Plaza mall), or take a cab (about C$12,000) and then walk across or take a *mototaxi* to the Venezuelan immigration office (four blocks to the right after the bridge).

You can change pesos to bolívars and vice versa at moneychangers all over Cúcuta, and in San Antonio and San Cristóbal, but not so easily away from the border area. Cash US dollars are the best currency to take with you into Venezuela, which is thirty minutes ahead of Colombian time. When leaving Venezuela, there is an **exit tax** to pay.

Terminal de Transportes in the north of town, just off Diagonal Santander on C 1 at Av 7–Av 8. Unfortunately the terminal is a notorious den of thieves and hustlers, and you need to keep your wits about you and your baggage with you at all times when passing through. If taking a bus or *colectivo* out, get your ticket from the office of the company itself, or from the driver, not from a tout. Note also that the area around the bus station is not safe at night. During the day there are buses (in town pick them up on Av 3). It is possible to avoid the bus station by going to the Copetran terminal out of town at Los Patios, but you will then be confined to using Copetran services. Local buses to Villa del Rosario and San Antonio del Táchira are best picked up along Av Santander in town.

Destinations Bogotá (10–12 daily; 15hr); Bucaramanga (every 20–30min; 5hr); Pamplona (every 40min; 2hr; plus *colectivos*); San Antonio del Táchira (every 15min; 30min).

ACCOMMODATION

Casablanca Av 6 No. 14–55 ⓦ hotelcasablanca.com.co. Cúcuta's top hotel, a modern four-star, where facilities include a rooftop restaurant and a pool, and there's a range of rooms and suites. Breakfast included. $$$

La Embajada de la Paz C 6 No. 3–48 ☏ 7 571 8002. A good budget choice, with everything you need. The rooms have fans or, for a little more, a/c, and there's a shaded outdoor bar and a small pool. $

Lady Di Av 7 No. 13–80 ☏ 7 572 5291. Not as cute as you might think from the name, although it does have photos of the late princess above the entrance and in the lobby. You have a choice of fan or a/c, and rooms on the top floor and the roof terrace are the best for light, noise and ventilation. $

EATING

Cevichería Sol y Mar C 7 No. 3–94 ⓦ bit.ly/solymarcucuta. Not much more than a hole in the wall, this popular little fish restaurant does an excellent ceviche and an even more excellent seafood *cazuela*. $

Doña Pepa Av 4 No. 9–61 ☏ 7 583 0150. A cool space with fans and tablecloths (admittedly with glass on top) where the house speciality is *cabrito* (roast goat), or you can be greedy and go for a *bandeja Doña Pepa* (like a *bandeja paisa* and then some). $$

La Embajada Antioqueña C 6 No. 3–48 ☏ 7 573 1874. A top spot for some hearty Paisa food, including a *bandeja paisa* (which they call "*típica campesina*"). They also do daily specials, and an *almuerzo ejecutivo*. $$

DIRECTORY

Banks and exchange Parque de Santander (the main square) has a handful of banks with ATMs, including Bancolombia at C 10 No. 5–06 on its north side, and a row of moneychangers on its west side, including Mekecambio at Av 6 No. 10–90, which will change pesos to bolívars or vice versa, and will also change dollars, euros or pounds. There are others in the plaza and the streets around; it's worth shopping around for the best rate.

Consulates Venezuela, Av Aeropuerto at C 17, Sector Corral de Piedra, Zona Industrial (ⓦ cucuta.consulado.gob.ve).

The Caribbean coast

- **126** Cartagena
- **140** Around Cartagena
- **143** Tolú
- **147** Capurganá and around
- **149** Mompox
- **155** Barranquilla
- **159** Santa Marta and around
- **171** Parque Nacional Natural Tayrona
- **174** Ciudad Perdida
- **176** Palomino and around
- **177** La Guajira
- **181** Valledupar

CARTAGENA

The Caribbean coast

From the untamed jungles of the Darién Gap to the arid salt plains of the Guajira peninsula, Colombia's Caribbean coast runs for sixteen hundred sweltering kilometres, a series of dazzling white-sand beaches, vast mangrove forests and ravishing colonial towns. It's where the country's beautiful blend of ethnicities is at its most diverse, from African, Indigenous, European and even Lebanese roots, and where life always seems far louder and more intense than Colombia's Andean heartland: car horns blare constantly, vallenato and beats boom out of every door, and temperatures remain high all year round. Even the language is different, an Español costeño ("Coastal Spanish") that can be difficult to grasp for other Colombians, never mind foreigners. Writer Gabriel García Márquez, who grew up here, loved the raucous, rebellious costeño culture: "the boarders from the coast," he writes in Living to Tell the Tale, had a "well-deserved reputation for rowdiness and ill-breeding".

Most trips begin in **Cartagena**, Colombia's booming colonial gem and, for all the tourist development, still one of South America's most intoxicating cities. To the south lie the pristine islands of the San Bernardo chain, the low-key resort of **Tolú** and a string of progressively wilder beaches all the way to Panama. To the east feisty **Barranquilla** is gradually regaining its position as cultural hub, while historic **Santa Marta** is undergoing a revival of its own, at the heart of an enticing area that includes the unspoiled jungles and beaches of **Parque Nacional Natural Tayrona** and backpacker hub of **Taganga**, one of the most inexpensive places in the world to learn to scuba dive. From here you can take a mesmerizing five-day trek to the **Ciudad Perdida** or explore the still undeveloped **Guajira peninsula**, home of the fiercely independent Wayuu people. Inland, the mighty Magdalena flows through the pancake-flat grasslands of the Depresión Momposina, where the spires and towers of **Mompox** rise like a sixteenth-century apparition. Closer to the Venezuelan border, near **Valledupar**, the Sierra Nevada massif is home to some of the nation's highest peaks and its most intriguing Indigenous groups. Wherever you go, prepare to sweat; the Caribbean coast is blisteringly hot, all year round.

Cartagena

One of Latin America's most beautiful cities, **CARTAGENA DE INDIAS** is an incredibly enticing blend of romantic colonial architecture, gourmet dining, all-night partying and beach life. Tourism has exploded in the last decade and large parts of the old town have been swamped by boutique hotels and galleries, yet the city that inspired *Love in the Time of Cholera*, and much of the oeuvre of long-time admirer **Gabriel García Márquez**, has somehow retained its rich, often irreverent Colombian character. Some of the most expensive boutique hotels on the continent still share street space with local beer shops and carts selling coconuts and ceviche; its gorgeous mansions are lined with tangerine-tinged Spanish balconies of carved wood, festooned with pink bougainvillea; the sound of salsa pervades the always scorching-hot streets, with peddlers trying to sell you all manner of tat; and black vultures lurk on rooftops. It's impossible not to be overwhelmed by the sheer magic of the place.

PLAYA TAROA, PUNTA GALLINAS

Highlights

❶ **Cartagena** Boutique hotels and hostels, blossom-lined streets and sunset cocktails on the battlements await in one of South America's most enchanting cities. See page 126.

❷ **Mompox nightlife** Boiling hot by day, this magical colonial city comes alive at night, with cobbled streets and plazas evocative of the novels of Gabriel García Márquez. See page 155.

❸ **Carnaval de Barranquilla** Colombia's most exuberant festival is a bacchanalian blend of parades, all-night parties and salsa. See page 158.

❹ **Parque Nacional Natural Tayrona** Hike through pristine jungles to scintillating tropical beaches, one after the other, in Colombia's most celebrated national park. See page 171.

❺ **Ciudad Perdida** A five-day hike through the jungle to the enigmatic "Lost City" of the Tayrona is one of the continent's most fulfilling – and spine-tingling – experiences. See page 174.

❻ **Punta Gallinas** Just getting here is an adventure, rewarded with nights in hammocks under the stars and the mind-bending dunes of Playa Taroa. See page 180.

HIGHLIGHTS ARE MARKED ON THE MAP ON PAGE 128

THE CARIBBEAN COAST

HIGHLIGHTS
1. Cartagena
2. Mompox nightlife
3. Carnaval de Barranquilla
4. Parque Nacional Natural Tayrona
5. Ciudad Perdida
6. Punta Gallinas

CARIBBEAN SEA

PANAMA

VENEZUELA

- Punta Gallinas
- Bahía Honda
- PARQUE NACIONAL NATURAL MACUIRA
- Puerto Bolívar
- Cabo de la Vela
- LA GUAJIRA
- Uribia
- Paraguachón
- Maicao
- Maracaibo
- Lake Maracaibo
- Salinas de Manaure
- Riohacha
- Santuario de Fauna y Flora los Flamencos
- Palomino
- Río Ancho
- SIERRA NEVADA DE SANTA MARTA
- Nabusimake
- Valledupar
- Balneario La Mina
- Alfonso López Pumarejo Airport
- PARQUE NACIONAL NATURAL TAYRONA
- Santa Marta
- Simón Bolívar International Airport
- Minca
- Ciénaga
- Aracataca
- Fundación
- Agustín Codazzi
- Ernesto Cortissoz International Airport
- Barranquilla
- Volcán de Lodo
- Río Magdalena
- El Carmen de Bolívar
- El Banco
- Ciénaga Candelaria
- San Bernardo Airport
- Mompox
- DEPRESIÓN MOMPOSINA
- Rafael Núñez International Airport
- Cartagena
- Islas del Rosario
- Tolú
- Golfo de Morrosquillo Airport
- Isla Fuerte
- Islas de San Bernardo
- Sincelejo
- Los Garzones Airport
- Magangué
- Ciénaga de Ayapel
- Caucasia
- Montería
- Medellín (140km)
- PARQUE NACIONAL NATURAL PARAMILLO
- Necoclí
- Turbo
- Apartadó
- Ocaña
- Sapzurro
- Capurganá
- Acandí
- Alcides Fernández Airport

0 — 100 kilometres

IN THE FOOTSTEPS OF GABO

Nobel Prize-winning novelist **Gabriel García Márquez** (1927–2014) had a long relationship with Cartagena, beginning with a stint as a journalist here in 1948. In the 1990s he built a large compound at the corner of Calle Zerrezuela and Calle del Curato (still owned by his family, behind peach walls), spending several weeks here each year, and famously set *Love in the Time of Cholera* (1985) in the city (the movie was also filmed here in 2006). In 2016, a deal with his family saw some of his ashes re-interred in Cartagena with much pomp and ceremony (see page 133).

Fans of Gabo should take the illuminating three-hour "**Route of García Márquez in Cartagena**" tour with expert (English-speaking) local guide Marelvy Peña-Hall (w tourincartagena.com).

Most visitors – rightly – focus on the walled **Centro Histórico** (including San Diego) and its atmospheric and grittier neighbour **Getsemaní**, in pockets of which shirtless men play dominoes and *cumbia* music blasts out in the plazas – it lacks some of the architectural grandeur of the walled city but offers a better taste of local life. The two districts are separated by **La Matuna**, an incongruous wedge of ugly modern buildings mitigated somewhat by its vibrant local street life (and especially its tasty street food). To the south lie the gleaming white skyscrapers of **Bocagrande**, Cartagena's middle-class beach neighbourhood, while most of the city's one million inhabitants reside in the vast conurbation to the west, stretching some 10km beyond the districts of Manga and Pie del Cerro.

Brief history

Founded in 1533 by Spanish Conquistador **Pedro de Heredia** in the Indigenous territory known as "Kalimari", Cartagena was one of the first Spanish cities in the New World and served as the main port through which the continent's riches were shipped off to the mother country. Not surprisingly, the city proved an appetizing target for English privateers (unequivocally "pirates" here). The most infamous attack was led by Sir Francis Drake in 1586, during which he held the town hostage for more than a hundred days. After "the Dragon" was paid a hefty ransom to withdraw, the Spaniards began constructing the elaborate fortifications that are now the city's hallmark. The city was brutally sacked again in 1697 by a French armada led by Admiral Bernard Desjean (aka **Baron de Pointis**), and buccaneer and governor of Saint-Domingue (Haiti) **Jean Baptiste Ducasse**, but in 1741 a large force of British and American colonial troops led by **Admiral Edward Vernon** were repulsed in a famous victory for Spain and the local militias.

Cartagena had prospered as a port primarily after the Canal Dique had connected the city to the Río Magdalena and the interior in 1650. Once the canal became permanently blocked with silt in 1821 the city slipped into a long period of decline, exacerbated by the cholera outbreaks of 1848 and 1849 that decimated the population. Recovery began with the arrival of the railway in the early twentieth century, but the old centre remained ramshackle, and half ruined until tourism ramped up in the 1990s. Today, locals worry that a glut of luxury hotel construction has pushed **gentrification** to a tipping point – beginning to force out the local life that makes Cartagena such an attraction in the first place.

Centro Histórico

In addition to holding the main points of interest for visitors, Cartagena's **Centro Histórico** is almost entirely surrounded by massively thick **walls** (La Murallas), built by the Spanish in the eighteenth century and a pleasant promenade from which to take in the sights and fresh sea breezes. You can walk along the top at all hours, for free (though it's best to avoid this late at night).

THE CARIBBEAN COAST CARTAGENA

Plaza de los Coches

Cartagena's former slave-trading square, the **Plaza de los Coches** faces the city's main formal entrance, the triple-arched **Puerta del Reloj**. Though the Baroque-style gate dates from the Spanish period, the iconic tower on top was completed in 1888 (the Swiss clock inside was added in 1937). In the centre of the plaza stands a statue of the city's founder Pedro de Heredia, while in the covered arcade, **Portal de los Dulces**, vendors adeptly pluck sweets of your choice out of a sea of huge glass jars; *panelitas* (milk candy with coconut), *cubanitos* (caramel spread between conical wafers), *melcochas* (marshmallows) and variations of *cocadas* (coconut sweets). In the evening, several lively bars open up above the arches.

Plaza de la Aduana

The largest and oldest square in the Centro Histórico, graced with a marble statue of Columbus unveiled in 1894, the **Plaza de la Aduana** was formerly used as a parade ground. The imposing Casa de la Aduana (Customs House) covers one whole side of the square and is thought to be the location of Pedro de Heredia's original residence – it now serves as the Alcaldía Municipal (City Hall).

Santuario de San Pedro Claver

Cra 4 No. 30–01 (Plaza San Pedro Claver) • Charge (English and Spanish speaking guides available) • w sanpedroclaver.co

Dominating the quiet plaza of the same name (studded with the modern wrought-iron sculptures of Eduardo Carmona), the imposing **Santuario de San Pedro Claver** comprises a church (with the giant dome clearly visible across most of the old city) and convent founded by Jesuits in 1603. This is where Spanish-born Jesuit priest **Pedro Claver**, now one of the patron saints of Colombia, lived and worked. Dubbed the "slave of the slaves" for his lifelong ministering to the city's enslaved population, aghast at the conditions in which they lived, the ascetic monk was canonized in 1888. Today the convent is part memorial to the saint, part **museum**, a grand whitewashed three-storey building surrounding a lush courtyard bursting with giant trees and greenery. As well as small and not especially interesting exhibits of religious art and pre-Columbian ceramics, upstairs there's a gallery of paintings depicting important events in the saint's life. On the mezzanine level you can visit the humble cell in which San Pedro Claver spent his nights, the infirmary where he died in 1654 and the old slave dormitory.

The **church** itself (included with Santuario admission; otherwise free during Mass only), is a cavernous but simply adorned space, with an elegant altar of Carrera marble created in 1884. The saint's skull and bones are guarded in a glass reliquary at the altar's base.

Museo de Arte Moderno

C 30 No. 4–08 (Plaza San Pedro Claver) • Charge • w mamcartagena.org

Housed in the seventeenth-century Almacén de Galeras (warehouses), all red-brick and original timbers, the **Museo de Arte Moderno** offers a refreshing break from Spanish colonial with a respectable collection of Colombian and Latin American art since the 1950s. Highlights include galleries dedicated to local boy **Enrique Grau** (1920–2004), whose curvy, lustrous images recall Botero and include the celebrated surrealistic triptych *Tríptico de Cartagena de Indias*; and (upstairs) the haunting images of local painter **Cecilia Porras** (1920–71), who was closely associated with Gabriel García Márquez and the Barranquilla Group (see page 156). There's also work by acclaimed artist **Alejandro Obregón** (who lived in the city from 1960 till his death in 1992), including the enigmatic *Dédalo*.

Museo Naval del Caribe

C San Juan de Dios No. 3–62 (Plaza Santa Teresa) • Charge • t 5 664 2440

The extensive **Museo Naval del Caribe** – contained within the grand former premises of the oldest Jesuit college in the Americas – is perhaps the best history museum in the city, exploring Cartagena's relationship with the sea from the Caribs of Kalamari, through all the major naval attacks from Drake in 1586 to Vernon's ignominious defeat in 1741, with detailed scale models and informative displays. Note the poignant exhibit on tragic hero **José Padilla**, who took part in the Battle of Trafalgar (for Spain) in 1805, was held prisoner by the victorious British for three years, later created the Colombian navy and won a stunning victory over Spain at Maracaibo in 1823 – only to be executed in 1828 after being (falsely) implicated in a plot to kill Simón Bolívar. There's also a section on the devastating **cholera epidemic** of 1848–49, and upstairs charts the history of Colombia's navy from 1810 to the modern day, including the oft forgotten Colombian contribution to the **Korean War** (1950–53). Almost everything is labelled in **Spanish only**; hire the services of a guide at the entrance to get the most out of it.

Plaza de Bolívar

Locals and tourists alike find respite from the heat in **Plaza de Bolívar**, a green, shaded square with a statue of **Simón Bolívar** as its centrepiece (the Liberator spent a few days in 1812 in a house nearby, on Calle de San Agustín Chiquita, just before his rise to glory). The plaza is surrounded by some of Cartagena's most opulent buildings, notably the old Palacio de la Inquisición, as well as several pricey emerald and jewellery stores.

Museo Histórico de Cartagena de Indias
Cra 3 No. 33–46 • Charge • W muhca.gov.co

On the west side of Plaza de Bolívar stands the Palacio de la Inquisición, a splendid block-long example of late colonial architecture now serving as the **Museo Histórico**. The seat of the dreaded **Inquisition** for two hundred years from 1610 until independence, what you see today mostly dates from the 1770s and is believed to be the site where at least eight hundred people were sentenced to death.

The lower floors of the museum focus on this grim legacy, with a particularly grisly display of torture implements, a room dedicated to witches and an outdoor area featuring a guillotine. Upstairs galleries chronicle the history of Cartagena, from the "Kalamari" settlements of the early Caribs through to the nineteenth century, with a handful of artefacts, scale models and enlightening panels (but very little in English) – if you can't read Spanish, consider **renting an audioguide** at the entrance, or perhaps skipping the museum altogether.

Museo de Oro Zenú
Cra 4 No. 33–26 • Free • T 5 664 6191

Though it's much smaller than its counterpart in Bogotá, the **Museo de Oro Zenú** contains some exceptional examples of goldwork from various pre-Hispanic cultures, particularly the **Zenú**, who flourished in the flat, swampy plains ("Las Llanuras") south of Cartagena from around 1500 BC through to 1100 AD (their descendants still inhabit the region). Especially striking are their delicate "woven" gold earrings, pendants and zoomorphic designs, as well as the remarkable funerary urns on the second floor from Tamalameque, adorned with geometric patterns and ghoulish faces.

Catedral Santa Catalina de Alejandría
Callejón Santos de Piedra No. 34–55 • Free • T 5 664 5308

Looming above the northeast corner of the Plaza de Bolívar is the fortress-like **Catedral Santa Catalina de Alejandría**, whose construction began in 1575, but which wasn't completed until 1612 due to setbacks such as its partial destruction by cannon fire in 1586 by Sir Francis Drake. The vast interior is airy and pleasantly austere, though the baroque wooden *retablo* is certainly ornate, embellished with gold leaf, and the black and white marble floors, stone columns, carved stone pulpit and timber ceiling are looking immaculate after a massive renovation. Opposite the cathedral, the handsome **Palacio de Proclamación** has been developed into a massive arts centre.

Iglesia de Santo Domingo
Plaza de Santo Domingo • Free • T 5 655 1916

On the lively **Plaza de Santo Domingo** and fronted by Fernando Botero's voluptuous "La gorda Gertrudis" sculpture (officially *Figurina Reclina 92*), sits the tangerine-painted **Iglesia de Santo Domingo**. Completed in 1579, the structure's simple interior (painted in ochre and blue), belies its status as Cartagena's oldest church. To the right of the Baroque altar, in its own niche, there's a venerated sixteenth-century calvary known as *Cristo de la Expiración*.

NH Galería
Centro Plaza de la Artillería, at Callejón de los Estribos (Cra 2) No. 33–36 • Free • ⓦ nhgaleria.com

Cartagena's contemporary and modern art scene is showcased at **NH Galería**, opened by New York art maven Nohra Haime in 2011 and since becoming a major force in the Colombian art world. Serious collectors come to buy, but art lovers are welcome to simply peruse the current exhibits (which usually rotate every two months).

Mausoleo de Gabo and Teatro Adolfo Mejía
Plazuela de la Merced • Mausoleo de Gabo • Free • Teatro Adolfo Mejía Enter on C de la Chichería • tours (1hr) • Charge

The grand edifice dominating tiny Plazuela de la Merced was once the Convento de la Merced, founded in 1619 and now part of the University of Cartagena. The old convent cloister is known as the **Claustro de la Merced**, best known for containing the **Mausoleo de Gabo**, featuring a giant bronze bust of the author – some of the ashes of Gabriel García Márquez were re-interred here in 2016 (the rest remain in Mexico). Next door, the stately **Teatro Adolfo Mejía** (also known as Teatro Heredia) was completed in 1911 on the spot where the convent church once stood. To see the artfully restored, lavish interior (including ceiling and curtain paintings by Enrique Grau) you have to take a tour (English-speakers usually available).

Las Bóvedas
In the northeast corner of the walled city, **Las Bóvedas** are 23 mustard-coloured vaults, built into the city walls between 1792 and 1796, and used variously as munitions storage, a jail and – their current incarnation – as craft and souvenir shops. At the far end you can wander down into the bowels of the Baluarte de Santa Catalina, through the dimly lit halls of the now defunct **Museo de las Fortificaciones** for free (the rooms are now empty) – the lower exit dumps you outside the walls.

Casa Museo Rafael Núñez
Real de Cabrero 41–89 • Free (English guides extra) • ☏ 5 660 9058

One of the most romantic houses in the city actually lies just outside the walls, where the **Casa Museo Rafael Núñez** is dedicated to the cartagenero who was Colombia's president four times in the nineteenth century (Rafael Núñez also helped frame the landmark 1886 constitution and wrote the national anthem). The gorgeous Antillean-style house dates from 1877, and has wraparound verandas and delicate woodwork throughout, with a handful of rooms decorated in simple period style and original wood floors. Displays chronicle the life and history of Núñez with old photos, paintings and personal effects (cuff links and the like), with a special section on Soledad Román, his common-law wife, disparaged as "la concubine" but incredibly influential on his life and work (the house belonged to her family). Note that labelling is Spanish only.

Núñez was buried in an elegant marble sarcophagus in the small, fairy-tale chapel across the street, **La Ermita de Nuestra Senora de Las Mercedes**, completed in 1885 (open for Mass).

Getsemaní

The most atmospheric part of the city, the narrow streets of **Getsemaní**, once an edgier section of Cartagena, are definitely worth exploring – strolling the streets is now perfectly safe during the day (take care at night, though). Indeed, gentrification is now the most pressing issue for the day for the district's remaining citizens.

The neighbourhood's focal point is languid **Plaza de la Trinidad**, one of the oldest squares in the city, though the humble **Iglesia de la Santísima Trinidad** is rarely open except for Mass – the plaza is especially lively at night, with food stalls and street performers. From here, peruse the increasingly prominent **murals** and **street art** in the neighbourhood (especially along C San Juan), or wander down gorgeous **Calle del Poz**, especially busy on Sundays and holidays with locals playing dominoes in the side streets; it ends at the small **Plazuela del Pozo** and the old well (*pozo*) for which it is named.

Castillo San Felipe de Barajas

Av Antonio Arevalo, Pie del Cerro • Charge; audioguides extra; English-speaking guides extra • W fortificacionescartagena.com.co/en • It's a short, safe but hot walk from the walls to the castle via Av Pedro de Heredia (you can't miss it), otherwise taxis will run you here from the Centro Histórico

The largest and most important fort defending Cartagena was **Castillo San Felipe de Barajas**, a mountain of stone looming just east of the walled city like a Maya pyramid. This incredible feat of engineering was built in phases beginning in 1657, and substantially reinforced in the 1760s. The panoramic views from the top, with the whole city visible, are worth the entry fee alone, but there's not much else to see other than multi-levelled gun batteries – exploring the dimly lit labyrinth of passages that run beneath the battlements can be fun, but to get more out of the experience it's best to pay for an **audioguide**. Alternatively, you can **hire one of the guides** who hang around the entrance.

Convento de la Popa

Cerro de la Popa • Charge; guides extra • Taxis 30–45min from El Centro; don't walk – robberies have been reported along the zigzagging road up the hill

For a real bird's-eye view of Cartagena, head to the **Convento de la Popa** (aka Convento de la Candelaria), which, wrote Gabriel García Márquez, "always has seemed on the verge of falling over a precipice". Lying atop a hill known as El Cerro de la Popa (148m), the restored whitewashed convent chapel, founded by the Augustinians in 1606, is clearly visible from almost anywhere in the city. On February 2, when the city celebrates the day of its patron saint, the Virgin of Candelaria, protector against pirates and the plague, a candlelit procession of pilgrims storms the hill.

Bocagrande

Buses every few minutes (TransCaribe T103); taxis available

The forest of shimmering white skyscrapers south of the Centro Histórico is **Bocagrande**, a densely populated peninsula jutting into the bay. Home to posh condos and hotels, popular primarily with Colombians, Bocagrande does have a beach, though it's mediocre at best and the water is usually too dirty to swim in. The scene can be a fun break from all things colonial, with *palenqueras*, women selling homemade African-style sweets – try the *ajonjoli* made with coconut – and a plethora of bars, shops and emerald marts. Aggressive vendors during the day, and a very visible prostitution problem (at night) have soured the experience for many in recent years, however – don't expect some tropical paradise. If you're looking for a really good beach, there are far more enticing targets further along the coast (see page 140).

ARRIVAL AND INFORMATION   **CARTAGENA**

BY PLANE
Aeropuerto Internacional Rafael Núñez Just 10–15min by taxi to/from the Centro Histórico – get a ticket from the official taxi "desk" outside the domestic terminal (it's actually just a yellow machine outside international arrivals) before taking a ride, to confirm the price (you pay the driver,

though). Locals pay less for the journey back from the centre, but you'll have to negotiate hard (no meters are used); fix the price first). TransCaribe bus T102 (which runs along C 70, one block west of the terminal), should whisk you to the Centro bus station on the edge of the old town; look for buses labelled "T102 Crespo" from Centro bus station to get back. On arrival at the airport you'll find a small tourist information booth in the baggage claim area (☎ 5 656 9200).

Destinations Bogotá (frequent; 1hr 25min); Bucaramanga (2 daily; 1hr 20min); Cali (3 weekly; 1hr 30min); Medellín (6 daily; 1hr 10min); San Andrés (2 daily; 2hr).

BY BUS

Terminal de Transportes de Cartagena To get from the city's rambling bus terminal, 12km west from the Centro Histórico (on the road to Barranquilla) take any local bus 2km to the Portal El Gallo TransCaribe bus stop (take anything labelled "Terminal de Transportes" from Portal El Gallo heading back to the terminal), then change to the T100 express to the Centro bus station. From the bus terminal, taxis charge set rates of into the centre and Bocagrande.

Destinations Barranquilla (every 30min; 2hr); Bogotá (every 30min; 20hr); Medellín (6 daily; 13hr); Mompox (1 daily; 6hr 30min); Riohacha (every 2hr; 7hr); Santa Marta (hourly–every 2hr; 4hr); Tolú (hourly; 2hr 30min).

Door to door For Barranquilla, Santa Marta, Taganga, Tayrona and Palomino it's much more convenient (if more expensive) to take a "puerta-to-puerta" (door-to-door) service, which will pick you up from your hotel anywhere in the city: MarSol Transportes (Cra 2A No. 43, Barrio El Cabrero; w marsol.com.co) is a reliable operator.

BY SAILBOAT TO PANAMA/SAN BLAS

Sailboats run between Cartagena and Panama via the remote islands of the San Blas archipelago. Trips take five to six days and can be arranged through Blue Sailing, C San Andrés No. 30–47 (w bluesailing.net) in Cartagena, which works with 25 independent boat captains, or through hostels such as *Mamallena* (see page 137); prices vary but include a bunk, three meals a day and snorkel gear. Note that this is more an adventure trip to explore the San Blas islands than a straight transfer between the two countries. Boats usually depart the Club Náutico in Manga (15min from the old city by taxi). Most boats only go as far as Porvenir and Carti in Panama (occasionally to Colón or Puerto Lindo). Between mid-Nov and mid-April the seas can be rough.

INFORMATION

Tourist information The most convenient information point lies outside the Puerta del Reloj in the Plaza de la Paz; there is another in Bocagrande, Carr 1 at C 4 (☎ 5 660 1583, w cartagenadeindias.travel).

GETTING AROUND

By bus TransCaribe, Cartagena's mass transport bus system, with dedicated stations based on the TransMilenio in Bogotá, offers by far the best way to get around by public transport. Buy smartcards at the station. Estación La Bodeguita and Estación Centro are the core stations in the heart of the city; the main lines run south to Bocagrande and east to Bazurto (for the market), Pie de la Popa (at the base of the Cerro de la Popa) and along Av Pedro De Heredia before terminating close to the main bus terminal (see page 135). The system also features a whole range of feeder routes (including T102 to the airport). The chaotic minibus system that compliments TransCaribe is not especially useful.

By taxi Most visitors get around the centre on foot, though the streams of taxis make a trip to the other end of town after a night out easy (Radio Taxis Cartagena; ☎ 5 677 0100). Taxis don't yet use meters in Cartagena, and are notorious for overcharging, despite prices for major routes being fixed by the city. Always fix the price in advance, though even locals often have trouble making drivers stick to "official" rates.

By bike Bike & Arts, C Media Luna No. 10–23 (☎ 313 506 4472) and Ciclo Sport 512, C Cuartel No. 35–36 (☎ 5 660 8438) offer rentals.

TOURS AND ACTIVITIES

Tours One of the best English-speaking guides in the city is Marelvy Peña-Hall (city day tours with an a/c van/car; w tourincartagena.com); Dora De Zubiria (☎ 300 808 9525, w cartagenatour.com) and Cartagena Connections Walking Tours (w cartagenaconnections.com), with Australian guide Kristy, are also recommended.

Diving Diving Planet has an office at C Estanco del Aguardiente No. 5–09 (☎ 320 230 1515, w divingplanet.org), and offers dive day-trips to the Rosario islands (see page 142).

Kitesurfing Cartagena Kitesurf School, C Ricaurte (Cra 3) No. 31–38 (☎ 300 461 9947) offers kite-surfing lessons and equipment rentals (Dec–April is the best season).

ACCOMMODATION

The most romantic, historic hotels are spread throughout **Centro Histórico** (the walled city), as well as **Getsemaní**, a short walk away. Prices during the high season (Dec–Feb) usually surge by ten to twenty percent, and in general, Cartagena is the most expensive place to stay in all Colombia. **"Hostel Row"** (C Media Luna) is the unofficial backpackers' strip in a lively part of Getsemaní; there's another cluster of hostels around Plaza de José Fernandez de Madrid in the San Diego section of the Centro Histórico. Beach hotels and resorts line the coast in **Bocagrande** to the south and **Marbella** and **La Boquilla** to the north, but unless you are desperate for some (mediocre) sea and sand, staying in the Centro Histórico is far more convenient and atmospheric. Note that airbnb (w airbnb.com), Oasis (which offers apartments with hotel services such as cleaning and linen changing; w oasiscollections.com) and Couchsurfing (w couchsurfing.org) have arrived in Cartagena in a big way; quality varies, so do your research before booking (and make sure you get a/c).

CENTRO HISTÓRICO

Casa del Arzobispado C del Arzobispado No. 34–52 w hotelcasadelarzobispado.com; map p.130. Stay in this gorgeous seventeenth-century palace, once the home of independence hero Antonio José de Ayos. The ten luxurious rooms have beautifully decorated beds and there's a romantic courtyard pool. $$$$

Casa Pombo C 5 No. 34–14 w casapombo.com; map p.130. This luxurious four-star hotel offers all the mod cons and services you'd expect. There's also a photo-worthy courtyard at the centre, complete with waterways and marble arches. $$$$

Casa Quero C 37 (C Quero) No. 9–53 w hotelcasaquero.com; map p.130. Plush boutique hotel with an all-white Neo-Baroque theme – period-style beds and furnishings with jacuzzis and plasmas TVs. $$$$

★ **Casa San Agustín** C de la Universidad No. 36–44 w hotelcasasanagustin.com; map p.130. One of Cartagena's historic gems, this justly popular luxury option is well worth a splurge, with colonial-era whitewashed buildings, original frescoes and timber beams. Rooms feature ironwork beds and chandeliers plus modern amenities (iPads, flatscreen TVs, free phone calls to the US), and there's an outdoor pool and soothing rooftop solarium. $$$$

Hostal Calamar Cra 3 No. 31–38 ☎ 5 665 2696; map p.130. Excellent value in the heart of the city, with comfy a/c rooms with balconies. The views from the roofdeck are magnificent. No breakfast or hot water, though coffee and cookies are free. $

República Hostel Cartagena Calle segunda de Badillo No. 36-45 ☎ 5 262 2364; map p.130. Gorgeous colonial property offering dorms with lockers (bunks in timber-beamed rooms) and plain but spotless private rooms (all a/c) with simple breakfast included. Guests can use a shared kitchen and a small pool. No children. Dorms and private doubles available. $

El Viajero Hostel Cartagena C 7 Infantes No. 7–35, San Diego w elviajerohostels.com; map p.130. At this sociable hostel, the a/c rooms and comfy dorms (with cold showers), are clustered around a narrow inner courtyard where everyone meets to socialize, so don't count on getting much sleep before midnight. The place is well run, but the basic doubles are rather overpriced for what they are. Simple breakfast included. Dorms $, doubles $$

GETSEMANÍ

Arsenal Hotel C Arsenal No. 8B–58, w arsenalhotel.com; map p.130. If Cartagena's colonial properties don't appeal, try this stylish, contemporary boutique hotel, usually a bit cheaper than its peers in the walled city. Rooms feature a sleek, all-white design (most look out over a cool vertical garden, with the more expensive rooms offering views of the city). The roofdeck and pool area is a great place to unwind. $$$

Casa Marta Cra 10 (C San Antonio) No. 25–165 ☎ 310 630 6003; map p.130. This family-run bed & breakfast (helmed by Marta herself) comprises just two beautiful a/c rooms with original Spanish tile floors, period furnishings, fridge, satellite TV and breakfast included. $$

Casa Villa Colonial C de la Media Luna No. 10–89 w casavillacolonial.co; map p.130. Quiet colonial house with spacious en-suite rooms (with a/c but cold showers), friendly staff (little English spoken) and attractive

---

BAZURTO MARKET

Trips to Cartagena's shambolic **Mercado Bazurto** (Bazurto Market), 3km beyond the city walls in Pie de Popa (Av Pedro de Heredia), have become something of a right of passage for adventurous travellers (and eaters: celebrity chef Anthony Bourdain visited on his US TV show). It's an odorous, unsanitary, garbage-strewn melange of food stands and cheap Chinese goods stalls, where pelicans huddle on the harbourside (at the back) waiting for scraps, and pickpockets often prowl the narrow alleys – definitely not a traditional tourist attraction. Nevertheless, it's an unusual spectacle, the vendors are generally friendly and some of the city's most lauded snacks are sold inside, from shark and octopus rice and fried *arepas* to *mondongo* (tripe braised with garlic, vinegar, peppers and tomatoes). If you take the usual precautions, during the day you should have no problems (take a taxi and leave valuables in your hotel).

communal areas to lounge around in. The small kitchen dispenses free coffee all day long (no breakfast, though). $\overline{\underline{\$\$}}$
Hostal el Balconcito C Media Luna No. 10–33 t 5 581 0455; map p.130. One of the best hostels in town, with wood bunks in clean dorms and simple private rooms (all with a/c), English-speaking staff, sunny bar/patio, shared kitchen and big lockers. Breakfast is included; laundry services are extra. It's a recommended place for arranging tours and onward transport. $\overline{\underline{\$}}$
Media Luna Hostel C Media Luna No. 10–46 w medialunahostel.com; map p.130. This super-hostel (with 160 beds) offers all the services discerning backpackers have come to expect (breakfast and laundry are extra). The dorms all overlook the central courtyard with pool and have good beds, there are plenty of tours on offer, and they rent out bicycles. Frequent parties on the enormous roof terrace, with a bar open until 4am. $\overline{\underline{\$}}$
Mystic House Hostel C Media Luna 10C–36 t 5 206 6677; map p.130. One of the brighter and more stylish of the options on hostel row, with simple, neat bunks in dorms (a/c or fan) and solid value en-suite doubles (with a/c) adorned with contemporary art. $\overline{\underline{\$}}$

EATING

Among Cartagena's greatest charms is its array of fine restaurants catering to all palates, though most are pricey compared to the rest of Colombia. Cheap street stalls and ceviche sellers are scattered throughout the city, with some of the best in **La Matuna** and on **Plaza de la Trinidad** in the evenings (try the fried delights at the *Fritos de Trinidad* cart; *empanadas*). If you want to gain kudos with the locals, grab a bottle of Kola Román, the much loved, bright red, fizzy drink invented in Cartagena way back in 1865 (though who knows what goes into the sugary contents).

CENTRO HISTÓRICO

Ábaco Libros y Café C de la Iglesia and Mantilla No. 3–86 w abacolibros.com; map p.130. Small coffee shop and bookstore, with tables squeezed in between the shelves in one brick-vaulted room, a bit like an old-fashioned library. It's a tranquil a/c retreat, with all Gabo's books stocked and a smooth jazz soundtrack. $\overline{\underline{\$}}$
El Balcón Plaza de San Diego (entry C de Tumbamuertos No. 38–85) t 311 753 9034; map p.130. Owned by Colombian-British couple Abdul Farah and Helen Pope, this is a solid spot for budget-friendly meals as well as early evening drinks. The second-floor balcony (above *La Tumbamuertos Burger Bar*), lined with stools, is the perfect place for plaza-watching. $\overline{\underline{\$}}$
★ **El Boliche Cebichería** C Cochera del Hobo No. 38–17, San Diego t 5 777 7889, w facebook.com/elbolichecebicheria; map p.130. Oscar Colmenares (who trained at Martin Berasategui's eponymous Basque restaurant) and Viviana Díaz run Cartagena's best ceviche joint, their locally-sourced fish flavoured with tamarind, sour cream or coconut (the coconut ceviche is sensational). Other highlights include the king prawns grilled with *butifarra* (a spicy local sausage) and quails' eggs. With room for just sixteen, reservations are recommended. $\overline{\underline{\$\$\$}}$
Carmen C del Santísimo (C 38) No. 8–19 w carmencartagena.com; map p.130. The place for a splurge, serving high-quality contemporary Colombian cuisine (with some Asian touches); try the "black fish" (the fish of the day in black olive oil and mango ravioli), or red snapper in yellow curry with local yams and bananas, or opt for the five-course tasting menu if you can. Helmed by the lauded (formerly Medellín-based) culinary team of Rob Pevitts and Carmen Ángel, it shares a space with *Moshi*, an upscale Japanese restaurant from the same couple. $\overline{\underline{\$\$}}$
La Cevichería C Stuart No. 7–14, San Diego w la cevicheriacartagena.com; map p.130. The buzz around this small seafood specialist, owned by Chef Jorge Escandon, has faded somewhat since appearing on Anthony Bourdain's TV show back in 2008 — it's still good, though, with innovative ceviche combos in coconut-lime and mango sauces. The tongue-tingling Vietnamese rice, smothered in coconut curry sauce, and the octopus with peanut sauce are standouts. $\overline{\underline{\$\$}}$
Estrella de la India C de la Universidad No. 36–152 t 315 705 1740; map p.130. Your best bet for a local-style canteen in the old centre, with an open-sided, no-frills dining area, cheap *empanadas* and plates of chicken rice, fried cutlets and fried fish. $\overline{\underline{\$}}$
La Esquina del Pan de Bono C Agustín Chiquita No. 35–78 t 5 498 3528; map p.130. Popular with students from the Universidad de Cartagena across the street, this is a rare find in the old centre, a local bakery and snack shop selling *cubanos*, airy *pan de bono* (cheesy buns), *pasteles* and *jugos*. $\overline{\underline{\$}}$
★ **Gelatería Paradiso** C de la Estrella at C el Cuartel t 5 660 4945; map p.130. The best of several gelato shops that have appeared around here. Venezuelan Maria Nevett's artisanal flavours utilize local fruits such as *zapote*, *maracuyá* and *lulo* (she also sells chocolate brownies, cookies and milkshakes). Take away or sample in the floral ice-cream parlour, allegedly a favourite of Juan Manuel Santos. $\overline{\underline{\$}}$
La Mulata C Quero No. 9–58 (next to Hostal Makako), San Diego t 5 664 6222; map p.130. This popular unhurried set-lunch (*corriente*) spot offers big portions and friendly staff; menus vary but dishes might include pork ribs, local red snapper or seafood casserole, washed down with coconut lemonade. $\overline{\underline{\$\$}}$
★ **La Palettería** C Santo Domingo No. 3–88 t 5 666 1579; map p.130. Mouthwatering *paletas* (popsicles, or lollies, on a stick), made with *agua* (water), *crema* (cream) or yogurt, in sensationally fresh flavours such as tamarind,

lulo (the local fruit), *salpicón* (fruit cocktail), mango, coconut and even Milo (the chocolate-malt drink). $

★ **Pastelería Mila** C de la Iglesia 35–76 Ⓦ mila.com.co; map p.130. Enticing French-influenced bakery and café from Chef Mila Vargas, with an elegant interior combining contemporary style with old colonial woodwork. Serves sandwiches and breakfasts, but it's the cakes that really zip: brownies, rich lemon pies, Key lime cheesecakes, amazing *churros* and cupcakes. Even the espresso is served in a special glass with a cup of flavoured water and a tiny piece of cake. $

Swikar Candy C Santo Domingo No. 3–30 Ⓦ swikarcandy.com; map p.130. This obviously isn't a place to eat a meal, but anyone with a sweet tooth will love the multicoloured sweets, and artisanal traditional treats on display ("hard candy" in the US). $

La Vitrola C Baloco No. 2–01 Ⓦ lavitrola.precompro.com; map p.130. This contemporary Cuban restaurant (part of the *Decameron* hotel) is one of the most hyped in Cartagena, but its blend of live Cuban *son* (sound), tasty mojitos and excellent menu can still make for a great night – reservations highly recommended. $$

GETSEMANÍ

Beer & Laundry C 31 No. 10–101 Local 2 ☎ 318 282 4918, Ⓦ facebook.com/beerandlaundry; map p.130. This small laundry has developed a cult following for serving cold beers and cheap pizzas while you wait for your washing (there are just a couple of tables inside). It's a great idea, and the friendly owners are a font of local information. $

★ **Café de Mural** C San Juan (Cra 9a) No. 25–60 ☎ 321 288 9323; map p.130. Tucked away in a tranquil corner of Getsemaní, this artsy café roasts much of its aromatic Colombian coffee (the best in the city) by hand, but also sells excellent shakes, hot chocolate and snacks. $

Caffé Lunático C Espíritu Santo No. 29-184 ☎ 320 383 0419, Ⓦ facebook.com/CafedelMural; map p.130. Small, chilled-out café and restaurant with relaxed atmosphere, open for brunch (Colombian breakfasts), coffee and predinner tapas and drinks. $

★ **La Cocina de Pepina** Callejón Vargas No. 9A–06 ☎ 5 856 5189; map p.130. Popular with nostalgic Colombian tourists who enjoy the slightly cramped, old-fashioned space (and the food their grandmothers used to make). Primarily Montería-style dishes; María Josefina's cheese-and-ham soup is a classic, as is the shrimp and coconut stew – the current menu is usually written on a board. $$

★ **Marea by Rausch** Centro de Convenciones, C 24 No. 8a–344 Ⓦ mareacartagena.com; map p.130. The city's premier waterfront dining option lies inside the conference centre (the testy guards should let you through, or you can walk along the water if the gate is open). Jorge and Mark Rausch serve exquisite seafood in a stylish, contemporary space with fabulous views across to the old town. Try the "three cup ceviche" (fish in coconut sauce with fried corn, shrimp in spicy tomato sauce and octopus in piquant creamy sauce with plantain chips), or the fried mojarra, a crispy delight. $$$

DRINKING AND NIGHTLIFE

Getsemaní tends to be the best bet for late-night partying, with **Calle del Arsenal** and **Calle Media Luna** the liveliest strips – "Visa por un Sueño" is a wildly popular party held on the roof of *Media Luna Hostel* (see page 137) every Wednesday from 10pm. Another option for a night out is a *chiva* ride ("Rumba en Chiva") – essentially a party bus in an old-fashioned, luridly decorated trolley that takes you on a late-night city tour fuelled by rum or red wine, fried regional finger foods and *vallenato* music. *Chivas* tend to depart at 8–8.30pm and return at midnight; any tour agency and most hotels will hook you up with a tour.

CENTRO HISTÓRICO

★ **Alquímico** C del Colegio No. 34–24 Ⓦ alquimico.com; map p.130. Extremely stylish bar over three floors of an old colonial mansion, specializing in craft beers and infused rums. There's a roof terrace and full dinner menu, as well expert mixologists cooking up all sorts of crazy drinks.

El Burlador Gastrobar C Santo Domingo (Cra 3) No. 33–88 Ⓦ elburladorgastrobar.com; map p.130. Restaurant best known for its nightly flamenco. The menu of classic Spanish dishes is also pretty good.

★ **Café del Mar** Baluarte de Santo Domingo Ⓦ cafedelmarcartagena.com.co; map p.130. Perched on the city's stone walls, with spectacular 360-degree views of the Caribbean and the old town, this is the ideal location to lounge on an open-air couch with a sunset martini surrounded by fashionable locals. Food is served until 1am and DJs take over from 10pm. Dress up.

★ **El Coro Lounge Bar** Santa Clara Sofitel, C del Torno No. 39–29, San Diego Ⓦ sofitellegendsantaclara.com; map p.130. Lounge on a luxurious white leather sofa with an exclusive cocktail at this hotel bar, housed in a former monastery dating from 1621 – it looks a bit like an old library. Well-heeled locals arrive for the quality live music and regular house DJs from Thurs to Sat nights. Gabo, who had a house nearby, was a regular.

Donde Fidel Portal de los Dulces No. 32–09 ☎ 5 664 3127; map p.130. This small local bar with outdoor tables, between the city wall and the Plaza de los Coches (next to *Hard Rock Café*), is the place to people-watch over a beer or rum cocktail. Thumping Cuban music from owner Fidel Leottau's extensive salsa collection is the soundtrack to which couples get romantic. Another of Gabo's favourite haunts.

La Movida C Baloco No. 2–14 ☎ 5 660 6126; map p.130. Popular Catalan-style tapas bar and club (the owner cut his teeth running bars in Barcelona), with one room dedicated to the usual electronica and another playing *merengue*, salsa, reggaeton and other Latin favourites. It's pricey (there's a cover charge), and tends to attract the city's upwardly mobile set.

Tu Candela Portal de los Dulces No. 32–25 (upper level) ⓦ tu-candela.cluvi.co; map p.130. One of Cartagena's wildest and most popular clubs, frequented by tourists and Colombian jet-setters, who dance the night away predominantly to salsa, though reggaeton, *merengue* and other genres creep onto the playlist.

GETSEMANÍ

Bazurto Social Club Av del Centenario (Cra 9) No. 30–42 ⓦ bazurtosocialclub.com; map p.130. Jorge Escadón's club venture showcases the city's Afro-based musical heritage with live bands, images of the country's first boxing world champion, Kid Pambelé, and the work of local graffiti artist Alcur. Try the machacao, the house cocktail made with fresh lime, soda, rum, grapefruit and honey.

★ **Café Havana** C de la Media Luna, at C del Guerrero ☎ 312 408 2896; map p.130. You'll be transported to 1950s Havana at this packed spot, where black-and-white photos of Cuban music legends line the walls and live Cuban beats get the crowd's hips swinging from around 11pm. Opening in 2006, the club is credited in sparking Media Luna's transformation from drug-and prostitute-addled strip to entertainment district. Cover charge.

Demente Plaza de la Trinidad No. 10–19 ☎ 5 660 4226; map p.130. Dimly lit bar carved out of a once crumbling eighteenth-century house off happening Plaza de la Trinidad, featuring exposed brick, rocking chairs and minimalist decor, decent drinks (they have Colombian craft beers in bottles) and tasty tapas (try the *patatas bravas*). It's a bit pricey – you're paying for the ambience and cool location.

Mister Babilla Av del Arsenal No. 8B–137 ☎ 302 441 0553; map p.130. Tacky jungle-themed decor aside, this massive multi-floor club will get you dancing to at least one of its music genres, be it salsa, rock or house. The party usually extends until the wee hours of the morning (it gets busy after midnight with *chiva* party buses). Cover charge.

Quiebra-Canto Camellón de los Mártires (C Media Luna) No. 25–110 ⓦ quiebracanto.com; map p.130. Another recommended club for traditional salsa, not far from the Puerta del Reloj – it's especially buzzing on Fri and Sat.

SHOPPING

Caribe Jewelry C 5 No. 2 51 Bocagrande ⓦ caribejewelry.com; map p.130. Jewellery shops specializing in Colombian emeralds are numerous in the Centro Histórico and Bocagrande, and this is a reasonable place to start, with reputable, English-speaking jewellers who won't rip you off (you won't get a bargain either), and an emerald museum (free) on site. Smaller branches in the Centro Histórico at C San Pedro Claver No. 31–18 and also on Plaza Bolívar.

Ketty Tinoco C Baloco, Edificio Piñeres Local 1 ⓦ kettytinoco.com; map p.130. The main boutique of celebrated local designer Ketty Tinoco ("La Dama del Lino") sells chic women's fashions as well as contemporary versions of traditional *guayaberas* (men's shirts), worn by Bill Clinton among others.

Librería Nacional C 2 (C Badillo) No. 36–27 ⓦ librerianacional.com; map p.130. This branch of the national book chain stocks some English-language titles, including all of Gabo's work.

DIRECTORY

Banks and exchange Several banks (including BBVA) with 24hr ATMs and casas de cambio are on the Plaza de la Aduana and adjoining streets, as well as along Av San Martín in Bocagrande. Major branches of Banco de Bogotá and Citibank can be found on Av Venezuela just beyond the city walls.

Festivals The best include Cartagena Festival Internacional de Música (early Jan; ⓦ cartagenamusicfestival.com); the Hay Festival, also in Jan (a literary fest modelled after the famous Welsh one; ⓦ hayfestival.com); Festival Internacional de Cine (film festival in March; ⓦ ficcifestival.com); and the Fiestas de la Independencia de Cartagena (Nov), a huge party to celebrate the city's declaration of independence from Spain on Nov 11, 1811.

Health Nuevo Hospital Bocagrande, C 5 No. 6–49 at Cra 6 (☎ 5 665 5270, ⓦ nhbg.com.co).

Laundry Hotels in the Centro Histórico tend to charge a fortune for laundry; hostels should be cheaper, but a convenient option is the small *lavandería* inside Opitours at C Media Luna No. 10–19, which charges by the kilogram for a 24hr turnaround. See also *Beer & Laundry* (see page 138), which is about two hours for a wash and dry.

Police Thanks to a large and visible police presence throughout, the Centro Histórico in Cartagena is generally safe. The main police office is in Manga at C Real No. 24–03 (☎ 5 660 9124).

Post office Your accommodation will recommend a good courier service. An official 4-72 post office can be found at C de la Moneda No. 7–94 and in La Matuna at Centro Comercial Galerías local 15.

Visa extensions Centro Facilitador de Servicios Migratorio, Cra 20b No. 29–18, Pie de la Popa (☎ 5 670 0555).

Around Cartagena

It's worth allocating a couple of days for day-trips **around Cartagena**, primarily the natural attractions and historic sites along the Caribbean coast. The spectacular beach at **Playa Blanca** is the most popular target, often combined with trips to the **Islas del Rosario** and evocative ruins at **Bocachica**. Boats – generally small and fast – to all three depart Cartagena's Muelle Turístico, better known as "**La Bodeguita**", just outside the city walls on Avenue Blas de Lezo. To the northeast, you can take a mud bath inside the **Volcán de Lodo El Totumo**.

Bocachica

To get a closer look at Cartagena's outer fortifications – and a glimpse of how the city's less fortunate live – take a boat to **Bocachica**, overlooking the channel of the same name on the southern tip of **Isla de Tierra Bomba**. With around 12,000 mainly Afro-Colombian inhabitants, Bocachica itself is a ramshackle, relatively impoverished village without running water or medical facilities, and a main street that floods at high tide – garbage lines the shores and muddy streets. The public boats terminate at the village dock (they might stop at several villages along the way), from where it's a relatively simple hike to two **forts** – there are no signs however, and it's a good idea to avail yourself of one of the **local guides** who will approach you on landing. Guides generally speak Spanish only, but they might be able to rustle up an English-speaker if you ask. The village is generally a safe place to wander, but the guides can be very pushy – insisting on a smaller tip or refusing them altogether may result in some aggressive remonstrations.

Fortificaciones de Bocachica
Free • ☎ 655 0277

Perched high above **Bocachica** on the Cerro del Horno, the **Batería del Ángel San Rafael** is a large gun battery built 1769 to 1778, with a line of hefty, rusting cannons on the battlements and stellar views of the surrounding area. The solid brick and stonework has been artfully restored, with the moat also intact. Further along the coast, overlooking a small beach popular with locals, the much more substantial **Fuerte de San Fernando** was built in stages 1753 to 1779 to better defend Bocachica, which, after a sandbar blocked Bocagrande in 1640, was the only access to the city's harbour. It's a remarkable structure, laid out in a typical star design common in the period and riddled with dark vaults and passages fluttering with bats. There are a few signs on doorways, but otherwise no information. This engineering feat included a heavy bronze chain dangled across the entrance, beneath the water, to the **Fuerte de San José**, built 1714 to 1725 and destroyed by Vernon in 1741 – what you see today was reconstructed in the 1750s (this fort is usually off-limits).

ARRIVAL AND DEPARTURE **BOCACHICA**

By boat Buy tickets for Bocachica at La Bodeguita Puerta 3; boat tickets are one-way (plus a tax paid on departure only, at Puerta 1), and depart regularly (around 20–30min one-way). Boats tend to leave only when full – normally every hour or so, but on weekday afternoons you might be waiting for over an hour to get back.

Playa Blanca

Gorgeous **Playa Blanca**, on the northwestern shore of **Isla Barú** (divided from the mainland by the Canal Dique), is one of the most popular beach destinations around Cartagena, a 3km strip of bleached-white sands and calm blue waters far more enticing than the beaches closer to the city. Having said that, Playa Blanca can be mobbed in high season (avoid weekends altogether) and like most Colombian beaches, expect plenty of vendors, hawkers, jetskis and ramshackle commercialization. Fried fish,

AROUND CARTAGENA THE CARIBBEAN COAST

snacks and the ubiquitous coco loco cocktails are delivered by a string of wooden beach shacks. To experience Playa Blanca after the tour boats depart, consider staying the night. Be sure to bring plenty of water and sunscreen.

Aviario Nacional de Colombia

Km 14.5 Vía Barú • Charge (plus additional parking charge) • W aviarionacional.co

Gaggles of macaws, toucans, peacocks, hawks and flamingos star at the **Aviario Nacional de Colombia**, just a five-minute drive from Playa Blanca (off the main island road; it's a straightforward but very hot 30min walk). The various enclosures are fairly naturalistic and spacious, with the two thousand inhabitants all rehabilitated or rescued from illegal traffickers (or descended from those birds).

ARRIVAL AND DEPARTURE   PLAYA BLANCA

By boat Booths sell a variety of tickets to the Islas del Rosario and Playa Blanca outside La Bodeguita Puerta 1. Boats to Playa Blanca should be a fixed fee, though agents will try and sell you a more expensive package if they can; most trips run 9am–4pm daily and include a cruise around the Rosario islands (meaning the bus is a better option if you aim to maximize time on the sand).

By shuttle bus You can take a convenient shuttle bus (45min–1hr) direct to Playa Blanca through *Hostel Mamallena* (see page 137): buses depart the hostel in Cartagena daily 8.30am and 1pm, returning 11am and 4pm.

By bus The cheapest way to the beach is to take a public bus to Pasacaballos (1hr 30min–2hr) from the Mall Plaza El Castillo (500m beyond the Monumento India Catalina, just outside the city walls, on Av Pedro de Heredia); in Pasacaballos take a *mototaxi* (negotiate them down before you set off) or *colectivo* taxis. To get back, *mototaxis* should be waiting (leave before 4pm), but note that some travellers have been mugged by *mototaxi* drivers on this route – go with a group.

By taxi City taxis should agree to take you to Playa Blanca for a set price one-way, but check your hotel for the latest rates.

ACCOMMODATION

Basic accommodation at Playa Blanca is budget-friendly if you don't mind a **hammock**, but note that you'll need a mosquito net or lots of DEET – the mozzies can be ferocious at night. Simple thatched **cabañas** (with shared bathrooms) are also on offer at the southern end of the beach (you might be able to negotiate a lower rate during quiet periods). If you have a tent, **camping** is permitted (for a fee) – wander towards the northern end of the beach, away from the cabañas, for a more tranquil experience. Electricity is usually only available 6am–6pm at Playa Blanca.

Islas del Rosario

Some 35km southwest of Cartagena lies an archipelago of small coral islands known as the **Islas del Rosario**, sunk in transparent turquoise waters. In total there are 27 islands, most of them private islets barely large enough for a bungalow; only two islands, Isla Tesoro and Isla Rosario (but much of the surrounding ocean), are protected within the **Parque Nacional Natural Corales del Rosario y San Bernardo**. Since 1950 over 100 structures and second homes have been constructed here – controversially, the government has been trying to reclaim the islands as national heritage since the 1980s, without much success.

Most travellers experience the islands on a day-trip from Cartagena's Muelle Turístico (see page 146), combined with Playa Blanca (see page 140), or one of the private beaches on **Isla Grande**, which provides a taster but tends to be fairly rushed and limited in scope. The only way to extend a stay is to pay for a private boat in Cartagena to take you to a less developed island, or stay the night at one of several hotels. Note that the national park also covers the southern half of Isla Barú, and several resort hotels (*Isla del Encanto*, for example) are actually located here rather than on the Rosario islands themselves.

Isla Grande

The biggest island in the archipelago is **Isla Grande**, with the main settlement of Orika. Most of the hotels are scattered around the coast on secluded bays or beaches; some tours from Cartagena will stop here, before heading back to the city, where the beaches and snorkelling are good and far less crowded compared to Playa Blanca; *Cocoliso*, *Isla del Sol* and *Gente de Mar* are popular (these might be described as "islands" but they are all resort hotels on Isla Grande), though you'll be expected to pay more for full use of the resort facilities. Some trips also take in privately owned **Isla Pirata** just off the east coast of Isla Grande, and *Coralina Island* on **Isleta**, one of the best and least crowded options.

ARRIVAL AND DEPARTURE — ISLAS DEL ROSARIO

Boat tours Basic return tickets to the Islas del Rosario range from the cheapest (on an ordinary boat) to the most expensive (on a fast boat) from La Bodeguita Puerta 1 (departing around 8–10am, returning around 3.30pm), plus the port tax; the fast boat is a much better option than the slow boat. It's rare to just buy a boat ticket – most of the ticket booths sell packages (including boat ride) which will include a short tour around some of the islands, a 1hr stop at the aquarium (admission is an additional fee), or a small beach (charge for snorkelling) for those who opt out; then a stop at Playa Blanca (see page 140) for lunch and a couple of hours on the beach before heading back. Note that if you stay the night anywhere on route you'll have to buy a completely new ticket for the return. Hotels sell more expensive day-trip packages to the private beaches (see above); these usually include pick-ups, boat transport, lunch and access to all facilities (but not diving).

ACCOMMODATION

Cocoliso Isla Grande ⓦ cocolisoresort.com.co. Popular all-inclusive option with contemporary-style rooms, pool, a very thin strip of beach and excellent snorkelling. Diving and kayaking available. Room only $$$, all-inclusive. $$$$

★ **Coralina Island** Isleta, off the west coast of Isla Grande ⓦ www.oralinaisland.com. One of the few resorts not located on Isla Grande and one of the most secluded, with just six beautifully decorated rooms and wooden decks tucked in between the mangroves (some sunset-facing). Rates include transportation and all three meals. $$$$

Hotel San Pedro de Majagua Isla Grande ⓦ hotel majagua.com. Hotel located on the site of French painter Pierre Daguet's former Isla Grande home, with stylish rooms featuring rattan and wood with sleek, minimalist furnishings, a/c and satellite TV. $$$$

Volcán de Lodo El Totumo

Galerazamba, 50km northeast of Cartagena • Charge (fee usually included in tours)

The small but utterly bizarre **Volcán de Lodo El Totumo** spews out thick, hot, grey mud, not lava, from a 15m-high cone. After dumping your clothes in a locker, you can clamber down into the crater for a refreshing wallow in the mud (you'll float around like it's the Dead Sea), which allegedly has therapeutic properties. Dextrous locals will offer to photograph you in your Creature from the Black Lagoon guise, and to give you an energetic but not terribly professional mud massage – after climbing back down you'll be directed to the nearby lagoon where local women will wash you clean. It's kooky fun but you are expected to tip each person at the end – though these services are not mandatory, as with many rural (and impoverished) Colombian communities, expect a fairly bad-tempered response if you turn any of them down.

Most hostels arrange trips to the volcano, but note that it can get very crowded since all the tours arrive at the same time (departures usually daily 8.30am & 1.30pm); it's not unusual to line up for thirty minutes or more to have a turn inside. Bring your own towel and small bills, and expect basic facilities and toilets.

Tolú

Popular with holidaying Colombians but practically undiscovered by overseas travellers, **TOLÚ** is a relaxed Afro-Colombian resort town on the Golfo de Morrosquillo, best known as the gateway to the beguiling beaches and island communities of the **Islas de San Bernardo**. It's a laidback, friendly place of around thirty thousand people, and its slightly down-at-heel charm definitely grows on you, provided you adjust your expectations; the town's **malecón**, lined with simple restaurants, bars and craft stalls, makes for a pleasant, breezy stroll, but its dark-sand **beaches**, shared with fishing boats, are fairly grim: small, often sprinkled with flotsam and litter, with murky, muddy water (though plenty of folks do swim here, it's not recommended). **Playas del Francés** (6km north of the plaza via Cra 2) and the sands 20km south at **Coveñas** are far better, but the San Bernardo islands are a much wiser choice if you're looking for idyllic Caribbean scenery.

The malecón and around

Tolú is one of the oldest towns in Colombia, founded by Spanish Conquistadors Alonso de Heredia and Pedro de Velasco in 1535, though nothing remains from that period. Most of the action today takes place along the **malecón** (aka Cra 1), and around the main square one block inland between Calles 15 and 16, shady **Plaza Pedro de Heredia**, dominated by the colonial-style **Iglesia de Santiago Apóstol**. Tolú is generally safe, but avoid walking north of the *malecón* late at night (beyond C 24).

The town's "famous" icon of Tolú is the brightly decorated **bicitaxi**, used to get around in lieu of car taxis or buses: though most of these are your standard pedicabs, the larger, souped-up versions that patrol the *malecón* and plaza from late afternoon onwards blare out reggaeton and salsa from speakers below the seats (it gets especially loud at the weekends).

ARRIVAL AND DEPARTURE

By plane Aerolínea de Antioquia (ADA) and SATENA run daily flights between Medellín (Olaya Herrera) and Golfo de Morrosquillo airport (1hr), at the southern end of the *malecón*.

By bus Most buses terminate or drop off at the petrol station (aka "Bomba") on the eastern edge of town (where C 16 meets the main road between Sincelejo and Coveñas), as opposed to "La Playa"; the bigger buses tend to be travelling between Montería or Medellín and Cartagena. From here bicitaxis will be waiting to whisk you to where you want to go, or it's around a 15–20min walk to the *malecón*. Moving on, you can buy tickets at the Expreso Brasilia office on Plaza Pedro de Heredia (or for Rapido Ochoa at *Punto B* restaurant on the plaza), though these buses will also depart from the petrol station. Transportes Luz and Torcoroma/Transportes Gonzalez have offices on C 16 near the petrol station. To get to Capurganá (see page 147) take a bus to Montería, then change for a bus to Necoclí (2–3hr), where you can take a *lancha* for the final leg.

TOLÚ AND AROUND

Destinations Bogotá (2 daily at 8am & 5pm; 20hr); Cartagena (hourly; 3hr); Medellín (4 daily at 8am, 10am, 4.30pm & 7pm; 10–12hr); Montería for Necoclí (hourly; 2–3hr); Santa Marta (5 daily at 7am, 8.30am, 4.30pm, 5pm & 6.30pm; 7hr); Sincelejo (hourly; 1hr).

To Mompox Travelling between Tolú and Mompox is straightforward, and things should be a lot faster once the new Río Magdalena bridges are open in 2019. First take a bus to Sincelejo, where all the main bus companies have terminals close to each other; if there are no direct buses to Mompox from here, catch a bus to Magangué (1hr 30min), where you should be able to make a relatively easy connection to Mompox.

GETTING AROUND

By bicitaxi The price for rides on a normal bicitaxi in town is fixed, though for rides to and from the buses (and at night) you'll usually be asked for double the usual fee, especially if bags are involved. Fix the price before you get in and note that the souped-up double-seaters are always more expensive.

By minibus Minibuses to the beaches at Coveñas (40min) depart frequently from the Cootranstol terminal on Cra 2, between Calles 16 and 17.

By taxi Taxis (cars) are available for longer trips from the main plaza.

ACCOMMODATION

Almost all Tolú's accommodation is located on, or near the *malecón*. Rooms are relatively cheap (especially if you've come from Cartagena). The high season runs from mid-December through January (and includes Easter); there's a slightly less busy/expensive shoulder season from mid-June to mid-August. Rates quoted below are for the high season, but they drop by over 50 percent during the rest of the year.

★ **Costa Linda** Km 7 Via El Francés ⓦ hotelcostalinda-tolu.com. North of town and facing the much more appealing sands of Playas del Francés, this is a popular choice for a relaxing stay. All nine rooms come with a private balcony and ocean view, with a/c. It's a little isolated, so there's not much choice for food – the in-house option is good, though, and pick-ups are included. English spoken. $$

Hostel Elena del Mar Cra 2 No. 12–17 ☎ 300 478 0073. With a great location near the waterfront, this hostel offers cheap, spotless rooms (with a/c and balcony access) and dorms, free drinking water and coffee all day. $

Hotel Mar de Plata Cra 2 No. 1850 ☎ 314 444 4095. Excellent budget option one block from the *malecón* containing simple but cosy en-suite rooms with TV and a/c. Breakfast included. $

La Mansión C 16 No. 3–52 ☎ 313 516 0941. Modern place just off the main plaza, with no-frills but clean rooms set around a central courtyard with inviting outdoor pool; all come with a/c, private bathroom and cable TV. $$

Villa Babilla C 20 No. 3–40 (between Cra 3 and 4) ☎ 312 677 1325. Three blocks inland from the *malecón*, this guesthouse features basic but airy, spotless rooms named after locations around the world (all with bathroom and fan). Those on the first floor are somewhat pricier, but they do come with a breezy terrace. There's free coffee all day, shared kitchen, laundry (charge per kg) and bike rental. $

EATING AND DRINKING

There are plenty of cheap **seafood restaurants** along the *malecón*, most serving fried fish and ceviche, while around the main plaza are several **bakeries** and *arepa* stalls, though hot-dog carts seem to outnumber them all (the stalls and carts get going from late afternoon). The Éxito supermarket (daily: high season 8am–10pm, low season 8am–8pm) on the main plaza is a solid option for self-catering, though its selection of fresh food is limited.

Punto B Plaza Pedro de Heredia (C 15 at Cra 2). Old-fashioned bar and restaurant on the main plaza, with shady interior and wooden tables poking through the colonial arcade. Good for a hearty breakfast, coffee or cold beer in the afternoon. $

La Red Av del Malecón No. 19–100, at C 20 ☎ 5 286 0782. Small seafood place on the *malecón*, serving all the usual Colombian dishes in addition to fresh shrimps, róbalo

(sea bass) and red snapper (pargo rojo) in a variety of styles and sauces. $
Terraza La 15 Av del Malecón, at C 15 • 5 288 6226. Laidback, covered restaurant and bar on the *malecón* serving a wide range of basic dishes, from fried fish and shrimp stew to chicken rice, though not everything on the menu is always available. $$

DIRECTORY

Banks and exchange There are various banks in town; note that the Banco Popular ATM (no branch) next door to Banco Agrario, just east of the plaza on C 16, only works with cards with chips.

Islas de San Bernardo

The ten principal islands that make up the **Islas de San Bernardo**, a short boat ride from Tolú (or longer journey direct from Cartagena), are wonderfully tranquil (when not overrun during Colombian holidays), and their teal waters and blinding-white beaches make for a fun day-trip or overnight stay. Settled by freed Afro-Colombian slaves in the nineteenth century, the area has been protected since 1996 within the **Parque Nacional Natural Corales del Rosario y San Bernardo**. The easiest way to get a taster of the islands is to take a full-day boat tour from Tolú, though you'll get more out of the experience by staying the night.

Isla Palma

The best snorkelling in the archipelago can be found off **Isla Palma**, which also has a glittering, narrow spit of sand at its southern end. Other than the aging *Decameron* resort, which owns the island, the main attraction on land was once the euphemistically named **Parque Ecológico**, with mostly caged animals, though at the time of writing its future looked uncertain. The flamingos that graze in the mangrove swamp and macaws you'll see squawking in the trees are one hundred percent natural to the island, however.

Isla Tintipán

Isla Tintipán, the largest of the San Bernardo islands, is around 3.5km wide and 1.7km long, though its boggy, mangrove-smothered coast and voracious mosquitoes makes it one of the least habitable. *Eco-Hotel Puntanorte* lies on the north side, while the privately owned **Playa Mar Adentro** is the best stretch of beach, an idyllic strip of chalky white sand (breezes keep the mozzies to a minimum). Just off the western coast lies the remarkable *Casa En El Agua* (see page 146).

Santa Cruz del Islote

The astonishing three-acre islet of **Santa Cruz del Islote**, in between Tintipán and Múcura, is completely smothered with shacks populated by fishermen and their families. Around 1200 people live here (though over a hundred kids are usually away at high school), with two small shops, one restaurant and primary school (electricity runs for just five hours/day) – it has no beaches, of course, and boat tours usually do a simple circuit around the edge, without stopping. To visit you'll have to ask one of the locals on Múcura or stay at the *Casa en el Agua* (see page 146); you can also check out the excellent documentary film *Santa Cruz del Islote* by Luke Lorentzen.

Isla Múcura

Tiny **Isla Múcura** features small, bone-white beaches dotted with palm trees, wonderful snorkelling in multi-hued blue waters and several places to stay. The small but relatively well-stocked shop sells beer, bottled water, tinned tuna and such like, and if you stay the night you'll be able to enjoy the main beach minus the boatloads of day-trippers from Tolú.

Isla Fuerte

Some 60km south of the main archipelago (but just 11km off the coast), the lesser-visited **Isla Fuerte** is gaining popularity for those looking to get off the beaten path. Covering just three square kilometres, the coral island is encircled by reefs and gorgeous sandy beaches and features yet another cave where the ubiquitous pirate Henry Morgan is said to have hidden treasure. The densely forested interior is crisscrossed by footpaths, with a colony of sloths near **Playa San Diego** and several ancient trees (including a giant ceiba, aka "*La bonga*", and a strangler fig known as the "Walking Tree"), still revered by the local Afro-Colombian community. There are no cars on the island, but it does have donkeys, the **Naui Dive Center** and several decent places to stay, with the tiny settlement of **Puerto Limón** offering basic eating options.

ARRIVAL AND DEPARTURE

Tours from Tolú Day-trip boats leave Tolú's Muelle Turístico (at the *malecón* between Calles 10 and 11) at around 8.30am, returning around 4pm. Recommended operator Club Náutico Mundo Marino (office between Calles 15 and 16; ☎316 297 7142) runs tours that start on Isla Palma before taking in Santa Cruz del Islote and Isla Múcura, where you get to linger the longest – around 3hr – to have lunch, sip a cold beer or go snorkelling. Buy tickets the day before or get to the pier before 8am. Club Náutico Mar Adentro (☎5 288 5481; w facebook.com/nauticomaradentro) offers a slightly different combo (same prices), with its longest stop on Playa Mar Adentro on Tintipán. Club Náutico Los Delfines (w facebook.com/clubnautico.losdelfines), opposite the Muelle at Cra 1a No. 11–08 also sells basic boat tours.

Overnight stays If you want to stay the night on Isla Múcura (see page 146) you'll need to take one of the tour boats that depart daily 8–8.30am – you must tell the tour agent/boat captain in advance so there will be space on the boat for the return trip. The price for a one-way trip on a tour boat does not include lunch, and you disembark before the snorkelling. Once here, local boatmen will zip you between the islands for a small fee.

ISLAS DE SAN BERNARDO

Public boat There's also a regular *lancha* to Tintipán and Casa en el Agua departing the Muelle around 8am daily (costs vary depending on the season), returning 3pm (call ☎315 889 0339 to reserve a seat).

By boat from Cartagena Speedboats depart La Bodeguita (Puenta 5) in Cartagena at 9am daily, taking around 2hr to reach *Casa en el Agua*, from where you can take another short speedboat ride (10min) to Isla Múcura. Boats return to Cartagena daily at 12.30pm from *Casa en el Agua* (you must reserve in advance).

To Isla Fuerte Take a bus to Lorica from Cartagena (direct Expreso Brasilia buses depart from 5am; 4–5hr), Medellín (10hr), Tolú (1hr) or Montería (1hr; also direct buses to Paso Nuevo 2hr–2hr 30min); then take a taxi to the fishing village of Paso Nuevo (30–45min). From here boats zip across to the island (30–45min) every few hours (or when full; get there before 1pm), though you can rent the whole boat. You might also be able take a boat direct from Fuerte (*La Playita*) to *Casa en el Agua* (see page 146); it's around two hours, but you must arrange this in advance at either hotel.

ACCOMMODATION

ISLA TINTIPÁN

★ **Casa en el Agua** w casaenelagua.com. Few hotels boast a more spectacular setting, with wooden, solar-powered *Casa en el Agua* set on a tiny sandbank just off Tintipán, seemingly adrift in the ocean. Basic dorm beds and private rooms are upstairs, with a bar and lounge downstairs, and wonderful snorkelling all round (coral has built up over the concrete foundations). Shared ecofriendly vault toilets and bucket showers conserve water. Breakfast included; no wi-fi. Advance reservations are essential, and only cash is accepted once you're here. Hammocks & dorms $, doubles. $$

ISLA MÚCURA

★ **Hotel Isla Múcura** ☎316 620 8660, w hotellisla mucura.com. One of the newer options on the beach, this is the island's best budget digs, with shady camping area, covered hammocks, simple wooden dorms (with fan), raised wooden "sky kiosks" for two (with fan) and larger cabins (for up to six people, with a/c). Meals are an extra fixed fee. Expect shared freshwater showers and 24hr solar-powered electricity. Hammocks, camping & dorms $, cabins $$-$$$

Hotel Múcura Club w mucuraclubhotel.com. Slightly more rustic option than the *Punta Faro*, with a choice of comfy rooms and luxurious suites, all fully inclusive, or cheaper cabañas with shared bathrooms which are a bit like dorms (doubles available). $$$

Punta Faro ☎317 435 9583, w puntafaro.com. Múcura's luxury option has access to the best beach on the island and features spacious, comfy a/c rooms with wooden beds, panelling and furnishings. Rates include all three meals (but not alcoholic drinks), tours to Tintipán and Islote de Santa Cruz, kayaks and snorkel equipment. Free wi-fi in public areas. Most rooms do not have hot water. Direct boat from Cartagena is extra (1hr 45min). Minimum two nights. $$$$

ISLA FUERTE
Isla Fuerte Ecolodge & Diving Center wislafuerte.com. Six luxurious cabins on the beach (for two, three or four people), fabulous food and a diving centre on site (packages including PADI courses available). Cell phone coverage, but no wi-fi. Rates include transfers from Paso Nuevo, boat tours and all three meals. Two-night minimum. $$$

★ **La Playita Hostel** wlaplayitaislafuerte.com. Right on the beach, with simple, clean double rooms (most en suite, all with fans and mosquito nets) and dorms, and an oceanfront bar. Breakfast included. Hammocks & dorms $, doubles $$

Capurganá and around

South of Tolú the development rapidly thins and the coast remains wild and relatively undiscovered territory all the way to Panama and the Darién Gap. The main exception is the growing beach and ecotourism hub of **CAPURGANÁ**, just a few kilometres from the Panamanian border on the western shore of the Gulf of Urabá, which cuts into mainland Colombia like an upside-down thumb. Here you'll find a relaxed Afro-Caribbean vibe, outstanding snorkelling and diving, and small but alluring beaches backed by virgin rainforest and waterfall-laced mountains.

Tourism was dealt a blow in 1999, when the area suffered a massive attack by FARC guerrillas, and until 2003 the lawless Darién region (a major narco-trafficking corridor) was host to a bloody power struggle between FARC guerrillas and right-wing paramilitaries. Things are far safer these days, with a permanent military presence, and though it's still not easy to reach (there are no motor vehicles), Capurganá does provide an adventurous route into Central America and the San Blas islands of Panama (see page 147). Note that there are no roads between Colombia and Panama's Darién province – attempting to cross the border solo, through the jungle, is extremely dangerous and invariably ends badly

The beaches

The main **beach** at Capurganá is **Playa La Caleta** at the northern end of the village, with honey-coloured sands and a barrier reef rich in tropical fish. You can also hike (1hr 30min) along the coast to **El Aguacate** (or take a boat; 10min), a gorgeous bay with turquoise waters, decent snorkelling and a small beach. The rocky headland here ends at the **Piscina de los Dioses** ("Pool of the Gods"), a natural ocean-fed pool you can swim in. Further south and only (safely) accessible by boat (30min) is **Playa Soledad**, a palm-fringed slice of delightful bone-white sand (hotels offer trips with lunch). For a break from

---

CROSSING INTO PANAMA FROM CAPURGANÁ

Getting to Panama from Capurganá is relatively straightforward, with boats departing the docks to Puerto Obaldía around 7.30am daily (charge; 45min). Make sure you get your **passport stamped** before you leave Capurganá at the Department of National Security of Colombia (DAS) office on the waterfront next to the police station (☏ 311 746 6234). Once you've cleared Panamanian immigration in Puerto Obaldía (you'll need another stamp and to show a certificate of yellow fever vaccination), aim to leave as quickly as possible (it's not an especially attractive place); AirPanama (wairpanama.com) flies direct (1hr) to Panama City.

Many travellers take a tour to the **San Blas islands** instead from Capurganá/Sapzurro (day-trips available), but you'll need a permit from the Panamanian consulate (Plaza Principal; ☏ 310 303 5285) in Capurganá if you intend to stay over; San Blas Adventures offers excellent four-day packages via Sapzurro (wsanblasadventures.com) that end up in Carti, Panama. While most of the islands are uninhabited, some of the larger ones are home to the native Guna people.

THE CARIBBEAN COAST CAPURGANÁ AND AROUND

> **DIVING CAPURGANÁ**
>
> The coral reefs off Capurganá are some of the most unspoiled on the Colombian coast, with around thirty major dive sites easily accessible by boat or from the shore – turtles, nurse sharks and octopus are commonly spotted. The **Dive & Green Dive Center** (wdiveandgreen.com), near the main pier, is a PADI-certified operator, with professional divemasters and new equipment. Note that between December and March the region experiences strong currents and poor visibility (May to November is best for diving).

the beach take a hike through the jungle to **El Cielo** (1hr 30min one-way; entry charge), a small waterfall surrounded by dense foliage visited by tropical birds, including toucans.

Sapzurro

Boats every 30min (or when boats are full); 10–15min • Charge

From Capurganá it's a short boat ride (or relatively steep two-hour hike through the jungle; go in a group to be safe) to the nearby bay and beach at **SAPZURRO**, an Afro-Colombian village of around three hundred people just across the border from Panama that's far less developed than its neighbour. From here you can take the gentle hike (20min) up through the jungle to the village of **La Miel**, across the border in Panama – you'll have to pass a very laidback border post (you might have to pay a fee here), so take your passport. **Playa Blanca** beach at La Miel is another strip of gorgeous white-sands fringed by palms and banana groves. From Sapzurro you can also walk (30min) to **Cabo Tiburón**, the promontory that marks the coastal borderline between Colombia and Panama, and officially, between South and Central America.

ARRIVAL AND DEPARTURE   CAPURGANÁ AND AROUND

By plane There are direct charter flights to Capurganá with TAC (☎313 722 8903); flights (1hr 10min) leave Medellín (Olaya Herrera) daily in high season (Mon & Fri only in low season). Buy tickets through walmar.com.co. The ADA service from Medellín (Olaya Herrera) to Acandí (1hr), is usually a bit cheaper. From Acandí you need to take a boat (30–40min) to Capurganá, departing around 1pm (the return departs Capurganá at around 7.30am). For reservations call ☎314 614 0704.

By boat Boats run to Capurganá from the ramshackle port towns of Turbo (reservations ☎312 701 9839) and Necoclí (reservations ☎315 687 4284), but the latter is recommended – the trip is shorter and the town is safer (robberies are common in Turbo). Boats leave both ports daily at around 8am; in high season there are usually several departures between 8am and 9am (get to the piers between 6am and 7am if you don't have reservations). The trip takes 2–3hr depending on sea conditions from Turbo, but only 1hr 30min from Necoclí. There is an 8kg luggage limit (with an additional fee per kilogram thereafter). Bin liners for your luggage (which are usually necessary) cost extra. Turbo (8–9hr) and Necoclí (9–10hr) are both accessible by bus to/from Medellín (Terminal Norte); Rapido Ochoa also operates a direct bus between Cartagena and Necoclí (9hr).

INFORMATION

Money There are no banks or ATMs in Capurganá, and few credit cards are accepted, so bring plenty of cash (Panama's official currency is the US dollar, and these are widely used in Capurganá and Sapzurro).

Wi-fi There is limited wi-fi in Capurganá, but none in Sapzurro (both places have mobile phone coverage).

ACCOMMODATION AND EATING

Book weeks in advance if you intend to visit over Easter or Christmas.

CAPURGANÁ

Acuali Eco Hostal wacualiecohostal.com. One of the best budget options, set on the edge of town amid lush jungle (on the trail to Sapzurro), so it's much quieter than the beach. Simple, clean en-suite rooms and dorms, with amazing shared showers (half outdoors). Breakfast is included, and there's a shared kitchen. Dorms $, doubles $$

★ **Bahía Lodge** El Aguacate wbahialodge.com. Idyllic hotel with four rooms and five thatched cabañas right on the beach at Aguacate, with breakfast and dinner included in the rates, along with free coffee and water. $$

La Bohemia Cra 1 No. 1–2 📞 318 633 399, ✉ labohemia capurgana@gmail.com. Fun, sociable hostel, with simple, blue-painted rooms and cosy dorms (it's a bit like a giant treehouse), with helpful staff, barbecue and garden but no wi-fi. Hammocks, dorms and doubles available. $

Hostal Capurganá C del Comercio (1 block from Playa La Caleta) 🌐 hostalcapurgana.net. Spacious, clean en-suite rooms with fans surrounding a flower-filled courtyard (no kitchen, though). The *hostal* prefers to sell packages that include pick-ups, tours and three meals, but you can opt for breakfast only. Unusually, accepts credit cards. $

★ **Josefina's** Playa La Caleta 📞 322 592 4812. Local beach shack where Josefina presides over delicious fresh fish, crab, squid, ceviche and lobster under shady trees overlooking the water; friendly service and laidback sounds. $$

Posada del Gecko & Café Bar C de Comercio 2 🌐 posadadelgecko.com. For a welcome break from Colombian staples, this congenial joint knocks out reasonably authentic Italian classics (Chef Alberto hails from Tuscany), from pizza to spaghetti, with large portions and candlelit tables in a pretty courtyard. $$

SAPZURRO

La Gata Negra C Principal 📞 317 438 0066, 🌐 facebook.com/sapzurrolagatanegra. Charming guesthouse just back from the beach run by congenial Italian owners Stefi and Giovanni. Shared outdoor kitchen and common area, cosy rooms (with shared bathrooms), plus languid house cats, hummingbirds and fabulous Italian food (not included). $

Zíngara Hospedaje Camino La Miel 📞 320 687 4678. Rustic wooden property located in the forest a short walk from the beach (on the path to Panama), with two simple, spotless rooms, wonderful views across the bay and hammocks on the balconies. Friendly owner Clemencia Camargo is a font of local knowledge. Rates include drinking water and coffee. $

Mompox

Viewed from the Río Magdalena, the elegantly weathered Baroque churches, palaces and domes of **MOMPOX** poke out above the palms and whitewashed colonial houses like an eighteenth-century mirage. Troupes of howler monkeys patrol the red-clay-tiled roofs, iguanas doze in trees and clouds of dragonflies hover over fragrant bougainvillea-draped balconies. For many years few places were as redolent of colonial South America, genuinely romantic or simply as magical as Mompox – and still today the spirit of Gabriel García Márquez, whose wife went to high school in the town, seems stronger here than anywhere else in the country. The 1987 movie of *Chronicle of a Death Foretold* was partly shot here (though the novella was inspired by several places), and Mompox has an important role in *The General in His Labyrinth*: José Palacios tells Simón Bolívar, "Mompox does not exist. Sometimes we dream about her, but she does not exist." Bolívar actually raised his army here in 1812, and visited the town six times thereafter (the final stay in 1830 is depicted in the novel).

The sense of time warp has faded dramatically in recent years, however, with a series of **road bridges** connecting Mompox to the rest of the country and a new **airport**. As a result, **tourism** is booming and the town is rapidly being renovated and restored to its former glory. One thing that hasn't changed is the stultifying **heat** – don't wander around during the day expecting to find much going on. The secret to appreciating Mompox is doing as the locals do, giving in to the **siesta spirit** between about 11am and 5pm, and going out when it's bearable – basically very early morning, when locals start walking their dogs at 5am, or late at night, when you'll discover something happening on every corner; deserted streets suddenly become colonized by tables,

> ### A STROLL ALONG THE MAGDALENA
>
> One of the best ways to spend an early morning in Mompox is to cross the **Magdalena** and wander up the opposite bank, chatting to local farmers and soaking up the glorious views of the old town (when the sun is in exactly the right place for photos). Small ferries transport people across the river just south of the football pitch (at the end of C 9) for a small fee – you can take another ferry back across the river opposite Plaza San Francisco, around 1.5km further north.

rocking chairs and bars, while kids ride tiny go-karts in the plazas. Many visitors don't go to bed before 6am.

Brief history
Marooned on a freshwater island in the Depresión Momposina, the vast low-lying wetlands of the Magdalena's eastern branch ("Brazo de Mompós"), Mompox (also spelt Mompós) was established in 1537 by **Don Alonso de Heredia**, the brother of Cartagena's founder. It served as the lynchpin for the mighty river's trade network between the Caribbean coast and the country's Andean interior, becoming one of Colombia's most prosperous commercial centres. Mompox was the first town in Colombia to declare complete independence from Spain in 1810, and two years later Simón Bolívar raised an army here. Mompox's long decline began in the mid-nineteenth century – like Cartagena it was ravaged by cholera in 1847, dramatically reducing the population. Things got worse when the main channel of the silt-heavy river changed its course in the early twentieth century, and port traffic moved to Magangué. Its beauty has remained practically untouched ever since and UNESCO declared it a World Heritage Site in 1995 in recognition of its outstanding colonial architecture.

The old town
Mompox's grid of streets stretches out alongside the river and is easy to explore on foot. Its sprawl of grand Catholic churches and enchanting colonial mansions is a constant reminder of the town's faded glory and wealth. The town is also famous for its wooden rocking chairs, which residents drag on to the streets in the evenings to watch the world go by, as well as filigree **silver** jewellery sold around Calle Real del Medio, and **Vinimompox** – fruit wines made from banana, guava, orange and tamarind. The best way to soak up the atmosphere is to simply wander the streets – these are gradually being paved, while a major beautification of the waterfront, the **Albarrada**, lined with old homes and palaces, makes this an especially enticing target for a promenade.

Plaza de la Concepción
The heart of the old town is **Plaza de la Concepción**, on the waterfront and dominated by its grandest church, the **Iglesia de Inmaculada Concepción**. The church stands on the location of Alonso de Heredia's original chapel of 1540, but has been enlarged and modified many times over the years (the latest restoration was completed in 1931). The marble image of "Our Lady of the Immaculate Conception" inside was brought from Paris in 1891. Opposite the church and facing the river is the old **Mercado Público** (the current market is on the main highway on the edge of town), built in 1910 and now occupied by *Crónicas*, the restaurant managed by students from the local *Escuela de Taller* (training to be chefs).

Plaza Bolívar
Simón Bolívar's statue graces the small namesake square, **Plaza Bolívar** (also known as Plaza del Tamarindo), a shady space behind the Iglesia de Inmaculada Concepción on Carrera 2. This was supposedly the location of the original Indigenous village of Mompoj, long since erased by the Spanish.

Plaza del Libertad
Tranquil **Plaza del Libertad** contains a statue of the goddess of freedom (aka Lady Liberty) erected in 1873, commemorating the town's proud claim to be the first to declare independence from Spain in 1810. The inscription on the plinth is a quote from Simón Bolívar (in Spanish): "To Caracas I owe my life but to Mompós I owe my glory."

THE FORGOTTEN THEATRE OF MOMPOX

Stroll down the alley off Plaza Santo Domingo (Callejón de la Faltriquera) and you'll come across a real Mompox treasure, a sight that's likely to become all too rare in the future. Here lies the once grand **Teatro Colonial**, completely abandoned more than twenty years ago, its roof partially collapsed and its faded grandeur now home to several local families – whose kids are usually glad to give you a free tour (in Spanish only) after 2pm (for a small tip). It's a totally bizarre-looking place, with home comforts lodged in between old balconies and velvet seating.

On the western side of the square lies the Alcaldía Municipal (Town Hall), housed in the old **Convento de San Carlos**, built in 1660 by the Jesuits as a school and convent.

Iglesia de San Francisco
Callejón de San Francisco (C 20) at the Albarrada (Plaza San Francisco) • Mass only

Featuring a typically humble all-wood interior and striking maroon facade facing the river, the **Iglesia de San Francisco** claims roots going back to the 1580s. Most of the church was rebuilt in the eighteenth century, however, with the tower added in 1886 and the adjacent Colegio Sagrado Corazón de Jesús opening in 1924.

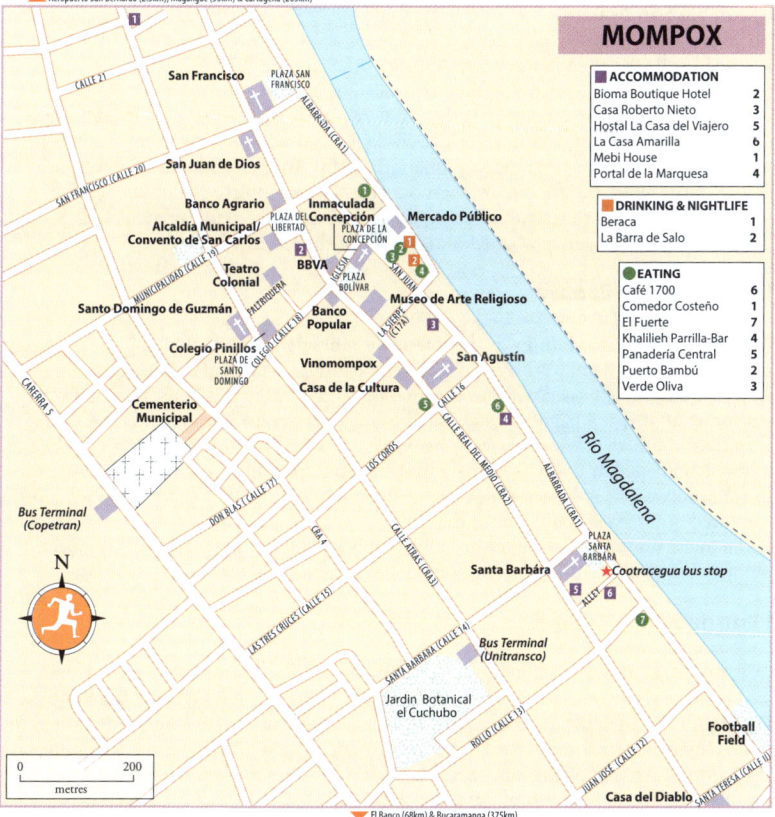

Museo de Arte Religioso
C Real del Medio (Cra 2) No. 17–07 • Charge • ☎ 5 684 0260

The **Museo de Arte Religioso** houses a small collection of religious art in the former home of Vicente Celedonio Gutiérrez de Piñeres, the pro-independence leader of the town in 1810 and one-time host of Simón Bolívar. The museum contains three moderately interesting galleries, showcasing gold and silver jewellery (sixteenth to eighteenth centuries), religious oil paintings of the seventeenth century, and a collection of images and documents associated with the local Easter *cofradías* (brotherhoods).

Casa de la Cultura
C Real del Medio (Cra 2) No. 16–25, opposite Iglesia de San Agustín • Charge, but often free

Housed in the eighteenth-century Casa Germán de Ribón, the **Casa de la Cultura** was restored in 2011 and contains a small exhibition of artefacts dug up from the town's plazas during restoration work. The most fascinating discovery was of Indigenous graves below Plaza Santa Bárbara, as well as 88 Spanish colonial burials under Plaza San Francisco. There's also a small silver workshop on site, with the whole thing set around a lush central courtyard and the spacious front hall, lined with old portraits of Simón Bolívar and original murals. The house once belonged to Ramón del Corral, and is where his son, future Antioquia independence leader **Juan del Corral** was born in 1778 – it was later acquired by the Germán de Ribón family (also strong supporters of independence).

Iglesia de San Agustín
Callejón de San Agustín (C 16), at C Real de Medio (Cra 2)

Founded in 1606, the **Iglesia de San Agustín**, officially the Basílica Menor del Santísimo Cristo Milagroso de Mompox since 2012, is now the town's main place of worship. It's especially venerated as the home of a miraculous image of the **Santísimo Cristo** ("Blessed Christ"), said to have been discovered mysteriously in the seventeenth century inside the *bodega* known as Albarrada de los Ángeles – it's the calvary at the centre of the altar. The church also harbours the **Santo Sepulcro** (an ornate, gold sepulchre, supposed to resemble St Augustine's), used in the traditional Semana Santa processions – it's usually protected under glass on the left as you enter.

Iglesia de Santa Bárbara
Callejón de Santa Bárbara (C 14) at the Albarrada (Plaza Santa Bárbara) • Charge for the tower

The finest church in Mompox is the **Iglesia de Santa Bárbara**, overlooking the riverfront plaza of the same name. With its magnificent Baroque octagonal bell tower and Moorish balcony adorned with ornate mouldings of flowers and lions, it vaguely resembles an oriental pagoda. Established in the early seventeenth century, the church is similar to others in Mompox with its simple, all wood interior, though it does boast a heavily gilded altar (with St Barbara in the centre), plus the Cruz de Mompox, used during processions at Easter – it's the archaic-looking, intricately carved wooden cross mounted on the wall to the left of the altar.

The tower was completed later in 1795, and is separate to the main hall – you can climb it but you might have to find someone to open the door.

Plaza de Santo Domingo
C de Atrás (Cra 3) at Callejón del Colegio (C 18)

Spacious **Plaza de Santo Domingo** is one of the town's liveliest squares, lined on one side by local shops, stalls and cafés, and on the other by the **Iglesia Santo Domingo de Guzmán**, most of which dates from a major reconstruction in 1856 and is dedicated to a miraculous incarnation of the Virgen del Rosario. The statue in the centre of the plaza is the *Monumento al Nazareno*, erected in 2010 (a tribute to "Nazareno Momposino", the main character in the local Easter celebrations).

Cementerio Municipal

C 18, at Cra 4 • Free

Mompox's **Cementerio Municipal**, the atmospheric cemetery, was established in 1831 and is where some of its more illustrious inhabitants were laid to rest. These include one of the godfathers of black Latin American poetry, **Candelario Obeso** (1848–1884; his memorial is on the left, with a marble bust), and liberation hero **General Hermógenes Maza** (1792–1847). It's a relatively small space, with beautiful white marble tombs typical of Latin America alongside more modest graves studded with fresh flowers and, bizarrely enough, inhabited by numerous (and very sleepy) feral cats.

Casa del Diablo

C Real Del Medio (Cra 2) No. 10–32/34, at Callejón de Santa Teresa

The long-abandoned, elegant mansion known as **Casa del Diablo** is infamous locally for having its own ghost; legend has it that construction started in the 1930s (it was supposedly going to be a club) but was never completed because of the demon lurking inside – today, as the town is spruced up, the property remains a conspicuous ruin.

ARRIVAL AND DEPARTURE — MOMPOX

By plane ASES offers nonstop flights between Cartagena and Mompox, making the city more accessible than ever before (ases.com.co). Aeropuerto San Bernardo lies just 3km northwest of the centre.

By bus The Copetran terminal is on the edge of town at Cra 5 (behind the Cementerio, between Calles 17 and 18). Unitransco services run from its terminal on Cra 3 just south of Callejón de Santa Bárbara (C 14). With one bridge over the Magdalena (between Santa Ana and Talaiga, the road between Santa Marta and Mompox) and a 12km highway linking Magangué and Mompox (including the 2.3km Roncador Bridge), bus travel times have been slashed between Cartagena and Mompox to 3hr 30min.

Destinations from Copetran terminal Bogotá (4 daily; 15–17hr); Bucaramanga (daily; 7–8hr); Medellín (daily; 10–12hr); San Gil (daily; 11–12hr); Santa Marta (daily; 6hr).

Destinations from Unitransco terminal Barranquilla (2 daily; 7hr); Cartagena (daily; 6hr 30min–7hr).

By minibus Cootracegua runs a convenient minibus route between Mompox and Maicao (3–4 daily; 7–8hr), via Valledupar, with onward connections to La Guajira (see page 177) and Maracaibo (Venezuela). These usually depart/drop off 400m south of Plaza Santa Bárbara on Cra 1.

Door to door A door-to-door van ("puerta-a-puerta") can be arranged from Cartagena with Toto Express (310 707 0838; around 6–7hr) departing at 4.30am; Omaira de la Hoz (311 414 8967) runs a similar service from Santa Marta (6–7hr) with 3am or 11am pick-up. Heading back, call *La Casa Amarilla* to book (see page 154), or ask for more information at your hostel.

To/from Tolú/Capurganá Frequent buses link Mompox and Magangué where you can make connections to Sincelejo (1hr 30min); from here there are onward buses to Tolú (1hr), and Necoclí (4–5hr), for the ferry to Capurganá.

ACCOMMODATION

Note that during the Jazz Festival (Sept), Easter, carnival (Feb or March) and the December/January school holidays, prices for hotels in Mompox usually triple and are **booked up** well in advance.

MOMPOX BOAT TOURS

Especially worthwhile if you're interested in local birds and wildlife, **boat trips** from Mompox are a fun way to spend an afternoon and are easily booked through your accommodation. Tours leave around 3pm and generally take three or four hours. Your guide will point out numerous animals and birds that live alongside the Magdalena, such as giant iguanas, monkeys, herons, fishing eagles and kingfishers, and there's usually an opportunity for a swim in one of the lakes, such as the **Ciénaga de Pjinon**, reachable by narrow channels from the main waterway. Returning by boat to Mompox after a quick sunset dip, you'll be greeted by a sixteenth-century vision of how the town would have appeared to new arrivals, with all six of its imposing churches facing the river to welcome you. A popular new tour, **La Valerosa** (312 618 8435) leaves Plaza de la Concepción at 4.30pm daily (2hr), turning into a party boat (especially in high season), with music, bar and dancing.

MOMPOX SILVER

Filigree silver, blending Spanish, Indigenous and Arabic techniques, remains a bargain in Mompox (for now), which has a long tradition of silver craftsmanship. For years travellers have purchased silver jewellery here and sold it back at home for a decent profit, though this opportunistic trade is unlikely to last much longer. Even if prices increase, getting silverware or jewellery made to order in Mompox is likely to be much cheaper than in your own country. The most respected **shops** are located on Calle Real del Medio below Plaza Bolívar: recommended stores include Filimompox at C 23 No. 3–23 (☏ 313 548 2322), and Magalys at C Real del Medio No.17–40.

Bioma Boutique Hotel C Real Del Medio No. 18–59 ⓦ bioma.co; map p.151. Artfully restored colonial home, with spacious, a/c rooms blending antique and contemporary furnishings set around a courtyard. The welcoming staff, lovely garden, tiny pool and rooftop jacuzzi are added bonuses. $$

★ **La Casa Amarilla** Cra 1 No. 13–59 ⓦ lacasaamarillamompos.com; map p.151. Beautifully restored, riverfront colonial building with ten stylish rooms, comfortable beds, colourful murals and laidback, friendly staff. The bright, plant-filled courtyard is great for an afternoon hammock snooze, and the open-air shared kitchen, rooftop terrace, bike rental, book exchange and cable TV are welcome extras. The Anglo-Colombian owners – Richard McColl and his wife Alba – are an excellent source of information and can arrange transport and tours. $$

Casa Roberto Nieto Albaradda (Cra 1) No. 16–43 ☏ 311 714 3145, ✉ martin@bignieto.com; map p.151. Hostel in one of the oldest houses in town, built on the riverfront around 350 years ago, with eight spacious rooms with high ceilings (all have fans or a/c, some with private bathroom) and a dorm with ceiling fan. There's also an apartment with kitchen and space for four to six people ($$$). Owner Martin Nieto is the grandson of the mansion's namesake. Dorms $, doubles $$

★ **Hostal La Casa del Viajero** C 10 No. 1–65 (Callejon de la Cruz) ☏ 320 406 4530, ⓦ hotelenmompox.business.site; map p.151. Spotless, comfortable budget option with super-friendly hosts Juan Manuel and Ligia, local karaoke and salsa experts (not much English spoken, though). The a/c rooms (shared bathrooms) are basic but comfy, and there's a five-bed mixed dorm (also a/c). Shared kitchen; breakfast extra. $

Mebi House Cra 4 No. 21b–56 ⓦ casa-mebi.negocio.site; map p.151. One of the newer budget options, just outside the centre, with clean six-bed dorm and private doubles (all with a/c) managed by the congenial Dimas and his family. $

★ **Portal de la Marquesa** Cra 1 No. 15–27 ☏ 5 761 1712; map p.151. Stylish riverside boutique hotel in another gorgeous Spanish mansion (and another former stopover for Simón Bolívar), with just four, huge, tranquil a/c rooms that overlook the river. Breakfast included. $$

EATING

Life in Mompox is all about the nights, when the temperature drops to bearable levels and everyone comes out to play. **Plaza de Concepción** is the best place to people-watch, while **Plaza Santo Domingo** bustles with popular food stands after 5pm.

Café 1700 Albarrada (Cra 1) No. 15–55 ☏ 313 533 7840; map p.151. Artsy café in a restored colonial house on the riverside, with great coffee (try the cappuccino, carefully prepared salads and tasty sandwiches. $

Comedor Costeño Albarrada (Cra 1) No. 18–45 ☏ 5 685 5263; map p.151. Informal, popular local restaurant, with tables inside an old home and on the breezy riverfront itself. No menus, just a series of special plates such as fried *bocachico* (a local freshwater fish), duck and mouthwatering *bagre* (catfish) with coconut rice, fried plantain and yucca – all come with non-alcoholic drinks. $

★ **El Fuerte** Albarrada (Cra 1), at C 12 No. 163 ☏ 321 818 7038, ⓦ fuertemompox.com; map p.151. The best pizza in the region is served at this stylish restaurant inside the so-called "Fuerte San Anselmo" (actually a colonial warehouse, not a fort), helmed by Austrian expat Walter Maria Gurth, with tables made of rattan and tree trunks shaded by banana palms and a *guadua* bamboo roof. The secret is the wood-burning oven that knocks out authentic thin-crust pizzas with toppings including house-made bacon, mozzarella and blue cheese. $$

Khalilieh Parrilla-Bar Albarrada (Cra 1) No. 17A–54 ☏ 311 603 4300; map p.151. Excellent falafel, Middle East-style roast meats and burgers in an old house on the waterfront, with exposed brick and original, ancient-looking wood doors. $

Panadería Central Cra 2 No 16–01 ☏ 310 373 1077; map p.151. Budget snack option conveniently open all day on Sun, this local bakery sells cakes, savoury pastries, coffee and beer – and has a few small tables inside. $

Puerto Bambú Plaza de Concepción ☏ 312 621 9458; map p.151. This local favourite sets up tables in the Plaza de Concepción every night, very popular with Colombians

for no-frills classics (grilled meats, burgers, *patacones*) and cheap prices. $
Verde Oliva Plaza de Concepción ☎ 318 659 6665; map p.151. The best place for vegetarians, with friendly owner Sandra offering a wide variety of veggie dishes, salads, sandwiches and pizzas (the four-cheese pizza is a speciality), and one of the best wine lists in town. $$

DRINKING AND NIGHTLIFE

Momposinos are well known for partying (any night of the week), and the town even has its own **cumbia** musical superstar in the form of Sonia Bazanta Vides, better known as "Totó la Momposina". Martin Nieto offers **dance classes** (salsa, *merengue*, *bachata*; charge) daily 4–8pm outside *Casa Roberto Nieto* (see page 154). The noisy **kiosks** on the river next to *Casa Amarilla* are a popular place for a beer under the trees, while you can purchase the local wine at **Vinomompox** on Cra 2.
Beraca Plaza de la Concepción (on the Albarrada) ☎ 316 868 2021; map p.151. Famed for its rocking chairs set up over the plaza and overlooking the river each evening, with a selection of local beers and music (and often blaring TV) that ranges from classical to more upbeat salsa at the weekend.
La Barra de Salo Albarrada (Cra 1) No. 17–69 ☎ 301 533 1780; map p.151. This stylish bar, set in an old house on the waterfront just off the Plaza Concepción, offers fabulous wines, foreign beers and microbrews – party nights with DJs make it more like a Latin dance club after midnight. Happy hour daily 4–8pm.

DIRECTORY

Banks and exchange There are several banks in the centre of town; the best for ATMs are Banco Agrario at Cra 2 and C 19, and BBVA on Plaza Bolívar (Cra 2 and C 18).
Festivals Mompox gets packed during the annual Festival de Jazz (early Sept); and during Holy Week (Easter; March/April).

Barranquilla

Despite being Colombia's fourth-largest city (with just under two million inhabitants), capital of the Atlántico *departamento* and its main port on the mouth of the Río Magdalena, **BARRANQUILLA** would be all but overlooked if it were not for its annual **carnival** – Colombia's biggest street party. Outside festival time this swelteringly hot, industrial city has traditionally attracted view tourists, but despite its grim reputation it would be a shame to skip "killa". Quite apart from its literary associations with the fame **Barranquilla group** (see page 156), the historic centre is starting to see signs of regeneration thanks to a booming economy, while the **nightlife** and **culinary scene** in the wealthier (and safer) northwestern districts are worth sampling. It's also just about the friendliest city on the Caribbean, its cultural mix enlivened by a large influx of Arabs (Syrian-Lebanese) and Jews in the late nineteenth century.

Paseo Bolívar

Anchored by **Plaza de Bolívar** in the north, **Paseo Bolívar** (C 33B) was once the central commercial avenue of Barranquilla, running south for a few blocks with a shady central reservation and lined with a mishmash of Republican buildings in varying states of restoration. The plaza itself features an equestrian statue of Simón Bolívar, erected in 1919. The streets either side of the paseo are crammed with shambolic **market stalls** giving the whole area a chaotic but vibrant feel – the area is heavily policed and safe during the day, but best avoided at night.

Iglesia de San Nicolás de Tolentino

Cra 42 No. 33–35 • Free • ☎ 5 340 2247

The historic heart of Barranquilla is **Plaza de San Nicolás**, a wide brick-lined space denuded of most of its character save the spectacular **Iglesia de San Nicolás de Tolentino**, an eye-popping twin-towered confection that was restored in 2011. A church has stood here since at least the 1730s, though the present peach-coloured edifice was

> **THE CAVE AND THE GRUPO DE BARRANQUILLA**
>
> The **Barranquilla Group** of writers, journalists and artists flourished here in the early 1950s, their rebellion against the conservative attitudes prevalent in much of the country making a huge impact on the subsequent development of Colombia. **Gabriel García Márquez**, Álvaro Cepeda Samudio, Germán Vargas and Alfonso Fuenmayor, among others, met, drank and debated together in Barranquilla from 1949; artists such as Alejandro Obregón, Enrique Grau and Cecilia Porras also became associated with the group. In 1954 **La Cueva** opened at Cra 43 No. 59–03 (wfundacionlacueva.org), a coffee shop destined to become a hangout of Márquez and his compadres until it closed in 1969. Reopened in 2002, the "Cave" is now a cultural centre, gallery, bar and restaurant (see page 159). Check out the four elephant footprints marking the spot Obregón rode an actual elephant to the door, his famous portrait *La mujer de mis sueños* (and the gun below it), various photos, paintings and bizarre nooks and crannies. Staff will play you a short video about the group (in English) if you ask.

built piecemeal through the nineteenth and twentieth centuries. The spacious interior contains little ornamentation (it was thoroughly looted during the Bogotazo riots in 1948), though the murals above the altar are exquisite.

Museo del Atlántico

Cra 39 (C Ricaurte) No. 35–21, between Calles 35 and 36 • Free

Housed in the elegant former local government building, the **Museo del Atlántico** is worth a quick peek, with a gallery of local contemporary artists upstairs and the white-arched cellar-like space downstairs dedicated to old photos of the city, temporary art exhibits and archaic printing presses (it's not a museum about the Atlantic Ocean). Originally built to be the home of a local banker, the building served as headquarters of

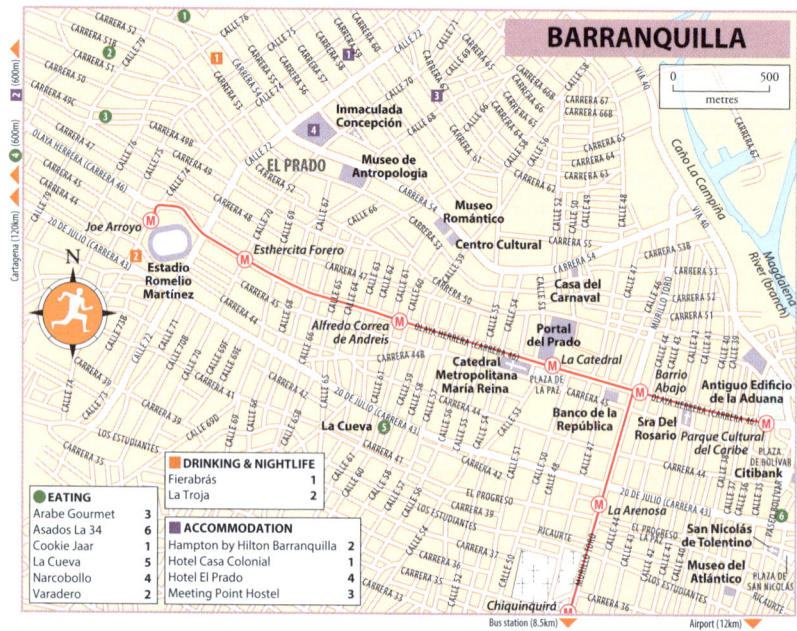

the Atlántico *departamento* between 1921 and 1963, and was restored in 2011. Some of the official government rooms have been preserved upstairs.

Antiguo Edificio de la Aduana
Via 40 No. 36–135 • W clena.org

The artfully restored Customs House, the **Antiguo Edificio de la Aduana**, a Neoclassical pile built in 1918, now serves several functions: part library, part historical archive and part Cámara de Comercio de Barranquilla (chamber of commerce). The complex also includes the old train station, the Estación Montoya, built in 1871 (with an old steam locomotive parked in the garden outside) and Alejandro Obregón's *Simbología de Barranquilla*, a mural created in 1956.

Catedral Metropolitana María Reina
Cra 54 No. 53–122 • Opening hours vary, usually Mass only • T 5 385 4690

Barranquilla's **Catedral Metropolitana María Reina** is a wholly modern edifice perched on the border between Centro and the El Prado neighbourhood. The harsh Modernist exterior, admired by Colombians more than foreign tourists – all triangles and concrete blocks – is mitigated somewhat by the sensational stained glass inside. Work began in 1955, but the behemoth wasn't complete until 1982. In front of the cathedral, the shady **Plaza de la Paz** was built in 1986 in celebration of Pope John Paul II's visit, a leafy, calm spot to escape the sun.

Museo Romántico
Cra 54 No. 59–199 • Charge • T 5 399 9000

Barranquilla's quirkiest attraction, the **Museo Romántico** is a large Spanish Revival mansion replete with period furniture and tiled floors, cluttered with all sorts of bric-a-brac from peeling photos to antiquated typewriters. The early twentieth-century home was once owned by the German-Jewish Freund-Strunz family, and donated as a museum in 1983 – you can still see two Stars of David at the back, and there's a room dedicated to local Jewish history upstairs. Other rooms are crammed with carnival costumes, and there are special exhibits dedicated to Gabriel García Márquez (including the Underwood typewriter on which he allegedly wrote his first novel, *La Hojarasca*), the poets of the Caribbean coast, and Simón Bolívar. Upstairs there's a more conventional gallery covering the various architectural styles prevalent in the city. Spanish labels only.

Museo Antropológico
C 68, between Cra 53 and 54, El Prado • Free • T 5 356 0067

Tucked away inside the handsome campus of the Bellas Artes faculty of the Universidad del Atlántico, the **Museo Antropológico** contains just one main gallery primarily of interest to aficionados of prehistory. Inside, all the main Indigenous cultures of the region are described, with rare ceramic pots on display (some from Tayrona), anthropomorphic images and a replica of the Piedra Pintada petroglyphs; there's also a small section on prehistoric water management technology. Labels are in Spanish only.

ARRIVAL AND DEPARTURE — BARRANQUILLA

By plane Frequent flights connect Barranquilla's Aeropuerto Internacional Ernesto Cortissoz with Bogotá and Medellín (Aerolínea de Antioquia, Avianca, LATAM and Viva Colombia); there are also flights to Cali (Avianca) and Valledupar (EasyFly). Copa Airlines Colombia flies to San Andrés. The airport is 12km south of Centro but much further from most of the better hotels in the north of the city – allow at least 1hr for the journey. Airport-based Asotaeba Taxis

CARNAVAL DE BARRANQUILLA

Four days before Ash Wednesday, the traditional start of Lent in the Catholic Church (Feb or March), Barranquilla drapes itself in a riot of vibrant colours, playful costumes and pulsating music: salsa, *cumbia*, *vallenato* and African drumming. Events ("Precarnaval") set off much earlier, often in mid-January, and once the festivities proper begin, the town converts into one huge street party, kicked off by traditional parades including the "Battle of the Flowers" and "Dance of the Caiman". Parallel to the festivities, the city-sponsored **gay carnival**, though less publicized, is equally bacchanalian. Although barely known outside Latin America, Barranquilla's festivities are second only to Rio's carnival in size. See W carnavaldebarranquilla. org. At other times of year you can visit the **Casa del Carnaval** (charge; T 5 370 5437), Cra 54 No. 49 B–39 (take a taxi), which holds an exhibition on the history of the festival (Spanish labels only).

(T 5 334 8476) charges fixed rates according to destination, with the current amounts clearly marked on boards at the taxi rank – get a ticket at the booth first (but pay the driver). Local buses also shuttle to/from the airport from the city.
Destinations Bogotá (hourly; 1hr 25min); Cali (2 daily; 1hr 25min); Medellín (3–4 daily; 1hr 10min); San Andrés (1–2 daily; 1hr 30min); Valledupar (2 daily; 40min).
By bus The huge bus terminal ("Terminal de Transportes") is 8.5km south of the city centre at Cra 14, C 62 (allow 30–45min by taxi). For Santa Marta/Taganga and Cartagena consider convenient puerta-a-puerta (door-to-door) minibuses via BerlinasTur (W facebook.com/Berlinastur Oficial) or MarSol (W transportesmarsol.com).
Destinations Bogotá (every 30min–hourly; 17hr); Cartagena (every 30min; 2hr); Medellín (hourly; 14hr); Mompox (2 daily; 7hr); Santa Marta (every 30min; 2hr).

GETTING AROUND

By taxi Try to always use radio taxis (T 5 322 2222 or T 5 386 8686). Taxis do not use meters – fix a price before you get in.
By bus Buses (no a/c) can be tough to work out on a short visit, though routes are posted in the front window on a small sign – you can flag them down anywhere on the street. Barranquilla's dedicated Transmetro (W transmetro. gov.co) service (similar to the Transmilenio system in Bogotá) is of limited use to tourists, but does provide a fast connection between the old centre (the cathedral) and the edge of El Prado (daily 5am–11pm); you need to purchase a rechargeable Transmetro card from any of the stations to use the system.

ACCOMMODATION

Arrange accommodation well in advance if you visit during **carnival**. **Centro** can be unsafe at night, but this is where you'll find the cheapest options – most of the better hotels lie several kilometres to the northwest in **El Prado** and beyond.
Hampton by Hilton Barranquilla C 85 No. 50–25, El Prado W hamptoninn3.hilton.com; map p.156. The best of the chain hotels in this part of town, with a sleek boutique feel and bright, contemporary-style rooms (plus gym and motel-style breakfast). $$$
Hotel Casa Colonial Cra 59 No. 72–129, El Prado W hotelcasacolonialbarranquilla.com; map p.156. Knowledgeable host Doña Amparo runs a cosy guesthouse offering cheaper rates than most El Prado hotels, located in a beautiful colonial-style home with a tranquil courtyard. Simple a/c rooms have flatscreen TVs. $$
Hotel El Prado Cra 54 No. 70–10, El Prado W hotelel pradobarranquilla.com; map p.156. This grand hotel, built in the 1920s, has been superseded by newer luxury options, but it's hard to beat for colonial atmosphere, with old-fashioned rooms (black-and-white-tiled floors, wood furnishings and high ceilings), huge breakfasts and a relaxing sun deck and pool. $$
Meeting Point Hostel Cra 61 No. 68–100, El Prado T 304 343 4299; map p.156. Backpacker hub in a family house with four- to eight-bed dorms and a/c singles and doubles in a busy, safe area, plus terrace with hammocks and shared TV room. Cash only. Dorms and doubles available. $

EATING

★ **Arabe Gourmet** Cra 49 C No. 76–181 W arabe gourmetrestaurante.co; map p.156. Set in what looks like an old colonial church, with beautifully prepared Lebanese and other Middle Eastern dishes, from succulent lamb and chicken kebabs to crispy falafel and minty salads. $$
Asados La 34 C 34 No. 43–110 (Paseo Bolívar) T 5 370 1566; map p.156. Best of the street canteens in the centre, with a few tables, benches and bar stools and knocking out delicious *pasteles* and more substantial plates of sausages (morcilla and *chorizo antioqueño*) and steaks. $

Cookie Jaar C 53 No. 41–46 ☏ 314 527 1081; map p.156. Tiny modern chain selling delicious American-style cookies, served warm and gooey. Flavours range from choc chunk and s'more to red velvet and Reese's (peanut butter). $

La Cueva Cra 43 No. 59–03 ⓦ fundacionlacueva.org; map p.156. The food here, once the famed social hub of the Barranquilla group (see page 156) is fairly typical Colombian Caribbean cuisine (fish, roast chicken, mango margaritas and the like), but the live music and historic ambience makes it worth the trip (it's a bit like eating in a lavish museum). $$$

★ **Narcobollo** Cra 43 No. 84–188 ⓦ narcobollo.com; map p.156. This iconic canteen chain is celebrated in Barranquilla for its delicious *bollo costeño* (a kind of traditional bun) in various flavours (sweet potato, coconut and corn, as well as various *fritos*, *pasteles* and *quibbe* (Lebanese kibbeh). $

Varadero Cra 51B No. 79–97 ☏ 5 385 5552, ⓦ varadero restaurante.co; map p.156. Enticing Cuban restaurant specializing in fresh fish and shellfish. Choose from ceviches and red snapper with *patacones* and coconut rice or seafood stew – or perhaps a Cuban classic like *ropa vieja* – and wash it all down with a tasty mojito. $$

DRINKING AND NIGHTLIFE

★ **Fierabrás** Cra 53 No. 75–64 ☏ 310 685 5333; map p.156. Barranquilla's very own microbrewery was founded in 2008, serving three main English-style beers on draft– María Antonieta (pale ale), Dulcinea (brown ale) and Juana de Arco (porter) – plus seasonal ales. Nachos, burgers and sandwiches are also available.

★ **La Troja** Cra 44 No. 72–263 ⓦ latroja.org; map p.156. This no-frills bar, with plastic tables and chairs spilling out into the street, morphs into one of the most popular salsa dance clubs in the city (it's been around since 1967 – look for the tributes to salsa legend Joe Arroyo). A classic Barranquilla experience, always packed with a mix of locals and visitors.

Santa Marta and around

Colombia's oldest city and the capital of Magdalena, **SANTA MARTA** lies at the heart of a region rich in attractions, from white Caribbean beaches and the backpacker resort of **Taganga** to the coffee plantations and refreshing mountain air of **Minca**, not to mention **Aracataca**, the birthplace of **Gabriel García Márquez** and the inspiration for the fictional Macondo.

Santa Marta itself is in the midst of a major transformation, though the development of tourism sits uneasily with its continued role as major coal and oil exporter. The **Centro Histórico** is certainly no Cartagena, but the narrow colonial streets and buildings that remain after years of neglect are gradually being restored, and the government is pouring millions into much needed regeneration. While parts of the old town remain run down, the blend of ramshackle mansions and unfiltered, salsa-soaked *costeño* street life oozes character, and the growing number of sensitively converted boutique hotels, hostels, restaurants and bars – not to mention the friendliness of the local *samarios* – makes this an enticing base for exploring the surrounding area.

Brief history

The Bahía de Santa Marta was discovered by Spanish Conquistador **Rodrigo de Bastidas** in 1501, but it wasn't until 1525 that he returned to establish a Spanish colony as governor, the first in Colombia. Things didn't go well for Santa Marta, however. Bastidas faced a mutiny almost immediately, and the city was continually attacked by Indigenous tribes – fighting with the **Tairona** went on till their final defeat in 1600 (when their leader Cuchacique was dismembered by the Spanish, and Tairona villages were razed to the ground). Add to that "pirate" assaults from the French and English (Francis Drake three times, Walter Raleigh once) – Santa Marta was attacked some 46 times between 1543 and 1779 – and it's no wonder the city remained in Cartagena's shadow for much of the colonial period, despite the importation of large numbers of African slaves. Santa Marta gained infamy as the place where **Simón Bolívar died** in 1830 (vividly re-created in Gabriel García Márquez's *General in His Labyrinth*), while a massive earthquake destroyed much of the old city in 1834.

THE CARIBBEAN COAST SANTA MARTA AND AROUND

> **SAFETY IN SANTA MARTA**
>
> Santa Marta – and even Taganga – has had a reputation for **street crime**, though in recent years a major police presence in both places had improved security. Nonetheless it pays to take care: the long-running, on-again, off-again conflict here between drug gangs rarely affects tourists, but Santa Marta is a city with a large indigent population, some of whom struggle to make a living and who resent the gentrification of the old centre; there's also a noticeable homeless problem. The streets are generally safe during the day, but take extra care at night; muggings by desperate individuals (or gangs) do occur. Stick to well-lit and busy streets, and do not wander around with tablets, smartphones or anything valuable – ask at your hostel or hotel about the latest situation. Official taxis are safe for trips in the city.

Things started to turn around in the 1840s (as Cartagena's fortunes waned), despite a devastating cholera epidemic in 1849. Santa Marta's port boomed as the surrounding plantations produced huge amounts of tobacco and later bananas, helped on by the arrival of railways in the 1880s and America's **United Fruit Company** in 1899 (which virtually monopolized banana production into the 1960s, despite a major strike and massacre of Colombian workers in 1928). Today it's palm oil that keeps the plantations booming, not bananas, while coal is the major export at the city's port. Santa Marta is also famous in Colombia for its **footballers**; it was the birthplace of **Carlos "El Pibe" Valderrama**, the eccentric midfielder with the unforgettable blond Afro, and current captain of the national team **Radamel Falcao**, aka El Tigre, who plays for AS Monaco.

Centro Histórico

Though Santa Marta's beach district of Rodadero attracts more Colombian tourists, the area of the city of most interest to foreigners is the **Centro Histórico**, still something of an acquired taste but which definitely grows on you – it's a boiling, ramshackle blend of colonial ruins and hip renovations, incessant salsa and *vallenato*, fruit sellers, a no-frills *malecón* and extremely laidback locals. The busier commercial section of town (and market) lies west of Carrera 5, the chaotic main north–south thoroughfare, while most of the historic attractions lie to the east. In the evenings tables fill the streets outside the restaurants and bars, and things stay busy late into the night; but note that most of the old town beyond these areas gets completely deserted after 6pm – stick to the main streets.

Catedral de Santa Marta
Cra 5 No. 16–30 (Plaza de Catedral) • Free • ☏ 315 678 2845

The stark, brick-paved **Plaza de Catedral** is dominated by the sparkling white **Catedral de Santa Marta**, with its Moorish bell tower and Neo-Romanesque stone portico dating mostly from the eighteenth century. The Neoclassical interior isn't especially interesting, but just to the left of the entrance is the marble monument to **Rodrigo de Bastidas**, the town's founder, whose remains are buried here (he actually died in Santiago de Cuba in 1527). Simón Bolívar was also interred here until 1842, when his body was repatriated to his native Caracas (Venezuela) – plaques mark the spot near the altar where his heart (allegedly) still remains. This is also the church where, in 1926, the parents of Gabriel García Márquez were married.

The elegantly faded Republican edifice on the north side of the plaza was built in 1914 as the Alcaldía (town hall), then served as the Concejo Distrital de Santa Marta (district council office) – a plan to convert it into a **Museo y Centro de Memoria** (commemorating Colombia's civil war) has been touted for years, without much progress.

Plaza de San Francisco
Cra 4, between Calles 13 and 14

Brick-lined **Plaza de San Francisco** is a smaller version of Plaza de Catedral, dominated by the modest colonial facade of **Iglesia de San Francisco** (C 13 No. 3–77; nominally daily 7am–8pm, but often closed; ☏ 5 421 0516), built in the 1770s but burned to the ground in 1962. The interior is a dreary modern replacement from the 1960s, but this is a much livelier church than the cathedral. Adjacent Calle 13 is lined with **art and craft stalls**.

Plaza de Bolívar
Calles 14 and 15, between Cra 2B and the Malecón (Cra 1)

The wide, largely empty space of **Plaza de Bolívar** stands on the location of Santa Marta's original Plaza Mayor, though nothing remains from that period. The main canary-coloured building on the north side is the old Palacio Consistorial (where Antonio Nariño was imprisoned in 1809), now the **Alcaldía** (city hall). The shady, park-like section at the western end contains an equestrian statue of Bolívar, while across Carrera 1 stands a noble image of Rodrigo de Bastidas himself.

The Malecón

The **Malecón** (boardwalk) stretches some 700m from the port to the marina in the south. It's a hot but pleasant place to stroll, despite the cranes of the container port looming just to the north – there's even a beach (Playa Santa Ana) at the southern end (swimming definitely not recommended). Some 3km offshore, the small island of **El Morro** once guarded the harbour (the fort is now a ruin, but the lighthouse is clearly visible).

Museo del Oro Tairona
C 14 No. 2–7, Plaza de Bolívar (entrance on Cra 2) • Free • ☏ 5 421 0251

The enlightening **Museo del Oro Tairona**, set inside the magnificently restored Casa de la Aduana (Customs House), is one of the best museums on the Caribbean coast, with everything labelled in English. On the ground floor, galleries feature an artfully curated ensemble of pre-Hispanic ceramics, nephrite jade pendants and copper and gold metalwork from the local **Nahuange** (200–900 AD) and **Tairona** (900–1600) cultures. There's also an intriguing room (and video, with English subtitles) dedicated to foreign explorers of the Magdalena region. Upstairs there's a comprehensive exhibit on the history of the region and its peoples, including the Indigenous Wintukua (Arhuaco), Kogi, Wiwa (Arsanio) and Kankuamo, as well as a section on the Customs House itself, which is a real gem. With wooden garrets underneath a pitched tile roof dating from 1730, it was built for local merchants the Jimeno brothers (it doesn't really date from the sixteenth century, as legend claims). It served as the customs house from 1819 into the 1820s, but was mostly used as commercial space (United Fruit was here in the 1920s), until 1979. **Simón Bolívar** stayed here briefly in 1830 before going on to the Quinta (see below), and his body lay in state in an upstairs gallery after his death. Another small exhibition on the first floor commemorates the association.

Museo de Arte
Cra 2 No. 16–44 • Free • 5 431 8536

The old Seminario San Juan Nepomuceno, dating back to the 1670s (but extended many times through to 1811), now serves as a cultural centre and the **Museo de Arte**, run by the Universidad de Magdalena and principally a showcase for local contemporary artists (exhibits rotate). Quality is usually quite good, and you'll get the chance to wander both floors of the cloister, a shady space lined with a small exhibition on Tairona culture (Spanish labels only).

Parque de los Novios
Calles 19 and 20, between Carreras 2 and 3

The regeneration of Santa Marta is most in evidence around shaded **Parque de los Novios** (also known as Parque Santander) and the adjacent pedestrianized strip of **Calle 19**, lined with bars, cafés and gourmet restaurants. The square itself features the delicate **Templete del Parque Santander** (which looks like an ornamental gazebo), completed in 1935, a statue of independence hero General Francisco de Paula Santander, and a bust of ex-president Manuel Murillo Toro.

On the south side of the plaza, the **Palacio Justicia** (C 20 No. 2A–20) is one of the city's greatest examples of 1920s Neoclassical design.

Quinta de San Pedro Alejandrino

Av Libertador (Via Mamatoco), 5km southeast of the Centro Histórico • Daily 9am–5.30pm (6pm in high season); last entry 1hr before closing • Charge; guided tours in Spanish (and sometimes English) included, but tips are expected • museobolivariano.org.co • Buses leaving the Malecón (Cra 1) for Mamatoco will drop you off – if you ask the driver– at the Quinta main gate (from where it's a short walk to the actual entrance); alternatively taxis run to this spot (just walk back to the main road to flag down buses or taxis heading back)

In 1830, a disillusioned and exhausted **Simón Bolívar** arrived in Santa Marta on his way to Cartagena and Europe, having resigned his presidency and all hopes for his "Gran Colombia". The old revolutionary got as far as the hacienda of **Quinta de San Pedro Alejandrino**, owned by rich (and sympathetic) Spaniard Joaquín de Mier, where he died of tuberculosis on December 17 – he was just 47 years old. As García Márquez wrote in *The General in His Labyrinth*: "I'm old, sick, tired, disillusioned, harassed, slandered, and unappreciated."

Whether or not you have a particular interest in South America's liberation hero, the former sugar plantation is an alluring half-day trip, set in lush, tranquil grounds, complete with an enchanted forest of twisted tamarind trees and creeping vines.

The hacienda

Founded in 1608 by a Spanish priest (who brought a holy image of San Pedro Alejandrino with him from Cádiz), the mustard-coloured buildings you see today were mostly constructed in the eighteenth century when the **hacienda** became a prosperous sugar plantation; the old house itself features a chapel, various period rooms (including a bathroom with original Italian-marble tub) and exhibits dedicated to Bolívar, culminating in the actual bedroom where the Libertador passed away – the clock was stopped at the exact moment, and the original camp bed (now draped with a Colombian flag) and red velvet armchair used by Bolívar have been preserved. Outside are the remains of eighteenth-century outhouses associated with the sugar cane industry, while the French saloon carriage used to bring Bolívar here from Santa Marta is preserved in the stables. Everything is labelled in English.

Altar de la Patria and Museo Bolivariano de Arte Contemporaneo

The modern section of the estate is anchored by the grand **Plaza de Banderas** and the **Altar de la Patria**, initiated in 1930 to mark the centenary of Bolívar's death. Though the grand marble monument of Bolívar inside the altar makes it look a bit like a mausoleum, it's not – he's buried in Caracas, Venezuela. Just to the right lies the **Museo Bolivariano de Arte Contemporaneo**, a series of small galleries featuring changing exhibits by contemporary Latin American artists.

El Rodadero

12km south of town • From Centro Histórico pick up buses on the Malecón (Cra 1) or C 22 (15–20min); in El Rodadero buses run along Cra 4, three blocks from the beach

A short ride south through a gap in the hills from downtown Santa Marta, **El Rodadero** has been the city's beach resort since the 1940s, with a mix of high-rise condos and hotels. A bit like Bocagrande in Cartagena (and the complete antithesis of budget Taganga), it primarily attracts Colombian tourists and gets totally swamped in December and January. The grey-sand beach (backed by a line of shady palm trees) isn't bad, and the water is calm and good for swimming, but the main reason to visit is to soak up the good-natured mayhem of a Colombian holiday resort: families playing in the sand, buskers from Argentina, pedalboats, *papayera* playing regional *vallenato* music, booming reggaeton bars and all sorts of seafood snacks and drinks being hawked up and down the promenade (Cra 1). It's fun (and well policed) at night, too.

Playa Blanca

Lanchas depart the far right-hand corner of Rodadero beach throughout the day (charge per person, min 5 people)

Pristine **Playa Blanca** lies just 15 minutes from Rodadero by boat near the Punta de Gaira, a wonderful strip of unspoiled, chalky white sand. Rent a cabaña when you arrive (there's otherwise little shade), and order food and drinks directly from the restaurants at the back of the beach. Though it gets crowded at weekends, the beach is much quieter during the week.

Acuario Rodadero

Taxi Marino office at Cra 1 No. 7–69, at C 8 • Charge, includes return boat transport; extra with Playa Blanca • ⓦ acuariosantamarta.com

Comprising thirteen saltwater pools, fifteen glass tanks and a small museum of various shark jaws, archeological items, dissected fish and even a section (randomly) on the *Titanic*, the **Acuario Rodadero** lies in a small bay (Ensenada Inca) a few minutes' boat ride from the main beach at El Rodadero, just south of Playa Blanca (boats depart near the ticket office). Sadly, the aquarium also features dubious dolphin "shows", which are definitely not recommended.

ARRIVAL AND DEPARTURE SANTA MARTA

By plane Santa Marta's Simón Bolívar airport is 16km south of the city centre. Taking a taxi into the city centre is straight forward (confirm the rate before getting in; no meters). Local buses also run up and down the main highway ("Aeropuerto") between the airport and the Centro Histórico via El Rodadero, but it can be a long, cramped and sweaty ride. Heading back, pick them up on the Malecón (Cra 1) or C 22.
Destinations Bogotá (12 daily; 1hr 30min); Medellín (3 daily; 1hr 30min).
By bus The Terminal de Transportes (main bus station) lies 5km southeast of the city centre at C 41 No. 31–17. For Barranquilla, Cartagena or Palomino consider convenient puerta-a-puerta (door-to-door) minibuses via MarSol (w transportesmarsol.com). Heading to Taganga, just take a local bus from the Centro Histórico (see page 161). Minibuses for Tayrona (see page 171), Palomino (see page 176) and Minca (see page 168) depart from their offices near the market.
Destinations Aracataca (every 30min; 1hr 30min); Barranquilla (hourly; 2hr); Bogotá (30 daily, mostly overnight; 17hr); Bucaramanga (3 daily; 10hr); Cartagena (hourly; 4hr); Medellín (11 daily; 15hr); Mompox (1 daily; 6hr); Riohacha (hourly; 3hr)
By car National Car Rental (w nationalcar.com) has branches at Santa Marta airport (t 5 422 8812) and at Cra 4A No. 11 in Rodadero (same contact).

INFORMATION AND GETTING AROUND

Tourist information Fontur operates a tourist office in the bus station, small kiosks at the airport and on the Malecón that sometimes have English speakers but not much printed info.
By taxi The city centre is small enough to explore on foot, but consider taxis for longer journeys, or for getting around the centre at night (when there is a chance of muggings). Official taxis are safe for trips in the city.

TOURS AND ACTIVITIES

Magic Tour C 16 No. 4–41 w magictourcolombia.com. Lost City (Ciudad Perdida) specialists (see page 174).
★ **Samoa Boat Trips** w hotelcasacarolina.com. Speedboat owned by the folks at *Casa Carolina* (see page 164) departing daily (8.30am–4.30pm) from the Marina to Tayrona National Park. Stops include at least one isolated beach – such as jaw-dropping Chengue (which you'll likely have to yourself) – Bahía Concha (where lunch is provided for an extra charge), plus snorkelling off Taganga. Minimum six people.
Santa Marta Dive & Adventure C 17 No. 2–43 w santamartadiveandadventure.com.co. The local dive school offers a full programme of dive courses and fun dives off Tayrona. Dive packages include hotel pick-up.
★ **Wi Make Tours** C 19 No. 3–121 w wimaketours.com. Small outfit specializing in magical hiking trips in the Sierra Nevada, including a two-day climb up Cerro Kennedy (3100m); one to four-day packages.

ACCOMMODATION

Hostels and hotels are plentiful in Santa Marta, but book well in advance in December and January, when **prices** can double.
Aluna C 21 No. 5–72 w alunahostel.com; map p.160. Peaceful hostel, beautifully designed around a 1920s villa by Dublin-born architect and owner Patrick Flemming. Paintings by local artists line the walls, rooms are spotless and fresh, thanks to wooden slats that allow air to circulate, and a bamboo roof offers welcome shade from the blazing midday sun. Excellent book exchange and a great little café on the premises (breakfast is extra). Pricier rooms have a/c. $\overline{\$}$
La Brisa Loca C 14 No. 3–58 w labrisaloca.com; map p.160. This sprawling converted mansion is owned by two party-loving Californian dudes and has firmly established itself as a backpacker party hostel, with spacious dorms, a roof terrace (and balconies overlooking the street), lively late-night bar and a well-used pool. It attracts a mostly younger international crowd; don't come here for a quiet time. The helpful bilingual staff are a plus. $\overline{\$}$
La Casa C 18 No. 3–115 w lacasadeltotumo.com; map p.160. Luxurious rooms in a variety of contemporary styles (inspired by themes as diverse as New York and Simón Bolívar), with a beguiling roof deck overlooking the cathedral and in-house massages. Breakfast included. $\overline{\$\$\$}$
★ **Casa Carolina** C12 No. 3–40 w hotelcasacarolina.com; map p.160. Fabulous boutique hotel carved out of an old colonial mansion, with a stylish wooden bar and restaurant (*Eli's*) – opening out onto an elegant central pool courtyard – and a roof deck with hot tub. Rooms are luxurious, from standards to suites, with cable TV and friendly English-speaking staff. Breakfast included. $\overline{\$\$\$}$
Don Pepe C 16 No. 1–92 w hotelboutiquedonpepe.com; map p.160. This lavish colonial palace contains just twelve stylish rooms combining exposed brick and period antiques with contemporary furnishings and amenities. The spa and roof deck are spectacular. $\overline{\$\$\$\$}$
Dreamer Hostel C 51 No. 26D–161, Magdalena w thedreamerhostel.com; map p.160. Some 5km out of town, but more than worth it for the atmosphere, this huge backpacker favourite has a pool in a hammock-bedecked courtyard, Italian food on the menu and a plethora of day-trips organized by the friendly staff. Breakfast is extra.

Dorms $, doubles $$.
Hostels Colombia Santa Marta C 14 No. 3–42 ☎ 5 430 4862; map p.160. Converted hostel with stylish dorms (each bunk has its own curtain for privacy), simple but spotless doubles (some en suite) with fans or a/c, and a tantalizing rooftop terrace with hammocks, showers, kitchen and sofas. Can be noisy at night. $

Hotel San Miguel Imperial C 21 No. 6–96 w hotelsan miguel.com.co; map p.160. This mid-range hotel with a rooftop pool has a view over the parkland next door and the rate includes a decent breakfast. It's not as luxurious as its neighbours but a good option if you won't be spending much time here away from sightseeing. $$$

★ **La Villana Hostel** C 17 No. 3–70 ☎ 350 821 4939; map p.160. Justly popular hostel, a small, cosy and artful renovation of a 1720 colonial house, with bright, Ikea-like dorms, a small pool and one simple en-suite double (the "pink room"). Dorms $, doubles $$.

EATING

While there are scores of places in town, eating in **El Rodadero** is a lot of fun in high season, with snacks on the beach, seafront bars and heaps of cheap places behind the *malecón*. Look out for *Tinto "Super Lucho"*, a tiny mobile coffee stall and something of a local institution on the *malecón* opposite C 6.

Bendito Café Cra 4 No. 16–16 (Plaza de Catedral) ☎ 5 432 2728; map p.160. This old-school café on the main plaza is an ideal a/c spot for coffee, coconut lemonade, smoothies, cakes and free wi-fi. $

★ **La Canoa Café Cultural** C 18 No. 3–75 ☎ 318 614 3260; map p.160. This inviting white-and-black themed café and French restaurant serves excellent róbalo (sea bass), breakfasts and huge stuffed paninis. $

Chucho Blu Cra 1, at C 3, El Rodadero ☎ 310 241 7325; map p.160. Stylish restaurant and lounge bar at the far end of the beach with potent cocktails, fresh seafood and nonstop music – come early to grab a table with the best views. $$

Ikaro Café C 19 No. 3–60 w ikarocafe.com; map p.160. Huge backpacker hangout for good reason – it's a spacious café with vegan/vegetarian/gluten-free dishes (mostly Thai and Vietnamese), free wi-fi and excellent Soul Seed Coffee (with almond, coconut or soy milk). The coffee is grown on their farm in the Sierra Nevada de Santa Marta, with the profits going to the Fundación Donama (dedicated to social and ecological projects). Lounge on recycled furniture or pallet couches and admire the hanging garden wall. $$

★ **Juancho Cevicheria** C 22, between Cra 1 and 2 ☎ 316 577 0439; map p.160. Serving seafood cocktails since 1973, this legendary food stall has moved into permanent a/c premises. Fresh cups of shrimp, octopus and conch (*caracol*) in zesty salsa come in four sizes of polystyrene cup, served with crackers. The main branch is a block south on Cra 1, between C 22 and C 24 $

Lulo Cra 3 No. 16–34 ☎ 320 476 8870; map p.160. Friendly owners Melissa Ford and David Alvarez whip up fantastic breakfasts at this bright café. Try the delicious "Ranchera" *arepa* made from natural corn, served with cheese, egg, beans and chorizo, or their ranges of paninis and pitas for lunch and juices and smoothies at anytime. Free wi-fi. $

Marc de Sabores C 20 No. 3–39 (just off Parque de los Novios) ☎ 5 422 6562; map p.160. Excellent seafood for reasonable prices, including wonderfully fresh and zesty ceviche, stuffed mojarra and creamy lobster rice. $$

Ouzo Cra 3 No. 19–29 (Parque de los Novios) w grupo ouzo.com/en/ouzo; map p.160. Quality Mediterranean-style cuisine with a focus, naturally, on Greek specialities like gyros, *keftedes* (meatballs) and meze, but also crispy wood-fired pizzas. Ideal location on the square, with indoor or outdoor tables shaded by the palms. $$$

Radio Burger Cra 3 No. 18–52 w radioburger.co ; map p.160. If not quite the best burger in Colombia, the best on the coast, though it's a little pricey. The building was once a radio station HQ, with the current decor reflecting its history (it also has very welcome a/c). $$

DRINKING AND NIGHTLIFE

Parque de los Novios and pedestrianized C 19 are the main **nightlife hubs** in the Centro Histórico, though things are always lively along the beach at **El Rodadero**.

La Bodeguita Pirata C 20 No. 3–16 ☎ 301 547 2123; map p.160. Opening in 2017, this French-Colombian joint quickly became one of the city's top party spots, with great music and potent cocktails.

★ **Charlie's Bar and Grill** C 19 No. 4–12 ☎ 321 686 0158, w facebook.com/charliesbarcolombia; map p.160. Delicious mojitos are a speciality at this congenial pub just off the Parque de los Novios, with a blend of antique and new furnishings, a breezy terrace and the indomitable Charlie (originally from Chicago) himself usually in attendance.

Addictive buffalo wings are served to accompany the booze **Crab's Bar** C 18 No. 3–69 ☎ 315 796 3636, w facebook.com/crabsbar; map p.160. Rock and blues pub with a small stage for live acts, brick-lined bar, terrace and pool table – the all-night rock'n'roll soundtrack makes a refreshing break from *vallenato* and reggaeton.

Mi Casa es Tu Casa Cra 3 No. 3–39 (Parque de los Novios) ☎ 304 526 7916; map p.160. A popular lounge bar and restaurant (it's better for drinks than food), with a cool open-air roof deck upstairs overlooking the plaza.

La Puerta C 17 No. 2–29 ☎ 317 384 8839; map p.160. Local students and foreign backpackers in their 20s and 30s frequent this jam-packed, sexy club. Salsa, electronica and international club hits will have you sweating on the narrow dancefloor that snakes into a warren of nooks and crannies. Cool off on the outdoor patio if the crowd gets too much. No cover.

★ **Siete Mares Santa Marta** Marina Internacional de Santa Marta Cra 1 no. 22–93 • 321 822 6020; map p.160. This venue in Santa Marta quickly garnered a loyal following thanks to its stylish lounge-bar vibe, house and electronica music and commanding views across the bay and marina.

DIRECTORY

Festivals Las Fiestas del Mar (The Festival of the Sea) is one of Santa Marta's biggest celebrations (late July and early Aug) with beauty pageants, parades and street parties. Other dates to note include Día de Brujitas (Halloween), which tends to be another big booze-up, and Día de las Velitas (Dec 8), the "night of candles" held to commemorate the Inmaculada Concepción (the traditional beginning of the Christmas period).
Post office C 22 No. 2–21; Servientrega is at C 13 No. 2–27.
Visa extensions Centro Facilitador de Servicios Migratorios, C 22 No. 13–A 88, Barrio Los Alcazares (• 5 421 7794).

Taganga

The ramshackle fishing village of **TAGANGA**, 4km north of Santa Marta (just over the hill), is a well-established backpacker hangout, where travellers come to dive, explore the Parque Nacional Natural Tayrona (see page 171) or just party, both before and after they tackle the Ciudad Perdida hike (see page 174). Its location is certainly picturesque, hemmed in by arid hills studded with cacti and facing a calm, deep blue horseshoe-shaped bay, but the actual **beach** here is fairly unappealing (though people do swim at the southern end). The village remains relatively good value, if a bit down-at-heel (most of the roads are dirt tracks, only very slowly being surfaced), inhabited by a mix of Colombian hippies, local fishermen and a smattering of international visitors – don't expect some sort of tropical paradise. Nightlife can get noisy and rowdy, and there have been security issues in the past (including muggings), though an increased police presence seems to have improved things considerably in recent years.

There's nothing to see in the village itself, though the simple adobe church of **San Francisco de Asís** on the tiny plaza (Cra 2 and C 14; only open usually during Mass) is certainly evocative of colonial Colombia (even though much of what you see today was reconstructed in the 1930s). Note that the village has no street signs as yet, but streets are informally numbered according to the typical grid, with Carrera 1 running along the bayfront between Calles 18 and 11.

The beaches

Playaca is an undeveloped beach some 2km from Taganga, back on the road to Santa Marta – buses between the city and Taganga will drop you at the dirt track, signposted, that leads down to the beach. Flag them down to get back.

Accessible by boat (5min) or on foot (20min) from Taganga, **Playa Grande** is modestly sized, heavily touristed and a bit pebbly, but still has the makings for a day of sun and sea. To get there follow the trail at the end of waterfront Carrera 1 (passing *Bahia Taganga* on the cliff), and walk through the hills.

ARRIVAL AND INFORMATION — TAGANGA

By taxi A taxi from the centre of Santa Marta is inexpensive but agree the price with the driver before you set off. If you're coming from the bus terminal, it will be a little extra. Taxi Taganga (• 5 423 0247) has a convenient booth with dispatchers on Cra 2, at C 18 (near the police station) in Taganga, with set prices to all destinations (include Tayrona, see page 171).

By bus Local minibuses zip regularly between Santa Marta and Taganga. In Santa Marta they usually head north along Cra 5, turn right on the Av del Ferrocarril and proceed to the market before turning north. In Taganga they pass along paved Cra 2 and terminate at the waterfront (Cra 1 at C 11) where the boats to Tayrona and Playa Grande depart. Daily minibus transfers to Tayrona National Park are best arranged through your accommodation.

Tourist information There's a tourist information kiosk on the waterfront (Cra 1, between C 17 and 18; daily 8.30am–6pm) operated by the tourist police, where you can pick up maps of Taganga (English is rarely spoken).

BOATS TO PARQUE NACIONAL NATURAL TAYRONA

Taganga makes a good base from which to explore Tayrona National Park (see page 171). Local **boats** depart the beach at the northern end of the village (at C 11) in the mornings up to 10.30am, with prices fixed and always including the return journey (check the times): Bahía Concha is one hour; Playa Cristal is one hour and 15minutes; and Cabo San Juan is one hour by speedboat. The park entry fee is extra and is paid on arrival. Book in advance with the boatmen on the beach (⊙301 566 6925), with tour agents or at your hostel, as spaces are limited.

ACTIVITIES AND TOURS

Ciudad Perdida treks, organized tours to Tayrona National Park and La Guajira, as well as various **dive trips** (see page 167) are offered by bigger agents on the main drag, and along the beach.

Magic Tours C 14 No. 1B–50 ⓦmagictourcolombia.com. Just up from the *malecón*, this reputable operator organizes treks to Perdida and various hikes and boat trips into Tayrona.

ACCOMMODATION

Casa Baloo Cra 2 No. 18–347 ⊙318 308 3719. Intimate, friendly digs with welcoming hosts and a huge terrace with expansive views across the bay. The rooms are quiet and clean, with free drinking water and breakfast included. $\overline{\$\$}$
Casa de Felipe Cra 5A No. 19–13 ⓦlacasadefelipe.com. Three blocks uphill from the beach, with beautiful views of the bay and a lush, greenery-filled garden, the rustic rooms at this long-time backpacker fave fill up quickly – book in advance. Plenty of information on exploring the area is available. They also offer private apartments for up to five people. Dorms & doubles $, apartments $\overline{\$\$}$
Casa Los Cerros Cra 2 No. 1–35 ⊙313 656 2026. Spotless a/c studios high above the village, with stellar views across the bay, kitchenettes (fridge, microwave) and hammocks. Breakfast included. $\overline{\$\$}$
Hostel Divanga B&B C 12 No. 4–07 ⓦdivanga.com. This French-run hostel has a small pool surrounded by hammocks, an upstairs bar, a sociable vibe and wonderfully friendly staff. Dorms and rooms (with fan or a/c) are compact but spotless and the on-site restaurant is one of the best in town. $\overline{\$}$
Taganga Beach Hotel Cra 1 no. 18–49 ⊙315 509 5443. Amazing location right on the beachfront, with basic but modern en-suite rooms featuring a/c and satellite TV, and the excellent *Taco Beach Bar* on site. Breakfast included. $\overline{\$\$}$

EATING

★ **Babaganoush** Cra 1 No. 18–22 (3/F, above the Tayrona Dive Center on road back to Santa Marta) ⊙314 651 8934. Diner overlooking the sea featuring the sumptuous culinary creations of Dutch-born chef Patrick Verdegaal, who whips up everything from Thai green curries to seafood spaghetti. $\overline{\$\$}$

★ **Divijuca Restaurante Bar** C 1 No.1210 (just off the malecón) ⊙300 700 9552. This no frills restaurant is always a popular spot. Mains include grilled chicken with plantains, rice and beans. $\overline{\$}$

Pachamama C 16 No. 1C–18 ⊙5 433 1144. On a backstreet just off the *malecón*, this tiki-bar-cum-tapas-bar serves some of the most imaginative offerings in town. The tapas plates are small, so you can have quite a few. Choose from the likes of *kefta* (spiced lamb meatballs), prawns wrapped in bacon, fish in passion-fruit sauce, scallop tartare

DIVING IN TAGANGA

One of the cheapest spots in the world for scuba certification, both PADI and NAUI, Taganga has so many **dive shops** that the prices and services offered by each are pretty competitive. Four- to six-day certification courses start at around C$850,000 and often include basic accommodation, English- or Spanish-speaking dive masters, and six dives (four open-water, two pool). Two tank dives in Tayrona National Park start at around C$280,000.

DIVE OPERATORS

Calipso Dive Center C 12 No. 1–40 ⓦcalipsodivecenter.com
Oceano Scuba Dive Center Cra 2 No. 17–46 ⓦoceanoscuba.com.co.
Poseidon Dive Center C 18 No. 1–69 ⓦposeidondivecenter.com.
Tayrona Dive Center Cra 1C No. 18A–22 ⓦtayronadivecenter.com.

and grilled Camembert. $\overline{\underline{\$\$}}$

El Reef Cra 1 No. 15–09 (malecón) ☏ 317 808 6664. Relaxed café on the waterfront, with outdoor tables under a *palapa*. It's popular for breakfast, sandwiches and ice cream flavoured with local fruits (*maracuyá* and *arequipe*, for example). $\underline{\$}$

Restaurante Bitacora C 1 #17-13 (malecón). Ranked among the best of the *palapas* that line Taganga's *malecón*, knocking out tasty daily specials – the menu (ceviche, fried fish, *arroz de coco*) is comparable to the other seafront spots, but the fish here is always wonderfully fresh. $\overline{\underline{\$\$}}$

NIGHTLIFE

Miradór de Taganga Cra 1 No. 18–107 ☏ 315 727 5250. The frisson sparked by the mix of locals and backpackers that fill this club (also a hostel) makes this place worth a trip even if you're staying in Santa Marta (taxis wait outside for the trip back). A disco with a scintillating view high above the bay (on the road back to Santa Marta), it throbs with mainstream pop. Things get going after midnight.

DIRECTORY

Banks and exchange The only ATM (Bancolombia), on Cra 2 next to the police station, often runs out of money (or won't accept foreign cards), so it's best to load up in Santa Marta.

Police The police post is on Cra 2 between Calles 16 and 17, just as you enter the village.

Minca

Just 20km southeast of Santa Marta, nestled in the foothills of the Sierra Nevada (660m above sea level), the small mountain town of **MINCA** awaits with its cool climate, hundreds of exotic bird species and yoga classes – it's rapidly becoming one of Colombia's most popular backpacker hangouts. Located at the beginning of Colombia's "coffee zone", Minca is a welcome respite from the heat of the coast, though there's not much to see in the town itself, a small settlement of around five hundred inhabitants. Other than soaking up the languid atmosphere, most visitors head out to waterfalls or coffee farms in the surrounding hills, taking refreshing dips in bubbling mountain streams.

Popular activities include a forty-minute hike (or short *mototaxi* ride) to **Pozo Azul** (free entry) a set of two enchanting swimming holes at the foot of a small waterfall, and **Las Cascadas de Marinka**, a larger waterfall (entry fee), a one-hour hike from the centre (15min via *mototaxi*). You can also tour the organic coffee farm **Hacienda La Victoria**, established in 1892 with English investors, thus the name (daily 9am–5pm; 1hr 30min; charge for tours; ⓦfacebook.com/LaVictoria1892). *Mototaxis* one-way take around 25 minutes, while 4WD jeeps take approximately 35 minutes; otherwise it's a 2hr hike.

ARRIVAL AND DEPARTURE — MINCA

By minibus Cootrasminca minibuses depart the small office on Cra 9, at C 12 next to the market area in Santa Marta; the trip takes around 45 minutes.

By taxi You'll have to negotiate a fixed rate with regular Santa Marta taxis. *Mototaxis* will usually take you for less (25min).

ACCOMMODATION AND EATING

Casa Loma 10min walk from the plaza ⓦ casalomaminca.com. Wooden hilltop house (it's a short but steep hike) with stunning views, five simple but cosy rooms, hammocks (which you can spend the night in), dorm beds and camping (tents available for rent). Congenial owners Jay (English), Anne (German) and Helena (French) are a font of local information. Cold showers and no wi-fi. The great on-site restaurant serves breakfast, lunch and dinner. Yoga classes (1hr 30min) are extra. Sleeping options in include camping (with own tent), hammocks, dorms and doubles. $\underline{\$}$

★ **Lazy Cat** C Principal No. 1–460 ☏ 300 748 2406. Alluring riverside cottage restaurant, with a relaxed terrace, free wi-fi, friendly Anglo/Colombian owners and superb food (from steaks and home-made burgers – to Thai-style noodles). Sunset happy hour daily 6–7pm. The name is in honour of the resident cats. $\underline{\$}$

★ **Masaya Casas Viejas** Hacienda la Victoria ⓦ masaya-experience.com/minca. This French-owned guesthouse on the Hacienda Victoria estate (6km from central Minca) is definitely worth the bumpy ride up for the spectacular views and simple, clean rooms and wonderful hot-water showers. There's no kitchen. but meals at the restaurant or the hacienda's *El Bistro de La Victoria* are all fresh and home cooked. Yoga classes and salsa lessons are also offered. Dorms $, doubles $$

★ **La Miga** Cra 66, next to Banco de Bogotá ☏ 313 537 2218. Amazing French bakery with some of the tastiest bread in Colombia, from sourdough to fresh baguettes, as well as home-made hummus, *pain au chocolat*, muffins and tasty ham-and-cheese sandwiches. $

Nevada Cervecería Hacienda la Victoria ☏ 310 232 3232. Craft brewery established inside an old chapel on the Hacienda Victoria estate (see page 168). Buy and sample the Happy Coca pale ale, Happy Tucan red ale and the Happy Nebbi golden pils.

El Paraíso de Tuki B&B Near the top of the mountain overlooking Minca ☏ 321 588 7985, w facebook.com/lacandelariacoffee.farm. Romantically located coffee and cacao farm offering rustic but clean and comfy digs (with fan and open-air showers) courtesy of friendly hosts Ana and Eugenio. It's a hard 45min–1hr hike from the centre, but *mototaxis* can take you there. Breakfast included. $

Aracataca

… Macondo was a village of twenty adobe houses, built on the bank of a river of clear water that ran along a bed of polished stones, which were white and enormous, like prehistoric eggs.

So begins *One Hundred Years of Solitude*, the novel that more than any other earned **Gabriel García Márquez** the Nobel Prize for Literature in 1982. Gabo principally based the fictional town of Macondo on **ARACATACA**, his oppressively hot birthplace some 80km south of Santa Marta (in *Living to Tell the Tale* he explains how he saw the name "Macondo" on a sign at a banana plantation near Aracataca). For Márquez fans the town is an essential pilgrimage, if only to see the **birthplace museum** here. There's not much else to do, though Aracataca is a pleasant, easy-going rural centre with a smattering of "Macondo" tributes (and an inordinate number of pool halls) – it's a working town and in no way a theme park (in 2006 a referendum to rename the town "Aracataca-Macondo" failed due to low turnout). Indeed, not everyone is happy with the Márquez connection, but on a witheringly hot, languid afternoon, with parrots squawking in the mango trees and locals dozing in hammocks, it's still possible to imagine the Macondo of Márquez's imagination.

Casa Museo Gabriel García Márquez

C 5 No. 6–35 • Free • ☏ 5 425 6588

Gabo's maternal grandfather moved to Aracataca in 1910 during the banana boom, and two years later he bought a simple house on a site now occupied by the **Casa Museo Gabriel García Márquez**. It was here Márquez was born in 1927, growing up amid that "lunatic house", with especially strong female role models (he was raised by his grandmother) and Wayuu servants from La Guajira, immersed in books, superstitions and ghost stories. Márquez left Aracataca for good in 1936, returning with his mother briefly in 1950 (another episode recounted in *Living to Tell the Tale*) when the town was a shadow of its former self – the house was by this time a dilapidated, creaking shell riddled with termites. What you see today is a series of whitewashed timber reconstructions built in a similar Antillean style to the originals in 2010.

A series of rooms, simply adorned with odd bits of period furniture and photos, quotes from *One Hundred Years of Solitude* and *Living to Tell the Tale*, chronicle the early life of Márquez here, and the family members who influenced him most – it's striking how many of his literary creations were inspired by real characters in this period of his life. Everything is labelled in English.

Other Márquez-related sights

Márquez fans will want to check out **Iglesia San José**, located on shady Plaza Bolívar (also called Parque Central), the slightly Moorish-looking church where Gabo was

GABO AND COLOMBIA

Most Colombians remain immensely proud of Gabriel García Márquez or "Gabo" as he is known, the Nobel Prize winner who – perhaps with the unfortunate exception of Pablo Escobar – became one of the best-known colombianos on the planet. In reality Gabo spent most of his life living overseas (primarily in Mexico) and had a complicated relationship with his home nation, raising some eyebrows with his left-wing political views and his close, somewhat bizarre friendship with Cuban dictator Fidel Castro.

EARLY YEARS

Gabo's father, Gabriel Eligio García, was a telegraph operator in Aracataca when he met Luisa Santiaga Márquez (the tragicomic story of their courtship would later be adapted in *Love in the Time of Cholera*), but little Gabito (born in 1927) was brought up by his maternal grandparents – his parents moved to Riohacha and later Barranquilla, and it's the house in Aracataca, presided over by the imposing figures of "Colonel" Nicolás Márquez – Liberal veteran of the Thousand Days War – and grandma Doña Tranquilina Iguarán Cotes, that had a lasting influence on the young Márquez. After Grandpa Márquez died in 1937, Gabito began a peripatetic life, with spells at boarding schools in Barranquilla, Zipaquirá and Bogotá – the family eventually settled in the town of Sucre but the young poet rarely spent time there. In the late 1940s he enrolled at law school in Bogotá, narrowly escaping the violence that shook the capital in 1948. He re-enrolled at university in Cartagena, but his heart wasn't in it.

THE JOURNALIST

After fleeing the capital in 1948, García Márquez spent his formative career as a journalist flitting between Cartagena, Barranquilla and Bogotá under the influence of the "Barranquilla Group" of artists and intellectuals (see page 156), initially cocooned from the political violence wracking the country. This was a difficult time for the young writer; surviving on meagre pay, he often

---

formally baptized in 1930 (usually open for Mass only). Behind the church on Calle 9, the **Casa del Telegrafista** (free) was where Gabo's father worked in the late 1920s; it is, now restored with its old telecom equipment on display, a collection of stamps dedicated to Gabo and miscellaneous antiques. Walk south along the train tracks (still used by freight trains), aka Carrera 1, and you'll come upon the old **Estación del Tren de Aracataca** (free) at Calle 3. Reopened as a museum, it has a shady patio and displays of local art, statues and objects associated with Márquez.

ARRIVAL AND DEPARTURE — ARACATACA

By bus The easiest way to get to Aracataca is to take a bus from Santa Marta's Terminal de Transportes; Berlinave operates fairly cramped, a/c minibuses every 30min (daily; 1hr 30min) – these are actually headed for Fundación (10km south of Aracataca), and they'll drop you on the main road that skirts the edge of Aracataca (C 7); bicitaxis (seemingly operated by kids), *mototaxis* or tuk-tuks will whisk you to anywhere in town, but it's just a 15min walk straight down C 8 to the centre. Flag down buses on the same stretch of main road heading back (to Santa Marta or Barranquilla). Heading to points south, take a minivan to Fundación and change there.

ACCOMMODATION AND EATING

Casa Morelli Cra 6 No. 6–24 ☏ 321 503 0239. This basic hostel is the main accommodation in town, with single or double rooms with a/c, cable TV and breakfast. $

Donde Ney Comidas Rápidas Cra 5 No. 7–36 ☏ 317 785 0305. This local canteen close to the museum serves hearty fast-food dishes, with plantains and breaded chicken featured across the board. $

★ **El Patio Mágico de Gabo y Leo Matiz** C 7 No. 4–57 ☏ 302 358 5054. The old home of lauded photographer Leo Matiz (1917–98) is the most atmospheric place to eat in town, littered with memorabilia and helmed by Doña Dilia Todaro (she'll show you her photos of Gabo). Meals (there are no menus) are eaten on communal tables in the lush garden (with caged parakeets); dishes of the day (grilled chicken or pork with rice, say) come with soup and lemon drinks. $$

slept in the street or in brothels (his early sexual exploits, though often described matter-of-factly in *Living to Tell The Tale*, might seem disturbing to modern readers – he lost his virginity at 13 to a much older prostitute, for example). A trip back to Aracataca with his mother in 1950 was the inspiration to start writing about his enchanted childhood – *The Leaf Storm* was published in 1955, beginning his gradual drift towards the genre known as "Magical Realism" (where magical or unreal events take place in otherwise realistic stories). From around 1954, García Márquez started reporting on Colombia's growing civil war – notably the "War of Villarrica" – and developed close ties with the local leader of the Communist Party. His Socialist leanings and articles, especially the piece that would become *The Story of a Shipwrecked Sailor*, started to attract Conservative criticism and even death threats, and in 1955 he left on assignment for Geneva, remaining in Europe for almost three years (mostly in Paris). The departure ends *Living to Tell The Tale* (García Márquez's only completed autobiography), and though told without much bitterness, there's a sense that the writer had finished with Colombia.

LATER YEARS

Márquez eventually took a job in Caracas, Venezuela, at the end of 1957, and though he flew back to Barranquilla briefly to marry his longtime sweetheart Mercedes Barcha in March 1958, he never again lived full-time in the country of his birth – the anti-communist persecution by the government of President Julio César Turbay from 1978 to 1982 made this exile permanent, though Márquez later owned a house in Cartagena and spent several weeks there each year, especially in the 1990s. García Márquez died of pneumonia in Mexico City in 2014, and was widely mourned in Colombia (even President Santos expressed his sadness); he was laid to rest in his adopted home, but some of his ashes were interred in Cartagena in 2016 (see page 133). The citizens of Aracataca, many of whom were highly critical of the writer's seeming indifference to his poverty-stricken birthplace over the years, held a bizarre symbolic funeral for him anyway, in the manner of one of his magical realist novels.

Parque Nacional Natural Tayrona

Main entrance around 40km west of Santa Marta at El Zaíno • Officially open to day-trippers 8am to 5pm; in high season visitors line up long before 8am (gates often open at 7am); 6900 visitors allowed/day; park closes one month/year, usually Jan or Feb • Charge (cash only); passport and yellow fever certificate required

Colombia's unspoiled tropical wilderness, **PARQUE NACIONAL NATURAL TAYRONA**, a 45-minute drive east of Santa Marta, is best known for its sensational **beaches**, with lush jungle running right down to the sand. The laidback attitude of the place sometimes makes it feel like a paradisiacal summer camp, and it does get totally **overcrowded** during the holidays – it's best avoided at these times. Tayrona stretches over 120 square kilometres inland, with an additional 30 square kilometres of marine reserve, but since much of the park isn't easily accessible, visitors find themselves sticking largely to the string of beaches that stretches for around 8km from the land entrance of the park, bounded by **Cañaveral** to the east and ending with **Cabo San Juan** to the west. The far west side of the park is more easily accessed by boat from Taganga. Note that the **park closes for one month every year**, for cleaning (and to allow Indigenous peoples access), usually January/February.

The beaches

Tayrona's **beaches** and the jungle that edges them are the irrefutable stars of the park. Arriving by road you'll pass the main park entrance at **El Zaíno**, where your bags will be searched for alcohol (which is banned). From here vans (charge per journey) run along the main park road 5km to **Cañaveral**, where the beach is ideal for sunbathing but the riptides make it unsuitable for swimming. From Cañaveral you can continue on foot (or ride mangy-looking horses for a fee), another hour or so west along a wooded, **muddy trail** to the long, beautiful, wave-lashed stretch of **Arrecifes**, where signs warn you that more than two hundred tourists have drowned; swimming is extremely dangerous due to riptides and strong currents (though you can spend the night here).

From Arrecifes, it's just a ten-minute stroll west to **La Aranilla**, a narrow strip of sand on a cove framed by huge boulders, fine for swimming, with another twenty minutes to **La Piscina**, an enchanting beach good for swimming and snorkelling, with calm, deep water. Thirty minutes' walk further west is **El Cabo San Juan de Guía** (also connected to Taganga by boat), an attractive pair of palm-fringed beaches where the majority of visitors stay; fifteen minutes further west into the park from here are two more beaches, the second being a **nudist beach** aka "Playa Nudista".

Bahía Concha

There's a charge to enter the beach (no need to pay park admission), but you'll be charged another fee for a cabaña and beach chair

Bahía Concha is a sheltered bay with a dazzling beach on the far western edge of the park, a bumpy twenty minutes by *mototaxi* from Santa Marta, boat from Taganga or by speedboat from Cabo San Juan – it's too far to walk safely. This is another spot that can be overwhelmed with visitors (and rubbish) during holidays (Easter, Christmas), when it's best avoided.

Playa Cristal

Park admission charged • Loungers can be rented by the day; snorkelling equipment can be rented in increments of 40 minutes

East of Bahía Concha and some forty choppy minutes by boat from Taganga, **Playa Cristal** feels extremely isolated, a pristine wedge of sand with beguiling snorkelling in translucent waters just offshore – the snowy peaks of the Sierra Nevada make a jaw-dropping backdrop. Note that in high season operators heading to Playa Cristal leave Santa Marta and Rodadero at around 3am in order to arrive before the daily quota of 350 persons is filled.

Pueblito

A beautiful but physically demanding uphill (3–4hr return) path leading from Cabo San Juan brings you to the archeological site of **Pueblito**, the ruins of a Tairona village also known as Chairama – it's definitely no Ciudad Perdida, though, with a few terraces, overgrown stone staircases and remains of circular houses (there are also contemporary Kogi huts here, but don't take photos without permission). Although it's possible to complete an Arrecifes–Cabo–San Juan–Pueblito circuit in one long, strenuous day, the trip is better made as part of a multi-day stay on the beaches in the park.

The Calabazo entrance

From Pueblito, you can also hike two hours through the jungle back down to the alternative park entrance at **Calabazo** and catch a bus back to Santa Marta there, instead of traversing your original route back to Cabo San Juan. **Entering the park** at Calabazo is also a good idea if you want to avoid the crowds (buses will drop you); note however, that it closes at 3.30pm and it's a fairly tough 4hr hike to Cabo San Juan from here.

ARRIVAL AND DEPARTURE   PARQUE NACIONAL NATURAL TAYRONA

By boat Regular speedboats run from Taganga to Cabo San Juan (1hr), arriving at around 11am and departing at around 4pm (see page 167). Rangers collect the park entrance fee when you disembark. From Taganga, Bahía Concha is 20min by boat and Playa Cristal is 40 minutes. If there's space on a boat you can usually negotiate a one-way ticket for the return journey, but boats are often full with day-trippers.

By bus Cootrans Oriente minibuses run from Santa Marta (every 30min; 1hr) from their small bus station behind the

market at the corner of Cra 9 and C 11 to El Zaíno, 34km away, which is the main entrance to Tayrona, where your passport will be checked, and entrance fee collected; the minibuses will also drop you at Calabazo if you ask, and usually go on to Palomino. Moving on, just flag the same buses down at El Zaíno or Calabazo in either direction. From Palomino the bus charges a flat fee to Tayrona.

By taxi Taxis run to Bahía Concha from Taganga or from Santa Marta, but most people get the same car to take them back.
By mototaxi The cheapest way to get to Bahía Concha is to take a local bus to "Bastidas" and then a *mototaxi* to the beach.

INFORMATION

Information Basic park information is available at El Zaíno and Cañaveral.
Services Bring plenty of cash, as much water as you can carry (it's very expensive in the park) and lots of insect repellent. The only internet access is in Cañaveral (the restaurant has wi-fi).

GETTING AROUND

Cañaveral is the end of the paved road; after here you continue on foot or on horseback.
By van Vans shuttle back and forth between El Zaíno and Cañaveral for a fee.

On horseback On arrival in Cañaveral you'll see locals offering horseback rides to Arrecifes, or to Cabo San Juan, though the horses are often in poor health.

ACCOMMODATION AND EATING

The two beaches offering the most accommodation are **Arrecifes** and **Cabo San Juan**; both offer the option of renting tents and hammocks, with basic cabañas a good alternative for medium to large groups at Arrecifes. Lockers are available, too. Note that for anyone not staying at one of the posher (and very expensive) options, budget accommodation is notoriously difficult to arrange in advance – aim to arrive early and nab a first-come, first-served spot (you can usually book something at the El Zaíno entrance). It's possible to stay the night in a tent on the beach at **Playa Cristal**. There are basic **restaurants** at Cabo San Juan, Arrecifes and Playa Cristal. You can bring in your own food (no alcohol), but note that there are no cooking facilities in the park.

Camping Cabo San Juan de la Guía Cabo San Juan ☎ 323 356 9912. The downside to the hammocks here – both on the beach and in a gazebo on a small hillock – is that they offer no mosquito netting, so bring your own, and that it can get quite chilly at night. Seek out the information hut next door to the restaurant (mains $), the only real building in sight. It cann get overrun during holidays and there are only four shared showers and four toilets. Camping/person with own tent $, hammock on the beach $, "VIP" hammock in gazebo $, camping/person with rented tent $, cabañas $$

Camping Don Pedro Arrecifes, a 10–15min walk inland from the beach ⓦ campingdonpedro.com. One of the cheapest accommodation options in the park, this spot has hammocks, simple en-suite cabañas and tents, and a no-frills restaurant (breakfast usually included, dinner is extra). Camping, hammocks & rented tents $, cabañas $$

Ecohabs Cañaveral ☎ 311 600 1614, ⓦ ecohabsparque tayrona.com. With large two-storey cabañas running uphill from the beach, the best accommodation in the park is a little overpriced – the higher your cabaña the more spectacular the sea view (you'll need to not mind steep stairs and the climb back down to the toilets). Cabañas feature mosquito screens, flatscreen satellite TV, ceiling fans, outdoor hammocks and window shutters. The on-site restaurant (mains $$), which has free wi-fi, is open 7am–9pm. The same outfit operates five similarly priced cabañas at Arrecifes. $$$$

Jasayma Parque Tayrona Km 1 Zaíno–Cañaveral ⓦ jasaymatayrona.co. Decent budget option, just inside the park (around 15min walk from El Zaíno). Rooms are rustic but clean, though there is no electricity in the main hotel block (or fans), so it can be very hot (there's a solar-powered charging station in the kitchen). Breakfast included. Limited wi-fi and shared bathrooms. Cash only. $\overline{\$\$}$

★ **The Journey Hostel** Ruta 90, Los Naranjos ⓦ journeyhosteltayrona.com. With a truly spectacular location on the hillside, this budget option lies a 20min walk from the El Zaíno entrance (on the road to Palomino), with comfy en-suite doubles and breezy dorms. Basic breakfast included, with the restaurant open for lunch and dinner. $\overline{\$}$

Posadas Ecoturísticas Seineken Ruta 90 Km 29 ⓦ ecoseinekentayrona.com. Four cosy wooden cabañas (with fans) run by the friendly Doña Lucila, some 500m outside the park entrance (a 5min walk from El Zaíno) and close to the tranquil Río Piedras. Breakfast included. $\overline{\$}$

Ciudad Perdida

The "Lost City" of the Taironas, **CIUDAD PERDIDA** ranks among South America's most mystical sights. More than a lost city, it's a lost world. Although its ruins are more understated than those found at Machu Picchu in Peru, thanks to its geographic isolation the once teeming city perched high in the Sierra Nevada de Santa Marta manages to preserve the natural allure that the overrun Inca capital lost years ago to tourism. While steadily climbing the sierra's luxuriant foothills, you'll get a chance to bathe in idyllic rivers, visit inhabited Indigenous villages and marvel at the swarms of monarch butterflies and beautiful jungle scenery. Founded around 660 AD, the former Tairona capital is less than 50km southeast of Santa Marta and is believed to have been home to around four thousand people before the Spanish wiped the Tairona out – the city was abandoned between 1550 and 1660. The ruins weren't "discovered" until the early 1970s, when a few *guaqueros* (tomb raiders) from Santa Marta chanced upon the city while scavenging for antiquities – archeological work didn't begin until 1976 and the site remained dangerous because of paramilitaries until relatively recently. Perched atop a steep slope 1300m high in dense jungle, the site comprises more than a thousand **circular stone terraces** – with more still being uncovered – that once served as foundations for Tairona homes. Running throughout the city and down to the Buritaca river valley is a complex network of paved footpaths and steep stone steps – more than 1350, if you're counting – purportedly added later to obstruct the advance of Spanish horsemen. Though the site has become busier in the last few years, the only way to get here is still via a five-day trek, meaning huge crowds are unlikely for the foreseeable future.

The hike

The trek covers 40km, with most hikers opting for the five-day version – joining a guided tour (see page 175) is mandatory. You get picked up in Santa Marta or Taganga for the three-hour drive to **El Mamey**, the village where the hike begins after lunch. From here it's four to five hours (6km) to **Camp 1** (usually **La Cabaña de Adán** or **Alfredo**) – mostly a steep uphill slog (520m elevation gain) with a long, steep descent

> **CIUDAD PERDIDA TIPS**
>
> There is no transportation (or road) to the **Lost City**, but the hike can be done all year round; the driest period is between late December and March, while during the wet months from May to November the trail can get exceedingly muddy. It's a fairly challenging trek lasting **four to six days**, and a reasonable level of physical fitness is required. Expect to get wet at any time of the year and pack everything you'll need, especially: a bottle of water for the first day; sturdy footwear suitable for river crossings (either waterproof trekking sandals or hiking boots and flip-flops); a towel; at least 5 percent DEET insect repellent; water-purifying tablets; antimalarial prophylactics (there's low risk of malaria but you should err on the side of caution); waterproof bag and poncho; and sunscreen. Bring a small amount for cash for snacks and drinks along the way.

> **THE KOGI (KOGUI)**
>
> Although now uninhabited, Ciudad Perdida is in many respects a living monument. It's surrounded by villages of the Kogi, who call the revered site **Teyuna**. You may be able to interact with the Kogis as they drift on and off the main trail you'll traverse as part of the trek. As it comprises only a fraction of the wilderness they call home, the Kogi are increasingly less present on this popular tourist trek. The men are recognizable by their long black hair, white (or off-white) smocks and trousers, a woven purse worn across one shoulder and trusty póporo, the saliva-coated gourd holding the lime that activates the coca leaves they constantly chew. Women also dress in white, and both women and girls wear necklaces; only the men own *póporo*. About nine thousand Kogis are believed to inhabit the Sierra Nevada region. When flower power was in full bloom in the 1970s, the Sierra Nevada became a major marijuana factory, and an estimated seventy percent of its native forests were burned to clear the way for untold amounts of the lucrative Santa Marta Gold strand. As the forest's prime inhabitants, the Kogis suffered dearly from the arrival of so many fast-buck farmers, one of the reasons why they're sceptical of the outside world; while Kogi children may well approach you, asking for sweets, **don't take pictures** of adults without their permission.

towards the camp. There's a swimming hole close to the start of the trail and another at Camp 1, where there are hammocks and basic huts with mosquito nets.

Day two's four- to five-hour hike (7km) to **Camp 2** (**Mumake or Tezumake**) is an hour's ascent followed by a steep descent, and an attractive flat stretch that takes you past the Kogi village of **Mutanyi**. At the camp there's good swimming in the river and relatively comfortable bunks with mosquito nets.

Day three consists of a four-hour hike (7km) that includes a narrow path overlooking a sheer drop and ups and downs along a narrow jungle trail, and a bridge across the main Río Buritaca. **Camp 3, Paraíso Teyuna**, tends to be the most crowded, and has hammocks, dorms with bunks and musty tents with mattresses. Weather permitting, some groups press on to Ciudad Perdida in the afternoon (four-hour round trip), involving an hour's ascent from Camp 3, most of it up a very steep bunch of uneven and slippery stone steps (660m elevation gain) – particularly challenging on the way down (there's supposed to be 1200 steps). And then it's there – your prize – stone terrace upon stone terrace, tranquil and overgrown with jungle, with splendid views of the main terrace from the military outpost.

On your return, you either stay overnight in Camp 2 at the end of **day four** or, if you made it to Ciudad Perdida on day three, you make the eight- to nine-hour hike from Camp 3 back to Camp 1. **Day five** is then either a very early start and a gruelling seven-hour hike from Camp 2 back to El Mamey before lunch or – if you're already at Camp 1 – a somewhat less gruelling four-hour slog, with the steepest part at the very beginning.

ARRIVAL AND DEPARTURE CIUDAD PERDIDA

Since 2008 the Lost City has been safe from **paramilitaries**, but you can only do the hike as part of an **organized group**. Several tour companies are authorized to lead tours, all with offices in Santa Marta (and most with branches in Taganga), though you may find that guides from different companies swap clients to accommodate those who wish to do the tour in more or fewer days, and during low season the companies tend to pool clients. The official price of the tour (4–6 days) is a set fee and includes all meals, accommodation along the trail (usually hammocks), travel insurance, the entrance fee to the ruins and transport to and from the trailhead. Guides generally don't speak much English. Groups consist of four to twelve hikers.

Expotur Cra 3 No. 17–27, Santa Marta (also in Taganga) expotur-eco.com. Professional outfit, with strong connections to the local Kogi community and (usually) bilingual guides.

Magic Tour C 14 No. 1B–50, Taganga; C 16 No. 4–41, Santa Marta magictourcolombia.com. One of the most reputable operators.

Palomino and around

The burgeoning backpacker hangout of **PALOMINO**, some 63km from El Zaíno, makes for a refreshing pit-stop between Tayrona and La Guajira, with an alluring **beach** and plenty of budget accommodation. The main part of the village lies along the highway between Santa Marta and Riohacha, with the beach a short 1.5km downhill walk to the north (you can also take a *mototaxi for a small fee*). Other than lazing on the sands (the rip currents make swimming dangerous) and dining on lionfish ceviche, the main activity is **tubing down the Río Palomino**, which most hostels can arrange (this involves a short jeep ride, followed by a 20min hike). An alternative inland stopover is nearby **Río Ancho**, and there are several quieter beachside options opening up along the coast towards Riohacha, including the small villages of **Dibulla** and **Boca de Camarones**.

Río Ancho

Some 12km east along the main highway from Palomino, **RÍO ANCHO** is a small town on the thickly forested river of the same name and the hub of a growing ecotourism scene that's far less developed than its seaside neighbour (there are no beaches here). *Riverside House* (see page 176) can help organize **rafting** and kayaking down the river to the sea (you'll likely see otters and howler monkeys), and **hikes** up into the hills, visiting traditional Kogi (see page 175) villages (around 4hr on foot).

ARRIVAL AND DEPARTURE   PALOMINO AND AROUND

By bus Cootrans Oriente minibuses run from Santa Marta (every 30min; 1hr 30min) from their small bus station behind the market at the corner of Cra 9 and C 11 to Palomino (via the Tayrona park entrance). Alternatively, any of the main buses travelling between Santa Marta bus station and Riohacha should be able to drop you in Palomino or Río Ancho (remind the driver). Moving on in either direction, just flag buses down on the main highway. Shared taxis charge per person and run between Palomino and Río Ancho (15min).

Door to door MarSol Transportes (5 656 0302, marsol.com.co) operates a convenient "puerta-to-puerta" service to Palomino from Cartagena via Santa Marta (around 5hr; charge).

ACCOMMODATION AND EATING

PALOMINO

★ **Aité Eco Resort** Playa Donaires aite.com.co. Luxurious boutique hotel with seven rooms and two cottages right on the beach, all with bathrooms, mosquito nets and electricity (free wi-fi in the main house). Three meals included in the rate. Doubles $$, cottages $$$$

Dreamer Hostel Playa Donaires thedreamer.com. No-frills but modern and large en-suite rooms with terraces as well as four small, basic dorms and a decent pool just off the beach – it tends to be a party place thanks to its popular bar (which closes at midnight) and dependable satellite wi-fi. The excellent buffet breakfast is also available to non-guests. Dorms $, doubles $$

★ **SUÁ Palomino** Av Troncal Caribe Km 70 (just off the main highway in town) 310 251 5738. Wonderfully fresh and wholesome dishes made with organic and locally sourced produce; the fresh bass (or lionfish when it's caught) in coconut sauce is sublime, but the ceviche, burgers and aubergine sandwich are all standouts. $

Tanko's Playa Donaires 323 453 3813. Friendly Australian/Colombian duo Franko and Natasha knock up delicious meals at this beachside spot (which also offers accommodation; dorms $), including lip-smacking pear-and-bacon "arrepizzas" and pastas. $

Tiki Hut Hostel Playa Donaires tikihutpalomino.co. The quieter alternative to the nearby *Dreamer* offers spacious dorms with mosquito nets and fans (basic cold showers), as well as comfy, rustic private en-suite cabañas and excellent food provided by your friendly hosts. Limited free wi-fi, breakfast extra. Dorms $, doubles $$

RÍO ANCHO

★ **Riverside House** C 1 No. 3–25 321 561 1898. Simple but well-maintained dorms (with single and double beds) run by affable Rafael and Diana. Camping is also available, in tents with air mattresses and dedicated toilets (shared). Shared kitchen for all guests, with food and drinks available in the restaurant. Camping, dorms and doubles available. $

La Guajira

Colombia's northernmost region, **LA GUAJIRA** has a hostile desert climate that has kept it largely isolated since colonial times. As a result it's one of those special places where independent travellers can still feel as if they're leaving fresh tracks; Gabriel García Márquez, whose ancestors hailed from here, simply called it "the province". Some 240km long and no more than 50km wide, La Guajira remains a barren peninsula virtually empty except for the seminomadic **Wayuu** and the odd herd of goats grazing under the sparse shade of acacia trees. More challenging to explore than the rest of the Caribbean coast, the Guajira Peninsula rewards those who make the effort with an end-of-the-world feel, though don't expect an untouched paradise – the region is blighted by poverty and lack of services, with Wayuu children regularly setting up impromptu roadblocks to beg for food and cash. It can also be hard to travel here without speaking good Spanish (even most Colombians struggle with the accent), though if you can and have a group, renting a car can make a huge difference. Though it is possible to get as far as the Wayuu fishing village and burgeoning resort of **Cabo de la Vela** on a day-trip from Riohacha, this is not recommended – you will almost certainly gain a negative impression and spend most of the time in a minivan. Try and spend at least one night here, taking in the otherworldly, mesmerizing dunes at **Punta Gallinas**.

Riohacha

Guajira's capital on the Caribbean coast, workaday **RIOHACHA** is slowly transforming its down-at-heel seafront, though its aim to become the next major Colombian resort seems a little ambitious. For now, a steady stream of visitors and tour groups pass through on the way to the upper Guajira Peninsula – as the main gateway to the region you'll likely spend at least one night here. The palm-lined stretch of the **malecón** (C 1) between Carreras 4 and 11 is a laidback combination of bars, no-frills seafood restaurants and craft stalls – mostly multicoloured Wayuu bags laid out on the boardwalk – overlooking a wide, often breezy and largely empty expanse of enticing white sand. The water is often choppy and muddied by silt, however, with little shade on the actual beach – the long **Muelle Turístico** (pier) provides an overview. The pier comes ashore at the striking *Identidad* monument, completed in 2010 and the main landmark along the *malecón*.

Parque Padilla

There's little to Riohacha beyond the *malecón*, with the main square, **Parque Padilla** (one block inland from the beach between Carreras 8 and 9) featuring the stately **Catedral de Nuestra Señora de los Remedios** (C 2 No. 7–13) and sellers of fresh

---

> **THE WAYUU**
>
> The **Wayuu** still dominate La Guajira, having resisted the Spanish throughout the colonial period (see page 341), and Christianity only taking tenuous hold in the twentieth century. Today most Wayuu are divided into matrilineal clans and still live in small, rural settlements known as **rancherías** centred around goat farming and weaving bags known as *susu*; they represent almost half the population of the province (with estimated numbers of around 145,000) and are also the largest Indigenous group in Venezuela, just across the border. Most still speak wayuunaiki, part of the Arawak language family, and though the Wayuu are subject to Colombian laws, the tribal justice system relies primarily on the **pütchipü'ü**, a mediator who is charged with solving local disputes through negotiation. The **Wayúu Tayá Foundation** (wayuutaya.net) was founded in 2002 by Wayuu actress and model Patricia Velásquez, primarily to improve access to education and health services.

LA GUAJIRA'S PINK FLAMINGOS

You can spot pink flamingos all along the Caribbean coast, especially in the wet season (Sept–Jan), but one place you'll definitely spy thousands of the long-legged beauties is the **Santuario de Fauna y Flora los Flamencos**, a nature preserve some 20km west of Riohacha (at other times of year it's much rarer to see them). Admission is free, but you'll need to take a taxi or Santa Marta-bound bus to get here, and then hire a Wayuu boatman to get close to the main flocks. Note also that the adjacent village of Camarones, 3.5km from the park entrance (Cabaña Guanebucane), is a relatively poor Wayuu community that rarely see any benefit from the trickle of tourists coming through.

---

coconuts, but otherwise ringed by unattractive modern buildings – the rest of the area behind the *malecón* remains a bit shabby and best avoided at night. Inside the cathedral, a Republican edifice with an interior of ersatz marble, lies the resting place of independence hero **Admiral José Prudencio Padilla** himself (his monument is to the right as you enter), a venerated image of Virgen de los Remedios and stained-glass incarnations of Mother Teresa and Pope John Paul II. A statue of Padilla also graces the square outside, the admiral nonchalantly grasping a sabre.

Playa de Mayapo
Take a taxi or *colectivo* from Mercado Nuevo

White-sand beaches and clear waters are on offer at **Playa de Mayapo**, some 20km northeast of Riohacha, part of a Wayuu reserve and a pleasant place to pass a day waiting to begin your Guajira tour (cheap meals are available).

ARRIVAL AND INFORMATION — RIOHACHA

By plane Aeropuerto Almirante Padilla lies 4km southwest of the centre (at C 29B No. 15–217), served solely by Avianca flights from Bogotá (1hr 30min). Taxis run from here to the centre.

By bus Riohacha's Terminal de Transportes is on the edge of the city at C 15 No. 11–38 (on the main ring road, Av 15). Taxis run to the *malecón* (and into the city). *Busetas* shoot around town, but routes are hard to follow – stick to taxis. Destinations Bogotá (1–2 daily; 18hr); Bucaramanga (2 daily; 12hr); Maicao (Venezuela border; hourly; 1hr); Santa Marta (hourly; 3hr); Valledupar (3–4 daily; 3–4hr).

To Cabo de la Vela Cootrauri (C 15 No. 5–39; ☏5 728 0000) runs *colectivos* to Uribía (1hr) where the driver will drop you off at the pick-up truck departure point for Cabo (Mercado de las Pulgas). The last trucks head for Cabo at around 3pm (1hr 30min–2hr). Coming back, trucks leave Cabo between 4 and 4.30am. Taxis will drive you direct to Cabo for a handsome fee.

Tourist information The main Guajira tourist office is right on the *malecón* (C 1 No. 4–42; ☏5 728 2046, w laguajira.gov.co), between carreras 4 and 5. They have maps, but rarely English speakers.

TOURS

Riohacha is the primary base for **Guajira tour companies** – try to contact these recommended operators in advance if you can. Prices are similar at each, but it's always worth shopping around.

Kaí Ecotravel Av 1A No. 4–49 w kaiecotravel.com. Reputable operator and pioneer in the area, with a very useful website and a full range of tours from one night/two days in Cabo to whole-week expeditions.

Tours Ramiro Vanegas C 18 No. 8–25 ☏315 759 3691, e tours-r@hotmail.com. Ramiro is one of the best local guides, offering genuinely informed commentary, context and a range of tour plans to suit every need.

ACCOMMODATION AND EATING

Don't leave Riohacha without sampling the fresh juices and seafood cocktails at **Los Kioskitos**, the collection of tiny, brightly painted huts lining C 1 at the western end of the main beach. Colombian tourists also like to snack and drink along the pedestrian section of Cra 8 at night (just off the *malecón*), lined with outdoor tables.

★ **Aliuuka** C 1 (Av La Marina) No. 4–77 (Taroa Lifestyle Hotel) ☏5 729 1122. This rooftop bar and restaurant (atop the *Taroa* hotel) is a must visit, even if it's just to check out the spectacular view along the coast. There's plenty of shade, but the breezes keep things cool anyway, and you can sip cocktails, beers and wines, or sample various local snacks and dishes. Food $$, accommodation $$

La Casa del Marisco C 1 (Av La Marina) No. 4–43 ⊕ 5 728 3445. One of the better restaurants along the seafront, specializing in fresh fish but also decent pastas. $$

Casa Patio Bonita C 7 No. 4–11 ⊕ 314 763 7221. Modern B&B a short walk (300m) from the seafront, run by Colombian-Canadian couple Glen and Claudia, with five spotless, cosy rooms with shared bathrooms. $

Hostal Santa Cecilia C 12 No. 317 ⊕ 315 344 4254. The best of the budget accommodation in the centre, with basic but comfy a/c rooms (shared bathrooms) and dorms (with fans). $

Malecón Bar C1 (Av La Marina) No. 3–47 (opposite Cra 4) ⊕ 316 285 1339. Beach bar right on the sands, not far from the tourist office, serving cocktails, light snacks and cold beers with booming Colombian sounds late into the night. $

Sazón Internacional C 1 (Av La Marina) No. 3–57 ⊕ 5 422 8624. Breezy two-deck *palapa* restaurant serving a mix of Colombian staples, seafood and international favourites. The seafood rice is always an appetizing choice, as is the variety of fresh fish. English menus. $$

★ **Taroa Lifestyle Hotel** C1 (Av La Marina) No. 4–77 ⊕ 5 729 1122. The best hotel in Riohacha lies in the centre of the main seafront strip, with the marvellous rooftop bar *Aliuuka* (see page 178), and a Wayuu theme. Rooms are bright and comfy, decorated with Wayuu textiles, and boasting cable TV and modern bathrooms; most have balconies overlooking the sea. Some English speakers. Breakfast included. $$$

DIRECTORY

Banks and exchange Banco de Bogotá has a branch and ATMs on Parque Padilla; BBVA is also on the plaza, while Banco Popular is on C 1 (Av La Marina) at Cra 7.

Consulates Venezuela, Cra 7 No. 3–08 (⊕ 5 727 4076).

Festivals Festival Francisco El Hombre, held every March, celebrates *vallenato* music (w facebook.com/Festival FranciscoElHombre).

Visa extensions Centro Facilitador de Servicios Migratorios, C 5 No. 4–48.

Uribía

The town of **URIBÍA** (some 94km northeast of Riohacha) is known as the handicraft capital of the country – or simply "Capital Indígena de Colombia" – though this is a little misleading. While Wayuu do live here, Uribía has become essentially a regional service centre (and supply station for Venezuelans), and sadly, often blighted with piles of uncollected rubbish. Tours often stop by nonetheless to check out the shops, and it's also the last good place on the journey north to stock up on water and snacks (or use an ATM). The best time to buy crafts (particularly Wayuu bags or *susu*) is during the **Festival de la Cultura Wayuu** (Festival of Wayuu Culture), usually held in May or August.

Salinas de Manaure

Most Guajira tours make an obligatory stop at the **Salinas de Manaure** (salt pans) on the way to Cabo de la Vela (114km from Riohacha), with mini mountains of glittering white salt that can be highly photogenic. Note though, that the locals who work here are extremely poor – many own or rent small pools of water used for harvesting salt, but for an incredibly meagre income. After a long legal struggle, the Wayuu became joint-owners of the main salt operation (SAMA) in 2004, but it wasn't until late 2014 that an agreement was reached with a private contractor to manage the business.

> ### CROSSING INTO VENEZUELA
>
> Passing between Colombia and Venezuela is relatively straightforward, though you should check the current **security situation** (especially in Venezuela). The main departure point in Colombia is the gritty Wayuu commercial centre of Maicao, some 76km east from Riohacha (hourly buses; 1hr). From here you can catch direct *colectivos* to the city of Maracaibo (every 30min) in Venezuela – make sure the driver stops at the Colombian border post at Paraguachón (8km east of Maicao), so you can have your **passport stamped**. At Venezuelan immigration most nationalities will get a ninety-day tourist card.

Cabo de la Vela

CABO DE LA VELA is a dusty and relatively impoverished one-street Wayuu settlement strung out along an aquamarine bay. Its main draw is the spectacular landscape that surrounds it: a long sliver of beach, rocky cliffs and cactus-studded arid plains that collapse into the Caribbean. In December and January the village is inundated with holidaying Colombians but the rest of the year it's a tranquil spot for sunset viewing (particularly from the lighthouse at the far end of the bay, **El Faro**), **kitesurfing** (1hr classes available; kiteaddictcolombia.com), or just lazing on the sands of **Ojo del Agua** (aka Lojou), the local dark-sand beach (you can walk to El Faro and Ojo del Agua in around 1hr 30min, or take a *mototaxi*). Tours tend to take in the wind turbines at the **Parque Eólico Jepirrachi**, but this is a dull prospect unless you've never seen them before.

Pilón de Azúcar

Looming high above the area is the **Pilón de Azúcar**, a small hill (around 120m), 7km north of Cabo and topped by a tiny shrine to the Virgin Mary (La Virgen de Fátima) – the hill is known to the Wayuu as Kama'ichi, a holy place (take a *mototaxi*; 15min one-way). The views over the sea and surrounding desert is mesmerizing, with the beach below, the **Playa de Pilón**, a strip of copper-coloured sands backed by jagged cliffs.

ARRIVAL AND DEPARTURE — CABO DE LA VELA

By colectivo and truck Most travellers visit the region on tours from Riohacha (see page 178), from where independent travel by public transport is also possible (see page 178).

By car There are no rental cars in Riohacha – the nearest place is Santa Marta – but if you do drive note that armed robberies do sometimes occur on the remote roads out here.

ACCOMMODATION AND EATING

There's plentiful **budget accommodation** in Cabo, comprising hammocks, traditional Wayuu *chinchorros* (warmer hammocks), Wayuu huts made of yotojoro (the inner core of the cactus) and basic concrete rooms. Showers tend to be bucket-style affairs. Most guesthouses have generators that only work between 6 and 10pm, and many double as **restaurants** serving goat and locally caught fish and lobster.

Hospedaje Jarrinapi Near the beachfront ☎ 310 835 6028. Simple but attractive yotojoro huts (with private bathrooms but no a/c), in a well-maintained Wayuu compound, with dependable electricity (6pm–6am), internet points and areas for cheaper hammocks. The restaurant turns out tasty Colombian staples. Food $, accommodation $

★ **Ranchería Utta** Vía al Faro (the road to the lighthouse) rancheriautta.com. This traditional Wayuu compound, replete with goats and gorgeous yotojoro huts (fans, bathroom and hammocks), offers an ideal taster of local hospitality, with simpler spaces for hammocks and *chinchorros* (with lockers) and all meals provided (expect to eat a lot of goat). Hammocks & *chinchorros* $, huts $$

Punta Gallinas

Even more remote than Cabo, **PUNTA GALLINAS** is one of the most alluring destinations on the Caribbean coast, where a series of giant sand dunes simply fold into the sea. Populated by a handful of very friendly Wayuu, this is the northernmost part of the South American continent and feels like a lost world.

The main attraction here is **Playa Taroa**, a short ride from the main settlement, a bizarre, enchanting place where you can slide down sandy mountains straight into the water – you are likely to have the beach to yourself.

ARRIVAL AND DEPARTURE — PUNTA GALLINAS

By tour Colombia's northernmost tip is most comfortably visited by organized tour – it's difficult to attempt the journey solo, even in a 4WD. The best option is Kaí Ecotravel in Riohacha (see page 178).

Independent travel It is possible to travel independently from Cabo: you can take a very bumpy jeep ride, departing around 5am (3hr 30min); heading back you'll leave at around 8.30am. Hostels in Cabo can help arrange the trip, and accommodation.

ACCOMMODATION AND EATING

Your options are understandably limited when it comes to Punta Gallinas, but finding somewhere to stay is relatively easy – most folks end up at the *ranchería* of **Doña Luz Mila** (📞 312 647 9881) with covered (but outdoor) hammocks (plus more comfortable *chinchorros*) and meals (it's hot but breezy at night). **Kaí Ecotravel** can arrange stays (see page 178).

Valledupar

The self-proclaimed "capital of *vallenato*" (the accordion-driven Colombian musical genre), **VALLEDUPAR** is a relatively affluent city of around half a million people. It's home to a small colonial centre, studded with trees ripe with mangos, but is best known for the sprinkling of natural attractions in the surrounding area. The city lies on the left bank of the **Río Guatapurí**, in the middle of a fertile valley anchored by two mountain chains – the **Sierra Nevada de Santa Marta** to the west and the **Sierra de Perijá** to the east, both providing relief from the heat in the form of several churning, pristine rivers. The Sierra Nevada is also the home of the Indigenous Wintukua (Arhuaco), Kogui, Wiwa (Arsanio) and Kankuamo – **Nabusimake** is an especially captivating Arhuaco village high in the mountains. Valledupar's chaotic but entertaining main shopping street is Carrera 7, south of Calle 15 and the main square, **Plaza Alfonso López**. Things heat up during the annual **Festival de la Leyenda Vallenata** (April), though actual temperatures rarely drop below 30 degrees during the day all year round.

Plaza Alfonso López

The heart of colonial Valledupar is leafy **Plaza Alfonso López**, sprinkled with lush mango trees and lined, in part, with low-slung adobe houses built in the 1780s. There are plaques (in Spanish) all the way around explaining which local luminary lived where, and a small church, the **Iglesia La Inmaculada Concepción** (usually open for Mass only), home to a venerated image of Santo Ecce Homo, patron of Valledupar. In the southeast corner of the square the expressive **Monumento La Revolución en Marcha** (1994) juts out into the plaza to commemorate beloved ex-president Alfonso López (1886–1959), while opposite, the art store **El Abasto** (C 16 No. 5–05) occupies the gorgeous 1802 colonial home of independence hero José Francisco Maestre.

Catedral Nuestra Señora del Rosario

Cra 7 No. 15–26 • 318 420 1563

The site of the sixteenth-century Convento de Santo Domingo is now the **Catedral Nuestra Señora del Rosario**, a largely uninteresting modern edifice built next to the far more attractive, former bell tower of the convent. The tower now serves as a curious little chapel, the Ermita de Jesús Sacramento.

Museo del Acordeón – Casa Beto Murgas

Cra 17 No. 9A–18 • Charge • 🌐 museodelacordeonvalledupar.com

To get to grips with Valledupar's musical heritage, visit the **Museo del Acordeón – Casa Beto Murgas**. Celebrating the work of José Alberto Murgas Peñaloza (aka Beto Murgas), one of the most beloved and successful *vallenatos*, it holds exhibits of personal effects, instruments and music (you need to speak Spanish to appreciate this, however).

Balneario Hurtado

Free

You could easily spend a pleasant afternoon bathing in the refreshingly cool waters of the **Balneario Hurtado**, a picturesque section of the Río Guatapurí near the road bridge at the north end of town. The site is overlooked by the benevolent gaze of *La Sirena del Río* (a gold-painted mermaid statue).

ARRIVAL AND DEPARTURE   VALLEDUPAR

By plane Aeropuerto Alfonso López Pumarejo is 5km south of the city, served by flights to Barranquilla (EasyFly) and Bogotá (Avianca and LATAM). Taxis run from the airport to the centre of Valledupar ("centro"); local buses to the centre depart from just outside the terminal. You can also rent cars here (Hertz has a desk at the terminal).
Destinations Barranquilla (2 daily; 40min); Bogotá (4 daily; 1hr 20min).

By bus The Terminal de Transportes lies 3km south of the main plaza at Cra 7 No. 44–156. Take a taxi to "centro" from here; local buses charge a standard flat fee throughout the city but route routes are complicated, and buses often very cramped.
Destinations Barranquilla (3–4 daily; 4–5hr); Bucaramanga (3–4 daily; 8hr); Mompox (3–4 daily; 7–8hr); Riohacha (3–4 daily; 3hr); San Gil (daily 7am; 10hr); Santa Marta (3–4 daily; 2hr).

ACCOMMODATION

★ **Casa de Los Santos Reyes** C 13C No. 4A–90 ⓦ hotelboutiquevalledupar.com. Contemporary boutique hotel in a colonial property, with just five beautiful period rooms with satellite TV, a tiny pool and a cache of bold local artwork. Breakfast included. $$

Hotel Boutique Casa Rosalía C 16 No. 10–10 ⓦ casarosalia.co. Beautiful and tranquil guesthouse combining lush gardens and period (a/c) rooms with contemporary art and furnishings. Hammocks available. Free national phonecalls; breakfast extra. $$

Hotel Nabu Valledupar C16A No. 6–63 ⓦ hotelnabu.com. This travellers' favourite is a well finished retreat near the main plaza, with modern and en-suite rooms (all with flatscreen TVs). $$

Hotel Tativan C 16a No. 9–50 ⓦ hoteltativan.com. Comfy business hotel with all the amenities you'd expect of a four-star; friendly staff, relaxing outdoor pool and modern rooms with a/c, cable TV and breakfast included. $$$

EATING AND DRINKING

The most central **Exito supermarket** stretches between Carreras 6 and 7 (between Calles 16A and 16C). When it comes to **drinking**, Valledupar is at the centre of the bizarre Colombian obsession with Old Parr Scotch whisky, the export-only blend that dominates the local market – during the *vallenato* festival crates of the stuff are shipped here.

Compai Chipuco C 16 No. 6–05 (just off Plaza Alfonso López, enter on Cra 6) ⓟ 605 589 8186. Part art shop, part bar and restaurant, this is a relaxing spot for lunch or just an afternoon drink, set in a quiet garden shaded by a giant mango tree. Lunch options include steaks, fried chicken or a variety of fish (red snapper, mojarra and catfish). $

Palenke Cra 5 No. 13C–52 ⓟ 315 235 4378. Bright, modern bar near the main plaza, adorned with contemporary and Indigenous art with a good mix of Afro, Cuban and Caribbean music (it makes a refreshing break from all the *vallenato* blaring on the streets), washed down with craft beers and fruity *micheladas* (blends of beer and mango juice).

Panadería La Mejor C 17 No. 8–15 ⓟ 5 574 3025. Old-fashioned café and cake shop established in 1979, with table service or takeaway, delicious *tortas*, cupcakes, *arroz con leche*, cheese breads and natural juices. $

★ **Varadero** C 12 No. 6–56 ⓦ varaderorestaurante.co. Superb Cuban seafood restaurant (with branches in Cartagena and Barranquilla, page 159), offering fresh ceviche and fish dishes as well as Cuban classics. $$

THE PEOPLES OF THE SIERRA NEVADA

The Sierra Nevada de Santa Marta is the traditional home to four main Indigenous groups (the **Kogi** are on the Tayrona side of the massif); logic (and local tradition) would suggest that these groups are descendants of the mighty **Tairona** civilization, but this has been hard to prove. The **Kankuamo** spoke the Kankwe language until a few decades ago (no longer), and live in twelve communities on the southeastern slopes of the Sierra centred around the village of Atánquez; most are coffee and sugarcane farmers and struggle to retain their traditions.

Like the other Indigenous peoples of the Sierra, the **Wintukuas** (Arhuaco) men carry the *póporo*, the saliva-coated gourd holding the lime that activates the coca leaves they constantly chew –the *póporo* symbolizes their partner in the spirit world, in whom they trust their thoughts and words; coca also helps them remember and recite myths, chants and genealogies during all-night sessions. The Wintukuas live in two reserves in the upper valleys of the Nabusimake, Chichicua, Ariguani and Guatapurí rivers; they speak Ijkan, a Chibcha language.

The **Wiwa** number around 13,000 on the southeast side of the Sierra, and they are the smallest of the Indigenous groups here – like all the peoples of the Sierra Nevada they too wear white and the men tend to grow their hair long.

SHOPPING

Centro Artesanal Calle Grande C 16 No. 7–18. This indoor arcade stretches between C 16 and Cra 7, packed with all sorts of arts and crafts stalls – quality is good and prices reasonable. Come here for backpacks (*mochilas*), hats, bags, bracelets, paintings and the *sombrero vueltiao*, Colombia's national hat, made to order from a local grass fibre called caña flecha (arrow cane, also known as wild cane or caña brava).

DIRECTORY

Festivals The Festival de la Leyenda Vallenata (April) sees the best in *vallenato* music performed in the main plaza (w festivalvallenato.com).

Visa extensions Centro Facilitador de Servicios Migratorios, C 11A No.15–42, Barrio Loperena.

Balneario La Mina

To enjoy a dip in the pure and invigorating waters of the **Río Badillo**, take a *colectivo* (see below) from Valledupar to **Balneario La Mina**, an idyllic spot some 40km to the north, inside the **Resguardo Indígena Kankuamo** (Kankuamo Indigenous Reserve), where the river snakes through an astounding landscape of silky smooth white rocks. It's a good place to swim because the current isn't that strong; be prepared for mosquitoes, though.

Atánquez

The twelve main Kankuamo communities lie around the village of **ATÁNQUEZ**, at the heart of the **Resguardo Indígena Kankuamo** high in the Sierra Nevada de Santa Marta (and a bit further up the road from La Mina). Around the cobbled main plaza the locals sell traditional crafts and really good coffee, but don't take pictures without permission.

ARRIVAL AND DEPARTURE   ATÁNQUEZ

By colectivo Unipueblos runs *colectivos* between Valledupar, La Mina and Atánquez, virtually every hour (daily; 1–2hr), from C 18 near the market and Cra 7 (you'll see Kankuamo waiting outside the *Sazón Vallenato* restaurant at C 18 No. 6–39).

Nabusimake

The spiritual centre of the Wintukuas (Arhuacos), **NABUSIMAKE**, meaning "land where the sun was born", is one of the most enigmatic and traditional Indigenous settlements in Colombia. It is a mystical place high in the Sierra Nevada de Santa Marta (at around 1800m), 39km beyond the village of Puerto Bello. From here, there is only one road into the village; it's pretty bumpy so come prepared if you suffer from car sickness. This is not a tourist attraction, but a real, sacred place (the buildings are actual dwellings), and outsiders are (understandably) limited in what they can see or do here (always ask first before taking photos as they may be prohibited). The traditional heart of the village is an incredibly atmospheric blend of thatched buildings and round-stone plazas – you are not allowed to enter the village by yourself and it is not guaranteed that you will be allowed in.

ARRIVAL AND DEPARTURE   NABUSIMAKE

By bus and jeep Take a Cootransnevada (t 317 883 1296) bus from Cra 7 (at C 18b and the Galería Popular mall) to Pueblo Bello (hourly; 1hr 30min), some 85km from Valledupar. From the Pueblo Bello bus terminal you can take a 4WD up to Nabusimake (a bumpy 2hr ride). There is an admission charge for the village.
On a tour Paseo Vallenato runs two-day tours from Valledupar (w paseovallenato.com).

ACCOMMODATION AND EATING

There should be at least three or four **places to stay** just outside the village proper – outsiders are strictly forbidden to spend the night inside the village. Electricity is limited here.

San Andrés and Providencia

186 San Andrés
199 Providencia

PRISTINE BEACH ON ISLA DE PROVIDENCIA

San Andrés and Providencia

A world apart from the rest of Colombia, both geographically and culturally, the islands of San Andrés and Providencia sit in the Caribbean Sea 220km off the coast of Nicaragua, with Providencia (74km north of San Andrés) atop the third-largest barrier reef in the world. Visitors come all this way for the glittering white-sand beaches, the best diving in Colombia and the unique Raizal culture; the Afro-Caribbean residents of Providencia in particular speak an English-based Creole with a Caribbean lilt that is reminiscent of Jamaican patois, and the influence of Bogotá seems remote indeed.

English is an official language alongside Spanish on both islands, but on larger, more developed **San Andrés**, the Raizal culture is much more diluted. For many Colombians, one of San Andrés' draws is its duty-free status, and tourism on the island is dominated by all-inclusive resorts and packages. Sleepy **Providencia**, with its empty beaches and protected reef is by far the more enticing destination – there's little point in coming to San Andrés without going on to its northerly neighbour.

Brief history
Providencia was first settled by **English Puritans** of the **Providence Island Company** in the late 1620s, a sister colony to Massachusetts Bay (modern-day Boston). Settlers arrived on San Andrés first (1628), which they dubbed "Henrietta" in honour of Henry VIII, before moving to "Providence Island", where they found a few Dutch privateers (today the island is also known as Old Providence – New Providence is in the Bahamas). The English introduced tobacco plantations and adopted privateering themselves in 1636 (plundering Spanish ships), finally provoking the Spanish into capturing the island in 1641 and ejecting most of the colonists. The Spanish did little to settle the islands however, and in 1670 pirates led by **Henry Morgan** essentially occupied Providencia; though the buccaneers had been flushed out by 1689, this period informs much of the island's romantic view of itself (and the tourist industry).

Both islands changed hands between the British and Spanish several times in subsequent years, though they were occupied by English-speaking Protestant cotton plantation owners (many of whom claimed descent from British pirates) and their Jamaican (Afro-Caribbean) slaves (the ancestors of today's Raizal population). **Slavery** was abolished in 1851, after which the **Raizal** population dominated life on both islands, replacing the cotton plantations with coconut groves. Most of the coconut palms were killed off during a blight in the 1940s; tourism began to transform San Andrés after military dictator Rojas Pinilla declared the islands a free port in 1953. Even today, very little farming is practised on either island – most food is imported. Marginalized for decades, Raizal culture got a boost in 2017 when *Bad Lucky Goat* – set in Providencia – became the first movie ever written and produced in the local Creole.

San Andrés

Colombia's very own Caribbean island of sandy cays, reggae bars and spectacular azure waters rich in marine life, **San Andrés** is a full-on resort destination for middle-class Colombians, especially busy during the long school holidays (December to January), Easter, and in July and August. **Diving** off San Andrés is absolutely sensational; the water is warm all year round, the visibility is (mostly) spectacular and the reefs are some of the richest and most beautiful in the Caribbean.

SCUBA DIVER EXPLORING THE CORAL REEF IN SAN ANDRÉS

Highlights

❶ Johnny Cay Lounge on the pristine beaches of this sandy, palm-smothered island just off San Andrés. See page 194

❷ Rondón The closest thing both islands have to a national dish, a sumptuous blend of seafood, plantains and coconut milk. See page 197

❸ Sunday gospel The gospel choirs of San Andrés' Baptist churches are a crucial pillar of the local Raizal identity – and a musical treat. See page 198

❹ Climbing The Peak Hike up to the highest point on Providencia to soak up mind-bending views across the island and the Caribbean. See page 200

❺ Crab Cay A protected islet just off Providencia on the edge of a massive reef, with fabulous snorkelling in the "sea of seven colours". See page 201

❻ Diving Providencia Experience some of the best diving in the Caribbean, with healthy reefs and a huge variety of marine life. See page 202

HIGHLIGHTS ARE MARKED ON THE MAP ON PAGE 188

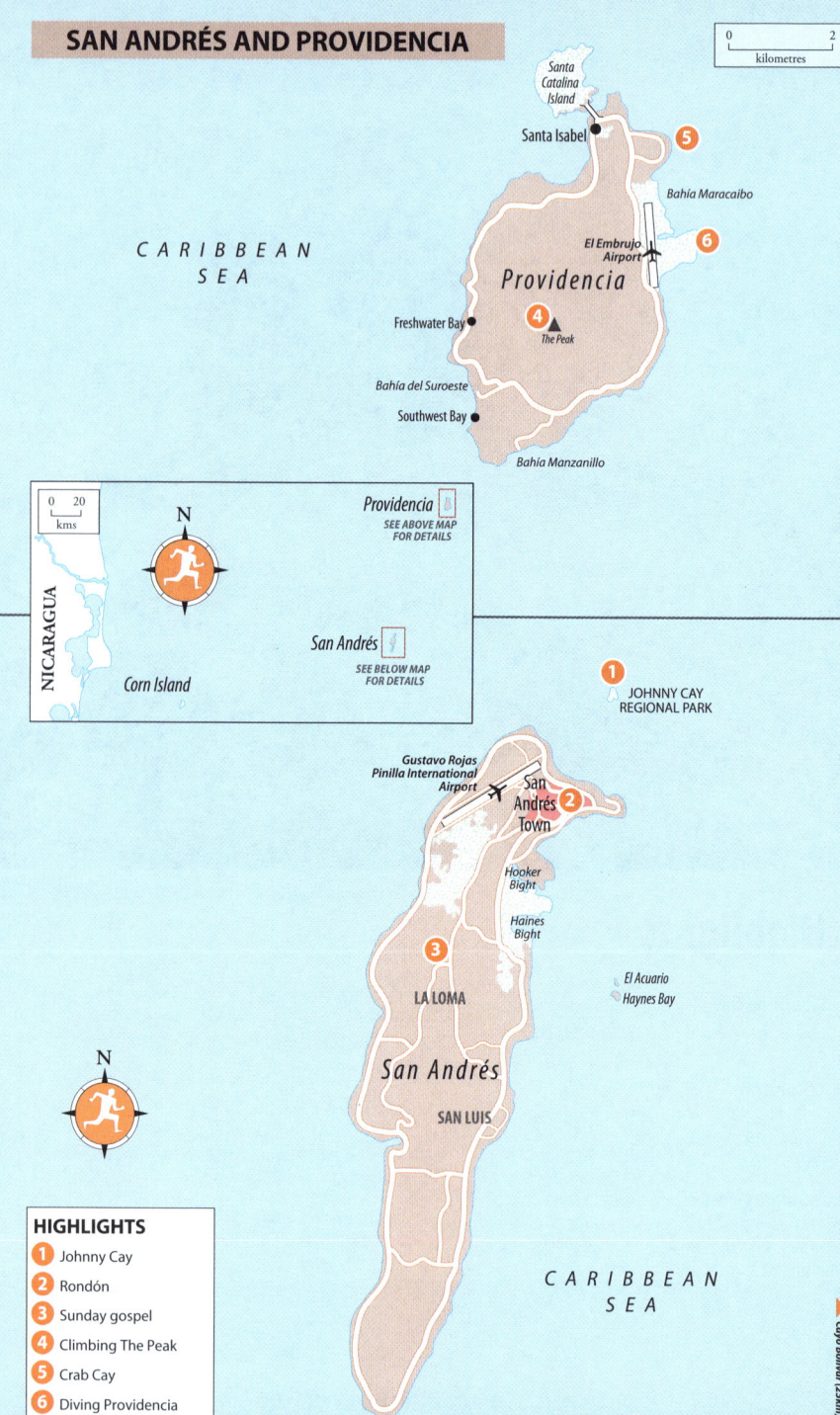

> **THE NICARAGUAN CLAIM**
>
> From 1803 the Spanish began to administer both San Andrés and Providencia from Cartagena (almost 800km away), which meant that they reverted to Colombian rule after independence in 1822. Nevertheless, **Nicaragua** (which is much closer) has never really given up its rival claim; in the 1980s the Sandinista government argued that Nicaragua signed the **Esguerra-Bárcenas Treaty** of 1928, which formally gave control of the islands to Colombia, under US pressure and military occupation. In 2001, Nicaragua filed claims with the **International Court of Justice (ICJ)**, and in 2012 the court finally decided in Colombia's favour, though granting Nicaragua control of the surrounding sea and seabed – a minor victory for Nicaragua that provoked fear in the islands that traditional fishing grounds might be lost (Colombia pulled out of the ICJ in protest). In 2013 Nicaragua filed a new case asking the court to rule on exact marine boundaries (it plans to start drilling for oil and gas in the area), though Colombia countersued in 2017 and Nicaragua also became embroiled with a similar dispute with Costa Rica – nothing is likely to be resolved soon. As you'll quickly notice, Colombia maintains a heavy military presence on both islands, just in case.

Though the **Raizal** here are now a minority thanks to immigration from the mainland, they continue to cling to a very distinctive Afro-Caribbean culture – everyone speaks Spanish, of course, but the locals also speak a Creole that has more in common with English, albeit with a West Indian twang. Beyond the **all-inclusive resorts** that dominate tourism on the island, parts of the interior remain surprisingly rustic, studded with old wooden houses with Antillean-style verandas. Indeed, two competing images loom large over modern San Andrés – **Bob Marley**, adopted saint of the local Raizal population (along with all things Jamaican, seemingly), and Johnny Depp's Captain Jack Sparrow, fictional hero of the **Pirates of the Caribbean** movie franchise and a symbol of everything "pirate" to the local tourism industry. It's a bizarre combination, certainly unique in Colombia.

Most accommodation is concentrated in **San Andrés Town**, the capital – a busy whirl of modern concrete buildings, **duty-free shops** and careering motorbikes. Visitors usually take at least one day to **tour the island**, sticking to the 30km coastal ring-road, though there are a few places where you can head inland. The souped-up **golf carts** are the most popular way to get around, but you can also rent scooters (see page 195). Travelling by public bus is possible, but not especially convenient if you want to see the whole island. Note, too, that the best beaches and snorkelling can be found on **Johnny Cay** and **Acuario**, which are only accessible by boat – much of the main island's coastline is rocky and devoid of sand and offers only mediocre snorkelling.

Note that the island's **tap water** is not safe to drink (it comes from desalinization plants) – make sure to stick to bottled water.

San Andrés Town

The capital of the archipelago, **SAN ANDRÉS TOWN** (aka "Centro") is a lively Colombian party town wedged onto a peninsula on the northern edge of the island, especially raucous during major holidays when domestic tourists (and increasingly, Brazilians) pack duty-free shops, cram the bars to watch live football and cheerfully carouse along the seafront promenades. Though the **town beach** (Playa Centro, or Spratt Bight) is often overcrowded, the buildings are uniformly modern concrete boxes and the streets are swamped with shoppers and death-defying scooter riders, it's not as grim as it sounds and can be lots of fun, as long as you adjust your expectations accordingly. San Andrés Town is where most of the island's hotels, bars and restaurants are located, so you'll probably spend at least your evenings here. The **promenade** (*malecón*) on the northern side (known as Av Colombia), with its clear view of Johnny Cay, is the best place for an evening or early morning stroll.

> **THE TOURIST CARD (TARJETA DE TURISMO)**
>
> Everyone who visits San Andrés and Providencia must complete a special "**Tourist Card**" (a bit like an immigration form); you'll be given these when you check in for your flight, where you'll also have to pay a **fee** (cash only; if you are flying from Panama City you can pay in US$-equivalent). On arrival in San Andrés or Providencia you will have this checked (with your passport) as if you are entering another country – your baggage will also be screened. You can spend a maximum of four months on the islands per year in total, regardless of how many trips you make.

Centro Cultural

Av Colón 2–74 • Free • ⓦ banrepcultural.org/san-andres

Opened by the Banco de la República, the stylish **Centro Cultural** is the town's arts hub, with a couple of rooms charting the island's history and local artwork, the Centro de Memorias Orales ("Oral Memories Centre") and a decent library, plus a programme of readings, live concerts and entertainment.

Rocky Cay Beach

As you head south from San Andrés Town along the east side of the island, the first attraction is **Rocky Cay Beach**, close to the road but not visible from it thanks to some dense vegetation and a couple of resorts. The small white-sand beach gets its name from a tiny island 100m offshore ("Cayo Rocoso" in Spanish) – the water is so shallow you can usually wade to the cay over the sandbank here. Note that the island itself is mostly jagged rock, so reef shoes are advised.

On the other side of the cay lies the rusting hulk of the abandoned freighter *Nicodemus*. Locals claim the boat was owned by shipping magnate Aristotle Onassis, and that around thirty years ago the ship was being towed to Cartagena when it split into three parts during a storm. Two bits sank to become artificial reefs, while the third section is what you see above the waves today. The wreck makes for a dramatic photo, but don't be tempted to board it – it's extremely dangerous. To access the beach look for the "Playa Rocky Cay" signs or walk through *Decameron Mar Azul* or *Hotel Cocoplum Beach* (the hotels are private but the beach is public, whatever the staff may tell you). You can rent lounge chairs, but hotel guests get priority.

San Luis

The somewhat impoverished village of **SAN LUIS** straggles for several kilometres along the east coast, encompassing a couple of decent restaurants (see page 198) and hotels. Towards the southern end, the main **beach** area is a pleasant slice of windswept white-sand that's often deserted, with decent snorkelling offshore assuming the waves cooperate – conditions here are often choppy and the coastline has been facing severe erosion and flooding in recent years.

Hoyo Soplador

Km 16 Crta Circunvalar • Free, but a "tip" for parking may be requested • "Cove/Loma" bus from San Andrés Town (every 20min; 40min)

Hoyo Soplador (literally "blowhole") at the southern tip of the island, is a natural blowhole in the jagged banks of old coral that form the coastline here; when the tide and wind conditions are right, a plume of water shoots up to 20m out of the fissure in the rock, soaking the hordes of squealing kids below. It's a bizarre sight, amplified by the carnival atmosphere most days, with makeshift bars, gift shops and restaurants surrounding the main attraction, and Jamaican dancehall pumping out of giant speakers.

La Piscinita

Km 13 Crta Circunvalar • Charge • Snorkel rental extra • "Cove/Loma" bus from San Andrés (every 20min; 40min)

Known as **La Piscinita** (or Piscina Natural), this Raizal-run attraction is where a crystal-clear cove of deep water has formed right on the rugged coral shoreline – the land has been owned by the local Pomare family for years. Entry includes bread with which you can feed large schools of multicoloured tropical fish (long accustomed to the practice), after climbing in via a wood ladder. It's fun (especially if this is your first experience of reef fish in the wild), but the snorkelling is otherwise unexceptional (rental snorkels are poor quality; bring your own). There's a basic restaurant on site and there's a fee to use the toilets.

West View

Km 11 Crta Circunvalar• Charge (life-jacket rental available) • 8 513 0341 • "Cove/Loma" bus from San Andrés Town (every 20min; 40min)

West View (sometimes confusingly also dubbed "Piscina Natural", like La Piscinita, a few kilometres to its south; see page 192) is a deepwater cove accessed by metal ladder, with vast numbers of tropical fish that will nibble bread (supplied) out of your hand. It's a similar setup – with a larger restaurant – to La Piscinita, and similarly, the snorkelling isn't that interesting beyond feeding the fish. Most Colombian tourists amuse themselves on the diving board and water slide, or sipping cocktails.

Cueva de Morgan and Pueblito Isleño

Km 7 Crta Circunvalar • Charge (each site) • 318 548 3468

Halfway up the west coast and just inland (signposted off the coast road), the **Cueva de Morgan** (Morgan Cave) is a kitsch tourist attraction run by the local Raizal. English-speaking guides will take you around the shady park-like site, beginning with the

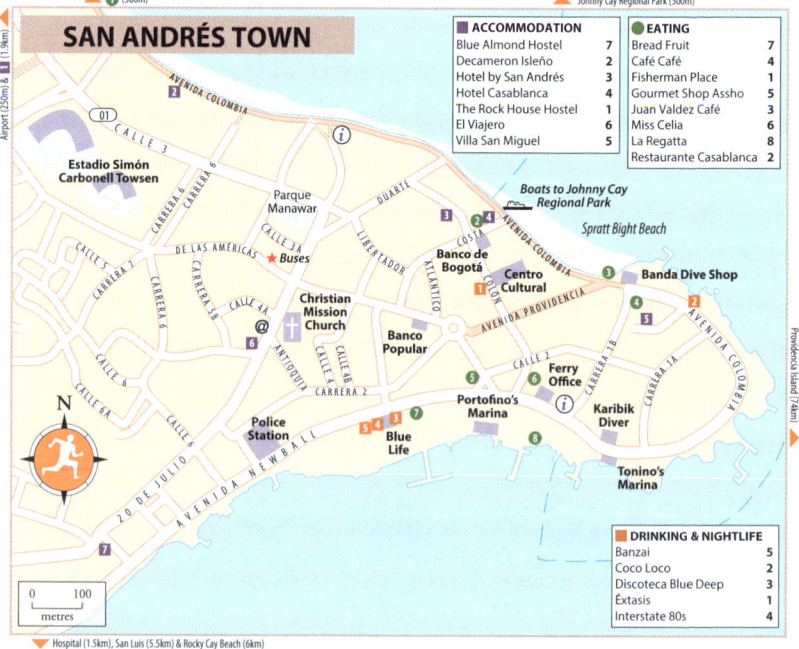

SAN ANDRÉS – THE ECOLOGICAL THREATS

Spend any time on San Andrés and it's obvious that the island is facing some fairly severe **ecological challenges**. A booming tourism industry and a growing population have put a huge strain on resources, causing pollution and poor waste management; refuse production on San Andrés is more than one hundred tonnes per day. The huge demand for water has led to the over-exploitation of local aquifers and the pollution of both groundwater and coastal waters. Beach erosion is a growing problem, and the island's waters are heavily fished by industrial ships. Global warming threatens to cause extensive bleaching of the coral reefs, already damaged by pollution, overfishing and hurricanes.

MOVING FORWARDS

Part of the challenge has been bringing the locals on board – since the 1960s, the Raizal population has been bypassed by the central government when it comes to development, leading to widespread poverty, a loss of traditional industries and an overreliance on tourism and imports. Locals need to make a living, and resent outsiders lecturing them on how to manage their island – the ongoing dispute over **Cayo Bolívar** (see page 194) is a sad example.

Since 1993, government-funded **CORALINA** has been working to reduce pollution in the islands, with some success (see ⓦcoralina.gov.co), and in 2000, UNESCO declared the San Andrés archipelago a biosphere reserve. The Colombian government established the **Seaflower Biosphere Reserve and Marine Protected Area in 2005**, while in 2011 the people of the main islands successfully united to stop a proposal to exploit oil in the territory. In 2017 and continuing to this day, the local **Bajo Tranquilo** started an initiative to deposit more than ten thousand live corals around the islands as a major reef restoration project (volunteers also continue to remove tonnes of rubbish annually from the surrounding waters).

---

cave itself (the end of a 200m limestone passage that connects to the sea, said to be one of Captain Morgan's treasure hideouts). Nearby lies an extremely crude "replica" of Morgan's ship *Sea Wolf*, a gallery of local artwork and a Museo del Pirata (Pirate Museum), full of Johnny Depp images and bric-a-brac salvaged from wrecks. Finally, the Museo del Coco (Coconut Museum) contains some truly enormous coconuts (no longer grown here), and endearing sculptures made from coconut shells.

Next door the **Pueblito Isleño** is a similarly half-hearted attempt to represent traditional Raizal life with wood huts and 35 life-size wood sculptures (hair-braiding, making music, playing dominoes, cooking and the like). The tour guides here can be enlightening, however, if you want to learn about local history.

Casa Museo Isleña

Km 5 Crta Circunvalar • Charge • ☏ 8 512 3419

Casa Museo Isleña on the northwest coast is a pretty, 200-year old, two-storey gem owned by the Guernica-Archibald family that offers the chance to get a brief look inside a typical island-style house. Its tiny rooms, with creaking floors and warped timbers, feature a handful of period items and you can also visit the outhouses in the garden; local dancers perform on demand as part of your admission. English-speaking guides are on hand for brief tours (included in admission).

First Baptist Church

La Loma Donation suggested; charge for tower • ⓦ lahispana.org • "Cove/Loma" bus from San Andrés (every 20min; 40min)

San Andrés is 65 percent Baptist (mainly thanks to the local Raizal population), and its oldest place of worship is the **First Baptist Church** (Primeria Iglesia Bautista), a clapboard beauty dating back to the 1840s. It's high above the coast in **LA LOMA** (aka

"The Hill"), a proudly Raizal village that straggles along the island's central ridge with Caribbean-style wooden homes and lush breadfruit trees. The plain interior is simply adorned, while the views from the cramped bell tower – over the whole island – are sensational. On Sundays, this is the place to witness one of the best **gospel choirs** in the archipelago (see page 198).

Jardín Botánico

Via Harmony Hall Hill (in front of Hotel Sol Caribe Campo), La Loma • Charge • facebook.com/JardinBotanicoSanAndres

Operated by the Universidad Nacional de Colombia, the shady **Jardín Botánico** makes for a pleasant break from the beach, with one-hour tours of the gardens (some English speakers) providing background on traditional medicinal plants, herbs and island ecology as well as local culture and history. Don't miss the expansive views from the 12m-high observation tower.

Johnny Cay Regional Park

Charge • Numerous boats depart from San Andrés beach (Spratt Bight) in the mornings around 8.30–10.30am; the last boats return around 4–4.30pm (make sure you remember which boat you came on)

The best San Andrés beach is actually on **Johnny Cay Regional Park**, the palm-shaded, iguana-inhabited island visible directly across the water from San Andrés Town. Gorgeous chalk-white sands surround the island's southern coastline, while the shimmering blue waters offshore are far more enticing for a swim than the main island (though currents can be strong). In high season expect the island to be swamped with visitors enjoying the fried red snapper and "coco loco" cocktails at the makeshift reggae bars here. You can usually avoid the crowds by strolling over to the northern side of the island, though the beach is smaller. Since 2017 only 1500 people can visit the cay daily, with no more than eight hundred on the island at one time.

El Acuario

Boat charge per return; combined with Johnny Cay; departures from Tonino's Marina (see map p.194) • Lockers, toilets and snorkel rental are extra

A tiny sandbank off the east coast of the main island, **El Acuario** is surrounded by water that is swimming pool-clear – though on busy days you'll find yourself fighting for space among the other visitors and its three shacks poking out of the water (one for snacks and drinks, one for lockers and one for toilets). Bring a snorkel and reef shoes if you intend to explore – the water is shallow enough to allow wading between tide pools, but the coral and rock can be sharp. You can also wade across to **Haynes Cay**, a small but more substantial palm-fringed islet occupied by popular restaurant *Bibi's Place*. The main marine attractions are the **manta rays** that often congregate here, especially towards the end of the afternoon, though sadly, some people feed them and even grab them for pictures.

Cayo Bolívar

By far the most idyllic stretch of white sand in the region lies on tiny **Cayo Bolívar**, made up of two small sandbanks (East and West Cays), some 25km southeast from San Andrés. The whole thing is just 6.4km long and 3.5km wide (there's a small military post on West Cay, but no tourist services).

Cayo Bolívar **was closed to tourism** in early 2016 to allow the authorities to develop a more sustainable plan after years of misuse. The government plan is to appoint a single operator to run tours to the island (around sixty people maximum/day), with regular closures throughout the year to allow the island to recover, but the local Raizal community opposes this and to this day, the situation remains at loggerheads, with tourism still off limits. When or if trips do resume, they are likely to be pricey. Be warned – the speedboat ride across (45min–1hr) can be very choppy.

ARRIVAL AND DEPARTURE SAN ANDRÉS

By plane Aeropuerto Internacional Gustavo Rojas Pinilla, just 1.5km northwest of the centre of San Andrés Town, is served by daily Avianca, LATAM, Viva Colombia, Wingo and Copa flights from the mainland and is connected to neighbouring Providencia by SATENA/SEARCA flights (use the SATENA website to book; if it doesn't work you will have to buy tickets from travel agents or in cash at San Andrés airport). You have to buy a tourist card on the mainland before checking in for your San Andrés flight (see page 191). On arrival there's a small tourist information booth (manned erratically) before the passport/tourist card check, then a line of travel agents and major hotel desks before the taxi rank – walk back into the main terminal if you need ATMs (BBVA and Banco de Bogotá are just to the right). Taxis from the airport to anywhere in San Andrés Town have a fixed fee, or else you can walk to the centre in around 15min. Always agree on the price before getting into a taxi.
Destinations Barranquilla (daily; 1hr 30min); Bogotá (4–5 daily; 2hr); Cali (daily; 2hr); Cartagena (daily; 1hr 25min); Medellín (daily; 1hr 45min); Panama City (2 daily; 1hr 20min); Providencia (2–4 daily; 15–20min).

By boat A catamaran runs between San Andrés Town and Santa Isabel on Providencia (weather permitting; 3hr 30min). Fares vary according to the low and high seasons (with online deals for return tickets). See w conocemosnavegando.com.

GETTING AROUND AND INFORMATION

By bus Local buses leave (from near *Hotel Hernando Henry* at Av Las Américas and Cra 5 in San Andrés Town every 20–30min). There are basically two routes: the "San Luis" bus (which runs back and forth along the coast to San Luis), and the "Loma/Cove" bus that runs all the way along the coast road to the Hoyo Soplador, then loops back inland to town via La Loma.

By bicycle/scooter Several outlets in San Andrés Town rent bicycles and scooters – your hotel should be able to recommend one. Cycling is a good way to explore the island,

---

DIVING SAN ANDRÉS

Some of the island's most jaw-dropping attractions are to be found under the sea, and San Andrés boasts numerous **diving outfits** that can introduce you to a whole new world, even if you're a first-time diver. The list below includes some of the more reputable operators (there are many amateur and ethically dubious operators here, so choose wisely). Most operators offer two dives per trip, but gear is not always included.

TOP DIVE SITES

The **Blue Diamond wreck**, off the eastern shore of the island (at around 10m) is one of the most fun and popular dives (you can swim through an open hatch in the hull).
La Piscinita (not to be confused with the sight on the west coast) is a solid choice for beginners, comprising a rich coral garden on a shallow plateau (10–20m), ending in a drop-off to more than 45m: expect to see angelfish, huge parrot fish, stingrays and lobsters.
Palacio de la Cherna – exciting wall dive southeast of San Andrés that drops from 12m to over 300m, with reef and nurse sharks, lobster and king crab among its denizens.
Pirámide – morays, stingrays, octopus and shoals of fish make this shallow reef dive one of the most exciting for beginners. It's also the only site open for night dives.

DIVE OPERATORS

Banda Dive Shop Hotel Lord Pierre, Av Colombia 1b–106, San Andrés Town w bandadiveshop.com. A friendly, central choice with some of the best rates for dives and courses.
Blue Life Hotel Sunrise, Av Newball 4–169, San Andrés Town w bluelifedive.com. Very experienced instructors (with good English) – lots of visitors get their Open Water Diver certification here.
San Andrés Divers Km 10 Crta Circunvalar w sanandresdivers.com. Located outside the main tourist areas, but particularly recommended for their professional approach.
Scuba San Andrés Km 8.5 Crta Circunvalar w scubasanandres.co. An incredibly professional operation located at *Hotel Playa Tranquilo* on the west side of the island. They offer free pick-ups from your hotel.

as the roads are paved and there's not much traffic. Most scooter rental places won't ask you for your licence and they won't provide you with a helmet, either; be prepared for some erratic local driving.

By golf cart (carrito) Golf carts are the transport of choice for Colombian tourists; you'll see numerous rental outlets along the seafront (avenidas Newball and Colombia) in San Andrés Town. Golf carts are not especially fast but can easily circle the island in a day, with stops.

By car Full-size cars are also available but not really worth it; try Rent-a-Car Esmeralda, Av Colombia 1 (❶8 513 1170).

Tourist information The official office ❶8 513 0801) is at Av Newball, almost directly opposite *La Regatta* restaurant in San Andrés Town, but it's not well supplied (English is spoken). There's a small booth (usually open the same times) on the north side of town on the seafront promenade (Av Colombia).

BOAT TRIPS AND TOURS

Arranging trips to **Johnny Cay** and **Acuario** is straightforward – most hotels can connect you with operators and prices are standardized (some hotels do get discounts, however). You can take shuttle boats to Johnny Cay from the beach on the north side of San Andrés Town, while most tour boats to Acuario/Johnny Cay leave from marinas on the south side of town (Av Colombia): Tonino's and Portofino's (near the Parque de la Barracuda; ⓦportofinocaribe.com).

Ecofiwi Turismo Ecológico Via San Luis, Sector de Mango Tree, Santa Isabel ❶316 567 4988, ⓔecofiwi@gmail.com. This small but highly recommended outfit runs enlightening tours of the mangroves (Old Point Mangrove Park) south of San Andrés Town (2hr), using standard but also two transparent kayaks (reserve these in advance); they also offer guided hikes and snorkelling trips.

Noche Blanca Portofino's Marina ⓦportofinocaribe.com. This party boat can be lots of fun, including an open bar of spirits and cocktails (not beer), a dinner buffet and DJ. Participants are encouraged to wear white.

ACCOMMODATION

San Andrés is littered with hotels, B&Bs and rental apartments, though most Colombian tourists tend to buy **all-inclusive packages** with the Decameron chain (ⓦdecameron.com), which has five properties on the island. Most hotels are in San Andrés Town, but there are several secluded resorts and *posadas* further along the coast – much more tranquil, but not as convenient (police won't let you ride golf carts or scooters south of town after 6pm). Airbnb (ⓦairbnb.com) lists more than three hundred properties on San Andrés and Couchsurfing (ⓦcouchsurfing.org) also operates here. Note that hot showers are quite rare.

SAN ANDRÉS TOWN

★ **Blue Almond Hostel** Los Almendros, Manzana 4, Casa 3 ❶8 513 0831; map p.192. Small, charming hostel run by the amicable Juan Velásquez (who speaks English) and Jenniffer Muñoz, around 15min walk from the town centre. There's a functional kitchen (no breakfast provided), four simple but clean rooms and dorms (fan only; some rooms with private bathroom for an extra fee) plus a communal computer and TV room. Free coffee, lockers (bring lock) and surfboards. Bike and snorkel rental available. Minimum two-night stay. $

Decameron Isleño Av Colón 6–106 ⓦdecameron.com; map p.192. The best place for a splurge at the flagship property of the Decameron stable. All the resort features you'd expect, with a vast complex surrounding a pool just behind the main beach offering a beach club, spa, fitness centre and watersports, plus access to all the amenities of the Decameron hotels on the island and the Rocky Cay Beach Club. Rooms are bright and modern (but not especially luxurious). All-inclusive packages only. $$$$

★ **Hotel by San Andrés** Av Colón 3–80 ⓦhotelbysanandres.com; map p.192. Cosy hotel with fifteen well-equipped rooms (a/c, satellite flatscreen TV and 24hr room service) and a boutique feel (the rooms have a vaguely Moorish style, with canopy beds). It offers especially good excursions and rentals. English-speaking staff. $$$

Hotel Casablanca Av Colombia 3–59 ⓦhotelcasablancasanandres.com; map p.192. Large, expensive and appropriately posh option right on the seafront, with stylish rooms (some with ocean views) sporting a fresh, white colour scheme, flatscreen TVs and contemporary art. Decent pool. $$$$

The Rock House Hostel C 8 No. 18A–59, Cabañas Altamar ⓦtherockhousehostel.co; map p.192. In a quiet residential area behind the airport, a 25min walk from the centre, Doña Luz and her family greet you with open arms for a bit of homely comfort. Double rooms with private and shared bathrooms, all spotless with a/c. Free airport pick-up. $

El Viajero Av 20 de Julio 3A–12 ❶8 512 7497, ⓦviajerohostels.com; map p.192. Thoughtfully designed, this lively HI-affiliated hostel occupies an entire multistorey building. Expect a/c dorms and doubles with private toilets, and all the perks you can think of – daily tours, a movie room, chill-out bar area, large guest kitchen and balconies to hang out on. Breakfast included. Can be noisy at night (bar open till 1am). Dorms $, doubles $$

★ **Villa San Miguel** Av Colombia (C 1) #1A–57 Interior, Barrio Punta Hansa (at Rent-a-Car Esmeralda) ⓦvillasanmiguelsanandres.com; map p.192. A series of sleek, modern studios and self-catering apartments (with kitchens) just off the main drag on the north side of town, with strong wi-fi, decent cable TV and friendly English-

THE REST OF THE ISLAND

★ Casa las Palmas Hotel Boutique Sector Elsy Bar 5–64, South End 📞 315 750 0263, 🌐 facebook.com/casalaspalmashotelboutique; map p.190. Secluded property amid lush gardens in the south of the island, its spacious, stylish rooms sporting a deluxe lodge theme using lots of wood, expansive bathrooms and outdoor pool. $$

Hostería Mar y Sol Sector Bowie Bay (Km 17), Punta Sur 🌐 hosteriamarysol.com; map p.190. Another tranquil property with a gorgeous pool in the south of the island, perfect for anyone looking to escape the crowds – it's quite a hike from the coast road and a long way from town. Rooms are compact and modern with clean tiled floors and flatscreen TVs. Tasty food on site and free transport into town. $$$

Playa Tranquilo Km 8 Crta Circunvalar (Via El Cove) 🌐 playatranquilo.com; map p.190. Enticing west-coast B&B with spacious rooms (from large suites with kitchens and outdoor showers to simple doubles with shared bathrooms), a good choice of breakfasts (included), scuba diving on site (no beach) and a relaxing pool. Two-night minimum. $$

★ Posada San Andrés United Crta Tom Hooker No. 8–75, South End 🌐 sanandresultd.com; map p.190. Relaxing hotel on the west coast, with friendly hosts, a spacious airy apartment with a/c, a cosy cottage, and two doubles with shared bathroom. Extras include a swimming pool, use of kitchen and bikes, and free glass-bottom-boat-rides. Two-night minimum. Doubles $$, cottage & apartment $$$

Sunset Hotel Km 13 Crta Circunvalar 🌐 sunsethotel.com.co; map p.190. West-coast hotel popular with families and divers, with basic but spotless a/c rooms, two pools and decent food on site (it's a long way to town from here; taxis available). Convenient dive shop, and easy access to snorkelling just in front of the hotel (no beach, though). Includes breakfast; full-board packages are available. $$$

EATING

San Andrés' speciality dish is **rondón**, a thick stew of fish, cassava, yams, pigtail, baked plantains and *domplines* (flour tortillas) cooked in coconut milk and seasoned with pepper (it's quite spicy). Look out also for *caracol guisado* (conch stew) and *árbol del pan* or *fruto de pan* (breadfruit), which is prolific on the island and usually served fried. Though **seafood** is common on restaurant menus here, don't assume the fish will be fresh, or even local – demand far outstrips the relatively small amount caught by local fishermen. Red snapper, shrimp, crab and octopus are usually local, but many other species are flown in from the mainland (freshwater tilapia is an obvious one). Tourist **restaurants** tend to be pricey; locals generally eat at the cheaper places serving Colombian staples further inland in San Andrés Town. Remember that **tap water** on the island is not drinkable – only drink bottled water.

SAN ANDRÉS TOWN

Bread Fruit Hotel Sunrise arcade, Av Newball 4–169 📞 8 512 6044; map p.192. Small café serving delicious pastries and cakes, Juan Valdez coffee and tasty breakfast sets. $

Café Café Av Colombia 1–51 (Edificio Hansa Coral) 📞 8 512 5894; map p.192. Popular US-style diner (with booths and TVs showing sports) and pizza joint that also knocks out decent pastas and burgers, plus draft beer. There's a small outdoor terrace on the main strip. $$

Fisherman Place (Cooperativa de Pescadores) Av Colombia, behind the airport 📞 8 512 2774; map p.192. Aka "El Pescadero", this is a large, casual, open-air restaurant, founded by local fishermen in 1975, and still serving the best of the local catch every lunchtime. With the grilled fish in garlic sauce with all the trimmings comes in a heaped platter, the *rondón* is flavourful and filling, and lobster is very reasonably priced. $

Gourmet Shop Assho Av Newhall, at Av Las Américas 📞 315 770 0140; map p.192. Outside there's a small bar with a few tables, while inside the restaurant proper features rustic oak tables and chairs, bottles hanging from the ceiling and high-quality steaks and seafood (try the prawn and octopus ceviche or red snapper with basil sauce). $$

Juan Valdez Café Av Colombia 1a–16; map p.192. The Colombian coffee chain runs a popular branch right on the main promenade, serving the usual range of coffees, breakfast and pastries to a well-heeled, tablet-wielding crowd throughout the day. $

Miss Celia Av Colombia, at C 2 (Av Colón) 📞 8 513 1062; map p.192. This friendly wooden seafood shack, with fishing nets hanging from the ceiling, nautical memorabilia and plastic fish aplenty, is the best place in town to sample *rondón*, though they often run out, and service can be hit-or-miss. If you're prepared to wait, you can't go wrong with the stewed crab, curried seafood or stewed conch. $$

★ La Regatta Av Newball (next to Club Náutico) 🌐 restaurantelaregatta.com; map p.192. The best place for a splurge, with quality seafood, top service and a dining room perched right over the water in the marina. Dine on seafood pasta, fresh lobster and fresh local fish. Expect inventive combos and sauces, big portions and delicious coconut pie. $$$

Restaurante Casablanca Av Colombia, at Av Costa Rica 3–59 🌐 hotelcasablancasanandres.com; map p.192. Posh restaurant on the promenade serving a delightful seafood casserole, lobster in curry sauce and red snapper in a variety of styles. At night, the restaurant ramps up the romantic vibes with a local band playing and candlelit tables. $$$

> **SAN ANDRÉS SUNDAY GOSPEL**
>
> The Raizal population on San Andrés remains proud of its cultural roots, and one of the strongest traditions is attending **Baptist church** on Sundays (services in English). Even if you are not religious, it's worth going along to experience the soulful **gospel choirs** that sing at the services – a magical experience.
>
> The best-known choir can be found at the **First Baptist Church** in La Loma (see page 193). Worship here is taken seriously and services (Sun 10.30am–1pm) are not designed as tourist attractions, but the congregation is very welcoming to non-members (you might be asked for your name at the entrance, and will be thanked during the service). Wherever you go, dress respectfully (definitely avoid tank tops, flip-flops or shorts) and remember that this is a religious service and not a show.

THE REST OF THE ISLAND

Donde Francesca Playas de Sound Bay (Crta Circunvalar), San Luis ☎ 318 616 8547; map p.190. No-frills seafood served on wood tables in cabañas right on the sand. Highlights include fresh shrimp and the tempura (fried) calamari – it's a bit pricey but you're paying for location as much as the food. $$

★ **The Grog** Rocky Cay Beach (next to Hotel Cocoplum) ☎ 311 232 3247; map p.190. Dreamy location on one of the best beaches on the island, with a few tables on the sand and delicious food, from pork ribs to addictive deep-fried coconut shrimp and coconut lemonade. $

El Paraíso Playas de Sound Bay 69–87 (Crta Circunvalar), San Luis ☎ 8 513 3881; map p.190. Large seafood restaurant (famed for its paella), with an indoor space but also chairs and umbrellas on San Luis beach. Also does excellent coconut lemonade and fried breadfruit. Popular with locals on Sun. $$

DRINKING AND NIGHTLIFE

For such a small island, San Andrés has had a huge impact on the Colombian **music and dance** scene, with local rap/reggaeton artists including Jiggy Drama and Rayo Y Toby.

SAN ANDRÉS TOWN

Banzai Hotel Sunrise arcade, Av Newball, Local 119 ☎ 8 512 3977; map p.192. Small surfer-themed bar with a good mix of well-heeled locals and tourists, a big selection of beer and cocktails, plus a reggae soundtrack.

Coco Loco Av Colombia (at Cra 1b) ☎ 316 701 7037; map p.192. This club is popular with a younger crowd (locals and tourists), with a pier overlooking the sea and a cover charge (ladies free on Wed). Expect the usual Latino mix of salsa, *bachata* and reggaeton.

Discoteca Blue Deep Hotel Sunrise, Av Newball 4–169 ☎ 8 512 3977; map p.192. Plush club with flashing lights, laser shows, a booming sound system, three bars and two sweaty dancefloors, with reggae nights Thurs and Sat from 9pm (cover charge).

Éxtasis Sol Caribe Hotel, Av Colón 2–77 ☎ 8 512 3043; map p.192. This local club sits on top of the *Sol Caribe Hotel*, with a decent sound system and TV screens for late-night sports. There's a cover charge, half of which goes towards food and drink.

Interstate 80s Hotel Sunrise arcade, Av Newball, Local 115 ☎ 8 512 9302; map p.192. This 1980s-themed bar is kitsch fun (it's the sister bar of the one in Medellín), with plenty of memorabilia (think early Nintendo hooked up to a black-and-white TV) plus decent pizzas and burgers.

THE REST OF THE ISLAND

Big Mama Original Reggae Bar Crta Circunvalar Km 11.5, Cove; map p.190. This enticing west-coast bar helmed by local Rasta Sol is the perfect place to enjoy a cold beer above the waves, watching the sunset and soaking up the chilled atmosphere.

★ **Black Zomombo Kella Reggae Bar** Crta Circunvalar, San Luis; map p.190. This long-running favourite (run by Kella Williams since 1980) is an old-style beach shack and reggae bar offering a real taste of the Caribbean with authentic reggae, dancehall music and a Rastafari vibe right on the shoreline. Things don't really get going till after midnight.

DIRECTORY

Banks and exchange There are several banks and ATMs in San Andrés Town: Banco Popular is at Av Las Américas 2a–69; Banco de Bogotá is at Av Colón 2–86.

Health Hospital Amor de Patria (Vía San Luis; ☎ 8 5512 3808) is San Andrés' main hospital, but for serious injury or illness you'll be transferred to Barranquilla. Heed warnings about the island's tap water, and make sure to drink bottled water only.

Police Av Newball 1–34 (☎ 8 512 3850); in an emergency call ☎ 123.

Providencia

Tiny **PROVIDENCIA** (Old Providence) is the antithesis of its sister island 74km to the south: a sleepier, friendlier place with a population of around five thousand, where everyone knows everyone else and where most speak an English-based Creole. It's the least Colombian part of Colombia, a beautiful island with a mountainous interior smothered with lush vegetation, and the world's **third-largest barrier reef** beckoning divers from all over the world. The island is circled by a 16km coastal road (the Circunvalar), so it's easy to see all the sights along it, though like San Andrés, a visit here is more about getting under the water or simply soaking up the island vibe.

The main settlement, at the northern tip of the island, is **Santa Isabel** (aka "Centro"), formerly New Westminster, with a smattering of old-style Caribbean buildings clustered attractively beneath lush hills and along the shore, home to ATMs, supermarkets and other services but not much else. Most of the accommodation can be found in **Freshwater Bay** on the west coast, which only has a small stretch of beach at the southern end (hemmed in by hotels); otherwise, tranquil **Southwest Bay** boasts the best beach with a smaller selection of hotels and restaurants. Note that between October and December it's likely to rain a lot on Providencia, and that virtually all the beaches (apart from Southwest Bay), get swallowed up by high tides at this time (diving is OK, however).

Santa Catalina Island

From the northern end of Santa Isabel a rickety, wooden, pontoon pedestrian bridge (known locally as "Lovers' Bridge") crosses the Canal Aury to tiny **Santa Catalina Island** – from late afternoon it's possible to see manta rays swimming under the bridge. Once across the bridge a concrete boardwalk leads right along the shore, between tangled mangroves and a ramshackle village to **Morgan's Cannon** (Cañones), a rusty old artillery piece said to be the place pirates were hanged and "protestants burned" by the Spanish.

Back at the bridge, the longer boardwalk to the left leads you along the shore then up the hill to the site of **Fort Warwick** (allow 15–20min). Little remains of the fort, established by the first English settlers in 1630 (and called Fuerte de la Libertad by the Spanish), though old cannons have been placed on top of the hill for effect, and the views are magnificent. Down the other side of the hill lies **Fort Beach** (Playa Fuerte), a small stretch of sand with another old cannon, wishing well, a submarine cave (also named for Morgan), and good **snorkelling** – note that this is a beach that can virtually disappear from October to January.

From the beach a narrow dirt track winds further along the steep, jungly shoreline (another 15–20min) to the jagged outcrop of **Morgan's Head** (Cabeza de Morgan). It's

> **THE BLACK CRABS OF OLD PROVIDENCE**
>
> As you'll soon realize, the Providencia **black crab** is a major staple on the island, appearing on most menus in soups, stews or fried in the shell – some twenty percent of the island's population make their living from the tasty crustacean.
>
> The crab is actually orange and black and lives on land most of the year (hiding in burrows in the hills and feeding at night). Between April 1 and July 31 the crabs descend en masse to the sea during their annual migration to lay eggs (the newly hatched juveniles then make the return journey) – it's sometimes possible to view this amazing spectacle on foot, but the army routinely closes and guards strips of the coast road to protect crossing crabs. In recent years, crab numbers have declined dramatically thanks to overexploitation and loss of habitat, but there has been some progress in making crab farming sustainable.

a tranquil, isolated spot ringed by coconut palms and enticing sapphire waters, though the sea is hard to access here because of the cliffs and thick vegetation.

The Peak (El Pico)

Towards the south of Providencia, a 7km hiking trail leads from **CASABAJA** village up **The Peak (El Pico)**, the island's tallest mountain (360m), with jaw-dropping 360-degree views from the top. The hike takes around one hour to ninety minutes one-way, through groves of cotton trees and tamarind, orange and mango trees that burst with fruit in season. Bring plenty of water and be sure to ask for directions – the path is signposted off the main road but it's a little difficult to find the actual trailhead through the village. Hotels can arrange guides for around C$50,000, but you don't really need one.

Manchineel Bay (Bahía Manzanillo)

From the village of Casabaja, a paved road leads 2km south to **Manchineel Bay (Bahía Manzanillo)**, a rustic, unspoiled stretch of palm-backed sand that can also become rough and extremely narrow during high tides in winter. The beach is named for the manchineel tree, which produces fruit that look like small apples but which are highly toxic. Other than chilling on the beach the main draw here is *Roland Roots Bar* (see page 203), but petty theft can be a problem so keep an eye on your stuff.

Southwest Bay (Bahía Suroeste) and Freshwater Bay (Aguadulce)

A short drive or walk off the main coastal highway, **Southwest Bay (Bahía Suroeste)** is the island's best beach, with a long stretch of fine white sand, palm trees and a couple of good places to stay and eat. It's also a major departure point for dive trips and boat tours (and subsequently for tour lunches). Be sure to check out the local **horseback riding competitions** on alternate Saturdays, a proudly maintained Raizal tradition. The main accommodation village, **Freshwater Bay (Aguadulce)**, on the west coast, only has a small stretch of beach at the southern end.

Almond Beach

Signposted off the main road between Freshwater Bay and Santa Isabel, **Almond Beach** is a secluded cove of sand with a small bar owned by the affable Delmar Robinson (selling drinks, coconuts and snacks). It's perfect for a quiet afternoon of lounging, though the beach is another that virtually disappears during winter high tides.

Parque Natural Nacional Old Providence McBean Lagoon

Much of the northeastern coast of the island and shore of **Maracaibo Bay** (Bahía Maracaibo) is protected within the **Parque Natural Nacional Old Providence McBean Lagoon**. Most of the park comprises **mangrove forests** that are hard to access without a guide (there's a small entrance off the main road, just south of the airport runway), but the most enticing section is Crab Cay, just offshore.

Crab Cay (Cayo Cangrejo)
Charge • ☏ 8 514 9003

Crab Cay (Cayo Cangrejo), just off the east coast of Providencia, is a tiny island with superb snorkelling in the spectacularly clear surrounding waters – you'll see plenty of small but multicoloured tropical fish, fans and corals here. The standard island **boat tours** (see box, page 202) always stop here for around two hours (you can stay longer if you rent your own boat, or rent a kayak, near *Deep Blue*; see page 203), but admission is rarely included, so bring cash. There's a small bar on the dock selling fresh coconuts and booze, and sometimes shrimp ceviche. You can also make the short climb to the cocoplum-smothered top of the cay for sensational views of the massive reef, "the sea of seven colours" (*el mar de los siete colores*) around it (where the sea seems to

> **THE LIGHTHOUSE**
>
> **Lighthouse Providencia** (w facebook.com/lighthouse.providencia.isla) in High Hill is a nonprofit arts and cultural association that operates a café (with locally sourced organic produce), art gallery and film theatre officially known as Muestra de Cine Ecocultural Seaflower – stop by to peruse the local art (for sale), or view thirty-minute video documentaries on the island and its people (charge).

gleam with several, if not exactly seven, shades of green and blue), and back over to the mountains of Providencia, rising into the clouds like a languid South Pacific atoll.

ARRIVAL AND INFORMATION PROVIDENCIA

By plane Searca and SATENA share the same tiny turboprop planes (use the SATENA website to book; otherwise you will have to buy tickets from travel agents or with cash at San Andrés airport) to shuttle between San Andrés and Providencia's El Embrujo airport (2–4 daily; more frequent Jan, July & Dec; 15–20min), 3.5km south of Santa Isabel and 8.5km from Freshwater Bay; there are no flights from the mainland, and services are often cancelled due to bad weather. You'll have your passport and tourist card (see page 191) checked on arrival. The luggage allowance is 10kg, and officially you'll be asked to pay for anything over this, though it often depends on how busy the flight is as to whether you'll be charged. Taxis (pick-up trucks) meet flights and will drop you off anywhere on the island for a non-negotiable fee (if there are several people going to the same place, costs can be shared). There are no car rental desks (or any other services) at the airport.

By boat A catamaran service (w conocemosnavegando.com) operates (weather permitting) between San Andrés and the main dock at Santa Isabel on Providencia (see page 199).

Tourist information The main office lies on the main road into Santa Isabel from Freshwater Bay (t 8 514 8054), but there's a more convenient kiosk by the bridge to Santa Catalina Island.

GETTING AROUND

By bus/colectivo *Colectivos* (basically pick-up trucks) make circuits around the island, but are not very reliable (they are supposed to run hourly) – just wave them down and get on and off where you like. It is also safe to flag down passing vehicles, which might give you a lift (confirm the price first).

By bike/scooter You can rent bicycles or scooters (negotiate cheaper rates for longer rental periods) from operators in Freshwater Bay and Santa Isabel.

By golf cart Souped-up golf carts (*mulita*) with off-road tyres are a fairly convenient option. Most hotels can organize one.

ACCOMMODATION

As with San Andrés, the Decameron group has a major presence on the island and is affiliated with five hotels and *posadas* (w decameron.com; packages including flights only), but there are plenty of independent options.

Cabañas Agua Dulce A short walk from the beach w cabanasaguadulce.com; map p.200. Clean and comfy rooms near the beach; the main appeal lies in the views from the *Ocean View Terrace* bar. All the cabins have hammocks on

PROVIDENCIA TOURS AND DIVES

Most hotels should be able to fix you up with standard **boat tours** around the island: resources are pooled, so it doesn't really matter who you book it with. Trips usually involve a speedboat ride around the whole island, with your captain pointing out various features (they'll speak English if asked). Stops usually include Santa Isabel, but the highlight is the two-hour visit to Crab Cay. Stops for lunch (not included) are almost always at Southwest Bay. If you've got the cash, you can see more sights, do more snorkelling and travel at your own speed by renting your own boat and captain.

DIVING

Diving off Providencia is even more spectacular than at San Andrés, with some of the highlights including the large southern stingrays (not mantas) that congregate at the "Manta City" dive site, and the snappers, goatfish and parrotfish that make you feel as if you're swimming in a giant aquarium at Tete's Place, off Southwest Bay. The water temperature is a balmy 26–28ºC, and visibility ranges from 23–33m: at most dive sites there is virtually no or very little current.

Note that **lionfish** are considered an invasive species here, so don't be shocked if you see your divemaster harpooning them. Recommended operators include:

Felipe Diving Center Cabañas El Recreo, Freshwater Bay w felipedivingshop.com. Top-notch equipment and professional divemasters.

Sirius Dive Center Sirius Hotel, Southwest Bay w siriusdiveshop.com. Diving excursions and PADI Open Water courses available.

the front porch, breakfast is included and there's free wi-fi in common areas. $$

Cabañas Miss Mary On the beach ⓦdecameron.com; map p.200. This Decameron-affiliated hotel, with eight rooms, is one of the only true beachfront hotels on the island. Rooms are all comfy and cool (with good a/c), though only four have sea views and patios. *Miss Mary* has hot water. $$

★ **Deep Blue** Maracaibo Bay ⓦhotelddeepblue.com; map p.200. This luxurious boutique was a game-changer when it opened and quickly became the best hotel on the island, with twelve stylish, contemporary a/c rooms with balconies, an excellent waterfront restaurant and bar and a rooftop pool. Free daily shuttle to beaches, and kayak use. $$$$

El Encanto Across the street from the beach ☎8 514 8295; map p.200. This bright pink hotel owned by friendly hosts offers simple but adequate rooms with free wi-fi, a/c, fans and fridge. This is the only island hotel that is wheelchair- and stroller-accessible. Breakfast included. $$

Hotel Old Providence Main road, Santa Isabel ☎8 514 8691; map p.200. Decent budget option, with no-frills, modern rooms in the centre of town (some with balconies), with a/c, wi-fi and small flatscreen TVs. There is a laundry on site, and mopeds are easy to rent here. No breakfast. $

Posada Enilda Aguamansa 2 ☎320 855 4912, ⓔposadaenilda@yahoo.com; map p.200. Justly popular B&B in the brightly painted yellow home of Enilda Chamorro, with sea views, pleasant terrace and modern, en-suite rooms with a/c, basic TV and fast wi-fi. $$

Posada Mister Mac By the water ☎318 695 9540, ⓔposadamistermack@hotmail.com; map p.200. This friendly option with seven large, simple cabañas by the sea has been a staple for years – "Mr Mac" himself passed away in 2013 but his daughter Laudina Robinson now manages the property. Ideal for self-caterers, as rooms come with kitchenettes (breakfast is usually included). Discounts for solo travellers. No wi-fi. $

Posada Nativa Sunshine Paradise Just across the bridge ⓦposadasunshine.com; map p.200. Lovely little B&B, run by Francisca and Fredy Robinson, in a rustic, sleepy setting – no traffic – overlooking the main island. Four spotless, modern, a/c rooms with hammock on the veranda. $$

EATING

The **seafood** on Providencia is usually fresher than in San Andrés if you stick to the local black crab (see page 199), lobster, shrimp, red snapper and octopus.

★ **Café Studio** Maroon Hill, 200m along the main road from Southwest Bay to Freshwater Bay ☎8 514 9076; map p.200. This humble-looking place is one of the best restaurants on the island, run by a Canadian/Raizal couple since 1996; try anything in Creole sauce. $$

Caribbean Place Freshwater Bay ☎8 514 8698; map p.200. Aka "Donde Martín" (after chef Martín Quintero) and adorned with empty bottles of booze, this has been a tourist staple since 1992. $$

★ **Deep Blue** Maracaibo Bay ⓦhoteldeepblue.com; map p.200. Stylish seafood restaurant, with arguably the best location on the island – it overlooks Crab Cay, with an outdoor terrace. $$

El Divino Niño On the beach, Southwest Bay ☎316 827 7489; map p.200. This local beach shack institution is best known for its awesome mixed plate (*plato mixto para dos*), with enough lobster, conch, shrimp, crab and fish to sink a ship. Look for the small statue of the Divino Niño (Jesus as a child) halfway along the sands. $$

DRINKING

Providencia is not a big party island, but there are a few low-key **reggae bars** on the beaches.

Richard's Place On the beach, Southwest Bay; map p.200. Laidback reggae and cocktail bar – tasty crab *empanadas* are also on offer. There is usually a beach fire on Fri & Sat nights.

★ **Roland Roots Bar** On the beach, Manchineel Bay ☎315 238 5980; map p.200. This Rasta-themed beach bar, with wooden shacks right on the sand, rocks to a thumping reggae soundtrack – there are even swings from which to fling yourself into the sea. Owner Roland Bryan Eden has become a minor Colombian celebrity after appearing on TV show *Desafío*.

DIRECTORY

Banks and exchange Banco Agrario and (more reliably) Banco de Bogotá have branches with ATMs in the centre of Santa Isabel.

Health Santa Isabel contains the island's small medical centre (near the Adventist Church in the centre of town; ☎8 514 8415), but for serious illness or accident you'll be transferred to Barranquilla.

Internet The island currently has two free wi-fi hotspots: in front of the grocery store in Freshwater Bay, and near the jetty and municipal office in Santa Isabel.

Police ☎8 514 8000. Posts in Santa Isabel and at the airport.

Medellín and the Zona Cafetera

206 Medellín and around
230 Zona Cafetera

VALLE DE COCORA, SALENTO

Medellín and the Zona Cafetera

The metropolis of Medellín has made a remarkable turnaround since its days as Colombia's murder capital in the early 1990s, and is now an attractive, cosmopolitan city. It sits in the middle of the huge, mountainous departamento of Antioquia (see page 209), whose capital it has been since 1826. Within striking distance is the previous capital, Santa Fe de Antioquia, which remains a lovely old colonial town and competes with lakeside Guatapé to attract day-trippers from the city. To the south of Antioquia, the compact departamentos of Caldas, Risaralda and Quindío form the Zona Cafetera, Colombia's main coffee-growing region.

Medellín is at the heart of **Tierra Paisa** – Paisa country. Although strictly speaking it means someone from Antioquia, the term "Paisa" can also by extension refer to people from the *departamentos* of Caldas, Risaralda and Quindío, which were largely created by immigrants from Antioquia. Paisas are alternately the butt of jokes and the object of envy for many Colombians. Their rugged individualism and reputation for industriousness dates back to the early nineteenth century, when they cleared Colombia's hinterland for farming in exchange for the government's carrot of free land. One of the Paisas' biggest contributions to Colombia has been their role in the spread of **coffee**.

The **Zona Cafetera** is based around the three modern cities of **Manizales**, **Pereira** and **Armenia**, all victims of earthquakes that have devastated them in modern times, yet each with its own charms in the way of scenery, innovation and entertainment. Easily accessible from Armenia or Pereira, the photogenic village of **Salento** is the gateway to some great hiking in the misty **Valle de Cocoro**. Along with Pereira and Manizales, Salento also makes a good base for exploring one of Colombia's most postcard-perfect national parks, **Parque Nacional Natural Los Nevados**, with its snow-capped peaks and ominously rumbling volcanoes. Out of town, many of the picturesque **coffee-growing fincas** – almost all established by Paisa homesteaders – have opened their estates to tourists. During harvest time you can partake in the picking process, and all year round you can learn about how the world's most popular drink is grown and processed.

Medellín and around

The second-biggest metropolis in Colombia, with a population of more than two and a half million people, Antioquia's capital, **MEDELLÍN** is a city reborn. Back in the 1980s, with some three thousand murders a year, it was the epicentre of the cocaine trade and the world's most violent city. Now, by contrast, Medellín is a source of pride, a showpiece of innovation whose regeneration is so dynamic you can almost feel it.

In today's Medellín, newly built tower blocks thrust skyward while fast, modern metro trains ply the city from north to south, and residents of the very poorest *barrios*, clinging by their fingertips to the steepest of the mountainsides around it, have an integrated system of cable cars giving them fast and easy access to the centre. Pleasant green spaces, interesting museums, a bustling (if sleazy) downtown area and thriving commercial zones make Medellín an exciting place to explore, while top-notch restaurants, vibrant bars and a pumping club scene provide nonstop fun until the early hours.

PLAZA BOTERO, MEDELLÍN

Highlights

❶ **Museo de Antioquia** Medellín's top art museum has some of the most important and most interesting works by local boy Fernando Botero, and a square full of his sculptures right outside. See page 211

❷ **Pablo Escobar tour** Learn about the local crime lord and politician who remains admired by so many despite having brought so much misery. See page 220

❸ **Guatapé** This delightful lakeside town, with its brightly painted houses, makes an easy and enjoyable day-trip from Medellín. See page 224

❹ **Santa Fe de Antioquia** Enjoy colonial elegance and beautiful warm weather in Antioquia's original capital. See page 226

❺ **Parque Nacional Natural Los Nevados** The most dramatic of Colombia's national parks, blessed with three snow-capped volcano peaks, high-altitude lakes, hot springs and jaw-droppingly beautiful scenery. See page 234

❻ **Coffee fincas** What better way to see how Colombia's excellent coffee is produced than to stay on a farm where it's done. See page 241

❼ **Salento** A popular weekend getaway, this lovely little town is a perfect base to visit the wax palm cloudforest of Valle de Cocora, eat fresh local trout, and dance to classic Colombian sounds in the main square. See page 243

HIGHLIGHTS ARE MARKED ON THE MAP ON PAGE 208

ANTIOQUIA

Older than Colombia itself, **Antioquia** was made a province of New Granada way back in 1576. Largely settled by Basques, the mountainous region was not well suited to agriculture, so its economy was based mainly on trade, a fact which goes a long way to explaining the famously entrepreneurial spirit of its people. In 1810, with Spain under Napoleonic occupation, the leaders of Antioquia's municipalities formed a junta and, while remaining loyal to the deposed Spanish king, created their own constitution, under which nearly all free male householders had the vote. In 1813, they declared independence, and Antioquia became a **republic**. The Spanish managed to regain control three years later, and when they were finally ousted by Simón Bolívar, Antioquia became part of Colombia. Nonetheless, the *departamento* and its people remain notably distinctive in their culture, their food and their manner of speech, and as late as the 1980s, politician and drug baron Pablo Escobar was still mooting the idea of Antioquian independence. The *departamento* stretches to the Caribbean coast, where the port town of Turbo is the jumping-off point for Capurganá (see page 147) near the Panama border.

Medellín sits in a valley surrounded by mountains at 1500m above sea level. Thanks to its moderate altitude and mild **climate**, it is known as the city of eternal spring. True, it rains quite a bit, especially around May and October, but for the most part Medellín is sunny and warm without ever being unbearably hot or freezing cold. Year-round temperatures average 24°C.

The town makes an excellent base for forays into more rural areas, particularly the beautiful colonial towns of **Santa Fe de Antioquia** and lakeside **Guatapé**, with its pretty painted houses, near the imposing natural rock formation of **"La Piedra"** ("the rock"). Either town is an easy day-trip, but both are well worth a longer stay if you have the time.

Brief history

In 1616, the Spanish explorer **Francisco Herrera y Campuzano** founded a village of eighty people at what is now Plaza el Poblado. Because the villagers were Indigenous, when a law enforcing **racial segregation** was passed in 1646, the Spanish administrators had to move to a new site at Aná, today's Parque Berrío.

In 1674, with a population of some three thousand people, Medellín became a fully fledged municipality, and in 1826 it was declared capital of Antioquia. What really put it on the map, however, was the discovery of coal deposits in the region and the arrival of the railway in 1875. With these resources and a bit of Paisa business savvy, Medellín established a **textile industry** that drove a huge expansion in the early twentieth century.

After 1948, the instability arising from the assassination of Jorge Eliécer Gaitán drove people from the countryside to Medellín as **refugees**. Most ended up squatting in deprived *barrios* on the mountainsides around the city, and within twenty-five years, the population had tripled to over a million. Although this boosted the textile industry, it also left many people unemployed. What moved in to fill the gap was **cocaine**.

Medellín's position as the cocaine trade's world capital, already established in the 1970s, was boosted by the civil war in Nicaragua – whose Contra rebels financed themselves with cocaine supplied by Pablo Escobar's **Medellín Cartel** – and by the rise of crack (see page 211). The resulting leap in demand brought in money, but also extreme violence and gang warfare. Only after the end of the Nicaraguan war were the authorities able to bring down the cartel, taking out its leaders one by one until they finally located and killed Escobar himself in 1993. His legacy remains controversial among Colombians to this day.

Twenty-first-century regeneration

From 2000, Medellín was the subject of a major urban **regeneration** project, starting with the initiation of the system of metro lines and cable cars but adding in grassroots initiatives from within local communities and based squarely on a policy of social inclusion. Not only public transport but also education, parks and libraries received huge investment and the result is the gleaming new city we see today. It still has its

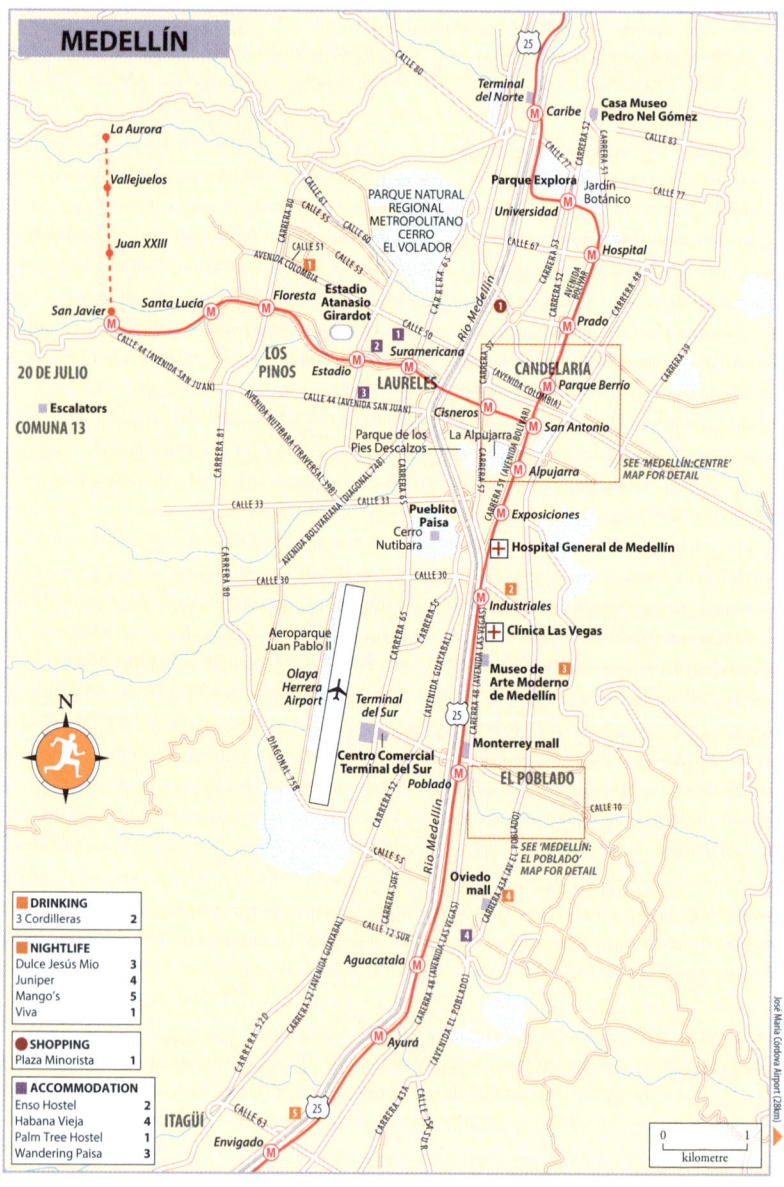

> ### COCAINE
> Cocaine is the main active chemical in the **coca leaf**, a traditional stimulant chewed historically by most of Colombia's Indigenous peoples. The chemical was first isolated in Germany in 1855 and found medical use as a local anaesthetic, before it became apparent it was highly addictive. From 1914 laws were brought in to control the drug and the trade was driven underground.
>
> From the 1920s to the 1970s, cocaine had a kind of glamour attached to it. Expensive and risqué, it was associated with the bohemian rich, and in particular with show business. But two new cocaine products on the scene put paid to that. Ordinary cocaine powder is actually cocaine hydrochloride, a water-soluble salt that's usually sniffed. When Nicaragua's **Contra rebels** started selling huge amounts of it in the US to raise funds in the early 1980s, they glutted the market and the price plummeted, shrinking away their profits, until one of their distributors hit on the idea of selling rocks of freebase cocaine (that is, without the hydrochloride bit) in LA's ghettos. Smoked, the new product, known as crack, was fast-acting, short-lived and almost instantly addictive. It swept the US and then the world, leaving a trail of misery behind it. Meanwhile, semi-refined cocaine paste, known as *basuco* (short for *basura de cocaina*, or "cocaine garbage") and also smoked, had long been bringing similar misery and addiction to the cities of South America, not least Bogotá and Medellín.
>
> Colombia is still a major cocaine producer today, and lots of people have their fingers in the till. Cocaine money has built shopping malls, condominiums, housing estates, sports centres and more. Guerrilla groups that started out with idealistic agendas are now little more than drug-dealing gangs. Paramilitary groups that set out to make war against the guerrillas have gone exactly the same way. The violent **drug wars** that so rent the country in the 1980s have moved on to Mexico, but the drug is still here, an unspoken, invisible source of power and wealth – and of strife.

problems, of course, and it certainly isn't crime-free, but compared with the Medellín of the 1980s, it's a different place altogether.

City centre
Although most of the sights are in the downtown **city centre**, it's quite a seedy area, with a lot of prostitution and drug dealing, and you certainly want to watch your step here, especially at night; even during the day, it's wise to keep snatchable items such as your phone or camera out of sight. For all that, the centre has a buzz that outlying areas don't, and the streets just west of the metro line between Parque Berrio and San Antonio stations have a bustling market vibe. The city centre is also the place to come if you're a fan of **Fernando Botero's works**, and in particular his sculptures.

Plaza Botero
Cra 52 at C 52 • Ⓜ Parque Berrío

Plaza Botero, otherwise known as Plaza de las Esculturas, a lovely, tree-shaded square is embellished with 23 bronze scultures by Medellín's favourite son, **Fernando Botero**, who gave them to his native city as a gift. The **sculptures** include several reclining – and some standing – nudes, a horse with a bowler-hatted rider and another without. There's a dog and a cat sticking their tongues out, a very un-Egyptian sphinx, and a Roman soldier wearing only a helmet, and managing to be both beefy and tubby at the same time. Feel free to touch the statues, by the way – not only was this Botero's original intention, but it's also supposed to be lucky.

Museo de Antioquia
Cra 52 No. 52–43 • Charge • Ⓦ museodeantioquia.co • Ⓜ Parque Berrío

On the west side of Plaza Botero, housed in a 1937 Art Deco pile that doubles up as the town hall, the **Museo de Antioquia** kicks off on its top floor with a gallery of works by **Fernando Botero**. The first painting of Botero's that the museum wanted was **Exvoto**, his entry for a biennial art competition in 1970, depicting the Virgin Mary holding in one hand a baby Jesus dressed in a sailor suit, and with the other dispensing the prize money (which Botero did not in fact win). When Botero heard that the museum wanted to buy the painting, he just gave it to them, and he's been giving them works of art ever since. Among them are bullfighting scenes, portraits of Cézanne and Velázquez, and **La Cocina**, a faintly disturbing kitchen scene in dirty white with a meaty-looking cat and a child dwarfed by the kitchen door. A darkened room of small works in oil contains the museum's most significant Botero works: **Car Bomb**, painted in 1999, and next to it, the **Death of Pablo Escobar**, created in the same year, and, as if to draw a line under the violence, **Pablo Escobar Dead**, dating from 2006, in which the bullet-riddled drug baron rests on a rooftop, looking almost as if he's just gone to sleep.

Also on the top floor is a **Sala Internacional** (International Hall) of works by modern artists including Rufino Tamayo and Rodin. Among the paintings on display, Frank Stella's colour-jarring *Doble Desmodulador Gris* boggles the eyeballs, Richard Estes's *Broadway Looking Towards Columbus Circle* plays with reflections in an almost photographically realistic New York street scene, and Arman's *Sinfonic Expansion* bursts forth in an explosion of paintbrushes and musical instruments.

The middle floor is devoted to twentieth-century Colombian art. Artists represented include Gregorio Cuartas, Eladio Vélez, Pedro Nel Gómez and Rafael Sáenz, but pride

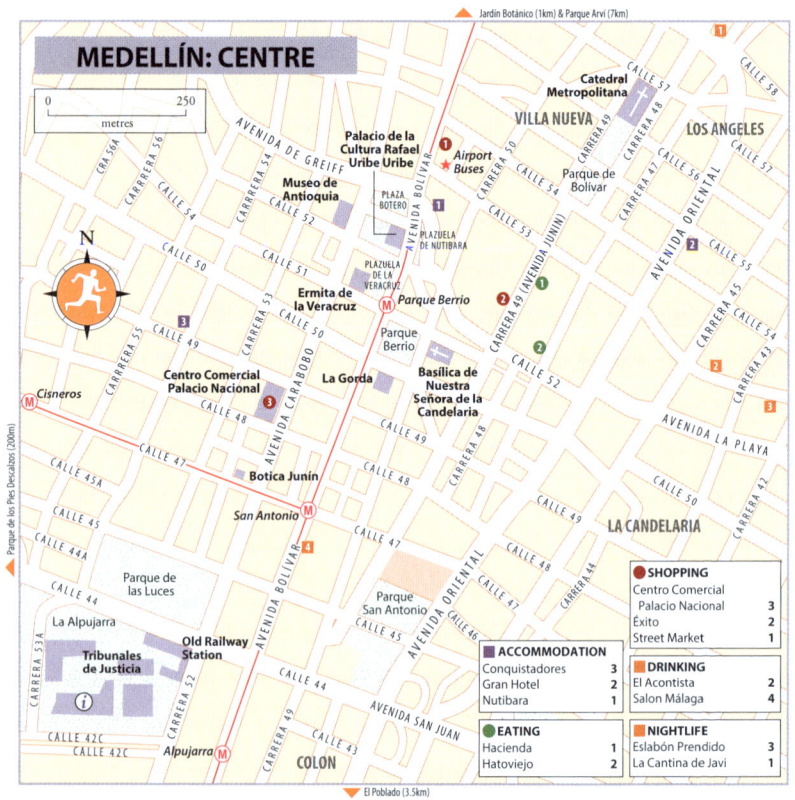

FERNANDO BOTERO

Medellín is the birthplace of **sculptor and painter** Fernando Botero, known for his often-satirical representation of all things podgy and rotund. Born here in 1932, Botero moved to Europe in his 20s, and now lives mostly in Paris, but he spends a month in Medellín every year. He's also been extremely generous, giving large numbers of his works to museums and open spaces in both Medellín and Bogotá, as well as donating his collection of paintings by other important modern artists to Bogotá's Museo Botero (see page 62).

Botero claims to find curvy models more attractive than slim ones, but as he has pointed out, what he's painting is not so much fat as a sensuality of form that also allows him to play with proportion and perspective. This in turn gives his work a naive, almost childlike quality, which contrasts with many of the subjects he depicts. True, he paints and sculpts a lot of cutesie-pie animals and buxom, rotund nudes, but Botero is also the man who painted Pablo Escobar being shot down on a rooftop, car bombs exploding in Medellín, the massacre of Mejor Esquino, and a whole series on the tortures of Abu Ghraib. Botero also revisits old masters, including Leonardo, Velázquez and – perhaps not too surprisingly – his fellow lover of plumpness, Rubens.

Medellín is particularly well endowed with Botero's paintings and sculptures, which you can see in Plaza Botero (see page 211), the Museo de Antioquia (see page 211) and Parque San Antonio (see page 215); in addition, Botero fans should definitely not miss the Botero Museum in Bogotá (see page 62), which houses some of his greatest works.

---

of place goes to four works by **Francisco Antonio Cano**. Among them, Cano's iconic 1913 **Horizons** is one of Colombia's most famous paintings, depicting a pioneering Paisa family gazing towards a new horizon to which the man is pointing with a hand whose pose mimics Adam's on Michelangelo's Sistine Chapel ceiling.

The museum's **annexe** (entry on the same ticket) contains works exhibited at three biennial exhibitions (1968, 1970 and 1972) sponsored by the local textile firm Coltejer. The works featured include Fernando Grillón's amusing dyptich of *Usurers Devoured by Panthers*, and a series of studies by Herman Braun on Velázquez's famous Spanish portrait, *Las Meninas*.

Palacio de la Cultura Rafael Uribe Uribe
Cra 51 No. 52–03 • Free • W culturantioquia.gov.co • M Parque Berrío

The impressive black-and-grey 1925 Neogothic pile in the southeast corner of Plaza Botero is the **Palacio de la Cultura Rafael Uribe Uribe**. Designed by Belgian architect Agustin Goovaerts, it was originally the seat of the Antioquia's *departamento* government, but it's now a cultural centre with a library, café and exhibition spaces. The iron dome – which is bolted rather than welded together – is today the ceiling of an in-house cinema. The *palacio* is named after the Liberal civil war general on whom Gabriel García Márquez based the character of Colonel Aureliano Buendía in *A Hundred Years of Solitude* (see page 214).

Ermita de la Veracruz
C 51 No. 52–58 • Free • T 604 423 6319 • M Parque Berrío

On what is really a southern branch of Plaza Botero, the Plazuela de la Veracruz, the beautifully Baroque **Ermita de la Veracruz** church was built at the start of the eighteenth century. By the end of that century, the church was so ruined that they had to tear it down and build it up again from the foundations, re-inaugurating it in 1803. If you can catch it open, pop in to see the interior, tastefully decorated in white and gold. The red **pillars** in front of the church are replicas of ones that stood there until being removed in the early twentieth century; they were restored by popular demand in 1968.

THE REAL COLONEL AURELIANO BUENDÍA

If you read only one Colombian novel in the whole of your life, it would have to be Gabriel García Márquez's *Cien Años de Soledad* (*A Hundred Years of Solitude*; see page 371). The book's main character, **Colonel Aureliano Buendía**, tall and slim with a thick black moustache and a stentorian voice, was based on one of the great characters of Colombian history, Liberal civil war general **Rafael Uribe Uribe**.

Born in the Antioquian town of Valparaíso, about halfway between Medellín and Manizales, Uribe made his name fighting for the Liberals in Cauca in the civil war of 1876. In 1884, he founded a leftwing newspaper, *El Trabajo*, before fighting again for the Liberal cause in 1885 and 1895, when, like Aureliano Buendía, he became a colonel. In peacetime he founded another newspaper, *El Autonomista*, but he took up arms yet again in the **Thousand Days' War** of 1899–1902, when he had overall command of the Liberal forces. In the wake of the Conservative victory at the Battle of Palonegro, Uribe fled to Venezuela but accepted an amnesty in 1902, becoming the Liberal Party's leader in 1907, a congress member in 1909 and a senator two years after that. In 1914 however, at the age of 55, his career came to a brutal end when he was hacked to death with axes – now in the Museo Nacional in Bogotá (see page 69) – by two carpenters who blamed him for the country's economic woes, possibly on the deliberate instigation of Uribe's political enemies.

Catedral Metropolitana
Cra 48 No. 56–81 • Free • ☎ 4 513 2269 • Ⓜ Prado

The fortress-like **Catedral Metropolitana** at the northern end of Parque de Bolívar, six blocks northeast of Plaza Botero, claims to be the largest church in the world built entirely of bricks – 1.12 million, if you're counting. Not only the outside, but also the rather dark interior, is completely faced with bare brick. The cathedral was designed in Neo-Romanesque style by French architect Émile Charles Carré. Construction started in 1875 but proceeded in fits and starts, and matters were not helped when the building was struck by a bolt of lightning in 1928, igniting a major fire. The cathedral was finally inaugurated in 1931. Although it's not the prettiest cathedral you'll ever see, it has some lovely stained-glass windows from Spain, designed by Giovanni Buscaglione and shipped over in 1921, as well as a fine German pipe **organ** which, should you attend Mass, you'll get to hear in action. A large **handicraft fair** is held on the first Saturday of every month in the **Parque de Bolívar** outside.

Parque Berrío
Cra 50 at C 51 • Ⓜ Parque Berrío

More a city square than a park as such, the **Parque Berrío**, two blocks southeast of Plaza Botero, is regarded as Medellín's geographical centre. It's named after Antioquia's nineteenth-century Conservative governor **Pedro Justo Berrío**, and an 1895 statue of him by Italian sculptor Giovanni Anderlini stands proudly in the middle. The square started life as an open space in front of the Basílica de Nuestra Señora de la Candelaria, whose congregation would socialize here after Mass. In the nineteenth century it became a marketplace where important public announcements were made, and also where public executions were held.

Apart from the statue of Berrío, the *parque* has three important artworks. In its southeast corner, **The Challenge**, by twentieth-century Antioquian sculptor Rodrigo Arenas Betancourt surges dynamically skyward, while all but unnoticed behind glass in the pedestrian walkway leading north alongside the metro line towards Plaza Botero, an ambitious **mural** by Pedro Nel Gómez depicts the history of Antioquia in twenty colourful panels. The most famous artwork, however, directly across Calle Colombia (Calle 50) from its south side, is Fernando Botero's sculpture *The Torso*, known universally as "**La Gorda**" ("The Fat Lady"). Fat and wide, as you'd expect from Botero, *La Gorda*'s lack of a head, arms and feet has not prevented her from becoming Medellín's favourite landmark and meeting point.

Basílica de Nuestra Señora de la Candelaria
Cra 49A No. 50–85 • Free • 604 231 4907 • Parque Berrío

Medellín's most important surviving colonial church is the **Basílica de Nuestra Señora de la Candelaria**, located directly opposite the east side of Parque Berrío. The basilica of today dates from 1778, but there's been a church on the site since 1649. It's dedicated to Our Lady of Candelaria, a manifestation of the Virgin Mary holding a candle, originally from the Canary Islands. The Virgin of Candelaria became the islands' patron saint, and her cult caught on in the Americas thanks to emigration from the Canaries in colonial times. The *barrios* of Candelaria in Bogotá and Medellín are both named after her. Her picture is high up on the *retablo* above the altar.

The church served as Medellín's cathedral from 1868 until 1931. It was declared a "minor basilica" by the pope in 1970, and narrowly escaped being burned down by a fire in 2014 which, luckily, was contained before it could do too much damage. The most impressive feature of the interior is a seven-tonne German pipe **organ**, which was shipped up the Río Magdalena in 1850 before being transferred here by mules.

Parque San Antonio
C 45 between Cra 46 (Av Oriental) and Cra 49 • San Antonio

Four blocks south of Parque Berrío, **Parque San Antonio** consists of a large, paved area on the north side of Calle 45, which pedants may insist is actually the *Plaza* de San Antonio, plus a greener area south of Calle 45, which the same pedants would agree really is the *parque*. Trees and flowers aside, the southern section's main attraction is the late nineteenth-century **Iglesia de San Antonio**, with its rounded, Romanesque-style interior and large dome.

The northern half boasts four sculptures by Botero (see page 213). One is his languid **Sleeping Venus**, and there's also a rather less rounded **Male Torso**, complete with chunky six-pack and tiny fig-leaf, all just a bit too squarely muscular for a Botero. Close at hand, and more reassuringly rotund, Botero's **Bird of Peace** is a replica of the original, which stands right next to it with its guts blown out. The damage was done by a **nail bomb** packed with ten kilos of dynamite, set off under it by persons unknown at a concert in 1995, killing 23 people. The perpetrators may have been the drug cartels, against whom Botero's son, then defence minister, had just declared war. Botero Senior asked that the mangled original be left in place in homage to the victims and as a protest against violence.

La Alpujarra and around
C 43 (San Juan) at Cra 52 (Carabobo) • Alpujarra

Four blocks southwest of Parque San Antonio, **La Alpujarra**, the administrative centre of Medellín and Antioquia and focal point for most of the demonstrations in town, is an open space surrounded by government buildings. In the middle, Rodrigo Arenas Betancourt's dynamic sculpture, the **Monument to the Race** is a writhing mass of battling bodies twisting skyward as good confronts evil across human history. Northeast, towards the old rail station, what look like two craggy lightning-struck trees belong to local sculptor Olga Inés Arango's monument to **Guillermo Gaviria** and **Gilberto Echeverri**, two prominent Antioquian politicians who in 2002, inspired by the likes of Gandhi and Martin Luther King, led a peace march into FARC-held territory to call for reconciliation with the guerrillas. FARC responded by seizing them, and later killed them when the army attempted a rescue. Arango's statues of four **street people** – a shoeshine boy, cigarette seller, hawker of lottery tickets and newspaper vendor – hang out in front of the town hall.

A block northeast of La Alpujarra, the **Parque de las Luces** is a space full of slender columns which, when lit up in the evening, become three hundred needles of light. Less high-tech and more touchy-feely, the **Parque de los Pies Descalzos** ("barefoot park"), directly west of the Alpujarra, has bamboo gardens and paddling pools where you're supposed to kick off your shoes to feel the textures of grass, sand, water and bamboo with your feet.

Pueblito Paisa
C 30A No. 55–64 • Free • ☎ 4 235 8370 • Ⓜ Industriales or Exposiciones

Two kilometres southwest of the centre, a hilly outcrop bearing the confectionery-like name of **Cerro Nutibara** is home to the **Pueblito Paisa**, a reconstruction of an early twentieth-century Antioquian village, complete with church, school and shops around a main square with a stone fountain. Of course, it's purely for tourists but it isn't completely phoney: as well as being built with all the proper materials, the *pueblito*, constructed in 1978, incorporates bits of real buildings from an old village that was being demolished at the time, and the church door, as well as its altar and baptismal font, come from a Medellín church of the right period. Even so, the best things about the *pueblito* are the amazing all-round **views** of Medellín, and the trees and greenery that surround it. There are **entrances** on Calle 30A (with stairs up, a 10min walk from the metro) and Calle 33 (accessible by buses heading west on Calle 33 from the centre), but to get to the top, if you don't fancy the climb, you'll need to take a taxi from the Calle 33 entrance.

On the slopes of Cerro Nutibara, a **Parque de las Esculturas** (sculpture park) was inaugurated in 1983 at the suggestion of then-president Belisario Betancur. Its ten works, mainly by Colombian and Latin American sculptors, are sparse and abstract. More fun is José Horacio Betancur's kitschy 1955 concrete statue of **Cacique Nutibara**, a local chieftain who led a brave but futile resistance against Spanish conquest in the region, and after whom the hill is named.

Museo de Arte Moderno de Medellín (MAMM)
Cra 44 No. 19A–100, 3km south of the city centre and 1km southeast of Cerro Nutibara • Charge • Ⓦ elmamm.org • Ⓜ Industriales or Poblado

Housed in an attractively restored industrial warehouse in Ciudad del Río, south of the city centre, the **Museo de Arte Moderno de Medellín** (or **MAMM**) features an impressive selection of contemporary art, largely local, including top Colombian artists such as Enrique Grau, Lucy Tejada, Leonel Góngora and Medellín's own Aníbal Vallejo. There are particularly good selections of work by prolific Antioquian painter Débora Arango (who has 233 works in the museum) and Cali's Hernando Tejada. As well as pieces from the permanent collection, which are rotated regularly, they always have at least one temporary exhibition.

El Poblado

Although most of the sights are in the downtown area, most foreign tourists prefer to stay in **El Poblado**, an upmarket neighbourhood in the southeastern part of town. This has the highest concentration of lodgings, restaurants and nightlife, including the city's **Zona Rosa**, which is centred on the Parque Lleras in the middle of the *barrio*.

Parque Arví
Vía Santa Elena, 7km east of Medellín • Guided tours (1–4hr) are offered in Spanish • Free (but specific sections cost extra; charge for tours) • Ⓦ parquearvi.org • Ⓜ Arví (Metrocable line L, accessed from Ⓜ Acevedo)

MEDELLÍN: EL POBLADO

■ ACCOMMODATION		● EATING				■ DRINKING		■ NIGHTLIFE	
Art Hotel	2	3M Gastro Bar	6	Mondongo's	4	37 Park	7	Babylon	2
Black Sheep Hostel	5	Ajiaco y Mondongos	5	Naan	10	Bogotá Beer Company	8	Donde Aquellos	3
Casa Kiwi	7	Azai Praia Lovers		Restaurante La Tienda		Niágara 5 Puertas	6	El Blue	1
Dann Carlton	4	vía Primavera	9	Del Vino desde 1999	3			Luxury	5
Lleras Green Hotel	3	Carmen	1	Señor Itto	2	● SHOPPING		Miró	4
Sites Hotel	6	Il Forno	8			Éxito	1		
Tiger Hostel	1	Hummus	7						

On the eastern slopes of the Aburrá valley, **Parque Arví** is an ecological nature reserve where you can walk pre-Hispanic trails and enjoy the fresh air and scenery. You shouldn't wander too far off the beaten track on your own, however; and note that some parts are off-limits altogether without a guide. The fifteen-minute cable car ride glides over the mountain ridge and into the park, affording spectacular views of the city, and a close-up of the shanty towns on the steep slope beneath. Additional attractions include **zip lines** and a **butterfly enclosure**. You could easily spend the day exploring this welcome bit of wilderness, and it's a good idea to get here early; they sometimes even limit the number of people entering, especially at weekends when it's busiest. Bicycles can be rented for free at the entrance, provided you leave ID.

Jardín Botánico

C 73 No. 51D–14, 2km north of the city centre • Free • W botanicomedellin.org • M Universidad

North of the city centre, near the University of Antioquia campus, Medellín's lush **Jardín Botánico** (Botanical Garden) is one of Colombia's oldest, dating from 1913. It's a very relaxing place to wander around, home to more than six hundred plant species, as well as a butterfly enclosure, and a large population of iguanas. It even has a **maze**. Don't miss the stunning **Orchideorama** – a weaving structure of steel trunks and towering wooden petals – where plants are showcased, and where the garden's annual orchid exhibition is held in August during the Feria de las Flores (Flower Festival).

Parque Explora

Cra 52 No. 73–75 • Charge (planetarium extra, reserve in advance) • W parqueexplora.org • M Universidad

Right next to the Jardín Botánico and a stone's throw from the university campus, kids will love the bold, modern, red-roofed **Parque Explora**, an interactive museum which they won't notice is educational because they're having so much fun. Outside there are **dinosaurs** – OK, not real ones, but they move, so who's quibbling – and inside there's an **aquarium** of Amazonian fish (which *are* real), and a **terrarium** full of reptiles, amphibians and bug-eyed creepy-crawlies. And that's before you even get on to the **interactive exhibits**, which are as hands-on as can be, illustrating physics and biology in a fun way, mostly with explanations in English as well as Spanish. The **planetarium**, which costs extra and needs to be booked in advance, is in Spanish only.

ESCOBAR'S LEGACY

Few individuals have had as great (and negative) an impact on Medellín in recent history as **Pablo Escobar Gaviria** – the most famous of Colombia's cocaine barons. A high-school dropout from a relatively middle-class background, Escobar began his career stealing marble gravestones, which he then sanded down and resold. He gained a foothold in the cocaine trade in the mid-1970s, as the drug was taking off in popularity in the US. By 1982, he had a well-established smuggling operation, just in time for the huge boost in the market caused by the rise of crack. By the mid-1980s, Colombia was shipping 70–80 tonnes of powder to the US every month, and eighty percent of the trade was in the hands of Escobar's Medellín Cartel.

To take advantage of diplomatic immunity, Escobar gained election to Congress in 1982 as a vice-representative. Anyone standing in his way was offered a choice of *plata o plomo* (silver or lead), and those who refused the *plata* got the *plomo*, including several judges and politicians. The Cartel's enforcers, young men on motorbikes known as *sicarios*, cruised the city shooting down whoever Escobar wanted dead. To remain in elected office however, Escobar curried favour with the poor, building homes and distributing money, to the extent that he was – and remains – hugely popular in some neighbourhoods. He's also believed to have financed Atlético Nacional football club in their successful 1989 Copa Libertadores campaign.

But Escobar's enemies were gathering: forming an organization called Los Pepes ("People Persecuted by Pablo Escobar"), his rivals started bombing Medellín Cartel properties, killing anyone who happened to be around at the time. Escobar naturally retaliated, equally arbitrarily. This was the time of the worst violence, from 1989 to 1992, when Medellín lived in fear. In 1989 Escobar infamously had a bomb placed on an Avianca passenger flight, killing 110 people, just to get politician César Gaviria Trujillo. Gaviria never took the plane, and went on to become president, determined to clamp down on all the cartels.

Eventually, to avoid extradition to the US in 1991, Escobar agreed to give himself up and be housed in a special luxury jail, La Catedral (no longer standing), but when the government decided to move him to a proper prison, he absconded and went on the run. He was finally traced by US and Colombian officials to a house at Cra 79B No. 45D-94 in the residential neighbourhood of Los Olivos, which still stands today. Cornered, he ran out onto the roof of the house behind, where he was shot. His remains lie in the Jardines Montesacro cemetery, in the southern *barrio* of Itagüí.

ESCOBAR TOURS

A couple of **tours** take visitors around the city to various Escobar-associated sights. You get to see the building he lived in, apartment blocks he had built, the rooftop on which he was shot and, finally, his gravestone. The best operators are **Paisa Road** and **Discovery Tours** (see page 220).

ESCOBAR'S HIPPOS

It's also possible to visit **Hacienda Nápoles** (whaciendanapoles.com), a huge farm 165km east of Medellín that was once Escobar's private kingdom, complete with mansions, menagerie of exotic animals, bullring and more. Once Escobar was on the run, his three hippos fled into the wild and bred; today they number over forty, and visitors can see them in a hippo park. Unfortunately, the mansion where Escobar used to live has now been pulled down, making this a rather less interesting excursion than it once was.

Casa Museo Pedro Nel Gómez

Cra 51B No. 85–24 • Free, but donations invited • W museopedronelgomez.org • M Universidad

In the *barrio* of Aranjuez, some 800m north of the Jardín Botánico along Carrera 52, the **Casa Museo Pedro Nel Gómez** was for 48 years the home of Antioquian painter, sculptor, engineer and muralist Pedro Nel Gómez, who bequeathed it to the people of Medellín when he died in 1984. The staff offer guided tours in Spanish around the house, the walls of which are decorated with huge **murals**, whose debt to Mexican muralists such as Diego Rivera is immediately apparent. The most impressive mural is Nel Gómez's epic 1940 *Homage to the Antioquian People*. Among the paintings displayed on the walls, the most poignant is *Spouses in the Window*, depicting the artist and his wife clearly very much in love.

The Comuna 13 escalators

4km west of the centre • Free • M San Javier (then bus to "20 de Julio"); it's also possible to visit Comuna 13 on a guided tour (see page 220)

To see one of the innovative projects that have helped rejuvenate the city, pop over to Las Independencias I in **Comuna 13**, a formerly gang-ridden, violent neighbourhood clinging to a hillside on the western edge of town. As part of the area's regeneration, the mayor's office have installed six flights of **escalators** (*escaleras eléctricas*) up the hillside, along with children's slides and fountains to play in on the streets, paint to brighten up the houses and youth clubs to keep local kids out of trouble. The result: a neighbourhood still poor, but with a better quality of life, less troubled and on the up. The escalators, installed in 2011, were among a number of projects called PUIs (Integrated Urban Projects), designed to improve life in the city, and uniformed staff, all local residents, will tell you with pride about the effect they have had.

On the way back, it's worth taking a detour to do a round trip on the **cable car** from San Javier station and to see how the cable car system has connected outlying areas to the city centre, cutting as much as an hour off journey times into town. It's certainly notable how, in Medellín, regeneration means improving life for the poor rather than shifting them out to replace them with the rich.

Laureles

The **Laureles** neighbourhood, within walking distance west of the city, is increasingly popular as a place to stay and to eat. Served by the metro (line 2), it doesn't have any tourist sights as such, but it's home to the **Atanasio Girardot sports complex**, including the home ground for both of the city's football teams.

ARRIVAL AND DEPARTURE   **MEDELLÍN**

BY PLANE

José María Córdova airport Medellín's José María Córdova airport (W aeropuertorionegro.co) lies a hilly 28km from the city along a scenic highway; it services all international and most domestic flights. There are buses between the airport and Cra 50A No. 53–13 in the city centre (T 4 511 4023, W bit.ly/combuses). Taxis are available from the airport into town; you may be able to share that as a *taxi colectivo*. From town, a good taxi firm with slightly lower prices is ACOA (W acoataxiaeropuerto.com.co).

Olaya Herrera airport A tiny handful of small domestic flights use the city's second airport, Olaya Herrera (W aeropuertoolayaherrera.gov.co), beside the southern bus terminal.

BY BUS

Depending on which part of the country you're coming from, long-distance buses arrive either at the Terminal del Norte or Terminal del Sur, almost equidistant from the centre. Terminal del Norte handles traffic to or from the north, east and southeast, while Terminal del Sur has buses to or from the south and west. For information, the two terminals share a single phone number (T 4 444 8020).

Terminal del Norte Cra 64C No. 78–580, best accessed by metro (M Caribe); failing that, a taxi will connect you to the centre or to El Poblado.

Destinations Barranquilla (13 daily; 14hr); Bogotá (every 10–12min; 9–10hr); Bucaramanga (18 daily; 8hr); Cartagena (10 daily; 13hr); Guatapé (every 30min; 2hr);

Magangué (for Mompox) (7 daily; 12hr); Santa Fe de Antioquia (every 12–20min; 1hr 30min); Santa Marta (9 daily; 15hr).

Terminal del Sur Cra 65 No. 8B–91, within walking distance of El Poblado and its metro station, but depending on what time of day you arrive and what you have with you, you should take a cab for safety.

Destinations Armenia (every 30min–hourly; 7hr); Cali (16 daily; 8–9hr); Manizales (every 15–30min; 5hr); Pereira (every 30min–hourly; 6hr).

INFORMATION

Tourist information The tourist office is in the Centro Administrativo la Alpujarra, C 44 No. 52–165 (📞 4 385 6966), but it's usually more convenient to visit one of the PiTs (Puntos de Información Turística) which are at both bus terminals, both airports, Parque de las Luces, Pueblito Paisa and Parque Arví.

Websites ⓦ guiaturisticademedellin.com is a tourist listings site run by the Viztaz Foundation and the mayor's office, while ⓦ medellin.travel, run by the city council's convention and visitor's bureau, covers activities for tourists in and around town.

GETTING AROUND

By metro and cable car The city's excellent metro system (charge; ⓦ metrodemedellin.gov.co) is clean and efficient; included in the price of a metro ride are cable cars that leave from Acevedo and San Javier metro stations (although not the one from Santo Domingo to Arví). To avoid queues, it's worth buying several journeys at once (all on one card, valid from any station to any station).

By bus and buseta The safety and efficiency of the metro means that you're far less likely to use buses, but they can be useful for extra savings. Bus #134 runs between Parque Berrío and C 10 in El Poblado, via metro Poblado, returning via C 10A.

By taxi Taxis are cheap and plentiful. Reliable cab firms include Flota Bernal Taxi (📞 4 444 8882, ⓦ flotabernal.com.co) and Coopebombas (📞 4 444 0000, ⓦ coopebombas. com), and Medellín is covered by Easy Taxi (ⓦ easytaxi.com) and, although not legally, by Uber.

By car Pico y placa (see page 30) applies over much of the city during morning and evening rush hours (7–8.30am & 5.30–7pm) – for details see ⓦ medellin.gov.co. Car rental is available (see page 224).

TOURS

Comuna 13 Tours ⓦ comuna13tours.com. A walking tour in English of Comuna 13 (see page 219), including the escalators and cable car, with explanation of the neighbourhood and its transformation; daily at 10am from El Poblado.

Discovery Tours Book via Black Sheep Hostel (see page 221). Excellent 3hr 30min Pablo Escobar tour run by people who actually knew him. There is no online presence as yet, but you can book through a couple of hostels, most notably *Black Sheep*, with departures from there most days at 8.30am.

Medellín City Tours ⓦ medellincitytours.com. A wide range of tours, excursions and activities, including a three-hour sightseeing tour of the city.

Paisa Road ⓦ paisaroad.com. A small local firm that organizes the original Pablo Escobar tour plus group visits to football matches, with pick-ups and set downs at various hostels around town.

Real City Tours ⓦ realcitytours.com. Excellent walking tours (4hr) in English and Spanish (Mon–Fri morning & afternoon), not a tour of the sights but a look under the surface of what goes on downtown. Book online; the tour is free, but donations are solicited. They also do a fruit-tasting tour for a fee.

Turibus ⓦ turibuscolombia.com. Daily hop-on hop-off city tour with buses following a loop of the city, leaving the Parque del Poblado (C9 at Cra 43A) four times daily and passing Plaza Botero, Estadio Atanasio Girardot, Parque de los Pies Descalzos and Cerro Nutibara. Tickets can be bought on board (for 24 or 48hr), and you can get on and off where you like. Turibus also offers a number of out-of-town and special-interest tours.

ACCOMMODATION

CITY CENTRE

Conquistadores Cra 54 No. 49–31 📞 350 318 9890; Ⓜ Parque Berrío; map p.212. A slightly drab but clean, friendly and respectable budget hotel on a grimy downtown street that's just a couple of blocks from the city's main sights. If you like a bit of daylight, it's worth asking for a room with an outside window. $

Gran Hotel C 54 No. 45–92 ⓦ granhotel.com.co; Ⓜ Parque Berrío; map p.212. The building doesn't look too great from the outside, but this is a decent option in the centre of town. The rooms are a good size, if not really modern in style, and there's a rooftop pool. Breakfast included. $$

Nutibara C 52A No. 50–46 ⓦ hotelnutibara.com;

ⓜParque Berrío; map p.212. Built in 1945 and grand in the slightly ponderous style of the time, the *Nutibara* feels like it's caught in a time warp, down to the linoleum tiles in the rooms and the bittersweet ambience of former grandeur gradually going to seed. That said, it's comfortable enough, and you can't get more central. Ask for a room on one of the top floors with a view over Plaza Botero. Breakfast included. $$

EL POBLADO
Art Hotel Cra 41 No. 9–31 ⓦarthotel.com.co; ⓜPoblado; map p.217. Medellín isn't exactly flush with boutique hotels but here's one that fits the bill. The rooms are large and warehouse-style modern, with lots of bare brick, and a bit dark, but they've got a/c and all the home comforts you need, and there's a jacuzzi and a gym. It's not as slick as it might be, but it's cool, stylish and friendly. Discounts available at weekends, with best prices from ⓦbooking.com. Breakfast included. $$$

★ **Black Sheep Hostel** Transversal 5A No. 45–133 ⓦblacksheepmedellin.com; ⓜPoblado; map p.217. This sociable backpackers' pad has all bases covered, including Spanish classes, a roof terrace and choice of other areas to hang out in, and weekly barbecues. The affable Kiwi owner has travelled extensively in Colombia and is happy to share his knowledge, the staff are super-friendly and super-helpful, and the metro is just a 10min walk away. Dorms $, doubles $$

Casa Kiwi Cra 36 No. 7–10 ⓦcasakiwi.net; ⓜPoblado; map p.217. Done out in the style of a bamboo beach hut, this popular party hostel offers clean dorms, DVD room, pool table, small pool, bar, kitchen and laundry service; the adjoining luxury wing has fancy doubles, some en suite. Dorms $, doubles $$

Dann Carlton Cra 43A (Av Poblado) No. 7–50 ⓦdanncarlton.com; ⓜPoblado; map p.217. The grandest hotel in El Poblado, one of the best hotels in town, unashamedly corporate and geared to business travellers, so service is punctilious rather than friendly. It has the usual premium facilities including a pool and gym, and a buffet breakfast is included. It's about 25 percent cheaper at weekends. $$$$

Habana Vieja C 10 Sur No. 43A–7 ☎350 318 9890; ⓜAguacatala; map p.210. An old-fashioned little house that's something of an island in a sea of steel-and-glass high-rises. More like a *pension* than a hotel, it's very homely, with Edwardian-style décor. Handy for the local shopping malls, although less so for El Poblado's Zona Rosa. Breakfast included. $$

Lleras Green Hotel C 9 No. 40–30 ⓦllerasgreenhotel.co; ⓜPoblado; map p.217. This modest hotel is functional but actually quite snazzy in its own little way; right by Parque de Lleras, it's very handy for El Poblado's nightlife. Rooms are bright and modern, with bathrooms separated off by frosted glass – there are suites and junior suites too, all at very decent prices. A bar and restaurant are in the works. $$

Sites Hotel Cra 45 No. 5–15 ⓦsitesmedellin.com; ⓜPoblado; map p.217. In a quiet and residential part of El Poblado, this luxury hotel and apartment complex includes a few quirky extras, such as a library complete with complimentary cheese and wine. $$$$

Tiger Hostel Cra 36 No. 10–49 ⓦtigerhostelmedellin.com; ⓜPoblado; map p.217. Right in the Zona Rosa, this is one of the liveliest hostels in town, with its own bar, lounge and pool table. The rooms are colourful but a bit basic – not that it matters, since you won't be spending much time sleeping. $

LAURELES
Enso Hostel C 47 No. 70A–73 ⓦensohostel.negocio.site; ⓜEstadio; map p.210. A small, low-priced hostel that's handy for the football stadium and public swimming pool, and just a block from the metro. Facilities include a kitchen, and bicycle and motorbike rental. Breakfast included. $

Palm Tree Hostel Cra 67 No. 48D–65 ☎300 241 9209; ⓜSuramericana; map p.210. A small and friendly hostel in a handy position, with a row of cafés and cheap restaurants just round the corner on C 49. Breakfast is included, but you have to cook it yourself. $

Wandering Paisa C 44A No. 68A–76 ⓦwanderingpaisahostel.com; ⓜEstadio; map p.210. On a quiet street off the busy C 44, this small hostel could be just the place if you're after somewhere a little bit out of the way. It's not a party hostel, but there's an on-site bar open in the evenings. $

EATING

CITY CENTRE
Hacienda Cra 49 (Junín) No. 52–98 ☎4 448 9030; ⓜParque Berrío; map p.212. A good place to sample top-notch local cuisine in relaxed surroundings. It's worth going for something traditional here, such as the *sancocho antioqueño* or a *bandeja de la Hacienda*, which is a full-on *bandeja paisa* and then some. $$

Hatoviejo Cra 47 No. 52–17 ⓦhatoviejo.com; ⓜParque Berrío; map p.212. Choose from a short menu of well-prepared Paisa dishes at this upstairs restaurant that's something of a retreat from the mean streets beneath, although you can watch them from the window. The *cazuela típica* is always a good bet, or you can opt for grilled chicken or trout with baked potatoes. On Fri and Sat nights, they have live music too. $

EL POBLADO

3M Gastro Bar Cra 36 No. 8A–92 • 322 569 0233; Ⓜ Poblado; map p.217. An excellent burger and sandwich joint that does lunches and breakfasts all day. $

Ajiacos y Mondongos C 8 No. 42–46 • 4 266 5505, W facebook.com/ajiacosymondongos; Ⓜ Poblado; map p.217. A top place for a seriously traditional feed. There are just three things on the menu here: *ajiaco*, *mondongo* or *cazuela*, and all are done well. $

Azai Praia Lovers vía Primavera C 8A No. 37A–78 • 311 703 2260; Ⓜ Poblado; map p.217. The decor here (especially upstairs) verges on being Scandinavian, but the food is authentically gluten free and vegan. The black bean burgers and the breakfast pancakes are especially good. $$

Carmen Gra 36 No. 10A–27 W grupocarmen.com; Ⓜ Poblado; map p.217. Book ahead for this top-notch contemporary fusion restaurant combining flavours from across the world, with strong European and Southeast Asian influences in particular. The list of dishes changes regularly, but there's always the option of a tasting menu. $$

Il Forno Cra 37A No. 8–09 W ilforno.co; Ⓜ Poblado; map p.217. A modern, open-air Italian place and El Poblado institution with plenty of mood lighting and satisfying pizza (five cheeses), home-made pasta (*spaghetti alla carbonara*) and salads. Other branches around town. $$

Hummus C 6 No. 43C–12 • 604 450 2751; Ⓜ Poblado; map p.217. Not only are there plenty of vegetarian options at this classy Lebanese restaurant, but their *limonada de coco* is easily the best in town and their *mezze* have that genuine Middle Eastern flavour. If you're extra hungry, go for the *mixto* platter – complete with *kofta*, *tabbouleh*, *shawarma*, *kibbeh* and rice. $$

★ **Mondongo's** C 10 No. 38–38 W mondongos.com.co; Ⓜ Poblado; map p.217. No prizes for guessing that the speciality here is *mondongo* (tripe soup), and this is one of the best places in Colombia to try it – it's a lot tastier than it sounds. Failing that, they do an awesome *típico antioqueño*, which is their version of a *bandeja paisa*, with all the trimmings and then some. The building was formerly the Medellín Cartel's administrative HQ. $$

Naan Cra 35 No. 7–75 W naansaboresdeindia.com; Ⓜ Poblado; map p.217. It's not every day you run across an Indian restaurant in Colombia and this one isn't bad, although purists may cavil. Meat curries include chicken tikka masala and pork vindaloo, or pricier lamb dishes such as *rogan josh*; veg options are a bit cheaper (*sag paneer*). $$

Restaurante La Tienda Del Vino desde 1999 C 9 No. 43B–93 • 604 311 5822, W facebook.com/restaurante bahiamar; Ⓜ Poblado; map p.217. A very popular little restaurant where traditional Colombian dishes are served alongside an extensive wine menu. There's also a good number of vegan and vegetarian options here. $$

Señor Itto C 9 No. 43B–115 • 4 314 0415; Ⓜ Poblado; map p.217. Some of the best Japanese food in town gets served up at this modest little place, with a lunchtime set menu, a choice of main dishes such as beef in eel sauce, or a bento lunch box. $

DRINKING

Clubs get busy from around 11pm, but a lot of people just hang out in El Poblado's **Parque Lleras**, buying beer in the shops at its western end – Lleras Park Minimarket at Cra 40 No. 9–21, for example – although drinking in the square and on the street is officially illegal. After closing time (under the local *ley zanahoria*), bars and clubs close at 4am), the throng tends to thicken, and street vendors are usually on hand with bottles of aguardiente.

3 Cordilleras C 30 No. 44–176 W 3cordilleras.com; Ⓜ Industriales; map p.210. Medellín's own local brewery opens its doors every Thurs afternoon for a tour with an explanation in Spanish of the brewing process; this is mostly an excuse for a booze-up in the bar, with your entry fee buying you a bottle of each of the brewery's five beers. Alternatively, for a cover charge, come along on a Fri evening, when there are live local bands.

37 Park Cra 37 No. 8A–04 W 37-park.cluvi.co; Ⓜ Poblado; map p.217 This bistro bar, spilling out into the little park by the river, is something of a chill-out zone amid the Zona Rosa's banging dance bars, and a good place to stop for a beer or a bite between nightspots. Or you could just come here during the day and treat it as an open-air restaurant.

El Acontista C 53 No. 43–81 W elacontista.com; Ⓜ Parque Berrío; map p.212. A sophisticated downtown café, bar, restaurant and (upstairs) bookshop, with live jazz music on Mon nights (except public holidays).

Bogotá Beer Company Cra 34 No. 7–165 • 4 311 3060; Ⓜ Poblado; map p.217. Fancy a quiet night at the pub rather than a rave-up? Well, the BBC's Medellín branch is right there by the Zona Rosa, with footie on the TV, pints of ale and a relaxed ambience. And you can always go dancing after you've had a pint or two.

Niágara 5 Puertas Cra 38 No. 8–11 • 4 268 8564; Ⓜ Poblado; map p.217. El Poblado's oldest bar, founded in 1946, is a real, authentic Medellín hangout, whose regulars have been coming here for years. It's a place to have a beer and a chat, meet up at the start of a night out, or just hang out and enjoy the company of friends.

Salon Málaga Cra 51 No. 45–80, Centro W salonmalaga.com; Ⓜ San Antonio; map p.212. A real old-school tango and *bolero* bar, where they play classic South American sounds dating from the 1930s to the 1960s, and even on occasion pull out the old wax 78s for a spin. The walls are lined with photos of tango greats, and there are a couple of ancient jukeboxes, too.

LGBTQ+ MEDELLÍN

Medellín has quite a thriving **LGBTQ+ scene**, albeit smaller than Bogotá's. Online information on bars, clubs and other locales can be found on *EgoCity Magazine*'s website at ⓦegocitymgz.com and on the *Guia Gay* website at ⓦguiagaycolombia.com/medellin.

LGBTQ+ BARS AND CLUBS

La Cantina de Javi C 58 No. 47–18, Prado ☎4 284 5370; ⓦfacebook.com/cantinadejavi; ⓜPrado; map p.212. Colourful city-centre bar with a Mexican *cantina* theme, a mix of Latin and electronic music, and a fun crowd. Cover charge.

Donde Aquellos Cra 38 No. 9A–26, El Poblado ⓦdondeaquellosbar.com; ⓜPoblado; map p.217. A well-established base for all branches of the LGBTQ+ community in El Poblado's Zona Rosa, with an outdoor terrace and a dancefloor where you'll hear everything from reggaeton to techno.

Miró C 9 No. 40–10, El Poblado ☎4 268 1211; ⓜPoblado; map p.217. Upstairs bar by Parque Lleras with music and cocktails. It tends to appeal more to the boys, but girls are welcome too.

Viva C 51 No. 73–100 ☎ 4 230 7943; ⓜEstadio; map p.210. Popular Sat night disco with two dancefloors: a bigger one downstairs for reggaeton and electronic music, and a smaller one upstairs for less energetic electronica, pop and Latino sounds. Cover charge.

NIGHTLIFE

Babylon Cra 41 No. 9–22 ☎316 876 7545, ⓦbit.ly/babylonmed; ⓜPoblado; map p.217. A hugely popular club where they'll mix anything from house to reggaeton, *vallenato* and even salsa. Thurs (ladies' night) and Fri are *barra libre*, which means you pay to get in and drink unlimited amounts of specific brands of beer, rum or aguardiente. On Sat, entry is free and you just pay for your drinks. Not in the least bit sophisticated but a lot of fun.

El Blue C 10 No. 40–20 ☎7 266 3047, ⓦfacebook.com/bluemedellin; ⓜPoblado; map p.217. A change from the usual dance music, this is a club dedicated to "alternative" sounds, which mostly means rock, but that seems to be just right for the friendly crowd of locals and backpackers who come here. There is usually a cover charge, but women are often given free admission till 11pm, and entry may cost more if there's a live band on.

Dulce Jesús Mio Cra 38 No. 19–255 (Km 2 Via Las Palmas) ⓦeslacarta.com/dulcejesusmio; map p.210. Every night is New Year's Eve at this kitsch club decorated with toys and cartoon characters representing a cutesie-pie version of an Antioquian town. The music is "crossover", and there's a stage with performers. Entry requires a cover charge, but drinks are expensive and you won't get a table unless you order a bottle of rum or aguardiente. Groups of men are not admitted without at least one woman.

Eslabón Prendido C 53 No. 42–55 ☎4 239 3400; ⓜParque Berrío; map p.212. This easy-going and friendly (if sweaty) little downtown salsa club is particularly worthwhile on Tues nights, when there's a live band from 10pm. They also run salsa dance classes. On the downside, the area's a bit sleazy, so it's best to arrive and leave by cab. Cover charge.

Juniper Cra 43a No. 130 ☎ 300 875 5888; map p.210. One of Medellín's more polished craft cocktail bars with weekly live jazz music, plus some of the best dressed people in Medellín. The entry fee depends on the night.

Luxury Cra 39 No. 8–45 ⓦreservasmedellin.com; ⓜPoblado; map p.217. This is where a young, tipsy crowd gets down and dirty to reggaeton, hip-hop and more. Luxury it ain't, but it sure is lively. There's usually a cover charge for men, and it's often free for women.

Mango's Cra 42 No. 67A–151, Itagüí ☎300 868 5854; ⓜEnvigado; map p.210. Medellín's biggest and glitziest club, with a Wild West theme, reggaeton and crossover music, and a well-heeled clientele. Entry fees vary, depending on the night.

SHOPPING

Centro Comercial Palacio Nacional Cra 52 No. 48–45 ☎4 513 4422; ⓜSan Antonio; map p.212. A mall, yes, but this one's in the former Palacio de Justicia, a very grand old building dating from the 1920s which once housed the offices of the law courts and has been carefully restored to retain all its original glory. Most of the shops are independent retailers selling sportswear, shoes or clothing, with a few selling DVDs, and a couple of cafés on the ground floor.

Éxito C 10 No. 25–43 ☎4 605 0145, ⓜPoblado, map p.217; Cra 49 No. 52–165, Centro ☎4 513 1253, ⓜParque Berrío, map p.212; ⓦexito.com. Medellín's two most useful supermarket branches, very handy for self-catering food supplies.

Plaza Minorista C 55A No. 57–80 ⓦplazaminorista.com/sitio/inicio; ⓜPrado; map p.210. A huge covered market, always busy, with lots and lots of food stalls, selling fruit and veg, fish and meat, juices, coffee and freshly made *arepas*, as well as others selling secondhand clothes and footwear, all at low prices.

Street Market Cra 51 between C 54 and C 60; ⓜ Prado; map p.212. A flea market stretching up Cra 51 under the metro line, and rather rough and ready, where you'll find anything from porn DVDs to new and used clothes, bric-a-brac and utter junk. Watch your step, as this isn't the most salubrious part of town.

DIRECTORY

Banks and exchange There are plenty of banks with ATMs around town, and all shopping malls have them. Casas de cambio include Interdolar, Cra 40 No. 10–19, El Poblado; Euroservicios (local 121); and several others in the forecourt of the Oviedo mall, Cra 43A (Av el Poblado) No. 6S–15.

Car rental Avis, C 9 No. 43A–31 (☎ 320 856 3561) and at the airport (☎ 4 536 0226); Hertz, Cra 43A No. 1A Sur–69 (☎ 4 319 1010); Localiza, Cra 48B No. 4 Sur (under the bridge) (☎ 4 268 2553), and at the airport (☎ 4 604 2900).

Cinemas One of the cheapest cinemas in town is Cine Procinal in the Centro Comercial Terminal del Sur, a shopping mall by the Terminal del Sur bus station. Another is Cine Monterrey in the Monterrey shopping mall on the junction by ⓜ Poblado.

Consulates Brazil, Cra 67B No. 43B–39 (☎ 4 559 9211); Panama, C 10 No. 42–45 (Edificio la Plaza), suite 266, El Poblado (☎ 4 312 4590); Peru, Cra 43B No. 16 –41 (STAFF Building), suite 1406, El Poblado (☎ 4 268 8059); Venezuela, C 32B No. 59–69 (☎ 4 444 0359).

Festivals The most exciting local festival is the Feria de las Flores (Flower Festival; ⓦ feriadelasfloresmedellin.gov.co), held over ten days in late July or early Aug, which features a series of processions, featuring everything from horses to *chivas* and vintage cars, but most importantly the *Desfile de Silleteros*, when flower growers display spectacular flower arrangements on contraptions strapped to their backs that were originally designed to carry people. July also sees a poetry festival (ⓦ festivaldepoesiademedellin.org) – mostly in Spanish, of course – and, on July 22–24, South America's biggest fashion festival, Colombiamoda (ⓦ colombiamoda.inexmoda.org.co).

Football Deportivo Independiente Medellín (home strip: red and blue) and Atlético Nacional (home strip: green and white) share as their home ground the Estadio Atanasio Girardot, most easily reached by metro (ⓜ Estadio). Tickets are not readily available and usually have to be bought from touts around the ground, so you need to check carefully before buying, especially the holographic panel, and you're best off enlisting local help. An easier way to go is with Paisa Road (see page 220) who organize football tours with pick-ups from various hostels.

Health Clínica Las Vegas, C 2S No. 46–55 (☎ 4 315 9000, ⓦ clinicalasvegas.com (ⓜ Industriales), has doctors and dentists. The local state-run hospital, Hospital General de Medellín, Cra 48 No. 32–102 (☎ 4 384 7300, ⓦ hgm.gov.co; ⓜ Exposiciones), also has a good reputation. Useful 24hr pharmacies include: Botica Junín, C 47 No. 50–80 in the centre (☎ 4 212 1212); Farmacia Pasteur, Cra 43 (Av el Poblado) No. 25A–4 in El Poblado (☎ 4 444 1400).

Internet Centro de Tecnología, local 202, Centro Comercial Veracruz, Cra 51 No. 51–47; Cibervoz, C 10 No. 36–51.

Laundry Todo Limpio, Cra 41A No. 10–9.

Police Tourist police, Pueblito Paisa (☎ 4 265 5907).

Post office C 49 No. 65A–10, city centre; Cra 43A (Av Poblado) No. 10–02, El Poblado.

Spanish courses Black Sheep Hostel (see page 221) can recommend local private teachers. Otherwise the Toucan Spanish School (Cra 41A No. 10–28; ⓦ toucanspanish.com), offers one week's tuition (20hr).

Swimming pools The Complejo Acuático Estadio Atanasio Girardot (C 48 at Cra 74; free; ☎ 4 436 0841) is a water park with an olympic-size pool in the same sports complex as the Estadio Atanasio Girardot football stadium. The city council also runs six other pools in the city's suburbs. Alternatively, the Aeroparque Juan Pablo II is a privately run water park next to Olaya Herrera airport (Cra 70 No. 16–04; charge; ⓦ aeroparquejuanpablo.gov.co), with six pools, plus games, slides and wave machines. Note that at any of these places you have to wear a proper swimming costume: cut-off shorts or other cotton clothing is not allowed.

Visa extensions Migración Colombia, C 19 No. 80A–40, Barrio Belén La Nubia (☎ 4 345 5500).

Guatapé and around

The gorgeous lakeside town of **GUATAPÉ** is just two hours out of Medellín. Many tourists come largely to see the nearby **Piedra del Peñol**, Colombia's answer to Sugar Loaf Mountain, but the town itself is a far greater attraction. Its picturesque little houses, painted in cheerful, bright pastels, with multicoloured wooden verandas, are famous for their decorative panels called *zócalos* (see page 225). Unsurprisingly, Guatapé is a big favourite with weekenders from Medellín, and it can get quite crowded come Saturday or Sunday, with many hotel prices rising sharply on Saturday nights.

Founded in 1811, Guatapé is older than the **lake** on whose shore it now stands, the Embalse del Peñol, which has only been there since the River Nare was dammed

> **GUATAPÉ'S ZÓCALOS**
>
> Guatapé's prettily painted houses are a far cry from the typical whitewashed buildings in most of Colombia's colonial towns, let alone Medellín's modern apartment blocks, but their most distinctive feature is their *zócalos*. These are colourful decorative panels, usually square, painted in relief along the base of the houses up to waist-height. Originally, they were all representations of the Lamb of God, and some do still have religious images on them. More commonly, however, they show rural scenes, geometric shapes, flowers, animals (not necessarily lambs, although there are still one or two), or new-fangled designs such as buses, *chivas*, cars or boats, or – if it's a business – things related to the services on offer, such as keys in the case of a locksmith, or sewing machines in the case of a tailor. You can spend hours wandering around town checking out the sheer variety.

to create it in 1972 (the dam now provides up to thirty percent of Colombia's electricity). The palm-lined *parque principal* (main square), **Plaza de Simón Bolívar**, is just a block off the lakeside, and must surely be one of the prettiest main squares in South America. On its north side, the **Iglesia del Carmen** church was originally faced with bare brick, but since the 1980s has been white with brick-red highlights. Those include its four *zócalos*, by local sculptor Mario Hernández, representing the four gospel authors – an angel for Matthew, a lion for Mark, an ox for Luke and an eagle for John.

Some of Guatapé's prettiest streets are off the **Calle del Comercio** (Calle 31), which leads east from the *parque principal*. Stairs opposite No. 29–9 lead down to the **Plazoleta de los Zócalos**, a lovely little square positively bursting with colour, and on past a row of little shops to the waterfront. Also full of painted houses and *zócalos* is the **Calle del Recuerdo** (Cra 28), with its little painted fountain of four *campesinos*, but bear off down any of the streets and you'll be rewarded with views taking in rows of jolly, *zócalo*-encrusted houses in bright, vibrant colours.

The lake

Boat rides • Charge per person (minimum of 20) • **Cable Paseo Guatapé** • Charge • 322 291 5470

Down at the waterside are a slew of boat companies offering three-hour **cruises** on the lake. During the week, the boats don't usually move until after lunch, but at weekends, when Guatapé throngs with visitors from Medellín, the boats fill up much faster, and there are departures throughout the day. *Lake View Hostel* also offers **lake excursions**, including a visit to the now largely submerged church from the old town of El Peñon (only its steeple protrudes above the water), and to a nearby abandoned *finca* that once belonged to Pablo Escobar.

If you prefer to zoom along above the water, have a go on the **Cable Paseo Guatapé**, which involves sitting in a harness and scooting across a zip wire above the lake.

La Piedra del Peñol

Embalse del Peñol, 3km west of Guatapé • Charge • Served by buses between Medellín and Guatapé (ask for "La Piedra"), or travel from Guatapé by *mototaxi*

Bearing a freakish resemblance to Rio de Janeiro's Sugar Loaf Mountain, 200m-high **Piedra del Peñol**, or simply "the rock", rises spectacularly from the edge of the lake. It's well worth climbing the 649 stone **steps** built in a natural cleft up to the rock's peak for phenomenal 360-degree views of emerald green peninsulas jutting into the azure water. There are shops and cafés at the top and bottom, as well as toilets, but food choices are limited.

Painted on the side of the Piedra are the letters GI. In fact, this was supposed to read "GUATAPÉ", but when the rock's proprietors started painting it in 1988, residents of El Peñon, the first town in the other direction (rebuilt on the lakeside after the original town was submerged in the lake), objected because they felt the rock belonged to them rather than to Guatapé. They complained to the local environmental authorities, who ordered the painting to stop because it would mar a feature of natural beauty. Only the first letter and one stroke of the second were completed, and remain.

ARRIVAL AND INFORMATION

By bus The bus station is by the lakeside on C 32 at Cra 30, with services to Medellín's north terminal every 30min (2hr). Note that buses back to Medellín fill up quickly on Sun afternoons and evenings, so it's worth buying your ticket ahead of time then, if possible.

Tourist information The tourist information office is inside the Palacio Municipal (Town Hall) in the northwest corner of the *parque principal* at C 31 No. 30–08.

GETTING AROUND

By bus and mototaxi The same buses that connect Guatapé and Medellín also stop at La Piedra, and are the cheapest way to get there. Alternatively, you can take a *mototaxi* from Plaza Simón Bolívar.

GUATAPÉ AND AROUND

ACCOMMODATION

Lake View Hostel Cra 22 No. 29B–29 ⓦ lakeviewhostel.com. This British-/American-run hostel by the lake (which also claims to be a "boutique hotel") has all sorts of activities on offer, including kayaking, cycling, visits to swimming spots and Pablo Escobar's old *finca*, as well as dorms and private rooms, a roof terrace and a good Thai restaurant on the roof. Dorms $\overline{\underline{\$}}$, doubles $\overline{\underline{\$\$}}$

Mi Casa Estadero la Mona ☏ 219 761 6677. A friendly hostel at the foot of La Piedra run by an English/Colombian couple offering rooms with either private or shared bathrooms. $\overline{\underline{\$}}$

Portobelo C 32 No. 28–29 ⓦ hotelportobeloguatape.com. A modern lakeside hotel with bright, fresh rooms, attractively furnished, each with a balcony overlooking the lake. A thirty-percent discount applies every day except Sat and *puentes* (a long weekend with Mon off). $\overline{\underline{\$\$}}$

EATING

La Fogata C 32 No. 31–32 (opposite the bus station) ☏ 4 861 1040; ⓦ facebook.com/lafogataguatape. A great restaurant with a covered terrace overlooking the lake, good beer and excellent service, just the spot for a lunch of charcoal-grilled trout or barbecue ribs. $\overline{\underline{\$}}$

Guatacrep' C 31 No. 27–58 (opposite the football pitch) ☏ 314 268 6322; ⓦ facebook.com/guatacrep. Healthy food, largely organic (sourced from a single permaculture farm), much of it vegetarian and all of it good. They do a great lasagne and crêpes for afters, and have a lunchtime set menu. They also make their own bread. $\overline{\underline{\$}}$

Martine Cra 29 No. 30–10 ☏ 4 861 0396. A pleasantly shaded little restaurant just above the Plazoleta de los Zócalos, and an excellent spot for lunch or a weekend supper. Vegetarians will particularly appreciate the veg crêpes. $\overline{\underline{\$}}$

★ **Pizzeria De Luigi** C 31 No. 27–10 (upstairs) ☏ 320 845 4552. The eponymous Luigi is Italian and it shows: this little place, run by Luigi and his wife, does some of the best pizzas in the country, and pretty much nothing else (pasta on Sun lunchtimes, but that's it). If you only eat one pizza in the whole of Colombia, eat it here. $\overline{\underline{\$\$}}$

DIRECTORY

Banks and exchange There's an ATM on the side of the town hall at Cra 30 No. 31–01, and another by the bus station at C 32 No. 30–27.

Festivals Guatapé shares with nearby Rionegro the hosting of a film festival, the Festival de Cine de Oriente every Oct or Nov (ⓦ facebook.com/cineoriente). There's also a small music festival, Mas que Sonidos (ⓦ facebook.com/MasQueSonidos), in late Nov or early Dec.

Internet Cyber Guatapé, C 31 No. 29-23

Santa Fe de Antioquia

Just 80km northwest of Medellín – but nearly 1000m lower in altitude, and therefore much warmer – the lovely whitewashed colonial town of **SANTA FE DE ANTIOQUIA** was the capital of Antioquia until that brash upstart Medellín usurped it in 1826. Since then Santa Fe has remained almost unspoiled. Many of its whitewashed houses still have their original stucco doorways with ornate decorations on the lintels in particular, while other buildings eschew the whitewash and stucco in favour of a bare but decorative stone and brick facade, a style called *calicanto*.

An easy journey from Medellín via the 4.6km **Tunel del Occidente** through the Cordillera, the town is a very popular weekend retreat from the city. During the week, things are much quieter, but on the other hand a lot of places are closed, with some bars and restaurants opening from Thursday to Sunday only, one museum open weekends only, and the churches generally open only for Mass.

Plaza Mayor
Cra 9–10 at C 9–10

Santa Fe's main square, **Plaza Mayor**, is as pretty a little colonial plaza as you could hope to find. Surrounded by colonial-era houses with wooden verandas, and stalls selling sweets, fruit and dried tamarind, its centrepiece is a statue of **Juan del Corral**, president of the Republic of Antioquia from 1813 until his death the following year, during which brief period he took the opportunity to declare the children of slaves free as a prelude to the abolition of slavery itself. On the southeast side of the square, the **Palacio Consistorial**, built in 1797 and now the town hall, is where del Corral declared Antioquia's independence and emancipation of the *pardos* (children of slaves).

Santa Fe's **Cathedral** (open for Mass; free), whose whitewashed facade overlooks the square from its northeast side, was inaugurated in 1837, forty years after its construction began, various political upheavals having intervened in the meantime. Its architect was Fray Domingo Petrés, who also designed Bogotá's cathedral (see page 60). If you can catch it open, it's worth popping in to see its triple-nave interior.

Museo Juan del Corral
C 11 No. 9–77 • Free • ☎ 4 853 4605

The main attraction at the **Museo Juan del Corral** is not so much its collection of archeological and historical artefacts and objets d'art as the beautifully restored nineteenth-century colonial mansion that houses them. The first of its six rooms display archeological finds from the region, and is followed by a colonial room dominated by religious works of art, and an altar room with still more. The Independence room is the most interesting, containing the table on which Juan del Corral signed Antioquia's Act of Independence back in 1813, and the last two rooms

> ### SANTA FE'S CHURCHES
>
> In addition to its cathedral, Santa Fe de Antioquia has three **colonial churches**. Unfortunately, they open only for Mass, around 7am and in the evenings at around 5.30pm or 6.30pm, but each is fronted by its own little square where you can hang out and admire the facade.
>
> **Iglesia de Santa Bárbara** C 11 at Cra 8. Even if you don't go in, do check out the wide 1795 Baroque Calicanto facade of this beautiful little church. Inside, the baptismal font, which dates from 1721, is the oldest in the region. The main altar and the pulpit are also eighteenth-century originals.
>
> **Iglesia de Nuestra Señora de Chiquinquirá** Cra 13 at C 10. Presiding over Santa Fe's Zona Rosa, such as it is, this nineteenth-century church, with its two towers, was erected in 1868 on the site of two ill-fated predecessors, one of which burnt down after being struck by a bolt of lightning.
>
> **Iglesia de Jesús Nazareno** C 10 at Cra 6. The narrow facade of this whitewashed Neoclassical church – commonly known as La Iglesia de Jesús mi Padre – was built in 1828 with Baroque touches and overlooks a square planted with palm trees.

are reconstructions of a dining room from the early republican era and a kitchen from colonial times. It won't take you more than thirty minutes to see it all, but it's time well spent.

Museo de Arte Religioso
C 11 No. 8–12 • Charge • ☎ 4 853 1086

Right next to the Iglesia de Santa Bárbara (see page 228), the **Museo de Arte Religioso** is housed in what was originally an eighteenth-century Jesuit house, although the upper storey wasn't actually added until the nineteenth century. It houses an impressive collection of paintings and sculptures, including works by Gregorio Vázquez de Arce, Colombia's most prominent artist of the colonial period. Taking up a whole room is the museum's most impressive exhibit, originally from Ecuador, a reconstruction of the Last Supper with life-size sculptures of Jesus and each of the disciples.

Puente de Occidente
6km northeast of Santa Fe de Antioquia • Round trip by tuk-tuk

South America's first ever suspension bridge, the **Puente de Occidente** (Bridge of the West) is a long walk or short tuk-tuk ride from town. The bridge was designed by the Antioquian engineer José María Villa, who learned his trade in New Jersey and worked on the Brooklyn Bridge before embarking on this project in 1887. Although he had many of the materials imported from Britain, Villa used wood for the actual roadway and sidewalks. As a result, and thanks to years of neglect, the bridge fell into some disrepair before being restored to its original state in 2014.

ARRIVAL AND INFORMATION — SANTA FE DE ANTIOQUIA

By bus and colectivo The bus terminal is on C 13 at Cra 10, and has regular buses (roughly hourly; 1hr 30min) and *colectivos* (every 20min; 1hr) to Medellín. The *colectivos* are faster and more frequent but cost more. After 8pm, you'll be dependent on buses passing through from further afield.

Bear in mind that buses fill up fast for the return to Medellín on a Sun.

Tourist information The office at the southern corner of the Plaza Mayor (☎ 4 853 1136) is very helpful, with a good map and information sheet on the town, but in Spanish only.

GETTING AROUND

There are taxis, tuk-tuks (auto-rickshaws) and motorbike taxis, none of which will be of much use in the compact town centre, although you may want to use them to get to the Puente de Occidente.

ACCOMMODATION

Prices quoted here are for **weekends**; in pretty much all of the town's hotels the price falls **midweek** but rises substantially for *puentes* (a long weekend with Monday off), Christmas and Easter.

Caserón C 9 No. 9–41 w caserondelparque.com; map p.227. Right on the Plaza Mayor, this lovely old colonial house has a variety of rooms (it's worth paying a bit more for an upstairs room at the back) and a good pool, but not all rooms are good for wi-fi (so, if you need it, ask for one that is). It's an absolute bargain midweek, when the price drops by over a third. $\overline{\$\$}$

Danhy's C 9 No. 10–56 ✆ 4 853 1091; map p.227. Nothing grand, but simple, decent rooms, each with its own bathroom, some a little bit dark, at this little budget guesthouse just off the Plaza Mayor. $\overline{\$}$

Franco Cra 10 No. 8A–14 ✆ 4 853 1654; map p.227. Just behind the Plaza Mayor, a funny little place with lots of pictures of macaws and strange objects strewn around the public areas, small but sweet rooms with ceiling fans and compact bathrooms, and coffee on tap all day. $\overline{\$}$

★ **Mariscal Robledo** Cra 12 at C 10 (Plazuela de Chiquinquirá) w hotelmariscalrobledo.com; map p.227. The town's top hotel, housed in a beautiful old seventeenth-century colonial mansion full of antique furnishings and interesting bric-a-brac. Indeed, the hotel's almost a sight in itself. The rooms are modern but retain a bit of olde-worlde style, and most have signs outside commemorating a (usually local) celebrity who's stayed in them. There are also modern amenities such as a pool. Breakfast included. $\overline{\$\$\$}$

EATING

La Comedia C 11 No. 8–03 ✆ 4 381 4462, w facebook.com/lacomediaabc; map p.227. This cool, arty bar and restaurant is a great place to hang out of an evening, and not a bad place to eat either, with decent *crêpes* (mushroom, spinach and cheese) and main courses (trout gratinée with prawns) as well as beers, spirits and cocktails. $\overline{\$\$}$

Portón del Parque C 10 No. 11–03 ✆ 4 853 3207; map p.227. This is Santa Fe's top restaurant. Its walls decked with portraits by local artist Olga, it offers a menu of well-cooked meaty dishes such as filet mignon or baby beef (heart of rump steak). $\overline{\$\$}$

Sabor Español C 10 No. 12–26 w restaurantesaborespanol.com; map p.227. A little place serving good Spanish food. You can go for a full-blown paella, or just get a jug of *sangría* and order some tapas. $\overline{\$\$}$

Santa Isabel Cra 10 No. 9–37 (on Plaza Mayor); map p.227. An excellent spot for a filling and economical breakfast or lunch. If you don't fancy the set menu, there's steak *au poivre*, or grilled sea bass with prawns and mushrooms. $\overline{\$}$

DIRECTORY

Banks and exchange Banco de Colombia, Cra 9 No. 10–72 has an ATM, and there are a couple more on Plaza Mayor.

Festivals Santa Fe hosts two annual film festivals: the Festival de Cine Colombiano in late July or early Aug, and the Festival de Cine y Video in early Dec (information on both w festicineantioquia.com).

Internet Telecom, C 10 No. 9–06 (east corner of Plaza Mayor).

Jardín

The pretty little nineteenth-century town of **JARDÍN** ("garden") is increasingly popular with visitors from Colombia and abroad. People from Medellín in particular like to pop down at weekends, making midweek the best time to visit if you want to avoid the crowds. The **Parque Principal** has a wonderful ambience, with an imposing grey and white basilica on its east side, and a row of cafés opposite where the town's old boys like to hang out of an afternoon. The **Casa Museo Clara Rojas**, a local museum on the square's south side, was closed at the time of research; it should be open in 2018, although hours and prices were not yet fixed. Surrounded by natural beauty spots, Jardín offers great hikes, including the **Sendero de la Lechuza**, a three-hour hike south of town. A longer hike north of town takes you to the **Cueva del Esplendor**, a cave with a waterfall coming in through its ceiling. It takes around three hours to reach on foot, and can only be visited on a tour; these must be booked in advance (charge; ✆ 316 515 2000).

Teleférico la Garrucha

C 12 at Cra 9A • Charge per round trip

At the southern end of Calle 12, the **Teleférico la Garrucha** is a home-made cable car built in 1995 by local resident Alejandro Vélez so that he could get into town from his home just across the gorge. Very soon, his neighbours were using it too, and then tourists cottoned on, and it's now a local attraction. Powered by the engine of a Ford 600 tractor, it takes five passengers. The wood-and-steel cabin, which looks a bit like a cattle truck on wires, has slats through which you can admire the view during the three-minute crossing.

ARRIVAL AND INFORMATION JARDÍN

By bus The two bus companies have offices facing each other across C 8 at No. 5–21 and 5–22; this is where buses pull in, serving Medellín (14 daily; 3hr) and Rio Sucio (3 daily; 3hr). For the Zona Cafeteram take the bus to Riosucio and change – if you're lucky you'll get a *chiva*; best views are on the right.
Tourist information There's a Punto de Información Turística (PiT) in the Casa Museo Clara Rojas on the Parque Principal at Cra 5 No. 9–31.

ACCOMMODATION

All the hotels in town drop their rates slightly midweek. Prices given here are for **weekends**.
Hostal las Flores C 12 No. 8–45 ☎314 845 3557. Painted in cheery colours, this little hostel has a pretty garden and offers horseback excursions. $

Hotel Casa Grande C 8 No. 4–33 ☎4 845 5487, ⓦbit.ly/hotelcasagrande. Bright, clean and neat as a new pin, with lots of vermillion-coloured paintwork, this friendly and respectable little hotel is handy for the buses and just a block off the Parque Principal. $$

EATING

Cafetería Jardín de Comidas Rápidas C 11 No. 5–02. A handy place for a cheap and filling breakfast or lunch. They also do a good *sancocho*. $
Dulces de Jardín de Comidas Rápidas C 13 No. 5–47 ☎4 845 6584, ⓦfacebook.com/dulcesdeljardin. Famous for its sweets, especially *arequipe*, as well as jams, macaroons and candied fruits, this is also a sweet place to have a coffee. $

Truchera la Argelia 1km northeast of town (take C3 to the end then turn left onto Cra 16, head over the bridge and continue for 1km) ☎4 845 5133. Jardín is surrounded by trout farms (*rucheras*), many of which, including this one, have attached restaurants where you can sit and eat their trout. You can have it cooked in various ways; trout with almonds is one tasty example. And if you fancy, you can pop out back and check out the trout ponds. $$

Zona Cafetera

The mountainous terrain and tropical climate of the **Zona Cafetera**, also called the *Eje Cafetera* ("coffee-producing axis"), is very well suited to growing arabica **coffee**. The entire region is lush and scenic, with cloudforests, wax palms and, of course, coffee estates, some of which you can visit and even stay on. In the fourth to seventh centuries AD, the area was inhabited by the Quimbayas, master workers in gold, who were responsible for some of the very best pieces in Bogotá's Museo del Oro (see page 66). Today, **Manizales**, **Pereira** and **Armenia** are the main centres of Colombia's Zona Cafetera, and coffee remains the economic mainstay.

Manizales and around

The wonderfully hilly city of **MANIZALES** is the capital of the Caldas *departamento*. It was founded in 1849 by a group of twenty Paisas fleeing from the Liberal–Conservative strife then wracking neighbouring Antioquia, but what really put Manizales on the map was the growth of the **coffee industry** at the end of the nineteenth century.

High in the mountains (altitude 2150m), Manizales owes its steep topography to the geologically volatile earth beneath it. **Earthquakes** occur with some frequency. In 1875 and 1878 they caused quite severe damage, but not as much as a huge fire in 1926, which largely destroyed the city centre. The result is that many older buildings in the centre date from the late 1920s when it was rebuilt.

The main thoroughfare in Manizales is **Carrera 23**, known for much of its length as **Avenida de Santander**. Running from east to west along the top of a ridge, it joins the city's two main hubs: the historic downtown **city centre** and the newer, brighter **Zona Rosa**, 3km to the southeast.

Though in places it's pretty scenic, much of Manizales' charm lies in its large student population, who help create a festive atmosphere, with night-time entertainment centred mostly on the Zona Rosa. The party comes to a head in the first weeks of January during the **Feria de Manizales** (see page 234). Manizales also makes an excellent base for exploring the surrounding **coffee farms** and the **Parque Nacional Natural Los Nevados**.

Plaza de Bolívar

The heart of the city centre is the main square, **Plaza de Bolívar**, which naturally features a **statue of Simón Bolívar**, but with a twist: here El Libertador is represented by a *Bolívar-Cóndor*, a creation of Colombian sculptor Rodrigo Arenas Betancourt, with the body of a man, the head and wings of a condor, and Bolívar's face as a detached mask.

The plaza is overlooked by a vast **Cathedral** (free) on its south side, officially named "La Catedral Basílica Metropolitana Nuestra Señora del Rosario de Manizales". Made of reinforced concrete, it was inaugurated in 1939 on the site of a predecessor that burned down in 1926. The new structure features a vertigo-

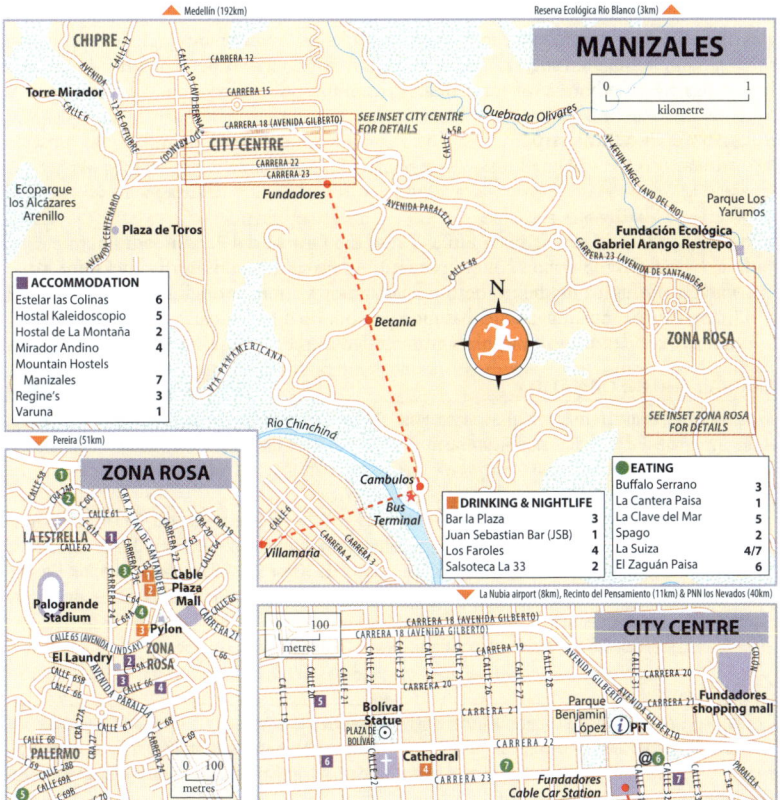

inducing, 106m-tall central tower that you can ascend as part of a **guided tour** (1hr 15min; charge).

Torre Mirador
Parque el Observatorio, Av 12 de Octubre, Chipre • Charge • 6 883 8311 • Bus showing destination "Chipre" from Cable Plaza along Av Santander

Northwest of town in the suburb of Chipre, the 45m-tall **Torre Mirador** (or Torre al Cielo) is the town's best lookout. It stands on a high bluff at the end of Avenida 12 de Octubre, and on a clear day, it gives a view over seven *departamentos* and three mountain ranges. The most popular time to come is at sunset, a view of which from this *barrio* so impressed the Chilean poet Pablo Neruda that he called Manizales the "factory of sunsets". As well as going up for the view itself, you can pay extra to do a *columpio extremo*, which involves swinging from a great height on a very long rope. Or you could just have a meal (or a drink) at the scenic restaurant instead.

Reserva Ecológica Río Blanco
3km northeast of Manizales • entry by appointment only – apply for permission from Aguas de Manizales (Av Kevin Ángel No. 59–181; 6 875 3950; reservarioblanco@aguasdemanizales.com.co), who will book the compulsory guides • Charge per person plus guide fee for up to ten people • Arrange a return trip taxi in advance

Northeast of town, the **Reserva Ecológica Río Blanco** is home to 380 bird species, including lots of hummingbirds and toucans (they have feeders to attract the hummingbirds), plus 180 butterfly species and more than sixty mammals. Tranquil orchid-lined uphill hikes through impressive cloudforest reveal dense jungle flora entwined in a battle for a place in the sun; if you're lucky, you may catch a glimpse of the reserve's endangered spectacled bear. You can do just a two-hour or a five-hour hike (mornings are usually best for this), or stay overnight or longer.

Recinto del Pensamiento
Km 11, Vía al Magdalena, 11km southeast of Manizales • Charge • 6 889 7073; recintodelpensamiento.com • Bus showing destination "Sera Maltería" from Cable Plaza along Av Santander (Cra 23) in the Zona Rosa (40min; can also be picked up downtown on Cra 20), or you can catch a taxi (20min)

Butterflies and birds are the main attraction at the **Recinto del Pensamiento** nature park, not far from the airport. As well as visiting the colourful butterfly enclosure, you can wander through a medicinal herb garden, enjoy a stroll through the orchid forest and marvel at the gigantic *guadua* bamboo gazebo, used for conventions and wedding ceremonies. Guides are compulsory and included in the admission price.

ARRIVAL AND INFORMATION

By plane La Nubia airport (6 874 5451) is 8km southeast of the city centre. Buses to "La Enea" from Cra 23 (Av Santander) in the Zona Rosa or Cra 20 downtown will drop you three blocks away.
Destinations Bogotá (3–6 daily; 1hr 5min); Medellín (10 weekly; 40min).
By bus The bus terminal (terminaldemanizales.com.co) is at Cra 43 No. 65–100. To get to the city centre, take a cable car (10min). For the Zona Rosa, walk over the road on the footbridge and take a bus showing the destination

MANIZALES AND AROUND

"Cable" (20min), or take the cable car to the centre and get a bus from there. The fastest services between Manizales and Medellín are the direct minibuses run by Flota Ospina and Tax la Feria.
Destinations Armenia (every 20–30min; 2hr 20min); Bogotá (24 daily; 8hr); Cali (every 30min; 5hr); Medellín (every 15–30min; 5hr); Pereira (every 15min; 1hr 15min).
Tourist information The PiT at Parque Benjamin López on the corner of Cra 22 and C 31 (6 873 3901) dish out maps and information about the city.

GETTING AROUND

The Zona Rosa is not served by the cable car but, confusingly, buses to the Zona Rosa show the destination "Cable", which refers to Cable Plaza, a large shopping mall by a square with a wooden pylon that originally held up an older, now defunct, cable car system.
By bus and buseta Buses and *busetas* ply the city's streets and you'll rarely have to wait more than a couple of minutes for one. The most useful services run along Cra 23 between

the historical centre and the Zona Rosa.
By cable car The Cable Aéreo (w cableaereomanizales.gov.co) connects the bus terminal (Cambulos station) with the city centre (Fundadores station), with one intermediate stop (Betania station), taking about 10min.
By taxi Taxis are the fastest way around town with an abundance of cabs running between the city centre and the Zona Rosa.

ACCOMMODATION

Estelar las Colinas Cra 22 No. 20–20, city centre w hotelesestelar.com; map p.231. This is just about the best bet for a mid-range hotel downtown. The building's ugly and the public areas are a bit scuffed, but the moderately sized rooms are decent enough, and the staff are very helpful. It's worth getting a room on the top floor for the view. Rates are usually lower if you book online, and about twenty percent less at weekends. Buffet breakfast included. $\overline{\$\$\$}$

Hostal Kaleidoscopio C 20 No. 21–15, city centre w kaleidoscopiohostel.com; map p.231. A small hostel in the middle of the downtown area; everyone gets a double bed and there's a well-lit central area to hang out in. Breakfast included. $\overline{\$}$

Hostal de La Montaña C 24 No. 36–58, Zona Rosa t 312 401 6961; map p.231. More like a homestay than a hostel, as you're sharing the family home and there are single and double rooms but no dorms. It's clean, friendly and quiet, bright and modern, and it's well located for the Zona Rosa bars and the football stadium. Breakfast included. $\overline{\$}$

★ **Mirador Andino** Cra 23 No. 32–20, city centre w miradorandino-hostel.com; map p.231. Just 100m from the cable car's Fundadores stop, this spacious hostel is a great city-centre option, immaculately clean, in a lovely old house with great views from the back rooms and the roof terrace, which is the perfect spot for a sunset beer. They can also organize multiple-day hikes to Los Nevados. $\overline{\$}$

Mountain Hostels Manizales C 66 No. 23B–91, Zona Rosa w mountainhostels.com.co; map p.231. A popular backpacker hostel in the backstreets behind the Zona Rosa, fun and sociable but possibly not the quietest place to stay in town. Breakfast included. $\overline{\$}$

Regine's C 65A No. 23B–113, Zona Rosa w regineshotel.com; map p.231. A boutique hotel in a quiet residential backstreet near the Zona Rosa, this friendly and relaxed option has a pretty little garden and fresh, bright rooms. Breakfast included. $\overline{\$\$}$

Varuna C 62 No. 23C–18, Zona Rosa w hotelvarunamanizales.com; map p.231. The best upmarket and modern choice in town, with large rooms, orthopedic mattresses, hydromassage showers and professional staff. The price includes breakfast and there are often discounts at weekends. $\overline{\$\$}$

EATING

Eating choices in the **city centre** are limited. Most restaurants are to be found in the **Zona Rosa** or in neighbouring *barrios* such as Palermo. If you're **self-catering**, try the branch of Éxito supermarket in Fundadores shopping mall at C 33 No. 20–72.

Buffalo Serrano Cra 23C No. 62–42, Zona Rosa t 301 652 8643; map p.231. A modern meat restaurant where the ingredients are slightly different, including – as its name suggests – buffalo. Starters include a delicious tilapia ceviche, and the house speciality is buffalo steak in chimichurri sauce, or you can just get a buffalo burger with all the trimmings (they have pork and beef too). $\overline{\$\$}$

La Cantera Paisa Cra 23 No. 58–40 La Estrella, Zona Rosa t 6 885 2952; map p.231. A good but basic diner where you can get a filling breakfast, a solid lunch or early supper. Nothing fancy, but cheap and cheerful. $\overline{\$}$

★ **La Clave del Mar** C 69A No. 27A–100, Barrio Palermo t 6 887 5528, w bit.ly/clavedelmar; map p.231. Excellent fresh seafood delivered from Tumaco or Buenaventura on the Pacific coast. Try the delicious *cazuela de mariscos* (seafood stew) or the *sancocho del bagre* (catfish soup with potato and cassava). They also do half-portions and takeaways. $\overline{\$}$

Spago C 59 No. 24A–10 La Estrella, Zona Rosa w spagorestaurante.com/index.html; map p.231. A stylish Italian restaurant that offers great home-made pasta (*fettuccine alla putanesca*) and wood-fired pizza (vegetarian). $\overline{\$\$}$

La Suiza Cra 23 No. 26–57, city centre; w lasuiza.com.co; map p.231. A superb bakery where you can grab breakfast (eggs Suiza-style, fried with bacon and parmesan), treat yourself to luscious pastries, or for true indulgence order a ginormous chocolate volcano with ice cream and cookies. They also have a Zona Rosa branch at Cra 23B No. 64–06. $\overline{\$}$

El Zaguán Paisa Cra 23 No. 31–27, city centre t 6 882 1395; map p.231. Enter through a long bamboo corridor for a hearty *menú del día* or specialities such as *bandeja paisa* or *plato montañero*, which is the same as a *bandeja paisa* except that the meat is pot-roasted instead of fried. $\overline{\$}$

DRINKING AND NIGHTLIFE

Most of the city's **nightlife** is centred on the **Zona Rosa**, where there are plenty of lively bars and clubs. In the city centre, the main nightlife attraction is **La Calle del Tango** ("Tango Street"), on C 24 between Cra 22 and Cra 23, where

A DEVIL OF A CARNIVAL

The Zona Cafetera's biggest and most spectacular festival is the biennial **Carnaval del Diablo**, held in early January of every odd-numbered year in **Riosucio**, 90km north of Manizales, with music, parades, dancing and costumes. It dates back to colonial times, but unfortunately, the little town is barely able to cope with the influx of visitors for the festival, and accommodation is extremely hard to come by, with many visitors resorting to sleeping on the streets.

---

there are more than half a dozen tango bars to choose from, some offering shows and classes as well as being places to go through your paces.

Bar la Plaza Cra 23B No. 64–80, Zona Rosa ☏ 6 885 2515; map p.231. Come the evening, this popular watering hole on the Cable Plaza is heaving with students downing cocktails from martinis to mojitos and dancing between the tables into the small hours.

Los Faroles C 24 No. 22–46, city centre ☏ 6 879 3097; map p.231. Other bars on this "Calle del Tango" may open more days of the week, may offer live shows or tango classes, and may not have annoying dress restrictions such as the "no trainers" rule, but this was the first of them and it remains the most classic.

Juan Sebastian Bar (JSB) Cra 23 No. 63–66, Zona Rosa ☏ 6 885 4736; map p.231. Popular with artists, writers and university lecturers, this intimate spot has great views of the city and fine cocktails. Charismatic owner Elmer Vargas has a passion for jazz and an awesome record collection.

Salsoteca La 33 Cra 23 No. 63–94, Zona Rosa ☏ 311 317 7678, ⓦ facebook.com/La33VIPManizales; map p.231. A fun but slightly tacky weekend salsa and reggaeton dance club. Fri is the big night, when there's a cover charge; entry is free on Thurs and Sat.

DIRECTORY

Banks and exchange There are a couple of banks with ATMs on opposite sides of Plaza de Bolívar, and a couple more in its northwest corner. You'll also find a handful strung out along Cra 23 in the Zona Rosa.

Festivals The Feria de Manizales in early Jan is a bullfighting festival and centres, unsurprisingly, on the city's bullring, the Plaza de Toros (C 8, at Cra 27), but there are also colourful parades and a beauty pageant in search of a new Coffee Queen. In Sept, the Festival de Teatro de Manizales, Colombia's answer to the Edinburgh festival, takes over the streets.

Football Local club Once Caldas – who stunned everyone by winning South America's Copa Libertadores in 2004 – play their home games at the Palogrande stadium on Av Paralela between C 62 and Av Lindsay, just beneath the Zona Rosa. Unfortunately, it's a multipurpose stadium, which means there's a running track between the crowd and the pitch. It's usually easy enough to buy tickets on the gate.

Internet Plotter, Cra 23 No. 60–70; Fundadores, Cra 23 No. 31–01.

Laundry El Laundry Cra 24 No. 65–61 (self-service).

Police Cra 12 at C 25 (☏ 6 880 6507).

Post office Cra 23 No. 60–36 and C 22 No. 23–57.

Parque Nacional Natural Los Nevados

40km southeast of Manizales or 61km northeast of Armenia • Zona Sul no time limits; Zona Central no time limits except in the area around Conejeras, Cueva, Potosí and Laguna del Otún (last entry 9am); Zona Norte (last entry 2pm) • Charge plus guide fee, though at present there is no ticket office at the southern end, so visitors entering and leaving via Salento or Ibagué escape the park entrance fee • ⓦ parquesnacionales.gov.co

Indisputably one of the crown jewels in Colombia's national parks system, the **PARQUE NACIONAL NATURAL LOS NEVADOS**, 40km southeast of Manizales, protects some of the last surviving snow-capped peaks in the tropics. That said, although the name Nevado implies perpetual snow, climate change has now lifted the snowline to almost 5000m on most peaks. Three of the five volcanoes are dormant, but **Nevado del Ruiz** – the tallest at 5321m – remains an active threat, having killed 22,000 people and buried the now extinct town of Armero when it erupted in 1985. It may be the most impressive area of the park, but the Nevado del Ruiz remains largely off-limits at present due to the risk of eruption.

The park has a variety of ecosytems which of course vary with altitude, and once you get up high enough, there's no plant cover at all. Typical **plant life** below that level includes the emblematic frailejón, well adapted to the high altitude, with its thick trunk, fat leaves and daisy-like flowers. Down in the cloudforest you'll find wax palms, Colombia's national tree. Indigenous **animals** include mountain tapirs and spectacled bears, and sharp-eyed birdwatchers may be rewarded with the sight of a majestic Andean condor soaring the thermals in search of prey.

The **best months** to visit the park are January and February, when clear days make for spectacular views of the volcanic peaks. March, July, August and December can also be ideal, while the rest of the year sees a fair amount of rain. Visitors are required to have a qualified **guide**, which the tour operators (see page 236) can arrange.

Nevado del Ruiz

The highest and most dramatic peak is the **Nevado del Ruiz**, which rises to 5321m and – despite global warming – still has the snowy head that caused the ancient Quimbayas to call it *Kumumbay* ("White Mountain"). As an active volcano, it is also potentially deadly, as the tragic 1985 eruption attested. As a result, it's carefully monitored, and a resurgence of volcanic activity **closed** it to the public. Weekly bulletins on its current status are posted (in Spanish) on the PNN (Colombian National Parks) website.

This means that, at present, it is not possible to climb the Nevado del Ruiz. Visitors in the northern (Brisas) section of the park may only proceed 5km from the park entrance, past Arenales, where there was formerly a lodge, up to Valle de las Tumbas (Desierto de la Soledad), at just below 4400m.

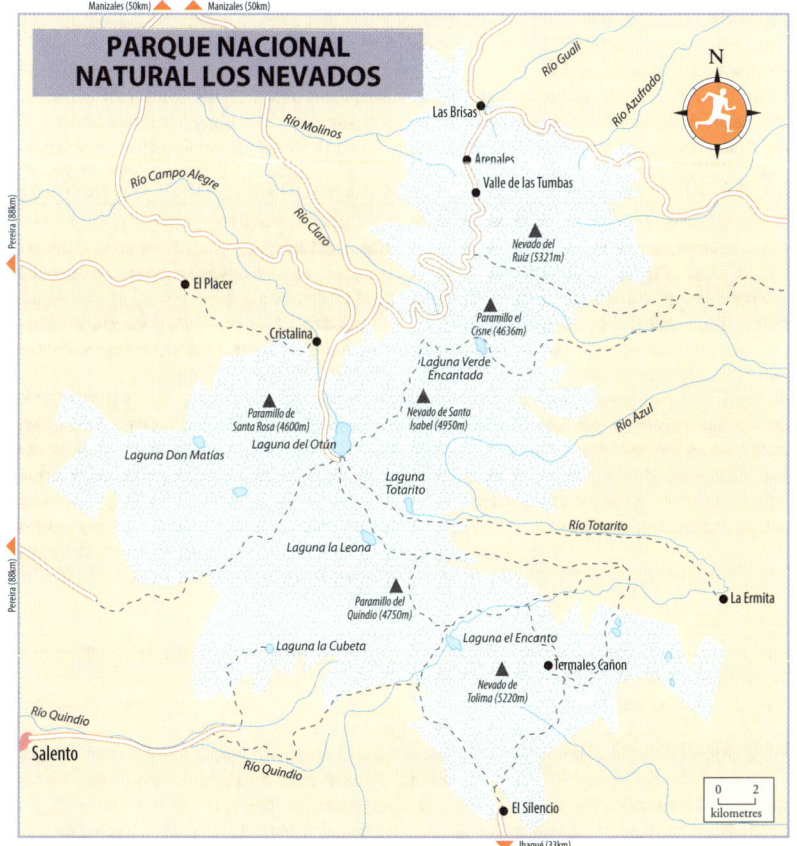

Nevado de Santa Isabel and Laguna del Otún

The **Nevado de Santa Isabel**, reaching to just under 5000m in altitude, is the lowest of the three snow-capped volcanoes, and can be reached in a day from Manizales. Given the right permits and equipment it is possible to climb it. Many people take it in on a single trip with the **Laguna del Otún**, a beautiful lake full of trout (fishing permitted), fed by meltwater from the Nevado de Santa Isabel. Reaching Laguna del Otún from Manizales involves an initial four-hour drive, taking in park highlights such as the extinct Olleta crater, Laguna Verde and Hacienda Potosí, before culminating in a two-hour trek to the lake. Otherwise, a visit to the Laguna del Otún from either Pereira or Ibagué would involve at least a two-day excursion, although you could alternatively approach it from Salento.

Nevado de Tolima

At 5220m, the park's second-highest peak is the **Nevado de Tolima**, in its southeast corner, which can be accessed from Salento or Ibagué, and is rated the park's most visually beautiful peak. Climbing it is no mean feat and would involve a four-day expedition with the right equipment and permits. From Salento, Páramo Trek (see page 236) can organize a three-day trek to the edge of the snowline. There are also hot springs on its slopes, most notably at Termales Cañón on its northeast side, which you can visit for a soak – very soothing after a hard day's trekking.

Paramillo del Quindio

At 4750m, the **Paramillo del Quindio** is now just below the snowline and no longer a *nevado* (snow-capped peak), but it's a relatively easy climb. The route to the summit leads above the tree line and vegetation across scree and rocks, taking some 14hr to reach the summit, which on a clear day affords views of Nevado del Ruiz, Nevado de Santa Isabel and Nevado de Tolima. It can be reached on a three-day excursion from Salento.

ARRIVAL AND DEPARTURE — PARQUE NACIONAL NATURAL LOS NEVADOS

Depending on which part you want to visit, the park can be approached from Manizales, from Salento, from Pereira or from the capital of Tolima *departamento*, Ibagué. Bear in mind that, if you go on a short trip from any of these, and particularly a day-trip, you'll be spending a large part of the time getting there and back. All visitors are required to use the services of an official **guide**.

By public transport Salento is the easiest entry as you can walk into the park from the Valle de Cocora, which is accessible from Salento by jeep (see page 247). There is no public transport up to the park from Manizales, Pereira or Ibagué, so from those you would need to have your own transport or go with a tour operator.

TOURS AND GUIDES

Asdeguias Caldas C 25 No. 20–25, Manizales w turismo asdeguias.com. A local guides' association for independent travellers who need a guide.

Ecosistemas C 20 No. 20–10, Manizales w ecosistemas travel.co. Offers a variety of routes, including one-day trips to Nevado Santa Isabel.

★ **Páramo Trek** Cra 5 No. 9–33, Salento w paramotrek. com. Friendly and well-informed operator offering easy two-day visits to the southern part of the park along with the Valle de Cocora, with discounts available for groups of more than two. They also offer more challenging three-day visits including the peak of the Paramillo del Quindio or the Nevado de Tolima snowline, again much reduced for groups of more than two.

ACCOMMODATION

There is **no accommodation** in the park. If you have a tent, you can camp, but bear in mind that in the northern sector you will need to get permission before pitching up.

Pereira and around

Capital of the Risaralda *departamento*, **PEREIRA** is an excellent base for exploring the Zona Cafetera. A busy city of nearly half a million people, it isn't a big tourist destination in its own right, but for all its lack of specific attractions, it's a lively place and certainly worth a look around. Its historic centre has been repeatedly destroyed by earthquakes, the most recent in 1999.

The city is quite compact, pretty much contained by the **Otún River** that runs along its north side and the **Avenida Circunvalar** (Cra 13), which belts it in to the south. In the centre, the bustling, crowded streets and narrow sidewalks are made narrower by the throng of vendors who set up shop along them, selling anything from clothes and accessories to fruit, juices and mobile phone minutes, but the density is pleasantly broken up by a scattering of open city squares and patches of greenery. Among them, **Parque del Lago Uribe Uribe**, between Carreras 7–8 and Calles 24–25, has a little lake in it, while the **Parque Olaya**, where Calle 19 meets Avenida Circunvalar, used to be the forecourt of the railway station, whose building still stands. The city's proudest modern landmark is the **Viaducto César Gaviria Trujillo**, a boldly designed cable-stayed bridge built in 1997 to link Pereira with the town of Dosquebradas across the Otún River, and quite an impressive a piece of engineering. A good day-trip from Pereira is to one of the **hot springs** in the surrounding countryside.

Plaza de Bolívar

Pereira's main square, **Plaza de Bolívar**, surrounded by mango trees, is also unfortunately surrounded by some rather ugly modern buildings. Its main draw is Rodrigo Arenas Betancourt's dynamic **statue of Simón Bolívar** nude on horseback, bearing the torch of liberty, Prometheus-like, to the people of South America. Controversial when first unveiled in 1963, the statue is now a beloved city symbol, since joined by a number of other audacious modern sculptures scattered around town, including Arenas Betancourt's striking **Monument to the Founders** on Avenida Circunvalar at Calle 13, put up in 1965 to celebrate the city's centenary.

Cathedral

C 20 No. 7–08 • Free

In the northwest corner of the Plaza de Bolívar, the city's silver-domed 1875 **Cathedral** may not look much from the outside, but its single-nave interior is as boldly bare as Arenas Betancourt's Bolívar, its unrendered brick walls supported by an elaborate latticework of twelve thousand wooden beams forming a canopy like a spider's web, leaving it with an interestingly unfinished look.

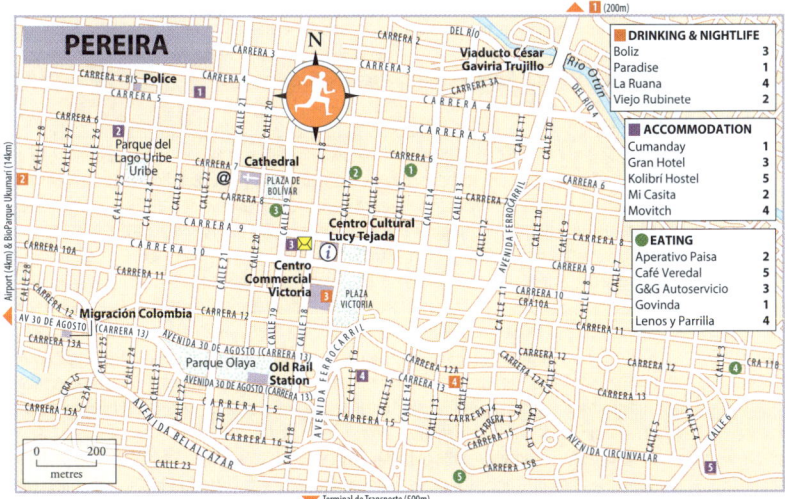

BioParque Ukumarí

Via Galicia (south of the Via Cartago (Hwy 29), 14km west of Pereira • Charge • ⓦ ukumari.org • Any bus heading to Cartago or La Virginia will drop you at the turn-off at Santa Barbara service station, 600m north of the zoo

Pereira's new out-of-town zoo, called **BioParque Ukumarí**, is pretty modern as zoos go. It's divided into areas, each representing a different type of wildlife habitat, but at the time of writing it was still incomplete, and only the Andean forest and African savannah areas were open. It's due to have a walk-through aviary, and enclosures separated from the public by reinforced transparent plastic, so you can come nose-to-nose with the animals. Many of the inmates were brought here from Pereira's old zoo near the airport, and some of the hippos, elephants and rhinos once belonged to Pablo Escobar. Other residents include toucans, flamingos and meerkats.

ARRIVAL AND INFORMATION

By plane Pereira's Matecaña airport (ⓦ aeromate.gov.co) is just 4km west of town, and reached by Megabús and (if you can squeeze your baggage onto your lap) by ordinary bus (#13 along Cra 4, or #26 on Cra 12 at C 17–18, destination "Matecaña" or "Aeropuerto").
Destinations Bogotá (14–19 daily; 50min); Medellín (2 weekly; 40min).

By bus The Terminal de Transporte bus station (ⓦ terminalpereira.com) is 1km south of the centre on C 17, with cabs available and frequent buses (destination "Terminal"),

PEREIRA AND AROUND

which you can pick up in town on C 18 at Cra 11.
Destinations Armenia (every 10min; 45min); Bogotá (every 15–30min; 9hr); Cali (every 10–12min; 4hr); Manizales (every 15min; 1hr 15min); Medellín (every 30min–hourly; 6hr); Salento (9 daily; 1hr); Santa Rosa de Cabal (every 5min; 25min).

Tourist information The friendly and helpful tourist office is on the bottom floor of the Centro Cultural Lucy Tejada on C 17 at Cra 10. They also have a desk at the airport.

GETTING AROUND

Walking is the best way to get around town, certainly during the day, although you'll probably want to **cab** it at night if heading to and from the Av Circunvalar's bars and clubs.

By taxi Cabs are cheap and easy in Pereira, and you'll rarely have to pay much for a ride in town during the day, but rates do increase at night. Easy Taxi and (not entirely legally) Uber cover Pereira, too.

By bus Orange minibuses ply the streets, charging a flat fee per ride. You're unlikely to use them much except perhaps to get to or from the airport or bus station. They don't tend to get too crowded as there are plenty of them, but travelling with a lot of baggage may be a challenge.

By Megabús Pereira has a BRT (Bus Rapid Transport)

system called Megabús (ⓦ megabus.gov.co), on the same lines as Bogotá's TransMilenio, if rather smaller and simpler. However, it's unlikely you'll use it – you need to buy a travel card before you even take your first journey, which will then cost you another fee on top, so all in all a taxi would cost less. There are three routes, all east–west, and the most useful service is to the airport, which you can reach by ordinary bus anyway.

By car Pereira operates a *pico y placa* scheme (see page 30), under which cars whose registration ends in certain digits are not permitted to drive in the city centre (Av del Rio–Cra 28 and C 50–Av Ferrocarril); for details see ⓦ movilidadpereira.gov.co.

ACCOMMODATION

Cumanday Cra 5 No. 22–54 ⓣ 301 625 3183; map p.237. Solid downtown budget option, and about your cheapest bet if you want a single room, with reliable hot showers, cable TV and a place to wash your dirty togs. The rooms are nice and fresh, but with a slightly chintzy touch; those at the back are the quietest, as ever. Single and double rooms available. $

★ **Gran Hotel** C 19 No. 9–19 ⓦ granhotelpereira.com; map p.237. If you want a hotel with character, this is the place. It may no longer be – as it was when it opened in 1938 – the poshest hotel in town, but the *Gran* still beats Pereira's more expensive options hands down when it comes to period charm and personality. Sensitively refurbished, the Art Deco building conserves most of its original features,

while keeping well up to modern standards comfort-wise, and the staff are super-helpful. Rooms at the front are more spacious but get one at the back if you need complete silence to sleep. Buffet breakfast included. $$$

Kolibrí Hostel C 4 No. 16–35 ⓣ 6 331 3955; map p.237. Super-clean, super-friendly hostel on a steep little side street off the Av Circunvalar, run by a Dutch/Colombian couple who also offer tours. There's a great terrace bar with mountain views, a covered patio, two kitchens, plenty of clean, modern bathrooms, wi-fi throughout, bicycle rental, coffee on tap, and really everything you could want from a backpackers' hostel. $

Mi Casita C 25 No. 6–20 ⓣ 6 344 6589; map p.237. A friendly little family-run hotel just off the Parque del Lago

Uribe Uribe. The rooms are small and immaculately clean, albeit rather kitschly decorated, and rather lacking in outside windows. $\overline{\$\$}$
Movitch Cra 13 (Av Circunvalar) No. 15–73 w movich hotels.com; map p.237. This business-class hotel on the southern edge of town is Pereira's top address, with all the five-star features you need, including a pool, gym, buffet breakfast, posh restaurant and room service. Lower rates are usually available, and the place positively crackles with snappy efficiency. Breakfast included. $\overline{\$\$\$}$

EATING

At **lunchtime** you'll find a group of places in the passage off the east side of Plaza de Bolívar by the Banco Caja Social with good value set menus. The most central branch of **Éxito supermarket** is at Cra 10 No. 14–71.
Aperativo Paisa C 17 No. 7–62, upstairs t 6 334 9522; map p.237. The walls are decorated with animal heads, horse saddles and old radios, the windows are big and always open, and the almost-veranda is a top spot to watch over the street below. Fill up on local specialities like a *bandeja paisa*, or come between 11am and 4pm for a set lunch. They also open for breakfast. $\overline{\$}$
Café Veredal C 11 No. 11–119 t 312 314 9278; map p.237. Fine Paisa grills are the mainstay at this Colombian restaurant, serving local cuisine a couple of blocks beyond the Circunvalar on the southern edge of town. $\overline{\$\$}$
G&G Autoservicio Cra 8 No. 19–17 t 6 335 6606; map p.237. A no-frills round-the-clock self-service cafeteria on Plaza de Bolívar. Handy for anything from daybreak caffeine cravings and solid, stodgy breakfasts to simple set lunches and basic dishes to satisfy late-night attacks of the munchies. $\overline{\$}$
Govinda C 15 No. 6–58, upstairs t 6 333 9650; map p.237. Vegetarians and anyone in need of a break from the meat and stodge will find this Indian-ish lunchtime veg restaurant something of an oasis. It also offers vegan dishes. $\overline{\$\$}$
Lenos y Parrilla Cra 12 No. 2–78 w lenosyparrilla.co; map p.237. "Argentine passion for meat" is their slogan, and this is the place to head to for the best steaks in town, done to whatever turn you desire, and quite reasonably priced. Top picks include the *bife chorizo* (sirloin strip, a favourite Argentine cut), and the mixed grill for two. $\overline{\$\$}$

DRINKING AND NIGHTLIFE

Bars playing **music** are concentrated on the Av Circunvalar (Cra 13) eastward from C 11, and the most popular thing to do is just head out there and bar-hop for the night. **Nightclubs** are concentrated in Popa, a *barrio* of the neighbouring municipality of **Dosquebradas**, which is just across the Viaducto César Gaviria Trujillo.
Boliz 5th floor, Centro Comercial Victoria, Cra 10–11 bis, C 17–18 t 6 324 2882; map p.237. A bar that's also a bowling alley, atop Pereira's most central shopping mall – a bit tacky but fun. The food (burger and fries) isn't much to write home about, but it's as good a place as any to sink a beer or a cocktail while you sink the skittles.
Paradise Cra 10 No. 14–75, Popa, Dosquebradas (behind Makro hypermarket) w discotecaparadise.com; map p.237. Pereira's (well, Dosquebradas's) biggest and glitziest nightclub, playing a mix of Latin and electronic sounds, depending on the evening and on who's spinning the music. There's usually a cover charge.
La Ruana Cra 13 (Av Circunvalar) No. 12–08 w laruana pereira.com; map p.237. By day this is a restaurant, handy for breakfast and lunch, but come nightfall it becomes a music bar, playing what they call "crossover" (a mix of musical genres, in other words), and a good place to begin a bar-hop along the Circunvalar.
Viejo Rubinete Cra 8 No. 28–83 t 6 326 1199; map p.237. A quirky little place, where old boys sup their beer to the strains of classic tango, *bolero* and other Argentine music from way back in the day, while pictures of the artistes smile down on them from the walls. From time to time they even dust off and play their original vinyl copies of the tunes, which they keep behind the bar.

WILLY JEEPS

The Zona Cafetera's most characteristic form of local transport – be it passenger or agricultural – is the **Willy jeep**, or, more correctly, the Willys jeep. Originally built for military use in World War II, and then sold off cheaply by the US Army in the 1950s, the Willy became an instant hit with local coffee farmers as just about the only motor vehicle that could negotiate the narrow tracks formerly used by donkeys. The fact that it could carry a lot more in the way of sacks of coffee than any donkey also rather helped matters. Today, even though the roads are now surfaced, the Willy remains a popular way to get around and is still used to transport agricultural produce, including coffee. Armenia has a parade every October (see page 243) to honour the vehicle, and in small towns such as Salento, the Willy is the best way to get around.

DIRECTORY

Banks and exchange There's no shortage of banks with ATMs – you'll find a row of them, for example, along the north side of Plaza de Bolívar. There are several money changers on C 18 at the corner of Cra 8.
Festivals The Fiestas de la Cosecha (Harvest Festival) is a series of concerts, activities and events, culminating with a big parade down Av Circunvalar. In Nov, the Festival del Despecho (Heartbreak Festival) is dedicated to those unlucky in love, with recitals of suitably sentimental music and poetry, and plenty of drink on hand in case you have any sorrows to drown.
Internet Cabina la Veintinueve, C 21 No. 7–38 (behind the Cathedral).
Police Cra 4 bis No. 24–39 (❶ 6 314 9800).
Post office Cra 9 No. 18B–15.
Visa extensions Migración Colombia, Av 30 Agosto (Cra 13) No. 26–37 ❶ 6 333 9898.

Termales Santa Rosa

Km 9.5 Vereda San Ramon, Santa Rosa de Cabal • Termales Balneario • Charge (discounts available outside of holiday time)

The closest hot springs to Pereira are the **Termales Santa Rosa**, set at the foot of a 25m-high waterfall and surrounded by lush greenery. The springs are easily reachable from **Santa Rosa de Cabal**, a town famous for its sausages, 9km northwest of Pereira. You reach **Termales Balneario** first, which has four thermal pools, with a visitor centre, cafeteria and massages on offer, and you can also take a dip in the natural pool directly beneath the waterfall.

A little further down the dirt road another group of hot springs is attached to the *Hotel Termales*, with one large pool and two thimble-sized hot tubs available to non-guests, set against a spectacular backdrop of three tall waterfalls. There's also a lavish spa on site.

ARRIVAL AND DEPARTURE — TERMALES SANTA ROSA

By bus and chiva Frequent buses run to Santa Rosa de Cabal from Pereira's Terminal de Transporte (30min). From the corner of Santa Rosa's *la galería* (marketplace), opposite the police station, *chivas* and buses (try to catch a *chiva* if possible) leave for the hot springs five times daily (45min), coming back pretty much straight after.
By jeep If you miss the bus from Santa Rosa, one of the Willy jeeps parked by the market will take you to the *termales* for a fee.

ACCOMMODATION

Hotel Termales By the springs ⓦ termales.com.co/termales-hotel. This hotel has its own thermal pool for exclusive use of hotel guests, as well as a spa, of course, and comes in three sections: the original "*casa finca*", which is the cheapest option; a chalet-style lodge called "Las Montañas"; and a new, modern building called "La Cabaña". $$

Termales San Vicente

Km 1 Vía Termales, 35km northeast of Pereira via Santa Rosa de Cabal • Charge • ⓦ sanvicente.com.co

The hot springs at **Termales San Vicente** feature a selection of steaming medicinal thermal pools scattered across some five square kilometres of cloud forest, river, waterfalls and luxuriant countryside. At 2330m, it gets pretty chilly up here, so it helps that the average pool temperature is 38°C. A variety of spa treatments is offered, including massage and mud therapy, while a range of packages include entry and different treatments.

ARRIVAL AND DEPARTURE — TERMALES SAN VICENTE

By bus and jeep At weekends, the easiest way to get to San Vicente is with one of the buses that leave at 9am from the springs' Pereira office at Cra 13 No. 15–62, returning at 5pm. This also runs during the week if there is a minimum of ten passengers. The price includes entrance, transport and lunch. Alternatively, you can make your own way to the spa by catching a bus to Santa Rosa from the bus terminal in Pereira and grabbing a seat on a Willy jeep from *la galería* (marketplace) for Termales San Vicente.

ACCOMMODATION

Termales San Vicente ⓦ sanvicente.com.co. Accommodation at the springs comes in five varieties. The cheapest option is camping, but failing that you can take a "traditional room" or a wooden "traditional cabin", or a deluxe cabin – only the first and last of these have breakfast included in the basic rate, but all prices include admission to the pools. Camping/person $\overline{\$}$, doubles $\overline{\$\$\$}$

Armenia and around

The capital of the Quindío *departamento*, **ARMENIA** was originally called Villa Holguín when founded in 1889. It was renamed just a few years later in memory of the quarter-million or so Christians murdered in sectarian massacres instigated by the Ottoman Empire in Turkish Armenia in 1894. Most tourists barely give the place a second glance as they pass through on the way to Salento, and it's hardly a city of quaint charm, having been largely flattened by an earthquake in 1999, and rebuilt using a lot of concrete. Even so, it's a friendly and bustling place, and worth a stopover.

The original centre is still the city's hub, but Armenia has expanded northward, beyond Calle 1, and into newer, smarter, uptown areas where the street numbers are qualified with an "N" for "north" (C 1N being the next one on from C 1). Armenia's main artery, **Avenida Bolívar** (Cra 14), is pedestrianized between Calle 21 (Plaza Bolivar) and Calle 11 (Parque de Sucre) to make a relaxed shopping zone in the heart of town planted with coffee bushes and interspersed with coffee stalls.

Plaza de Bolívar
Cra 13–14 at C 20–21

Since the city centre's almost total wipeout in the 1999 earthquake, the main square has been revamped in modern style. Its 1930 **statue of Simón Bolívar** now stands atop a 5m-high square concrete column, and is joined, across the square, by a typically dynamic Rodrigo Arenas Betancourt sculpture, the **Monument to Effort**. The monument's two figures, depicted stretching skyward, represent the pioneering Paisa peasant farmers of Francisco Antonio Cano's much-loved 1913 painting, *Horizons* (see page 213).

> ### STAYING ON A COFFEE FARM
>
> A number of coffee *fincas* in the Zona Cafetera are open for visits, from traditional **estates** still attended by their owner to deceptively modern **rural hotels** where the only coffee you'll find comes served with breakfast. The farms look out on lush slopes, overgrown with the shiny-leaved coffee shrubs and interspersed with banana plants and bamboo-like guadua forests. Many will arrange horseriding and walks, and they make an ideal base to explore the region's attractions. The tourist offices in Manizales (see page 232) and Pereira (see page 238) will have further information.
>
> **FINCAS**
>
> **Hacienda Guayabal** Cra 3 No. 15–72 Chinchiná ☏ 314 772 4856. Runs tours, in English, of their postcard-perfect coffee farm (1hr; bookings by WhatsApp only). Guests can stay in the main house, where accommodation rates include breakfast, a tour and use of the swimming pool. To get there, take a bus from Manizales or Pereira to Chinchiná (30min), and then travel the last 3km by taxi or catch a bus from in front of the church to the farm.
>
> **Hacienda Venecia** Vereda el Rosario ⓦ hacienda venecia.com. This fourth-generation, family-owned working coffee farm is an essential stop for anyone who wants to learn more about the trade in general. Tours (3hr; fee includes pick-up from Manizales) allow visitors to observe the production process from start to finish; you could also spend a night at the guesthouse, swinging in a hammock on the veranda, firefly-spotting and listening to the croaks of happy frogs in the swimming pool. Accessible from Manizales by taxi, or they'll pick you up if you get to Puente de San Peregrino (on the Manizales–Pereira bus route via Autopista del Café) between 10am and 5pm. Breakfast included. Dorms $\overline{\$}$, doubles $\overline{\$\$}$

Presiding over the plaza, Armenia's **Cathedral** (C 21 No. 12–20; free), rebuilt from scratch after the earthquake, is a slightly ponderous concrete affair, cross-shaped with a triangular facade and modern stained-glass windows. It isn't the prettiest cathedral you'll ever see, but it's a welcome change from the usual colonial-style basilicas.

Museo del Oro Quimbaya

Cra 14 (Av Bolívar) No. 40N–80 • Free • W banrepcultural.org/armenia/museo-del-oro-quimbaya • Any bus with destination "Limites", "Museo" or "Oro negro" on Cra 18 at C 16–20 or Cra 14 (Av Bolívar) north of C11

In a low-rise brick building amid greenery at the very northern end of town, the **Museo del Oro Quimbaya** covers the archeological history of the region. It's got some interesting pre-Hispanic ceramic figures, but what you really come to see is the gold, which takes the form of little figurines, containers for lime to dab on coca leaf when chewing it, and of course jewellery, including earrings, nose-rings and a lovely little necklace of gold frogs. The exhibits have captions in Spanish and English, as well as more detailed explanation cards that you can take round with you.

Jardín Botánico del Quindío

Av Centenario No. 15–190, Km 3 Vía al Valle, Calarcá • Charge • W jardinbotanicoquindio.org • Local bus to Calarcá from Parque de la Constitución (Cra 12 opposite No. 9–20)

The **Jardín Botánico del Quindío** is a 15-hectare botanical garden southeast of town. Consisting largely of forest, it has more than two hundred species of palm tree, plus ferns, guadua forest, a maze and a butterfly-shaped butterfly house that's rated one of the best in the world. There's also a suspension bridge and a seven-storey lookout tower. Entry comes with a compulsory guided tour in Spanish; tips are appreciated.

Parque Nacional del Café

Km 6 Vía Montenegro, Pueblo Tapao, around 15km west of Armenia; Armenia office at Mocawa Plaza, suite 503, Cra 14 (Av Bolívar) No. 9N–16 • Charge • W parquedelcafe.co • Pueblo Tapao buses leave Armenia's terminal every 15min or take a taxi from Armenia

The **Parque Nacional del Café**, between the villages of Montenegro and Pueblo Tapao, isn't really a national park, but a slightly incongruous combination of an educational museum and natural site with a funfair. The educational and cultural side includes scenic walks, an old Quimbaya cemetery, a coffee museum and quite a spectacular daily "Show del Café" around lunchtime, featuring folk dances from around the country. On the funfair side, there's a carousel, roller coasters, train rides, a cable car and a chair lift. It's a fun family day out, but it gets rather crowded at weekends, when there are long waits for many of the rides.

ARRIVAL AND DEPARTURE

By plane Armenia's El Eden airport (T 6 747 9400) is 15km southeast of town.
Destinations Bogotá (2–3 daily; 55min); Fort Lauderdale (2 weekly; 3hr 50min); Medellín (1–2 daily; 45min); Panama City (3 weekly; 1hr 15min).
By bus Armenia's bus terminal is towards the western end of town at C 35 No. 20–68 (W terminaldetransporte.gov.co/destinos/armenia). City buses between the terminal and

ARMENIA AND AROUND

the centre include #1, #2 and #18. For Salento and Filandia, you can pick your bus up in town on Cra 20 at the corner of C19.
Destinations Bogotá (every 15–30min; 7hr); Cali (every 10–15min; 3hr); Filandia (every 15min; 45min); Ibagué (every 15–20min; 3hr); Manizales (every 20–30min; 2hr 20min); Medellín (every 30min–hourly; 7hr); Pereira (every 10min; 45min); Popoyán (9 daily; 10hr).

ACCOMMODATION

Bolívar Plaza C 21 No. 14–17 T 6 741 0083. Be right at the heart of things in this snazzy modern building overlooking Plaza de Bolívar – indeed, it's worth asking for a room with a little balcony and a vista over the square, although these are of course not the quietest rooms in the hotel. There's a rooftop restaurant, and the staff are extremely helpful. Breakfast is included. $$
Casa del Parque Cra 14 No. 12–26 W castell

anogermanoc.wixsite.com/website. A bright and friendly little hotel on the Parque de Sucre, with decent-sized rooms, bright orange bed coverings, wi-fi, cable TV and all mod cons. Breakfast included. $$

Casa Quimbaya C 16N No. 14–92 ⓦcasaquimbaya.com. A clean and friendly hostel in a quiet uptown area, which you may or may not consider an advantage. Breakfast included. $

Casa Real Cra 18 No. 18–36 ☏6 734 0606, ⓦhotelcasarealarmenia.wixsite.com/home. A welcoming little place and the best deal among the city centre's numerous cheap hotels. Nearly all the rooms have private bathrooms attached, albeit mostly lacking outside windows (so it's worth specifying if you want one). $

EATING

Chung Wah Cra 14 No. 6–07 (opposite Unicentro mall) ☏6 746 4603. None of Armenia's chop suey houses are particularly outstanding, but this is one of the most popular, and the servings are certainly generous, with half-portions of most dishes available. $$

La Fogata Cra 14 No. 14N–39 ⓦlafogata.com.co. A good, if slightly pricey, uptown locale for nicely done meat dishes, be it ribeye steak or fine *osso buco* with tagliatelle. They also offer a selection of good beers, although you may find that only a few are actually available. $$

La Fonda Antioqueña Cra 13 No. 18–59, upstairs ☏6 744 1927. A block off Plaza de Bolívar above a karaoke bar, this is one of the best spots downtown to get stuck into the local cuisine without putting too much of a dent in your wallet. They do *bandeja paisa*, obviously or, as they describe it themselves, a super *mondongo*. $

La Parillada Cra 14 No. 7–47 (opposite Universidad de Gran Colombia) ☏6 732 5732. A little way north of the centre but better than most of the grimy diners downtown, with similar prices. There's *chorizo santarosano* (a sausage speciality from Santa Rosa de Cabal, near Pereira) and they do a good lunchtime set menu, and breakfast too. $

DIRECTORY

Banks and exchange There are plenty of banks with ATMs around town, including three in Plaza de Bolívar, and facing each other across C 21 between Cra 16 and Cra 17, the Banco Popular and Banco de Bogotá have several ATMs each.

Festivals The Yipao is a huge parade of Willy jeeps (see page 239) held in mid-Oct every year and not to be missed if you're in the area. The jeeps, dating from the 1950s, are loaded up with agricultural produce, household furnishings, everything but the kitchen sink (and even that on occasion) and paraded along Av Bolívar in their hundreds.

Internet Comunicaciones del Centro, Cra 15 No. 19–18; Ciudad Virtual, Cra 13 No. 17–30.

Post office C 15 No. 22–38.

Salento and around

In the heart of coffee country, 24km northeast of Armenia, the adorable village of **SALENTO** is one of the region's earliest settlements, founded in 1842 on the old colonial road from Popoyán to Bogotá (which still exists as an unsurfaced trail). Its slow development means the lifestyle and buildings of the Paisa journeymen who first settled here have barely been altered since then, and rural workers clad in cowboy hats and *ruanas* (Colombian ponchos) are a common sight to this day. The colourful, wonderfully photogenic one-storey homes of thick adobe and clay-tile roofs that surround the plaza are as authentic as it gets.

Salento is a popular spot with tourists both foreign and domestic, and at weekends it can get quite busy, still more so on *puentes* (long weekends when the Monday is a public holiday), but during the week, not much disturbs the tranquil charm. The presence of foreign tourists – mostly backpackers – does however mean a good variety of eating places, and a large number of good-value hostels (though no upscale hotels).

The village itself doesn't have much in the way of **sights**. Its main street, Calle Real (Cra 6), lined with shops and cafés, ends at six flights of steps, painted green, yellow and blue, and marked by posts representing the Stations of the Cross. At the top, a big wooden cross marks the **mirador**, which – weather allowing – affords panoramic views over the town. For all this, Salento's real draw is the surrounding countryside, including the **Valle de Cocora**, as well as the **coffee farms** round about; it's also an excellent base for visits to **Filandia** (see page 247) and the Parque Nacional Natural Los Nevados (see page 234).

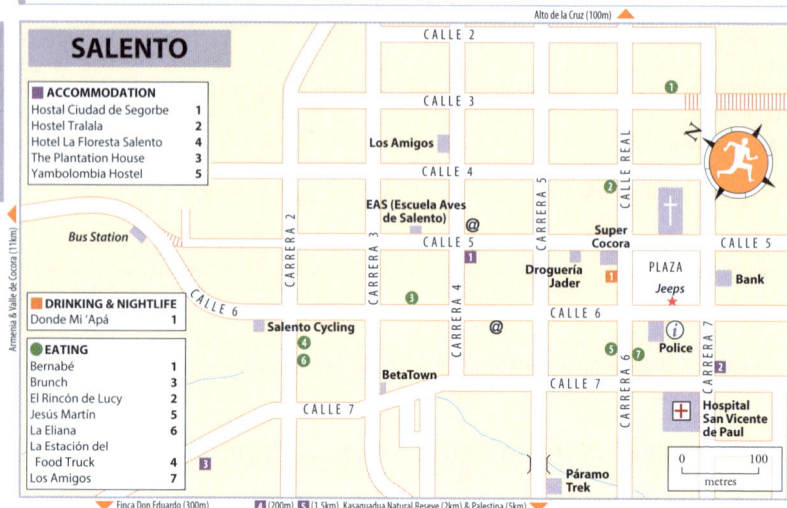

Finca Don Eduardo

Camino National, Vía Salento–Boquia • Charge • Tours (3hr) daily (with discounts for guests at *The Plantation House*, where the tour starts) • w theplantationhousesalento.com/coffee/coffeefarmtours

Of the coffee farm visits which you can make from Salento, the tours of **Finca Don Eduardo** are the easiest, the most informative and the closest to town. They also have the advantage of being conducted in English. Tim from *The Plantation House*, who owns the farm, gives a comprehensive explanation of the different types of coffee, how they're grown and how they're processed, and is happy to answer questions. You also get to taste and compare two varieties of coffee in low-, medium- and high-roast versions, to see for yourself how they're different, something which no other tour offers. If it's muddy, they'll even lend you a pair of Wellington boots.

Kasaguadua Natural Reserve

Km 2.4 Vía Palestina (continuation of Cra 5), 600m past Yambocolombia • By appointment; tours (2hr 30min) • No set fee, but donations requested • w kasaguaduanaturalreserve.org

The **Kasaguadua Natural Reserve** is a privately owned reserve containing twelve hectares of Andean rainforest. The two owners (one British, one Colombian) offer guided walks in English through three different types of forest, including guadua (see page 246), accompanied by enthusiastic explanations of the local wildlife and ecology. More than just a pleasant walk in the woods, the tour gives a real insight into how the local ecosystems work, and an explanation of the different kinds of forest, with opportunities for bird- and animal-spotting along the way. Questions are positively welcomed.

ARRIVAL AND DEPARTURE   SALENTO AND AROUND

By plane *The Plantation House* (see page 245) offers an airport transfer service for slightly less than a taxi (for both Armenia airport and Pereira airport), regardless of whether or not you are staying with them; you need to book it in advance.

By bus The bus station is on C 6 at the entrance to town. Buses between Armenia and Filandia or Pereira will leave you at the Salento turn-off on the main road, but it's not a great idea to get stuck there after dark, when it's hard for bus drivers to spot you waiting, and walking the last 12km in pitch darkness is no fun. Especially on buses from Pereira, keep a close eye on your baggage. For Manizales, either change at Pereira, or get an Armenia-bound bus to Los Flores on the main road, cross the road and pick up an onward bus there.

Destinations Armenia (every 15min; 45min; last departure from Armenia 8pm); Pereira (9 daily, but every 30min on Sun and public hols; 45min).

By taxi Taxis are available between Armenia and Salento, but agree on the fee before you set off.

INFORMATION

Tourist information You'll find the Punto de Información Turística (PiT) in the town hall on Salento's main square.

ACTIVITIES

EAS (Escuela Aves de Salento) C 6 No. 3–61 w escuela avesdesalento.com. Birdwatching trips in La Carbonera and further afield, which include one-day trips to La Carbonera.

Salento Cycling C 6 No. 1–30 w salentocycling.com. Mountain biking trips incorporating a 30km downhill ride from La Carbonera (3400m cloudforest), through beautiful scenery and a variety of ecosystems ("you don't have to pedal once", they say), as part of a 5–6hr excursion. The fee includes transport, support, guide, picnic lunch, equipment and insurance.

ACCOMMODATION

Hostal Ciudad de Segorbe C 5 No. 4–06 w hostal ciudaddesegorbe.co; map p.244. Although it calls itself a hostel, this is really a hotel, and one of the best in town. It's in a beautiful nineteenth-century house, lovingly restored with the proper materials (wooden floors and *bareque* walls keep it cosy in cold weather), well-kept and with a pretty central courtyard. Breakfast included. Rates rise over Christmas, New Year, Easter and long weekends. $\overline{\$\$}$

Hostel Tralala Cra 7 No. 6–45 t 314 850 5543; map p.244. The Dutch owner has worked hard to convert this traditional Paisa-style house into a beautiful, modern hostel. The spotless rooms with ultra-comfortable beds and smart bathrooms retain original features, including wooden floors and furnishings. There's also a fully equipped guest kitchen, DVD lounge, library and sun terrace. $\overline{\$}$

Hotel La Floresta Salento Cra 5 No. 10–11 t 312 888 1808, w lafloresta hotel.com.co; map p.244. A cheap and cheerful hotel over the yellow bridge on the way out of town, homely and friendly, and in a quiet location. The small garden at the back offers great views and they rent out bicycles. $\overline{\$\$}$

★ **The Plantation House** C 7 No. 1–04 w the plantationhousesalento.com; map p.244. Amid gardens and trees, with access to a fantastic viewpoint at the owner's house close by, and the option to stay down in the valley on the hostel's working coffee farm (the Finca Don Eduardo), this is Salento's first backpackers' hostel and the best place to stay in town if you want local information, of which the British owner has loads that he's happy to share. The hostel also runs tours, and daily visits to their coffee farm (see page 244), on which guests get big discounts. $\overline{\$}$

Yambolombia Hostel 1.5km out of town on the Palestina road (Car 5) t 320 756 5036; map p.244. This spacious and clean hostel is set amidst lush farm grounds with male and female only, and mixed dorms available. There's also private rooms with en-suites, and glamping nearby as an option to boot. Breakfast is included. $\overline{\$}$

EATING

Los Amigos Cra 6 No. 6–21 t 313 502 4453; map p.244. Fresh trout from the farm in Cocora is on the menu in all Salento's restaurants, but here's where you'll find the biggest selection of trout dishes, cooked twelve ways, be it plain pan-grilled, in mango sauce, or *au gratin* with prawns and mushrooms. $\overline{\$\$}$

PALESTINA COFFEE TOURS

A number of *fincas* in the village of **Palestina**, 5km from Salento, offer coffee tours. Getting to Palestina is a bit of a hike, but that's half the fun – head south out of town on Cra 5, across the yellow bridge and straight on. It's quite a steep descent (especially the last bit), and as steep an ascent on the way back (especially the first bit). You don't need to make an appointment – just turn up and ask. Afterwards, you can drink a cup of their coffee, and of course buy some if you want to.

FINCAS

Las Acacias Km 3.5 t 310 463 8585. Another good tour, with the advantage of being higher up on the road, so less far to walk. They'll give you more information here on how the coffee is processed, and they speak a bit more English. Alternatively, you can just stop off for a cortado on the way down to Don Elías's. Tours (2hr), charge.

Finca Don Elías Km 5 t 315 606 1113. On the right, about 200m past the prominently signposted El Ocaso coffee farm, this was the first *finca* to offer tours and is still one of the best. One of Don Elías's sons – or Elías himself if you're lucky – will show you round with gusto (but with explanations mostly in Spanish). Tours (2hr), charge.

> ### COLOMBIA'S VEGETABLE STEEL
> **Guadua** is the only species of bamboo native to the Americas. It's also the strongest type of bamboo. It's been used for centuries to make handicrafts, fences and huts, but only lately has its versatility and sustainability brought it to prominence as a potential fuel source. Because it's so light and so strong, guadua also makes an excellent building material. It's pretty much **earthquake-proof**, no small thing in a country like Colombia. In some quarters it's even being called the "vegetable steel". Untreated, it isn't very durable, but new processes are now becoming available which can extend its useful life.
>
> Guadua grows very fast, and when harvested carefully, it can be a sustainable crop. Because water rises up it, like the tide, when the moon is waxing, it needs to be harvested under a waning moon. Technology for building with guadua is still being developed, with permaculture enthusiasts leading the way, but many **handicrafts** are already made with guadua, from mats and furniture to cups and ashtrays. Because it grows so fast without depleting soil, it is also potentially a sustainable source of biofuel. Certainly, it's an important resource and many people think that guadua is the future: watch this space.

Bernabé C 3 No. 6–03 ⊕ 315 596 1447; map p.244. You can stop at this excellent little place for just a single-variety coffee prepared in any way you choose, be it filter, espresso or even Turkish, but it's also a restaurant where you can try dishes made with coffee, such as succulent pork medallions in passion fruit and coffee sauce, or aubergines in tomato sauce with parmesan gratinée. $\overline{\$\$}$

Brunch C 6 No. 3–25 ⊕ 311 757 8082; map p.244. American-run burger bar (Boquía burger topped with their own sauce plus lettuce, tomatoes, onions, cheese and mushrooms, and proper French fries on the side), where you can seriously stuff yourself at breakfast, lunch or supper. They even make and sell their own peanut butter, and claim to be the "home of the peanut butter brownie" – you can pig out on a very large one with ice cream. $\overline{\$\$}$

La Eliana Cra 2 No. 6–45 ⊕ 314 660 5987; map p.244. If you're pining for a curry then look no further: choices include chicken tikka masala, chicken jalfrezi or even a Thai green curry (chicken or veg). $\overline{\$\$}$

La Estación del Food Truck Cra 2 at C 6; map p.244. An open-air food court, where half a dozen food trucks between them offer a choice of Middle Eastern, Mexican or Venezuelan fast food, burgers or cocktails. $\overline{\$}$

Jesús Martín Cra 6 No. 6–14 ⓦ cafejesusmartin.com; map p.244. A very refined coffee bar where they use top-notch, fresh-ground beans. The list of lattes, espresssos and cappuccinos – all made exactly right – includes a beautiful creation called an *angélica* (espresso half-and-half with condensed milk). They also serve sandwiches and light snacks, and they have a coffee shop on C Real (Cra 6) at C 3 where you can try their coffees before choosing which to buy. $\overline{\$}$

El Rincón de Lucy Cra 6 No. 4–02 ⊕ 314 255 7964; map p.244. A favourite with locals, out-of-towners and foreigners alike, Lucy serves the best-value set lunches in town. With the set menu you get juice, soup and a heaped plate of beans, vegetables and fish or meat. $\overline{\$}$

DRINKING

★ **Donde Mi 'Apá** Cra 6 No. 5–24; map p.244. The town's most atmospheric watering hole, right on the main square and chock-a-block with bric-a-brac, including a knackered old jukebox, a bull's head and Charlie Chaplin film stills. The main illumination is a neon sign reading "*música vieja*", which fairly describes the 18,000-odd rare and classic vinyl records of Colombian and South American tunes they keep behind the bar and play (usually now from digitized recordings) to a crowd of good old boys supping beer and *aguardiente*.

DIRECTORY

Banks and exchange There are two ATMs on the main square.
Health Hospital San Vicente de Paul, C 7 No. 6–60 (⊕ 6 759 3000, ⓦ hospitalsalento-ese.gov.co) is little more than a first aid post, but will get an ambulance to Armenia in cases of urgent need. The best pharmacy is Droguería Jader, C 5 No. 5–44 (daily 7.30am–9.30pm).
Internet I@ Esquin@, C 5, at Cra 4; Inter Rapidísimo, C 6 No. 4–50.
Laundry Lavandería Yola, Cra 3 No. 6–25.
Police C 6 No. 6–30 (on the main square; ⊕ 6 759 3050).
Post office Droguería Jader doubles as the local post office.
Tejo Los Amigos, Cra 4 No. 3–32 (⊕ 312 792 8486), is the best place in the country to learn *tejo* – they speak English, are used to tourists, and are very happy to help beginners pick up the game. You can also play *tejo* at BetaTown, C 2 No. 6–20 (ⓦ beta.com.co), which has a restaurant and various other facilities.

Valle de Cocora

Salento sits atop the **VALLE DE COCORA**, which contains a thick forest of the skyscraper **wax palm**, Colombia's national tree. The world's tallest palm tree, it grows up to 60m high and lives for as long as 120 years. The valley, which offers picturesque hikes, is easily explored in a day-trip from Salento.

The hamlet of **Cocora**, 11km east of Salento, has a handful of restaurants, small shops and hotels and from here a well-trodden path leads into misty, pristine cloud forest, scattered with the remains of pre-Columbian tombs and dwellings. Orchids, bromeliads and heliconias are just some of the **plant** species that thrive here, and the **animal** life includes spectacled bear, native deer and puma, along with hundreds of **bird** species such as toucans, eagles and motmots.

A five- to six-hour loop walk starts in Cocora from a blue gate onto a muddy track. The trail passes a trout farm – whose denizens you'll very likely be tucking into at one of Salento's restaurants – and runs through farmland for around 45 minutes before reaching the park entrance. After that, you'll be following an uneven, slippery trail through cloud forest. The trail eventually branches, with one track leading up to the extremely worthwhile **Reserva Acaime** (entrance charge), home to eighteen species of hummingbird that flock to its bird feeders. The entrance fee includes a large mug of revitalizing hot chocolate and a chunk of locally produced cheese. You then retrace your steps to the main trail that crosses nine rickety wooden Indiana Jones-style bridges over the Río Quindío before the Finca La Montaña branch culminates at a mountain-top viewing platform with exhilarating valley views. The way down along a wide gravel road takes you past an especially large cluster of wax palms.

ARRIVAL AND DEPARTURE — VALLE DE COCORA

By jeep Willy jeeps leave from Salento's main square every hour. The ride to Cocora takes 20min. Alternatively, you can charter a jeep each way for up to eight people.

Filandia

Just 23km west of Salento, its sister village of **FILANDIA** is just as pretty – arguably more so – but has a quieter and more refined air. At any rate, it gets far fewer visitors, and those who do come, so the locals reckon, are a cut above the hoi-polloi who flock to Salento. The village was founded in the 1870s by people seeking refuge from the political strife in Antioquia, and many of the houses in the village date from the late nineteenth or early twentieth century, the oldest being at Carrera 6 No. 5–63, which now houses the Droguería Bristol.

Filandia's main square, the **Parque de Filandia**, is certainly better preserved than Salento's, and has several places to relax with a coffee while taking it in. On the east side of the square, the blue and white parish church, the **Templo La Inmaculada Concepción**, built in 1905, is worth popping into for a look, as it's even prettier on the inside than it is on the outside. Otherwise, Filandia's main sight is the strange-looking hexagonal wooden **Torre Observatorio** (charge), a 27m-high lookout tower a kilometre west of town (head out along Cra 4), which affords great views of the surrounding countryside, weather allowing of course. The main local handicraft is **basketwork**, which you can check out and buy in a craft shop on the way to the Torre Observatorio.

ARRIVAL AND INFORMATION — FILANDIA

By bus Buses run to Filandia from Armenia (every 15min until 8pm; 45min). From Salento, get an Armenia-bound bus to the junction with the main road, cross over and pick up the Filandia bus there.

Tourist information Casa de la Cultura, Cra 5 No. 6–40, on the main square (☏ 6 758 2172).

ACCOMMODATION

Hostal Colina de Lluvia Cra 4 No. 5–15 ☏ 321 715 6245. An informal little hostel just a block off the main square. It's very friendly, family run and an excellent hangout if you're looking for a bit of peace and quiet. Breakfast included.

Hostal Tibouchina C 6 No. 5–05 • 6 758 2646, 🌐 hotel tibouchina.hotelonia.com. A quirky – and creaky – little place in a great old house with a balcony overlooking the main square, wooden floors and wooden walls to match, lots of character and an excellent location. Breakfast included. $$

EATING

Choripollo C 7 No. 4–57 • 316 514 6015. There's trout and *bandeja paisa* on the menu at this immaculate little restaurant just off the main square, or you can opt for the *menú del día*. $$

Helena Adentro Cra 7 No. 8–01 🌐 helenaadentro.com. All the food is fusion cuisine at this café-bar-restaurant decorated with bric-a-brac and old photos, where specialities include a smoked hummus platter or *marranitas* (cornbread balls stuffed with meat). $$

Ibagué

Tolima's state capital, **IBAGUÉ** was founded by the Spanish in 1550, at a site 42km to the west (where the town of Cajamarca now stands); it was forced to relocate the following year due to opposition from the local Pijao people. Its main square, **Parque Bolívar**, complete with grass, trees and cherubic water features, is dominated by a pretty white and gold cathedral, forming the heart of the central La Pola *barrio*. Two blocks south, the **Parque de la Música** lies behind the **Conservatorio de Música**, Ibagué's internationally renowned music school. Featuring modern sculptures of musicians, and views of the mountains, the park is dotted with benches that make a favourite meeting place for young lovers, especially around dusk. Along with Salento and Pereira, Ibagué is a point of access to the Los Nevados national park, especially the Nevado de Tolima (see page 236).

Cañon de Combeima
Via al Nevado de Tolima • Bus #48 from C 14 at Cra 1

Ibagué's main tourist attraction, the **Cañon de Combeima**, is out of town on the way up to the Nevado de Tolima. It's outside the Los Nevados national park (see page 234), but shares some of its landscapes and animal and plant life. The bus will take you as far as **Juntas**, 18km north of town, where you can walk to a **mirador** with good views of the Nevado. You can also climb down into the canyon and scramble along it. There are hot springs further up the canyon at **El Rancho**, but they are not reached by public transport. At **Villa Restrepero**, 3km before Juntas, you'll find places to eat and to stay, and you can stop off to check out the local waterfalls.

Jardín Botánico San Jorge
Via las Nieves (up C 19, right onto Cra 10, bearing left after 500m) • Charge • • 313 378 3055

North of town, around a 40min walk from the centre, the **Jardín Botánico San Jorge** is more a scenic park than a botanical garden as such. Largely untended, it has three trails you can follow on a 5km hike through the country on a hill above town. There isn't much else up here, so bring drinking water with you.

Orquidiario del Tolima
Cra 30 Sur No.13–35, Barrio Darío Echandía • Charge • 🌐 orquideasdeltolima.com • Bus #7 or #40 from the city centre

Dedicated to the conservation of Colombian orchids, the **Orquidiario del Tolima** boasts around 170 species on its 54-acre site, located 5km southwest of the city centre, along with other flowering plants such as bromelias, heliconias ("lobster-claws") and fruit trees. They also reckon to have 150 species of birds, and in particular hummingbirds. It's a popular local beauty spot, where you can walk on trails around the site to admire the flowers and the wildlife, with guides on hand; there's even a swimming pool.

ARRIVAL AND INFORMATION

By bus The bus terminal is just east of the junction of C 20 with Cra 1. There are regular bus departures for Armenia (every 15–20min; 3hr), Bogotá (every 15–30min; 4hr) and Medellín (every 20min–hourly; 6hr).

IBAGUÉ

Tourist information The Punto de Información Turística (PiT) in the bus terminal gives out ad-filled pamphlets on tourism in Tolima, and dispenses advice, but doesn't have any decent city maps.

ACCOMMODATION

Hotel Dann Combeima Cra 2 No. 12–37 ⓦ hoteles dann.com/dann-combeima. A good central hotel for those who value comforts and amenities such as a/c, bar and restaurant. You have the option of a suite or junior suite, but even the standard rooms are quite spacious. Breakfast is included. $\overline{\$\$}$

El Imperio Cra 3 No. 18–47 ⓦ hotelimperioibague.com. A good-value budget hotel near the bus station, overlooking a large square, the Parque Andrés López Galarza. Functional but modern, bright and clean. $\overline{\$}$

EATING

Anfield Pub Cra 3 No. 8–09 ☏ 8 261 2253. Despite the name, this cosy little bar-restaurant doesn't have too much in common with a Scouse boozer, although it does have a British theme, serves beer, and often shows English football on the TV. They'll also do you a plate of fish and chips (*un escocés*, as they call them), a burger (*un americano*) or a pitta-type bread filled with pulled beef (*un árabe*), and they have great cakes, juices and yogurt drinks. $\overline{\$}$

Jus'so Café La Pola Cra 7 No. 2–60 ☏ 316 409 2617. A little coffee shop where you can buy single-farm coffees from across Colombia, and they have a choice of five varieties every day to drink, accompanied by oat biscuits and organic *panela*. $\overline{\$}$

Yerba Buena Cra 5 No. 6–28 ☏ 8 273 1204. Overlooking the Parque Centenario, this is the best restaurant around the city centre, specializing in steaks, including baby beef or *bife chorzo*. At weekday lunchtimes they offer a set menu. $\overline{\$\$}$

Cali and the southwest

252 Cali and around
270 Popayán and around
279 Tierradentro
283 San Agustín and around
289 Desierto de la Tatacoa
291 The far south

POPAYÁN

Cali and the southwest

Ravishing colonial cities, the mystifying remnants of pre-Hispanic civilizations, Indigenous markets, a raw, untouched Andean landscape and the booming salsa-soaked city of Cali await in Colombia's southwest. Though the Pan-American Highway down into Ecuador sees a steady stream of travellers, much of the region remains lightly visited and unless it's a Colombian festival or holiday, you are likely to see very few tourists – for now. Indeed, few regions boast so much tourism potential, from the painted subterranean tombs of Tierradentro and ancient, haunting statues of San Agustín, to Indigenous cultures that have retained a distinctive character to the present day, from the Nasa to the Guambiano.

Though it's something of an acquired taste, if you like big cities you'll love **Cali** and its dizzying nightlife, with day-trips out to the microbrewery at **Buga**, kitesurfing at **Calima** and refreshing mountain streams at **Pance**. Further south, across the vast plains of sugar cane in the Valle de Cauca – between the cordilleras Occidental and Central – lies the elegant town of **Popayán**, known for its blindingly white colonial architecture and surrounding hot springs, snow-capped volcano and **Guambiano market**. Heading deeper into the Andes, **Pasto** is the capital of Nariño, a region ripe for adventure travel and littered with remote, crystal-clear lagoons, foaming waterfalls and smouldering volcanoes all the way to Ecuador.

Cali and around

For most visitors (and most Colombians) **CALI** means one thing: **salsa**. Colombia's third-largest metropolis, with a population of 2.4 million, the city stakes a powerful claim to being **Colombia's party capital**, and you'll hear **Colombian-style salsa** blaring throughout the day and night. Dance schools are cheap, clubs stay open till dawn and every month *Delirio* offers an extravaganza of salsa, cabaret and pure adrenaline. During the day Cali doesn't boast any major sights, though its **centro histórico** has plenty of character, a blend of shabby streets, modern skyscrapers, colonial museums and market vendors; to the south **San Antonio** is an attractive historic residential district now littered with hip restaurants, cafés and shops, while to the north affluent **Granada** is crammed with bars and clubs.

The city was founded in 1536 by Spanish Conquistador Sebastián de Belalcázar, but only shed its provincial backwater status in the early 1900s, when the profits brought in by its sugar plantations prompted industrialization. It remains one of Colombia's most prosperous cities, in part because of its central role in the drug trade since the dismantling of the rival Medellín cartel in the early 1990s; however, Cali is now more famous for its salsa dancers than white powder. Indeed, the large numbers of African slaves brought to work the sugar mills left a notable impact on Cali's culture (the Afro-Colombian population is almost 25 percent), nowhere more so than in its music.

Today, despite the scary crime statistics, Cali is generally safe for tourists (take the usual precautions at night), and *Caleños* are likely to be some of the friendliest people you'll meet in the whole country. At weekends it can seem like the entire city descends on nearby **Pance** and **Parque Nacional Natural Farallones**, the colonial gem of **Buga**, and huge **Lago Calima**.

LAGUNA DE LA COCHA

Highlights

❶ Cali salsa Colombia's party city is the home of salsa, with mesmerizing shows like *Delirio*, excellent dance schools and plenty of sizzling clubs open till dawn. See page 257.

❷ Popayán Soak up the colonial heritage in the "White City", a gorgeous ensemble of Baroque churches, adobe homes and intriguing museums. See page 270.

❸ Parque Nacional Natural Puracé Climb an active volcano and spot majestic condors in this vast slice of untouched Andean wilderness. See page 277.

❹ Tierradentro Explore these mystical pre-Hispanic underground tombs, surrounded by the bewitching scenery of the Central Cordillera, home of the Nasa. See page 279.

❺ San Agustín In this mountainous region sprinkled with towering waterfalls, one of South America's great pre-Hispanic civilizations created thousands of enigmatic stone statues to guard their tombs. See page 283.

❻ Laguna de la Cocha Take a boat ride to the jungle-smothered island in the centre of this pristine Andean lake, then dine on fresh trout in the Quillacinga village of El Puerto. See page 296.

❼ Santuario de Las Lajas Bizarre and completely unexpected, this magnificent French Gothic basilica is perched dramatically at the bottom of a precipitous gorge. See page 297.

HIGHLIGHTS ARE MARKED ON THE MAP ON PAGE 254

Plaza de Caycedo

The heart of Cali's **centro histórico** has always been the palm-filled expanse of **Plaza de Caycedo**, anchored by a modest bronze statue of independence hero Joaquín de Caicedo y Cuero (1773–1813). Today it's a workaday space surrounded by mostly unattractive modern buildings, the exceptions being the **cathedral**, the grand French Neoclassical **Palacio Nacional** (completed in 1933 and still home to the local judiciary) and the **Edificio Otero** next door, another French *Belle Epoque* gem completed in 1926. Once a posh hotel and restaurant, the latter building gained notoriety on December 3, 1984, when an assault on the *Diners Club* inside ended with nine people dead ("**Masacre del Diners Club**"). It was restored by Banco BBVA in 2009 and now functions as a bank.

Catedral Metropolitana de San Pedro Apóstol
Plaza de Caycedo (C 11 No. 5–53, at Cra 5A) • Free • ☎ 2 881 1378

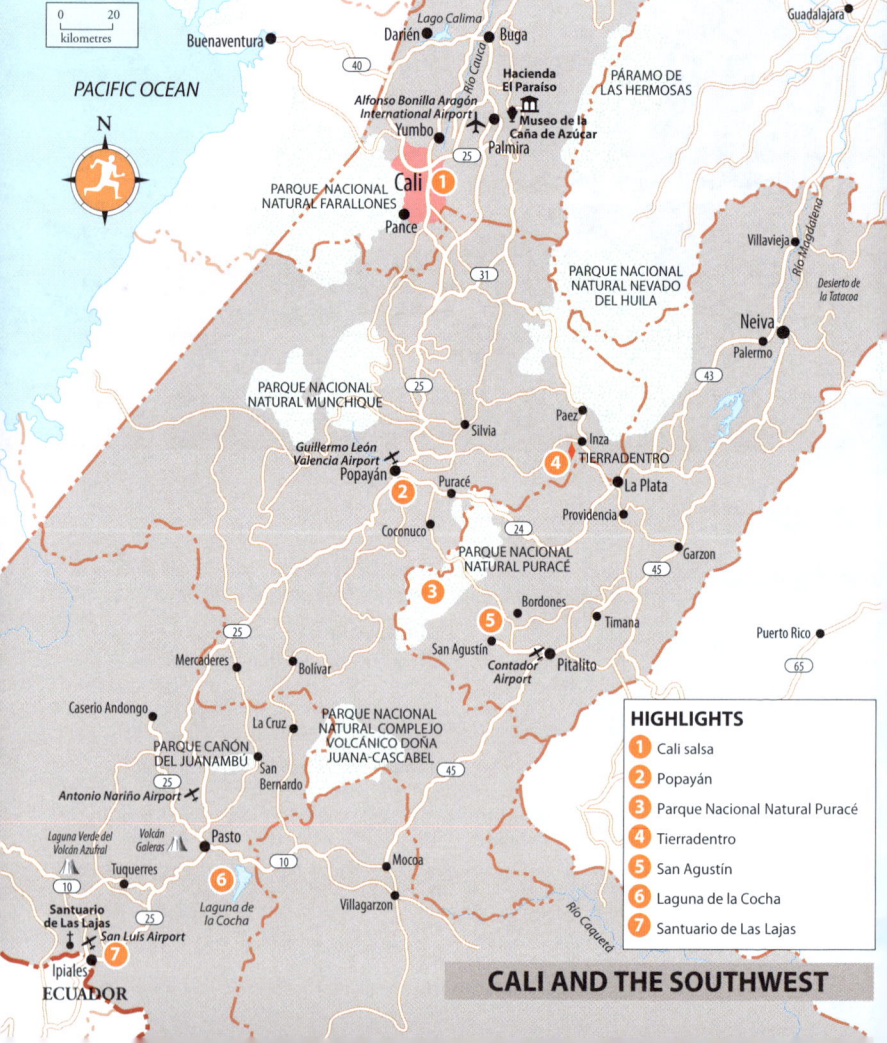

> **CALI WEATHER**
>
> Cali is a low-lying and extremely **hot** city (with an average high of 34ºC) straddling the Río Cali, a tributary of the Río Cauca, and surrounded by the sugar plantations of the marshy Valle de Cauca and craggy Farallones de Cali to the west. The dry seasons go from December to March and from July to August; the steamy rainy seasons run from April to June and September to November.

Built between 1782 and 1802 in a grand Neoclassical style, the **Catedral Metropolitana de San Pedro Apóstol** was damaged in several earthquakes over the years, and much of the facade and choir were rebuilt in brick and concrete in the late 1920s. The interior is an attractive blend of painted arches and stained glass, but the most venerated image here is the **Señor Caído**, a Quiteño school woodcarving of a prostrate Jesus (on the left side of the nave). The image only leaves the church during the annual Good Friday procession, and is surrounded by votive plaques donated by the faithful.

Iglesia La Ermita

Cra 1A at C 13 • Free • ☎ 2 881 8553

A gorgeous wedding-cake confection overlooking the Río Cali, the **Iglesia La Ermita** is all Gothic turrets and pinnacles, built between 1930 and 1942 on the ruins of an earlier church. On the left side of the nave is the original eighteenth-century painting of **El Señor de la Caña** (a bloodied Jesus holding a sugar cane); many miracles are attributed to the image.

From the church the pedestrianized **Bulevar del Río** runs west along the Río Cali, a beautification project completed in 2014 – you can stroll along here towards the Gato de Tejada and La Tertulia (see page 259).

Iglesia de San Francisco

Cras 5 and 6, at Calles 9 and 10 • Free

The **Iglesia de San Francisco** is the centrepiece of a grand, red-brick Franciscan religious complex that looks like its been transported to Cali from medieval Italy – it's easily the most photogenic structure in the city. The church itself, mostly constructed between 1803 and 1827 (but much damaged by earthquakes) sports a beautiful, turquoise, painted interior, with a grand Baroque *retablo*. The central dome, featuring images from the life of St Francis of Assisi, was painted by Colombian artist Mauricio Ramelli, while the dimly lit, medieval-style chapel to the right of the altar contains a trio of revered images (the Cristo Muerto, Nuestra Señora de las Angustias and Juan el Evangelista). To the left of the altar is a rare image of Mary in her guise as La Inmaculada de las Apocalipsis, an exquisite Quiteño-school carving with ornate tiara and wings of silver.

The most striking feature of the complex is the **Torre Mudéjar**, a 23m tower constructed around 1757 in a distinctive Mudéjar (Spanish Moorish) style (closed to visitors), while in between the tower and the church lies the **Capilla de la Inmaculada** (same hours) dating from 1764, with an intricate Mudéjar exterior but relatively plain interior. The biggest part of the complex is the **Convento de San Joaquín** behind the church, still in operation and closed to visitors.

La Merced

Cra 4, between C 6 and C 7 • Guides (free) are available at the museums (and will include the church), but are usually Spanish-speaking only

Once an important monastery, **La Merced** religious complex lies in the most attractive part of downtown Cali, where the colonial-era buildings have largely

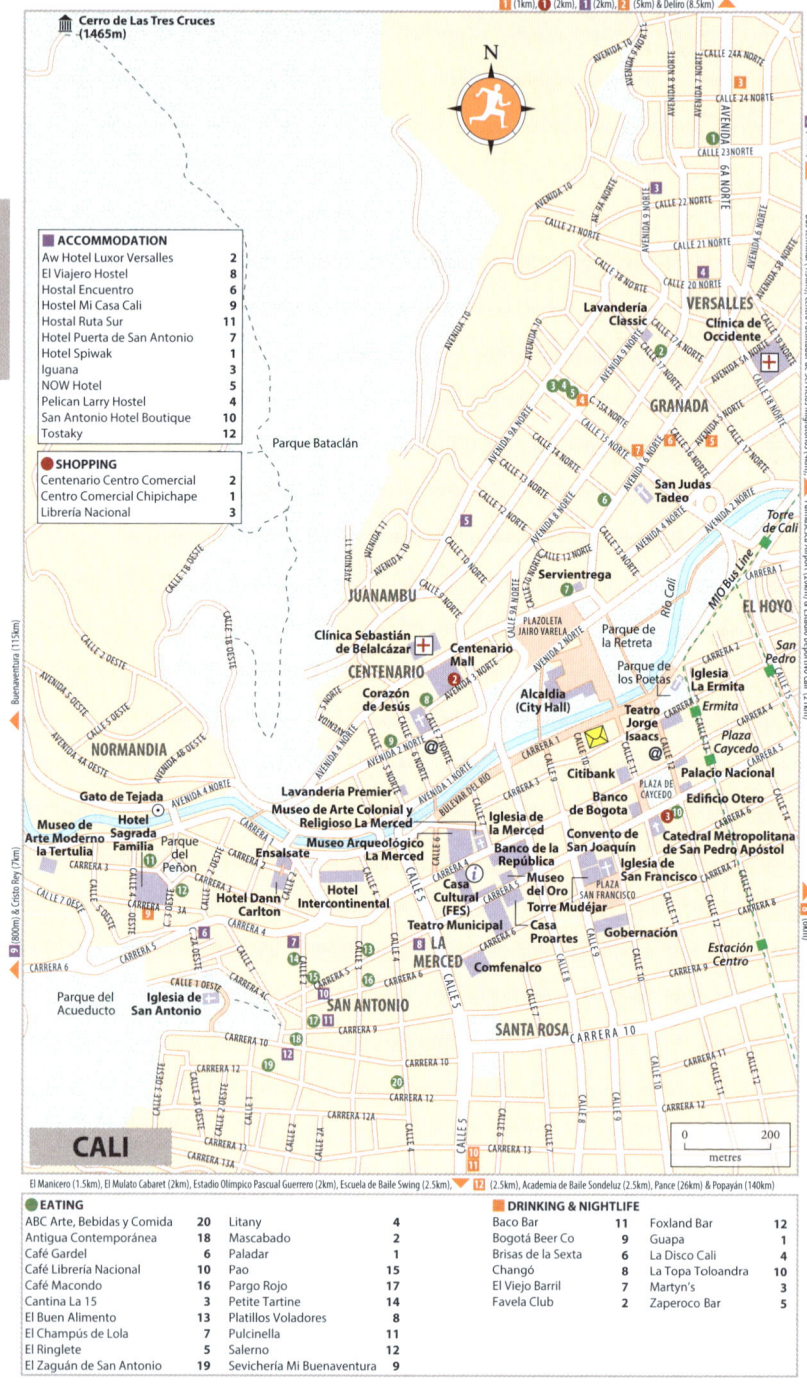

remained intact. The complex was home to the Orden de la Merced (a Catholic religious order) until 1813, when it passed into the hands of the Order of Augustinian Recollects. Today La Merced comprises the oldest **church** in the city and two small **museums**.

Iglesia de la Merced
Cra 4, at C 7 • Free • ⓘ 2 880 4737

The humble **Iglesia de la Merced** was built from adobe around 1678, with unpolished stone floors and timber ceilings. Its unusual L-shape comprises two main chapels: the simple all-white altar of the **Capilla de la Virgen de los Remedios** features a revered image of Mary with a crown donated by Pope John Paul II during his visit in 1986,

THE SALSA CAPITAL OF THE WORLD

Salsa music and dance permeates the fabric of Cali like nowhere else; as a result the city likes to think of itself as the "**salsa capital of the world**". That said, the genre has its origins in New York, created by Cuban and Puerto Rican musicians, blending jazz with Cuban styles such as son, cha-cha and mambo. In 1968 New York stars Ricardo "Richie" Ray and Bobby Cruz performed at the Feria de Cali, creating a salsa sensation that has never really gone away. The Cali style was primarily developed by an Afro-Colombian dancer from Buenaventura known as **Watussi**; he taught in Cali from 1972 (winning the Salsa World Championship with the equally legendary **María Tovar** in 1974), and today Cali-style salsa (*salsa caleño*) features more rapid footwork and high kicks than other versions.

There are several ways to experience *salsa caleño*: the most obvious is to visit throbbing **salsa clubs** like *Chango* (see page 263), but there are also "**party buses**" or *chivas*, old buses done up like clubs that crawl the streets on Friday and Saturday nights: contact Chivas Tours (ⓘ 5 680 3535, ⓦ chivasrumberascali.com). For the real deal, serious salsa fans head out to the poorer neighbourhoods (by taxi) on the fringe of the city (see page 263).

CLASSES

Cali is home to many **dance schools** where you can learn to swing those hips, and though having some Spanish will help, it's not essential. Note that Tin Tin Deo (see page 264) offers free beginners' lessons around 8pm most nights.
Escuela y Academia de Baile Sondeluz (Sondeluz Academy) Cra 28 No. 6–118, Barrio El Cedro ⓦ sondeluz.co. Renowned studio (the home of several salsa champions), with classes covering the entire Latin ballroom genre; *bachata*, *bolero*, tango, *milonga*, *merengue* and salsa.
Escuela de Baile Swing Latino Fundación (Swing Latino) Cra 31 No. 7–25 ⓦ swinglatino.com.co. The most famous salsa academy in the city, founded in the late 1990s by Luis Eduardo Hernández, aka "El Mulato". Classes most afternoons and evenings and all day Sat.
El Manicero C 5 No. 39–71 ⓦ elmanicero.negocio.site. Fun group *salsa caleño* lessons at two hours per session.

SPECIAL EVENTS AND SHOWS

Every September the city goes even more salsa crazy during the **Festival Mundial de la Salsa**. At the end of December, the **Feria de Cali** features a *salsodromo* parade of local salsa troupes.
Delirio Centro de Eventos Valle del Pacífico (off the Cali–Yumbo Autopista) Cra 25 No. 12–328 ⓦ delirio.com.co. If you're in Cali on the last Fri of the month, splash out on *Delirio*, which features some of the best salsa dancers and performers in the country. Shows are described as a Colombian "Cirque de Soleil", which is a little misleading – it's more like a wild cabaret, with audience participation encouraged. It's incredibly fun, a bit kitsch, and gets better the more you drink. Shows take place in a giant tent in northern Cali.
El Mulato Cabaret Cra 32 No. 7–43 ⓦ facebook.com/MulatoCabaret. Purists should check out the shows put on by Swing Latino; their "Sunday socials" at 4pm are a delight.
Ensalsate Hotel Dann Carlton, Cra 2 No. 1–60 ⓦ ensalsate.co. *Delirio* has competition in the shape of this similar show that runs on the second Fri of the month at the *Hotel Dann Carlton*. It's a full-on celebration of salsa, mambo, cha-cha and *bolero*. (ⓦ vive.tuboleta.com).

> **THE CALI CARTEL**
>
> Rival to the more infamous drug gangs in Medellín, the **Cali Cartel** was active from the late 1960s to the late 1990s. Founded by the Rodríguez Orejuela brothers, Gilberto and Miguel, as well as associate José Santacruz Londoño, the cocaine smuggling syndicate became one of the most powerful criminal gangs in the world in the 1980s, when it controlled a multi-billion-dollar empire. Violence – of course – was part of the deal, and the cartel not only murdered rivals (it attempted to kill Pablo Escobar at least twice) but also Cali's *desechables* ("discardables"), mostly street kids, prostitutes and homosexuals, whose bodies were often dumped into the Río Cauca. By 1995, most of the cartel's leaders had been killed or arrested – the Rodríguez brothers were extradited to the US and in 2006 were sentenced to thirty years in prison (Londoño was killed in a police shoot-out in 1996). Though the cartel was largely finished after this, various successors have risen to prominence, such as the **Norte del Valle Cartel**, active until at least 2010. In subsequent years a war between neo-paramilitary groups **Los Rastrojos** and **Los Urabeños** has had some impact on Cali, with the collapse of Los Rastrojos in 2011–12 leading to a spike in violence. Despite dropping more than six percent in recent years, to historic lows, Cali's murder rate remains one of the highest in Colombia.

while the gold and redwood altar in the **Capilla de la Virgen de las Merced** is dedicated to the patron of the city (another incarnation of Mary).

Museo de Arte Colonial y Religioso La Merced
Cra 4 No. 6–117 • Charge • 2 888 0646

Part of the former Merced convent holds the **Museo de Arte Colonial y Religioso La Merced**, a religious art museum set in creaky wooden-floored galleries around a pretty colonial cloister. The exhibits are relatively modest – eighteenth- and nineteenth-century religious paintings, old vestments, silver chalices and the like – but it's artfully presented and the building drips with historic character.

Museo Arqueológico La Merced
Cra 4 No. 6–59 • Charge • 2 885 5309

The other half of the old Merced convent contains the **Museo Arqueológico la Merced**, comprising five themed rooms featuring artefacts from all the major pre-Hispanic cultures in the southwest: Calima, Nariño, Quimbaya, San Agustín, Tolima and Tumaco. There are remarkable anthropomorphic pots and sculptures, a wide range of patterned ceramics and exhibits dedicated to religious belief and death – funerary urns, a replica hollowed-log coffin and a slightly ghoulish (real) mummified body. Labels are in Spanish only, but you can grab a written English guide at the entrance.

Museo del Oro
C 7 No. 4–69, at Cra 5A • Free • banrepcultural.org/cali/museo-del-oro-calima

This small museum in the back of the Banco de la República (officially **Museo del Oro Calima del Banco de la República**) contains a couple of galleries showing temporary exhibits of local art, though the main attraction is the vault-like room holding its collection of pre-Columbian **gold**. Though not as impressive as the cache at its namesake in Bogotá, the collection contains some astounding pieces – masks, breastplates, diadems and ornate necklaces – as well as a large ensemble of ceramic pots and jars. The artefacts were dug up in the Calima region north of the city, primarily from the early settlement (to 1500 BC), Ilama (1500 BC–100 AD), Yotoco-Malagana (200 BC–200 AD) and Sonso (700–900 AD) cultures. Spanish labels only.

Museo de Arte Moderno La Tertulia

Av Colombia No. 5–105 • Charge • W museolatertulia.com

The main galleries of the **Museo de Arte Moderno La Tertulia** show a rotating selection of high-quality contemporary art from the museum's permanent collection of over 1500 pieces – mostly painting, but also photography, sculpture and mixed media, with big names from Colombia (Ignacio Gómez Jaramillo, Édgar Negret and Hernando Tejada among them) and throughout the Americas (including one of Robert Indiana's *Love* images). The adjoining **Cinemateca** screens art-house films (charge). The museum is a pleasant twenty-minute walk along the Río Cali from La Merced, via the **Gatos del Río** (see below).

Iglesia de San Antonio

Colina de San Antonio, C 1 Oeste, at Cra 10 • 📞 2 883 8790

High above the old city atop the **Colina de San Antonio**, the humble **Iglesia de San Antonio** boasts scintillating views across Cali – it's an easy walk and much more convenient to get to than the other *miradores* (see page 261).

The church itself dates back to 1747, and contains rare *tallas quiteñas*, seventeenth-century wooden statues of the saints, carved in the style of the Quiteño school. In the evenings the slopes come alive with an **arts and crafts market**, while the **San Antonio** area below the hill features artsy boutiques and quality restaurants (see page 262).

Miradores de Cali

Cali is ringed by a series of spectacular **miradores** (viewpoints), beloved by locals and visitors alike. The two main ones are similar – the **Cerro de Las Tres Cruces** is the best to climb, while **Cristo Rey** offers a slightly more expansive view. You can take a taxi to either but set the price in advance (including waiting time on top). Both hills are safe during the day, with police posts nearby manned 8am to 11pm.

Cristo Rey

Cerro de Los Cristales (7km southwest of the centre) • 24hr • Free • **Fundación Andoke** Parcelacion la Reforma Km 6 • Tours (1hr) daily • Charge • W andoke.com.co

Completed in 1952, the 26m-high **Cristo Rey** ("Christ Redeemer") statue looms over the city at 1474m above sea level – on a clear day the views are astounding. It's possible to hike up here, but most people take a taxi, admiring the expressive **sculptures** of Carlos Andrés Gómez along the road and visiting **Fundación Andoke**, with its Mariposario ("butterfly house"; more than fifteen Colombian species) and lush gardens buzzing with hummingbirds.

Cerro de Las Tres Cruces

Free

The hike up **Cerro de Las Tres Cruces** (1465m) is one of the highlights of Cali, a relatively straightforward but energetic climb that takes around two hours. The three crosses on

---

> ### CATS OF THE RIVER
>
> Hernando Tejada's cute purple cat sculpture, "**Gato de Tejada**", has become a city mascot since it debuted in 1996, overlooking the Río Cali on Avenida 4A (opposite C 3 Oeste). The 3.5m bronze image marks a small park of similar cat sculptures, also created by Tejada (the "**Gatos del Río**", cats of the river). You'll find more of them along the section of river known as the Bulevar del Río in the old centre near the Iglesia La Ermita (see page 255). Tejada was a Colombian sculptor who spent much of his life in Cali and died here in 1998.

> ### CALI'S ART MARKETS
>
> Every evening the slopes of the **Parque Artesenal Loma La Cruz** are lined with a selection of Cali's alternative arts and crafts sellers – it's a safe and relaxed scene, and at weekends you'll see local street performers known as *cuentachistes* (comedians/storytellers). The market gets going daily from around 6pm – it's in the San Fernando district, on Carrera 15 near the Santa Librada MIO station. San Antonio (see page 259) has a smaller but similar market, while the Parque El Peñón hosts a high-quality contemporary art market on Sundays from 10am to 6pm.

top were completed in 1938 (the central cross is 26m tall), with intoxicating views across the city and mountains beyond. The story goes that monks placed the first bamboo crosses here back in 1837, in an attempt to subdue a demon dwelling here known as "Buziraco". A cleansing pilgrimage to the top takes place every Easter and on May 3.

To find the path up, cross the Río Cali near the *Hotel Intercontinental* on Avenida Colombia, turn left along Avenida 6, then right up steep Calle 1B Oeste – the path begins on the right of this street further up the hill. It's best to start early to avoid the heat (and with fewer people in the afternoon/evening, it's not as safe). Take lots of water.

ARRIVAL AND DEPARTURE — CALI

By plane Cali's Aeropuerto Palmaseca (☎ 2 666 3200) lies 20km northeast of the city. The cheapest way into the centre is to catch one of the regular minibuses that run to and from the bus terminal, aka Terminal de Cali (every 15min; 30–40min). Taxis charge a fixed rate into the centre: Asotaba (☎ 2 666 3435) has a monopoly at the airport – get a ticket at the taxi window outside the terminal confirming the rate (pay the driver on arrival). Note that if you arrive on a domestic flight there are no ATMs or banks (just Localiza, Hertz and Avis car rental desks) – exit the baggage hall and walk left to re-enter the main terminal building for ATMs and cafés.

Destinations Bogotá (daily; 50min); Cartagena (2–3 weekly; 1hr 25min); Medellín (4 daily; 40min); Pereira (4 daily; 30min); Pasto (2 daily; 1hr); San Andrés (daily; 2hr). Also nonstop international departures for Lima, Madrid, Miami, Panama City and Quito.

By bus The giant Terminal de Cali at C 30N No. 2AN–29, 2km north of the old centre, can seem confusing at first, though it's relatively well organized. Level 1 is crammed with snack stalls, cafés and shops (including a supermarket), and there is also a small tourist information booth; level 2 is where most ticket offices are located, and where some minibuses depart; level 3 is where bigger buses and other minibuses depart (you can buy some tickets up here also). Numerous companies compete for routes – services range from bigger, comfortable buses to minibuses of various sizes (*microbús* and the slightly bigger *buseta*) and even large cars (*camionetas*, *aerovans* or just "KIA" and so on). Though some vehicles are definitely worse than others, for short trips the difference between companies is marginal – take a look before you buy just to be sure. If you are heading to Bogotá, Buga, Pasto, Popayán or Medellín you won't have to wait long. Taxis wait for passengers on the south side of level 1. Further along, past the taxi rank, you can walk through the pedestrian tunnel to Av 3A and the nearest MIO bus station (Las Américas), a 15min walk (minibuses to Pance leave from this side, too).

Destinations Armenia (hourly; 4hr); Buenaventura (hourly; 2–3hr); Buga (every 30min; 1–2hr); Darién (hourly; 2hr 30min); Bogotá (hourly; 12–15hr); Manizales (hourly; 5hr); Medellín (16 daily; 8–9hr); Pasto (hourly; 9hr); Pereira (several daily; 4hr); Popayán (every 30min; 2hr 30min–3hr).

GETTING AROUND

Much local sightseeing can be done on foot, provided you're staying in the Granada or San Antonio neighbourhoods and are prepared to **walk** a lot.

By bus The efficient MIO network of electric buses (w transmilenio.gov.co), a replica of Bogotá's TransMilenio (using dedicated street lanes and metro-like covered stations), runs along the river, and also passes through the centre and along Av Quinta (Av 5). You can pay for single trips or buy a prepaid card (*tarjeta básica*) at the *taquilla* (ticket office) at the station entrance. MIO also runs a network of feeder routes throughout the city, using normal bus stops (same cost; prepaid cards only).

By minibus Most of the city is served by cramped minibuses known as *busetas*, with destinations marked at the front and stopping anywhere they can be flagged down; almost all charge a flat fee per ride.

By taxi Cali taxis use meters that measure units, not currency; a chart in the taxi should clearly show what is the current equivalent in C$/unit, but most taxi meters automatically calculate the total at the end of your ride. Always take a taxi at night. Try Taxi Libres (☎ 2 444 4444), Radio Taxis (☎ 2 664 0000) or Taxis Val Cali (☎ 2 333 3333).

Uber (w uber.com) is available in Cali – it's safe and cheap, but you'll need to speak good Spanish and have your smartphone on roaming to use it (and preferably be in a group, just in case).

INFORMATION AND TOURS

Tourist information Fontur operates a small information office (❶ 2 885 6173) in the Centro Cultural de Cali (aka "FES") near La Merced on Cra 4 at C 6, with English speakers and basic information; there is another at the Terminal de Cali (see page 260).

Tours Free Tour Cali offers illuminating, free guided strolls in English from Ermita Church (see page 255) through central Cali (❶ 302 438 3348, w facebook.com/freetourcali).

ACCOMMODATION

Cali's backpacker **hostels** are concentrated in two clusters, one around the **Granada** neighbourhood with good access to nightlife on Avenida 6N and the restaurants around Avenida 8N, and the other in the characterful (but slightly less secure at night) colonial neighbourhood of **San Antonio**. Mid-range **hotels** tend to focus on the more affluent districts (in Granada and to the north). Note that airbnb (w airbnb.com) and Couchsurfing (w couchsurfing.org) have arrived in Cali in a big way.

GRANADA AND NORTHERN CALI

Aw Hotel Luxor Versalles C 23N No. 5AN–37 w hotelesbyaw.com; map p.256. Justly popular boutique hotel, with a warm, contemporary theme, helpful staff and comfy rooms (small bathrooms; cable TV with English channels), set in a quiet neighbourhood of homes and businesses a short stroll from the MIO station and main bus terminal. Cooked breakfast included. No lift. $$$

Hotel Spiwak Av 6D No. 36N–18 w spiwak.com; map p.256. A few steps from Chipichape Mall, this incredible-looking hotel with a space-age atrium (inspired by New York's Guggenheim Museum) boasts luxurious rooms with chic decor (some with fully equipped kitchens and marble bathrooms), and a large outdoor pool. Breakfast included. $$$$

Iguana Av 9N No. 22N–22 ❶ 2 382 5364; map p.256. A friendly youth hostel with all the vital backpacker facilities spread over two floors: small, cosy dorms, bargain doubles, garden barbecues, plus loads of information on the region. $

NOW Hotel Av 9AN No. 10N–74 w nowhotel.com.co; map p.256. Cali's most creative boutique hotel, with a quirky, contemporary design concept (featuring the work of Colombian artists), stylish, spacious doubles (with flatscreen TVs on metal poles) and a rooftop bar and pool with panoramic city views. $$$

Pelican Larry Hostel C 20N No. 6AN–44 w thepelicanlarry.com; map p.256. The big beds, DVD room and twice-weekly barbecues at this fabulous location in Granada make this hostel popular with younger backpackers who are in Cali to party. Breakfast included. $

SAN ANTONIO

★ **Hostal Encuentro** C 2 Oeste No. 4–16 w hostalencuentro.com; map p.256. One of the city's best hostels, with helpful staff, stylish dorms and doubles (with comfy beds) plus a tranquil terrace and delicious breakfast included. $

Hostel Mi Casa Cali Cra 24e Oeste No. 6–41 ❶ 304 540 1100; map p.256. Cheap hostel with clean dorms (bamboo bunks), simple doubles, a well-equipped shared kitchen, and a tranquil garden. $

Hostal Ruta Sur Cra 9 No. 2–41 w hostal-ruta-sur.hotelsincali.com; map p.256. Popular budget hotel with six en-suite rooms in a lovely old house adorned with plants, regional artwork and hammocks, centred on a tranquil courtyard. Breakfast extra. Cash only. $

Hotel Puerta de San Antonio C 2 No. 4–14 w hotelpuertadesanantonio.com; map p.256. Sleek, modern hotel, with black-and-white colour scheme and grand murals of historical Cali scenes. $$

San Antonio Hotel Boutique Cra 6 No. 2–51 w hotelboutiquesanantonio.com; map p.256. Old property given a gorgeous makeover in the heart of San Antonio, with ten modern, stylish (soundproofed) rooms with satellite TV and free calls to the US and Canada. Breakfast included. $$$

Tostaky Cra 10 No. 1–76 ❶ 300 355 1650; map p.256. There's a refined atmosphere at this French-run hostel in San Antonio, which probably has something to do with the coffee bar, complete with chess sets, in the front room. The guest kitchen for self-catering is a bonus. Breakfast is extra. $

El Viajero Hostel Cra 5 No. 4–56 w viajerohostels.com; map p.256. This fun hostel, part of a chain, entices travellers to its simple dorms and doubles with free breakfast, pool, free daily salsa classes and a genuine attempt at sustainability (solar-powered hot water, recycled rainwater and recycled trash). HI members receive 15 percent discount. Dorms $, doubles $$

EATING

The centre of Cali is crammed with the standard Colombian bakeries, fried snack stalls, juice sellers and fruit carts, but the most enticing places to eat lie in **San Antonio**, nearby **El Peñon**, or along Avenida 9 in **Granada** to the north, all of which are relatively safe neighbourhoods. Note that shopping malls like Centenario (see page 264) and Chipichape (see page 264) have huge indoor food courts and supermarkets.

CENTRO

Café Librería Nacional Cra 5 No. 11–50, Plaza de Caycedo ⓦlibrerianacional.com; map p.256. Small, simple café inside the bookstore on the main plaza, with cosy booths and tasty desserts. Highlights include the addictive banana split and cheesecake, but there are also hefty sandwiches, from simple cheese to steak, salads and *malteadas* (milkshakes). $

El Champús de Lola Av 2N No. 10–129 ☎2 660 3991; map p.256. Come to this no-frills local place just across the river to try a Valle del Cauca speciality: *champús*, the refreshing meal-in-a-drink made with brown sugar syrup, crushed maize, marinated pineapple, cinnamon bark and cloves, best accompanied with an *empanada* or plantains with *chicharrón* (fried pig skin). *Champús* also includes the local fruit known as *lulo*, rare to find beyond Colombia (a cross between a tomato and persimmon, with a lime taste). $

★ **Platillos Voladores** Av 3N No. 7–19, Barrio Centenario ⓦplatillosvoladores.com; map p.256. Chef Vicky Acosta's award-winning contemporary Colombian restaurant combines local produce with a variety of regional and international dishes, from the traditional prawn soup with coconut to *pad Thai*, salmon macadamia and the spring-roll-like *rollitos de chontaduro*. $$

GRANADA AND NORTHERN CALI

Café Gardel Av 6N No. 13N–83 ☎310 529 2012; map p.256. Named in honour of 1920s tango legend Carlos Gardel, this old-school café with shady trees is a laidback retreat despite being on the main drag, attracting local old boys who like to chat over the superb coffee in the afternoons. Also serves pastries, sandwiches and freshly baked *pan de bono* (cheese bread). $

★ **Cantina La 15** C 15N No. 9N–62 ⓦcantinala15.com; map p.256. Glamorous contemporary Colombian/Mexican restaurant, with stylish decor, live bands and DJs making it more like a club as the evening wears on. Taco plates are the most budget friendly and mains include beef tenderloin, and grilled octopus. Reservations recommended. $$

Litany C 15AN No. 9N–35 ☎316 449 9843; map p.256. Flavour-starved foodies should make a beeline for this acclaimed Lebanese ("Comida Árabe") restaurant from Lebanese chef Malaki Alil Ghattas, which serves up mouthwatering platters featuring *tabouli*, falafel, vine leaves and top-notch *shawarma*. $$

★ **Mascabado** C 17N No. 8N–30 ⓦmascabado.com.co; map p.256. Popular with backpackers and anyone seeking quality, healthy meals – traditional home-made breads and cakes, fresh fruits, salads and sandwiches. English menus and friendly service, and even pots of Early Grey tea. $$

Paladar Av 6AN No. 23–27 ⓦpaladar.co; map p.256. This is an excellent, relatively upscale cafeteria (go upstairs for a/c), where you choose your dishes on trays – delicious plates of home-made lasagne, stews, seafood rice and shrimp. The desserts are well worth sampling, from guava tarts to *tres dulce* puddings. $$$

★ **El Ringlete** C 15N No. 9N–31 ⓦrestaurante-ringlete.kyte.site; map p.256. The best traditional Colombian restaurant in the city, specializing in the cuisine of the Valle de Cauca or "Nueva Cocina Vallecaucana": dishes include *marranitas* (pork and plantain balls), *aborrajados* (deep-fried plantains stuffed with cheese), *fritanga* (meat, sausage and vegetables), *tamales*, mamey fruit desserts and a luscious chicken stew on Sun. $$

Sevichería Mi Buenaventura Av 2N No. 5–21, Centenario ☎310 413 1382; map p.256. Quaint little hole in the wall, serving good Columbian fare, with a focus on seafood. Portions are large and can easily be shared. $

SAN ANTONIO

ABC Arte, Bebidas y Comida C 4 No. 10–24 ☎323 346 8953; map p.256. Restaurant-cum-art gallery, with the kitchen set up like a stage. The food is excellent, featuring anything from barbecue ribs and pork chops to hummus and rice pudding. $$

★ **Antigua Contemporánea** Cra 10, at C 2 No. 1–39 ☎2 893 6809; map p.256. Gorgeous but pricey ivy-clad restaurant surrounded by gardens, with a cosy interior featuring old wooden doors and tables and contemporary art. The Mediterranean-inspired mains include salmon and pasta dishes, but you can also pop in for a coffee and a slice of cake. An attached shop sells designer furniture. $$

El Buen Alimento Cra 5 No. 3–23 ⓦvinapp.co/el-buen-alimento; map p.256. Elegant colonial property with several rooms and a pretty courtyard with a fountain, housing one of the best vegetarian restaurants on the continent. Feast on lasagne with plantains and corn, tasty soups, falafel and spiced apples; they also serve large fresh juices and breakfast plates. $$

Café Macondo Cra 6 No. 3–03 ⓦmacondocafe.blogspot.com; map p.256. This cosy café with a jazz and blues soundtrack offers sandwiches, salads and veggie burgers plus delicious cakes and a decent list of coffees (made from ground local beans and stronger tipples. $$

★ **Pao** C 2 No. 4–128 ☎2 379 8215; map p.256. Tiny café serving excellent coffee, refreshing lemonade flavoured with ginger and cucumber/mint and tasty breakfasts, plus *pan de bono* and brownies. Free wi-fi. $

Pargo Rojo Cra 9 No. 2–09 ☎2 893 6949; map p.256. Seafood restaurant with a cult following – the food is excellent but service can be hit-or-miss. The flavours are inspired by the Afro-Colombian cooking of the Pacific coast, with set lunches featuring a traditional fish soup. $$

★ **Petite Tartine** C 2 No. 4–38 ☎2 892 1334; map p.256. This is a real surprise – a genuine French bistro, part art gallery, with reasonable prices for tasty dishes such as home-made chicken pâté, pork, rabbit, fresh salads and

French onion soup. Cash only. $

★ **El Zaguán de San Antonio** Cra 12 No. 1–29 ☎ 2 893 8021; map p.256. This San Antonio institution serves high-quality traditional *vallecaucana* food – which means there's plenty of meat. The fresh juices are sensational and on Sun it prepares *sancocho de gallina* (free-range chicken soup) cooked the traditional way over a wood fire. The food is fantastic but the real reason to come is for the amazing view from the rooftop, which is also a great place for a drink. $$

EL PEÑÓN
Pulcinella Cra 3 Oeste No. 3–28 ☎ 317 670 3093; map p.256. Cute little French and Italian restaurant, serving all the classics from snails in garlic to luscious cannelloni; there's authentic Alsatian *tarte flambee*, delicious pizzas and pastas and a decent crème brulee. $$

Salerno C 3 Oeste No. 3–35 ⓦ pizzeriasalerno.co; map p.256. *Salerno* has several branches in Cali but this is the most atmospheric, set in an old hacienda right on the square. Stick to the Italian classics – grilled rosemary chicken, *pizza pantalón* (pocket pizza) – and the fresh orange juices. $$

DRINKING AND NIGHTLIFE

Much of Cali nightlife is dedicated to **salsa** clubs and shows (see page 257) – people don't often go out solely to drink, and most bars, such as they are, double as cafés (locals will also sit and drink outside their local grocery stores). The clubs along **Avenida 6N** are liveliest at the weekends (the area can be sketchy at night, so take taxis), especially between Calles 15 and 17. Single male travellers should find themselves a mixed group to go out with or risk being refused entry. **Juanchito** in the east is the traditional salsa heartland. To get there, you cross a bridge over the Río Cauca, immortalized by the salsa classic *Del puente para alla es Juanchito* – locals will often refer to "over the bridge". **Menga** and **Yumbo** in the north are the newer areas, with at least twenty clubs. The main reason for the late-night exodus, apart from the classic, old-school salsa bands at these places, is that clubs inside Cali city limits must close at 3am – clubs in the 'burbs can close at 6am (or later). Visitors seeking a more subtle experience can start with a *viejoteca* (a club technically for seniors), where there's more actual dancing, less physical drama and generally less chaos.

SAN ANTONIO AND EL PEÑÓN
Baco Bar C 5 No. 13–23, San Antonio ☎ 318 363 9742; map p.256. Chilled-out locals' bar on the edge of San Antonio that morphs into trendy dance club (hip-hop, house, electronica) at the weekends. Cover charge.

★ **Bogotá Beer Co** C 3 Oeste No. 3A–49, El Peñón ☎ 2 345 0453, ⓦ instagram.com/bogotabeercompany; map p.256. Colombia's leading micro-brewer has opened an outpost in Cali, a spacious beer hall with all the best pours on tap plus snacks and burgers. Shows most of the big European football matches.

★ **La Topa Toloandra** C 5 No. 13–27, San Antonio ☎ 323 597 2646, ⓦ facebook.com/Latopabar; map p.256. Happening salsa club with a convenient location that welcomes dancers of all skill levels – everyone is friendly and it's easy to find a (more skilful) dance partner. Wednesday is an especially popular night.

AVENIDA 6N AND AROUND
Brisas de la Sexta Av 6N No. 15N–94 ☎ 314 515 2764, ⓦ facebook.com/brisascafebar; map p.256. Popular café, bar and club on the main strip, with a second-floor veranda, big dancefloor and a vast menu of neon-coloured cocktails.

El Viejo Barril Av 6N No. 15–14 ☎ 316 407 1898, ⓦ elviejobarril.blogspot.com; map p.256. Classic Colombian salsa bar, with a no-frills dimly lit interior, open sides and street seating.

★ **Zaperoco Bar** Av 5N No. 16–46 ☎ 2 661 2040, ⓦ facebook.com/zaperocobar; map p.256. Known as one of the best salsa bars in Cali. *Salseros* flock here to dance the night away (look for the two giant cacti outside); the vintage interior adorned with photos of salsa legends and Cuban flags adds to the distinctive atmosphere.

GRANADA AND NORTHERN CALI
La Disco Cali Av 9N No. 15–39 ☎ 316 873 8176; map p.256. The best salsa and dance club in Granada, with its celebrated sunroof adding a starry element and DJs spinning a wide range of salsa classics. Cover charge.

Guapa C 28N No. 2bis–97 ☎ 2 653 5389; map p.256. There's rock, pop and electronica at this large, rowdy disco, but the live bands, who usually blast out salsa, are the biggest draw. Cover charge.

Martyn's Av 6AN No. 24N–22 ☎ 2 667 3296; map p.256. Popular – and straightforward, non-salsa – rock'n'roll bar in an ornate building, around since 1983. Cash only.

JUANCHITO
★ **Changó** Km 3 Vía a Cavas ☎ 311 734 0088; map p.256. Legendary club named after the African god of virility and leisure, overlooking the Río Cauca at the entrance to Juanchito. Skilled salsa dancers regularly fill its two dancefloors, and so the clientele are less forgiving of gringos with two left feet than at some other places.

MENGA
Favela Club Cra 32 No. 10–59 ☎ 310 547 2957; map p.256. One of the current trendsetters in Menga, with elaborate stage shows, resident DJs and a decent sound system.

SOUTHERN CALI
★ **Foxland Bar** C 5 No. 1–26, San Fernando ☎ 300 894 3977; map p.256. Unpretentious salsa and sports bar, with regular happy hours and a decent enough food menu.

ENTERTAINMENT

Casa Proartes Cra 5N No. 7–02 ⓦproartescali.com. Movie theatre, art gallery and concert venue in the heart of the old city (the building was once the Conservatorio de Música).
Teatro Jorge Isaacs C 12 at Cra 3 ☎ 2 880 9027, ⓦfacebook.com/teatrojorgeisaacs. This grand French Neoclassical confection opened in 1931 and still hosts a varied programme, from ballet and salsa concerts to stand-up comedy and magic festivals. Prices vary according to event.
Teatro Municipal Cra 5N No. 6–64 ⓦcali.gov.co/teatromunicipal. Gorgeous venue opened in 1927, with a dynamic programme of musical and theatrical performances.

SHOPPING

Centenario Centro Comercial Av 4N No. 7N–46 ⓦcentenariocc.com; map p.256. Cheap cafés at ground level and a third-floor food court, a big screen that shows sports (including European football), Citibank ATMs, pharmacies and a cinema.
Centro Comercial Chipichape C 38N No. 6N–35 ⓦchipichape.com.co; map p.256. Huge mall with more than three hundred shops, a food court, banks, cinemas and a casino. Joyería Carmenza Yanguas de Linares is a dependable dealer in Colombian emeralds here.
Librería Nacional Cra 5 No. 11–50, Plaza de Caycedo ⓦlibrerianacional.com; map p.256. Bookshop selling some international magazines and a small selection of English-language books, including most of the Márquez oeuvre. There's a café inside, too (see page 262).

DIRECTORY

Banks and exchange It's easy to find banks and ATMs in Cali. Banco de Bogotá has a branch right on Plaza de Caycedo and Citibank has several branches in the city, all with ATMs that work with international cards: at C11 No. 3–50, just off Plaza de Caycedo (ATMs 24hr), and in Chipichape mall.
Couriers Deprisa, C 9 No. 4–55, local No. 101 (☎800 051 9393); DHL, Cra 5 No. 10–17 (☎2 486 0037); FedEx, C 13 No. 65C–34 (☎800 011 0339).
Festivals La Feria de Cali (ⓦferiadecali.com.co) has been celebrated from Dec 25 to 30 since 1957, with an opening *cabalgata* (parade of horseback riders), salsa concerts, bullfights, parades and cultural exhibitions. The Festival de Música del Pacífico Petronio Álvarez is usually held in Sept (ⓦpetronio.cali.gov.co), as is the Festival Mundial de la Salsa, with live salsa bands, street parties and free lessons all over the city.
Football Cali's two fanatically supported football teams are Deportivo Cali (ⓦdeportivocali.co) in Primera A, which plays at the Estadio Deportivo Cali (near the town of Palmira, north of Cali), and América de Cali (ⓦamericadecali.co) also in Primera A, which plays at the Estadio Olímpico Pascual Guerrero (near Estadio MIO station). The fiery matches between them are known as the "Clásico Vallecaucano".
Health Clínica de Occidente, C 18N No. 5–34 (☎2 660 3000).
Internet access Cali offers free wi-fi access in several spots across the city – look for "Zona Wi-Fi" signs. There are still plenty of internet cafés around: Internet Llamadas is near Plaza de Caycedo (C 12 No. 3–46).
Laundry Lavandería Premier, C 5N No. 1N–26 (☎2 524 2447); and Lavandería Classic, Av Colombia No. 1A–50 (☎2 892 7449) and Av 9N No. 17N–14 (ⓦclassiclavanderia.com).
Left luggage There's a left luggage office at the outside (west) of the Terminal de Cali bus station, level 1 (24hr; charge per 12hr).
Police Emergencies ☎112; Cali Police (Policía Metropolitana de Cali; ⓦwww.policia.gov.co) have posts at the bus terminal (☎2 661 3850), and throughout the city.
Post office Cra 3 No. 10–49 (☎2 881 3327).
Visa extensions Centro Facilitador de Servicios Migratorios, Av 3N No. 50N–20 (☎2 397 3510).

Pance and Parque Nacional Natural Farallones

Just a short drive west of Cali, the **Río Pance** tumbles out of the Farallones de Cali mountains through a series of waterfalls, gentler cascades and natural pools, surrounded by lush forests, bamboo groves, blossoms and lemon trees. The whole area is a popular trip for Caleños on Sundays, when thousands flock here to enjoy a cool swim, refreshing beer and *sancocho*, a savoury chicken stew with plantains, potato and yucca. On weekdays not much is open, but you'll probably have the valley to yourself.

"Pance" tends to be used as an umbrella term for the whole valley, though the village of **Pance** proper lies at the end of the road, on the edge of the pristine Parque Nacional Natural Farallones. The higher you get, the more scenic and wild it becomes – you can take the bus up and walk down, stopping at various pools, restaurants and private parks or "clubs" along the way, though there are plenty of raw, undeveloped stretches of river to enjoy. When the mist comes down – more likely in the rainy seasons – you'll really feel like it's another world.

Ecoparque Río Pance
Vía Pance • Free (parking charge) • 2 555 0717 • Buses stop at all four entrances

The first major stop along the valley, some 7km from Universidades MIO station, is **Ecoparque Río Pance**, a family-friendly reserve with four main entrances (*entradas*) along the road, connected by a 4km trail and paths along the riverbank. It's a pleasant spot to enjoy the river, lined with trees and bamboo groves alive with birds and butterflies, though the scenery is more enticing further up the valley.

La Vorágine
The mountain village of **LA VORÁGINE** (pronounced "la bora-henay"), another kilometre on from the Ecoparque and where most buses terminate, is packed with restaurants and bars that can get quite lively on Sundays. At the top end of the village the **Centro Recreacional Los Arrayanes** (charge; losarrayanesrecreacional.com) is a family-friendly water park – much more fun during the week when it's often empty.

La Chorrera del Indio
Vía Pance • Charge (cabins available $$$) • 2 312 6993

Around 3.5km beyond La Vorágine, **La Chorrera del Indio** is an enticing target with natural pools along the river, a photogenic 35m waterfall and plenty to eat and drink on site. It's around half a kilometre before the small village of **SAN FRANCISCO**, where locals have built numerous (and precarious looking) footbridges over the torrent.

Pance
Some 2.5km on from La Chorrera, the road splits at a bridge over the river: the left fork goes to Topacio (see below), while the right fork continues for another kilometre to **PANCE** ("Pueblito Pance"), a pleasantly cool mountain village with a handful of places to eat and stay. This is the end of the line for buses, but hikers can continue on towards El Pato (for the park-like **Reserva Natural Anahuac**; entry and camping charges; reservanaturalanahuac.com) or to La Castellana.

Parque Nacional Natural Farallones – Sector El Topacio
From the left fork at the bridge (see above), a bumpy track runs for around 2.5km into the **Parque Nacional Natural Farallones** at the **Sector El Topacio** (around 1700m above sea level). The scenery is much wilder up here, with dense forest, swirls of mist, chirping birds and the constant swish of running water. You'll come to the **Centro de Educación Ambiental**, not a centre as such, but more an area, beginning with a guard post and bamboo huts overlooking a very picturesque pond and bamboo grove – rangers here can guide you to the waterfalls. The nearest attraction is the **Cascada Topacio**, an entrancing flume of water plunging some 130m into the forest, though the hike up **Pico de Loro** (2832m) is a real highlight – the climb takes around three hours up and the views on a clear day are well worth the effort. Though the views are equally spectacular, scaling **Pico Pance** (4100m) is a different proposition entirely, taking around four days to hike. Both peaks can only be tackled with an authorized group or guide (see page 261).

ARRIVAL AND DEPARTURE   **PANCE**

By car The Pance valley is accessible by just one road, which begins as Cra 122 at Av Cañasgordas in the south of Cali (Ciudad Jardín), 3km from the Universidades MIO station. From here it's another 13km up the mountain to Pance village (beyond La Vorágine the road is an unsurfaced track). **By bus** Minibuses (*busetas*) depart the roundabout to the west of Terminal de Cali bus station (on Av 3N, through the tunnel from the bus terminal) daily, though more frequently on Sundays (one-way 1hr 30min). The bus should say "Recreativos" on the front; most just go as far as La Vorágine, so get on a bus with a "Pueblo Pance" sign to go all the way to the top. You can pick up the same buses near the Universidades MIO station. MIO feeder bus #A14B also runs up to La Vorágine from Universidades MIO station.

By taxi Taxis are available from the Terminal de Cali bus and from the Universidades MIO station.

ACCOMMODATION AND EATING

Árbol de Cerezo Vía El Pato (just beyond Pance) • 2 556 4634. The "Cherry Tree" restaurant (it's also a hotel) specializes in paella and local trout – the main dish is presented in numerous ways. Cash only. $

La Fonda Pance Vía Pance (200m before Topacio turn-off) • 2 558 1818. Restored historic hacienda with a selection of small, simple doubles (some with shared bathrooms), cosy dorms and space for camping. There's a laundry, jacuzzi and a small pool. English spoken. $

Hostería El Manantial Km 6.4 from La Vorágine • 2 558 1905. Beautiful property on the river, with simple, comfy doubles and dorm rooms, hot water, restaurant, pool table, access to natural pools, TV and free wi-fi. $

Rancho Super Cheers On the Topacio road • super cheers.wixsite.com/supercheerspance. Bucolic camping spot high in the mountains, just below the national park, with friendly dogs running around and meals provided if required (for an extra daily fee). $

Hacienda El Paraíso

Vía Santa Elena–El Pomo (36km northeast of Cali) • Charge • inciva.gov.co • Get here on a tour (see page 261) or take a taxi (see page 267)

Beautifully restored and wonderfully evocative of nineteenth-century plantation life, most Colombians know the **Hacienda El Paraíso** as the setting for beloved romantic novel *María* by **Jorge Isaacs**, adapted into TV series and movies many times. The plantation house with its surrounding canals and gardens is loaded with historic character and rustic charm, but you'll get the most out of a visit if you've read the novel (or seen the film) and understand Spanish – nothing is labelled in English and guides only speak Spanish.

The hacienda was built between 1816 and 1828 by Víctor Cabal, a former Cali mayor, and was purchased by Isaacs's father in 1854. Today the rooms inside the house have been designed to resemble the (fictional) novel (Efraín's room, María's room and so on), albeit with genuine period details.

Museo de la Caña de Azúcar

Hacienda Piédechinche (42km northeast of Cali) • Guided tours (45min) every 30min • Charge • museocanadeazucar.com • Get here on a tour (see page 261) or take a taxi

Similar to the Hacienda El Paraíso (and best visited on the same trip), tranquil Hacienda Piédechinche dates back to 1715 and now serves as the **Museo de la Caña de Azúcar**, monument to the immensely lucrative sugarcane industry that still dominates

> ### PARQUE FARALLONES PERMITS
>
> To visit **El Topacio** you must officially get a **permit** (charge) from the Corporación Autónoma Regional del Valle del Cauca (CVC) headquarters in Cali, Cra 56 No. 11–36, about 1km east of the Plaza de Toros MIO station (cvc.gov.co). Your hostel or hotel can help, but at weekends if you arrive early (6–8am), you'll probably be allowed to hike without a permit (but if the quota has been met you will be turned away).
>
> You are officially not allowed to **camp** inside the park, but hiking is allowed from the Sector El Topacio access point (see page 265). The latest rules allow for only fifty people a day to climb Pico de Loro (237/day in the rest of the park), with climbers obliged to depart before 8am and to go with a guide. PicoLoro Ecotourism (picoloro.co) arranges excellent guided hikes up the mountain for a fee (including van ride to the entrance from Panadería Dulce Adicción, Cra 105 No. 15A–45 in Cali).

> **THE TRAGEDY OF MARÍA**
>
> **Jorge Isaacs** (1837–1895) wrote just one novel, but *María* (published in 1867) is regarded as one of the finest examples ever of Latin American romantic writing. Much of the story was autobiographical, set at the Hacienda El Paraíso (see page 266), with María herself based on a cousin of the author. The plot is a fairly straightforward romantic tragedy – María and her cousin Efraín fall in love, but are kept apart by family and duty. First, Efraín is sent to Bogotá for six years to study; when he returns the couple manage to live together for just three months before Efraín is forced to go to London to study medicine. By the time he returns two years later María has died of illness, leaving a hapless Efraín brokenhearted.

the Valle del Cauca. As at El Paraíso, you'll need to speak Spanish to make the most of this, though most of the outdoor exhibits (nineteenth-century sugar-making apparatus), the main Casa Colonial (restored in period style) and the gorgeous grounds can be appreciated without explanation. All visits are conducted by guided tour.

ARRIVAL AND DEPARTURE: THE HACIENDAS

By tour or taxi Most people visit both haciendas from Cali by car, on a tour (see page 261), or by booking with a Cali taxi firm.

By minibus and taxi Cheaper than a tour or taxi is taking a minibus from Cali's bus terminal towards Cerrito or Amaime and ask to get off at "la parada Crucero del Placer" (or "el puente peatonal del Placer" after the footbridge over the road); here taxis will be waiting to take you there and back (17km to Paraíso and 8km to Piédechinche). If you arrive in the morning taxis will usually be here, but you can also call one of the drivers in advance to make sure (Spanish only): try Nelson Martínez (☎ 311 647 8686), Mauricio Reyes (☎ 313 612 7093) or Segundo (☎ 311 612 4822).

Buga

Sweltering in the heart of the Valle del Cauca some 70km north of Cali, surrounded by shimmering fields of maize and sugarcane, **BUGA** is a small colonial gem, where wandering shoe-shiners and horse carts share space with modern boutiques and fast-food joints, mobile phones and pilgrims. Thanks to the miracle-granting **Señor de los Milagros** the town is a celebrated religious site in Colombia, though backpackers tend to be more impressed by the exceptional **microbrewery** here, one of the nation's finest.

Basílica Menor del Señor de los Milagros

Cra 14 No. 3–62, at C 4 • Free • ⓦ milagrosodebuga.com

The rose-tinted, twin-towered **Basílica Menor del Señor de los Milagros** is a massive Neo-Romanesque pile, always humming with visitors and with an atmosphere interior more akin to a low-grade carnival than a religious site – be prepared for flashing lights and loud, inspirational music. Built between 1892 and 1907, the church replaced a much older shrine, versions of which have stood here since 1573. The cavernous interior is relatively plain (other than the exquisitely painted cupola), the focus completely on the revered image of **El Señor de los Milagros** – Christ on a silver cross – above and behind the altar. You can join the lines of faithful to walk up to *al camarín* (the special chapel that contains it) to get a closer look (enter left of the altar). The venerated image is said to have been discovered in the river by an Indigenous woman in the sixteenth century, and has been healing the sick and performing miracles ever since.

Museo del Señor de los Milagros

Cra 14 No. 3–37 • Free • ☎ 2 228 2823

Just across the street from the Basílica, the small **Museo del Señor de los Milagros** adds some context to the religious site, though you'll need to read Spanish to make the most of it. Most of the exhibits comprise holy relics and memorabilia associated with the statue and the church, while votive plaques on the wall give thanks to El Señor de los Milagros. Check out also the 18m **Torre de la Ermita Vieja** on the street outside, completed in 1830 and the only remaining section of the old church (which was demolished in 1918).

Catedral de San Pedro Apóstol
C 6 No. 14–41, at Cra 15 (Parque José María Cabal) • ☏ 2 227 7532

Overlooking the lush main plaza, **Parque José María Cabal**, the **Catedral de San Pedro Apóstol** is a complete contrast to the Basílica, a humble colonial relic of low-slung adobe (mud brick) and timber beams with a cool, quiet interior. Most of what you see today dates back to a massive reconstruction in the 1770s.

Monumento a Alejandro Cabal Pombo
C 1A, at Cra 15 • Charge

South of the Basílica on the banks of the Río Guadalajara, the **Monumento a Alejandro Cabal Pombo** (aka "El Faro") is an incongruous, slim tower that looks vaguely Art Deco (it's not really a lighthouse), offering a wonderfully scenic panorama over the red roofs of the town, its churches, the Basílica and the whole Valle del Cauca – it's a short but strenuous climb up 134 steps. The tower was built in 1954 in honour of Dr Alejandro Cabal Pombo, who was instrumental in getting the highway across the mountains to Buenaventura completed a few years before.

ARRIVAL AND INFORMATION BUGA

By bus Terminal Guadalajara de Buga is located just off the Cali highway on the western edge of town. It's a 15min walk straight down C 4 to the Basílica from here – otherwise taxis and local *busetas* are an option. Numerous companies compete on the minivan/minibus route to Cali (62km "via Rozo") – recommended operators include Líneas de la Fe (⊛ lineasdelosandes.com.co) and Expreso Palmira (⊛ expresopalmira.com.co). For Lago Calima and Darién your only option is TransCalima (⊛ transportescalima.com).

Destinations Armenia (hourly; 2hr 30min); Bogotá (6 daily; 7–8hr); Buenaventura (hourly 5am–6pm; 2hr 30min); Cali (every 15min; 1hr); Darién/Lago Calima (every 30min; 1hr); Medellín (6 daily; 7–8hr).

Tourist information The information booth on Plazoleta Lourdes in front of the Basílica (on C 4; Thurs–Sat 8am–5pm) has maps and leaflets, but rarely English speakers.

Services There's a Banco Popular ATM near the information booth.

ACCOMMODATION AND EATING

El Arriero Paisa #2 C 4 No. 16–61 ☏ 315 682 1094. Restaurant serving a wide range of Colombian staples; it is best known for its quirky bamboo furniture and decor, and the graffiti on the walls. $

★ **Buga Hostel** Cra 13 No. 4–83, at C 5 ☏ 2 236 7752, ⊛ facebook.com/brew.hostel. The best budget option in town, with English-speaking owners and a microbrewery on site (see page 267). Spacious dorms, doubles – some with private bathroom, and one private twin with a shared bathroom and a balcony overlooking the street. Shared kitchen and roof-top terrace and coffee. Breakfast, laundry and bike rental available. $

★ **Holy Water Ale Café** Cra 13 No. 4–83 ☏ 2 236 7752, ⊛ facebook.com/brew.hostel. *Buga Hostel*'s on-site restaurant and bar makes its own tasty microbrews (under the title The Water Blessing Co), bread, sandwiches, pizzas and pastas, and is also great for espresso, wine and desserts – the balcony is a perfect place to relax. $

Hotel Casa Escobar C 7 No. 11–72 ⊛ hotelcasaescobar.com. Lovely historical building from 1900, with its Republican architecture carefully restored and simple modern rooms tastefully decorated with contemporary art and Spanish-style tiled floors. Breakfast included. $$

Jazz Hostal Real C 6 No. 9–43 ☏ 300 279 0576. Small, friendly hostel in the centre (behind a café/bar/disco), with bright dorms and simple en-suite doubles (with TVs) set around a quiet colonial patio. Breakfast is extra. $

Lago Calima and Darién

One of the largest artificial lakes in the country (it's actually a reservoir constructed in the early 1960s, some 13km long and 1.5km wide), **Lago Calima** has become a wildly popular weekend destination for Caleños. Though the location is pleasant, surrounded by mountains, and the heat tempered somewhat by the afternoon breezes, it's not

KITESURFING AND BOATING CALIMA

The main reason to come to Lago Calima is to get on the water, and that means boating, windsurfing and especially **kitesurfing** – the conditions are perfect and prices reasonable. Getting around can be tricky without your own transport, but the operators below will be able to help with accommodation and pick-ups.

Barco Bonba Muelle Puerto Plata (next to Comfandi) ☎ 315 555 4745. Daily boat rides (45min–1hr30min) around the lake.

★ **Calima Kitesurf School** Next to Hotel Los Veleros ⓦ calimakitesurf.com. Kitesurfing lessons (1hr or five-day package available, with accommodation and lessons in English). Also offers budget cabañas (dorms), with breakfast included. Dorms $, doubles $$

Calima Windsurf Club ⓦ calimawindsurfclub.com. Windsurfing and kitesurfing lessons, jet skiing and horseriding. Camping charged per person. $

El Centro Recreativo Comfandi El Lago ⓦ comfandi.com.co. Built like a Swiss village at the western end of the lake, this is a plush kitesurfing base. Rooms include breakfast and entry to the adjacent Centro Recreativo water park; lessons and rentals are extra. $$

Entrada No.5 2km from Darién. Base for all manner of watersports, including various boat rides via Calimarina (☎ 2 253 3943) and paratrike or paragliding with certified pilots from Destino Aventuras (☎ 315 488 0668).

---

especially scenic (the best views are from the south side) and the main reason to visit is the array of watersports on offer, especially **kitesurfing** – the lake boasts some of the best conditions in the world for the sport.

The main hub is **DARIÉN**, a small but surprisingly busy little town above the lake on its northern side. Other than the small museum and shady Plaza Principal, surrounded by a mishmash of bright colonial houses with balconies and a plain church, the Nuestra Señora del Perpetuo Socorro, there's not much to see. Most of the waterside action takes place along the northern shore several kilometres to the west, towards the dam at the far end of the lake, beginning with **Entrada No. 5**, a watersports hub 2km from Darién.

Museo Arqueológico Calima
C 10 No. 12–50 • Charge • ☎ 2 253 3496 • The museum lies in the upper section of town – walk up C 10 (next to the church) until you see it on the left

The only attraction in Darién itself is the **Museo Arqueológico Calima**, a tiny museum dedicated to pre-Hispanic Calima cultures such as the Ilama, Yotoco and Sonso. Though the collection – mainly ceramics, anthropomorphic jars and funerary urns, labelled in Spanish only – will primarily appeal to aficionados, the gardens around the museum are beautifully maintained, studded with blossoming bird-of-paradise flowers.

ARRIVAL AND INFORMATION   LAGO CALIMA AND DARIÉN

By bus Lago Calima lies just 42km west of Buga, and around 100km north of Cali – the new Buga–Buenaventura highway winds high above the southern shore, but most of the action, and the main town of Darién, is on the north side, connected to the highway by a winding, narrow loop road. Buses go to Darién "via Jiguales" on the east side (the fastest route), or "via Lago" on the longer western route – these latter buses pass all the main resorts and surf schools. Getting to the lake from Darién means negotiating a rate with one of the local jeep "taxi" drivers (expensive), *mototaxis* (cheaper) or catching the "via Lago" buses.

Destinations TransCalima (ⓦ transportescalima.com) operates minibuses between Darién and Cali (every 30min; 2hr) and Buga (every 30min; 1hr 30min).

Information The folks at Calimadarien.com (ⓦ calimadarien.com) have an office on Cra 7, a couple of blocks west of the plaza with basic maps and information.

ACCOMMODATION AND EATING

When it comes to staying the night the best accommodation options in the area tend to be tied to **kitesurfing packages** (see page 269). Darién features the usual array of cheap **canteens** serving Colombian staples, though the better restaurants are beyond the town along the lake road, only accessible by car or taxi.

Al Carbón C 8A, at Cra 7A (a few blocks west of the plaza in Darién). This popular local grill is a no-frills kitchen in an old colonial-style house, knocking out steaks, stews and cold beers. $$

★ **Mesón llama** On the lake road west of Darién w mesonilama.com. Local and international cuisine (lake trout, tilapia, chicken stew, pizzas, etc), plus its own ice cream shop. Dining $$, accommodation $

Pirata de los Vientos Calima Windsurf Club (opposite Condominio Mónaco) t 311 757 4120. Excellent Argentine steakhouse, with sizzling slabs of meat accompanied by *chimichurri* and red wine. $$

Popayán and around

The capital of the Cauca region and one of the most tantalizing cities in Colombia, **POPAYÁN** boasts a historic core of handsome streets flanked by colonial terraces, exquisite Baroque churches and grand, whitewashed mansions – it's nicknamed the "Ciudad Blanca" for good reason. The city remains remarkably undeveloped, with only a trickle of visitors and few concessions to tourism. Indeed, Popayán is very much a working place, with its historic properties interlaced with government offices, small businesses and the faculties of the Universidad del Cauca. Though it's worth spending a couple of days soaking up the architectural charms and museums, Popayán also makes an excellent base from which to explore the surrounding terrain of the Valle de Pubenza (aka the Upper Cauca Valley) – the market at **Silvia**, the **Puracé volcano** and the thermal springs at **Coconuco**.

Brief history

Founded in 1537 by **Sebastián de Belalcázar** (see page 339) on his march northwards from Quito, the "White City" was a powerful counterweight to Bogotá's dominance during the colonial era and a bastion of Spanish loyalty during the wars of independence. For most of the Spanish period the city was under the jurisdiction of the Real Audiencia de Quito (now in Ecuador), and Quiteño-style art had a major influence on its churches and mansions. Since **independence** Popayán's aristocrats have remained very active in politics, and no fewer than fifteen presidents have emerged from their ranks.

Earthquakes ravaged the city in 1564 and again in 1736; in 1983, when another disastrous tremor destroyed most of the historic centre, collapsing the cathedral's roof onto the worshippers just before the Maundy Thursday celebrations, residents banded together to rebuild over the subsequent decade.

Catedral Basílica de Nuestra Señora de la Asunción de Popayán

Parque Caldas (C 5 No. 6–71) • Free • t 2 823 0340

The town's leafy main square, **Parque Caldas**, is an elegant, rather austere place, anchored by a modest statue of independence hero Francisco José de Caldas, added in 1910. The plaza is overlooked by the **Catedral Basílica de Nuestra Señora de la Asunción de Popayán**, dedicated to the city's patron saint (another incarnation of the Virgin Mary). Architecturally it's the least important church in town, however, built between 1856 and 1906 on the site where two earlier structures stood – the interior is rather bare and modern compared to other city churches. Pope John Paul II visited the cathedral in 1986 – several photos of the pontiff decorate the interior, while a modern sculpture of Christ adorns the altar. Next to the cathedral, the **Torre del Reloj** (clocktower) is a local landmark built between 1673 and 1682 and dubbed the "*Nariz de Popayán*" ("nose of Popayán") by local poet Guillermo Valencia (see page 272).

Iglesia de San Francisco

C 4 No. 9–32, at Cra 9 • Free • t 2 824 0160

The largest colonial church in the city, the late eighteenth-century **Iglesia de San Francisco** is a dazzling Baroque edifice, with a delicate, pale yellow facade artfully

ACCOMMODATION		EATING				DRINKING & NIGHTLIFE	
Hostel Caracol	6	Capriccio	10	Oromo	5	Bar La Iguana	2
Hostel El Jardín	3	Caracol Café	9	Pita	8	Bogotá Beer Co	1
Hotel Camino Real	7	Doña Chepa	1	Restaurante Pizzeria Italiano	3	El Sotareño	6
Hotel Lili'	5	La Cosecha Parrillada	4	Restaurante Vegetariano Maná	11	La Tarima Café Rock	4
Hotel La Plazuela	4	La Tienda de Carmelita	6	Tequila's	7	Restaurante Bar Buffalo Rock & Food	5
Hotel Los Balcones	2	Mora Castilla	2			Wipala	3
Hotel Villa Blanca	1						

restored after the 1983 earthquake. The main highlights inside are the intricately carved Plateresque-style pulpit, the high altar and painted wood side-altars, but for a more ghoulish experience ask the security guard on the right side of the church to take you up to the roof. Up here, on view, are two preserved nineteenth-century **mummies**, still in their burial clothes – alleged to be German architect Simón Schenher and Italian monk Fran Germán Barbetti, designers of the Puente del Humilladero (see page 272).

Museo Guillermo León Valencia

C 5 No. 9–82 • Free • 2 824 1555

The life of the 21st President of Colombia (from 1962 to 1966) is celebrated at the **Museo Guillermo León Valencia**, former home of the eponymous politician. Guillermo León Valencia Muñoz (1909–71) was the son of local poet Guillermo Valencia (see page 272), and the museum charts his life with displays of photos, portraits, medals and personal effects.

Museo Negret and Museo Iberoamericano de Arte Moderno

C 5 No. 10–23 • Charge • 2 8244546

The elegant former home of Modernist artist **Edgar Negret** (1920–2012), the **Museo Negret** is now a museum set around a flowery courtyard exhibiting his work, from abstract prints to his twisting, layered, painted aluminum sculptures. You can also see old photos, portraits, antique furniture and personal effects of the artist, who was born in Popayán. A modern annexe (Sala MIAP) contains the **Museo Iberoamericano de Arte Moderno**. Here you'll find work owned by Negret, primarily by Colombian, Spanish and Latin American Abstract artists such as Eduardo Chillida, Carlos Rojas, Darío Morales and Beatriz González, though the highlight is an untitled watercolour by **Pablo Picasso**. The house itself was built in the nineteenth century and bought by the Negret family in 1930.

Casa Museo Mosquera

C 3 No. 5–14 • Charge • 2 820 1129

If you're interested in a glimpse of the salon society of the colonial and early independence era, visit the **Casa Museo Mosquera**, the childhood residence of **Tomás Cipriano de Mosquera** (1798–1878), four times Colombia's president. Completed in 1788 for José María Mosquera (Tomás's wealthy father), the single-storey adobe home is arranged around a charming courtyard, with rooms dedicated to the president but also colonial art, much belonging to the Quito school (Arte Quiteño). On a macabre note, Mosquera's heart is kept in an urn in the wall.

Museo Nacional Guillermo Valencia

Av 6 No. 2–36 • 1hr tours every 30min • Free • 2 824 1555

The former home of beloved Colombian poet **Guillermo Valencia Castillo** (1873–1943), father of Guillermo León Valencia (see page 271), the **Museo Nacional Guillermo Valencia** has been preserved, shrine-like, as memorial to the great man. Guided tours (Spanish only) take you through the elegant rooms of his impressive, creaky-floored mansion, filled with antique furniture, ornately carved beds, aged photos, portraits, letters and various honours received. The Valencia family tomb is at the back of the house, with his most famous poem, *Josephina*, engraved on the mausoleum walls (dedicated to his wife, Josefina Muñoz). The house actually belonged to Josefina: built at the end of the eighteenth century, it was later purchased by her father and occupied by the poet and his wife from 1908 to 1943.

Puente del Humilladero

Cra 6, at C 2

Completed in 1873, the **Puente del Humilladero** has become one of the symbols of the city, traversing the Río Molino with twelve arches and a span of 180m. Today it's a well-used footbridge, originating at a pleasant garden and plaza where craft stalls set up during the day.

Iglesia de Santo Domingo

C 4 No. 4–15, at Cra 5 • Free • 2 824 0533

Largely rebuilt after the devastating earthquake of 1736, the **Iglesia de Santo Domingo** still feels like a much older, colonial church, with its rose stone floor, red-brick arches, timber beams, lavishly carved pulpit and gilded wood altars. Its Baroque stone portal is an especially good example of Spanish New World architecture.

Museo de Arte Religioso

C 4 No. 4–56 • Charge • 2 824 2759

To gain some insight into the significance of Popayán over the centuries visit the **Museo de Arte Religioso**, a showcase for religious art from the seventeenth to nineteenth centuries and set in a grand mansion that once served as the home for the wealthy

Arboleda family. The quality of work is much higher than the usual offerings in collections like these, beginning with an opulent silver *expositorio* (mobile shrine) and a large statue of Mary as the Inmaculada Apocalipsis carved in 1788. Upstairs rooms are dedicated to the Quito school, featuring its signature vivid colouring, including the work of Bernardo de Legarda (his intricate sculpture of the *Virgen del Apocalipsis*) and Manuel Chili "Caspicara". A whole room is dedicated to the dark, crimson-tinted vision of the *Last Supper* (1782) by Bernardo Rodríguez, while other galleries contain work from the José Cortez de Alcoser brothers and even some Italian religious art from the eighteenth century attributed to Giovanni Battista Piazzetta and Marco Alvise Pitteri. Labelling is in Spanish only.

Iglesia de La Ermita
C 5 and Cra 2 • Free

The city's oldest standing church, dating from the late sixteenth or early seventeenth century and perched romantically at the eastern end of Calle 5, **Iglesia de la Ermita** features a simple single-naved chapel comprised of wooden ribbing and a golden Baroque altar.

Museo de Historia Natural
Cra 2 No. 1A–25 • Charge • 2 820 9800

Aficionados of old-fashioned natural history museums will enjoy the Universidad del Cauca's dusty collections at the **Museo de Historia Natural**. Three floors overflow with taxidermied animal, fish, insect and bird species, most of which are endemic or at least native to Colombia (ignoring the polar bear, obviously), from anteaters and sloths to snakes, condors, parrots and jaguars. Other rooms highlight the minerals and precious stones of Colombia, fossils such as trilobites and dinosaur bones, and archeological remains such as pottery and anthropomorphic images from the Calima, Quimbaya and Tierradentro cultures, as well as artefacts discovered on Cerro de Morro.

Cerro de Morro
Cra 2, at C 7 • Free

For magical views of the old city and the surrounding Andes ranges, climb the **Cerro de Morro** (also known as the Morro del Tulcán), a short but steep hill at the northeastern corner of the centre. Once thought to be a pre-Hispanic pyramid, excavations since the 1950s have proved that it is a natural feature used and developed by Indigenous groups as a sacred ritual site – human bones, pottery and other artefacts have been dug up on its slopes. On top stands an equestrian statue of city founder Sebastián de Belalcázar, inaugurated in 1937.

Rincón Payanés
C 7 • Free

Just beneath Cerro de Morro is **Rincón Payanés** (aka "Pueblito Patojo"), a slightly bizarre set of buildings that are smaller copies of Popayán's most famous landmarks (La Ermita and the Torre de Reloj, for example), serving as a small arts and crafts market (there are local snack stalls here, too).

Capilla de Belén
C 5 (street entrance)

The hilltop chapel of **Capilla de Belén**, accessible via a steep cobbled path from the eastern end of Calle 4, is a tremendous viewpoint across the city, but robberies have been reported here and the climb is best attempted in a group (and not in the evenings at all) – it's often very quiet on top. Founded in 1681, the church was destroyed by an earthquake in 1885 and was rebuilt with donations from the congregation (it was badly damaged by another tremor in 1925).

ARRIVAL AND INFORMATION POPAYÁN

BY PLANE
Tiny Aeropuerto Guillermo León Valencia (Avianca and EasyFly) is a few minutes' walk from the bus terminal on C 4N, north of the centre, with a basic café and little else. Taxis will take you to anywhere in the centre (Sundays and nights at the more expensive rate), but you'll have to walk to the bus terminal to get a local bus.
Destinations Bogotá (3–4 daily; 1hr 20min).

BY BUS
Popayán's Terminal de Transportes is just off the Pan-American Highway, a 20min walk from the historic centre (walk over the footbridge across the Pan-American, and continue straight along Cra 11). There are ATMs, cafés and a police post. Note that although security is much improved, it's best not to travel between Popayán and Pasto/Ipiales/Ecuador overnight.
Taxi and bus to the centre Taxis (Radiotaxis ☎2 823 1111) charge a flat fee to anywhere in the centre, while buses labelled "Centro" (try #3 or #5) should take you to the historic centre (take any bus labelled "Terminal" or "Exito" on the way back).
Bus companies The usual array of companies compete on the busy Cali and Pasto routes (Tax Belalcázar, ⓦtax belalcazar.com, is reliable and fast). Transtimbio runs minibuses to Coconuco daily (6am–4.30pm), while Sotracauca (camionetas 7am & 11.30am; microbus 2.30pm; ⓦsotracauca.com) and Cootranshuila (every 2hr; ⓦcootranshuila.com) run to San Agustín; Sotracauca also runs direct to Tierradentro at 10.30am (the buses at 5am, 8am, 1pm & 3pm drop you 2km short of the village), and La Plata via Puracé national park – nominally at 5am only (to Cruce de la Mina 2hr; to San Juan Termales 2hr 30min). Convenio Silvia runs to Silvia (daily 5am–5pm; you can pay extra for the faster KIA buseta).
Destinations Bogotá (5 daily; 12hr); Cali (every 15min; 2hr 30min–3hr); Coconuco (hourly; 30–40min); Ipiales (hourly; 8hr); Medellín (1 daily, 8pm; 10hr); Pasto (hourly; 6hr; travel during daylight hours); San Agustín (6 daily; 5–6hr); Silvia (every 30min; 1hr 30min); Tierradentro (2–4 daily; 5–6hr).

INFORMATION AND TOURS

Tourist information Your best bet for comprehensive information on the city, tours, and onward travel is Café Caracol at Hostel Caracol (see page 274). The information office operated by the tourist police on Parque Caldas at Cra 7 No. 4–36 (☎2 822 0916) hands out free city maps but little else. The official Oficina de Turismo is at Cra 5 No. 4–68 (☎2 824 2251).
Bike rental Popayán Tours organises cycling trips with the cost of bike rental included in the price.
Walking tours Free walking tours leave from the information office on Parque Caldas, hosted by enthusiastic (bilingual) students and volunteers from "Get Up and Go Colombia" (ⓦfacebook.com/getupandgocolombia).
Popayán Tours In addition to the Coconuco bike ride (see page 275), this outfit has a great range of tours including a Volcan Puracé climb (see page 278) and a scintillating climb/biking Volcan Puracé package (minimum five people), where you climb the volcano then bike down it (54km with a descent of around 3000m, all in day). Ask too about the trip to the more remote Salinas and Pozo Azul hot springs.

ACCOMMODATION

Popayán boasts a good selection of budget options, including several excellent **hostels**, as well as plenty of mid-range and more expensive places, often in colonial **haciendas**. Accommodation is particularly expensive during **Semana Santa**; book well ahead. Note that airbnb (ⓦairbnb.com) and Couchsurfing (ⓦcouchsurfing.org) have a small but growing presence in the city.
★ **Hostel Caracol** C 4 No. 2–21 ⓦcasacaracolcadiz. com; map p.271. Hostel Trail's offshoot is popular with travellers who like a quiet place to retreat to at the end of the day, with three cosy dorms and eight private rooms – six with shared bathrooms, two with private – clustered around a covered courtyard. Free bike rental, plus Caracol Café has all the information you need on the area. Laundry is extra, although there is an express 4hr turnaround. $
Hostel El Jardín C 4 No. 1–60 ☎310 373 3317; map p.271. Cosy, spotless and central hostel with small dorms and modern, bright private rooms (with shared bathroom), a shared kitchen and lounge. $
Hotel Los Balcones Cra 7 No. 2–75 ☎2 824 2030; map p.271. Shabby chic option, with plenty of historic charm – the property was built in 1798 for former president Joaquín Mosquera – but it could do with a renovation. Decent breakfast included. $$
Hotel Camino Real C 5 No. 5–59 ⓦhotelcaminoreal. com.co; map p.271. Converted historic property (which

THE COCONUCO DOWNHILL

The most popular day-trip from Popayán is Popayán Tours' **Coconuco Downhill Cycling trip**, which runs daily with a minimum of two people (charge per person includes transport to the pools, entrance fees, mountain bike rental, helmet and puncture kit; ⓦpopayantours.com). Guests are collected from the centre of Popayán at 10am and driven to Coconuco where they can bathe in the hot thermal springs at Hirviendo (see page 279). You make your own way back to Popayán along 30km of mainly paved, downhill roads from here by bike, with very little traffic – it's an easy, refreshing way to experience the beauty of the Cauca countryside. Most cyclists stop at the venerable *Estadero Don Luis* restaurant to sample the celebrated cheese bread (*almojábana*) and hot chocolate, 2km outside of Popayán (they also cook up local trout and offer delicious blackberry juice).

allegedly dates from 1591) set around a gorgeous colonial courtyard. In a superb central location with comfy rooms, flatscreen cable TV and a hearty home-cooked breakfast included. $\overline{\underline{\$\$}}$

Hotel Lili C 7 No. 7–14 ☏305 335 8543; map p.271. This simple but clean hotel in the center of Popayán has rooms that slighter on the smaller side, however you won't find better when it comes to value for money in this neighborhood. The floral window boxes and cactus displays in the main foyer is a nice touch. $\overline{\underline{\$\$}}$

★ **Hotel La Plazuela** C 5 No. 8–13 ⓦhotellaplazuela.com.co; map p.271. Handsome eighteenth-century colonial mansion with cosy rooms around quiet cobbled courtyards, all with cable TV and small but stylish modern bathrooms. Simple cooked breakfast in the atmospheric restaurant included. Not much English spoken. $\overline{\underline{\$\$}}$

Hotel Villa Blanca C6 No. 0–52 ☏304 345 7070; map p.271. Relatively modern option, with stylish rooms combining modern furnishings with prints from local artists. $\overline{\underline{\$\$}}$

EATING

For self-caterers, there's an enormous **Éxito supermarket** next door to the bus station. On Sundays the historic centre virtually shuts down and the whole town seems to spend the day inside the **Centro Commercial Campanario**, Cra 9 No. 24AN–21 (ⓦcampanariopopayan.com), a lavish shopping mall north of the centre – it contains a large food court, plus a plaza of kiosk-type bars where locals merrily drink away the afternoon and evening.

Capriccio C 5 No. 5–63 ☏2 820 5334; map p.271. Small café with an old-world feel (wooden tables with dried coffee beans under the glass tops), fabulous *granisados* (iced coffee drinks) and cakes. Locally roasted coffee too. $\overline{\$}$

Caracol Café C 4 No. 2–21 ⓦelcaracol.co; map p.271. Grind your own coffee beans on an antique machine at this travellers' hub (part of *Hostel Caracol*, but open to non-guests), where you can peruse information and even get your laundry done (in 4hr). $\overline{\$}$

La Cosecha Parrillada C 4 No. 7-79 ⓦlacoshechaparrillada.com; map p.271. Popular steak joint with sizzling slabs of meat, but also excellent grilled trout and pricey bottles of wine. $\overline{\underline{\$\$}}$

★ **Doña Chepa** C 2 No. 4–46 ☏2 824 0071; map p.271. Small shop in a family home, selling locally celebrated *aplanchados* (crispy wafer cakes) to a recipe created by Josefina Muñoz in the 1930s – pictures of the matriarch adorn the walls. You'll see the cakes sold all over Popayán. $\overline{\$}$

★ **Mora Castilla** C 2 No. 4–44 ⓦmoracastilla.com; map p.271. Gem of a restaurant with two floors serving a range of classic Popayán snacks: *tamal de pipián* (tamale with the local potato, tomato and peanut filling), *patacón con queso* (fried plantain with cheese) and the best *salpicón payanés* in the city (a smoothie of blackberry, lulo and guanabana). $\overline{\underline{\$\$}}$

★ **Oromo** Cra 5 No. 3–34 ☏310 257 1219; map p.271. Excellent café in historic digs, specializing in Colombian small-batch coffee and fascinating ways of preparing it (siphon/vacuum-produce coffee). Excellent espresso and cappuccinos. $\overline{\$}$

Pita Cra 2 No. 3–58 ☏300 662 7867, ⓦfacebook.com/pitartesanal; map p.271. This superb Lebanese joint makes for a pleasant break from typical Colombian restaurants, with a simple menu that involves an array of fresh toppings on toasted pita bread. Board games and magazines add to the laidback ambience. Cash only. $\overline{\$}$

Restaurante Pizzeria Italiano C 4 No. 8–83 ☏2 824 0607; map p.271. A two-floor, Swiss-owned restaurant serving good Italian standards as well as fondues (with real Italian cheese) – try the "steak café de Paris" a 300g slab of meat smothered in a divine garlic butter sauce. $\overline{\underline{\$\$}}$

Restaurante Vegetariano Maná C 7 No. 9–56 ☏320 671 3856; map p.271. Great value and a welcome break from red meat and fried food, with items for lunch and dinner – choose from soups, salads, dishes such as lentil meatballs or curried broccoli and cauliflower, and fresh juices (written on the white board – write down what you want on slips of paper provided). Very popular and very crowded at lunchtime. $\overline{\$}$

Tequila's C 5 No. 9–25 • 2 822 2150; map p.271. A jaunty Tex-Mex café that is not going to win any fine dining awards, but does get a prize for its burritos and *quesadillas*, cheap beer, good cocktails, lively music and very friendly service. $

La Tienda de Carmelita C 5 No. 9–45 • 2 824 4862; map p.271. This is a classic old Popayán canteen best known for its delicious *tamales de pipián*, as well as *salpicón*, *mecato payanés* (bite-sized traditional cakes) and hearty breakfasts. $

DRINKING AND NIGHTLIFE

Bar La Iguana C 4 No. 9–67 • 316 281 0576, W facebook.com/LaIguanaAfroVideoBar; map p.271. This dimly lit salsa bar has a decent cocktail list, a funky, loud salsa soundtrack, a projector screen for showing videos and a mainly student clientele. Gets busy after 10pm at weekends, when couples come to dance.

Bogotá Beer Co Cra 9 No. 14N–1 • 2 824 4835; map p.271. Colombia's leading microbrewer opened a warehouse-like pub here; it's out of the centre on the main highway, 1.7km north of Parque Caldas, but still worth the taxi fare/hike for its array of tasty craft beers.

Restaurante Bar Buffalo Rock & Food C 6 No. 8–87 • 322 567 72248101; map p.271. Quirky rock bar and restaurant with an almost deafening playlist of the classic rock anthems. Popular with students, there's no cover charge.

★ **El Sotareño** C 6 No. 8–05 • 2 808 8571; map p.271. Frozen in time since the 1960s, this old bar is renowned for owner Agustín Sarria's huge vinyl collection of vintage salsa, tango and other Latin music (the man himself is usually working behind the bar). Order a cold beer, bag one of the booths then sit back and listen as the tunes are spun. *El Sotareño* is a classic "bambuco" song composed by Francisco Diago in 1928 (Sotará is a region of Cauca just south of Popayán).

La Tarima Café Rock C 3 No. 4–84 • 312 671 2759; map p.271. Popular student bar that tends to play 1980s and 1990s rock (including Spanish rock), with coffees, beers and cocktails available from early evening.

★ **Wipala** Cra 2 No. 2–38 W wipala.com.co; map p.271. Cool bar and café, set around a lush guayabilla tree (a wild guava used in traditional *hervidos* drinks), with exuberant contemporary art on the walls and hummingbirds fluttering around the sugar feeders. Beers, organic coffee, juices and decent wine served.

DIRECTORY

Banks and exchange Banco de Bogotá has a branch on Parque Caldas, and on C 2 overlooking the Río Molino; Banco de Occidente, Bancolombia and several other banks have branches on Parque Caldas.

Festivals During Easter week the city is cordoned off to make way for thousands of parading worshippers brandishing candles and colourful flowers; Popayán's Semana Santa celebrations are the second largest in the world, after Seville's in Spain. The Congreso Gastronomico food festival (W gastronomico.org.co) is in September.

Health English-speaking doctors practice at the Clínica La Estancia, C 15N No. 2–256 (• 2 823 3950, W laestancia. com.co); otherwise the best public hospital is Hospital Universitario San José (Cra 6 No.10N–142; • 2 823 4508, W hospitalsanjose.gov.co).

Internet access Try La Red at C5 No. 7–11, or the internet café at the bus station.

Laundry Hostel Caracol (see page 274) will do laundry (including for non-guests) for a fee, with a 4hr turnaround.

Post office C4 No. 5–74.

Visa extensions Centro Facilitador de Servicios Migratorios, C 4N No. 10B–66, Barrio Modelo (• 2 839 1051).

Silvia

The rural village of **SILVIA**, 60km northeast of Popayán, is best known for its vibrant Tuesday **market**, when the streets fill up with members of the **Guambiano** Indigenous group from the surrounding villages – the men in blue skirts with fuchsia trim and felt bowler hats, the women with deep blue woollen shawls (taking photos won't make you any friends and might be met with aggression). The market itself focuses on fruit, veg and basic household goods rather than tourist-friendly handicrafts, but the presence of the Guambiano makes it a great opportunity for people-watching. There's not much to see in Silvia the rest of the week, but if the Guambiano have piqued your curiosity you can visit their villages further up the mountain on other days.

Guambía

From Silvia it's possible to rent horses a block from the central plaza (near the *Confrandi Hotel*), and ride up to the village of **GUAMBÍA** (1hr), where your guide will take you to visit Guambiano strawberry, blackberry and trout farms: at the latter it's usual to fish for trout straight out of the pond and have your hosts fry it up for a small charge. Though the "Switzerland" comparison is pushing things a bit, at around 2600m it's pleasantly cool and as the countryside is completely undeveloped it's your best chance to experience genuine Indigenous Cauca culture.

ARRIVAL AND DEPARTURE SILVIA

By bus Buses (every 30min; 1hr 15min) leave for Silvia from Popayán's bus terminal. If coming from Cali, take a Popayán-bound bus to Piendamó (2hr), then grab a bus to Silvia (30min).

Parque Nacional Natural Puracé
58km east of Popayán • Charge; guides extra

The **Parque Nacional Natural Puracé** encompasses 860 square kilometres of awe-inspiring volcanoes, snow-capped Andean mountains, bubbling natural springs, roaring waterfalls, jagged canyons, trout-stuffed lagoons and wind-swept grasslands. In September and October the *páramo* (high tundra) is drizzled with the spectacular yellow blooms of the *frailejón* (espeletia) shrub.

Much of the park lies in a **Kokonuko** Indigenous reserve, home to around 4500 Kokonuko (or Coconuco) people, closely related to the Guambianos (see page 277), but culturally unique, though their language has been lost. In late 2013, a long-standing dispute between the Kokonuko and the government-run park administration resulted in the formal closure of the national park – however, attractions that lie within the reservation are now under the control of the Kokonuko, meaning that visitors no longer have to register with the national parks office. The Kokonuko community also runs the condor viewing and feeding, and provides guides for the climb up the Puracé volcano. The parks administration will tell you the whole park is closed – not true. It is possible to visit independently, but you'll need to be flexible and leave Popayán very early.

Puente Tierra
Travelling by bus from Popayán, get off at the **Cruce de la Mina** (11km beyond the actual village of Puracé on Hwy 24), where the Kokonuko have their park entrance post – they have renamed the entrance area, previously known as Pilimbalá, as **Puente Tierra**. You pay your admission fee here, plus hire a compulsory guide regardless of

> ### THE GUAMBIANO
> One of the southwest's many Indigenous groups, the **Guambiano** (or Misak) share a cultural and linguistic heritage with the Kokonukos and the Nasa (see page 282), though their population is smaller and younger (the average age is a startling 21). Though once thought to have originated in Peru, the Guambiano have worked hard to prove a millennia-long and spiritual connection with their current homeland in the Colombian mountains east of Silvia, based around the origin stories of "Mama Manuela Caramaya", the founding *cacica* or chieftainess of Guambía. Most of their land was lost to Spanish coffee plantations in the nineteenth century, despite the village of Guambía being given *resguardos* (protected territories) status by the Spanish monarchy as far back as 1700. Though the Guambiano participated in the creation of **CRIC** (Consejo Regional Indígena del Cauca) in 1971 (see page 282), they later split from that Nasa-dominated organization and created the **Autoridades Indígenas de Colombia (AICO)** in the 1980s to focus more on their specific needs. Guambiano leader Floro Tunubalá became the governor of Cauca in 2000.
>
> Traditional healers known as *mirbik* still occupy an important place in Guambiano society – you may see them at the market in Silvia – though most Guambiano remain simple hill farmers. There are thought to be around twenty thousand Guambiano today.

where you want to go in the park. The hike up the volcano begins here, but note that your guide won't supply transport to the other attractions – you are reliant on public transport, lifts or (more likely) hiking.

Volcán Puracé

The park's literal high point is **Volcán Puracé** (4650m), which last blew its top in 1956 – this is currently the only active, steaming volcano you can climb in Colombia. It's a lung-straining four-hour climb (7km; allow 3hr to descend) to the steaming crater where, on a clear day, there are eye-popping views of Cadena Volcánica de Los Coconucos – a chain of forty volcanoes. The climb is not technical, but the change in altitude makes it hard going. The volcano can be tackled year-round: though July to August is windy on top it's generally much drier underfoot which makes it good for climbing; October and November are the wettest months, so the lower slopes are very boggy; December and January are the best for clear skies and views. Warm/waterproof clothing and sun protection is essential, and water, food and snacks should be bought in advance as there are no facilities. Note that the last **bus** back to Popayán passes the Cruce de la Mina at 5pm (be there by 4.30pm), but the timetable isn't reliable and hikers often have to hitch a lift on a passing truck.

Condor observation and feeding point
Hwy 24 Km 25

Visits to the popular **condor observation and feeding point**, just under 2km further along Hwy 24 from the Cruce de la Mina, are also managed by the Kokonuko, with **feedings** now taking place daily at 10am (included in your park fee). It can be a spellbinding experience: the condors sometimes swoop down just 2m from the viewing point. In 2002, eleven Andean condors were introduced into the park – sadly only a handful still remain, and it is feared that these are unable to reproduce, perhaps due to farm pesticides – see them while you can.

Termales de San Juan
Hwy 24 Km 37

The rustic natural springs known as the **Termales de San Juan** (12km east of the condors) are about the closest you'll get to untouched Andean beauty in the region, with verdant green mosses and crimson lichens lining the rock walls, mini geysers and boulders in the river stained yellow from the minerals. Note that there is **no swimming** here, as the thermal pools are too toxic, hot and unpredictable. The hot springs are still nominally patrolled by the national park administration, and are officially not open to the public, but if you are with a Kokonuko guide (solo or with Popayán Tours) the park guards will let you in.

ARRIVAL AND TOURS PARQUE NACIONAL NATURAL PURACÉ

By bus At the time of writing only one Sotracauca bus departed Popayán for La Plata daily, passing Cruce de la Mina (2hr; other La Plata buses take a faster route) and other locations along the main national park road (2hr 30min to San Juan Termales). This leaves the bus station at 5am, making it a tough trip to do independently. The bus back to Popayán passes El Cruce between 4.30pm and 5pm.
Tours Popayán Tours (see page 274) offers guided hikes up the volcano with private transport (minimum five people), and can tailor trips to other parts of the park.

Coconuco and the thermal springs

There's little to detain you in the village of **COCONUCO**, 26km from Popayán on the road to San Agustín, but it's a short hop from here to some rudimentary but refreshing outdoor **thermal springs**. It's best to avoid visiting at weekends (especially Sunday), when local families swamp the pools and the local van and *moto* drivers tend to hit the booze. Alternatively, you can check out **Termales Agua Tibias**, 5km southwest of Coconuco.

These springs were closed at one point due to a long-running dispute between the private owners and the local Kokonuko community which turned violent in 2017 after protestors clashed with police outside the springs – a Kokonuko journalist was shot and killed. However, at the time of writing, the springs were open to the public.

Agua Hirviendo
Charge • ☎ 321 800 1383

The Kokonoko-run **Agua Hirviendo**, 4km east of Coconuco on a side road, is less picturesque than Agua Tibias (it's a basic, all-concrete affair) but it's open around the clock (though buses only run till 6pm), its sulphur-reeking pools are far toastier (they also have cold pools and makeshift saunas) and the icy freshwater showers are a refreshing shock to the system. Basic cabins are available for rent and a restaurant serves meals until late (there is no place to lock up valuables, however).

Pozo Azul and Salinas
In recent years more remote springs have opened up beyond Coconuco, notably the pristine bubbling waters at **Pozo Azul** and **Salinas**, where you can bathe in natural hot spring pools. Salinas is accessible by 4WD only (best via Popayan Tours, page 274), from where you can hike up (1hr 30min) to the more remote Pozo Azul, the "blue well", considered sacred by the Kokonuko (who manage both sites).

ARRIVAL AND DEPARTURE	COCONUCO
By bus To get to Agua Hirviendo take the Transtimbio minibus from Popayán bus station to Coconuco (hourly; every 30min at weekends; 45min), from where it's a 4km walk (or pay for a *mototaxi* ride, or a jeep journey one-way)	to the springs (on a side road to the left, just out of the village). **Tours** Popayán Tours' downhill bike trip (see page 275) starts at Hirviendo.

Tierradentro

The mystical, magical underground tombs of **TIERRADENTRO** form part of Colombia's most treasured archeological complex, though they are far less visited than the equally venerated San Agustín. Off-limits for years due to guerrilla activity and poor road links, the site is now safe for tourists and is starting to attract more visitors, primarily backpackers, to its collection of **pre-Hispanic hypogea**, dating back over a thousand years. Tierradentro means "Inner Land", an appropriate name to describe its rugged countryside of steep valleys and saw-toothed peaks in the Central Cordillera. The archeological site is close to the Nasa village of **San Andrés de Pisimbalá**, though the nearest big town is **Inzá**, some 100km northeast of Popayán, high above the Río Ullucos.

Brief history
Tierradentro is best known for its underground **tombs** (or hypogea), some as deep as 9m and reachable by steep, smooth original steps through trapdoors, and often decorated with elaborate geometric iconography – the best-preserved tombs, with zoomorphic and anthropomorphic designs in red and black paint on a white background, are truly dazzling works of art. Monumental statues have also been found here, indicating a cultural influence from San Agustín, though little is known about the tomb-building civilization other than that it flourished around 600–900 AD. The sites were abandoned before the thirteenth century, and modern occupation gradually uncovered the tombs, many of which were opened and looted during the eighteenth and nineteenth centuries. No large population centres have been discovered, lending credence to the belief that the original inhabitants belonged to a dispersed group of loosely related farmers, though the scale of the tombs suggests the existence of a hierarchical social and political structure based on chiefs with priestly functions.

Though the tombs were considered spiritual places by the **Nasa (Páez)** long before being requisitioned for tourism, until quite recently the modern Nasa population, 25,000 of whom live in the surrounding hills (see page 282), denied any physical link to their creators. Today younger (and more politically conscious) Nasa tend to emphasize their common ancestry with ancient Tierradentro and its culture.

Parque Arqueológico Nacional de Tierradentro

Closed first Tues of every month • Charge, ticket good for two days • ⓦ icanh.gov.co • The main entrance and museums are 2km along the road from El Cruce de San Andrés, the junction on the main Popayán–La Plata highway

The **Parque Arqueológico Nacional de Tierradentro** is a protected area spread out over a sublime mountain landscape and comprising five key Tierradentro burial sites. It's possible to visit all **five tomb sites** on a full-day hike that runs in a 14km loop from the museums, with Pisimbalá making a convenient lunch stop. It's best to do the loop anticlockwise, since a clockwise route would mean tackling a long, tough uphill climb first thing. Exploring the park solo has become fairly safe, though it's always better to hike in a group if you intend to cover the entire loop.

Museums

The main park trail begins behind the **Museo Etnográfico** at the main entrance, where you pay the park entry fee and receive a wristband, valid for two days. The well-presented displays in the museum focus on the history and customs of the Indigenous Nasa, while the **Museo Arqueológico** across the road has an archeological display including funerary urns, some statues and information about the park's burial sites. Both museums are worth a stop before you visit the tombs themselves.

Tomb sites

Be sure to bring your own **torch** to explore the **tomb sites**, as some are unlit (the guards at each site who open the tombs for you will answer most questions, in Spanish, but may not have a torch).

Alto de Segovia

The **Alto de Segovia** (1800m; 20min walk uphill from the museums, above the Quebrada de San Andrés) is the most important of the tomb locations. There are 29 pits here and 64 tombs; guards will open the most jaw-dropping examples (T10, T11, T12 and multicoloured T30), most of them illuminated by electric lights. You'll descend into the trapdoors and down large, steep, stone steps to peer into the gloom; incredibly, vivid black, red and white patterns on the walls have survived the centuries.

From Segovia, it's a fifteen-minute stiff hike (600m) up to **Alto del Duende**, a smaller site with thirteen tombs (five open), though with very little colour remaining on the walls.

El Tablón

From Duende it's a 25-minute walk to **El Tablón** (2000m) – where you'll find nine weatherworn stone statues, which look similar to the ones found in San Agustín (see page 283). To get here, follow the path up from Duende to the main road and turn left; El Tablón is signposted (it's hard to spot: look up) on your left ten minutes or so further on. From here to Pisimbalá you can either go back to the main road or descend down the muddy trail that joins the other road into the village from the museums. The best place for lunch on the full Tierradentro loop is *La Portada* in San Andrés de Pisimbalá (see page 283).

Alto de San Andrés

After eating in Pisimbalá you can pick up the trail again along the side of *La Portada*. A ten-minute walk gets you to **Alto de San Andrés** (1850m), its seven open tombs boasting well-preserved wall paintings, including a human face in SA5.

Alto del Aguacate

From San Andrés, it's a good ninety minutes (2km) to the last and most remote site, **Alto del Aguacate**, a ridge with stupefying views over the valleys of the Quebrada San Andrés and Río Ullucos. A total of 62 tombs (42 open, unattended, with a style of tomb painting not found at the other sites) run along a precipitous 250m ridge high above the town (at 2100m), best experienced with your own torch – with rarely another soul in sight, this is a real Indiana Jones moment. Allow plenty of daylight time for the ninety-minute walk back down to the start of the trail, as there have been several robberies along this isolated path.

San Andrés de Pisimbalá

The main village at Tierradentro is tiny **SAN ANDRÉS DE PISIMBALÁ**, 4km from El Cruce de San Andrés (and 2km beyond the park entrance). San Andrés once had a picturesque, seventeenth-century thatched-roof **chapel**, the last of several colonial, thatched churches in the region. Tragically burned to the ground by arsonists in 2013, the chapel may eventually be restored – at the time of research a temporary zinc roof covered the nave. San Andrés is a Nasa (Páez) village, though plenty of Hispanic Colombians live here – you'll get a different interpretation of what happened to the church depending on who you talk to.

La Pirámide

Donation requested • The site is a long walk from Pisimbalá; arrange transport at your accommodation or take a *colectivo* to Inzá and ask to be dropped off

Located on private land, high above the Pisimbalá–Inzá road, **La Pirámide** is a curious, stepped pyramid-shaped peak thought to have been significant to pre-Hispanic cultures, though little research has been done and no one really knows how much of the pillar-like rocks on the summit (like Giant's Causeway in Northern Ireland)

THE NASA (PÁEZ)

Colombia's largest Indigenous group, with over 120,000 members, the **Nasa** (also known as the **Páez**, a hispanicization of the name of a Nasa chief at the time of the Spanish conquest) are scattered across the Central Cordillera and Cordillera Occidental of the southwest, dominating the region around Tierradentro and the Páez river basin. Most Nasa still speak their own language, Nasa Yuwe, which is even taught in schools, and shamans known as "thê' wala" remain figures of authority in the community (most Nasa also practice some form of Evangelical or Pentecostal Protestantism, rather than Catholicism). Given their size, it's no surprise that the Nasa have also taken a lead in fighting for Indigenous rights in Colombia. Peasant leagues inspired by Communism were active here in the 1930s and 1940s, and La Violencia (1948–58) was especially bloody in Tierradentro. The Nasa heartland has remained fertile ground for FARC recruitment until relatively recently, though this is a very touchy subject – most Indigenous people are working hard to change the perception that there is a link between the two, and in 1974 the Movimiento Armado Quintín Lame (MAQL) was created to defend Indigenous communities against all violent groups (they demobilized in 1991). In 1971 CRIC (Consejo Regional Indígena del Cauca) was established to represent all Indigenous people in Cauca but in practice has been dominated by the Nasa. Since 1999 Nasa activists have resorted to blocking the Pan-American Highway several times in what's known as a "*paro*" (literally a "block"): a protest against lack of government services but also the *promesas incumplidas* (broken promises) of the Colombian state – as tourism picks up in the region, this is also likely to become a point of contention. Some believe the church in Tierradentro (see page 279) was burned down as protest against Hispanic Colombians making too much money out of tourists in what is essentially the Nasa homeland.

THE 1994 EARTHQUAKE

The Nasas' biggest tragedy of modern times was the 1994 **Páez river earthquake**, which caused a mudslide that destroyed the small town of Páez and several villages, killing an estimated 1100 people and leading to a small migration from the region. In response, the government created the **Corporación Nasa Kiwe** to take care of Nasa affairs (wnasakiwe.gov.co), help rehouse displaced victims and improve infrastructure in *resguardos*, though this process has had mixed success.

---

were shaped by human interaction. Today it's a short, steep climb from the road (signposted), behind the home of a local family, with stupendous views across the Ullacos valley. Just below the peak are some large tunnels, said to have been created at the time of the Spanish conquest (though again, no one really knows who made them, or why). The tunnels have electric lighting, but this can be temperamental, so bring a torch.

ARRIVAL AND DEPARTURE — TIERRADENTRO

Tierradentro is 113km from Popayán along a rough mountain road that's been undergoing improvement for years – once complete, the journey should take 3hr or less (4hr at the time of writing). In the other direction, the road from La Plata (36km) is good to Valencia and the Río Páez (marking the Huila/Cauca border), and the road is gradually being surfaced for its entire extent.

To/from Popayán There is one direct bus daily (5hr 30min) from Popayán to San Andrés de Pisimbalá and the park entrance via Sotracauca, and three daily buses that stop at El Cruce de San Andrés, a road junction. From here it's a 2km walk to the park entrance and museums, and a further 2km uphill to San Andrés de Pisimbalá (unless you can hitch a ride; there is no fixed public transport). There's a direct bus back to Popayán daily from Pisimbalá, and from El Cruce de San Andrés. *Mototaxis* charge a fixed fee between the village and the Cruce de San Andrés and for the journey to Inzá, where you can take a *colectivo* to Popayán.

To/from La Plata Battered old *chivas* and pick-ups (*carpati*) run also from San Andrés de Pisimbalá to La Plata (2hr) where you can pick up connections to San Agustín (via another change at Pitalito or Garzón), and Bogotá, via Neiva (for Tatacoa).

INFORMATION

Services Note that the best place to eat (*La Portada*) and basic shops (which close around 7pm) lie in the village of San Andrés de Pisimbalá, a 2km walk from the park entrance (those extra 4km can make a big difference when added to the 14km loop). Note also that there are no banks or ATMs here – bring plenty of cash.

ACCOMMODATION

There are several basic **guesthouses** of comparable standards very near the two museums and park entrance; meals are available on request in most places. You'll find guaranteed **hot water** and **wi-fi** only at Portada (though hot water is becoming more standard in guesthouses) and **electricity** that runs until 9pm or 10pm only.

Hospedaje Ricabet A short walk up from the museums ⓦ hospedajetierradentro.com; map p.280. Small, basic rooms with shared or private bath, set around a pretty cobbled courtyard. Breakfast is extra. No wi-fi. Cash only. $

Hotel El Refugio A 2min walk from the main park entrance ☏ 321 811 2395; map p.280. This hotel with a refreshing pool (often full of locals) and somewhat musty rooms is the swishest option in Tierradentro, though water is often cold. Breakfast is usually included, with a set dinner and lunch option for an additional fee. No wi-fi. Camping $, doubles $$

★ **La Portada** Main road, central Pisimbalá ⓦ la portadahotel.com; map p.280. Attractive, clean rooms – the cheapest have shared bathrooms with cold water, while others have private bathrooms with reliably hot showers – in a modern, bamboo annexe. The excellent, home-cooked food in the pretty restaurant (breakfast included) is the best in town and the gregarious owner is a treasure-trove of local knowledge (Spanish only). Free wi-fi. Cash only. $

San Agustín and around

Around two thousand years ago, the people who lived around the town known today as **SAN AGUSTÍN**, 140km southeast of Popayán, started marking their tombs with large stone statues – adorned with grinning mouths, pointed fangs, birds eating snakes and huge, round eyes. Today many of these remarkable sculptures are preserved within the **Parque Arqueológico Nacional de San Agustín**, with hundreds more littered across the hillsides on either side of the Río Magdalena. The area's appeal is enhanced by a dizzying landscape of coffee farms clinging to the sides of mountains, vertigo-inducing cascades and the plunging cliffs of the Magdalena gorge, though there's not much to see in the town itself, a sleepy place that primarily caters to the – so far – trickle of tourists coming through. North of the town, bone-jarring Vía Estrecho winds its way down to the Magdalena and on to

---

THE YANACONA

The San Agustín area is home to the **Yanacona**, one of Colombia's Indigenous communities. They chose their official name in the 1980s to reflect the belief many of them were transported here from Peru and Ecuador as *yanaconas* ("slaves") by the Incas or the Spanish (Yanacona in the south are still ethnically Quichua/Kichwa). Numbering around 45,000 today, the group now only speaks Spanish and has often struggled for recognition within Colombia; many Hispanic Colombians still regard the Yanacona in Huila as somewhat disingenuous (made up of people of various, mixed backgrounds), their fight for acceptance politically and economically motivated (being "Indigenized" means otherwise private land can be claimed and designated a *resguardo* or reserve by the community).

In September 2014 the Yanacona effectively closed the San Agustín Parque Arqueológico with a *paro* (roadblock) protest about access to their farms and ancestral *maloka* (spiritual hall), as well as the long history of *promesas incumplidas* (broken promises) made by the government – the dispute with the park has been raging for more than ten years, with park officials worried about damage caused by Yanacona using the park roadways. At the time of writing, the Colombian High Court had ruled against the Yanacona, who are not expected to accept the decision – check the latest situation in advance if you can.

the village of **Obando**, while further north the town of **Bordones** is staging point for a spectacular waterfall.

To see San Agustín and its surroundings properly, you ideally need **three days**: one for the archeological park, one for a day-long jeep tour of the outlying sights, such as the **Alto de los Idolos**, and one for a **horseriding tour** of El Tablón, La Chaquira, El Purutal and La Pelota.

Brief history

No one really knows who made the **stone sculptures** of San Agustín, and experts still disagree on the evidence, though the surreal imagery of sex-crazed monkeys, serpent-headed humans and other disturbing zoomorphic glyphs suggests that the hallucinogenic San Isidro mushroom may have been working its magic when the statues were first created. What is known is that San Agustín's vast network of pre-Hispanic ceremonial sites, settlements and large earthen burial mounds, connected to one another by terraces, paths and causeways, were mostly constructed between 1 AD and 900 AD (though relatively advanced farming communities had been in the valley since at least 1000 BC). The statues are thought to depict gods or supernatural beings, an expression of the link between deceased rulers and priests and their supernatural power. The San Agustín sites were abandoned by 1350 (possibly due to pressure from the **Inca**, whose empire stretched into southern Colombia). The Spanish colonial settlement of San Agustín began in 1608 with the foundation of a Catholic missionary school for the Indigenous people, but the statues weren't officially discovered until the mid-eighteenth century, when most of the tombs were looted. Scientific research began in 1913 and the park was created in 1931.

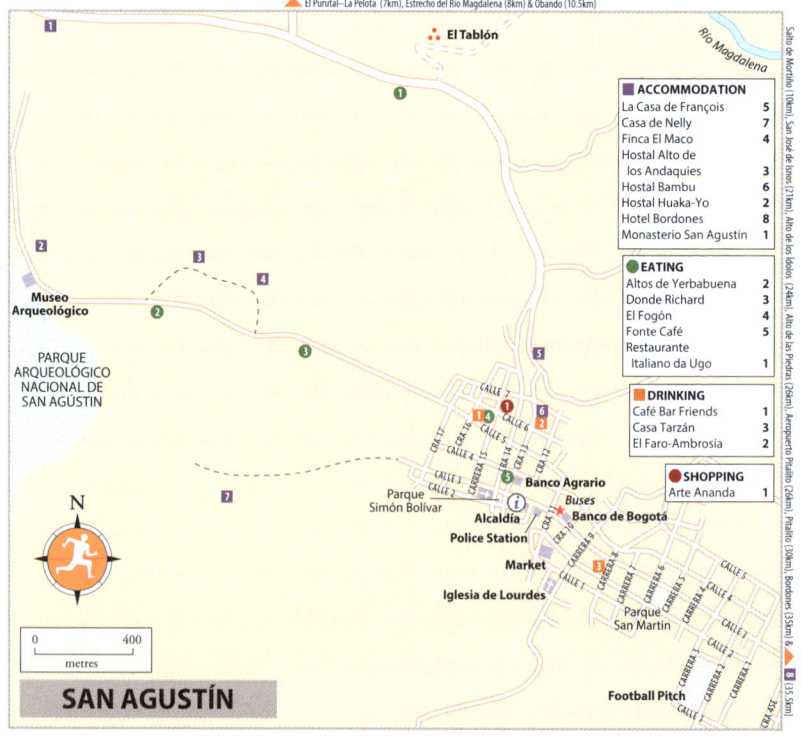

Parque Arqueológico Nacional de San Agustín

Ruta Quinchana • Charge, ticket valid for two days (guides at the entrance charge extra) • W icanh.gov.co • Take a taxi or bus #1 from C5 and Cra 14 (every 30min)

The most concentrated collection of statues in the region lie protected in the beautifully manicured **Parque Arqueológico Nacional de San Agustín**, some 2.5km west of San Agustín town (45min walk). The park contains more than a hundred stone creations, many of them left as they were found. Give yourself at least two hours to do the park justice, though you'll appreciate it more if you allow double that – hire a guide at the entrance to get the full experience.

Museo Arqueológico
Included with park admission

The park's **Museo Arqueológico**, at the main entrance, contains pottery, jewellery, smaller statues and background information on the San Agustín culture with bilingual labelling throughout; visit it before hitting the statue sites if possible.

Bosque de las Estatuas

Just inside the main park entrance lies a wooded sector known as the **Bosque de las Estatuas**, where around 39 giant statues from various locations (including some liberated from homes and the town plaza) have been rearranged and linked by an 800m interpretive trail. The statues are beguiling – their fanged faces, the animal-human hybrids, the stylized animal carvings – and all very much intact.

Las Mesitas (A, B and C)

The main section of the park comprises three *mesitas* (literally "tables"), concentrations of tombs and statues linked by easy-to-walk cobbled paths. **Mesita A** is the biggest and most impressive site, settled as a village some two thousand years ago and converted into a burial ground 300–800 AD. **Mesita B** was inhabited around 1000 BC and contains three funerary mounds and some captivating statues, including one of the tallest (a slightly disturbing image of two opposed bodies and heads, with the upper body holding a child by the legs), a monstrous fang-toothed head and a giant bird with a snake in its beak (a visitor favourite). **Mesita C** originally comprised a single funerary mound surrounded by fifteen statues (some of these are now in the Bosque de las Estatuas) and around 49 tombs.

Fuente de Lavapatas

From Mesita C it's a short walk down to the river and the **Fuente de Lavapatas**, not a "fountain" but an ingenious series of carvings made into the rocks of the riverbed itself (now protected by a roof). It can be hard to see them at first – check out the patterns shown on the information boards and you'll start to make out various features: a maze of terraced pools, smothered with images of reptiles and human figures, thought to have been used for ritual ablutions. Discovered in 1937, this must have looked astonishing when it was carved more than one thousand years ago.

Alto de Lavapatas

Beyond the river, and up a short, steep path, the **Alto de Lavapatas** is the oldest of the sites (people were living here in 3300 BC), with statues sitting forlornly on a hilltop (1750m), their brooding gaze sweeping over the countryside. There's a *Doble Yo* statue here (a warrior combining human and animal features), similar to the one at Alto de las Piedras (see page 287). On the way up you'll pass private homes and farms that serve delicious, locally grown coffee with a view.

La Chaquira and El Tablón

Vía Estrecho, 4km north of San Agustín • Free

La Chaquira is a small but important collection of rock carvings primarily worth visiting for its gasp-inducing location, 200m above the sheer walls of the Río Magdalena gorge, with at least four waterfalls visible, tumbling down its sides. Small farms cling to the cliffs, with coffee bushes planted on impossibly steep terraces. It's a bumpy 2km along an unsurfaced track (off the Vía Estrecho) to the parking area, where you continue on foot down a short but very steep path to the rock itself.

The site of **El Tablón**, on the way to La Chaquira but just 300m off Vía Estrecho, lies at the bottom of a small hill, with five statues under a roof (you can see it from the road). The farmhouse nearby doubles as the **Museo Etnográfico Vereda El Tablón** (charge), with old farm tools and artefacts from Indigenous cultures in the region.

El Purutal–La Pelota

Vía Estrecho, around 7km northwest of San Agustín • Free

The combined site of **El Purutal–La Pelota** lies at the end of a bumpy track 5km off the Vía Estrecho. From a wooden shack selling fresh juices, it's a short climb up to La Pelota, an arrangement of three stone sculptures, then a walk along a 230m earth causeway to El Purutal, where you can see the **only painted statues in situ**, dating from the sixth century. Gazing at the two images, daubed with red, blue, yellow, black, ochre and white, you gain a sense of their original appearance, though someone painted (illegally) over them – what you see today is what remained after the attempt to remove the added colours.

Estrecho del Río Magdalena

Vía Estrecho, 14km north of San Agustín • Free

The **Estrecho del Río Magdalena** is where Colombia's longest river churns and foams through a narrow 2.5m gap in the rocks – it looks small enough to jump, but don't try it. It's a tranquil spot, only busy when the tour vans come through, with the sheer sides of the gorge topped with dense jungle.

Museo Arqueológico de Obando

Parque Principal, Obando • Charge • ☏ 320 273 5258 • Camionetas from San Agustín

Around 5km beyond the Río Magdalena and the "*estrecho*", the small Andean village of **OBANDO** contains the locally run **Museo Arqueológico de Obando**. The site contains five underground tombs in situ (similar to those in Tierradentro; you can walk down and take a peek), while the modest, thatched museum building displays artefacts discovered inside the burial chambers (some English labels) and fascinating photographs of how many of the San Agustín statues were put to use by local villagers before the national park was created.

Salto de Mortiño

400m off the San Agustín–San José de Isnos road, 11km from San Agustín • Charge

The jaw-dropping **Salto de Mortiño** marks the spot where the Quebrada de Mortiño tumbles into the Río Magdalena, some 300m below. The rickety, privately owned viewing point lies just off the main road to San José de Isnos, next to a huge plantation of lulo fruit trees.

Alto de los Ídolos

4km southwest of the town of San José de Isnos (26km northeast of San Agustín) • Admission with Parque Arqueológico ticket (charge) • ⓦ icanh.gov.co • Some travellers hike all the way here, but you can also catch a regular San Agustín to Isnos camioneta and take a mototaxi from Isnos

The area's second most important site after the Parque Arqueológico, the **Alto de los Ídolos** is another beautifully maintained, well-policed park easily explored in around one hour – though getting here can be tough if you don't join a tour. The small **Casa Museo Juan Friede** at the entrance is essentially a display of information posters (in English and Spanish), highlighting the pioneering work of archeologists around San Agustín over the years (the building was constructed in the 1940s by researcher Juan Friede). The most remarkable aspect of the site itself – two connected plateaus on top of a hill – are the seven tombs in situ, huge stone chambers built like Stone Age barrows in Europe (there are around 23 modest statues in front of the tombs). The site does boast the region's tallest statue, 4m high and known as "the bishop" or "the midwife"; there are also two rare statues of crocodiles (which, intriguingly, are not native to this region).

Alto de las Piedras

6km north of Isnos (28km from San Agustín) • Admission with Parque Arqueológico ticket (charge) • Ⓦ icanh.gov.co • Join a tour or take a *mototaxi* from Isnos

The small but significant **Alto de las Piedras** occupies a low hill north of Isnos, its highlight being the **Doble Yo**, a statue that is half-man, half-beast. If you look closely, you'll see that there are four figures carved on that rock.

Bordones

Beyond the Alto de las Piedras, on the same bone-jangling track some 15km from Isnos (which should be paved by 2019), sits the coffee and sugarcane farming town of **BORDONES**, an odd little place that seems completely cut off from the rest of the country. The main attraction here (another 1km out of town) is the **Salto de Bordones**, at 270m (and 1600m above sea level), Colombia's tallest and most intoxicating waterfall. The best place to see it is from the **Hotel Bordones** (see page 288). From here a footpath leads down into the gorge for a closer look at the falls (40min). Getting to the hotel independently means taking a 4WD *colectivo* from Isnos to Bordones (hourly) and walking the rest of the way.

ARRIVAL AND INFORMATION   SAN AGUSTÍN AND AROUND

BY PLANE

SATENA flies from Bogotá (1 daily; 1hr 25min) and Cali (1 daily; 1hr 10min) to tiny Aeropuerto Pitalito Contador, 5km west of Pitalito and 26km east of San Agustín.

BY BUS

Buses arrive and depart in the centre of San Agustín near the corner of C 3 and Cra 11, where there is a cluster of bus company offices. The once notorious road to Popayán is now safe and much improved, though work has stopped indefinitely on the final 40km gravel section.

To/from Popayán Most buses from Popayán are bound for Pitalito and drop off at the Cruce de Isnos (aka "kilometro 5") – from here pick-up truck *camionetas* shuttle passengers the 5km into San Agustín itself (cost included in your ticket).

To/from Bogotá Buses to and from Bogotá usually go straight to the centre.

To/from Pitalito and Tierradentro Getting to Tierradentro from San Agustín involves two bus transfers, which can extend the journey time to around 7hr. The first transfer is usually at Pitalito, where you change for La Plata (3hr). From La Plata it's 1hr 30min to El Cruce de San Andrés,

---

SAN AGUSTÍN WHITEWATER RAFTING

Though they play second fiddle to the archeological attractions, **whitewater rafting** and **kayaking** are also possible in San Agustín, thanks to ready access to the Class II–IV Río Magdalena. Viajes Colombia/Magdalena Rafting (Ⓦ viajardecolombia.com/Inicio) offers excursions; trips can be arranged via your guesthouse. The same outfit can arrange canyoning/rappelling expeditions.

then a 2km walk to the park in Tierradentro (followed by another 2km uphill to the village of San Andrés itself). There are many more buses to destinations (including Mocoa) from Pitalito (30km).

Destinations Bogotá (5 daily; 10–12hr; afternoon and evening only); Neiva (5 daily; 4–5hr); Pitalito (several daily; 45min); Popayán (at least 7 daily; 4–4hr 30min).

GETTING AROUND AND TOURS

By taxi Taxis charge a fixed rate for destinations in town; for sights outside the rates should be agreed before you set off.

Tours Unless you have your own transport, or hire a taxi, getting to see all the major sights beyond the national park usually means joining a tour. Though these are pricey, most visitors find that riding through spectacular scenery is one of the highlights of San Agustín, and knowledgeable guides, booked through your accommodation, can shed light on what you are seeing. English-speakers are rare but available – make sure you check in advance. Prices (and itineraries) tend to be standardized. Tours on horseback usually take in La Chaquira, El Tablón and El Purutal–La Pelota: you need to pay for both your horse, your guide and their horse. Jeep tours usually take in Alto de los Ídolos, Alto de las Piedras and Bordones.

INFORMATION

Tourist information The helpful tourist office (C 3, at Cra 12; ☎ 8 837 3062) is inside the Alcaldía (town hall) on Plaza Cívica. Anything else that claims to be an "information" point is just a tour office.

Services Banco de Bogotá is located near the buses at C 3 No. 10–61.

ACCOMMODATION

SAN AGUSTÍN

La Casa de François 250m along Vía Estrecho (Cra 13) ⓦ lacasadefrancois.com; map p.284. Situated on a bluff overlooking the city, this ecologically friendly and sociable place offers airy dorms (one with fantastic views), an excellent communal kitchen and a couple of private doubles. The enthusiastic owner offers home-made bread, jam and other goodies, plus hearty breakfasts. $

Casa de Nelly Vía la Estrella (1.5km along Av 2) ⓦ hotelcasadenelly.co; map p.284. Tricky to find, as the route along a poorly lit dirt track from town is not brilliantly signposted, but lovely once you've made it. Romantic cabins (some en-suite) surrounded by trees make this a great spot for those who want to hide away and relax for a couple of days. There's a restaurant serving breakfasts (for an extra charge) and "whatever's available" for dinner. $

Finca El Maco 750m along the road to the Parque Arqueológico and then 500m up a rough road ⓦ elmaco.ch; map p.284. This working organic farm with a gaggle of friendly dogs offers a range of sleeping options from simple dorms to luxurious *casitas* (literally "small houses"). The restaurant serves good-value Thai curries, great *crêpes* and massive breakfasts. Alternatively, you can buy home-made bread, cheese, pasta sauces and yogurt and make your own meals in the basic communal kitchen, then retire to a hammock and admire the surrounding hills. $

Hostal Alto de los Andaquíes Vía Vereda Nueva Zelanda, 1km from town, beyond Finca El Maco ⓦ andaquies.com; map p.284. This hotel on an old coffee farm is justly popular, surrounded by lush gardens and with four exquisite properties in traditional Andean style. There's an attractive adobe colour-scheme in the spotless rooms, with Indigenous art on the walls. Free coffee and breakfast included. $$

Hostal Bambu Cra 13 No. 6–78 ⓦ hostalbambu.com; map p.284. Popular hostel with spacious doubles and triples, adorned with bright local artwork and murals, either en-suite or with shared bathrooms, as well as cosy dorms (no bunks) and ample hot water. The terrace offers sensational views of the town and surrounding area. Vegetarian breakfast available. $

Hostal Huaka-Yo Vía Quinchana (200m beyond the Parque Arqueológico) ⓦ huaka-yo.business.site; map p.284. Sensational property 4km out of town but just 200m from the Parque Arqueológico, a grand colonial-style place with simple but spacious en-suite rooms and a cool veranda – definitely the place to get some peace and quiet. Breakfast included. $$

★ Monasterio San Agustín Off the road to the Parque Arqueológico ⓦ monasteriosanagustin.com; map p.284. Classy German-run option just outside town, with spectacular views. Built to resemble a Spanish colonial monastery, this modern boutique hotel offers luxurious rooms, a relaxing pool, friendly hosts, professional service and an excellent on-site restaurant (breakfast included). $$$

BORDONES

Hotel Bordones Vereda Salto de Bordones ☎ 313 833 2706, ⓦ facebook.com/bordoneshotel; map p.284. You'll get the best views of the Salto de Bordones (see page 287) waterfall from this totally incongruous architectural marvel, where you can grab coffee or even spend the night. $

EATING

The town's fruit-and-veg **market**, on the corner of C 2 and Cra 11, is open daily but liveliest when the *campesinos* come to sell their wares. There's also a handy **supermarket** on Parque Simón Bolívar (near the church).

★ **Altos de Yerbabuena** C 5 (1.5km along the road to the Parque Arqueológico) ☏ 310 370 3777; map p.284. Halfway between San Agustín and the park, this gem of a *parrilla* is gaining a cult following for its affordable steaks, trout, excellent wine list and wonderful service. $$

★ **Donde Richard** C 5 No. 23–45 (750m along the road to the Parque Arqueológico) ☏ 312 432 6399; map p.284. The best spot to chow down in town serves high-quality, carnivore-friendly food such as barbecued pork, chicken, beef and fish, all cooked on a big grill at the front of the restaurant. Don't miss the Sunday special of *asado huilense* (slow-cooked pork marinated overnight). $$

El Fogón C 5 No. 14–04 ☏ 320 834 5860; map p.284. Extremely popular restaurant with an open kitchen, family feel and cooks fussing over the boiling pots. They serve a better-than-average *menú del día* to scores of hungry locals every day of the week. Specialities include *cuy* (guinea pig), trout and *asado huilense* (traditional pork dish). $$

Fonte Café Cra 13 No. 3–63 ☏ 322 358 7979; map p.284. One of the newer options in the centre, with a creative menu featuring beautifully presented dishes, from tasty vegetarian crêpes (*tortillas*) to steaks and chicken and mushroom pasta. Also fresh juices and wonderful coffee. The set breakfast and lunches are great deals (dinner is a la carte only). $$

Restaurante Italiano da Ugo Vereda El Tablón ☏ 321 487 5123 ⓦ facebook.com/restauranteitalianoilpastaio; map p.284. A short taxi ride out of town, this authentic Italian spot delivers consistently good dishes, including home-made pasta, which have earned the praise of Italian and non-Italian travellers alike. $

DRINKING

Café Bar Friends C 5 No. 14–2 ☏ 313 428 1208; map p.284. Fun bar with an international theme that attracts plenty of locals as well as travellers, with friendly owners, cocktails (top mojitos), live football, local coffee and salsa dancing.

Casa Tarzán C 2 No. 8–16 ⓦ casatarzan.com; map p.284. This bizarre Tarzan-themed bar (also a hotel) is quite fun, the interior decked out like a jungle hut with hammocks, slide-down fireman's poles and even rope swings, over several levels.

El Faro-Ambrosía Cra 13 No. 6–60 ☏ 311 287 7696; map p.284. On the pretty stretch of street known as the Calle de la Locería, this is one of the few bars in town. It's part of the *Ambrosía* restaurant (serving wood-fired pizzas) with live music and a varied programme of cultural events.

SHOPPING

The town has plenty of standard arts and **crafts shops**, but look out for the distinctive jewellery made of local "dalmatian beans", coffee beans and orange peel.

Arte Ananda C 5 No. 13–46 ☏ 311 510 5039; map p.284. A good place to shop for jewellery and to look for local crafts and souvenirs.

Desierto de la Tatacoa

The peculiar **DESIERTO DE LA TATACOA** (Tatacoa Desert) makes for a worthwhile detour between Bogotá and San Agustín or Tierradentro. A relatively small but otherworldly blend of sun-scorched rocks, giant cacti, orange-and-grey sand dunes, old lava flows, dried *arroyos* and towering red rock formations, it's a landscape that seems more like northern Mexico than the rest of Colombia, and makes for a jarring contrast to the cloud forests of the Andes. Located just outside the town of **Villavieja**, Tatacoa's arid topography is all the more astonishing because it lies just 37km northeast of **NEIVA**, the gritty modern capital of Huila, encircled by fertile coffee and rice plantations. The best time to explore the desert is early morning before the heat becomes intolerable (temperatures frequently reach 40°C and above) – and at night the sky explodes with stars.

Villavieja

The sleepy colonial town of **VILLAVIEJA** is a baking hot but a surprisingly green and friendly oasis. The town, which contains just under seven thousand inhabitants, is centred around the leafy Plaza Principal (where local guides tout for business) and its simple white and blue church, the Iglesia del Perpetuo Socorro, and the seventeenth-century Capilla de Santa Bárbara. There's not much else to see in the town itself, though aficionados will enjoy the fossil museum.

Museo Paleontológico

C 3 No. 3–04 (Plaza Principal) • Charge • 314 347 6812

A tiny sample of the fossils the Tatacoa desert is renowned for are on display at the **Museo Paleontológico**, with three small galleries containing giant tortoise shells, monstrous caiman jaws and the remains of a *megaterio*, a giant sloth that spanned 5m (check out the life-size model in the middle of the plaza). Labelling is in Spanish only.

Observatorio Astronómico del Desierto de la Tatacoa

6km from Villavieja • Charge • 310 465 6765 • A *motocarro (tuk tuk)* from Villavieja to the observatory can take up to three people

The tiny **Observatorio Astronómico** at the heart of the Tatacoa desert area is 6km from Villavieja on a paved road – a stiff walk that would be easy enough if it weren't for the heat. During the day a small snack and drink stall operates here, with some celestial photos on show, but the main event takes place in the evenings, when local astronomer Javier Fernando Rúa Restrepo leads a star-gazing show via three powerful telescopes. The clearest night skies are usually July to October, then late December to January.

Laberintos de Cusco

Across the road from the Observatorio Astronómico is a lookout point over the **Laberintos de Cusco** – a maze of crinkled red rock formations reminiscent of the Badlands of South Dakota (locals call this the "red desert"). A 45-minute trail runs down through this labyrinth and loops back to the main road.

Los Hoyos

6km beyond the Observatorio Astronómico • Charge • 311 536 5027 • On foot or by tour (*motocarro*; charge)

The most enticing destination in the desert is the isolated swimming pools (*piscinas*) at **Los Hoyos**, another 6km on a dirt track from the observatory in what locals call the "grey desert". As you walk down from the car park through a sandy gorge, two concrete pools and a thatched restaurant appear tucked between the craggy sandstone formations, accessible by steps of tyres. Avoid weekends, when the pools get mobbed, and go during the week, when you'll have the place to yourself.

ARRIVAL AND TOURS — DESIERTO DE LA TATACOA

By plane The closest airport is Neiva's modern Aeropuerto Benito Salas (Avianca and EasyFly), just north of the city centre, with a small information booth and cafés, but no ATMs. Taxis charge a flat fee to Neiva bus terminal (La Terminal de Transportes).
Destinations Bogotá (daily; 45min).
By bus Villavieja is 1hr by bus from Neiva, which in turn is 6hr by bus from Bogotá and 5hr from San Agustín on the main Bogotá–San Agustín road. Coomotor minivans from Neiva's Terminal de Transportes run frequently to Villavieja early in the morning and late in the afternoon (1hr).

Tours Touts will greet you on arrival at Villavieja's informal bus terminal on the main plaza: tours of the desert by *mototaxi* are the most affordable option, with *motocarro* (tuk-tuks) charging more (for up to three people) – the guide (Spanish only) will drive you to all the main attractions of the desert for 3–4hr. This is your only option to go further into the desert, bar walking (a very hot proposition). Hotels in the desert will provide tours at a much cheaper rate. Chopo Taxi (run by Faiver Martínez Perdomo, aka "Chopo") is a recommended operator (313 865 8710).

ACCOMMODATION AND EATING

Villavieja has a few **hotels** and a handful of basic **restaurants** on the plaza and Calle 4, the main drag, but since one of Tatacoa's chief attractions is the amazing night sky, it pays to stump up for one of the bare-bones four-walls-and-a-corrugated-iron-roof deals in the **desert** itself; accommodation is scattered along the road just past the observatory, the desert's focal point. Accommodation tends to be basic and overpriced for what it is, though with some negotiation you can bring the prices down. Most hotels will provide meals if required, with the local *chiva* (goat) featuring on most menus, though the meat can be too tough and fatty for most foreign palates. Note that you can **camp** at the observatory (see page 290) for a fee, using the cold showers and toilets on site.

VILLAVIEJA
Hotel Boutique Yararaka Cra 4 No. 4–43 ⓦ facebook.com/HotelBoutiqueYararaka. One of Villavieja's top options, with twelve comfy en-suite rooms dressed with a blend of contemporary and Indigenous styles (the property is all thatched, with wood-and-cane ceilings). Breakfast included $$
Villa Paraíso C 4 No. 7–69 ⓦ hotelvillaparaisovillavieja.com. Centrally located in Villavieja, with basic rooms arranged along a lush tropical garden with a mango tree. No breakfast, but there's a shared kitchen open to guests. Doubles with fan $, doubles with a/c $$

THE DESERT
Noches de Saturno 200m beyond the observatory ☏ 313 305 5898. Very basic rooms and camping; there's a small swimming pool (non-guests can use this for a fee), and meals available. Options include camping and doubles. $
Rincón del Cabrito 500m past the observatory ☏ 312 528 1729. If you are determined to try the local "delicacy" (goat), this is the place, with a wide variety of goat (and lamb) dishes on the menu (*pepitoria* or *cordero asado*), as well as fresh goat's milk (*leche de cabra*), goat's milk desserts and drinks. $$
Sol de Verano Doña Lilia 400m past the observatory ☏ 313 311 8828. Popular with groups and the easiest accommodation to walk to/from the observatory; very basic solar-powered cabins (with fans), hammocks and camping available (with access to shared toilets and showers), as well as meals on request (lunch is extra). No wi-fi. Accommodation options include camping with your own tent, hammocks, dorms and cabins. $

The far south

Bordering Ecuador, the department of **Nariño** in the far south of Colombia is a land rich in untapped adventure and ecotourism potential, with sky-scraping volcanoes, isolated Indigenous villages, plunging canyons and roiling rivers slicing through snaggle-toothed Andean ranges. Hostels are beginning to offer paragliding, mountain biking, kayaking, canyoning and rafting, but there are plenty of more sedate attractions, beginning with bucolic Laguna de la Cocha, accessible from the likeable mountain city of **Pasto**, and the remarkable Catholic sanctuary of **Las Lajas** near Ipiales. Note that the **Laguna Verde del Volcán Azufral** has been closed since 2017, after protests by the local Indigenous community over damage caused by tourism, and is unlikely to reopen any time soon.

Pasto

Nestled in the Valle de Atriz in the shadow of the massive, emerald cone of (active) **Volcán Galeras**, the Andean city of **PASTO** is the capital of Nariño, a bustling commercial hub of half a million with a small but attractive historic core. At 2527m above sea level, it's a lot cooler here than in Cali (Colombians tend to think it's like going to the Arctic, but it's not *that* cold), though don't be fooled – the sun can be incredibly strong (Pasto is only 135km north of the Equator).

Like Cali, Pasto was founded by the unstoppable Sebastián de Belalcázar in 1537, and today the heart of the old town is **Plaza Nariño**, ringed by a blend of Republican-style and newer buildings and anchored by a modest statue of independence hero General Antonio Nariño himself. From here narrow Calle 18 cuts south through mostly historic buildings to the wide expanse of **Plaza del Carnaval**, a modern, rather soulless square created on the space occupied by the old bus terminal. The plaza comes alive in January for the **Carnaval de Blancos y Negros**, one of the country's most exuberant festivals.

Templo de San Juan Bautista
C 18A No. 25–17 (Plaza Nariño) • Free • ☏ 2 723 5440

The oldest building on the main plaza is the Romanesque **Templo de San Juan Bautista**, a Spanish colonial gem dating back to around 1669 (though it's been remodelled many times since). Its Mudéjar (Moorish) touches are remarkable, with the altar and apse seemingly transported straight from the Alhambra. To the left of the nave, the Capilla de San Miguel contains the tomb of **Agustín Agualongo** (1780–1824), a *pastuso* who fought for Spain and was executed in Popayán during the independence wars – his body was re-interred here in 1983. Unlike most of Colombia, Pasto was intensely loyal to Spain during Bolívar's rebellion, with pro-Spanish guerrillas fighting on here until 1826.

Catedral de Pasto
Cra 26 No. 17–23 • Free • ☎ 2 723 3328

One block north of Plaza Nariño, the twin-towered red-brick **Catedral de Pasto** was built in Neoclassical style between 1899 and 1920, replacing a ruined Franciscan church that once stood here. The interior is very grand, noted chiefly for the ornate, painted ceiling, its *nariñense* artwork, the venerated image of the Sagrado Corazón de Jesús in the altar and the painting of (and chapel to) the Virgen de Guadelupe on the left side of the nave.

Museo Taminango de Artes y Tradiciones Populares de Nariño
C 13 No. 27–67 • Charge • ☎ 2 723 5539

Pasto's most enticing historic sight is the **Museo Taminango de Artes y Tradiciones Populares de Nariño**, housed within a colonial home with original mud walls, thatch roof and creaky wood floors. Built around 1623 (next to Nuestra Señora de Lourdes church), the Casona Taminango was artfully restored, beginning in the 1970s, and its rooms now contain small exhibits on local "mopa-mopa" designs (see page 295), traditional weaving, a smithy, *nariñense* woodwork and a printing press belonging to local hero **Leopoldo López Álvarez** (1891–1940), professor, judge and humanist. Guides (Spanish only) will show you around.

Templo de la Merced
Cra 22 No. 17–24 • Free • ☎ 2 721 5681

OFF THE BEATEN PATH IN NARIÑO

If you're looking for adventure, you've come to the right place. Nariño is studded with dazzling, untouched natural wonders largely devoid of tourists. Hostels and tour agencies can help with trips to the less visited attractions, though with time (and good Spanish) you can visit just about everywhere independently. One enticing target is the **Parque Nacional Natural Complejo Volcánico Doña Juana-Cascabel** (accessible from the town of La Cruz, 90km northwest of Pasto), encompassing three massive volcanoes (Doña Juana, Ánimas and Petacas) in a forbidding landscape of lava fields, forests and waterfalls, home to endangered species like the Andean condor, the tapir, spectacled bear and puma. Perhaps the most spectacular destination is the **Parque Cañón del Juanambú** (50km north of Pasto), a deep, twisting gorge, hemmed in by lush cloudforest, where you can go rafting under a ruined arch bridge (Puente Histórico de los Arcos). Note that climbing still-active Volcán Galeras (4276m) is strictly forbidden.

MOCOA: YAGÉ AND THE "TRAMPOLINE OF DEATH"

Another less-travelled route is the bone-jarring but gasp-inducing ride 130km across the Andes from Pasto to **Mocoa** (in Putumayo, on the edge of the Amazon basin) via the "trampoline of death" – one of the most dangerous roads in the world (yes, buses do make the trip). From here you can continue north to Pitalito (see page 287) and San Agustín (see page 287). The Mocoa area is the main centre in Colombia for the herbal concoction known as **yagé** (ayahuasca) and the shamanic rituals it has inspired for thousands of years (see page 39).

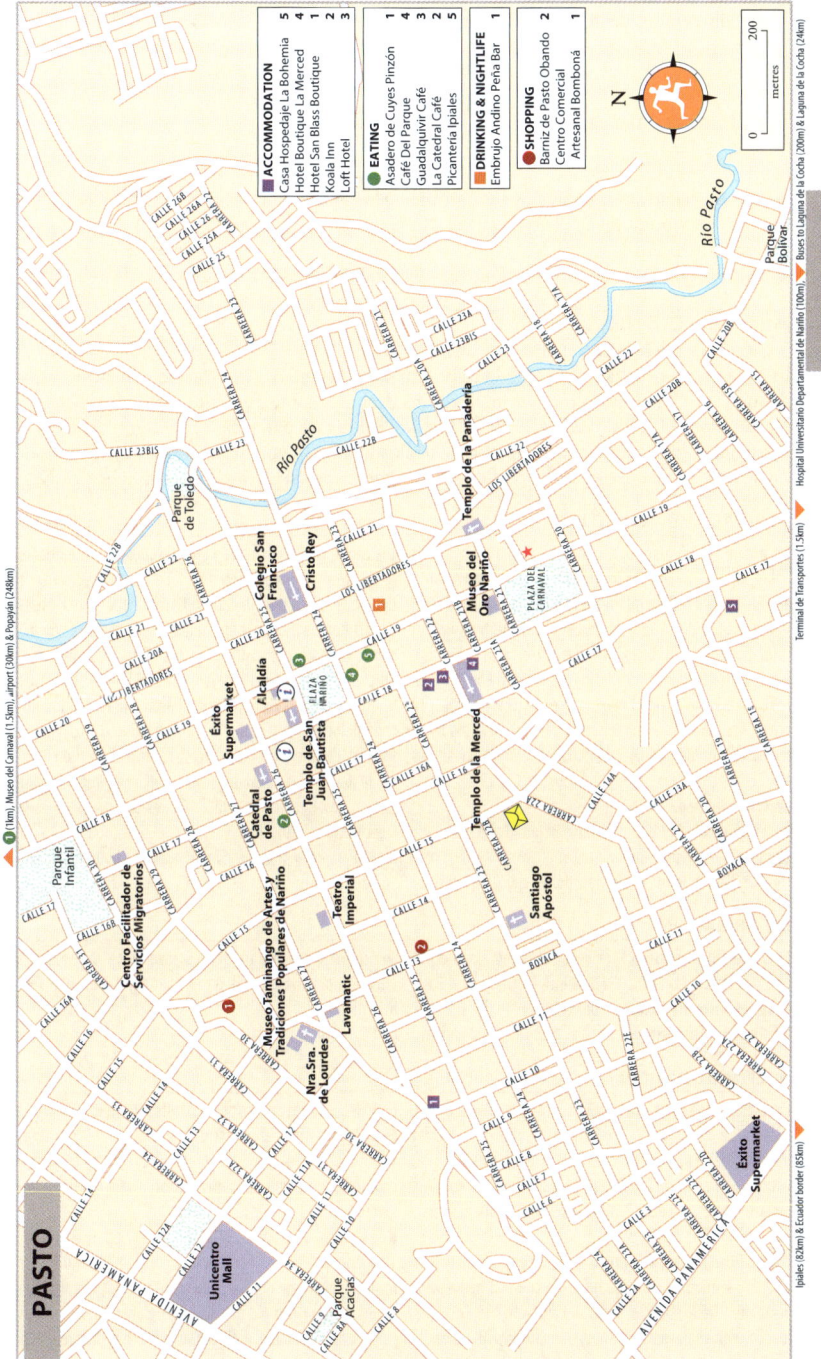

The giant **Templo de la Merced** is adorned in a wedding cake Neoclassical style, best known for its large, commanding image of an all-white **Nuestra Señora de las Mercedes** (Virgin Mary) set in the grand altar, one of the most revered icons in the city.

Templo de la Panadería
C 21 No. 20–20 • Free

An incongruous confection of neo-Gothic and Spanish *Modernisme*, the Templo de San Sebastián, commonly known as the **Templo de la Panadería** was built in 1936, dedicated to Nuestra Señora del Rosario de la Panadería (another incarnation of the Virgin Mary). The rare oil painting of the Virgen del Rosario, left of the nave, was once venerated in local mills and bakeries. Check out the lavish stained glass throughout the church.

Museo del Oro Nariño
Centro Cultural Leopoldo López Álvarez, C 19 No. 21–27 • Free • ☎ 2 721 5777

Inside the fortress-like Banco de la República, the **Museo del Oro Nariño** doesn't actually contain much gold, but its two small rooms do boast some exquisite pieces from Nariño's pre-Hispanic cultures. Items include some rare pan pipes, tiny figurines from Valdivia, gold fish hooks from Tumaco, freaky-looking Capuli anthropomorphic jars, intricate gold necklaces and a replica tomb replete with skeletons. Spanish labels only.

ARRIVAL AND DEPARTURE — PASTO

By plane Pasto's Aeropuerto Antonio Nariño is a winding 35km north of the city. Avianca flies to Cali and both Avianca and SATENA fly to Bogotá. There's nothing in the arrivals hall – walk out and turn left to go back into the terminal for cafés, shops and ATM. Taxis charge a fixed rate to the city centre (30–40min); *colectivo* vans operated by Cochachagüí (☎ 315 552 2594) run between the airport and the city centre daily (35min; minimum four people). Heading back, the *colectivos* depart La Corporación de Transportadores Nariñenses (the Esso garage forecourt at Cra 19 and C 23) every 20min or so.
Destinations Cali (1 daily; 45min); Bogotá (4–5 daily; 1hr 15min).
By bus Pasto's Terminal de Transportes lies 2km south of the centre on Cra 7. There's a *guardaequipaje* (left luggage) here (see page 296). Minivans (*micros*) and *colectivo* taxis depart from section (*módulo*) 1, while the larger buses depart from section 2. There's not a lot of difference when it comes to short trips, with numerous companies competing on the route to Ipiales, Popayán, Cali and Tumaco. Note that it's best not to travel between Popayán and Pasto at night, though the threat of robberies is much reduced. Taxis charge fixed rates (there are no meters) for trips into the centre while local buses marked "Centro" or #C11 charge a flat fee per journey. Heading back take #C1 or #C2.
Destinations Cali (hourly; 9hr); Ipiales (hourly; 2–2hr 30min); Mocoa (hourly; 5hr); Popayán (hourly; 6–7hr); Tumaco (hourly; 5–6hr); Túquerres (hourly; 2hr).

INFORMATION

Casa de Don Lorenzo Your best bet is this small office on Plaza Nariño (☎ 2 722 3717), which has maps and basic information, but few English speakers.
Oficina de Turismo The official tourism office, around the corner from Casa de Don Lorenzo on C 18 No. 25–25 (w turismo.narino.gov.co), is more like a gift shop, with less information.

ACCOMMODATION

Casa Hospedaje La Bohemia Cra 18 No. 16–2 ☎ 301 390 3408; map p.293. Friendly farmhouse-style hostel near the centre managed by fun hosts Anthony and Monica, with one small dorm (five beds) and six basic but spotless private rooms, shared bathrooms (with hot showers), common kitchen and TV room. $
Hotel Boutique La Merced C 18 No. 21B–11 ☎ 311 650 9154; map p.293. Beautiful old colonial home with verandas overlooking a central courtyard, six doubles loaded with character and good, hot showers. The friendly owner is a font of information, hot water bottles are provided at night and tasty breakfasts are included. $$
Hotel San Blass Boutique C 26 No. 11–89 w hotel sanblass.com; map p.293. Modern, bright hotel with a cool roof deck, well appointed rooms and a good on-site restauarant. $$
Koala Inn C 18 No. 22–37 ☎ 300 225 4860; map p.293. This long-established backpackers' guesthouse, two blocks from the main square, is a convenient spot for travellers on a budget. Set in an old mansion, there are fifteen spacious private rooms (some with bathrooms), hot showers and cable TV. Pancake breakfast is extra, but no kitchen access.

CARNAVAL DE BLANCOS Y NEGROS

Pasto explodes into life each January during the annual **Carnaval de Blancos y Negros**, when thousands descend on the city for some serious partying. The festival officially kicks off on January 2 with a parade, followed by a children's carnival (Carnavalito; Jan 3), "Black's Day" (Día de los Negros; Jan 5), commemorating the one day of the year when slaves were allowed to let loose (everyone paints themselves black), and "White's Day" (Día de los Blancos; Jan 6), when everyone gets painted white for the Grand Parade of vast, elaborate floats and costumes. While this could be problematic in other countries, it is seen as a celebration of equality and diversity in Colombia. Be prepared to be sprayed in paints, talcum powder, chalk, ink and a variety of liquids both days. At other times of year, you can visit the Museo del Carnaval, C19 at Cra 42 (Centro Cultural Pandiaco; free; ☎ 2 731 4598), to get some sense of what goes on.

Laundry available. $
★ **Loft Hotel** C 18 No. 22–33 ⓦ lofthotelpasto.com; map p.293. Luxurious choice in central Pasto (next door to *Koala Inn*) with stylish, contemporary rooms, cable TV and free snacks in your room. Breakfast included in the posh restaurant downstairs. No lift. $$

EATING

Central Pasto overflows with **cafés** serving coffee, cake and sometimes light meals and sandwiches. Self-caterers can visit the conveniently located **Éxito** supermarket, at the corner of C 18 and Cra 26.

Asadero de Cuyes Pinzón Cra 40 No. 19B–76, Palermo ☎ 2 731 3228; map p.293. Palermo district, on the outskirts of town, is celebrated for its restaurants specializing in *cuy* (guinea pig). Cra 40 is home to several, including this lauded *asadero*, which roasts guinea pigs with liver, potatoes and *chilli peppers*. $$

Café Del Parque Cra 24 No. 18–56 (Plaza Nariño) ☎ 2 723 7857; map p.293. Popular spot next to the casino, with tables under the portals and the best views of the plaza. Serves excellent Nariño coffee, cakes and juices. Friday nights feature live jazz, classical or salsa. Great place for a beer or glass of wine, too. $

La Catedral Café Cra 26 No. 16–37 ⓦ cafelacatedral.com; map p.293. Similar to *Guadalquivir* but a much more refined, quieter retreat, set in an old building with timber ceilings and carnival memorabilia (posters, paintings, masks) on the walls. Serves *tamales*, excellent cheesecake, *empanadas*, Nariño coffee and a huge range of pastries. $

Guadalquivir Café C 19 No. 24–84 (Plaza Nariño) ☎ 7 239 5043; map p.293. This café, decorated with posters from the carnival, is open on Sun, which is rare for places on the plaza. Classics here are the *empanada anejo* (fried *empanadas*) and *quimbolitos* (a bit like suet pudding). $

Picantería Ipiales C 19 No. 23–37 ⓦ picanteriaipiales.com; map p.293. Most of Pasto's major restaurants are located outside the centre, but this is a decent exception, serving classic Nariñense dishes such as *lapingachos* (potato pancakes) served with pork, chicken or chorizo sausage. $$

DRINKING AND NIGHTLIFE

★ **Embrujo Andino Peña Bar** Cra 23 No. 19–58 ⓦ embrujoandinobar.business.site; map p.293. Bar and discoteca specializing in Son Cubano, tropical and Andean musical genres – videos are shown on a giant screen and there are live performances on weekends (dance lessons Wed nights). Cash only.

SHOPPING

Pasto is best noted for the ancient craft of **mopa-mopa**, or *barniz de Pasto*, a technique using the natural resins of the mopa-mopa plant to decorate wood carvings (see page 46). The town's woodcarvers are also renowned.

Barniz de Pasto Obando Cra 25 No. 13–04 ☎ 301 490 3551; map p.293. Small but exclusive store that stocks very high-quality mopa-mopa work.

Centro Comercial Artesanal Bomboná C 14 No. 28–109 ☎ 2 722 5392; map p.293. Large market hall mostly given over to clothes stalls, but there are some excellent arts and crafts sellers, notably Artesanías Yalty. Also known for the snack stall *Hornado de Albita*, serving roasted pork Mon–Fri for more than forty years.

DIRECTORY

Banks and exchange All the main banks have branches and ATMs on or around Plaza Nariño including Citibank, Banco de Bogotá and Banco Popular.

Health Hospital Universitario Departamental de Nariño, C 22 No. 7–93 (☎ 2 733 3400).
Laundry Lavamatic, Cra 27 No. 12–96.

Left luggage At the Terminal de Transportes bus station (charge per bag/24hr).
Post office C 15 No. 22–05.

Visa extensions Centro Facilitador de Servicios Migratorios, C 17 No. 29–70 (📞 2 722 9393).

Laguna de la Cocha

A vast, pristine expanse of blue tucked in between mist-topped mountains, **Laguna de la Cocha** is just 25km from central Pasto but feels like another world. At 2800m above sea level it gets genuinely chilly here, so bring a jacket. The lake is wildly popular with Colombian tourists, who come to enjoy the enchanting wooden chalets, blossoms, rickety bridges, narrow canals and brightly painted boats of **El Puerto**, an ethnic Quillacinga village on the wetlands at the mouth of the Río Encano (**El Encano** itself is a small town, 2km inland). While El Puerto is certainly touristy, with almost every home along the main street converted into a restaurant serving lake trout, the village has retained a rustic charm, and it never seems that busy. From here most visitors take a quick boat ride out to the unspoiled reserve of **Isla La Corota**.

Isla La Corota
Santuario de Flora Isla Corota • Charge (boat to island; 10min) • 📞 2 732 0493

Buses from Pasto terminate at the main river dock at El Puerto, where boatmen await to whisk you out onto the lake on simple motor *lanchas* to the **Isla La Corota**, a national park where a magnificent slice of Andean cloud forest has been preserved. On disembarking you'll pass the wood-and-stone **Templete a Nuestra Señora de Lourdes** (a chapel and pilgrimage site built in 1986), before reaching the ranger station where you pay the entry fee. From here an easy-to-follow path (it can be muddy) dubbed the **Sendero El Quiche** rises gently upwards for 550m, through dense forest littered with flowering bromeliads to a viewpoint on the other side of the island. The boat will wait and take you on a spin around the island on the way back.

ARRIVAL AND DEPARTURE   LAGUNA DE LA COCHA

By minivan and colectivo Transport to El Encano and the lake is operated by Cootranar (📞 2 721 8989), which runs small white minivans and white *colectivo* taxis from its base on Cra 7 at C 22, next to the hospital and opposite the Alkosto hypermarket. The journey takes 30–40min, and unless you pay for the whole vehicle, you'll have to wait until it fills up (usually not long). All transport runs through El Encano village and terminates at El Puerto near the lake and the *lancha* dock; the last transport back departs around 6pm.
By taxi A yellow Pasto city taxi will take you to the lake but you'll pay a premium each way.

EATING

Restaurante La Casona Next to bus terminal. El Puerto is lined with numerous attractive, wood-chalet restaurants, all generally offering the same basic menu – La Casona is close to the bus stop/dock, with a pleasant upper deck overlooking the river and the boats. Order the fresh trout: it's mostly fried (and good enough), but the best version is *trucha ahumada* (smoked trout). $

Ipiales

There's little point in stopping at the scruffy border town of **IPIALES**, some 80km south of Pasto and just 2km from Ecuador, at a heady elevation of about 2950m, other than to organize a trip to **Las Lajas** – easily done on the way to the frontier or even as a day-trip from Pasto. The road between Pasto and Ipiales is mesmerizing, as it winds up the precipitous canyons of the **Río Guáitara** – sit on the left side of the bus going south for the best views. Remember to carry your **passport** (or at least a good photocopy) when travelling anywhere south of Pasto – frequent police and military roadblocks stud the main highway, and being caught without your ID can result in lots of hassle and even a hefty fine.

CROSSING INTO ECUADOR

Ipiales lies just 2km from the historic Rumichaca Bridge, which connects Colombia with **Ecuador** over the Río Guáitara/Carchi – *colectivo* taxis shuttle back and forth from Ipiales bus terminal. There is no through transport.

Border formalities (24hr) occur on each side of the bridge, though heading into Ecuador usually takes a lot longer than the other way round, so make sure you allow plenty of time. Once you've crossed the bridge (on foot) and cleared immigration, shared taxis and minivans run to the Ecuadorean town of **Tulcán**, 7km from the bridge (20min). From here you can take buses (or fly) to Quito and elsewhere. Check the safety situation on the Ecuadorian side before travelling. There are moneychangers on both sides of the border on and close to the bridge (Ecuador uses the US dollar as its national currency).

ARRIVAL AND DEPARTURE IPIALES

By bus The Terminal de Transporte de Ipiales lies about 1km northeast of the city centre, replete with cafés, ATM, *guarda equipaje* (luggage storage) and even a small tourist information kiosk – taxis charge a fixed rate anywhere in the city but there's not much point in staying here. *Colectivo* taxis to the Ecuador border (labelled "Rumichaca") depart from just outside the terminal (US dollars usually accepted).

Expreso Las Lajas handles transport to the Santuario de Las Lajas, with shared taxis also departing just outside the bus terminal or from their base at Cra 6A 3–118, at C 4, in the centre of Ipiales.

Destinations Cali (hourly; 10hr); Pasto (frequent; 2–3hr); Popayán (hourly; 8hr); Tumaco (hourly; 5hr); Túquerres (every 2hr; 1hr).

Santuario de Las Lajas

Vía Ipiales–Potosí, 9km from Ipiales • Free • ⓦ laslajas.org

Few sights in Colombia are more unexpected as the extraordinary **Santuario de Las Lajas**. The church was built between 1916 and 1949, though it commemorates a much older event: the story goes that in 1754 a local Indigenous woman called Maria Mueces (and her deaf-mute daughter Rosa), took refuge between giant "lajas" rocks during a storm. Here Rosa is supposed to have seen an apparition of the Virgin Mary (aka **Nuestra Señora de Las Lajas**), and in time the site became a popular pilgrimage spot. The current edifice rises 100m from the bottom of the canyon and is connected to the opposite side by a bridge over the Río Guáitara; a pretty waterfall. The interior of the church is rich in stained glass, though the altar, actually built into the rock face, is the main focus, adorned with a painted image of the Virgin Mary, marking the location of the miracle (the faithful believe this is the actual image that appeared to Rosa).

Teleférico de Las Lajas

Vía Ipiales–Las Lajas Km 4 • Charge • ⓦ laslajas.co/teleferico.html

The **Teleférico de Las Lajas**, a 1.5km cable car, zips across the Río Guáitara gorge (15min) twice on its way to the Santuario de Las Lajas. The main station lies on the road between Ipiales and Las Lajas, around 2.5km before you reach the Santuario.

ARRIVAL AND DEPARTURE SANTUARIO DE LAS LAJAS

By shared taxi *Colectivo* taxis shuttle between Ipiales bus terminal and Las Lajas (10–15min). You'll be dropped at the car park where the church is a short, steep stroll down the hill through a gauntlet of snack stalls and souvenir shops. If you'd rather take the cable car down, ask to be dropped off at the station before Las Lajas.

ACCOMMODATION

Casa Pastoral Just below the main car park ☏ 318 203 1710. The classic pilgrim accommodation (run by nuns) is also one of the cheapest here, with great views of the church, cheap rates, basic but clean rooms and very hard beds. $

Hotel Danny Opposite Lajas taxi rank ☏ 317 664 6935. For a little more comfort consider this small hotel set right on the road down to the church, with comfy rooms, cable TV and hot showers. $

The Pacific coast

- 300 Bahía Solano and around
- 304 El Valle and around
- 306 Parque Nacional Natural Utría
- 307 Nuquí and around
- 310 Buenaventura and around
- 315 Isla Gorgona
- 317 Tumaco

NUQUÍ, CHOCÓ

The Pacific coast

Welcome to Colombia's wild west coast, where empty volcanic beaches, palm-fringed islands, isolated Indigenous villages and a vibrant Afro-Colombian culture make for a dramatic contrast to the Andes – made all the more vivid by the rainy, humid and steaming hot climate. Author Gabriel García Márquez, who toured the Chocó departamento in the 1950s, called it "the most forgotten region in the country", a "magical homeland of flowering jungle and eternal downpours" in *Living to Tell the Tale*. Even today tourism has yet to make a big impact, though the region's ecotourism potential is beginning to be ramped up. Getting here can be time-consuming and expensive, but you're likely to have much of the place to yourself.

Until relatively recently, much of the coast was considered dangerous, riddled with guerrillas, paramilitary groups and drug-runners. Though blackspots remain, the situation has much improved and you are highly unlikely to encounter any problems. Indeed, communication and transport will probably be your biggest headaches, as the region still lags far behind the rest of the country; roads only connect the coast with the interior at **Buenaventura** and **Tumaco**, and access is otherwise by cargo boat, basic *lanchas* or tiny turboprop planes. Electricity is rarely available 24 hours (be prepared for cold showers and candles), internet and wi-fi are hard to find and mobile phone coverage is extremely limited. Lounging on one of the region's wide, empty beaches, backed by jungle-smothered mountains, it's easy to feel you've travelled back to the eighteenth century.

An **Afro-Colombian culture** dominates most of the settlements along the coast, but you'll also encounter members of the **Emberá** and **Wounaan** Indigenous peoples – visiting their villages is possible, a genuinely enlightening experience that for now at least, remains uncommercialized.

Yet most people come for the ruggedly beautiful landscapes and natural attractions of the Pacific coast: the endless beaches of the **Bahía Málaga**, **Bahía Solano** and **Nuquí**; pristine reserves such as the **Parque Nacional Natural Utría**; whales and dolphins frolicking just offshore; hot spring pools; and enough parrots and hummingbirds to fill a football stadium.

Bahía Solano and around

The northern section of Colombia's Pacific coast is anchored by **BAHÍA SOLANO**, a sleepy town in the rain-drenched Chocó region, best known for sportsfishing and **whale-watching** (July to October) and accessible by boat from Buenaventura but also more conveniently by plane from Medellín – there is no land connection. The town itself has a population of around 13,000, made up primarily of Afro-Colombians but also Indigenous Emberá and Hispanic-Colombians from Medellín.

Travelling here still feels like an adventure: facilities are basic and foreign visitors are few. There's little to see in the town itself (also known as "Ciudad Mutis"), which was only officially founded in 1962, and most travellers head out to the more appealing stretches of sand short boat-rides away around the bay, or at **El Valle** (see page 304) facing the Pacific, though there are cheap hotel options in Solano near the waterfront.

CAPUCHIN MONKEY, ISLA GORGONA

Highlights

❶ Playa El Almejal This volcanic black-sand beach just north of El Valle is the perfect place to chill out or use as a base to explore the wild jungle interior. See page 304.

❷ Parque Nacional Natural Utría Pristine reserve smothered in dense tropical forest, with an unspoiled coastline rich in marine life and a rare white-sand beach at Playa Blanca. See page 306.

❸ Nuquí The bay around Nuquí is sprinkled with enchanting Afro-Colombian villages, hot springs, isolated Emberá communities and untrammelled rainforest. See page 307.

❹ Playa Juan de Dios The most enticing, most isolated and least visited of the beaches around the Bahía Málaga. See page 312.

❺ Whale-watching See hundreds of humpbacks along the Pacific coast between July and December, with the Bahía Málaga the best place to see new-born calves. See page 312.

❻ San Cipriano Take a hair-raising ride along the rails on a *brujita* to this languid Afro-Colombian village and nature reserve in the jungle. See page 314.

❼ Isla Gorgona For a real adventure organize a trip to this Pacific island some 35km off the mainland, home to monkeys, a ruined prison, sloths and whale sharks offshore. See page 315.

HIGHLIGHTS ARE MARKED ON THE MAP ON PAGE 302

BICHE

Spend any time in the Colombian Pacific and you are likely to come across "*biche*" (or *viche*), the potent **traditional tipple** of Afro-Colombians and the Emberá people and regarded as something of an elixir for centuries. Distilled from sugar cane and tasting a bit like moonshine it certainly packs a punch, though its alleged health and aphrodisiac qualities seem a little dubious. Locals sell bottles of *biche* for as little as C$10,000 (you won't be served it in a normal bar, just local dives known as *vicheras*) – an unusual souvenir or gift, but one you need to enjoy with care.

The beaches

The best **beaches** near Bahía Solano line the U-shaped bay of the same name beyond the town, beginning with **Playa Mecana**, a quiet 2km stretch of sand anchored by a small village and the refreshing waters of the Río Mecana. You can take a *lancha* here (15min), or simply walk northeast along the beach from Solano at low tide (allow 1hr 30min).

Other beaches include **Playa de los Potes** (30min north of Solano by boat) and beyond to tranquil **Playa de la Paridera**, really a small, jungle-ringed cove on the Punta Nabugá, where **humpback whales** give birth between July and October. There's only one hotel here (see page 304), and it arranges its own boat transport.

On the isolated, northwestern side of Solano bay lies **Playa Punta Huina**, a beautiful reddish sand beach with wreck diving offshore (the World War II-era *San Sebastián de Belalcázar* was sunk here intentionally), and a handful of resorts and lodges – these will organize airport pick-ups and the boat ride (20min) from Solano.

Jardín Botánico del Pacífico

Playa Mecana • Free; charge for guided walks (7km, 2hr; 9km, 7hr) • ⓦ jbdp.org

On the northern bank of the Río Mecana, stretching inland from the beach, the **Jardín Botánico del Pacífico** is a gorgeous 170-acre slice of preserved tropical forest, brimming with palms, heliconia blossoms and orchids, home to howler monkeys and sloths, and laced with four trails of varying difficulty. Kayaks are available to rent for a half day.

ARRIVAL AND DEPARTURE — BAHÍA SOLANO AND AROUND

By plane You can fly from Medellín with SATENA into Bahía Solano's tiny Aeropuerto José Celestino Mutis (which lies 1.5km south of the waterfront and "downtown"), though flights are very much weather-dependent. Departing flights incur a per person tax.

Destinations Medellín (2–3 weekly; 1hr 15min).

By boat It's usually possible to take a cargo boat all the way along the coast between Solano and Buenaventura. Captain Óscar Restrepo (📞 314 6178859) runs Transportes Renacer (📞 2 242 4785 or 📞 313 7936522) on the route, usually departing Muelle El Piñal in Buenaventura on Tuesday and returning from Solano on Saturday. The journey generally shouldn't take longer than 24hr; three meals a day and a bunk bed included. Boats sometimes stop in Nuquí (24hr from Buenaventura, 10hr from Solano) along the way, though it's best to catch a *lancha* from El Valle to here (see page 306).

By jeep You can take a jeep taxi to El Valle (via 7km of paved road and 7km of unpaved track; 45min) from the airport or opposite the school (45min).

GETTING AROUND AND INFORMATION

By chiva and mototaxi *Colectivo chivas* (improvised buses) and *mototaxis* run between the town, airport and El Valle.

Tourist information There is no tourist office – your accommodation will be your main source of information.

Services There is a bank and ATM in Solano (Banco Agrario at Cra 3A No. 2–10), and another ATM at the airport, though don't count on either having cash or accepting your card. Internet cafés can usually be found in town (try Bahia.com; hours vary); there's also a police station and at least four reasonably stocked pharmacies.

ACCOMMODATION AND EATING

Note that most hotels will charge a premium during the **whale-watching season**, roughly mid-July to mid-October.

BY BOAT TO PANAMA

Serious travellers have always found a way to travel between **Solano and Jaqué** in Panama by boat – it's not that difficult, but still requires some planning. Boats (usually just small *lanchas*) vary what they charge for the 10hr trip – your hotel should know which boat is currently making the journey, though times are not set and captains will want to have plenty of passengers before departing. You'll need to get your passport stamped by Colombian immigration before leaving or entering the country; coming into Colombia boats tend to stop at Juradó on the way to Solano, where migración officials at the Alcaldía Municipal (town hall); ❶ 8 521 3845) will do the job; leaving Colombia you can visit the office in central Solano before you go (Cra 3A at C 1A; ❶ 4 682 6984). You will also need to have a yellow fever certificate to show the authorities when you arrive in Panama. Needless to say, security in Panama's Darién region is sketchy at the best of times, so check the latest before making the trip.

BAHÍA SOLANO

Posada del Mar Bahía Solano Cra 3 at C1 ❶ 314 630 6723. Excellent deal, with several basic but comfy en-suite cabañas within a lush garden with hammocks. The friendly hosts are a font of local information and can arrange dive trips. All cabañas come with fan, mosquito net and flatscreen TV. Free wi-fi; breakfast usually. Cash only. $

★ **Rocas de Cabo Marzo** C 3, at Cra 1 ❶ 310 205 7135. B&B-type place owned by friendly Colombian–American couple (Enrique is an expert on local fishing and diving). Rooms come with fan, ocean views and bathrooms. Breakfast and wi-fi included. Cash only, but you can book via ⓦ airbnb or ⓦ booking.com. $$

THE BEACHES

Choibaná Playa Punta Huina ⓦ choibana.com. Lodgings on a private cove beyond the main Playa Huina, with beautiful views, surrounded by jungle. Three simple wood cabañas, each with private bathroom and hammocks on the terrace; rates include breakfast (transfers available from Solano dock for two people minimum). Electricity 24hr daily but no wi-fi, TV or hot water. Offers set meals and sandwiches/salads for additional fixed rates per day. $$

Mapara Lodge Playa de la Paridera ❶ 314 700 4824, ⓦ facebook.com/Maparalodge. Secluded resort with five simple but comfy cabins right on the beach, all with gorgeous sea views. Full range of activities on offer, from whale-watching to diving. Rates include airport transfers and all meals. No internet/wi-fi. $$

Mecana Ecohotel Playa Mecana ⓦ jbdp.org. En-suite cabins with terraces overlooking the beach, with hammocks, fans and mosquito nets, perfectly integrated within the surrounding botanical gardens. Rates include three meals a day, airport transfers and wi-fi. Can arrange trips to the Indigenous community of El Brazo along the Río Valle (4–5hr), as well as local waterfalls. $$$

Pacific Sailfish Ecolodge Playa Punta Huina ❶ 314 375 0941. Gorgeous wooden cottage with six rustic, all-wood-and-palm rooms facing the ocean, with mosquito nets, private bathrooms and free wi-fi. There's a common room with satellite TV. English spoken. Breakfast and airport transfers included. $$

Playa de Oro Lodge Playa Punta Huina ⓦ playadeoro lodge.com. Most luxurious of the area's hotels, with four blocks of eight spotless wooden cabañas, each with balcony, fans and hammock – some have sea views, while others have rainforest views. Breakfast included and free wi-fi in public areas. Excellent restaurant *Cardumen* on site. Food $$, accommodation $$$

El Valle and around

Some 14km by road southwest of Bahía Solano, the Afro-Colombian village of **EL VALLE** is a convenient base for visiting **Parque Nacional Natural Utría** (see page 306), where it's possible to see **whales** close to the shore during calving season (mid-July to mid-Oct). In El Valle itself, there's some fine **surfing**, and you may see **turtles** nesting (Sept–Dec) at nearby **Estación Septiembre**.

The main beach area (and where most of the hotels are), **Playa El Almejal** lies just north of the village (20min walk or 5min by *mototaxi*). In addition to surfing or lounging on the volcanic black sands (rimmed by an end-of-the-world-feeling jungle), you can take several enticing **day-trips** organized by hotels (including whale-watching in season) and explore the **Reserva Natural del Almejal**, operated by *Ecolodge El Almejal* (see page 306), a preserved section of tropical rainforest crisscrossed with trails and aflutter with multicoloured butterflies.

Río Tundó

Of the many standard tours and trips offered from El Valle, make time for the guided canoe ride up the **Río Tundó** (a tributary of the Río El Valle), a four-to five-hour trip through an untouched slice of tropical wilderness. Guides point out wildlife and flora, from kingfishers, toucans and bat-sized butterflies to blooming orchids and sprouting bromeliads.

Boroboro

The Emberá village of **BOROBORO** (actually within the northern section of Parque Nacional Natural Utría but best accessed from El Valle), is likely to be the closest you'll get to experiencing Indigenous life in Chocó, though the effect of greater tourism may change things. For now, **tours** involve motorized canoe rides (2hr) up the Boroboro arm of the Río El Valle (you can also hike up in 6hr; 1hr downriver by canoe). The picturesque village is home to around one hundred people, living in thatched huts on 2m stilts (*palafitos*), and selling local crafts and paintings decorated with the black juice of the jagua, a local fruit.

Cascada del Tigre

Charge • The hike from Playa El Almejal is 3–4hr one-way, or 30min by boat

From El Valle you can hike north through the jungle and along the shore to the **Cascada del Tigre**, a magnificent waterfall that crashes on to the beach and a refreshing waterhole (if hiking, a guide is recommended). Boat trips usually also visit the pristine beach at the mouth of the **Río Juná** further along the coast.

Reserva Estación Septiembre

Playa Cuevita, 5km south of El Valle • Donation requested • ⓦ natura.org.co • You can walk (1–2hr) or hire a *mototaxi* (6min)

> **THE EMBERÁ AND WOUNAAN**
>
> The Chocó region is the ancestral home of the Indigenous **Emberá** and the **Wounaan** (or Waunaan) peoples, two closely related ethnic and linguistic groups with around 70,000 members in Colombia and slightly fewer in Panama's Darién. Far more research has been done on the communities in Panama, and even today little is known about the tribes in Colombia – it's very common to confuse the two groups, though there are key differences. The Indigenous people of Ladrilleros and Cocalito associate with the Wounaan, who were traditionally skilled artists (the Emberá were noted warriors), and even today their reputation for fine craftsmanship is well deserved: you'll see their carvings, baskets, handicrafts and vases made out of *wérregue* wood all along the coast, though the Emberá now produce similar items.
>
> Like the Wounaan, the Emberá are a river people, historically living in family groups. Only since the 1950s have the Emberá started living in villages and towns, though even these communities are located along riverbanks. You can visit Emberá villages from El Valle and Nuquí (see page 309).
>
> Colombia's recent violent history has taken a huge toll on both peoples – as late as 2011 Emberá leaders were being murdered by paramilitary groups seizing tribal land for illegal mining and logging operations. **OREWA** (officially the Asociación de Cabildos Indígenas Wounaan, Emberá Dovida, Katío, Chamí y Tule del Departamento del Chocó) was established to support all the Indigenous peoples of Chocó, and especially the ongoing struggle for land rights.

Between September and December, it's possible to observe **turtles** nesting, laying eggs and hatching at **Reserva Estación Septiembre**, a visitor centre and sanctuary at **Playa Cuevita**. Created to protect the 400m-long nesting site, the reserve is visited by green, hawksbill and leatherback, but mostly olive ridley, turtles.

ARRIVAL AND INFORMATION — EL VALLE

By jeep To reach El Valle from Bahía Solano take a jeep from opposite the school (1hr). *Mototaxis* and *chivas* also run from the airport (see page 303).
On foot You can walk from Bahía Solano in around 3hr, following the road.
By boat Boats from Buenaventura only go to Bahía Solano (see page 303) – take land transport from there. Small, fast boats (*lanchas*) travel between El Valle and Nuquí (see page 309).
Services At the time of writing, the wi-fi in El Valle was unreliable, though this might change in the near future. No banks/ATM machines. Electricity is often only turned on for limited hours or not at all.

ACCOMMODATION

Ecolodge El Almejal Playa El Almejal ⓦ almejal.com.co. The most expensive hotel on the beach features twelve luxurious stone-and-wood cabañas, a whale-watching tower, 24hr electricity, pleasant communal areas and a butterfly garden. Rates include all meals and airport transfers. No internet. $$$$
Hotel Playa Alegre Playa El Almejal ⓦ playaalegre.com.co. Ten beautiful, private wood-and-brick cabins with bathrooms, some with sea views and others arranged around a small shrimp pond, next door to the *Ecolodge* (see above). Includes three meals, excursions and airport transfers – no internet. Minimum stay three nights. $$$$
★ **Humpback Turtle** Playa El Almejal ⓦ humpbackturtle.com. Run by a friendly American/Colombian couple, this sociable hostel comes with beach bar, two comfy cabaña-style doubles, six dorm beds in a rustic cabin, campsite with hammocks, a plethora of tours, surfboard rental, shared kitchen and an on-site restaurant. They can organize whale-watching trips (2–3hr). Breakfast included (lunch and dinner extra, featuring local fish); no internet. Hammocks, dorms and doubles available. $

Parque Nacional Natural Utría

Charge (usually not included in tour prices) • ⓦ parquesnacionales.gov.co

Roughly halfway between El Valle (see page 304) and Nuquí (see page 307), covering some 545 square kilometres, the exceptional **PARQUE NACIONAL NATURAL UTRÍA** is another precious slice of untrammelled mangrove swamp and tropical rainforest rich in flora, fauna and marine life. The park shelters marmoset and capuchin monkeys, agoutis, foxes, ocelots, deer and peccary, while humpback whales and turtles graze offshore. Some 80 percent of the park falls within three Emberá reservations – you'll often see Emberá fishermen in the streams and rivers here.

Most visitors end up around the large inlet (Ensenada de Utría) at the northern end of the park, though **day-trips** – easy to arrange – are frustratingly short, only scratching the surface of the coastal section. Staying the night and visiting independently will give you a lot more time to explore. You can also consider a trip to the Emberá village of Boroboro (see page 305) from El Valle.

The park

The **park headquarters**, halfway up the eastern side of the Ensenada de Utría, comprises simple lodgings, a restaurant and the **Centro de Interpretación**, with displays on the region's ecosystems. Most day-trips begin nearby with a guided stroll along an 800m elevated boardwalk into the coastal **mangroves** (guides are knowledgeable but usually only speak Spanish). After this a boat will take you across the bay, where you hike the 990m-trail through lush jungle to **Playa Cocalito**, a deserted beach on the other side of the Peninsula Utría and a refreshing place to swim. From here your boat usually makes a fifteen-minute trip south to a small privately owned island known as **Playa Blanca**, with a pristine white coral-sand beach and a small restaurant run by the Caizamo family. The restaurant stands on top of a small hill, with spectacular views. Later you can snorkel around the reefs off the beach, before returning to El Valle or Nuquí by boat.

ARRIVAL AND DEPARTURE

By boat Boats travel to the park from El Valle daily (30–40min). From Nuquí boats take around 1hr (1hr 30min from Guachalito).

On foot You can walk to the park along an easy trail, 9.5km from El Valle (allow 3hr), but to reach the park headquarters you must arrange for a boat to pick you up at the end of the Ensenada de Utría (ask at your hotel). You can arrange a guide for a fee when you arrive – you are not officially allowed to explore the park trails without one.

PARQUE NACIONAL NATURAL UTRÍA

Tours Nuquí-based Chocó Community Tourism Alliance offers 7hr day-trips out of Guachalito (see page 308). Four-night packages (for two people) available. Mano Cambiada (⌾ manocambiada.org) handles the park's lodging and food services and also runs tours.

ACCOMMODATION AND EATING

Centro de Visitantes Jaibaná ⌾ manocambiada.org. Mano Cambiada operates the only lodging in the park, with three simple but comfy cabañas (one with five doubles, all with bathroom; one with three large rooms with bathroom; and another with eight beds and one shared bathroom). Cheap meals are served at the restaurant. All-inclusive available. **$$$**

Nuquí and around

South of the Parque Nacional Natural Utría, **NUQUÍ** ("new-key") serves as the focus for some of the most enticing stretches of the Pacific coast, though there's little to see in the town itself. Established on the Golfo de Tribugá as a remote trading post in 1917, it now boasts a population of around 7500, mostly poor Afro-Colombian fishermen and farmers.

The airport and docks are here, along with a small clinic and basic supermarkets (and 24hr electricity), but the best hotels are scattered along beaches to the north and south, especially in **Guachalito**, a short boat ride away. This is another excellent place to see humpback whales during the breeding season (July to October).

Shops in town sell local crafts such as *wérregue* vases, *totumo* utensils and *tagua* necklaces, but the town beach – Playa de Nuquí – is usually littered with driftwood and not a good place to relax. More enticing is **Playa Olímpica**, an enormous 5km-swathe of sand stretching south to Panguí, a small village on the Río Panguí. The beach starts a short walk to the southwest of town, across the river and the promontory known as the **Morro de Nuquí** (you can walk on the sand and wade across at low tide, otherwise accessible by speedboats and kayak). To the north of town lies the 8km near-deserted stretch of **Playa de Tribugá**.

Coquí

The first major *lancha* stop as you head southwest along the bay from Nuquí (15min by boat), **COQUÍ** is a small fishing community of around 250 right on the beach, slowly

> ### SURF NUQUÍ
>
> Still unknown to most international surfers, the beaches and bays around Nuquí offer some of the most spectacular **surfing** on the Pacific, with breaks for all levels, from flat, sandy beaches with gentle waves suitable for beginners to gnarly breaks of up to 6m. Hotels should be able to hook you up with an experienced local if you are looking for lessons. The bad news is that board rental is usually expensive, with lessons a lot more. In Guachalito the scene is dominated by the guys at *El Cantil Ecolodge* (see page 309). Experienced surfers will appreciate the more challenging waves at Cabo Corrientes, Pela Pela, Juan Tornillo and El Derrumbe.

developing its ecotourism potential. For now, this means languid *chingo* rides (a dugout canoe powered by long poles like a gondola) through some of the most dense and pristine mangrove forest in Colombia, replete with tangled roots loaded with rare birds and tropical plants (Spanish-speaking guides only). Most hotels will be able to arrange tours. There are two small restaurants in the village and two small *posadas*, as well as a shop in the centre that sells bottled water and cold beer. The village usually gets electricity between 5pm and 10pm only.

Joví

Fifteen minutes by boat southwest along the coast from Coquí (you can walk in one hour or so), **JOVÍ** is another small Afro-Colombian fishing community of around four hundred people, lining the beach and along the Río Joví. Local guides offer illuminating trips up the river by *chingo* deep into the rainforest where giant, curving pichindé trees form leafy tunnels over the water. After about an hour, you arrive at the junction of another small stream where it's a ten-minute hike to the **Cascada Chontadura** and a natural pool in the jungle, perfect for a refreshing dip. From here it's another hour hike up the mountain to the more impressive **Cascada Antaral** deeper in the forest (also with deep pool for swimming). Most hotels will be able to arrange tours.

Guachalito

Ten minutes beyond Joví by boat (or a 20min walk) lies **GUACHALITO**, its coffee-coloured sands home to the area's best hotels (see page 317). Lounging on the beach is the biggest activity here, though you can also stroll through the jungle (around 15min) to the crystal clear **Cascada de Amor**, a double waterfall with an inviting waterhole for swimming.

Termales

TERMALES, around fifteen minutes beyond Guachalito by boat (1hr on foot), is a pretty fishing community of around two hundred people, its beachfront houses surrounded by small gardens overflowing with blossoms. The locals here have also created flowery arches across the main street, and gardens sprouting from old canoes raised on stilts (known as *azoteas*). Termales usually gets electricity between 6pm and 11pm daily, though this can be temperamental.

The hot springs
5min walk from the beach • Charge

Termales is named after the large **hot springs** (*aguas termales*) just outside town. Managed by locals, the site is clean and well maintained, with a medium-sized man-made pool containing the piped-in spring water, a small "spa" where you can enjoy a mud facial, and a simple restaurant.

Cascada de Cuatro Encantos

Other than the hot springs, the other main attraction near Termales is the **Cascada de Cuatro Encantos**, a picturesque waterfall with four tiers forming a wide, deep pool where you can swim. The falls lie at the end of a pretty trail through the jungle, best accessed with local guides.

Cabo Corrientes

Beyond Termales and the next village of **Arusí**, the promontory known as **Cabo Corrientes** is a serious surf destination, with a decent beach break and a spectacular point break for advanced surfers. Boats will usually take you for the day from Guachalito (find other surfers to share the cost).

Jurubirá

JURUBIRÁ is a picturesque Chocó fishing village just outside the boundary of Utría national park (see page 306), around 45 minutes north of Nuquí on an unsurfaced road (30min by boat). Attractions include the *azotea* gardens (in old canoes raised on stilts) and relaxing **hot springs** just outside town (similar to Termales; charge). You can organize boat trips to visit the nearby **Emberá communities** up the Río Chorí (Puerto Jagua, Puerto Indio and La Loma) or hike the Sendero Dos Boca trail (1hr 30min) – it's an enchanting experience, more like something you'd expect in the remote Amazon.

Morromico

MORROMICO is a gorgeous, tranquil and isolated bay at the southern end of Utría National Natural Park (see page 306). There are several hiking paths in the dense jungle around the bay, some to beaches in the park and others to nearby Emberá villages – the owners of *Cabaña Morromico* (see page 310) can help arrange guides. All pass by waterfalls with natural jungle pools good for swimming.

ARRIVAL AND DEPARTURE · NUQUÍ AND AROUND

By plane Tiny Aeropuerto Reyes Murillo is in the middle of Nuquí, a short stroll from the only hotels, and from the boat dock where you catch *lanchas* to the beaches. At the time of writing only SATENA served Nuquí, with flights from Medellín via Quibdó on a small, eighteen-seat turboprop plane. Note that the 10kg check-in and 5kg hand baggage weight limits are strictly enforced. Buy tickets in advance, especially in high season. There is an arrival tourist tax charged per person.

By boat Fast boats to El Valle depart Nuquí at around 6am on Mon and Fri (one-way; 1hr 30min), returning at around 11am. It's also sometimes possible to pick up the cargo boat travelling between Bahia Solano and Buenaventura in Nuquí – call Captain Óscar Restrepo (☎ 314 617 8859).

GETTING AROUND

By lancha *Lanchas* go up and down the coast around Nuquí each day; Marcos Salas (☎ 314 714 4752) boats head south to Arusí via all the main villages on route (usually 1–1.30pm Mon–Sat, returning 6.30am–7am from Arusí). If you want to travel at other times you'll have to charter a boat. Note that if you are travelling to El Valle (see page 304) from Guachalito you must contact the boat captain in advance so he will wait for your connecting boat in Nuquí (your hotel should be able to do this for you).

TOURS

Chocó Community Tourism Alliance (Alianza de Turismo Comunitario del Chocó) Nuquí ☎ 320 348 8400, w facebook.com/visitchoco. Collective representing local guides in Termales, Coquí, Jovi and Playa Blanca.

ACCOMMODATION AND EATING

There are only a few **hotels** in Nuquí itself, with the rest of the accommodation spread out around the bay, though budget options are rare. Nuquí has a handful of **restaurants** offering fish, chicken, meat and local produce, but most visitors eat at their lodgings – packages usually include all meals.

NUQUÍ

Hostal Claus ☎ 311 302 4409. Budget accommodation in the village, with very basic but clean en-suite rooms, all with TV and free drinking water. Housed in a nondescript modern building, above a small local restaurant. $

Nuquimar Hotel Av La Playa w hotelnuquimar.com. Nine comfortable cabin-like wood rooms with sea views, fan, TV and private bathrooms, within walking distance of shops and restaurants (100m from the beach). Rates include airport pick-up. Breakfast included. $$

GUACHALITO

La Cabaña de Beto y Marta ☎ 300 639 7279, w facebook.com/betoymartanuqui. Small, enticing hotel with four cosy cabañas set around a lush garden on the beach (each has a private bathroom and 24hr solar-powered electricity). The garden contains an outdoor kitchen, and an

open-air dining room with views of the beach. Rates include three meals, guided walks and airport/boat transfers. $$$$
Ecolodge Mar y Río ☎ 313 745 9579, ✉ elmardediego@gmail.com. Operated by the friendly Diego González on the northern beach of Guchalito beach (where the river flows into the ocean), this budget option offers two simple but comfy rooms in the main palm-and-bamboo beach house (with veranda and hammocks), plus a private cinderblock cabaña with private bathroom. Rates include all meals and transfer from Nuquí, plus free wi-fi. Diego can help organize whale-watching tours and snorkelling equipment. $$$
★ **La Joviseña** ⓦ lajovisena.com. This trio of simple, thatched cabañas with doubles and private bathrooms (cold water) lines a blooming tropical garden full of butterflies, hummingbirds and fresh fruits you can pick right off the trees. The open-air kitchen knocks out three sumptuous home-cooked meals a day (all included), enjoyed outside. Owners provide snorkelling equipment and plenty of good advice. Electricity and mobile phone connection 6–10pm only; no internet. $$
Pijibá Lodge ⓦ pijibalodge.com. Tranquil but ageing cabañas (very basic double rooms) surrounded by beach and rainforest, with an excellent restaurant and sea views. Electricity just 6–9pm (and not in the rooms; sockets available in the restaurant) and no hot water. Price includes airport transfers and all meals, but no internet. $$$

TERMALES
Cabañas Refugio Salomon ☎ 322 608 8431. Large stone house close to the beach, with simple but adequate single, double and triple rooms on the second floor, all with mosquito nets (two with private bathrooms, the rest shared). Prices include three meals a day, with electricity 6–10pm daily. $$$

CABO CORRIENTES
Punta Brava Arusí ⓦ puntabravachoco.co. One of the most remote lodges, between the small village of Arusí and Cabo Corrientes, this is also one of the most rewarding, surrounded by pristine beaches and jungle with super-friendly owners. The property comprises five cosy rooms and two shared bathrooms, with three meals included. Transfers from Nuquí not included. $$$

MORROMICO
★ **Cabaña Morromico** ⓦ morromico.com. This is the real thing: an enchanting, rustic family lodge with the breezy main building containing four all-wood bedrooms on three floors (two shared bathrooms). Fabulous meals (included) cooked by owners Javier and Gloria are shared on one long wooden table, while hammocks are strategically placed around the property. Electricity 24hr. Rates include meals and airport transfers. No TV or internet. $$$$

DIRECTORY
Banks and exchange There are no banks or ATMs in Nuquí – bring lots of cash.
Internet and phone Internet is available in a couple of cafés in Nuquí, but mobile phone and wi-fi service is poor. There's no internet and only sporadic mobile phone service in the communities around Nuquí (Movistar is the best provider).

Buenaventura and around

The sweltering, salsa-imbued big city of the Pacific coast, **BUENAVENTURA** is also one of the country's largest Afro-Colombian centres (85 percent of the 600,000 population), giving it a street life and cultural flavour quite unlike anywhere else. It's definitely an acquired taste: though attempts have been made to improve things (see page 311), your first impression is likely to be of a chaotic, gritty port city ringed by shantytowns and blighted by poverty. While it's true that this is statistically one of the most violent cities in Colombia, the grisly reports of "chop houses" (use your imagination) are a little misleading – the area of **Isla Cascajal** (downtown) near the **Muelle Turístico** (tourist wharf) and major hotels is reasonably safe, as is the waterfront Parque Néstor Urbano Tenorio and *malecón*. For tourists Buenaventura is primarily the gateway to stellar **beaches** and **whale-watching** opportunities, as well as a potential gold-mine of **ecotourism** trails and activities – the urban sprawl is surrounded by dense jungle, rivers, pristine mangroves, Indigenous villages and spectacular beaches. Many of the latter are scattered around **Bahía Málaga**, a deep bay that cuts into the mainland a short boat ride to the west, much of it protected within the Parque Nacional Natural Uramba Bahía Málaga. Just inland, the laidback community of **San Cipriano** is linked to the rest of the world by rail carts known as "**brujitas**", one of Colombia's quirkiest sights. But most of all, the locals here are likely to be some of the friendliest and fun of any you'll meet in Colombia.

HOPE FOR BUENAVENTURA?

Buenaventura has a grim **reputation** in Colombia. Though it remains statistically the country's most violent city, the truth is that most trouble is confined to specific areas well beyond the main tourist zone on Isla Cascajal (downtown), where there are always plenty of people, police and soldiers patrolling the streets. Buenaventura's problem is **cocaine**, and the rival gangs that control the lucrative trade in it – originally the local branch ("Banda Local") of national cartel Los Urabeños and La Empresa (affiliated with Los Rastrojos, the sworn enemies of Urabeños). These gangs emerged from paramilitary groups originally formed to fight FARC in the 1990s. In 2014 the government sent hundreds of troops to the city to fight the gangs, and "El Mono", the "Pablo Escobar of Buenaventura", was captured. That same year, the central government pledged money and resources to help turn things around: the aim is to transform the city, with the "Proyecto Malecón Bahía de la Cruz" an ambitious plan to beautify the whole southern shore of Isla Cascajal (though locals would prefer basic improvements to city infrastructure). The *malecón* (boardwalk), and new sports facilities in waterside Parque Néstor Urbano Tenorio, are among the most recent additions.

The **roots of the problem** run deep: strikes and peaceful protests in the city have turned violent, locals frustrated at the lack of progress. In 2018, 60 percent of the population still lived in poverty, unemployment in some neighbourhoods was also above 60 percent and, with no public hospital or water treatment plant, sewage was flowing directly into the bay. Though killings have certainly declined, little has changed for the majority and gang wars have continued, this time between new groups such as the "La Gente del Orden", and the Clan del Golfo and even the ELN.

Piangüita and La Bocana

The closest beaches to the city, **PIANGÜITA** and **LA BOCANA**, can be reached only by a twenty-minute boat ride west along the Bahía de Buenaventura. Piangüita has dark sands and murky water (from sediment, not pollution), but is cleaned every morning and can be lots of fun at weekends, with beach bars blaring salsa and cheap restaurants backed by dense jungle. There's no dock here, so disembarking requires jumping over the side into the water and wading to the beach. From Piangüita, there's a rough road to La Bocana, a more rustic grey-sand beach and fishing village 2km back towards the city. This beach is not cleaned daily, so the flotsam (basically trash from the city) tends to build up, but the hotels here are usually cheaper. Basic packages are sold at the Muelle Turístico in Buenaventura.

Juanchaco

A small fishing village on the Istmo de Malaguita, some 40km northwest of Buenaventura, **JUANCHACO** is the gateway to the Parque Nacional Natural Uramba Bahía Málaga (see page 312). Though it is also the access point for Ladrilleros and La Barra, there's little to see in the village itself and the beaches can be rather dirty. It's a genuine working place, with music blaring from the bars and shrimp nets drying in the sun. Juanchaco boasts around five hotels, but it's not worth staying here unless you plan to take a lot of boat tours.

Ladrilleros

Surfers are especially drawn to single-street **LADRILLEROS**, a short 2.5km ride (5min) or walk (30min) west from Juanchaco on the other side of the Istmo de Malaguita, where enormous 2–3m waves lash the shore during the August to November rainy season and where you can stay in a number of basic digs. Ladrilleros is also a popular weekend beach getaway for Caleños, and there are a growing number of posher places to stay and eat on the steep cliffs above the beach. Sadly, the beach itself (which was never that big) was almost totally **washed away** by a storm – it's still beautiful during low tide, but can disappear during high tide (the sands at La Barra, a short stroll north, were unaffected).

Seafood dominates in Ladrilleros (tasty shrimp *empanadas* are a speciality), though plenty of small restaurants serve the Colombian staples of rice, chicken, beef or fried fish. Ice-cold beer is served everywhere. That said, most visitors end up eating in their hotels, where meal packages are only slightly more than the cost of a room.

La Barra

A small fishing village and beach of the same name, **LA BARRA** is justly regarded as one of the most beautiful swathes of sand in Colombia, just a couple of kilometres north of Ladrilleros. The walk takes about 45 minutes to one hour (*mototaxis* are also available); an easy-to-follow coastal path links the two villages, and you can also stroll along the beach, but only at low tide – make sure you check the tide times in advance. The sand is a dark, greyish colour, but clean, generally devoid of people and hemmed in by untrammelled rainforest.

Playa Chucheros and Playa Juan de Dios

If you really want to get away from civilization, the best beaches in the area lie on Istmo Pichidó on the other side of Bahía Málaga from Juanchaco. **Playa Chucheros** is a largely undeveloped and usually empty 3km-long beach, with a 10m-high waterfall that forms a freshwater pool on the sands. Further south lies **Playa Juan de Dios** (wplayajuandedios.com), a gorgeous natural reserve with the only white-sand beach in the area and basic accommodation (45min by fast boat by Buenaventura).

Parque Nacional Natural Uramba Bahía Málaga

The **Parque Nacional Natural Uramba Bahía Málaga** encompasses much of the precious biodiverse waters of the bay itself, some 470 square kilometres in total. Best known for **whale-watching** (see below), most tour agencies in Buenaventura also offer trips to attractions in and around the park, including the **Archipiélago de La Plata** at the northern end of the bay. These islands are home to the Afro-Colombian community of La Plata and offer opportunities for clam fishing and diving; the clams are especially fresh at *Sazón Malagueño* (see page 314). On the east side of the bay the **Cascadas de la Sierpe** comprises two beautiful waterfalls tumbling some 65m to form a pool of fresh

> ### WHALE-WATCHING IN BAHÍA MÁLAGA
>
> Parque Nacional Natural Uramba Bahía Málaga is home to hundreds of frolicking Southern Ocean **humpback whales** that breed here from June to November, fleeing the Antarctic winter some 8500km to the south, in what locals call the "Fiesta de la Migración". During their stay the whales mate, give birth, then feed and teach their young how to breathe and hunt. Observing the whales at this time of year can be a magical experience, with adults 18–30m in length (at birth, calves measure around 6m), and humpbacks especially prone to crowd-pleasing displays of breaching and slapping the water. Humpbacks are also famed for their "songs", those otherworldly, spine-tingling underwater cries produced by forcing air through their massive nasal cavities. They were once highly endangered, but the global moratorium on hunting humpback whales introduced in 1966 has boosted numbers, though threats from fishing and pollution still exist.
>
> **Whale-watching tours** usually depart Buenventura (see page 313) or the pier in Juanchaco (which are cheaper). Though the whales arrive in June, whale-watching is only permitted from 1 July to 1 November.

water mixed with salt water, surrounded by dense rainforest. Just north of the park, deep inside the jungle, the **Comunidad Indígena Cocalito** is the home of the Indigenous Wounaan people, on the Río Bongo, while downriver lies **Puerto España**, an Afro-Colombian fishing town on the Pacific Ocean. Crabs are the speciality here (you can sample fifteen different kinds).

ARRIVAL AND DEPARTURE   BUENAVENTURA AND AROUND

By plane Aeropuerto Gerardo Tobar López, around 16km southeast of downtown, only receives flights from Bogotá (3 weekly; 1hr 30min) on SATENA. Taxis meet flights and connect visitors to downtown/Muelle Turístico.

By bus Buenaventura's Terminal de Transportes is in the heart of the tourist zone on Isla Cascajal (Cra 5 No. 7–32), a short walk from the main hotels and the boats at the Muelle Turístico. Numerous *busetas* (minibuses, the cheapest), *microbuses* and *camionetas* (big cars, the most expensive option) run between Buenaventura and Cali, and you can stop in San Cipriano (see page 314) on the way.

Destinations Armenia (hourly; 4–5hr); Bogotá (3–4 daily; 11–12hr); Buga (every 30min; 2.5hr); Cali (every 15–30min; 2hr 30min–3hr); Medellín (hourly; 9–10hr); Pereira (hourly; 5–6hr).

By boat It's usually possible to take a cargo boat all the way along the coast between Buenaventura and Solano (see page 300), departing the Muelle el Piñal, 3km east of the Muelle Turístico.

To Isla Gorgona Vive Gorgona (see page 317) can arrange boat transport from the Muelle Turístico in Buenaventura (3hr 30min). Otherwise, cargo boats (*barco de cabotaje*) depart from the Muelle el Piñal, typically taking 10–12hr to Gorgona. Try Barco Andrés Paola (☏ 315 551 7162). You can also take speedboats (3hr 30min) from the Muelle Turístico in Buenaventura to Guapí and continue on to Gorgona from there.

GETTING AROUND

By taxi and minivan Taxis in Buenaventura will charge a flat fee for destinations within the city.

By boat Speedboats and *lanchas* for various coastal destinations leave from the Muelle Turístico, on the western edge of the waterfront on Isla Cascajal (C 1, at Cra 2). Times vary, but most boats usually depart daily at 8am, 10.30am, 1.30pm and 4pm to Juanchaco (45min–1hr), Chucheros and Juan de Dios (return valid for ten days), with boats returning at 8am, 1pm and 4pm (during holidays and busy periods boats leave every 2hr, when full). Various companies compete on the main routes, but Lanchas Bahía Mar (☏ 2 242 6041, w facebook.com/bahiamarlanchas) is a safe bet. To reach Chucheros or Juan de Dios you can also take a *lancha* from Juanchaco (10min).

By mototaxi and tractovía Between Juanchaco and Ladrilleros, get a ride on the back of a *mototaxi* or on a *tractovía/tracto-chivas* (a bus pulled by a tractor).

INFORMATION AND TOURS

Tourist information There is a small tourist information kiosk at the entrance to the Muelle Turístico (C 1, at Cra 2).
Ecomanglar (La Asociación Comunitaria Ecomanglar) w ecomanglar.org. Various trips from Buenaventura and Juanchaco along the Bahía de Buenaventura and the Bahía Málaga.

ACCOMMODATION

BUENAVENTURA

In Buenaventura, as the cheapest digs in town are downright unsavoury, it's worth paying a little more for comfort.

★ **Cosmos Pacífico Hotel** C 3 No. 1A–57 w hotelescosmos.com. This five-star behemoth is the best hotel in Buenaventura, with stylish rooms, glass balconies and luxurious bathrooms, plus a gym, rooftop deck and outdoor pool. Free wi-fi. Huge buffet breakfast included. $$$$

Hotel Cordillera Diagonal 3 No. 3B–51 w cordillerahotel.com. Huge, excellent-value hotel in the centre of town, with clean, modern rooms (some with sea views) equipped with flatscreen cable TV and free wi-fi (there's also a gym and internet room). Breakfast included. $$

Hotel Tequendama Inn Estación C 2 No. 1A–08 w booking.com. Buenaventura's chic historic hotel was built in 1925 overlooking the water, next to what used to be the train station (now an art school). The plush rooms feature flatscreen TVs, balconies and free wi-fi, and there's an outdoor pool. Breakfast included. $$

LADRILLEROS

Prices here range wildly between high (Christmas & Jan; Easter; July & Aug) and low season. Ladrilleros boasts around fifteen hotels; most of the year you can just turn up and check rooms before paying (which is cheaper than buying a package at the Muelle Turístico in Buenaventura).

Hotel Bahía Del Sol w hotelbahiadelsol.com.co. Basic but comfortable standby, with reliable a/c rooms with bathrooms (also with fans) and TV in small wooden cabins (some rooms have shared bathrooms). Basic rates include wi-fi, ferry from Buenaventura, breakfast and dinner (packages that include lunch also available). $$$

Hotel Palma Real w hotelpalmareal.com. Luxurious option with lovely cabañas (with a/c) and a small pool tucked away in the palms above the shore. Breakfast included (most packages also include transport and all meals). $$$

Papagayos Beach Hotel w hotelenladrilleros.com. One of the cheaper resorts, popular with Caleños, with simple but comfy rooms with a/c (and cheaper options with fans), all with TVs and buffet breakfast included. All-inclusive packages available. $

★ **Reserva Agua Marina** w reservaaguamarina.com. Plush hotel perched on the cliffs, with a choice of simple, clean motel-like doubles with a/c and cheaper cabañas (fans, no a/c and cold showers outside), all with free wi-fi, great views and access to a pool, decent restaurant (breakfast included) and bar. Whale-watching tours and all-inclusive packages available. $$

PLAYA JUAN DE DIOS

Reserva Natural Juan de Dios w playajuandedios.com. The reserve maintains two cabañas *nativas*, shared rustic, open-sided cabins with several basic beds and hammocks, and two private *bohíos* (huts) with doubles and mosquito nets, as well as a camping area (with showers and toilets). Prices include three meals a day and the boat transfer from Buenaventura with Bahía Mar. Camping $$, *bohíos* $$$, cabañas $$$$

EATING

BUENAVENTURA

Seafood is, unsurprisingly, king here, with locals justly proud of the huge range of dishes on offer.

★ **Café Pacífico** C 1 No. 5A–15 w cafepacifico.com.co. Artsy café on the waterfront, specializing in strong coffee and traditional Afro-Colombian food; ceviche, *patacones* with shrimp, *cazuela de mariscos* (sefood stew), local cakes such as *torta de chontaduro* and coconut ice drinks. Also hosts an intriguing array of cultural events, from poetry readings to dance. Cash only. $$

Restaurante Brassa Mare C 1 No. 5–96 t 314 682 1984. Right on the seafront, with an outdoor patio, this is the best choice for seafood or drinks, though it also serves plenty of chicken and beef dishes. Specialities include *langostinos gourmet* (shrimp stuffed with crab), *cazuela de calamar* (squid stew with clams, crab and a secret house sauce) and fried snapper. $$

ARCHIPIÉLAGO DE LA PLATA

Sazón Malagueño La Plata w ecomanglar.org. The local community runs this simple restaurant by the waterside, specializing in fresh fish, *sancocho de pescado* (fish stew), *tamal de mariscos* (seafood *tamales*) and a huge range of clams (*piangua*). $

San Cipriano

Set in the sizzling tropical jungle at the confluence of the Escalarete and San Cipriano rivers, 20km inland from Buenaventura, the Afro-Colombian village of **SAN CIPRIANO** seems like another world, a sleepy collection of ramshackle wooden houses lined with *muchillá* (freshwater shrimp) traps, toddlers chasing butterflies and bare-bones bars with old boys sipping beers. In the lush **Reserva Natural San Cipriano** you can swim or go tubing in crystalline waters, hemmed in by palms, blossoms and a vast array of tropical birdlife.

What makes San Cipriano really unique, however, is its **transportation**. There's no road and only a forest-flanked railway line linking San Cipriano with Córdoba, 6.5km

---

THE PIANGUA

Spend any time on the Pacific coast, especially around Buenaventura, and you'll encounter the humble but tasty **piangua** (also known as the "*concha negra*" or "*chucheca*"), the ubiquitous clam harvested from the mud beneath local mangrove forests and tossed into everything from *tamales* to soups. It's always been central to the Afro-Colombian communities along the coast (and in neighbouring Ecuador), but only 15 percent of the harvest is sold to inland Colombia. Ecomanglar (see page 313) organizes special *piangua* tours to the La Plata archipelago in the Bahía Málaga, with a meal at *Sazón Malagueño* (see page 314) to sample fifteen different varieties.

away. With the passenger trains long gone, inventive locals have attached motorcycle-powered wooden carts to the tracks; these "**brujitas**" (literally, "little witches"), whisk you between the two villages at hair-raising speed. It's a single-track railway, but riders simply stop and remove their carts to allow oncoming traffic to pass (they make it look much easier, and lighter, than it must be) – those with heavier loads (or small kids) get to stay on the tracks.

Reserva Natural San Cipriano
Charge

From the San Cipriano *brujitas* "station", follow the main road through the village (the river will be on your right) and you'll soon reach the entrance to the **Reserva Natural San Cipriano**. From here the track continues up the valley for around 10km (the first kilometre is still village); the further you get the more lush, pristine and enticing the scenery becomes. The main attractions along the way are well-signed swimming areas or "*charcos*", usually bends and natural pools in the river with small accessible banks or beaches. The water is clear, clean and refreshing, with lots of fish swimming around. Around 5km up there's a waterfall, with a deeper pool you can dive into. In the village you can rent **giant tubes** ("*neumático*"), walk up the valley, jump in where you like and float back down (as many times as you like). Around halfway up there's also a trail that takes you over to the **Río Zabaletes**, an even more pristine river (you'll need to stay the night in San Cipriano to tackle this properly).

ARRIVAL AND DEPARTURE · SAN CIPRIANO

By bus To reach San Cipriano, you have to get to Córdoba first. Minivan (*colectiva*) #5 shuttles back and forth from downtown Buenaventura to Córdoba station (around 45min) frequently during the day, but you can also ask to be dropped off by any Cali-to-Buenaventura bus service – these will drop you on the main highway from where it's around a 1km walk down to the Córdoba station.

By train cart (brujitas) From Córdoba station carts (*brujitas*) usually leave on demand for San Cipriano throughout the day. As a foreigner you'll probably be asked to pay a lot more than the advertised rate, but be firm – you may have to wait until the cart is full, but maintain a sense of humour and you'll eventually be let on (pay on the way back). The trip takes about 15–20min.

ACCOMMODATION AND EATING

Many places in the village offer very **basic accommodation** (breeze-block cells with a mattress and maybe a fan, single light bulb, shared bathrooms – you get the idea). If you do plan to spend the night, bring a mosquito net. A number of **restaurants** serve meals in the village but there's little to distinguish them – pork, chicken or fresh tilapia (the best option) tend to grace menus, served with rice and plantains, but opening times are at the whim of the owners. The celebrated *encocado de muchillá* (the local freshwater shrimp cooked in coconut milk) is rarely offered, but is a fabulous treat. Look out also for the potent local tipples: *viche* (liquor made from sugar cane), *tumbacatre* and *arrechón* (the "Pacific Viagra").

Hotel David Beyond the entrance to the reserve (200m on the right) ☏ 312 815 4051. The simple rooms here come with fans, mosquito nets and shared or private bathrooms with cold water only; the food is hearty and tasty. Breakfast not included; no internet. $\underline{\$}$

Isla Gorgona

One of the most enchanting adventure destinations in Colombia, **ISLA GORGONA** is a blessedly isolated nature reserve, 35km off the west coast. Visiting the island requires advance planning (and plenty of cash), though it's worth the effort: it offers the chance for a real wilderness, back-to-nature experience.

Gorgona is roughly 9km long and 2.5km wide (giving an area of around 26 square kilometres) and other than groups of tourists and researchers, completely uninhabited. The island was privately owned by the D'Croz and Payán families until 1960, when President Camargo ordered its seizure – Gorgona subsequently served as a Devil's Island-style high-security prison until 1984, when it became the **Parque Nacional**

Natural Gorgona. Most of the prison is now ruined, though the old hacienda of the Payán family acts as the interesting **Museo Payán** and **Museo del Antiguo Penal**. Ancient petroglyphs have also been found carved into the island's rocks.

Otherwise the island is smothered with tropical jungle replete with cheeky, white-faced capuchin monkeys, boobys, caimans, frigatebirds, pelicans, sloths, tortoises and snakes (rubber boots are available for rent). A handful of structures comprises the settlement known as **El Poblado**, with all the amenities on the island (hotel, dive shop) – beyond this area you need to be accompanied by a **guide** (you'll usually be assigned one on arrival).

The island's palm-backed **beaches** are generally empty, and the **coral reef** offshore is rich in barracudas, jacks, sea turtles, killer whales, whale sharks and whitetip sharks. From June to November it's a fabulous place to view **humpback whales** and their offspring. No surprise that **diving** and **snorkelling** are the main activities here.

ARRIVAL AND DEPARTURE — ISLA GORGONA

By boat from Guapí The port town of Guapí is just 1hr 30min by fast boat from Gorgona, though Guapí itself is inaccessible by land from the rest of Colombia. The easiest way to get there is with SATENA flights from Cali (1 daily; 45min); taxis connect the airport to the boat pier. TAC (wtaccolombia.com) also offers charter flights from Popayán. The Isla Gorgona resort (wislagorgona.co/en/tour-item/plan-vivegorgona) arranges boat transport to the island (free for package customers), usually departing Mon, Wed & Fri at 12.30pm (boats return at 7am on the same days). These boats will wait if flights are delayed. At other times private boat owners should be able to take you across, but it won't be cheap.

By boat from Buenaventura The Isla Gorgona resort (see page 317) can arrange boat transport for a minimum of ten people from the Muelle Turístico in downtown Buenaventura, with boats departing Mon, Wed & Fri at 8am (call 314 751 6944 to see if you can join a group) – this is typically sold as part of a three-night package. These boats take 3hr 30min to reach Gorgona. Otherwise, cargo boats (*barco de cabotaje*) depart from the Muelle el Piñal in Buenaventura (see page 313), typically taking 10–12hr to Gorgona. Call 314 378 9710 or 321 874 5663. You can also take speedboats (3hr 30min) from the Muelle Turístico in Buenaventura to Guapí, to connect with boats to Gorgona.

Liveaboard dive tours All-inclusive four- to five-day dive trips usually depart Buenaventura's Muelle Turístico (including accommodation on board, meals and park entry fees). These trips can be arranged through the various dive shops in Cali and Buenaventura. Contact Embarcaciones Asturias (2 404 0483, barcoasturias@yahoo.com) or Colombia Dive Adventures (wcolombiadiveadventures.com).

By organized tour The Isla Gorgona resort (wislagorgona.co) sells all-inclusive packages that include boat transfers from Guapí to the island (you have to arrange flights to Guapí yourself) plus food and accommodation (minimum three nights) and dives – not a bad idea if you are short of time. The island entry fee is not included. All-inclusive whale-watching packages (mid-July to Sept) are also available.

SHARKS OF ISLA MALPELO

Experienced divers should consider a trip to **Isla Malpelo**, a rocky outcrop and protected marine reserve some 500km west of the mainland, only accessible via week-long liveaboard dive trips (it's forbidden to land on the islet).

The **sharks** are the main attraction at Malpelo; schools of up to five hundred scalloped hammerhead sharks, silky sharks, whale sharks, Galapagos sharks and even the rare smalltooth sand tiger shark are often sighted by divers. Only one dive boat is allowed to visit the island at a time, ensuring that the waters remain pristine, though illegal fishing remains a problem. The Colombian government has controversially banned dive ships from neighbouring countries, notably Panama, from visiting Malpelo. Though Buenaventura is an obvious base (a 30hr voyage from the island), few companies have been willing to arrange dive trips from there due to the security situation (see page 317). At the time of writing the most dependable option was Colombia Dive Adventures (wcolombiadiveadventures.com) operating the Ferox, under Captain Anthony Cruzveragara. Expect to pay a premium for a ten-to eleven-day all-inclusive trip. The Colombian authorities require all divers to have Advanced Open Water certification and minimum 25 dives.

TUMACO'S FIRE CARNIVAL

Tumaco's biggest fiesta is the **Carnaval del Fuego** (Fire Carnival), held in the five days leading up to Ash Wednesday (the beginning of Lent, usually February or March). Like other traditional carnival celebrations, this features parades, live music, parties and lots of boozing (as well as copious amounts of flour and water thrown in the streets). While you'll also see plenty of daredevil fire-eaters (*tiradores de fuego*), making a fiery spectacle once the sun goes down, the carnival name is actually a reference to the financial support it provides to the local volunteer fire-fighting department.

INFORMATION AND ACTIVITIES

Admission fee There is a charge for foreigners, paid in advance with the cost of accommodation. The Isla Gorgona resort (wislagorgona.co) manages the facilities on Gorgona; even if you don't take a package with them, you'll have to book your accommodation with them in advance.
Rules Note that smoking, making fires and alcohol is strictly forbidden on Gorgona, as are aerosols (don't bring mosquito spray cans). Rubber boots can be rented – it's mandatory to wear these to hike beyond El Poblado.
Internet and phone There is limited internet on the island, and mobile phone reception.
Diving Wetsuit, snorkels and diving equipment can all be rented here by the day. The Isla Gorgona resort all-inclusive diving packages for two people include all dive equipment, making this the cheapest option if you intend to dive every day. PADI courses are also offered.

ACCOMMODATION AND EATING

There is just one resort on the island (no camping), which is attached to the one **restaurant** – the food is good enough, generally seafood and rice.
Isla Gorgona Short walk from Playa Pizarro wisla gorgona.co. Basic but adequate rooms and two-person cabañas, with modern toilets and showers (no a/c, TV or phones). Prices usually include three meals plus transfers from Guapí, boots and tours on the island; minimum two nights. Outside of peak season (mid-Dec to Jan, Easter, mid-June to Aug) expect a significant discount. $$$

Tumaco

Close to the border with Ecuador, the beaches and resorts of **TUMACO** are already popular with Colombian tourists, and though the ramshackle island city, surrounded by stilt hut shanties, can seem unappealing, there are a few reasons you might consider a diversion to the "Pearl of the Pacific". Like Buenaventura, Tumaco is a hot, steamy Afro-Colombian city with a reputation for drug-running, an immense (as yet) untapped ecotourism potential, excellent whale-watching and untrammelled mangrove islands all around. The city's enticing black-sand beach area lies on the **Isla del Morro**, connected to the city (itself on the Isla de Tumaco) by a bridge. The best beaches are on the nearby **Islas de Bocagrande**, a thirty-minute boat ride away from the city.

ARRIVAL AND DEPARTURE   TUMACO

By plane Aeropuerto La Florida is on the Isla del Morro (4km from downtown), close to the main beach area. Avianca and SATENA connect Tumaco with Cali (3 daily; 1hr).
By bus Tumaco is connected to the Pan-American Highway south of Pasto by a 284km paved road. Most *camioneta* services (large cars) arrive and depart company offices along C 13 between Cras 8 and 9 (Transipiales is at C Las Mercedes/C 13 no. 4–35). The Cootraner minibus terminal is on C 13 at Cra 8.
Destinations Cali (hourly; 14–16hr) via Popayán; Ipiales (every 30min; 6hr); Pasto (every 30min; 5–6hr).

ACCOMMODATION AND EATING

The **Isla del Morro** is the best place to stay, eat and drink – far less frantic and much safer than the city centre.
Los Corales Isla del Morro whotelloscorales.com. The best hotel on Isla del Morro is a big, three-storey modern place, featuring small but comfy rooms with a/c, sea-view balconies and free wi-fi. Breakfast included. $$
Villa del Sol Isla del Morro ☏2 727 1587. Large resort complex, offering a decent pool and comfy rooms. $$

Los Llanos and the Amazon

320 Los Llanos
324 Leticia and around
332 Tabatinga (Brazil)
333 Isla Santa Rosa (Peru)
334 Puerto Nariño

BABY SLOTH IN THE AMAZON

Los Llanos and the Amazon

Accounting for around a third of Colombia in size and largely inaccessible to visitors, the Amazon basin feels unlike any other part of the country, with its pristine rainforest, fantastic wildlife and Indigenous peoples living deep in the jungle, their cultures still preserved intact. The capital of the Amazonas province, the steamy jungle town of Leticia is only accessible by air and river, and thus retains a somewhat isolated feel. Travellers head to Leticia for a taste of jungle adventure, to cross over into Brazil or Peru, and to visit the charming little eco-town of Puerto Nariño.

The Amazon region is separated from the rest of Colombia by the vast tropical grasslands known as **Los Llanos** ("The Plains"). Most of this belongs to another great river system, that of the Orinoco, and indeed it is officially called La Región de la Orinoquía. Largely inaccessible to visitors, it is now gradually opening up, but there are few roads in the region, and much of it is accessible only by air, or sometimes by river. The main gateway to the Llanos region is **Villavicencio**, 75km southeast of Bogotá. For the Amazon, most visitors fly in to **Leticia**, at the very southern tip of Colombia, where it meets Brazil and Peru. This point is known as the **three-way frontier**, and if you're heading into Brazil, it's somewhere you may end up staying for a few days waiting for a boat. It is possible to reach Leticia without flying, travelling by river via Ecuador and Peru, but it's a journey of some weeks, which you'd have to be pretty intrepid to embark upon. The other possible base in the Amazon region is **Mitú** in Vaupes, which is reachable by plane, and from neighbouring areas of Colombia and Brazil by riverboat, but has very little tourist infrastructure at present.

Los Llanos

LOS LLANOS, the vast grasslands of the Orinoco Basin comprise Colombia's cowboy country, and as wild as the West ever was. Residents – Llaneros – are known for their horsemanship and cattle driving, and are to Colombia what gauchos are to Argentina. All over Colombia, you'll see Llanero restaurants, invariably serving meat cut from huge hunks cooked on wooden stakes around an open fire.

It is now possible to **travel** safely on your own into Los Llanos: all the areas we cover here are gradually opening up to tourism, and the local tourist infrastructure can be expected to expand in the future. For now however, they remain off the beaten track, and you may well feel rather intrepid for getting to them. The best season for spotting **wildlife** is December through July, when dry conditions induce animals to gather at waterholes; you may be lucky enough to spot capybaras, jaguars, giant anteaters, anacondas, caimans and even the endangered Orinoco crocodile, as well as spectacular birds such as the scarlet ibis.

Villavicencio

The workaday city of **VILLAVICENCIO**, Los Llanos' transport hub, is the main base for tours into the region. There isn't much to see in town, but it does have a tourist office (☏ 8 673 1313, ⓦ turismovillavicencio.gov.co), and hosts a rodeo-based **Llanero Festival** in early December. The main appeal is what lies on the outskirts of the city where you will find spectacular scenery and plenty of hiking routes.

THE AMAZON RIVER IN LETICIA

Highlights

❶ **Leticia** Colombia's corner of the three-way Colombia/Brazil/Peru frontier, a jungle town with a sultry climate and a friendly, laidback vibe. See page 324

❷ **Jungle trips** Venture into the rainforest by boat, spotting caimans and freshwater Amazonian dolphins. See page 330

❸ **Amazon river fish** From piranhas to pirarucú, some of the freshest, tastiest fish you'll ever eat, big and sweet-fleshed, straight out of the world's biggest river. See page 331

❹ **Caipirinha sundowner in Tabatinga** Cross the border into Brazil to watch the sunset while sipping Brazil's national cocktail, a heady mix of lime, sugar and cane spirit. See page 324

❺ **Ceviche in Isla Santa Rosa** Peru's piece of the frontier doesn't have much of a town but it's well worth the short boat ride over from Leticia for a memorable ceviche lunch. See page 334

❻ **Puerto Nariño** Colombia's most ecofriendly town, where you can kick back and enjoy the lush tropical setting undisturbed by any motor traffic bar the odd outboard fishing boat. See page 334

HIGHLIGHTS ARE MARKED ON THE MAP ON PAGE 322

Puerto Gaitán and Puerto Careño

PUERTO GAITÁN, in the Meta *departamento*, is another transport hub and an excellent base for dolphin-spotting and birdwatching on the Meta River. *Mototaxis* and tour operators can take you to local beauty spots. In dry season it is possible to continue by rough road (or otherwise, to fly from Villavicencio) to **PUERTO CAREÑO**, in the northeast corner of Meta, which is another good base for wildlife-spotting.

Caño Cristales

The **Serranía de la Macarena**, in the south of Meta, where the Andean, Orinoco and Amazonian regions meet, is home to one of the Llanos' biggest attractions: **Caño Cristales**, otherwise known as the "rainbow river" due to the algae which turn it a bright pinky-red during the rainy season (Aug–Nov). A number of tour operators from

Bogotá and Villavicencio make the trip; the main local base is the town of **La Macarena** (served by flights from Bogotá and Villavicencio).

Tuparro

The national park at **Tuparro** (w bit.ly/Tuparro), in the west of the region, by the Venezuelan border, is home to exotic animals such as armadillos and tapirs, not to mention 320 bird species and the Orinoco River's Maypures rapids. The best way to get to the park is with a tour operator from Bogotá or Villaviciencio.

Hato La Aurora

Hato La Aurora, in Casanare, is another good base for exploring Los Llanos; it can be reached by road from Tunja (4WD) or you can get there with Colombian Highlands (see below) from Villa de Leyva. Its local, privately run, 42,000-acre **nature reserve** is home to animals such as capybaras, caimans, anacondas, and lots of birds.

Inírida

INÍRIDA (or Puerto Inírida), the capital of Guainia *departamento*, where the Inírida and Guaviare rivers meet, is accessible from most of Colombia only by plane, although there are local connections by boat. Here you can go dolphin-spotting on the local waterways, and the town has its own flower, which residents will be happy to point out. The large number of local Indigenous peoples here gives the place a special flavour. From Inírida you can charter a boat (get a group together to share the cost) to the **Cerros de Mavecure**, a group of three enigmatic black hills featured in the movie *El Abrazo de la Serpiente*; it's possible to climb them if you have your own camping equipment.

ARRIVAL AND DEPARTURE — LOS LLANOS

Many people fly to a base from where you can use local transport or tour operators to visit nearby attractions.

Via Villavicencio The main gateway is Villavicencio, 75km from Bogotá and easily accessed from there by bus. This is the chief base for tours and the best place to pick up air transport: most flights into the Llanos start in Villavicencio (usually small planes with great views), and even those that originate in Bogotá tend to stop off here.

Via Puerto Gaitán Puerto Gaitán, in the Meta *departamento* can be reached by surfaced road.

GETTING AROUND

By plane The easiest way to get around is on small planes, either with SATENA or on cargo flights from Villavicencio; indeed, to some destinations this is the only transport available. All of the cargo flight companies have desks at Villavicencio's airport, which is just north of town, across the river.

TOURS AND ACTIVITIES

When travelling in the region, check your government's **travel advisories**; various parts of the Llanos formerly controlled by guerrilla groups are now safe to travel in, but you will not be covered by travel insurance if you venture into areas that your government advises you not to visit.

Colombian Highlands Cra 10 N° 21–Finca Renacer, Villa de Leyva, Boyacá w colombianhighlands.com. This small operator associated with a hostel in Villa de Leyva (see page 99) runs tailor-made trips to parts of the Llanos and Amazon regions that other firms don't get to.

Ecolodge Juan Solito Hato La Aurora w juansolito.com. A lodge in the reserve at Hato La Aurora which organizes local excursions, safaris, treks and fishing trips.

Ecotourism Sierra de la Macarena 2nd floor, Aeropuerto Vanguardia, Villavicencio w ecoturismomacarena.com. A Villavicencio-based operator offering tours to Caño Cristales and to the eastern part of the Llanos region.

De Una Colombia Tours Cra 26A No. 40–18, suite 202, La Soledad, Bogotá w deunacolombia.com. The leading tour operator in the Llanos run tours to the national parks at Tuparro and Serranía de la Macarena, as well as wildlife-spotting trips in the *departamentos* of Casanare and Guaviare.

Leticia and around

The compact riverside town of **LETICIA** was founded in 1867 by the governor of Peru's Loreto province, whose main concern was stopping Colombia getting hold of the area. After its foundation, Leticia remained part of Peru until it was ceded to Colombia in 1922, in exchange for Colombian recognition of the Peruvian claim on the region to its west (see below). A den of iniquity and sin (well, drug trafficking) in the 1970s, Leticia had to clean up its act when the Colombian army moved in, and today it's safe and traveller-friendly, though still a centre for contraband (the town's several casinos wash the money), and visitors are warned not to wander into the outskirts after dark.

If you've just flown in from Bogotá, you'll appreciate the tropical climate and tranquil pace; it's hot and humid until the heavens open and the whole place is doused in a tepid downpour and half the streets turn into rivers. Leticia's streets buzz with a fleet of scooters and motorcycles and the busy waterfront is fun to wander around, but the main appeal for tourists is the opportunity to take excursions into the jungle, and in particular up the **Río Yavarí** (see page 328).

The town is located on the **three-way border** between Colombia, Brazil and Peru, and there's free access between Leticia on the Colombian side, Tabatinga on the Brazilian side (see page 332) and Isla Santa Rosa on the Peruvian side (see page 333) – to the extent that you can easily pop over to Peru for a ceviche lunch and then to Brazil for a Caipirinha sundowner.

Parque de Santander

The **Parque de Santander**, Leticia's main square, unlike most of Colombia's so-called *parques principales*, really is like a little park, with grass, trees, fishponds – one of which even has a bridge over it – and a basketball court. In the daytime there are food and juice stalls, but it's at dusk that the *parque* really becomes animated, as local residents gather here to enjoy the cool of the evening. Nor is it just the people: half the town's

> **THE LETICIA TRAPEZIUM**
>
> It looks strange on the map, that wedge of land jutting out of the southernmost corner of Colombia to encompass **Leticia**, but there are historical reasons why it's there. Back in the nineteenth century, when there were barely any communications with this part of the jungle, the frontier between Peru and Colombia was still ill-defined. As the need for a clear border became stronger, however, Peru and Colombia staked rival claims, and in the early twentieth century they came to blows.
>
> **Three Amazon tributaries** divided Peru from Colombia: the Caqueta to the north, the Putumayo in the middle and the Napo to the south. Colombia reckoned the Napo was the border, but Peru thought it was the Caqueta. From 1911 to 1922, the two countries squabbled, with sporadic fighting. In 1922 however, following negotiations, they signed a treaty under which both sides withdrew their troops, and the Putumayo became their mutual border, except that Colombia was given the trapezium so as to have access to the Amazon.
>
> Not everyone in Peru was happy with this. In 1932, a group of Peruvian nationalists took over the city of Iquitos and launched an **invasion** of Leticia, demanding support from their government. Peru's military junta, which had taken power in a coup and disliked the 1922 treaty, were unable to resist all the flag-waving patriotism, and sent in troops. Colombia mobilized its army in response, and occupied a slew of Peruvian towns further west, while Brazil attempted in vain to intercede. The dispute eventually ended when Peru's army-appointed president, Colonel Luis Miguel Sánchez Cerro, was assassinated. Unwilling to continue the expensive and rather pointless war, his civilian successor made peace with Colombia and restored the 1922 treaty.

parrot population also make a beeline to the trees to roost, and the square is filled with the sound of their screeching – it's really quite a spectacle.

Museo Etnográfico Amazónico
Cra 11 No. 9–43 • Free • ⓦ banrepcultural.org/leticia

In a modern, salmon- (or rather, Amazon dolphin-) pink library building at the southwest corner of the Parque de Santander, the Banco de la República maintains a one-room exhibition, the **Museo Etnográfico Amazónico**, illustrating aspects of local Indigenous culture. Although the exhibition is small, it's extremely interesting, with explanations in Spanish and English.

Exhibits include mortars used to pound *yarumo*, a local plant that is dried and pulverized together with coca leaf to make a powder called *mambe*. This is placed in the mouth, moistened with saliva to make a ball on the tongue, and then pushed up between the lip and gums, the *yarumo* taking the place of the lime ash used to alkalize coca-leaf quids elsewhere in Colombia.

Also on display are the blowpipes traditionally used by local peoples for hunting – you can see the ammunition, too: darts tipped with curare, a debilitating poison made from local plants and animals, including arrow frogs. However, pride of place goes to the splendid (and scary) monster-like ceremonial costumes used in shamanic ceremonies by the Yakuna and Ticuna peoples.

Galería Arte Uirapuru
C 8 No. 10–35 • Free • ☏ 321 340 3757

The **Galería Arte Uirapuru** is a craft shop (see page 332), which keeps a museum at the back. Many of the objects here are similar to those in the Museo Etnográfico Amazónico (see page 326), but displayed in a more higgledy-piggledy fashion, without the explanatory captions. For all that, and perhaps because of its musty, lost-in-time feel, the little museum is really quite fascinating. One of the shop assistants will

---

THE TICUNA PEOPLE

The **Ticunas** – also known as Maguta – are the most important Indigenous ethnic group in the three-way border region. They number around fifty thousand people, most of whom (some 36,000) live on the Brazilian side, with only eight thousand or so in Colombia and another five thousand in Peru. Traditionally, they live in large *malocas* (open-sided huts) adjoined by a fruit garden and cassava patch. The Ticuna **language** is tonal, so words have different meanings depending on the tone you use, as in Chinese. Unlike Chinese however, Ticuna does not seem to be related to any other spoken language.

Ticuna **handicrafts**, particularly string bags and hammocks, can be bought in Leticia and Puerto Nariño. Crafts such as ritual masks and bark paper paintings are very popular with visitors, but visitors aren't always popular with the Ticunas. The Ticuna village of Nazareth **banned tourists**, who they felt were intrusive and dirtied up the place, while profits from their visits never seemed to go anywhere near Indigenous people. A long history of disrespect for Ticuna culture and attempts at forcible integration has not helped matters. On the Brazilian side in particular, Ticunas have faced **problems** even in the recent past from people such as loggers and rubber-tappers. In 1988, in Benjamin Constant, very near to Leticia, four people were murdered and nineteen wounded (and ten disappeared, whereabouts still unknown) when gunmen hired by loggers attacked a Ticuna meeting called to discuss demarcation of their land by the Brazilian government. Thirteen years later, thirteen men were finally convicted of genocide for the attack, but the timber-mill owner accused of organizing the massacre got off on appeal, when the rest had their sentences cut.

> **BARBED AMAZONIAN NASTIES**
>
> You may have heard the story: a man is innocently having a pee in the Amazon, when a slender, eel-like creature called the **candiru fish** swims up his urine stream and hooks itself onto the inside of his penis using sharp, pointed barbs. Because of its barbs, the fish cannot be removed, causing septicemia and gangrene, and driving the man mad with such excruciating pain that eventually his only remedy is to cut off his own penis.
>
> So much for the myth; here's the truth. Firstly, the candiru fish does exist, and yes, it does live in the Colombian Amazon, and it does have backward-pointing spines to hook onto its victims. Generally however, it hooks itself onto the gills of larger fish. In reality, the fish cannot scent urine, and it cannot swim up a urine stream of someone weeing in a river (or anywhere else, come to that).
>
> Cases have actually occurred – although they are extremely rare – of candiru fish entering the vagina. Despite the spines, removing them is in fact a relatively simple matter, but it does require medical help. In 1997, a man in Brazil had to have an operation to remove a candiru fish lodged in his penis, which he claimed had swum in while he was urinating in a river, although investigators have cast doubt on this, and it remains the only known case.
>
> Lurid stories about the candiru fish have nonetheless been perpetuated by the likes of Beat novelist William Burroughs, whose favourite creatures also included another local species, the **machaca** (lantern fly), which he called a "xiucutil". According to Burroughs if it lands on you, it releases such a strong aphrodisiac that it causes instant death unless you have sex with the nearest person immediately. Even in genuine local legend, if it bites you, you must have sex within 24 hours to survive. In reality however, the creature is harmless.

take you around, showing you the aquarium tanks with local fish, including an electric eel, as well as cases of mummified fish and insects, including the infamous *machaca* lantern fly (see above), plus blowpipes and shamanic costumes. Of course you're encouraged to buy in the shop as well, but it isn't obligatory.

Mundo Amazónico

Km 7.7 (off the Tarabaca road) • Charge • W mundoamazonico.com

Mundo Amazónico is an educational, ecological theme park, divided into five "routes"; you can easily spend a day here doing all of them, enjoying a lunch of Amazon fish in the restaurant in between. Routes 1–4 take about thirty to 45 minutes, depending on how quickly you want to cover them. Route 1 covers **ethobotany**, with a tour to see different medicinal plants, and a chance to try teas made with several of them. Route 2 is a survey of **sustainable productive processes**, mainly focusing on jungle fruits and plants used for crafts by local Indigenous peoples. Route 3 is on **cultural activities**, with the chance to shoot a blowpipe and a bow and arrow like the locals. Route 4 comprises an **aquarium** where you can see 47 species of local fish, including electric eels and all the river fish served in local restaurants. Route 5 is a **jungle trail**, with the choice of short (45min) or deeper (2hr) versions. You can take as many of the routes as you like; all in all, the park makes a very enjoyable and informative excursion.

Reserva Omagua

Km 10 (on the Tarabaca road) • Charge for walk and canopy access • ☎ 310 337 9233 W facebook.com/omaguareserva

The **Reserva Omagua** is a small, private reserve where you can take an undemanding 600m stroll through the forest, with a guide to tell you about the flora and fauna. Then you can climb up 35m to the tree canopy, to scream down zip lines and totter across walkways through the foliage.

> ### SOME OF THE AMAZON'S STRANGER CREATURES
>
> Here in the forest, you'll find animals you may have heard about but perhaps didn't quite imagine were real. Along with the candiru fish and the *machaca* lantern fly (see page 327) these beasts really do live in the jungle, and better still, you may even get to see them, although you shouldn't necessarily expect to.
>
> **River dolphins** The Amazon's famous pink dolphins (see page 357) are the world's largest freshwater species of dolphin, and are as playful as their marine cousins. You'll often see and even hear them coming up for air, and your jungle trip, if it features a boat ride, is sure to take you to places where you can spot them.
>
> **Tree sloths** Lazy, lovable and very, very slow, sloths don't do much except hang upside-down from the tree tops munching leaves. If you're very lucky, you may spot one, but it isn't an everyday occurrence. Sloths do occasionally come down from the canopy, mostly to go to the loo; they can't run, but when necessary they can swim.
>
> **Anacondas** If you don't like snakes, look away now: the anaconda isn't venomous but it can grow to well over 5m in length, and maybe longer, and over 1m in circumference. A constrictor, the anaconda crushes its prey, not so much to strangle it as to make it easier to swallow. You'll be lucky to see one in the wild, but some jungle tours visit places where they are kept as pets.
>
> **Piranhas** It's said that these sharp-toothed, voracious little predators can strip a human to the bone in seconds, but that's an outrageous exaggeration. On many jungle trips you'll be fishing for and eating piranhas, rather than the other way round. However, they have been known to take a nip out of people on occasion, and they do hunt in packs and, like sharks, they indulge in feeding frenzies.
>
> **Electric eels** Not really an eel, although it looks like one, the electric eel – which can grow to as much as 2m in length – is, however, really electric, and can deliver a shock of 600 volts to stun its prey. Such a shock could in principle kill you, or cause you to drown, but as they tend to live in muddy creeks or on the river bottom contact with one is unlikely.
>
> **Vampire bats** Yes, they really do exist, and they inhabit not Transylvania but South America, especially the rainforest. They can run along the ground, and usually attack by jumping up and biting the bums of cows and horses. Very occasionally they have been known to bite humans, and even more occasionally to transmit rabies. Since they are one of the commonest types of bat, you're quite likely to see them.

The reserve also rescues injured animals to heal and rehabilitate them, so depending on what they've found, there are also wild animals on site. You should also be able to spot some exotic birdlife while you're up in the trees, and perhaps even the odd toucan.

Reserva Natural Tanimboca

Km 11 (on the Tarabaca road) • Charge for guided walks, zip lines and kayaking, one-day all-in ticket available • ⓦ tanimboca.com

The **Reserva Natural Tanimboca** is a private reserve where you can zip through the tree canopy, take guided forest walks by day or by night, with explanations of the plants and animals (and maybe a taste of some of the wild jungle fruits), or go kayaking in the local river. It's also possible to stay the night, either in a tree house or a hammock under an open shelter. The staff are friendly and knowledgeable; it's a lot of fun.

Río Yavarí

For the most popular of the jungle tours from Leticia head up the **RÍO YAVARÍ** (Javari River), which starts off in Peru, and then, further up, forms the border between Peru and Brazil. The shorter trips (two to three days) generally go up as far as the **Zacambú Lagoon**, where you can swim, see the dolphins, fish for piranhas, and maybe go caiman-spotting in the evening. Numerous tour agencies in Leticia (see page 330) can organize jungle and river trips of virtually any length, taking in flora, fauna and the area's Indigenous communities. Some have their own lodges here, or else have an agreement with local residents who run lodges; there's also usually the option of camping out in the jungle – except at the height of the wet season (March to May), when this whole "low forest" area is flooded and the only way to get around is by boat. Since the Amazon is such a vast area, odds are you won't see any big mammals except for monkeys and dolphins, but you'll see numerous bird species, and a three-day stint in the jungle is great exposure to a unique environment.

ARRIVAL AND INFORMATION LETICIA AND AROUND

By plane Aeropuerto Nacional Alfredo Vásquez Cobo is 1km north of town on the continuation of Cra 10. From the airport, you can walk (20min) or catch a taxi into town. All travellers flying in by plane must pay a tourist tax on arrival in Leticia. LATAM and Avianca operate daily flights from Bogotá (2hr), while SATENA and some charter firms have weekly flights from Leticia to a few remote spots in the jungle.

By boat Boats leave from the dock at the western end of C 8. Boats to Isla Santa Rosa (10min) don't usually run at night, so you'll need to make prior arrangements (or go to Tabatinga) to make the 3am Iquitos boat (see page 332). There are three daily fast boats from Leticia to Puerto Nariño (see page 335) or you can go to Caballo Cocha in Peru (2 daily; 2hr).

Tourist information The tourist information office at C 8 No. 9–75 (📞 312 506 0645 🌐 facebook.com/amazon asmidestino) gives out a map of Leticia and Tabatinga and is happy to answer questions; there is also a desk at the airport (open daily to meet incoming flights).

GETTING AROUND

By public transport In town you can walk to most places, including the border and the airport, but there are tuk-tuks and *mototaxis*. To get up to the reserves, take a *mototaxi*, or a "Km 11" bus from Parque Orellana. Buses to Tabatinga (some only to the centre, others all the way to Comara) start from C8 at Cra 11, and can be picked up along Av Internacional.

By bike The city council is trialing a scheme where you can

THE THREE-WAY BORDER

You can travel between Leticia (Colombia), Tabatinga (Brazil) and Isla Santa Rosa (Peru) without restriction, although you should carry your passport with you anyway, but if travelling further into Brazil, Peru or (if coming from either of them) Colombia, you must complete **border formalities**. You're allowed 24 hours between getting your exit stamp from the country you're leaving and getting your entry stamp for the country you're entering, and you need to do both. Note that the **time** on the Brazilian side of the border is officially an hour ahead of Peru and Colombia; many businesses in Tabatinga run on Colombian time, but boat companies don't.

COLOMBIAN FORMALITIES

Although **Migración Colombia** have an office in town (see page 332), it does not issue entry or exit stamps. To complete border formalities, you must go to the immigration post either at Leticia airport or on a boat moored at the port. If entering from Brazil, you may be required to show a yellow fever vaccination certificate.

BRAZILIAN FORMALITIES

Brazilian entry and exit stamps are issued by the **Policía Federal**, Av Amizdade 26 in Tabatinga (📞 97 3412 2180). You may well be required to show a yellow fever vaccination certificate, so bring it along.

PERUVIAN FORMALITIES

The **immigration office** on Isla Santa Rosa (near *Brisas del Amazonas* restaurant) is open daily. You won't be able to get an entry stamp in the early morning when the boat leaves for Iquitos (see page 332), so get it the day before.

PARQUE NACIONAL NATURAL AMACAYACU

Around one hour thirty minutes upstream from Leticia, the 3000-square-kilometre **Parque Nacional Natural Amacayacu** is a spectacular slice of wilderness, home to five hundred bird species, plenty of crocodiles, anacondas and other reptiles and 150 mammal species, including big cats. The park is officially closed at present due to flooding, but it is possible to visit parts of it with guides from the neighbouring villages of San Martín and Mocagua. A particularly worthwhile visit is to the **Fundación Maikuchiga**, a project for rehabilitating monkeys – visits can be arranged through *La Jangada* hostel (see page 331).

---

borrow bicycles for free for up to 3hr in the morning, 2hr in the afternoon on weekdays; how long it will continue remains to be seen, but it's based at C 9 No. 10–86, opposite *Café Sesan*. You'll need to leave a copy of your ID.

By moped and scooter Rentals at JW, Av Internacional No. 7–31 (☎ 321 230 3991); J&J, Av Internacional No. 9–27 (☎ 312 214 9337).

TOURS AND ACTIVITIES

The exact **price** of your tour will depend on what package you choose, but a typical choice will be a three-day, two-night trip. There are a lot of companies offering tours in Leticia, many of which take very large groups and often cut corners in terms of what they offer their customers, what they pay their employees, and how much they respect local Indigenous people, wildlife and the environment. At the very least, make sure you've agreed on exactly what's included, and avoid pushy "guides" who accost you in the street. Many tours visit a place on the Peruvian side of the river called **Puerto Alegría**, where animals taken from the wild are held in captivity for tourists; firms which include this on their itinerary are also worth avoiding.

Amazon Jungle Trips Av Internacional No. 6–25 ⓦ amazonjungletrips.com.co. Going strong after more than 25 years, and offering a popular three-day, two-night tour with a bit of everything (swimming in a lagoon, dolphin spotting, fishing for piranhas, looking for caimans), as well as longer tours that include birdwatching, and a six-day tour that includes the Tupana Arü Ü, a "high forest" area (which doesn't get flooded in the wet season) on the Colombian side of the Amazon.

La Jangada Cra 10 No. 6–37 ⓦ lajangadamazonas. com. Run by the hostel of the same name (see page 331), with English-speaking guides, offering a variety of trips including a popular (and very good) three-day, two-night "bit of everything" tour, longer and deeper forays into the jungle, stays with a Ticuna family in a Ticuna village where you can learn about their traditional lifestyle, and visits to the Fundación Maikuchiga's monkey rehabilitation centre.

Omshanty Omshanty Lodge, Km 11 ☎ 311 489 8985. For those who want to go deeper, foregoing comfort for serious adventure, Omshanty offers jungle tours to places that aren't commonly visited, including a seven-day trip up the Rio Calderón, staying in jungle camps and tracking and spotting animals, including jaguars. They also have a very privileged arrangement with a few members of the hunter-gatherer Matiz people who are prepared to meet outsiders on their land and give them a taste of their way of life, as part of an in-depth eleven-day excursion.

Tanimboca Cra 10 No. 11–69 ⓦ tanimboca.org. English-speaking guides and five different tours ranging from five to eight days, including such options as canopy tours, staying in a tree house and visits to nature reserves, Indigenous communities and a reptile zoo.

ACCOMMODATION

★ **Amazon B&B** C 12 No. 9–30 ⓦ amazonbb.com; map p.325. In the style of an upmarket safari lodge, with a choice of spacious rooms and even more spacious bungalows. They don't have a/c or a pool, but there are ceiling fans and a jacuzzi, crisp white sheets and a peaceful garden space, as well as a variety of local tours. Breakfast included. $$

Anaconda Cra 11 No. 7–34 ⓦ hotelanaconda.com.co; map p.325. In the middle of town on the Parque Orellana, this package-style hotel is getting a bit long in the tooth but still has plenty going for it: a large pool, not to mention large, airy rooms, a/c and a restaurant. Wi-fi is available only in the lobby, however. Breakfast included. $$$

Anaira Hostel Cra 10 No. 7–16 ☎ 312 760 1980 ⓔ reservas@anairahostel.com; map p.325. A small hostel with a big dorm opening onto a small garden, a handful of private rooms and a pool. $

Decameron Cra 11 No. 6–11 ⓦ decameron.com; map p.325. The most expensive hotel in town by a very long chalk, and the best, by a rather shorter one. The rooms are spacious, with a/c and ceiling fans, hot water and a safe; there's a big pool, and some local tours are included in the price. Half-board $$$$

Hostal la Esperanza C 6 No. 17–10 ☎ 317 372 7957;

map p.325. This backpacker lodge out towards the airport offers simple but clean rooms (some with hammocks as well as beds) in a quiet neighbourhood. Rooms with a/c are extra. $

La Jangada Cra 10 No. 6–37 ⓦ lajangadamazonas.com; map p.325. Top marks for friendliness and helpfulness to this long-running travellers' hostel. The fan-cooled rooms and dorms are clean and airy, you can book your jungle adventures here, and the kitchen whips up a simple breakfast, which is included. They also have a forest lodge at Km 15, where you stay in the woods, check the local birdlife, and swim in a natural pool. $

Leticias Guest House Cra 11 No. 4–06 ☎ 322 754 4596 ⓔ leticiashostel14@gmail.com; map p.325. A big pool is the main thing this bright little hotel has going for it, although the rooms are decent enough (the cheapest have shared bathrooms – a room with a private bathroom is extra). $

Waira Suites Cra 10 No. 7–36 ⓦ wairahotel.com.co; map p.325. There are two pools and two restaurants at this rather chic little establishment, all done out in white, with splashes of colour in the rooms that change with the seasons. They have a/c and hot water. The best rooms are upstairs at the front, with big balconies. Breakfast included. $$$

EATING

In Leticia you'll find culinary delicacies you won't encounter elsewhere in Colombia – an abundance of **river fish** and a vast variety of Amazonian **fruit juices**. The most delicious fish include *gamitana* and pirarucú, but you should avoid eating the latter during its breeding season (mid-Nov to mid-March), when fishing it is banned to conserve stocks, and ordering it in restaurants encourages illegal fishing. On **Sunday mornings**, a lot of places, including private houses, sell suckling pig and rice on the street.

Amektiar Cra 9 No. 8–15 ☎ 8 592 6094; map p.325. This spick-and-span modern restaurant has indoor and outside seating, and offers a range of international dishes. The menu includes BBQ ribs, or you can order *pinchos* (small kebabs), with a choice of chicken or beef. $

Café Sesan C 9 No. 10–85 ☎ 8 592 5971; map p.325. Leticia's best bakery doubles as a bright little café that's great for breakfast (eggs of your choice plus coffee, toast and jam), or a snack or a juice morning or afternoon. Oddly though, it closes for lunch. $

El Cielo Avenida Internacional No. 6–11 ☎ 315 612 8663; map p.325. A pioneering restaurant serving what they call "fusión amazónica" – essentially, experimental modern cuisine using traditional local ingredients. You can start with *canoas* (plantain stuffed with prawns) or, if you want to be more adventurous, *canajois* (*mojojoy* jungle grubs stuffed with meat), before moving on to the house speciality, *casabes*, consisting of a cassava-bread base, served pizza-style, with a choice of locally inspired meat, fish or vegetable toppings). $$

Punto Lounge C 5 No. 4–70, Barrio Gaitán ☎ 316 833 2537; map p.325. The best place in town for charcoal-grilled meat. Try the quarter-kilo baby beef (heart of rump) or the *punta de anca* (sirloin tip). On Sun they do executive lunch dishes. $$

Street grills C 7 at Av Internacional; map p.325. Every evening, this row of street stalls grills fish, sausages or spatchcock chicken over charcoal and serves them with rice and cassava. Very cheap, very filling and pretty damn good. $

★ **Tierras Amazónicas** C 8 No. 7–50 ☎ 8 592 4748 ⓦ facebook.com/Tierras-Amazonicas-296256393854271; map p.325. Cool, open-fronted restaurant serving large portions of perfectly cooked fish, with a choice of local species and preparations. The *pescado a la pupeca* (fish fillet steamed in a banana leaf) is particularly succulent, and you can wash it down with juices such as *borojó, copoazú* or *kamu-kamu*. $$

Tierras Antioqueñas C 8 No. 9–03 ☎ 314 224 4056; map p.325. Maybe not quite as Antioquian as the name suggests, but this relaxed restaurant with wooden tables lining the street can rustle up a decent *bandeja paisa*, or a fish cooked in coconut milk. It's also a top spot to have a breakfast *caldo* with *patacones*. $

DRINKING AND NIGHTLIFE

BarBacoas Cra 8 No. 8–28 ☎ 8 592 5000; map p.325. At the back, this is a billiard hall where the Colombian version of pool is played. At the front is a relaxed little bar serving coffee by day and beer by night, accompanied by old-school tango and *bolero* music.

Legends Cra 9 No. 5–123 ☎ 320 428 5242, ⓦ facebook.com/NochesLegends; map p.325. A rock bar (and grill) where a friendly crowd down cold beers to the sound of American rock, with occasional live bands. Their burgers are rated the best in town.

Mossh Cra 10 No. 10–08 ☎ 8 592 7097; map p.325. Quite a refined music-bar at the southeast corner of the Parque de Santander, where well-dressed Leticians sip cocktails inside or on the sidewalk to the latest Colombian and Brazilian pop videos.

SHOPPING

Artesania Sibundoy C 8 No. 11–82; map p.325. A musty little shop with a strong whiff of *palo santo* incense, hidden away down an alley; visiting it is an adventure in itself. Crammed in there are all manner of medicinal herbs, spices, lucky charms, religious figurines, bits of old bones, textiles, trinkets and carvings – a veritable Aladdin's cave.

Galería Arte Uirapuru (the Pink Shop) C 8 No. 10–35 ☎ 321 340 3757; map p.325. The best, albeit not the cheapest, of the town's craft shops – with its own little museum at the back (see page 326) – where you can buy medicinal plants, including *mambe* (see page 326), blowpipes and darts in both authentic hunting and tourist souvenir versions, not to mention carvings, pottery, basketware, paintings in natural pigments on tree bark, and jewellery made from orange forest beans and pirarucú scales.

Hiper C 8 No. 9–29 ☎ 8 592 8067; map p.325. Leticia's main supermarket, and a good place to buy anything from a can of beer to a piece of fruit (a different selection from the local fruit sold in the market by the port or the fruit stalls by Parque Orellana). A bigger branch is due to open on Av Vasquez Coro at C 15.

DIRECTORY

Banks and exchange There are banks with ATMs dotted around town – Bancolombia, for example, at Cra 11 No. 9–52. Moneychangers are concentrated on C 8 by the port; on any given day they'll offer varying rates for pesos, reales, soles, dollars and euros, so shop around.

Consulates Brazil, C 11 No. 8–104 (☎ 320 846 0637); Peru, C 11 No. 5–32 (☎ 8 592 7755).

Festivals Anniversary of Foundation, April 25, celebrated with a parade in Parque de Santander; Festival de la Confraternidad Amazónica (Amazon Fellowship Festival), July 15–20, with sporting events and tournaments, including a beauty contest, between Colombia, Peru and Brazil; Golden Pirarucú Music Festival, last week of Nov (four days), in which music from the region is performed in the Parque Orellana.

Health The public hospital (San Rafael) is at Cra 10 13–78 (☎ 8 592 7826, **w** esehospitalsanrafael-leticia-amazonas. gov.co). There's a private clinic, Clínica Leticia, at Av Internacional (Cra 6) No. 6–01 (☎ 8 592 7718).

Internet Connectivity in Leticia has traditionally been dire, but all being well a new network should have been installed by the time you read this. Internet cafés include Centel.net, C 9 No. 9–09 and Servientrega, C 8 No. 9–50.

Laundry Aseo Total, Cra 10 No. 9–32.

Police C 11 No. 12–32 (☎ 8 592 4896).

Post office Av Internacional 8–28.

Visa extensions Migración Colombia is at C 9 No. 9–62 (☎ 8 592 6001), but to get your Colombia entry or exit stamp you have to go to the port or the airport (see page 329). The easiest way to extend your visa is to (officially) leave the country for a few days in Brazil or Peru and then re-enter.

Tabatinga (Brazil)

Pretty much just an extension of Leticia across the Brazilian border, **TABATINGA** is not the most exciting of towns, and it can be quite dodgy, especially at night. Generally speaking, you're better off staying in Leticia, but Tabatinga does have the advantage of boats to Manaus and night-time ferries over to Santa Rosa for the Iquitos boat (indeed the boat companies have offices here). If you're heading further into **Brazil**, or coming from there, Tabatinga is also the place to complete Brazilian entry (or exit) formalities.

ARRIVAL AND INFORMATION   TABATINGA (BRAZIL)

By boat to/from Manaus Boats downstream to Manaus leave from the port at the end of Travessa Doze in Tabatinga on Tues, Wed, Fri and Sat (double-check times in advance), taking four days and three nights to get to Manaus. After buying your tickets you'll have to to sling your own hammock (get there a few hours early if you want a good spot), or pay extra for a double cabin; coming upstream (six days and five nights) the hammock and the cabin costs the same. There are also fast boats leaving Tues, Thurs, Sat and Sun, which take 34hr. Tickets can be bought at the port; the boats are run by different firms, who take turns selling their tickets, but Sol Viagens' office (☎ 97 99154 2597 or ☎ 97 98121 9711) should sell tickets for all of them, as (for slightly more) do travel agencies in Leticia. Whichever boat you take, expect thorough searches for drugs.

By boat to/from Isla Santa Rosa and Iquitos Boats across the river to Isla Santa Rosa run 24hr and take 10min for the crossing. The cost goes up at night. Companies running boats from Isla Santa Rosa to Iquitos (see page 333) have offices in Tabatinga where you can make your bookings (as you can, for slightly more, at travel agencies in Leticia). Transportes Golfinho, Rua Marechal Mallet 306 (☎ 97 3412 3186, Colombian mobile ☎ 322 289 3297), leave Santa Rosa on Tues, Thurs and Sat. Amazonas I, Rua Marechal Mallet 35 (☎ 97 99150 6898, Colombian mobile ☎ 315 813 7990) runs boats on Wed, Fri and Sun. The journey takes around 12hr and prices include breakfast and lunch.

By plane Tabatinga's airport is at the southern end of town. You'll want to take a cab or a *mototaxi*, especially to or from Leticia, although some buses from Leticia do come down this far. The only regular flight is Azul's daily departure to Manaus (1hr 55min), where you can change for points beyond.

Tourist information Centro de Informação Turística, Av Amizdade 1930.

ACCOMMODATION

Brasil Rua Marechal Mallet 306, ☎ 97 3412 3186, ✉ gcabrera@transportegolfinho.com; map p.325. Next door to, and associated with, boat company Golfinho (see page 332), so a handy place to stay if you're taking their boat to Iquitos. Rooms are simple, but clean enough, and have their own bathrooms, but breakfast isn't included and there's no wi-fi. $

Takana Rua Osvaldo Cruz 970, ⌂ sites.google.com/view/hotel-takana/inicio; map p.325. Tabatinga's nicest hotel, complete with a/c and a swimming pool, a restaurant and a bar. Most upstairs rooms have balconies, and the suites have big ones (not to mention king-size beds). A good breakfast is included. $$

EATING

Bella Época Rua Pedro Teixeira 589, ☎ 97 3412 2478; map p.325. A typical Brazilian *por kilo* restaurant, where, from 11am onwards, you serve yourself from a selection of salads and vegetable dishes and pick up a few slices of *churrasco* (barbecued meat) from the grill before putting your plate on a scale and paying by the kg. $$

São Jorge Av Amizdade 1941, ☎ 97 3412 5148; map p.325. A good spot for a lunch of ceviche or *tacu-tacu* (rice and beans with fish). They even have a few Chinese dishes. $

DRINKING AND NIGHTLIFE

Comara Show Club Rua São Sebastião, Bairro de Comara; map p.325. By the waterfront, out past the airport on the very southern edge of town, this is the perfect spot – if the weather is right – to sip a caipirinha while watching the sun go down over three countries. On Sun they have a jolly party, with singers and dancers, and finally adult cabaret (of both sexes), for an entry fee.

Scandalo's Dance Av Amizdade, at Rua Pedro Teixeira ☎ 97 99151 8777; map p.325. Tabatinga's main dance club, a lot of fun but a bit rough – it makes Leticia's nightlife look tame by comparison. You're advised to arrive and leave by taxi (or at least *mototaxi*), and do watch your step: many of the patrons will be armed, and this is not a place where you want to start any trouble. Cover charge.

DIRECTORY

Banks and exchange There's a moneychanger right on the border, and the Banco do Brasil and Bradesco, both with ATMs, face each other across Av Amizdade by the junction with Rua Marechal Mallet.
Consulates Colombia, Rua General Sampaio 623 (☎ 97 3412 2104, ⌂ tabatinga.consulado.gov.co).
Internet Café L@tino, Rua Marechal Mallet 522; Vivian, Av Amizdade 326.
Post office Av Amizdade 1086.

Isla Santa Rosa (Peru)

There isn't much on **ISLA SANTA ROSA**, the island on the Peruvian side of the river that's the starting point for boats on the 500km journey to **Iquitos**, and it's rather poor and run-down compared to Leticia and Tabatinga. But even if you don't need to catch the boat, you may want to drop in for ceviche and a cold Peruvian beer. And if you *are* taking the boat, you'll need to pop over the day before to get your passport stamped. Soles and Colombian pesos are accepted in Santa Rosa, but you'll often get better prices if you pay with Brazilian **reales**.

ARRIVAL AND DEPARTURE   ISLA SANTA ROSA (PERU)

By boat to/from Iquitos Fast passenger boats for Iquitos leave at 5am every day except Mon, taking around 12hr. You'll need to buy your ticket in advance, preferably from the boat companies in Tabatinga (see page 332), although agencies in Santa Rosa also sell them, and you'll need to get an exit stamp the day before in Leticia (or, if officially you've been in Brazil, in Tabatinga) and also to get a Peruvian entry stamp the day before from the immigration office in Santa Rosa. Arriving from Iquitos, you'll need to get an exit stamp here before you get stamped in to Colombia or Brazil. There are also cargo boats between Santa Rosa and Iquitos that are cheaper, but they take around three days, are uncomfortable, none too clean and have sometimes been targeted by pirates (you'll need to keep an eye on your baggage anyway); they tend to leave in the evenings from around 6pm.

By boat to/from Leticia and Tabatinga There are frequent informal ferries across the river and during the day so you should have no trouble finding boats at the dock in Santa Rosa, Leticia or Tabatinga to do the crossing, but at night and sometimes in the dry season, boats run from

ACCOMMODATION

Hotels in Santa Rosa are pretty **insalubrious** and may leave you feeling itchy (bed bugs are rife here), but they do have the advantage of being right where the boat leaves, so you'll get a good extra hour's shut-eye if you stay here rather than in Leticia or Tabatinga.

Hospedaje Yauyino Av Mi Perú, by the market ☏ 065 830423 (Colombian mobile ☏ 322 438 0669), ✉ jennypj_@hotmail.com. The best of the rather rudimentary choices along the main street. Rooms are reasonably clean and most have their own bathrooms. $

Hostal Sin Fronteras (aka Hotel Gamboa) Near the dock ☏ 313 497 6277 (Colombian mobile), ✉ antonio amazonas1@gmail.com. This wooden hotel with a corrugated roof, by the road from the dock into town, is the best place in Santa Rosa to stay. It looks rather ramshackle but the rooms are clean (and fumigated) and have private bathrooms, it has its own *mirador* (lookout tower) and it's very handy for the boat. $

EATING

★ **Brisas del Amazonas** Centro. The best ceviche in the three-way border zone, well worth popping over from Leticia or Tabatinga to sample. A huge plate of mixed ceviche for two to four people is a good deal here. For extra entertainment, parrots and macaws frequent the restaurant. $

Puerto Nariño

Lush and steamy **PUERTO NARIÑO** sits around 75km upstream of Leticia and makes a great excursion. It's possible to visit on a day-trip, but more rewarding to spend a night or two. Puerto Nariño is super-chilled and extremely relaxing, the only motorized vehicle in town being the tractor that pulls the trash cart. In fact, this is Colombia's most ecologically aware community: rubbish is carefully segregated for recycling and many places collect rainwater for reuse. Puerto Nariño was only founded in 1961, and most of its residents belong to the local Indigenous peoples, the Ticunas, Yaguas and Cocanas. There isn't a lot to do in the town itself, but with its thatched wooden houses dotted among tropical vegetation, it's a great base for boat trips to spot Amazonian pink dolphins and other wildlife, or just to completely unwind for a couple of days.

Fundación Natütama
East of C 4 near the dock • Voluntary donation • ⓦ fundacionnatutama.org

The **Fundación Natütama** is a nonprofit local project working to conserve the local ecosystem and to manage its resources sustainably. Visitors take off their shoes to be taken on a guided tour that includes a re-creation of the flooded rainforest with life-size wooden models of local animals to illustrate how the local ecosystem works. *Natütama* is Ticuna for "underwater world" and your guide will explain (in Spanish) how the annual flooding is vital for the life cycles of local animals and how the forest's plant and animal species are dependent on each other.

The mirador
C 7, at Cra 4 • Charge

On Calle 7, an old water tower has been converted into a **mirador** (lookout point), where you can climb a rickety wooden staircase to the top for great views of the surrounding countryside, tree canopy and neighbouring lagoons. Also at the top is a souvenir shop selling local wood carvings, and just across the street you can buy delicious **ice creams** made by hand with jungle fruits such as *coapoazá* and *arazá*, as well as (relatively) more conventional flavours such as coconut or passion fruit.

Lago Tarapoto

10km southwest of town (20min by boat)

Most visitors to Puerto Nariño take an excursion to **Lago Tarapoto**, a beautiful lagoon located west of town, where you may, if you're lucky, see pink dolphins, giant Victoria Regia water lilies, pirarucú fish and the noisy Amazonian bird the horned screamer, known locally as a camungo, which is an onomatopoeic name derived from its distinctive call. To get to the lagoon, you'll need to arrange a trip with local boat owners at the waterfront, who may well approach you to offer their services. A three-hour excursion can take up to six people. Depending on the season, you may be able to sail through flooded forest on the way, and you should have time for a swim too.

ARRIVAL AND INFORMATION   PUERTO NARIÑO

By boat Boats between Leticia and Puerto Nariño are operated by three local companies: Transportes Amazónicas (☏ 8 592 5999), Líneas Amazonas (☏ 8 592 6711) and Expresos Unidos Tres Fronteras (☏ 8 592 4687), who take it in turns to run the day's services. All have offices in Malecón Plaza by the port in Leticia, and at the dock in Puerto Nariño, and there are three services daily in each direction (2hr), leaving from Leticia and Puerto Nariño. It's a good idea to buy your ticket a day in advance if possible. Note that tourists have to pay a tax on arrival.

Services The tourist information office is at Cra 1, at C 5 (☏ 314 269 0788) and at the dock. Note that there are no banks here, so do bring all the cash you'll need. Wi-fi used to be confined to the area around the Alcaldía (town hall) but should now extend to the whole town; there's an internet café called N6Utapa at C 5 with Cra 2.

ACCOMMODATION

Hospedaje Wóne Cra 1, by the dock ☏ 311 517 9493. A simple little place by the dock, nothing fancy, but neat, tidy and reasonably priced. The rooms are small, but each has a bed and a hammock and its own bathroom. ‾S‾

Lomas del Paiyü C 7 No. 2–26 ☏ 313 871 1743. Set in a verdant little garden near the mirador, this is a slightly more sophisticated choice than most of the town's lodgings. Each room has its own bathroom, there's a choice of local tours, an upstairs veranda with hammocks, and even an in-house restaurant. Breakfast is extra. ‾SS‾

Paraíso Ayahuasca C 4 No. 5–71 ☏ 320 244 0187. As you might guess from the name, this is a place to learn about local psychoactive and medicinal plants, but it's also an extremely friendly and very laidback little retreat, entwined with yagé vines, where the walls on four sides are mainly just mosquito netting, and the common space upstairs affords great views. ‾S‾

Refugio Eware 1.5km west of town ☏ 321 988 0095, ⓦ facebook.com/Ewarerefugioamazonico. A short ride upriver from town (they'll come and collect you if you book in advance or call – otherwise it's a 30min walk), this forest lodge is on the Loreto Yaco river, visited by dolphins twice daily, as well as lots of birds, and has a large swimming pool and a *mirador*, all in a peaceful, verdant setting. Breakfast included. ‾SS‾

Waira Selva Cra 2 No. 6–72 ⓦ wairahotel.com.co/waira-selva. Run by the same firm as the *Waira Suites* in Leticia, this is the nearest thing to luxury in Puerto Nariño, and it's pretty comfortable in a modest kind of way. The well-kept rooms are quite spacious and all have private bathrooms, there's a *mirador* at the very top of the hotel with views of the countryside around. Breakfast included. ‾SS‾

EATING

Doña Luz C 6 at Cra 5 ☏ 321 248 8401. A hearty set meal of soup followed by fish, meat or chicken with all the trimmings, at a fixed price. ‾S‾

Las Margaritas C 6 No. 6–80 ☏ 311 276 2407. A great-value buffet restaurant where they have a little bit of everything – fish, meat, salads, beans – including their speciality, *yucaditas* (crispy fried croquettes of sweetened cassava flour), plus soup, juice and coffee.

SHOPPING

Tachiwa At the dock ☏ 312 309 3576. Pick up local Indigenous crafts – carvings, paintings, basketware – at prices rather lower than you'll find in Leticia.

SIMÓN BOLÍVAR

Contexts

337 History
355 Natural Colombia
360 The music of Colombia
366 Religion in Colombia
370 Books
373 Spanish

History

Like much of the New World, little is known about Colombia before the arrival of the Spanish in the early sixteenth century, with its great Indigenous civilizations largely destroyed by the Conquistadors and leaving no written records. The long colonial period saw the Spanish language, Catholicism and African slaves introduced to Colombia, but it's the years since independence was proclaimed in 1810 that have had the most impact, with the new nation blighted by violence and civil wars until relatively recently.

First peoples of Colombia

South America's **first human inhabitants** most likely arrived from North America, having crossed the Bering Strait land bridge from Siberia around 12,000 to 14,000 years ago. These **Paleo** (or "Early") **Indians** lived hunter-gatherer existences – the spear tips they used are widely found across the central and northern parts of Colombia, though many of these peoples were simply moving through to other parts of the continent. Between 2000 and 1000 BC (about the same time the Olmecs were flourishing in Mexico and Andean civilizations blooming in Peru), advanced cultures began to develop and settle permanently in Colombia (including the ancestors of the Wayuu, Ticuna and Emberá), notably the **Taironas** along the Caribbean coast, and the **Muiscas** in the Andes near modern-day Bogotá. The Muiscas are thought to have migrated to central Colombia between 5500 and 1000 BC from Central America, with their most ancient settlement dating to 1270 BC. By the time the Spanish arrived a Muiscan Confederation had evolved, loosely divided into two parts, one centred on Bacatá (now Bogotá) and the other at Hunza (now Tunja). **Ciudad Perdida** – the Tairona's largest city – was built between 660 and 800 AD, but abandoned during the Spanish conquest (today's Arhuaco, Kogi and Wiwa peoples claim ancestry from the Tairona).

Elsewhere, **Calima** cultures flourished in the Valle del Cauca between 200 BC and 400 AD, while the **Quimbaya** people, noted for their sophisticated gold work, dominated the northern Andes between the fourth and seventh centuries. To the far south in the area known today as **San Agustín** another advanced civilization emerged around 1000 BC, with the complex of earthen mounds, tombs and statues that survive today constructed between 1 and 900 AD – the sites were abandoned around 1350 long before the arrival of Europeans, and little is known about the people who built them. The tombs of **Tierradentro**, built from 600 to 900 AD, may have been related to the San Agustín culture, but as these too were abandoned in the thirteenth century, little is known about their creators.

When the Spanish arrived in 1509, they nevertheless found a flourishing Indigenous population estimated at around 1.5 million to 2 million people, divided into hundreds of tribes speaking largely mutually unintelligible languages. With no written script of any kind, our knowledge of these peoples is largely based on (deeply biased) contemporary Spanish sources and archeology.

10,000 BC	1200 BC–1525 AD	660–800
Earliest evidence of human habitation at El Abra in Bogotá.	Indigenous cultures – including the Tairona, Calima, Muisca, Quimbaya, Nariño and others – dominate Colombia.	The Tairona build Ciudad Perdida.

> **WHO ARE THE COLOMBIANS?**
>
> The majority (49 percent) of the Colombian population is classified as **mestizo**, of mixed European and Indigenous ancestry, with 37 percent European (predominantly of **Spanish** origin), around 10 percent **Afro-Colombian**, and 4 percent **Indigenous**. The latter group comprises some 87 different ethnicities (speaking around 67 languages), with Indigenous reserves (*resguardos*) covering 27 percent of the country. Most Afro-Colombians are descended from slaves brought over in the sixteenth and seventeenth centuries (slavery was abolished in 1851), with the largest populations on the Caribbean and Pacific coasts: the department of Chocó is more than 80 percent Afro-Colombian.

The Spanish conquest

After Christopher Columbus discovered the "New World" in 1492, the **Spanish** began to carve out a vast empire in the Caribbean and Central America. In 1499, **Alonso de Ojeda** (a companion of Columbus on his second voyage to the Americas), became the first European to make landfall at what is today Colombia (at Cabo de la Vela in La Guajira). In 1502 he founded a colony at **Bahía Honda** (dubbed Santa Cruz), but this lasted a mere three months (after Indigenous attacks and fighting between settlers). Ojeda raided the coast of Colombia again in 1509, devastating Indigenous villages near present-day Cartagena and Turbaco. In 1510 he founded a fort at **San Sebastián de Urabá** (today in the *departamentos* of Antioquia and Chocó), but this too was burned down by Indigenous tribes (one of Ojeda's commanders was **Francisco Pizarro**, future conqueror of the Incas). Ojeda died in Santo Domingo (now the capital of the Dominican Republic) in 1515, like many old Conquistadors seemingly repentant for the crimes he had committed against Indigenous peoples.

Santa Marta and Cartagena

Conquistador **Rodrigo de Bastidas** (another companion of Columbus on his second voyage to the Americas), sailed into Santa Marta Bay in 1501, and went on to discover the Magdalena River and Panama. Bastidas returned in 1525 to establish the first permanent Spanish settlement in Colombia at **SANTA MARTA**. The colony barely survived the early years, with mutinies, epidemics and Indigenous attacks ensuring that the population remained low and growth stagnant. Bastidas himself was mortally wounded by Spanish mutineers in 1527, and fighting with the **Tairona** along the coast went on until their final defeat in 1600. After a brief period in charge of Santa Marta following Bastidas' death, **Pedro de Heredia** founded Cartagena in 1533, defeating the local Indigenous inhabitants of "Kalimari". Heredia quickly conquered the areas around Turbaco and the Magdalena River near Cartagena, looting graves in the Sinú River area – his spoils allegedly included a solid gold porcupine weighing 60kg (Heredia spent his remaining years trying to acquire more territory and feuding with other Spanish leaders).

The conquest of the Muisca

Enticed by stories of **El Dorado**, the "city of gold", new Spanish Conquistadors arrived on the Caribbean coast determined to press inland. In 1536, **Gonzalo Jiménez de**

1499	1525	1533
Alonso de Ojeda lands at Cabo de la Vela, the first European to visit Colombia.	Rodrigo de Bastidas establishes the first Spanish settlement in Santa Marta.	The Spanish establish Cartagena.

Quesada led an army south from Santa Marta along the Magdalena River into the Andes. A lawyer by training, Quesada is a fascinating, complex figure, one of the few Spanish intellectuals of the *conquista* and a possible model for Cervantes' *Don Quixote*. Nevertheless, when it came to conquest, Quesada was as ruthless as his contemporaries. Exploiting a civil war between the two pre-eminent leaders of the **Muisca**, he was swiftly able to subdue both the Bogotá and Tunja Muisca kingdoms, establishing **Santafé de Bogotá** on the site of the Muisca village of Bacatá in 1538.

Sebastián de Belalcázar

Two rival Spanish forces arrived in Colombia at around the same time as Quesada. Marching north from Quito, Ecuador – the city he founded – **Sebastián de Belalcázar** had been one of Pizarro's captains in Peru, notorious for his massacre of Inca women and children. He founded Cali in 1536, and Pasto and Popayán in 1537. **Nikolaus Federmann**, a German mercenary in the employ of Spain, was also intrigued by the stories of El Dorado, and set off from Venezuela in 1536. He founded Riohacha before heading south to Bogotá, helping Belalcázar mop up resistance to the Spanish.

All three captains desired to control what was being called "New Granada" (after the southern Spanish city and province) – in what now seems an incredible display of restraint, they decided to petition King and Holy Roman Emperor Charles V (back in Europe) rather than fight it out. In 1540 Charles appointed Belalcázar governor of Popayán, though disputes with other Spanish rivals dogged his premiership until his death in 1551.

Quesada returned to Colombia in 1550 intending to live the quiet life of a colonist, but was to lead a disastrous expedition to conquer the Llanos east of the Colombian Andes in 1569–72. Federmann returned to Europe and died in a Spanish prison in 1542.

New Kingdom of Granada (1549–1717)

The region was originally placed under the direct control of the Viceroyalty of Peru, but the long distances from Lima soon deemed this impractical and in 1549 Santafé de Bogotá became the capital of the **New Kingdom of Granada**, governed by the president of the Audiencia of Bogotá (though it remained nominally subordinate to Peru).

The colonial economy

The Spanish developed the interior of Colombia relatively slowly with **gold and copper mining** the staple of the colonial economy. Agricultural output was initially limited beyond providing basic subsistence for the colony, but developed in the 1600s and replaced mining as the core of the Colombian economy by the eighteenth century; **sugar** and **tobacco** were the first major export commodities. As throughout the Spanish Americas, Colombia was governed by the *encomienda* system, where Spanish landowners were permitted (by the Crown) to use local Indigenous communities as free labour (in return for their religious and moral "welfare"). As many Indigenous people fled the Spanish colonies or simply died off, **African slaves** were imported to work

1537–38	1586	1611
Gonzalo Jiménez de Quesada wrests power (and staggering amounts of gold and emeralds) from the native Muisca and founds Bogotá.	Sir Francis Drake sacks Cartagena.	The Inquisition is established in Cartagena.

Spanish plantations and mines, primarily through Cartagena. The Spanish enacted laws to separate the slaves from the Indigenous people so the two groups would not join together to resist them, though many slaves did rebel, forming independent *palenques* (towns) beyond Spanish control.

Colonial society
Colonial society was highly stratified, with the elites at the top known as *peninsulares*, those of Spanish descent actually born in Spain. Below them were the *criollos*, those of Spanish descent born in the colonies – in the late eighteenth century it was this group that led the fight for independence. Next in importance and the most numerous were the *mestizos*, individuals of mixed Spanish and Indigenous ancestry who were free but could never hope to gain positions of authority. Indigenous people who refused to assimilate were treated the same as black African slaves – given no rights and important only as a source of labour: this despite a massive **missionary** effort by the Catholic Church, with Franciscans, Dominicans, Capuchins, and later the Jesuits (from 1604) and Augustinians all competing for converts in Latin America.

English and French attacks
It didn't take long for the English and the French to start pillaging the riches of the Spanish New World, and the Colombian colonies on the Caribbean coast were prime targets. **Cartagena** was an especially enticing prize, rapidly developing into a major slave market and portal for the export of gold and silver from the mines in New Granada.

French corsair **Jean-François Roberval** kicked things off by attacking Santa Marta in 1543 and Cartagena in 1544; Santa Marta was to be attacked another 44 times up to 1779. The English under **John Hawkins** failed to take Cartagena in 1568, but **Francis Drake** succeeded in 1586, destroying vast swathes of the city in the process (he was paid to leave).

The most serious attack on Cartagena occurred in 1697, when the city was sacked by a French force led by Admiral Bernard Desjean (aka **Baron de Pointis**), and buccaneer and governor of Saint-Domingue (Haiti) **Jean Baptiste Ducasse** – the "Raid on Cartagena" ended with the latter's pirate army plundering the city, making off with a fortune in gold and treasure.

Viceroyalty of New Granada (1717–1811)
In 1717, the **Viceroyalty of New Granada** (encompassing today's Ecuador, Colombia, Venezuela and Panama), was created, making the region officially independent of Peru (it was re-established in 1739 after a short interruption). Though Bogotá was ostensibly the capital of this vast territory, in practice the older **Audiencia of Quito** (in today's Ecuador) retained authority in the south, and in 1777 the autonomous **Captaincy General of Caracas** was created to rule modern-day Venezuela – when independence came, these long-standing regional differences proved critical. The territories of Venezuela in particular boomed in the eighteenth century, mostly thanks to cocoa and tobacco exports, produced by slave plantations.

1687	1717	1741
Cartagena sacked by a French force led by Baron de Pointis and pirate Jean Baptiste Ducasse.	Viceroyalty of New Granada created (covering today's Ecuador, Colombia, Venezuela and Panama).	British under Admiral Edward Vernon fail to capture Cartagena.

The Battle of Cartagena (1741)

In 1739 **Sebastián de Eslava** was named viceroy of New Granada. In 1741 he faced one of his greatest challenges when Cartagena was attacked by a large force of British and American colonial troops led by **Admiral Edward Vernon**. The **Battle of Cartagena** (part of the infamous War of Jenkins' Ear) at first went badly for the Spanish, but the British were eventually repulsed by a combination of ferocious local resistance and a devastating yellow fever epidemic. Even today there's much local pride in the victory.

Incidentally, Lawrence Washington, **George Washington**'s half-brother, took part in the siege on the British side – he named the now hallowed **Mount Vernon** estate in Virginia after his commander (George inherited the plantation in 1761 and led America to independence in 1776).

Spanish consolidation

Eslava's successor as viceroy, **José Solís Folch de Cardona** (1753–1761) fortified the royal mint, built roads and bridges, established Catholic missions and held the first census of the colony. Development continued under his successor, **Pedro Messía de la Cerda** (1761–73), though he presided over the expulsion of the Jesuits in 1767 and disastrous military campaigns against the Wayuu (the indigenous people who inhabited the Venezuelan coast and La Guajira) in 1761 and 1768.

The Guajira rebellion (1769)

The **Wayuu** of **La Guajira** had never really been conquered by the Spanish. Conflict flared throughout the eighteenth century, and in 1769 a major rebellion was precipitated by the Spanish abducting 22 tribesmen to help strengthen the fortifications at Cartagena. In response the local church in El Rincón, near Riohacha, was burned down, killing two Spaniards who had taken refuge inside. A punitive Spanish force led by José Antonio de Sierra was defeated, with Sierra himself killed – this success encouraged an all out **Guajira rebellion**, with a large Indigenous force burning virtually all the Spanish settlements and Capuchin missions in the region. The rebellion only ended when factions within the Wayuu began to fight each other, and Spanish reinforcements were able to mop up the remainder. Another rebellion in 1776 effectively ended Spanish attempts to colonize the area.

Revolt of the Comuneros (1781)

Usually regarded as a precursor to the independence movement, the **Revolt of the Comuneros** pitched the colonial inhabitants of New Granada against the Spanish government, particularly over increased taxes and stricter colonial controls (including a hugely unpopular two real hike in the price of tobacco and aguardiente, on which the state had a monopoly). The revolt began with protests over taxes in Socorro, and central committees or *comúnes* were organized under the leadership of **Juan Francisco Berbeo**, a *criollo* (Spanish, but born in Colombia). Berbeo marched on Bogotá where his army was able to force concessions from the colonial government; once the army had dispersed, however, the government reneged, and most rebel leaders were eventually imprisoned (Berbeo managed to somehow avoid serious punishment and died in 1795). Rebel hero **José Antonio Galán** tried to continue resistance but he was also captured and executed in 1782.

1769	1781	1810	1811–14
Guajira rebellion.	Revolt of the Comuneros.	War of Independence against Spain begins.	The First Republic.

THE GREAT LIBERATOR

The independence of Colombia would have been impossible without **Simón Bolívar** (1738–1830), a Venezuelan by birth but venerated today across South America as the liberator of the continent – almost every city and town in Colombia (and Venezuela) has a bust or statue of the great man in the main square. Bolívar was an unlikely revolutionary, born into an aristocratic Spanish family that had settled in Caracas back in the sixteenth century. Though his childhood was certainly privileged, his parents died when he was very young, and Bolívar entered the local military academy when he was just fourteen – after a spell in Europe he returned to Venezuela in 1807, and partly inspired by what he had seen in France, became involved in the early independence movement three years later (see page 342). His initial involvement in the civil wars that followed saw him rise to the rank of colonel, but it wasn't until he arrived in New Granada (Colombia) in 1813 that Bolívar achieved real success. After raising troops in Mompox (see page 149) and issuing his **"Decree of War to the Death"** (calling for the death of any Spaniard not actively supporting independence), he was able to capture Caracas and was proclaimed as "**El Libertador**". Though the Spanish recaptured Caracas in 1814, Bolívar fought on in Colombia, liberating Bogotá. With Spain resurgent, Bolívar was forced to flee to Jamaica and then Haiti in 1815, but he never lost sight of his ultimate goal, and in 1817 he returned, capturing Angostura (now Ciudad Bolívar in Venezuela). It took two more years of campaigning, but victory at the **Battle of Boyacá** in 1819 assured the independence of New Granada (Colombia) – Venezuela was liberated after the Battle of Carabobo in 1821, and Bolívar became president of a united Gran Colombia. The fighting wasn't over however: Ecuador was only freed in 1822, after which Bolívar met with Argentine general and equally revered independence hero **José de San Martín** to hash out a final strategy. Peru and Bolivia were liberated in 1824, Bolívar briefly becoming leader of both countries (Bolivia, formerly "Upper Peru", being named for him).

The rise of Nariño

Beginning in the 1790s (and influenced by the American and French revolutions), the *criollo* elites in New Granada were increasingly divided over their allegiance to Spain. In 1794, **Antonio Nariño** (1765–1824), an aristocratic idealist from Bogotá, published a Spanish translation of the French *Declaration of the Rights of Man* – he was promptly arrested and exiled. Nariño was eventually able to return to Colombia (in 1797 and again in 1811), and began to work towards the goal of South American independence.

Independence

By the early nineteenth century Spain's vast American empire was beginning to crumble, a trend exacerbated by the invasion of Spain by **Napoleon** in 1808. While Spain's **King Ferdinand VII** remained imprisoned by the French, who would govern his colonial empire?

Rebellion (1809–10)

In 1809 the *criollo* elites in Quito formed their own *junta*, or ruling council, in opposition to the Spanish government-in-exile, and asked Bogotá to join them. Most locals were in favour but the Spanish viceroy **José Amar y Borbón** was opposed – he sent troops to Quito to quell the rebellion. After the failure of several small

1812	1819	1828
Simón Bolívar publishes Cartagena Manifesto.	Bolívar defeats Spanish forces at the Battle of Boyacá; Republic of Gran Colombia created with Bolívar first president.	Gran Colombia–Peru War.

> It wasn't until 1827 that Bolívar returned to Bogotá, but divisions within his Gran Colombia were already showing. Bolívar himself admired the young nation of the USA (though he was staunchly anti-slavery), but believed that a similar federal system would not work in South America – instead he advocated strong, almost monarchial central government, something many of his contemporaries rejected.
>
> After a constitutional convention at Ocaña failed to solve the problems in 1828, Bolívar was effectively made dictator, surviving an assassination attempt a few weeks later – his vice president Santander was implicated in the plot. After two years of opposition and rebellion, the now exhausted Liberator agreed to stand down, and to the partition of Gran Colombia in 1830. Aiming to live quietly in Europe, Bolívar died of tuberculosis in Santa Marta before he could set sail (see page 158) – he was just 47 (his last days beautifully reimagined in **Gabriel García Márquez**'s *The General in His Labyrinth*). He was survived by his partner, Manuelita Sáenz; Bolívar never married Sáenz, having sworn not to wed again when his wife, María Teresa, died in 1803 after only eight months of marriage. On his deathbed, he told his aide-de-camp, Daniel Florence O'Leary, to burn his papers; luckily, O'Leary disobeyed him and they survived, giving us a huge trove of information on his life and ideas. Understanding their significance, Manuelita Sáenz gave O'Leary all of her letters from Bolívar before her own death in 1856. In 1842 Bolívar's remains were transferred to Caracas, where his tomb remains a national shrine.
>
> Though he is less known outside of South America, the potency of Bolívar's legacy was emphasized in 2008, when then-president of Venezuela **Hugo Chávez** set up a commission to investigate whether the Liberator had actually been poisoned (Chávez had long presented himself as the continent's heir to the freedom-fighting hero). In 2011 it was decided there was no proof of foul play.

uprisings and anti-Spanish plots, Colombian cities began to organize their own councils in 1810: Cartagena, Cali and finally, Bogotá itself. On 21 July 1810 an autonomous ruling body was created for the capital and all of New Granada (now regarded as Colombia's first act of independence). Borbón was deposed, though the *junta* was technically still loyal to Ferdinand VII (Mompox was the only town to declare complete independence from Spain).

The First Republic (1811–14)

Colombia's initial phase of independence was crippled by disagreement and infighting among the provinces, and between anti- and pro-Spanish forces – as conflict emerged between Federalists and Centralists the period became known as **La Patria Boba** ("the Foolish Patriotism").

The **Republic of Cundinamarca** (covering the region of modern central Colombia loosely centred on Bogotá) was proclaimed in February 1811 as a constitutional monarchy, with elected president **Jorge Tadeo Lozano** (1771–1816) proposing a federal system for the former provinces of New Granada. This was vehemently opposed by independence hero Antonio Nariño, newly returned from exile – he was elected president of a new entity (claiming the same territory), the **United Provinces of New Granada**, in late 1811 after Lozano had resigned. A bloody civil war between the

1830	1839–41	1853	1858–62
Ecuador and Venezuela secede from Gran Colombia. Bolívar resigns and dies in Santa Marta.	War of the Supremes.	Colombia adopts a constitution that confirms the abolition of slavery.	Granadine Confederation.

United Provinces, the supporters of Cundinamarca and the royalists (now based in Panama) ensued, with the United Provinces emerging victorious in 1814, thanks primarily to Venezuelan commander **Simón Bolívar** (Nariño took Popayán in 1814, but was subsequently captured by the Spanish and remained in prison till 1821). Bolívar had been a low-level officer when Caracas declared its de facto independence in 1810, but enlisted in the New Granada army in 1812 after publishing his **Cartagena Manifesto** (which tried to analyse why the movement had initially failed in Venezuela).

Spain fights back (1815–19)

Napoleon's defeat meant that Ferdinand VII returned to Spain in 1814, cracking down on liberal political movements and initiating a period of absolutism – he also intended to bring South America to heel. Spain's army, led by **General Pablo Morillo** ("*El Pacificador*"), captured Santa Marta and then Cartagena in 1815 – the siege of the latter was especially devastating, with up to six thousand civilians (half the population) dying. Morillo took Bogotá the following year, initiating a reign of terror against pro-independence supporters (Jorge Tadeo Lozano was one of many executed). Bolívar fled to Jamaica and then Haiti, and it wasn't until 1817 that he secured a foothold in Venezuela, declaring himself "Supreme Chief of the Armies". Bolívar was finally able to liberate Bogotá after the decisive victory at the **Battle of Boyacá** in 1819. Morillo signed a treaty with Bolívar in 1820 and returned to Spain – minor Spanish resistance did continue (Bolívar only freed Caracas in 1821 after the decisive **Battle of Carabobo**), but from now on Colombia was effectively an independent nation.

Gran Colombia: the Second Republic (1819–30)

The **Republic of Gran Colombia**, a union of New Granada (with Panama and Ecuador) and Venezuela, was created in 1819, with a constitution agreed at the **Congress of Cúcuta** in 1821 (known as "The Cúcuta Constitution"). Bogotá was decreed capital with **Simón Bolívar voted president** by the congress (defeating Antonio Nariño, who died in 1824), but because he continued to campaign against Spanish armies in Peru and Ecuador until 1827, vice president **Francisco de Paula Santander** (1792–1840) effectively ran the country. Venezuelans resented the power given to Bogotá however, and with differences also emerging between Bolívar and Santander it was soon clear that Gran Colombia would not last. Bolívar became dictator in 1828, surviving an assassination attempt soon after (Santander was implicated and exiled in the aftermath). The **Gran Colombia–Peru War** began the same year (essentially over political boundaries), and by the time Bolívar had returned in 1830 Congress had approved a new constitution, with Venezuela and Ecuador deciding to secede from the union. Bolívar resigned and agreed to go into voluntary exile, dying a broken and bitter man in Santa Marta in December 1830 before leaving the country. A short civil war followed, but by 1832 the independence of Venezuela and Ecuador had been confirmed, Colombia becoming the **Republic of New Granada** with Santander its first president.

The Republic of New Granada (1830–58)

Santander began his presidency of the **Republic of New Granada** in 1832, having returned from exile in New York. Building a modern nation was to prove a long,

1863–86	1886	1899–1902	1903
The United States of Colombia.	The Republic of Colombia proclaimed, after Christopher Columbus.	The War of a Thousand Days.	With the support of the US, Panama secedes from Colombia.

RODRÍGUEZ: COFFEE ENTREPRENEUR

The Conservative president overthrown in 1861 (see page 346), **Mariano Ospina Rodríguez** is perhaps better known as one of Colombia's earliest and most influential **coffee** entrepreneurs. He founded an experimental plantation in 1835, in Fredonia, Antioquia, largely credited with introducing high-quality Arabica beans and modern farming practices to the country. Though Ospina Rodríguez was imprisoned by Mosquera, he escaped in 1862, finding sanctuary in Guatemala – by 1865 he had founded several coffee plantations there, becoming a coffee pioneer in Central America. Rodríguez was able to return to his Colombian plantations in Fredonia in 1871, and went on to write an influential manual for coffee-growing, published in 1880, before dying in Medellín in 1885. In 2011 UNESCO declared Colombia's main coffee growing region a World Heritage Site.

gruelling and often grisly task – one of Santander's first acts was to execute all remaining Spanish prisoners. Much of Colombian politics thereafter was to be dominated – well into the twentieth century – by the division and conflict between **Conservatives** and **Liberals**, with Bolívar's supporters eventually forming the Conservative Party (1849) and Santander's becoming the forerunners of the Liberal Party (1848). The Conservatives wanted strong, centralized government in alliance with the Roman Catholic Church, while the Liberals believed in a federal, decentralized system, with the state taking a leading role in areas like education, rather than the Church. Individual allegiances remained fluid however, with nominally independent politicians often changing sides or forming temporary alliances with the opposition.

War of the Supremes (1839–41)

José Ignacio de Márquez succeeded Santander as president in 1837, but just two years later the nation was rocked by a rebellion in **Pasto** known as the **War of the Supremes**. The revolt was precipitated by the government order to close monasteries in the Pasto area, an especially strong Catholic region, but the uprising soon became a fight between Centralism (Conservatives) and Federalism (Liberals), with **General José María Obando** eventually emerging as rebel (and Liberal) leader. After Ecuadorian troops helped defeat Obando, the rebellion escalated into a national conflict, with twelve provinces declaring independence under various *jefes supremos* ("supreme leaders"). However, the movement remained disunited, and Conservative government forces under **General Pedro Alcántara Herrán** were able to rally; Herrán returned to Bogotá victorious in 1842, and was sworn in as the new president – Obando fled into exile. In 1845 nominally independent **Tomás Cipriano de Mosquera** (1798–1878) was elected president with the support of the Conservatives, but his policies (such as separating the Church and State) gradually moved closer to the Liberal position.

The end of slavery (1851–53)

A former Bolívar lieutenant but supported by the Liberals, **José Hilario López** (1798–1869) was elected president in 1849 determined to carry out the Liberator's wishes and **abolish slavery**. In 1821 a law had been passed that freed children born in New Granada to slave mothers once they reached the age of eighteen, but this was

1927	1928	1932	1932–33
Gabriel García Márquez born in Aracataca.	The Banana Massacre in Ciénaga near Santa Marta.	Fernando Botero born in Medellín.	Colombia–Peru War.

conditional on their "masters" issuing a certificate of good conduct; special *juntas* were supposed to buy the freedom of adult slaves, but in practice very few were released. López ordered that slave owners be compensated (with around 2 million pesos) for their loss of "property", and Congress formally abolished slavery on 1 January 1852 – this provoked a Conservative uprising in Cauca, easily crushed by government forces.

Meanwhile, **Obando** had returned to Colombia in 1849, and in a remarkable turnaround of political fortune was elected Liberal president in 1853. His first order of business was to confirm the abolition of slavery in the **Constitution of 1853**, an incredibly progressive document for the time that also extended the suffrage to all married men aged 21 and older, and provided for freedom of religion. A period of unrest followed, and Obando was removed by **José María Melo** in a bloodless coup in 1854 (Melo himself only lasted a few months).

Granadine Confederation (1858–62)

The 1853 Constitution had paved the way for a greater degree of federalism in New Granada (a policy favoured by the Liberals), and in subsequent years provinces began declaring their sovereignty. In 1858 their relationship was formalized in what was dubbed the **Granadine Confederation**, with a new constitution and the federal capital in Bogotá, but provinces wielding a high level of autonomy.

Conservative factions within the Granadine Confederation remained unhappy with the new federal structure, however, and when Conservative president **Mariano Ospina Rodríguez** (president 1857–61) and the national Congress began to push back, passing laws that increased central power, the states rebelled. Full **civil war** erupted in 1860 when ex-president Tomás Cipriano de Mosquera – now fully converted to the Liberal Party – declared himself leader of an independent Cauca.

The United States of Colombia (1863–86)

After fierce fighting Mosquera captured Bogotá in 1861 and became Liberal president of the whole country; a loose federal system was confirmed by the **Constitution of 1863** when the name of the confederation was officially changed to the **United States of Colombia**.

Mosquera served two terms as elected president, leading Colombia to victory in a **short war with Ecuador** in 1863 but removed in an 1867 coup after disagreements with the Catholic Church. Mosquera contested the 1870 election but was defeated by radical Liberal candidate **Eustorgio Salgar** (1831–85), a modernizer who founded the country's first railway company and pegged the Colombian peso to the French franc as part of the international gold standard. Exports of gold and coffee rose as tobacco declined, but the economy remained almost completely dominated by agriculture, with very little industry.

The Republic of Colombia

Liberals had dominated politics since the 1850s, but **Rafael Núñez** (writer of Colombia's national anthem) was elected president for the second time in 1884

1935	1943	1948	1953
Argentine tango legend Carlos Gardel killed in plane crash in Medellín.	Colombia enters World War II on the side of the Allies.	The assassination of Jorge Eliécer Gaitán triggers El Bogotazo and La Violencia.	General Rojas Pinilla seizes power in a military coup; gradually restores peace and order.

with the support of the Conservatives. Núñez was leader of the Independent Liberal faction, but supported the **Regeneración** movement that called for a stronger central government to develop the economy. After a Liberal rebellion was defeated in 1885, Núñez sponsored a new Centralist constitution that abolished the United States of Colombia and created the **Republic of Colombia** in 1886 – he was elected as first president. The formerly sovereign states of Colombia were reorganized as departments firmly under the control of the central government, cordial relations were re-established with the Catholic Church and the new **National Party** was formed. Núñez won a fourth term as president in 1892, this time as National Party candidate, but due to ill-health ceded power to his vice president **Miguel Antonio Caro**. With Caro cracking down on the Liberal Party yet another **civil war** broke out in 1894, ending in complete government victory a year later. Núñez died in 1894, while Caro remained president until 1898.

The War of a Thousand Days (1899–1902)

National Party candidate **Manuel Antonio Sanclemente** was elected president in 1898, but it was a result the Liberal Party, antagonized by almost two decades of Centralist policies, refused to accept. In 1899 the Liberals launched the latest in a long line of tragic and bloody civil wars, this one dubbed the **War of a Thousand Days**. The war lasted for three years and left thousands dead. The Conservative government emerged victorious at the end of 1902 (**José Manuel Marroquín** had replaced Sanclemente as president in a 1900 coup). The short-lived National Party was dissolved and the **Conservative Party** dominated politics for the next thirty years.

Panama secedes (1903)

Still regarded with much bitterness in Colombia today, the **secession of Panama** in 1903 was a bitter blow, leaving the modern-day country as the last remaining rump of Bolívar's "Gran Colombia". Panama became independent because of the US desire to build a canal between the Atlantic and Pacific oceans, a project conceived as far back as the sixteenth century. The first attempt to construct the **Panama Canal** began in 1881 under Colombian control and the leadership of **Ferdinand de Lesseps**, French builder of the Suez Canal. This attempt had failed completely by 1889. In 1903 the US and Colombia signed a treaty transferring construction rights to the US (the US would build and operate the canal on a renewable lease in return for a down payment of $10 million and royalties of $250,000 per year). Colombia's Congress refused to ratify the agreement, however, and fearing loss of control US president Theodore Roosevelt changed tactics, openly supporting Panama's nascent independence movement (separatists had been gaining ground since the 1880s). When the Panamanians duly declared independence from Colombia on 3 November 1903, the US government swiftly recognized the new nation, making it clear that it would not tolerate Colombian attempts to quell the rebellion. Roosevelt also signed a new treaty with Panama permitting the US to build and indefinitely administer the **Panama Canal Zone** and its defences (for essentially the same terms as the first treaty). Work on the canal resumed in 1904 and it opened in August 1914 (Panama resumed full control of the canal only in 1999). Colombia recognized the sovereignty of Panama in 1914

1954	1957	1958	1964
Women win the right to vote.	Pinilla is deposed.	The Conservative and Liberal parties become a united National Front, agreeing to share power.	Military attacks on rural communities provokes the creation of the FARC and ELN guerrilla groups; civil war rages.

THE BANANA MASSACRE

The "Masacre de las bananeras", a massacre of workers at the **United Fruit Company** on 6 December 1928, had a huge impact on Colombian politics into the 1930s and beyond (indirectly leading to La Violencia and the rise of FARC), and even influenced the work of Gabriel García Márquez (who was just a baby when it happened, but who grew up in nearby Aracataca hearing stories of the tragedy). The massacre occurred in **Ciénaga** near Santa Marta, after the Conservative government decided to send the Colombian army to end a month-long strike organized by the local workers' union (they were trying to improve their medieval working conditions). It's still not known how many workers were killed (the army opened fire with machine guns, and anywhere from fifty to two thousand workers may have been hit), but it is known that the US had pressured the Colombians to take action in order to protect the interests of the hugely influential United Fruit Company.

in a treaty with the US, though the payment of US$25 million in compensation and a formal US apology for the incident wasn't ratified by the US Congress until 1921.

Limited reconciliation (1903–30)

To a large extent the devastation that resulted from the War of a Thousand Days had utterly discredited both the Liberals and the Conservatives, and as a consequence a rare **period of peace** lasted into the early twentieth century. Although **Conservatives** were nominally in control, they tended to form coalition governments involving key Liberal politicians and civil war was avoided. **General Rafael Reyes** was elected president in 1904 and pursued a combination of political reconciliation and authoritarianism (including a protectionist trade policy); his economic polices initiated a return to the gold standard, restored Colombian credit abroad and attracted foreign capital (Reyes resigned in 1909 over Congressional rejection of his treaty with the US). Between 1900 and 1910 Colombia started to industrialize, with textile industries in Medellín, ceramic plants in Caldas and breweries in Itagüí and Bogotá leading the way, and the US replaced Britain as Colombia's key financial and commercial partner. **Coffee** came to dominate 80 percent of exports. The Conservative administration of **Pedro Nel Ospina Vázquez** (1922–26) oversaw the reorganization of the banking and financial sectors, creating the **Banco de la República** in 1923. Social tensions increased throughout the Conservative administration of **Miguel Abadía Méndez** (1926–30), with Colombian workers gradually organizing unions and a decisive strike at Unified Fruit Company in 1928 (see above).

The Liberal Hegemony (1930–45)

In 1930 the Liberal Party finally regained power when **Enrique Olaya Herrera** was elected president, ushering in a period of "**Liberal Hegemony**" in Colombian politics (in part a reaction to the Banana Massacre; see page 348), with Liberal Party candidates dominating the presidency until 1945. It wasn't good a time for a comeback. The 1929 Wall Street Crash had sparked a global **Depression** that hit Colombia – still dependent on commodity exports – especially hard, and in 1932 **conflict erupted with Peru** (see page 349).

1970	**1974**	**1982**
Fraudulent election of Misael Pastrana Borrero.	National Front ends; radical leftist guerrilla group Movimiento 19 de Abril (M-19) founded.	Gabriel García Márquez wins the Nobel Prize for Literature.

COLOMBIA IN WORLD WAR II AND KOREA

Colombia had remained neutral during World War I (1914–18), but in November 1943 it declared war on Germany and Japan in support of the Allies in **World War II**. Its army did not participate in any fighting, but the Colombian navy did see action fighting German U-boats in the Caribbean (some Colombian ships were sunk).

Colombia also sent a force to aid the US and its allies under the guise of the United Nations in the **Korean War** (1950–53), when the "Colombian Battalion" numbered 4314 men (plus one naval ship, the *Amirante*). The last troops came home in 1954, but the fate of veterans remained a controversial issue for many years.

Nevertheless, **Alfonso López Pumarejo**'s first administration (1934–38) enacted far-reaching reforms, nationalized education, supported the creation of labour unions and also passed a law allowing for the government seizure of private property if deemed to be in the "social interest". The **Communist Party of Colombia** was formed in 1930 and generally supported the Liberal Party, further alienating Conservatives. Pumarejo was re-elected in 1942 but this time Conservative opposition was stronger; after a failed military coup in 1944 (when he was briefly held prisoner in Pasto), Pumarejo resigned in early 1945, and Conservative **Mariano Ospina Pérez** (grandson of former president Mariano Ospina Rodríguez), ruled from 1946 to 1950.

Colombia–Peru War (1932–33)

In 1932 **conflict erupted with Peru** over the Colombian Amazon port of **Leticia**. Unhappy with an earlier border treaty (signed in secret), Peruvians had occupied the town expecting a mild Colombian response. In fact, spurred on by public outrage, the Colombian navy managed to assemble a fleet to sail up the Amazon and its rudimentary air force bombarded Peruvian positions (with little success). However, when the Peruvian president was assassinated in 1933, hostilities were quickly brought to a halt, the Peruvians withdrew and a new agreement confirmed the old borders.

La Violencia (1948–58)

In 1948 the assassination of the working class's greatest advocate, Bogotá's populist mayor, **Jorge Eliécer Gaitán**, led to the massive rioting known as **El Bogotazo** in the capital. Gabriel García Márquez was a student at the time and witnessed the lynching of the lone gunman accused of committing the crime – one Juan Roa Sierra – harrowingly described in *Living to Tell the Tale*. Like many others then and now, Márquez believed the lynching was orchestrated by Conservative elements in an attempt to protect the real perpetrators (by coincidence, a 20-year-old Fidel Castro was also in Bogotá that day). The ten hours of riots and looting that followed resulted in thousands of deaths. The protests spread across the country, and led to a decade of partisan blood-letting dubbed **La Violencia**. At least 200,000 died, with many victims horribly tortured; quartering, beheading, crucifixions, hanging, mass rapes, the murder of infants and scalping became commonplace. Márquez later wrote "On April 9, 1948, the twentieth century began in Colombia". The Conservative Party managed to hold

1983	1985	1986	1993
Popayán devastated by a massive earthquake.	M-19 takes over the Palace of Justice in Bogotá; volcanic eruption leads to Tragedia de Armero.	Pope John Paul II visits Colombia.	Drug kingpin Pablo Escobar is shot dead evading arrest.

onto power until 1953, cracking down on Liberals in what was essentially a civil–military dictatorship.

Martial law (1953–58)
Frustrated with the violence – and with the tacit support of leading Colombian oligarchs – **General Rojas Pinilla** led a military coup to overthrow Conservative president Laureano Gómez Castro in 1953. Pinilla held on to power until he too was forced to resign after massive national protests in 1957. During his premiership most of the armed groups (dubbed *bandoleros*) of "La Violencia" were demobilized during an amnesty (a small number that fought on were brought to heel in 1954). Rojas also gave the **right to vote to women** for the first time, and introduced **television** to Colombia (both in 1954).

However, in 1955 Rojas Pinilla ordered a military offensive against rearmed rural workers, triggering a confrontation known as the **War of Villarrica**, and he started to lose popular support.

The National Front (1958–74)
After Rojas Pinilla was deposed a military Junta assumed control of the nation, but in 1958 things seemed to be looking up for Colombia when the Conservative and Liberal parties created a united **National Front**, agreeing to share power, with each party holding office alternately for four years. Liberal Party leader **Alberto Lleras Camargo** was elected first president. Though it seemed that the worst of the violence was over, underlying problems – rural poverty, inequality, Indigenous rights, land rights and social issues – remained, and **guerrilla movements** (mostly inspired by Communism) emerged in the early 1960s. The National Front system itself eventually began to be seen as a form of political repression, especially after the fraudulent election of Conservative candidate Misael Pastrana Borrero (president 1970–74), which resulted in the defeat of the relatively populist candidate Gustavo Rojas.

Civil War begins – again
In the early 1960s Colombian army units loyal to the National Front began to attack rural communities they suspected of Communist sympathies, but it was the US-backed attacks in 1964, especially on the community of Marquetalia, that led rural workers, liberal and communist militants to reorganize into the **Fuerzas Armadas Revolucionarios Colombianos (FARC)**, with a political platform of agrarianism and anti-imperialism. In contrast, the smaller Communist **National Liberation Army (ELN)** was founded in January 1965 by primarily ex-student radicals in the cities, led by charismatic orators like Camilo Torres Restrepo. The **19th of April Movement (M-19)** emerged in 1974 espousing a similar blend of revolutionary socialism and populism, primarily in response to the Borrero election (on 19 April 1970; see page 348), and by the end of the National Front period there seemed little hope of ending the violence.

Post-National Front period (1974–90)
From 1974 until 1990, Colombia's **civil war** rumbled on, while at the same time the drug trade in **cocaine** boomed, creating a whole new front of criminal activity.

1997	1999	2001
Creation of the United Self-Defense Forces of Colombia (AUC); the Mapiripán Massacre.	Plan Colombia, aimed at tackling the country's cocaine production, is launched, with backing from the US.	Colombia hosts and wins its first Copa América football tournament.

When the National Front officially expired in 1974, Liberal candidate **Alfonso López Michelsen** easily won the presidency, though his premiership was marred by violent protests and strikes in 1977. The Liberals held on to the presidency 1978 to 1982 through **Julio César Turbay Ayala**, who continued the crackdown on guerrillas, particularly M-19, and in 1981 made homosexuality legal in Colombia for the first time. During the Conservative administration of **Belisario Betancur** (1982–86), Popayán was devastated by a massive **earthquake** in 1983 and two years later over 20,000 people were killed by flooding in the wake of the eruption of the Nevado del Ruiz volcano, dubbed the "**Tragedia de Armero**". The visit of **Pope John Paul II** to Colombia in 1986 gave the country a much-needed boost, but the economy remained weak and the civil war seemed to have no end in sight. The Liberal presidency of **Virgilio Barco Vargas** (1986–90) saw peace talks initiated with M-19 (see below), but the drug gangs appeared to be out of control.

The rise of the drug cartels

In the 1980s **cocaine** became Colombia's biggest export (mostly due to a surge in demand from the US), creating immensely powerful **drug cartels**. The world gradually came to know of **Pablo Escobar**, head of the dreaded **Medellín Cartel** (see page 218), who had started cocaine smuggling in the 1970s and by 1990 was a US$ billionaire, bribing cops and politicians, fixing elections and football matches. In the early 1980s Escobar helped create a paramilitary organization dubbed **Muerte a Secuestradores** ("Death to Kidnappers") or MAS, ostensibly to fight left-wing guerrillas but mostly to provide protection for the corrupt elites Escobar was bribing and to protect the gang's now considerable economic interests. Escobar became increasingly involved in what was essentially **terrorism**, his MAS death squads murdering hundreds of community leaders, elected officials and farmers. High-profile murders include **Rodrigo Lara Bonilla**, Minister of Justice, killed on a Bogotá highway in 1984; **Jaime Pardo Leal**, presidential candidate and head of the Patriotic Union party killed in 1987; **Antonio Roldan Betancur**, governor of Antioquia, killed by a car bomb in 1989; and **Luis Carlos Galán**, presidential candidate, killed by gunmen during a rally in 1989. Also in 1989, Escobar ordered the bombing of **Avianca Airlines Flight 203**, which was destroyed just after takeoff from Bogotá with the loss of all 107 people on board (see page 218). The **Cali Cartel** also grew immensely powerful in the 1980s (see page 258), initiating a bloody feud with Escobar and the Medellín Cartel.

The end of M-19

Despite attempts by Betancur to make peace, guerrillas from **M-19** took over the **Palacio de Justicia** (Supreme Court) in Bogotá in a spectacularly audacious attack in 1985; Colombian security forces laid siege to the building and then raided it. In the resulting firefight all the M-19 attackers and eleven judges were killed. In the aftermath M-19 suffered a series of setbacks, with several leaders killed; **Carlos Pizarro** took over and reopened negotiations with the government. In 1990, the M-19 demobilized and almost all remaining militants joined a legitimate political party known as "**Alianza Democrática M-19**" (many former guerillas have since become elected politicians, including founder Antonio Navarro Wolff). FARC and the ELN fought on.

2002	**2006**	**2010**	**2011**
Álvaro Uribe Vélez is elected president.	AUC paramilitaries officially disarm; Uribe re-elected.	Juan Manuel Santos is elected president.	Former leader of the M-19 guerrillas, Gustavo Petro, becomes mayor of Bogotá; US signs free-trade agreement with Colombia.

The 1990s

In the early 1990s Colombia's left-wing guerrillas were increasingly overshadowed by the violence of the **drug cartels**. In 1990 the Colombian government started re-implementing a controversial extradition treaty with the US (which had been ruled invalid by the Colombian Supreme Court in 1986), prompting Pablo Escobar and the group he called **Los Extraditables** to step up their war on the government (knowing that it would now be easier for the American government to take them to trial). The murder rate in Colombia exploded, and in mid-1990 Escobar ordered the **kidnapping** of several high-profile journalists, including **Diana Turbay** (recounted in Gabriel García Márquez's nonfiction book, *News of a Kidnapping*). Most of the journalists were released in 1991 (though Turbay was killed during a bungled rescue attempt), and the Liberal government of **César Gaviria** persuaded Escobar to surrender, just as the new **Colombian Constitution of 1991** prohibited extradition. Escobar was able to run the Medellín Cartel from a luxurious private prison, "La Catedral", but escaped in 1992 when it seemed likely his cushy deal was about to end – he was hunted down and killed in 1993, and the leadership of both the Cali and Medellín cartels was largely wiped out or arrested by the late 1990s. In 1997 **extradition was restored** during the Liberal government of **Ernesto Samper** (1994–98), while the Conservative administration of **Andrés Pastrana Arango** (1998–2002) initiated the US-backed **Plan Colombia** in 1999, authorizing the spraying and destruction of thousands of acres of coca fields, along with normal food crops that got in the way (US financial support for Colombian anti-narcotic initiatives has continued ever since).

The rise of right-wing militias

Meanwhile, Colombia's civil war was being fuelled by the rise of **right-wing militias**, beginning in the 1980s when drug gangs and rogue elements of the police and armed forces encouraged militias to combat left-wing rebel kidnappings and extortion. A merger of such forces established the notorious **United Self-Defense Forces of Colombia (AUC)** in 1997, which almost immediately carried out the **Mapiripán Massacre**, the brutal murder of an estimated thirty civilians in the Llanos region. At its peak the AUC claimed some 20,000 members and was funded primarily through drug smuggling and kidnapping. Leader **Carlos Castaño** was killed in 2004, and most of the AUC was disbanded in 2006 (see below).

The Uribe presidency

In 2002 ex-Liberal **Álvaro Uribe Vélez** was elected president on a platform of law and order and defeating FARC under the independent "**Colombia First**" umbrella. By this time FARC seemed to be growing ever stronger, with four years of peace talks failing to make any headway, violence rife and **kidnapping** out of control. True to his word, Uribe did make some progress against the guerrillas (and remains popular today thanks to reforms that kick-started the economy), with FARC much diminished by the end of his premiership. However, his deal to disarm AUC paramilitaries in return for lenient sentences for massacres and other human rights abuses in 2006 was harder to assess, with many regrouping as neoparamilitary groups such as **Los Rastrojos** – the drug trafficking, murders and land grabbing continued.

2012	2014	2014
FARC begins negotiations with the Colombian government in Cuba.	Gabriel García Márquez dies in Mexico City; Colombia's James Rodríguez becomes top scorer at the World Cup in Brazil (Colombia reaches the quarter-finals for the first time).	Santos is narrowly re-elected president.

Thanks to a constitutional amendment, Uribe was able to stand for a second term in 2006; he was re-elected with around 62 percent of the vote, one of the largest landslides in Colombian history.

The Andean diplomatic crisis

In 2008, former vice presidential candidate Clara Rojas and former congresswoman Consuelo González were freed after nearly six years in FARC captivity; a few months later the killing of FARC leader **Raul Reyes** by the Colombian military on Ecuadorean soil precipitated the **Andean diplomatic crisis**, primarily due to an incensed Venezuelan president **Hugo Chávez** (though his country wasn't directly affected, he had been acting as a go-between with FARC). Chávez closed the Venezuelan embassy in Bogotá and even mobilized troops before things were calmed down at the Rio Group summit – for Uribe the whole incident was a huge victory, and a severe blow to FARC. A few months later Operation Jaque rescued high-profile politician and one-time presidential candidate **Ingrid Betancourt** along with fourteen other FARC hostages – the rebels seemed to be in full retreat. Uribe ended his presidency in 2010 with another Venezuelan crisis, precipitated by his accusation that the Chávez government was actively permitting FARC and ELN guerrillas to seek safe haven in its territory (relations were only restored after the Colombian elections).

Falso Positivos

Uribe's government (though seemingly not the president himself) was tainted somewhat by the "**Falso Positivos**" scandal between 2008 and 2012. In 2008 it was discovered that some members of the military had been murdering innocent civilians since the 1990s in order to present "false positive" figures on the numbers of rebel fighters killed (making them look more successful than they actually were). A 2012 report by the International Federation for Human Rights suggested there had been over three thousand civilian victims – several members of the military have since been imprisoned, but no senior politicians have been implicated.

The Santos presidency

Following Uribe's failed attempt to run for a third term, former Defence Minister and leader of the Partido Social de Unidad Nacional, or "Party of the U", a centre-right coalition, **Juan Manuel Santos** was elected president in 2010, promising to continue the armed offensive against all rebel movements. FARC actually stepped up attacks in the south, but their leader Víctor Julio Suárez Rojas – aka **Mono Jojoy** – was killed in September; his successor **Alfonso Cano** was also killed by security forces in 2011. Seemingly weakened and tired of fighting, FARC released most of its remaining hostages in 2012, announced it would **end the practice of kidnapping** for ransom and began **peace negotiations** with the Colombian government in Cuba.

Not everyone approved of the ostensibly conciliatory approach Santos took with the rebels. In 2013 former allies such as Álvaro Uribe broke away to form the **Centro Democrático** ("Democratic Centre"), a relatively conservative coalition opposed to the negotiations with FARC. In 2014 Santos was **re-elected president** with

2016	2017
FARC signs a ceasefire accord with Santos in Havana, but the peace deal is rejected in a national referendum. Santos wins Nobel Peace Prize.	Revised peace deal with FARC approved by Congress; FARC disarms and reforms as a legal political party, the Common Alternative Revolutionary Force.

51 percent of the vote, defeating Centro Democrático candidate Óscar Iván Zuluaga – Santos remained premier until 2018.

One policy that unites most mainstream politicians in Colombia is the country's close **relationship with the US**, which since signing a **free-trade agreement** in 2011 has never been stronger – this in stark contrast to other South American nations such as Argentina, Venezuela, Ecuador, Bolivia, Paraguay and Uruguay, where politics has veered to the left in the last decade and relations with the North have been strained.

Peace with FARC

FARC finally signed a **peace deal** with Santos in 2016, though in a stunning reversal, the deal was rejected by the Colombian public in a subsequent **national referendum** (50.24 percent voted against). Santos received the **2016 Nobel Peace Prize** nevertheless, and swiftly negotiated a revised agreement with FARC; not risking another referendum, this time Santos had the deal approved directly by Congress. In 2017, FARC disarmed, reforming as a legal political party, the **Common Alternative Revolutionary Force**. Negotiations with the ELN, however, dragged on, with a ceasefire ending in early 2018 with no agreement reached.

In the **2018 presidential election**, the first round of voting saw **Iván Duque Márquez**, a conservative and Uribe protégé (representing the Democratic Center Party and the "right coalition") who aggressively opposes the FARC peace deal, taking the largest share of the vote (39 percent), though short of the 50 percent required to win. Instead, he faced **Gustavo Petro** – a left-wing former mayor of Bogotá and ex M-19 member (who came second with 25 percent as the "Progresistas" candidate) – in a runoff vote. Duque was finally elected president in June, after defeating Petro 54 percent to 42 percent in the second round. Duque stated his priorities as being to diversify Colombian's exports away from oil and agricultural crops, and also to promote tourism and what he calls the "orange economy" – goods and services related to creativity.

Colombia today

In the **2022 presidential election**, the first round of voting led to a runoff after neither candidate obtained 50 percent. Former president **Iván Duque** was ruled out as a contender due to term limits and in a surprising turn of events, Gustavo Petro (the 2018 runner-up), defeated Rodolfo Hernández Suárez, making history in the process. Petro's victory made him the first ever left-wing candidate to be elected president of Colombia, alongside his Vice-President Francia Márquez — the first Afro-Colombian elected to the position.

Despite its ongoing political wranglings, Colombia is now far safer than it's been for decades, with almost all forms of crime and violence in decline, the **economy booming** and **tourism** growing rapidly for the first time. Poverty, access to basic services like clean water and garbage collection, and poor infrastructure (especially the appalling road network) remain major issues, however, and the legacy of civil war runs deep: an estimated 220,000 people died in the conflict between 1958 and 2013, most of them civilians; and more than five million civilians were forced from their homes between 1985 and 2012.

2018	2022	2023
Truce with Marxist ELN rebels expires. Iván Duque defeats former liberal mayor of Bogotá Gustavo Petro in second round of presidential election.	Gustavo Petro becomes first ever left-wing candidate to be elected president of Colombia.	Colombia's Congress approves a 19 percent increase in the 2024 budget, the highest in the country's history.

Natural Colombia

The biggest surprise for most visitors to Colombia is the sheer diversity of ecosystems on offer, from empty, arid deserts and tropical beaches to frigid Andean altiplano and some of the thickest Amazon jungle in South America. Colombia is also gaining recognition for being one of the richest countries in the world when it comes to biological and cultural diversity, especially in relation to its birdlife.

Many factors contribute to the unusual diversity of **ecosystems** found in Colombia, the most obvious being **topography** and latitude: while the country sits just north of the Equator, accounting for the tropical nature of its coastline, the Andes cut a massive swathe across the centre where just a few inches in elevation drastically affects what grows. The mountain barrier effectively separates Colombia's eastern Amazon provinces from the rest of the country, a region dominated by giant waterways and jungles.

The Andes

Colombia's largest cities are located within the valleys of the **Andes** in the heart of the country, the mighty mountain chain that runs down the spine of South America. The Andes enter Colombia from Ecuador to the south in what's known as the Colombian Massif in the *departamentos* of Cauca and Nariño, a vast, thinly populated region of volcanoes and snowy peaks. From here the Colombian Andes divide into three branches: the **Cordillera Occidental**, running along the Pacific coast and including the city of Cali (the highest peak is Cerro Tatamá at 4250m); the **Cordillera Central**, running through the heart of the country between the Cauca and Magdalena river valleys, with the highest peak Nevado del Huila (5364m) and including the city of Medellín; and the **Cordillera Oriental**, extending northeast all the way to the Guajira Peninsula and the Caribbean, and including Bogotá and Bucaramanga (its highest peak is Ritacuba Blanco at 5410m).

Climate and vegetation vary considerably according to altitude, but the region is best known for its Andean cloud- and rainforests, and **páramo** (the alpine tundra zone), dominated by distinctive tussock grasses and laced with the spectacular yellow blooms of the *frailejón* (espeletia) shrub between September and November.

The Caribbean coast

The **Caribbean region** of Colombia features mostly lowland plains running all the way between the borders of Venezuela and Panama, characterized by a broiling hot, tropical climate. There are a number of quite different ecosystems here, from jungle and savannah to wetland and desert, including one of the largest swamps in Colombia, the **Ciénaga Grande de Santa Marta**. The main river is the **Río Magdalena**, which cuts through the marshy **Depresión Momposina**, the pancake-flat floodplains south of Santa Marta. To the east lies the **Guajira Peninsula**, a vast desert wilderness, made arid thanks to the rain shadow of the **Sierra Nevada de Santa Marta**, an area of snow-capped peaks that are isolated from the main Andes ranges.

The Pacific coast

The **Pacific coast** or "Chocó Biogeographic Region" is a biodiversity hotspot but is perhaps more popularly known for having the **highest rainfall in the world**. It's generally flat, steaming hot and covered by dense rainforest, rivers, swamps and mangroves, extending from the Gulf of Urabá in the north to the border with Ecuador in the south. The humidity and rainfall dominate life here, with an average of 4000mm per year and some areas that receive as much as 12,000mm annually. The coastal lowland forests of Chocó are among the most biodiverse on the planet, home to 7000–8000 species, with over 2000 endemic plant species and 100 endemic bird species.

Los Llanos

Also known as the **Orinoquía** region, **LOS LLANOS** is the swampy plains region of the Orinoco River watershed Colombia shares with Venezuela. Its primary ecosystems are tropical savannah with some forests and wetlands along the rivers – it's also a region rich in oil and sparsely populated. During the rainy season (May–October), parts of Los Llanos can flood up to a metre, creating temporary wetlands that teem with life (comparable to the Pantanal of Brazil). It's the best part of Colombia to see water birds, including the scarlet ibis and rare white-bearded flycatcher.

The Amazon

The vast **Amazon region** of Colombia comprises largely uninhabited rainforest dominated by a web of great rivers feeding into the Amazon basin: the Caquetá, Inírida, Guaviare and Putumayo among them. Most of the area is smothered in tropical moist broadleaf forest, rich in wildlife, though this is also the region hardest to access and the most threatened environmentally.

Flora

Given the nation's ecological diversity it's no surprise that over 130,000 species of **plant** have been described within Colombia. The national flower is a type of **orchid** (Colombia has the largest number of orchids in the world), while the national tree is the **Quindío wax palm**.

Trees and flowers

Though travellers rarely see evidence of this, many Colombian **tree** species are highly endangered due to the high quality of their wood (especially Colombian mahogany) and the exploitation of the timber industry, often in very remote areas. Other than various types of **palm** tree and **coconut** tree along the coast (and in the Cocora Valley), major tree species include ceibas, kapoks and banyans in the jungle, with colourful **bromeliads** often smothering trees in Andean cloud forests. Throughout the upland zones you'll see **coffee** plantations tucked in between the vegetation. **Orchids** are Colombia's most celebrated floral wonder, but even in the cities flowers are common all year round (only the Netherlands actually exports more fresh flowers than Colombia): the ubiquitous bougainvillea, orange-red tubular flowers, Victoria amazonica flowers, banana flowers, heliconia, water lilies, roses, gerberas, ginger and sunflowers are all grown here.

Fruits

As well as vast plantations of bananas, mangos, passion fruit (maracuyá), pineapples, guavas and avocados, all sorts of exotic tropical **fruits** are grown in Colombia, many quite unfamiliar to foreigners. Perhaps the most famous is **lulo**, popular in juices and a bit like lime; the pulpy borojó, known for its aphrodisiac qualities; the curuba, which looks like a banana but tastes like passion fruit; the more tart, earthy-tasting feijoa; the granadilla, packed with slimy seeds; the mamoncillo (Spanish lime); the custardy guanabana (soursop); zapote (which tastes like a tart papaya) and the incredibly popular tomate de árbol (tamarillo or tree tomato).

NATURAL COLOMBIA **CONTEXTS** 357

Fauna
Though Colombia has been a favourite of birdwatchers for years, and its coral reefs attract plenty of divers, it's otherwise not well known for **wildlife**, with most of its larger species hiding deep in the jungles or mountains.

Birds
Colombia has long been eulogized as a birdwatcher's paradise, with over 1800 **bird species** spotted here (more than the number of existent bird species in North America and Europe combined). Birds vary greatly according to which region you visit. Some of the biggest stars include toucans in the Amazon, the yellow-eared parrot in the Cocora Valley, the red-striped Colombian woodpecker, the brightly plumed golden-headed quetzal, the hard-to-spot harpy eagle, the brilliant orange Andean cock-of-the-rock in the Andean cloudforests and the Andean condor, though this is now rare in Colombia (see page 278). You'll see doves, parakeets, green jays and hummingbirds all over the place.

Reptiles and amphibians
The Colombian coastline is visited by several **turtle** species (on both the Caribbean and Pacific sides), though almost all are endangered: green, hawksbill, Kemp's Ridley, leatherback, loggerhead and Olive Ridley. Mud turtles, pond turtles, snapping turtles, wood turtles, side-necked turtles and tortoises are far more common inland, especially in the Pacific region and in the Amazon jungles. **Caimans** are also a common sight on Colombia's rivers (especially in the Amazon), though **crocodiles** are becoming endangered (the Orinoco crocodile critically so). **Lizards** and **snakes** are common throughout the country. **Salamanders**, **toads** and **frogs** are also commonplace, with new species of frog being discovered in the Amazon in recent years; Colombia holds one of the most diverse **amphibian** communities in the world, with more than 750 species currently recorded.

Mammals
It can be tough to spot larger **mammals** in most parts of Colombia, with by far the most diverse habitat the remote Amazon jungles. Anteaters, sloths and armadillos are relatively common but shy, while tapirs and peccaries (small pigs) are slightly less skittish. You'll see **monkeys** however, all over the country (even in Mompox town centre), from capuchin and howler monkeys, to marmosets and tamarins. Guinea pigs and agoutis populate the Andean forests but again, these are rarely seen by hikers in the wild. It's very rare (but possible) to see the larger predators: **cougars** and **jaguars** in the jungle (even on the hike to Ciudad Perdida), and the **spectacled bear** in the Andes. Colombia also boasts a vast number of **bat** species throughout

---

> **THE AMAZON'S PINK DOLPHINS**
>
> One of the most remarkable creatures in South America is also one of the most endangered. The pink dolphins (*botos*) of the **Amazon** and **Orinoco** river basins can be found within Colombia but also Brazil, Peru, Bolivia, Ecuador and Venezuela. Until relatively recently, mercury pollution, over-fishing, excessive boat traffic and habitat loss were thought to have threatened the species with extinction, though numbers now appear to have stabilized (no one really knows for sure). In Colombia and Brazil river dolphins are often deliberately killed to use as bait for the lucrative catfish industry.
>
> Seeing them in the river for the first time can be startling; the largest females can range up to 2.7m in length (males are a little smaller), and though some are just light grey in colour, the carnation-pink individuals that give rise to the popular name are magnificent (scientists remain baffled as to the purpose of the colouring).

the country, including **vampire bats** (that do actually bite, especially in Huila, and can carry rabies).

Whale-watching along Colombia's Pacific coast has become increasingly popular in recent years (see page 312), with flourishing populations of **humpback whales** from Antarctica coming to Colombia to mate in July, staying till around early November.

Marine life

Colombia's **marine life** is richest off the Caribbean islands of San Andrés and Providencia, with the latter home to the world's third largest barrier reef. The protected waters of Tayrona National Park (see page 171), and Capurganá (see page 147) near Panama, are also ideal for diving. Lobsters, grouper, crabs, sponges, anemones, cardinal fish, parrotfish, angelfish, squirrel fish and dozens of tropical species are common. In the Pacific, Isla Gorgona (see page 315) and Malpelo (see page 316) are remote but incredible dive destinations – Malpelo especially attracts hundreds of **hammerhead sharks** and silky sharks, as well as the rare **smalltooth sand tiger** shark.

Environmental issues

Colombia has come a long way when it comes to environmental awareness and protection, but the challenges are considerable. **Deforestation** remains a major problem along with soil erosion, soil and water contamination and air pollution (especially in Bogotá) from vehicle emissions. As you travel around you'll also notice many locales still struggling to organize effective rubbish collection and disposal; clean drinking water is often not supplied to poorer neighbourhoods. Coastal flooding along the Caribbean and around San Andrés – in part due to erosion, part due to rising sea levels – means many beaches disappear entirely at certain times of year, and many villages have little or no defence against high tides. Colombia did introduce environmental protection legislation in 1991, and numerous protected forest and marine zones and national parks have been created since then, though enforcement of regulations has been patchy.

Deforestation

Deforestation in Colombia is mainly the result of the over-exploitation of the Amazon and Chocó forests, as well as wholly illegal logging that can be tough to

---

> **THE JAGUAR IN COLOMBIA**
>
> Considered sacred by many of the nation's Indigenous cultures (a symbol of power and strength), the once common **jaguar** is now designated a "near-threatened" species by the International Union for Conservation of Nature (IUCN) and its numbers are declining in Colombia. Oil palm plantations have been blamed as the primary cause of the jaguar's habitat loss; forced onto the plains in search of cattle, jaguars are regularly killed by ranchers, though hunting of jaguars has long been prohibited.
>
> The jaguar is the third-largest big cat after the tiger and the lion, and the biggest in the Americas, with the largest populations in the rainforests of the Amazon basin and Central America. Panthera, a big cat conservation organization, has proposed a wildlife corridor ("Paseo del Jaguar") between Mexico and Argentina but this is a long way from becoming reality. However, Panthera did sign a deal with the Colombian government to establish and protect corridors in the country; USAID's Conservation Landscapes Program helped to create an 18km natural pathway to protect jaguars crossing through the Colombian Andes (using electric fences and relocating farms). The Rainforest Trust and ProAves successfully raised enough money to establish El Jaguar Nature Reserve in the Meta *departamento* of Colombia's Amazon region.

monitor. Ranching, mining, hydroelectric projects, road building, illegal cocaine production and rural farming also take their toll. Part of the problem was the **Plan Pacífico**, initiated in the late 1980s to develop the economy of the Pacific coast region; vast swathes of forest were cleared to make way for factories, roads, gold mines and plantations. Even today, palm oil and sugar cane production continues to expand. Coca farming also remains a problem, especially in the Andean regions, where an estimated 73 percent of forest has been affected by drug cultivation. Though Indigenous communities have the right to manage their own natural resources, especially in the Amazon it's been hard in practice to crack down on illegal loggers and ranchers; land-based conflicts usually end with the deaths of Indigenous people. Though accurate figures are impossible to verify, UN estimates claim between 2000 and 3000 square kilometres of forest were being lost annually in the 1990s and 2000s. In 2014 the Colombian government released an **annual report on deforestation** for the first time; in 2016 the report revealed that deforestation had increased 44 percent compared to the previous year, primarily due to coca cultivation, large-scale agriculture, road infrastructure projects and illegal mining. In 2014 the government also joined the **20-20 Initiative**, which aimed to restore 200,000 square kilometres of forest to Latin America by 2020. Despite some early setbacks and deadline extensions, the initiative was renewed in 2020 and the work continues.

Endangered species

Around 22 percent of all mammal species in Colombia are endangered or critically endangered, mostly due to human activity. Deforestation and the destruction of plant and animal habitats is the biggest single factor, though pollution is a problem across the country. Special cases include the **cotton-top tamarind**, one of the world's most endangered primates; local initiative **Proyecto Tití** (Ⓦproyectotiti.com) was established in 1985 to help preserve the species. The **Andean bear** (aka spectacled bear) is highly endangered in Colombia, where its habitat is largely unprotected, as is the **Andean condor**, despite attempts to reintroduce it to the south. Numerous species of plant, frog, bat and bird are struggling to survive, while almost all the species of **sea turtle** that visit Colombia are endangered, as are **crocodiles** and the **pink dolphins** of the Amazon basin (see page 357).

The music of Colombia

Life in Colombia would be unthinkable without music. The country has a long and vibrant history of musical excellence linking the first colonial troubadours with globally celebrated superstars such as Shakira. Homegrown genres such as *cumbia* and *vallenato* waft out of doorways and blare from shop windows, cars, buses, hotel lobbies and along beaches, while Colombians have adapted salsa, pop, rock, reggaeton and rap to great success, creating their own distinctive interpretations of international trends.

When it comes to forms of folk music, Colombia's regions each have their own very different regional traditions, from the Afro-Colombian rhythms of the Caribbean and Pacific coasts, to the ancient melodies and instruments of the Andes and the various Indigenous forms of music throughout Los Llanos and the Amazon. The following are the most popular and influential Colombian genres, though there are many others.

Cumbia

Cumbia is one of Colombia's most traditional and popular musical genres, a blend of Spanish, Indigenous and African music that emerged on the Caribbean coast in the nineteenth century. *Cumbia* is thought to have started as a courtship dance among African slaves, with the moves said to recall the shackles worn around the ankles and the rhythms related to dances from West Africa – this was gradually influenced by the melodies and instruments of various Indigenous tribes, with the guitar, flute and accordion thrown into the mix later in the nineteenth century (the core beat is created by drums and claves). *Cumbia* songs also tend to feature earthy lyrics (using lots of local slang), with a focus on Colombian customs and everyday life.

Originally confined to small villages and towns along the coast, the **golden age of cumbia** was the late 1940s and 1950s, when it spread inland to Colombia's cities, influencing the big-band sound of the period under band leaders and musicians such as **Pacho Galán** (1906–79) and **Lucho Bermúdez** (1912–94), who also made *cumbia* popular in Cuba and Mexico in the early 1950s. **Discos Fuentes**, the largest and most influential record label at the time (founded in 1934 in Cartagena), was instrumental in promoting *cumbia* groups like **La Sonora Dinamita**, established in 1960 in Cartagena but re-formed in the 1970s under the direction of Julio Ernesto Estrada "Fruko" Rincón, the artistic director of the label – the group continues to perform today. Since then *cumbia* has continued to evolve into several subgenres, including Peruvian or "*chicha*" *cumbia*, *cumbia sonidera* in Mexico City, *tecnocumbia* in Mexico, *cumbia villera* in Argentina and Chilean *cumbia*. Even today **Cumbia Cienaguera** remains one of the most popular songs in Colombian history (listen to the radio long enough and you will hear it), often considered Colombia's unofficial national anthem. Major *cumbia* artists include the collective known as **Los Gaiteros de San Jacinto**, active since the 1940s, Medellín-based **Los Black Stars**, popular in the late 1960s and 1970s, **Los Golden Boys** (another aging group still going strong), Mompox-born diva **Totó la Momposina** and the award-winning **Los Corraleros de Majagual**, founded in 1962 and still making music today. Legendary accordionist **Aniceto Molina** died in 2015, having moved to Texas in the 1980s. **Bullerengue** is another musical style and dance from the Caribbean coast based on *cumbia*, but traditionally sung exclusively by women.

Porro

Evolving along the Caribbean coast as a subgenre of *cumbia*, **Porro** is a type of big band or orchestral music that developed first around the Sinú River area and was most popular between the 1940s and 1970s. Driven by large brass ensembles, *porro* is primarily a ballroom dance music, with *porro palitiao* (with its distinctive cowbell sound) born in Córdoba and *porro tapao* emerging around Cartagena (El Carmen de Bolívar). Major *cumbia* artists such as Pacho Galán and Totó la Momposina also tended to dabble in *porro*, with other stars including **Matilde Díaz** (1924–2002), **Banda de 11 Enero** and **Orquesta Climaco Sarmiento**.

Vallenato

Spend any time in Colombia, especially along the Caribbean coast, and you'll become very familiar with **vallenato**, the incredibly popular accordion-driven genre that gets blasted into the streets day and night. The birthplace of *vallenato* is **Valledupar** (see page 181), where a major **festival** still takes place in April, though it's been popular all over the country since the 1980s. It's another genre that has origins in *cumbia*, with the sound created primarily by the bass guitar, *guacharaca* (traditional percussion instrument that looks like a stick, played with a wire fork) and the *caja vallenata* (a larger version of the bongo drum) in addition to the accordion. *Vallenato* comprises four beats or rhythms: *son* (very slow), *puya* (the oldest and played faster), *merengue* (not related to the Dominican dance) and *paseo* (the most popular), though they can be hard to distinguish for the untrained ear.

Vallenato artists

Co-founder of the Vallenato festival in 1968, **Rafael Escalona** (1927–2009) is generally regarded as one of the all-time greats of the genre along with **Alejo Durán** (1919–89), winner of the first competition held at the festival. Other influential *vallenato* artists include controversial but wildly popular **Diomedes Díaz** (1957–2013), aka "*El Cacique de La Junta*", (literally, "overlord of the board" but more like "boss of the bosses"), Latin Grammy award winners **Los Hermanos Zuleta**, renowned singers **Jorge Oñate** and **Iván Villazón**, accordion player **Alfredo Gutiérrez** (who has won the annual competition at the Valledupar festival three times), the group **Binomio de Oro de América** (formed in 1976 but still performing) and finally multi-award-winning **Carlos Vives**, who is probably the most famous *vallenato* performer living. His 1993 album *Clásicos de la Provincia* was a major landmark, fusing *vallenato* with rock, pop and other Colombian genres – it scandalized purists but thrilled audiences worldwide. His massive hit *La Bicicleta* – performed with Shakira – featured *vallenato*, pop, reggaeton and *cumbia* and won two Latin Grammy Awards.

La Nueva Ola and sub-genres

The *vallenato-pop* of Carlos Vives led to more experimentation within the genre and the new generation of *vallenato* groups and orchestras emerging in the twenty-first century were dubbed **La Nueva Ola** ("the new wave"). **Martín Elías** (1990–2017) and **Kaleth Morales** (1984–2005) were considered pioneers of the movement with hits such as *Vivo En El Limbo* before their tragic premature deaths (both in car accidents). La Guajira native **Silvestre Dangond** is now considered the leader of the movement, with his first album a big hit in 2002 and his latest, *Gente Valiente*, released in 2017 (his eleventh to date). Rival singer **Jorge Celedón** has won several Latin Grammy awards.

Other subgenres of *vallenato* include **vallenato-protesta**, which is known for its social and political themes, and **charanga vallenata**, which was created by Cuban exiles in the US in the 1980s.

Currulao

With its roots among the Afro-Colombian communities of the Pacific coast, **currulao** is a style of music heavily influenced by African traditions, usually played by a group of four musicians; instruments include the narrow drum known as a *cununo*, a shaker called a *guasá* (a hollow cylinder filled with seeds or rice) and the Colombian marimba (a wooden xylophone). Current exponents include **Grupo Socavón** and **Grupo Bahía Trio**, performing since 1992, with Buenaventura native **Baudilio Cuama Rentería** one of the region's marimba pioneers.

Bambuco

Colombia's Andean regions are home to many forms of Indigenous music, with the slow-paced sounds of **bambuco** (similar to the waltz) said to have originated from the Muisca people (see page 99). It remains popular, though *bambuco*'s heyday was the 1920s to 1940s. Famous exponents of the genre include **Jorge Villamil** (1929–2010), guitarist **Gentil Montaña** (1942–2011), the **Trío Morales Pino**, **Luis Enrique Aragón Farkas** and the collective **Cantadoras del Pacífico**, who still perform. "*El Sanjuanero*", a *bambuco* tune written in 1936, is one of Colombia's most popular folk songs (it's another one still played on the radio today), and the anthem of the annual **Festival Folclórico y Reinado Nacional del Bambuco**, held in Neiva at the end of June.

Joropo

The **joropo** musical style falls under the *música llanera* umbrella, the harp-led genre from the Los Llanos region popular throughout Colombia (it's also been the national dance of Venezuela since 1882). *Joropo* is a bit like the waltz, with the accompanying dance having African and European influences, and is traditionally played with an *arpa llanera* (harp), *bandola* (type of mandolin), *cuatro* (guitar), and maracas. Leading artists include **Arnulfo Briceño** (1938–89), **Grupo Cimarrón**, an all-star collective of instrumentalists and singers led by Carlos Rojas Hernández, Cuban-born **Alfredo Rolando Ortiz** and Latin Grammy winner **Orlando "Cholo" Valderrama**.

Colombian salsa

Salsa music may have originated in New York in the 1960s – the genre was cooked up by Cuban and Puerto Rican musicians, blending jazz with older Cuban styles such as son, cha-cha and mambo – but it has flourished in Colombia. Arriving in 1968 in Cali (see page 257), the genre soon developed a distinctive Colombian flavour; Cali-style salsa (*salsa caleño*) features more rapid footwork and high kicks than other styles, and Colombian dancers have gone on to dominate the Salsa World Championships. Today salsa remains the dominant sound in Cali, but is also popular in Barranquilla and along the Caribbean coast – you'll hear it played at clubs and on radios all over the country.

Salsa artists

The Colombian king of salsa was Cartagena-born **Joe Arroyo** (1955–2011), whose records remain wildly popular. Arroyo initially sang with salsa pioneers **Fruko y sus Tesos** (led by Julio Ernesto "Fruko" Estrada) formed in 1970 and still performing today, as is **Grupo Niche**, the Cali-based band established in 1978 (**Orquesta Guayacán** was formed by ex-band members). **La Misma Gente** is another popular Cali-based band, while **Los Titanes** hails from Barranquilla and **La Sonora Carruseles** from Medellín. **Charlie Zaa** has been active since the 1990s, blending salsa, *bachata* (a dance style from the Dominican Republic) and *bolero* (a genre of slow-tempo Cuban/Spanish music).

Colombian rock

Though you won't hear much of it on the streets, Colombia is home to a thriving **rock'n'roll** tradition, beginning in the 1960s with bands like **Los Speakers** and **The Flippers**. One of the most influential bands was **Génesis** (totally unrelated to the UK outfit led by Phil Collins), active 1972 to 1992, which blended traditional genres (like *cumbia*) with rock. Founded in Medellín in 1983, **Kraken** became the first true heavy metal band in Colombia (and is still going strong), while thrash metal **Ekhymosis** followed in 1987 – in 1997 Juan Esteban Aristizábal, better known as **Juanes**, left the band to begin an incredibly successful solo career (see below). In 1992 **Andrea Echeverri** and **Héctor Buitrago** teamed up in Bogotá to form the phenomenally successful **Aterciopelados**, one of the first Colombian rock bands to gain international recognition and still one of the country's top acts. In 2005 Echeverri debuted her first eponymous solo album. Barranquilla-based alternative rockers **Los de Adentro** started out in 1994, performing on-and-off since then. One of the originators of "*electro cumbia*", **Sidestepper** is another Colombian band with a modicum of international success, formed in 1996 by English DJ/producer Richard Blair and Colombian singer Iván Benavides, while **Diva Gash** has been pioneering electronic soft-rock in Bogotá since 1997.

The new millennium

Since 2000, Colombia has seen a boom in punk rock and alternative rock bands. Punk band **Tres de Corazón** has remained at the heart of the Medellín scene since forming in 2002, while **Don Tetto** formed in Bogotá a year later, with their eponymous *Don Tetto* (2014) winning much acclaim. Several bands have a distinctive Britpop influence (blended with more local sounds), including **Soundacity** and Bogotá-based **The Mills** (2007) and **The Hall Effect** (2004), whose last album was *¿Y Por Que No?* (2014). Originally formed in Colombia, **Palenke Soultribe** fuses traditional folk music with electronica, and is now based in Los Angeles. Established in 2012, **Diamante Eléctrico** went on to win a Latin Grammy for their rock album *La Gran Oscilación*.

Colombian pop

Colombian pop music has always borrowed heavily from traditional genres such as salsa, *cumbia* and *vallenato* and has given rise to "tropipop". Former rocker **Juanes** has been one of the most successful pop-rock performers since winning three Latin Grammy awards for his debut album *Fíjate Bien* in 2001. He has since become popular internationally with a string of hits such as *La Camisa Negra* (his latest album is *Mis Planes Son Amarte*) and numerous Latin Grammies, as well as his lauded charity work for the victims of anti-personnel mines. Juanes remains something of a hero in Colombia, despite living in Key Biscayne, near Miami. Buenaventura-born **Marbelle** has been knocking out romantic ballads since 1996 while **Anasol** (aka Anasol Escobar) has been making sugary pop since 1999. Another major solo star is **Fonseca** (born Juan Fernando Fonseca in Bogotá), making records since 2002 – blending pop, *vallenato* and *cumbia*, his *Homenaje* (2016) won yet another Latin Grammy. **Maía** (aka Mónica Andrea Vives Orozco, born in Barranquilla) is a major contemporary female star, releasing her first album in 2003, while crooner and Medellín-born **Lucas Arnau** has been cutting pop records since 2004. Newer artists include **Miranda & The Soul Band**, **Paula Arenas** and model **Naty Botero** – the latter releasing her popular hit song *Feliz* in 2023. Other major names in Colombian pop include **Manuel Medrano** who won two Latin Grammy Awards, **Esteman** who rose to fame on YouTube, with his blend of pop, reggae and 1980s disco, **Sebastián Yatra who** released his hit *Traicioner*, and **Paula Arenas** who released her first debut single *Nada* and was later nominated for a Latin Grammy. However, when it comes to Colombian pop, one name continues to dominate the international market like no other – **Shakira** (see page 364).

> ### SHAKIRA
> Barranquilla-born superstar **Shakira** (officially Shakira Isabel Mebarak Ripoll) made her first record at the age of 13. She rose to success with her *Pies Descalzos* album in 1996 before crossing over to the English-language market with 2001's *Laundry Service* and the song *Whenever Wherever*, a major international hit. The blend of pop with Andean beats and panpipes proved wildly popular, and Shakira's seventh album, *Oral Fixation, Vol. 2* (2005) spawned the monster hit *Hips Don't Lie*, her first **US number one** (fusing salsa, reggaeton and pop). In 2010 Shakira was the somewhat controversial choice to create the official song of the FIFA World Cup in South Africa (she did collaborate with South African group Freshlyground) but returned to her Latin roots for ninth album *Sale el Sol* later that year. Though her popularity has waned somewhat since then, Shakira remains the **highest-selling Colombian artist** of all time by a large margin. She released her eleventh studio album, *El Dorado*, in 2017 and continues to collaborate with other global hit artists to this day.

Champeta

Emerging from the Afro-Colombian communities in and around Barranquilla and Cartagena, **champeta** is perhaps the genre of Colombian folk music most directly influenced by African traditions. However, the genre is a relatively recent phenomenon: the name *champeta* itself originally denoted a curved knife, and was only applied to a specific kind of dance in the 1970s (set to up-tempo versions of salsa, *jíbaro* and reggae) and a form of music in the 1980s (influenced by African genres such as *soukous* from Congo and highlife from Ghana, as well as music from Haiti and the Caribbean). Today *champeta* is a heavily bass-driven sound, utilizing percussion, electric guitars, bass, conga drums and often synthesizers. Performers have traditionally had less exposure overseas than other Colombian genres, with major stars including John Eister Gutiérrez Cassiani, aka "**Jhonky**" who was murdered in 2005, **Papo Man** (Milton Torres) and **El Michel**, who started to create more religiously inspired music. Today, *champeta urbana* sounds more like reggaeton and dancehall, with artists such as **Elio Boom** (behind 1990s mega-hit *La Turbina*) influenced by Jamaican ragga.

Colombian hip-hop, reggaeton and reggae

Hip-hop arrived in Colombia in the 1980s from the US, finding an audience in the poorer neighbourhoods of Medellín, Cali and Bogotá, though it wasn't until the 1990s that Colombian rappers started to make albums. Bogotá-based **La Etnnia** released their first tape in 1994 and are considered the pioneers of Colombian hip-hop (their last album, *5-27 Internacional*, was issued in 2015), along with fellow *bogotanos* **Gotas de Rap**, which disbanded in 1998. Both groups tended to focus on social, economic and political themes, protesting the violence, corruption and inequality of life in the capital's poorer quarters. Formed in Cali in 2000, **Asilo 38** developed a more commercial sound, while **ChocQuibTown** has been gaining popularity since releasing their first album *Somos Pacífico* in 2006. The rapping trio hail from Chocó in western Colombia, but started performing in Cali and Bogotá, blending traditional Afro-Colombian rhythms with modern hip-hop; their latest album *Sin Miedo* was released in 2018. The other shining star of Colombian rap is **Jiggy Drama** from the island of San Andrés, who is somewhat controversial thanks to his colourful lyrics. Colombia also boasts an active if small-scale underground scene, with artists such as **JhonFor** based out of Pasto.

Reggaeton

The bass-thumping, car-rattling rhythms of **reggaeton** became the defining sounds of Puerto Rico in the late 1990s, rapidly spreading all over Latin America. Though rapping is a crucial element, reggaeton is more than just Spanish hip-hop, with a distinctive back-beat known as "dem bow" that is part Jamaican dancehall, part salsa: the "reggae" part of the name is a bit deceptive, and the genre owes more to Shabba Ranks than Bob Marley.

In Colombia reggaeton has been pioneered by groups and performers based in **Medellín**, including **Tres Pesos** (formed 2001 and still a major force), **Reykon** (whose single *Secretos* was a big hit, only later to be matched by *Dejame Te Explico*), **Yelsid** and **J Balvin** (recording since 2009, his album *Energía* won a Latin Grammy) – the city has been so important to reggaeton's development that many artists from Puerto Rico have spent time working, recording and making videos here.

Other major acts include duo **Rayo Y Toby**, from San Andrés (who scored a big hit with *Ninfómana*), Medellín-based **Sebas & Migue**, **Saga Neutron**, **Wolfine**, **Maluma** (best known for *Obsesion* and *Felices los 4*) and Cali-based **Kofla**.

Reggae

Reggae has been popular on the Colombian Caribbean islands of San Andrés and Providencia since the late 1970s, and there remains a strong rasta and Jamaican influence among the local Raizal population; Spanish reggae from Panama is more popular on the mainland. Colombian artists include Bogotá-based **Voodoo Souljahs**, **Nawal** (around since 1999) and **Alerta Kamarada** (since 1996).

Religion in Colombia

Colombians, on the whole, are very religious people, with church services often packed out, even during weekdays, and religious festivals an important part of local culture. Though Catholicism dominates, other faiths are present here and Colombia is an extremely tolerant place, with religious conflict (and extremism) very unusual. Colombia has been a Roman Catholic country since the Spanish conquest, with around 75–80 percent of the population Catholics and just 17 percent Protestants. Thanks to the 1991 constitution the Catholic Church is no longer the state church and freedom of religion is guaranteed.

Catholicism and the saints

Like all Christians, Catholics believe the central tenets of the Bible's New Testament, but one of the unique aspects of Catholicism is the **worship of saints**. In the Middle Ages, saints were regarded as powerful sources of material and spiritual favours, thanks to their proximity to God in heaven: not only did saints make the mysteries of the Church seem more human, it was believed that they were far more likely to take pity on wretched sinners than God himself. Only the **Pope** in Rome can confer sainthood: the process is known as **canonization** and cannot begin until at least five years after a person's death. At least one miracle is required for **beatification**, the first stage, while a second miracle is required before sainthood is declared – both must be certified by a series of meticulous Church investigations. Miracles can be anything from an apparition after death to curing terminally ill patients.

In Colombia, most churches you visit will be dedicated to a saint (or at least filled with shrines dedicated to them). In addition, most of the country's municipalities have patron saints, each with an annual feast day, usually celebrated by a boisterous *fiesta*.

The Virgin Mary

Mary is the most important saint in the Catholic Church, the "mother of God", whose Immaculate Conception (*Inmaculada Concepción*) is at the heart of the New Testament. In Catholic churches, you'll tend to see more people praying to Mary than at the main altar, the idea being that she is more compassionate than even Christ and, as his mother, is in the best position to intercede on your behalf. As Catholic scholar Richard McBrien says, "Christ locks the front door of heaven to keep out unworthy sinners, while Mary lets them in through a side window."

In practice, the worship of Mary can seem quite confusing to non-Catholics. Colombian churches and shrines tend to honour specific **incarnations** of Mary that have appeared over the years, each with their own special name and set of accompanying miracles and powers. In Spanish, any dedication that begins with **Nuestra Señora** ("Our Lady") or **La Virgen** refers to an incarnation of Mary.

La Virgen de la Candelaria

This tradition of Mary originated in the **Canary Islands** and was brought to Colombia by immigrants in the eighteenth century, becoming patron saint of Cartagena, Magangué and Medellín. This apparition is said to have appeared to shepherds around 1400 in Tenerife, and became associated with the Feast of the Purification of Mary or **Candlemas** held on February 2.

La Virgen del Carmen
One of the most popular incarnations of Mary during the Spanish conquest, **La Virgen del Carmen** is patron saint of the armed forces of Colombia, the national police, firemen, truck and bus drivers (it's common to see small shrines to her on the road), Salento (Quindío) and El Carmen de Bolívar. Her origins lie within the **Carmelite Order**, originally a community of monks based on Mount Carmel in Israel, established in the twelfth century – their dedication to Mary gradually led to the association of the name, though it became popularized thanks to the cult of English saint Simon Stock who died in the thirteenth century. Simon (who was a Carmelite) is said to have been given a **scapular** (two pieces of material joined together by two ribbons over the shoulders, worn as a symbol of salvation) when Mary appeared to him in 1251. Though the modern order considers this story pure legend, scapulars are still worn by the faithful. Her feast day is July 16.

Nuestra Señora de la Monserrate
This version of Mary stems from a sacred statue, said to have been carved by St Luke around 50 AD and brought to Spain. Lost until 880, it was discovered on **Montserrat** north of modern Barcelona, which has since become a major pilgrimage site: in the Middle Ages the statue was said to have miraculous powers, its face remaining black despite constant cleaning. During the Spanish conquest, numerous churches in the New World were named in honour of **Nuestra Señora de la Monserrate** (the Spanish rendering of the Catalan original) and today she has a major sanctuary above Bogotá (see page 68), with her feast day on September 8 (also the birthday of Mary).

Nuestra Señora del Rosario
Our Lady of the Rosary or **Nuestra Señora del Rosario** is associated with the Catholic devotion known as the **Rosary**, referring to both a set of prayer beads and the prayer itself, which comprises 150 Hail Marys. The story that an apparition of Mary gave the first Rosary to St Dominic in 1208 is now viewed as myth by the Church, and the first Feast of the Rosary was established by the Pope in 1573 to celebrate the victory over the Turks at Lepanto (attributed to diligent recital of the Rosary). Today she is primarily remembered in Colombia as the **Virgen de Chiquinquirá**, patron saint of Colombia, with her feast celebrated on July 9, and **Nuestra Señora de Las Lajas** (see page 297), another wholly Colombian incarnation dating back to 1754.

San Juan Bautista (St John the Baptist)
John the Baptist is a seminal figure in the New Testament, a mystical prophet who predicts the rise of Jesus and later baptizes him – infamously beheaded by Herod Antipas on the behest of Salome, he was later venerated as one of the most important saints. Christopher Columbus was particularly fond of St John, and today he is patron saint of Pasto. His feast day is June 24.

San Francisco (St Francis)
One of the most popular saints in Colombia, numerous churches are dedicated to **San Francisco**, aka **Saint Francis of Assisi**, the Italian Catholic friar and preacher born around 1182. Popularly known for his love of animals and nature, he is also venerated for receiving the stigmata (the wounds of Christ) and founding the Franciscan order of monks. In Colombia he is the patron saint of Quibdó (capital of Chocó).

Santa Bárbara (St Barbara)

The worship of **Santa Bárbara** has been officially discouraged by the Church since 1969 (experts have questioned whether she ever really existed), despite being patron saint of Santa Fe de Antioquia and of the most famous church in Mompox (see page 152). She is traditionally thought to have lived in modern-day Turkey at the time of the Roman Empire, and was martyred around 303 AD. After her father killed her for becoming a Christian, he was struck by lightning, and today she is thought to offer protection from not only lightning, but also explosives and fires – she remains the patron saint of firefighters, artillerymen, architects and builders.

Santiago Apóstol (St James the Apostle)

One of the original twelve disciples of Jesus, **St James** or **Santiago Apóstol** was one of Christ's closest followers and the first apostle to be martyred. Despite being buried in Jerusalem, a tradition emerged that he had either visited or was reburied in Spain, at the town of **Compostela**. As his cult grew, the town became one of the most important pilgrimage sites in the Catholic world, James honoured as the **patron saint of Spain**. Invoking his name in battle was so efficacious he became known as Matamoros ("Moor-slayer") in the Middle Ages for his supposed help in defeating the Moors, and in the sixteenth century Spanish colonists brought his cult to Colombia. Today he is patron saint of Chile, Guatemala, Nicaragua, pilgrims, pharmacists, labourers and even sufferers of arthritis. In Colombia he's the patron of Cali, Tunja and Tolú.

San Antonio de Padua (St Anthony of Padua)

Regarded as one of the greatest ever Church teachers, **San Antonio de Padua** (1195–1231) was born in Lisbon, became a Franciscan friar and later preached all over northern Italy. Buried in Padua, he became patron saint of Brazil, Portugal, travellers and the poor, but is best known for being the **finder of lost articles**. His feast day is June 13.

San José (St Joseph)

San José, the husband of the Virgin Mary and the adoptive father of Jesus, is another immensely popular saint, patron of workers, fathers of families and a "happy death". His main role in the Bible is to take in Mary after the Immaculate Conception, and he rarely appears in later sections of the New Testament, suggesting he died before the public ministry of Jesus began. He is the patron saint of Cúcuta in Colombia, as well as Canada, Mexico, Peru and the Mission to China. His primary feast day is March 19.

San Miguel Arcángel (St Michael the Archangel)

In Catholic tradition **San Miguel Arcángel** is the leader of the angels and protector of the people of Israel, a powerful figure who appears primarily in the Old Testament and the Book of Revelations. He is traditionally considered the patron saint of Mocoa in Colombia, as well as of soldiers, the sick, grocers and police officers. His feast day is September 29, also known as **Michaelmas**.

Santo Domingo (St Dominic)

St Dominic or **Santo Domingo**, often called Dominic de Guzmán (1170–1221), was a Spanish priest and founder of the Dominican Order of monks, an especially humble outfit committed to begging for alms. He remains one of Colombia's most popular saints – you are bound to come across a church named for him somewhere (there's a major one in Cartagena; see page 132). Buried in Bologna, Italy, he's also the patron saint of astronomers and the Dominican Republic. His feast day is usually August 8.

San Agustín (St Augustine)

San Agustín, aka St Augustine of Hippo (354–430), is one of the most distinguished Christian theologians and philosophers, whose writings were especially influential in the development of the Catholic Church and Western philosophy. He became the bishop of Hippo Regius (in modern-day Algeria) in 395 (during the late Roman period) and is regarded as one of the most important early Church Fathers (he died during the siege of Hippo by the Vandals). His feast day is normally August 28.

San Pedro Apóstol (St Peter)

San Pedro Apóstol (St Peter) was the first disciple and one of the twelve apostles of Jesus, originally a fisherman on the Sea of Galilee known as Simon. He became a foremost leader of the early Christian Church after the death of Jesus – in Catholic tradition he was the first pope, and later founder of the Church of Antioch and Rome, where he was crucified (upside down) around 64 AD (he's thought to be buried under the current St Peter's Basilica in Rome). He's a popular saint in Colombia with numerous churches dedicated to him.

Books

Colombia's perennial state of social and political flux has always promised rich material for historians and journalists eager to pin the place down. Rarely have they managed this, though the picture of the region's unpredictable evolution that emerges can make for compulsive reading. The giant of Colombian literature – if not the whole of Latin America – is of course Gabriel García Márquez (see page 170), whose stories so beautifully evoke the nation's history, tropical landscapes and cultural soul. His best are listed below, but it's worth reading just about anything in his considerable oeuvre. There's far more to Colombian fiction than Márquez however, though many of the earlier giants of the craft – Tomás Carrasquilla and José María Vargas Vila for example – have rarely been translated into English. In the following list the ★ symbol signifies titles that are especially recommended.

HISTORY AND POLITICS

★ **Marie Arana** *Bolívar*. Colombia's liberation hero was born in Venezuela, but raised his first successful army in Mompox, won his most famous victory in Boyacá, was the first president of "Gran Colombia" and died in Santa Marta. Arana's excellent biography is exhaustively researched and compulsive reading.

★ **Mark Bowden** *Killing Pablo*. The gripping tale of how feared Medellín Cartel boss and billionaire cocaine smuggler Pablo Escobar was hunted down and killed between 1992 and 1993 by elements of both the Colombian and US special forces.

David Bushnell *The Making of Modern Colombia*. Published in 1993, this remains the standard reference text (in English) for students of Colombian history, beginning with the struggle for independence and ending with the cocaine wars and guerrilla conflicts of the late twentieth century.

★ **Ann Farnsworth-Alvear (ed)** *The Colombia Reader*. This is a fabulous compendium of Colombian historical writings and commentaries, with much of the contents appearing in English for the first time. Assorted journalistic reports, songs, artwork, poetry, oral histories and government documents shed light on Colombian history since the colonial period.

Tom Feiling *Short Walks from Bogotá: Journeys in the New Colombia*. Feiling's book sounds like a travelogue but in fact explores Colombia's slow and difficult transformation from violent narco-state to modern democracy. Feiling's "walks" take place in areas once deemed off-limits thanks to conflict, and cover themes such as Colombia's poor record on workers' rights and human rights abuses. See also Feiling's excellent *The Candy Machine: How Cocaine Took Over The World*.

Gabriel García Márquez *News of a Kidnapping*. Márquez's lauded true-life account of a series of prominent kidnappings orchestrated by Escobar's Medellín Cartel in the early 1990s, including the abductions of Diana Turbay and Maruja Pachón. Gripping descriptions of the day-by-day emotions of not just the captives but also the young, reckless kidnappers.

Michael J Larosa & Germán R Mejía *Colombia: A Concise Contemporary History*. This history of Colombia from 1800 to the modern day, written by two Colombian historians, is divided thematically rather than chronologically, with essays on politics, society and culture.

David McCullough *The Path Between the Seas*. The loss of Panama in 1903 remains a traumatic event in Colombia's history, with this erudite but readable account of the creation of the Panama Canal (1870–1914) the best introduction to the whole affair.

Silviana Paternostro *My Colombian War*. Published by a Colombian-American journalist who returned to her homeland (she grew up in Barranquilla and left as a teenager in the 1970s) – the book is part memoir, part grim history of the civil war through local interviews, portraits and anecdotes.

★ **Álvaro Uribe Vélez** *No Lost Causes*. Arguably Colombia's most successful and most popular modern president in his own words; Uribe's memoir outlines the risks and challenges of his presidency (2002–10). Obviously biased, but fascinating stuff nonetheless for its insights into Uribe's character, and a must for political junkies.

FICTION

James Cañón *Tales from the Town of Widows*. Tragicomic tale set in the small Colombian mountain village of Mariquita, in the wake of a temporary occupation by anti-government guerrillas – all the men of the village are taken away and the remaining women and children must somehow carry on.

Jorge Franco *Rosario Tijeras*. Probably the most popular of this Medellín-born novelist's works (it's been made into a film and a TV series), this book begins when the beautiful Rosario is shot in the gritty, cocaine-laced streets of Medellín in the late 1980s. The story of her troubled life is thereafter told through the eyes of admirer Antonio in vivid, lively prose, though Franco (in translation at least) does have a penchant for melodrama.

★ **Santiago Gamboa** *Necropolis*. One of the most innovative voices in Colombia today, Gamboa is yet to be widely translated into English, but this novel, in turns brutal, shocking and incredibly spellbinding is one of his best, a murder mystery set in Jerusalem.

Tomás González *In the Beginning Was the Sea*. Published in Spanish in 1983 but only translated (beautifully) into English in 2014, this was the first novel from González, the lauded writer born in Medellín. The book charts the story of a couple from Medellín who have moved to the coast in the 1970s to escape the problems of the city, but right from the beginning González makes it clear their venture is doomed to failure.

Jorge Isaacs *María*. The giant novel of the Colombian nineteenth century (published in 1867), this romantic classic follows the tragic story of María and her cousin Efraín, set on a country estate loosely based on the real-life Hacienda El Paraíso (see page 266). Heavy going but essential for fans of Colombian history (and romanticism).

Jaime Manrique *Cervantes Street*. The world of renaissance Spain is explored in this intriguing tale by the popular poet, novelist and journalist from Barranquilla, a sort of homage to the original *Don Quixote* that re-creates the remarkable life of classical Spanish novelist Cervantes.

★ **Gabriel García Márquez** *The General in His Labyrinth*. Márquez charts the final days of Liberator Simón Bolívar in this masterful work of fiction, loosely based on real events and ending with the general's death in Santa Marta. Essential reading for travellers to the northern half of Colombia.

★ **Gabriel García Márquez** *Love in the Time of Cholera*. First published in 1985 and perhaps one of Márquez's most popular novels, *Love in the Time of Cholera* is the quintessential portrayal of colonial Cartagena, a tragicomic love story based on the author's own parents set in the sweltering, tropical streets of the Caribbean capital.

★ **Gabriel García Márquez** *One Hundred Years of Solitude*. Published in 1967, this was the novel that made Márquez and introduced the fictional Macondo (based on Aracataca; page 169) to a wider world. It's the complex, Magical Realist story of six generations of the Buendía family (loosely based on Rafael Uribe Uribe; see page 214), a scintillating and often comic retelling of Colombian history and some of the key events of the early twentieth century.

Laura Restrepo *Delirium*. One of Colombia's foremost contemporary female writers (born in Bogotá), Restrepo sets this gripping novel in the cocaine-fuelled 1980s, when Aguilar, an unemployed professor, comes home to find his wife Agustina gone mad – the story gradually unearths the source of Agustina's "delirium". An evocative depiction of the lawless Bogotá of the period.

★ **José Eustasio Rivera** *The Vortex*. Rivera's only novel, published as *La Vorágine* in 1924, is considered a modern classic in Latin America, charting the fictional adventures of the poet Arturo Cova and his lover Alicia in the Colombian Amazon. Though the natural world of the jungle is beautifully described, Rivera also exposes the appalling conditions experienced by workers in the rubber boom and the treatment of Indigenous tribes. In the end, "the jungle devoured them!".

Fernando Vallejo *Our Lady of the Assassins*. Like Márquez, Medellín-born Vallejo moved to Mexico for political reasons but writes about Colombia; this is his most celebrated novel, centred on a fictional return to the city of his birth and his subsequent relationships with two teenagers caught in the local cycle of violence (made into a film in 2000).

★ **Juan Gabriel Vásquez** *The Sound of Things Falling*. Bogotá-born Vásquez has become a sort of anti-Márquez, critical of Magical Realism, and this novel, published in English in 2013, showcases his cold, bleak style. Set in 1990s Bogotá, this is the gripping story of a young professor named Antonio, who tracks down the history of a mysterious man he befriends in a pool hall but whom is shot soon after – it's essentially about how the drug trade affects not just those who are involved in it, but everyone around them.

Juan Gabriel Vásquez *The Secret History of Costaguana*. Here Vásquez takes aim at Joseph Conrad and his 1904 novel *Nostromo*, in which the country of Costaguana was loosely based on Colombia. In this clever reimagining of actual events, Conrad is inspired by the life story of Colombian exile José Altamirano, who regales the author with tales of his homeland but is dismayed when he reads about Conrad's fictional creation a few months later: as narrator, he then goes back thirty years to tell the real story of Colombia.

MISCELLANEOUS

Ximena Diego *Shakira: Woman Full of Grace*. Accessible biography of Colombia's very own musical superstar, Barranquilla's Shakira Isabel Mebarak Ripoll, born to a Lebanese father and Colombian mother. Sure to appeal to fans.

Gabriel García Márquez *Living to Tell The Tale*. Dream-like and even whimsical at times, Márquez's autobiography charts the author's early life in Colombia from birth in 1927 through to his departure to Europe in 1955. It's a fascinating portrait of the early artist (or at least, how Márquez saw himself) written with the same rich language and metaphors that sprinkle his novels. Essential reading for anyone travelling to Aracataca (see page 169).

Steven L Hilty & William L Brown *A Guide to the Birds of Colombia*. When it comes to birding guides this remains the standard text, though it hasn't been reprinted for many years (and can be expensive on-line). More than 1700 species are clearly described, with beautiful illustrations and introductory chapters highlighting Colombia's geography, climate and vegetation. San Andrés and Providencia are also covered.

★ **Michael Jacobs** *The Robber of Memories*. Poetic memoir and travelogue centred around a boat journey along the length of the country's longest river, the Río Magdalena – the title is also a hint at the dementia which afflicts the British writer's mother as he sets off and preoccupies him throughout. Jacobs starts in Cartagena with a brief meeting with an ageing Gabriel García Márquez, and later has several scary encounters with FARC guerrillas.

Gerald Martin *Gabriel García Márquez*. The best biography of Colombia's Nobel Prize-winner so far, and a completely different experience to reading the author's autobiography – Martin adroitly chronicles Márquez from his upbringing in rural Aracataca and his early journalism career, through to the publication of *One Hundred Years of Solitude* and the fame that followed in later years.

★ **Patricia McCausland-Gallo** *Secrets of Colombian Cooking*. Colombian cuisine often gets short shrift on the international scene but this cookbook provides an enticing introduction, with 175 classic recipes from hearty *sancochos* (stews) from different regions to exotic Caribbean dishes such as lobster in coconut sauce.

★ **Alan Weisman** *Gaviotas: A Village to Reinvent the World*. In the late 1960s a young Colombian development worker named Paolo Lugari initiated a remarkable project in Los Llanos to create a genuinely sustainable village in what was considered an inhospitable wilderness. The book chronicles that project, one of the most successful (and hope-inspiring) environmental tales ever told – Gaviotas is still around and thriving.

Spanish

Spanish is relatively straightforward to learn. Being understood, of course, is only half the problem – getting the gist of the reply may prove more difficult, but it's worth the effort. Spanish varies from region to region in Colombia, in particular between the Caribbean coast, the Eastern Cordillera (including Bogotá) and the Western Cordillera (notably Antioquia), but Colombian Spanish in general is clearly spoken and usually easier to understand than, for example, that of Spain or Argentina.

Pronunciation

The rules of **pronunciation** are straightforward and strictly observed. Unless there's an accent, words ending with a vowel or "n" or "s" are stressed on the second-last syllable, and all others on the last. All **vowels** are pure and short; combinations have predictable results.

A somewhere between the A sound of "back" and that of "father".
E as in "get".
I as in "police".
O as in "hot".
U as in "rule" (but see "G").
C is like "s" before E and I; otherwise, hard; sometimes people lisp the "s" sound slightly, but not as much as in Spain.
G a breathy "H" sound before E or I, a hard G elsewhere: gigante is pronounced "higante"; a silent "u" is sometimes inserted between "g" and "e" or "i" to harden it, and if the "u" has two dots on it (ü), it's pronounced like a "w".
H is always silent.
J the same sound as a soft G: jugo is pronounced "hoogo", except that the "h" is breathier than in English.
LL sounds like a Y: Medellín is pronounced "Medeyeen".
N is as in English unless it has a tilde over it (Ñ), when it becomes NY: mañana sounds like "manyana".
QU is pronounced like an English K.
R is rolled, RR doubly so.
S as in "dose", never as in "rose".
V sounds more like B, vino becoming "beano".
X has an S sound before consonants, but sounds like a Spanish "j" before vowels; it's rarely seen in Colombian Spanish.
Z is the same as a soft C, so cerveza becomes "serbaysa".

If you're travelling for any length of time a dictionary or phrasebook is obviously a worthwhile investment. If using a **dictionary**, bear in mind that in Spanish Ñ is a separate letter that comes after N, and some dictionaries (particularly from Spain) count CH and LL as separate letters that come after C and L respectively. For a plural, add an -s to words ending with a vowel, or -es if they end in a consonant. Adjectives agree with nouns, and in Spanish even inanimate objects are assigned a masculine or feminine gender, so adjectives which end in -o for a masculine thing will change it to -a for a feminine one, and add an -s for the plural.

WORDS AND PHRASES

BASICS

Yes, No, OK Sí, No, Vale
Please, Thank you Por favor, Gracias
Where? When? ¿Dónde? ¿Cuándo?
What? How much? ¿Qué? ¿Cuánto?
This, That Esto, Eso
Here, There Acá/Aquí, Allá/Allí
Now, Later Ahora, Luego
Open, Closed Abierto/a, Cerrado/a
Push, Pull Empuje, Jale/hale
Stop, Go ahead Pare, Siga
With, Without Con, Sin
Good, Bad Buen(o)/a, Mal(o)/a
Great/brilliant/cool Chévere
Cheap, Expensive Barato, Caro
Hot, Cold Caliente, Frío
More, Less Más, Menos
Today, Tomorrow Hoy, Mañana
Yesterday Ayer

GREETINGS AND RESPONSES
Hello, Goodbye Hola, Adiós
Good morning Buen día, Buenos días
Good afternoon Buenas tardes
Good evening/night Buenas noches
How's it going? ¿Qué tál?/¿Cómo va?/¿Quiúbo?
Nice to meet you Mucho gusto
See you later Hasta luego
Sorry Lo siento/Disculpéme
Excuse me Perdón/Con permiso
How are you? ¿Como está (usted)?
I (don't) understand (No) Entiendo
Thank you (very much) (Muchas) gracias
You're welcome Con gusto
Do you speak English? ¿Habla (usted) inglés?
I (don't) speak Spanish (No) Hablo español
My name is … Me llamo …
What's your name? ¿Como se llama usted?
(I am) American (Soy) estadounidense
… Australian …australiano/a
… British …británico/a
… Canadian …canadiense
… English …ingles/esa
… Irish …irlandés/esa
… a New Zealander …neozelandés/esa
… Scottish …escocés/esa
… South African …sudafricano/a
… Welsh …galés/esa

HOTELS AND SHOPPING
Do you know …? ¿Sabe (usted) …?
I don't know No sé
How much does (this) cost? ¿Cuánto vale (este)?
There is (is there?) … (¿)Hay(?) …
Give me (one like that) Deme (uno así)
I/we would like… me/nos gustaría …
Do you have …? ¿Tiene …?
… a room (for one person/two people) … una habitación (para una persona/dos personas)
… with two beds/ a double bed … con dos camas/cama doble
… with a (private/shared) bathroom … con baño (privado/compartido)
for one night/week para una noche/semana
It's fine, how much is it? Está bien, ¿cuánto es?
It's too expensive Es demasiado caro
Do you have anything cheaper? Tiene algo más barato?
Can one camp (near) here? ¿Se puede acampar aquí (cerca)?

DIRECTIONS
Where is …? ¿Dónde está …?
… the bus station … el terminal de transportes
… the toilet … el baño
Left, Right, Straight on Izquierda, Derecha, Siga derecho
Is there a (hotel/hostel/ATM) near here? ¿Hay un (hotel/hostal/cajero) aquí cerca?
Where does the bus to … leave from? ¿De dónde sale el bus para …?
Is this the bus for Bogotá? ¿Es este el bus para Bogotá?
What time does it leave/arrive ¿A qué hora sale/llega?
What's the time? ¿Qué hora es?
What is there to eat? ¿Qué hay de comer?
What's that? ¿Qué es eso?
What's this called (in Spanish)? ¿Como se llama esto (en español)?

NUMBERS AND DAYS
1 un/uno/una
2 dos
3 tres
4 cuatro
5 cinco
6 seis
7 siete
8 ocho
9 nueve
10 diez
11 once
12 doce
13 trece
14 catorce
15 quince
16 diez y seis
20 veinte
21 veintiuno
30 treinta
40 cuarenta
50 cincuenta
60 sesenta
70 setenta
80 ochenta
90 noventa
100 cien(to)
101 ciento uno
200 doscientos
500 quinientos
1000 mil
first primero/a
second segundo/a
third tercero/a
fifth quinto/a
tenth décimo/a
Monday lunes
Tuesday martes
Wednesday miércoles

Thursday jueves
Friday viernes

Saturday sábado
Sunday domingo

FOOD AND DRINK

BASICS
Desayuno, Almuerzo, Cena Breakfast, Lunch, Supper
Cuchillo, Tenedor, Cuchara Knife, Fork, Spoon
Botella, Vaso, Taza Bottle, Glass, Cup
La carta, La cuenta The menu, The bill/check
Menú/Almuerzo ejecutivo/corriente Lunchtime set menu
Plato del día Dish of the day
Sal, Pimienta, Azúcar Salt, Pepper, Sugar
Ají, Hogao Hot salsa, Tomato and onion salsa

COOKING TERMS
A la plancha Pan-grilled
Al carbón Charcoal-grilled
Al horno Baked
Asado Roast
Crudo Raw
En salsa In sauce
Frito Fried
Parrilla(da) Grill(ed)
Relleno Stuffed
Salpicón Mixture (fruit salad, for example)

SOUPS (SOPAS) AND STEWS
Sopa (de pollo/marisco/arroz) (Chicken/seafood/rice) soup
Caldo (de costilla/pescado) (Beef rib/fish) broth
Ajiaco Hearty soup with big pieces of chicken, potatoes and corn
Cazuela Chowder-like stew, usually of fish
Changua Milk soup with an egg poached in it
Mondongo Tripe and vegetable soup/stew
Sanchocho Meat soup with potato, plantain and/or cassava
Viudo de pescado Soup of river fish with plantain and cassava

FISH (PESCADOS) AND SEAFOOD (MARISCOS)
Atún Tuna
Bocachico A medium-sized river fish
Bagre Catfish
Calamar Squid
Camarón/langostino Prawn
Ceviche Raw fish marinated in lime juice
Corvina Sea bass
Langosta Rock lobster (crawfish)
Mero Grouper
Mojarra Tilapia
Pargo Snapper
Pulpo Octopus
Róbalo Snook (a type of sea bass)
Salmón Salmon
Trucha Trout

MEAT (CARNE) AND POULTRY (AVES)
Baby beef Heart of rump
Cabro, cabrito (con pepitoria) Goat, kid (with a black-pudding-like mash made from its blood and offal)
Cerdo Pork
Chicharrón Fried pork rind, usually cripsy
Chorizo Chunky pork sausage or sirloin strip steak
Churrasco Grilled sirloin steak
Hamburguesa Hamburger
Higado Liver
Jamón Ham
Lechona Suckling pig
Lengua Tongue
Lomo Loin (usually beef)
Milanesa Breaded meat
Pechuga Breast (usually chicken)
Pollo Chicken
Punta de anca Sirloin cap
Res Beef
Sobrebarriga Flank steak
Solomito Sirloin steak

VEGETABLES (VERDURAS Y LEGUMBRES)
Aguacate Avocado
Arroz Rice
Batata Sweet potato
Cebollas Onions
Champiñones Mushrooms
Choclo Sweetcorn
Coliflor Cauliflower
Espinacas Spinach
Frijoles Black beans
Garbanzos Chickpeas
Lentejas Lentils
Maíz Sweetcorn
Papas Potatoes
Patacón Squashed fried plantain
Pepino Cucumber
Plátano Plantain
Tomate Tomato
Yuca Cassava (manioc)
Zanahoria Carrot

FRUIT (FRUTAS)

Banano Banana
Breva Fig
Carambola/o Starfruit
Chirimoya Custard apple
Ciruela Plum
Coco Coconut
Curuba Banana passion fruit
Durazno Peach
Fresa Strawberry
Grenadilla Sweet yellow passion fruit
Guanábana Soursop
Guayava Guava
Gulupa Small purple passion fruit
Higo Prickly pear
Limón Lime
Mamoncillo Guinep (Spanish lime)
Manzana Apple
Maracuyá Big yellow passion fruit
Mora Local variety of blackberry
Naranja Orange
Nispero Sapodilla (chicu)
Piña Pineapple
Pitaya Dragon fruit
Sandía Watermelon
Tomate de árbol Tamarillo (tree tomato)
Toronja Grapefruit
Uchuva Cape gooseberry (physalis)
Uva Grape

OTHER COMMON FOODS

Arepa Grilled cornflour-like bread
Bandeja paisa Antioquian dish consisting of a huge plateful of beans, rice, sausage, *chicharrón*, *patacones*, fried egg and more
Huevos (pericos) Eggs (scrambled with tomato and onion)
Panela Unrefined sugar
Queso Cheese
Tamal Cornmeal cake, stuffed (usually with meat) and steamed in a banana leaf

SWEETS AND DESSERTS (DULCES Y POSTRES)

Arequipe Caramelized condensed milk (*dulce de leche*)
Bocadillo A fairly dense guava jelly
Cocada Coconut macaroon
Cuajada con melado Curd cheese with syrup made from *panela*
Helado Ice cream
Matrimonio *Bocadillo* with white cheese
Merenguito Small meringue
Oblea Round, sweet wafer, usually served with a sweet topping
Roscón Sweet bread ring stuffed with *bocadillo*

DRINKS (BEBIDAS)

Agua de panela Hot water with *panela*
Aguardiente Cane spirit, usually flavoured with aniseed
Café Coffee
Cerveza Beer
Champús Sweet, thick corn drink with fruit and spices
Chicha Alcoholic brew made from fermented corn
Guarapo Cane juice
Jugo Juice
Limonada (de coco) Real lemonade (made with coconut milk)
Mazamorra Cold drink made from milk boiled with corn and *panela*
Pintado *Tinto* with milk
Ron Rum
Té Tea or infusion
Tinto Black coffee (usually filter)
Vino Wine

Glossary

Ayuntamiento Local council, town hall
Barra libre Free bar at a nightclub, meaning that the entrance fee includes unlimited drinks, but usually only Colombian spirits
Barrio Neighbourhood (not necessarily a poor one)
Bogotano/a Someone from Bogotá
Buseta Minibus
Cacique Pre-Hispanic local ruler or tribal chief
Caleño/a Someone from Cali
Campesino Country person, especially a peasant farmer
Casa de cambio Bureau de change, currency exchange
Chalupa Small boat
Chiva Traditional rural bus, usually brightly painted, with rows of benches
Colectivo Shared taxi, usually a minibus
Cordillera Mountain range (Colombia has three: eastern, central and western, all branches of the Andes)
Costeño/a Someone from the Caribbean coast
Criollo (in colonial times) Someone of Spanish ancestry born locally
Crossover (at a nightclub) A mixture of different music
Autodefensas (= *paramilitares*) Right-wing paramilitary groups in armed opposition to left-wing guerrillas
Dar papaya (literally: "give pawpaw") To make yourself an easy mark for criminals
Departamento Administrative division of the country, like a large county, but lacking significant autonomy

ELN (Ejército de Liberación Nacional) Marxist guerrilla group

FARC (Fuerzas Armadas Revolucionarias de Colombia) Colombia's biggest guerrilla group, Marxist-Leninist, with several splinter groups

Finca Farmstead or villa

Gringo Foreigner (not necessarily American, nor necessarily white, nor necessarily derogatory)

IVA (Impuesto al Valor Añadido) VAT, sales tax

Ley zanahoria Stiffs' law: municipal regulation imposing a compulsory closing time on bars and clubs, usually 3am (*zanahoria*, literally "carrot", is a derogatory term for someone conventional)

M-19 (Movimiento 19 de Abril) Guerrilla group that existed 1970–89

Mestizo/a Mixed-race, including anyone of mixed indigenous-Hispanic ancestry: the ethnic majority

Mirador Viewpoint, lookout tower

Muelle Quay, dock

Nevado Snow-capped mountain

Paisa Someone from Antioquia, and by extension Caldas, Risaralda and Quindío

Paramilitares Right-wing paramilitary groups in armed opposition to leftwing guerrillas

Param(ill)o High-altitude zone immediately below the snowline; also a mountain whose peak is in that zone

Parque In principle a park, but often just a city square

Perico Scrambled eggs with tomato and onion: coffee *tinto* with milk; cocaine (slang); literally: "parakeet"

Pico y placa City-run scheme under which cars whose registration numbers end in specific digits are banned from driving in town on certain days

PiT (*punto de información turística*) Tourist information point, often just a little kiosk

Plata Literally, "silver"; slang for money

Plaza Town square

Pueblo Population, meaning "the people", but also a town or village ("*pueblito*" if it's a little one)

Puente Literally, "bridge"; a long weekend when Monday is a public holiday

Raizal English-speaking Afro-Caribbean people of the San Andrés and Providencia

Retablo Altarpiece, the stand of holy images behind the altar of a church

Reggaeton Originally reggae with Spanish lyrics, but now its own genre influenced by dancehall, hip-hop and Latin beats

Rumba; rumbear Night out; to party

Tagua Palm seed; "vegetable ivory"

Taita Shaman; herbal or spiritual healer in indigenous communities

Tejo Traditional game involving throwing an iron puck at a clay target

Vallenato Caribbean troubadour dance music, usually played with an accordion

Zona Rosa uptown area of shops, bars and nightlife

Small print and index

379 Small print
379 About the authors
381 Index
388 Map symbols

A ROUGH GUIDE TO ROUGH GUIDES

Published in 1982, the first Rough Guide – to Greece – was a student scheme that became a publishing phenomenon. Mark Ellingham, a recent graduate in English from Bristol University, had been travelling in Greece the previous summer and couldn't find the right guidebook. With a small group of friends he wrote his own guide, combining a contemporary, journalistic style with a thoroughly practical approach to travellers' needs.

The immediate success of the book spawned a series that rapidly covered dozens of destinations. And, in addition to impecunious backpackers, Rough Guides soon acquired a much broader readership that relished the guides' wit and inquisitiveness as much as their enthusiastic, critical approach and value-for-money ethos. These days, Rough Guides include recommendations from budget to luxury and cover more than 120 destinations around the globe, from Amsterdam to Zanzibar, all regularly updated by our team of roaming writers.

Browse all our latest guides, read inspirational features and book your trip at **roughguides.com**.

Rough Guide credits

Editor: Lizzie Horrocks
Updater: Robert Savage
Cartography: Katie Bennett
Picture Editor: Piotr Kala
Picture Manager: Tom Smyth
Layout: Pradeep Thapliyal
Head of DTP and Pre-Press: Rebeka Davies
Head of Publishing: Sarah Clark

Publishing information

Third edition 2024

Distribution

UK, Ireland and Europe
Apa Publications (UK) Ltd; mail@roughguides.com
United States and Canada
Two Rivers; ips@ingramcontent.com
Australia and New Zealand
Woodslane; info@woodslane.com.au
Worldwide
Apa Publications (UK) Ltd; mail@roughguides.com

Special Sales, Content Licensing and CoPublishing
Rough Guides can be purchased in bulk quantities at discounted prices. We can create special editions, personalized jackets and corporate imprints tailored to your needs. mail@roughguides.com.

roughguides.com

EU Representative
LOGOS EUROPE, 9 rue Nicolas Poussin, 17000, LA ROCHELLE, France; Contact@logoseurope.eu; +33 (0) 667937378

Printed by Finidr in Czech Republic

ISBN: 9781839059964

This book was produced using **Typefi** automated publishing software.

A catalogue record for this book is available from the British Library.

All rights reserved
© 2024 Apa Digital AG
License edition © Apa Publications Ltd UK

No part of this book may be reproduced, stored in a retrieval system, or transmitted in any form or by any means – electronic, mechanical, photocopying, recording, or otherwise – without prior written permission from Apa Publications.

No part of this book may be used or reproduced in any manner for the purpose of training artificial intelligence technologies or systems.

Every effort has been made to ensure that this publication is accurate, free from safety risks, and provides accurate information. However, changes and errors are inevitable. The publisher is not responsible for any resulting loss, inconvenience, injury or safety concerns arising from the use of this book.

Help us update

We've gone to a lot of effort to ensure that this edition of **The Rough Guide to Colombia** is accurate and up-to-date. However, things change – places get "discovered", transport routes are altered, restaurants and hotels raise prices or lower standards, and businesses cease trading. If you feel we've got it wrong or left something out, we'd like to know, and if you can direct us to the web address, so much the better.

Please send your comments with the subject line **"Rough Guide Colombia Update"** to mail@roughguides.com. We'll send a copy of the next edition (or any other Rough Guide if you prefer) for the very best emails.

Acknowledgements

Thank you to everyone at the Ministerio de Comercio, Industria y Turismo for their help throughout the update. Thanks also to my editor Lizzie Horrocks and to my husband, Mohamed Bounaim.

ABOUT THE AUTHORS

Daniel Jacobs has worked on Rough Guides to Morocco, Tunisia, Egypt, West Africa, Kenya, India, Bolivia and Brazil. He lives in London.

Stephen Keeling worked as a financial journalist and editor in Asia for seven years before writing his first travel guide and has written numerous titles for Rough Guides, including books on Puerto Rico, Brazil and Mexico, and The Rough Guide to South America on a Budget. Stephen lives in New York City.

Robert Savage is a Yorkshire-born travel writer who lives in St Petersburg, Florida. He has covered destinations for Rough Guides since 2017, has contributed to the Guardian, Le Monde and Der Spiegal, and has written more than 20 guidebooks.

Photo credits

(Key: T-top; C-centre; B-bottom; L-left; R-right)

Banco de la República 19C
Dreamstime.com 184/185
iStock 12, 14T, 19B, 20, 124/125
Shutterstock 1, 2, 4, 9, 11T, 11B, 13TL, 13TR, 13C, 13B, 14B, 14C, 15T, 15B, 16T, 16B, 17T, 17BR, 17BL, 18B, 18T, 19T, 23B, 22T, 23, 54/55, 57, 84/85, 87, 127, 187, 204/205, 207, 250/251, 253, 298/299, 301, 318/319, 321, 336
Ulita/Dreamstime.com 24

Cover: Carnival in San Pedro **Shutterstock**

Index

A

accessibility 47
Accessible travel 47
accommodation 31
addresses 30
adventure sports 36, 108, 115
Agua Hirviendo 279
aguardiente 35
Agua Tibias hot springs 278
altitude sickness 41
Alto de las Piedras 287
Alto de los Ídolos 286
Amacayacu National Park 330
Amazon wildlife 328
Antioquia 209
Aracataca 169
Arhuaco people 182
Armenia 241
Arusí 308
Atánquez 183
ATMs 49
ayahuasca 39

B

Bahía Concha (Tayrona) 172
Bahía Solano 300
Balneario La Mina 183
Banana massacre 347
Barichara 110
Barra 312
Barranquilla 155
Barú Island 140
Battle of Boyacá 94
beer 35
Belalcázar, Sebastián de 339
biche 303
bicycles 31
Bocachica 140
Bocana 311
Bogotá 56
   accommodation 76
   airport 73
   Archeological Museum 64
   arrival 73
   banks 83
   bars 80
   bicycle tours 74
   bicycles 75
   Botero Museum 62
   British Cemetery 71
   buses (intercity) 74
   buses (local) 75
   cabs 75
   Candelaria 58
   Capilla del Sagrario 61
   car rental 75
   Casa del Florero 61
   Casa de Moneda 63
   Casa de Nariño 62
   Casa Museo Jorge Eliécer Gaitán 71
   cathedral 60
   Cementerio Central 70
   Cerro de Monserrate 68
   Chapinero 71
   Chicó 72
   Chorro de Quevedo 65
   churches (historical) 65
   city centre 65
   Colonial Art Museum 64
   consulates 83
   Costume Museum 64
   crime 59
   cycling 75
   downtown area 65
   drinking 80
   driving 75
   eating out 78
   embassies 83
   Emerald Museum 67
   festivals 83
   football 83
   Gaitán Museum 71
   Gold Museum 66
   graffiti tour 74
   health 83
   history 56
   hospitals 83
   hotels 76
   immigration office 83
   internet 83
   La Candelaria 58
   La Macarena 69
   laundry 83
   LGBTQ+ Bogotá 81
   Macarena 69
   MamBo 68
   markets 82
   mint (Casa de Moneda) 63
   Mirador Torre Colpatria 69
   Modern Art Museum 68
   moneychangers 83
   Monserrate 68
   MUSA 64
   Museo Arqueológico 64
   Museo Botero 62
   Museo Colonial 64
   Museo de Arte del Banco de la República 63
   Museo de Arte Moderno 68
   Museo de la Esmeralda 67
   Museo del Chicó 73
   Museo del Oro 66
   Museo de Trajes Regionales 64
   Museo Histórico de la Policía Nacional 64
   Museo Jorge Eliécer Gaitán 71
   Museo Militar 63
   Museo Nacional 69
   National Museum 69
   nightlife 80
   Palacio de Justicia 59
   Palacio de San Carlos 63
   Parque 93 72
   Parque de Santander 66
   pico y placa 75
   Plaza de Bolívar 59
   Plazoleta del Chorro de Quevedo 65
   police 83
   Police Museum 64
   post office 83
   presidential palace 62
   Quinta de Bolívar 68
   restaurants 78
   safety (from crime) 59
   shopping 82
   soccer 83
   Spanish classes 83
   taxis 75
   tejo 83
   Terminal de Transporte 74
   Torre Colpatria 69
   tourist information 74
   tours 74
   TransMilenio 74
   transport 73, 74
   Tren Turístico 73
   Usaquén 73
   visa extensions 83
   Zona G 71
   Zona M 69
   Zona Rosa 72
   Zona T 72
Bogotazo 67, 349
Bolívar, Simón 342
   assassination attempt 63, 122
   Bogotá residence 68
   elected president 344
   in Mompox 149, 151

in Santa Marta 162
military victories 94
residence in Tunja 92
rivalry with Santander 122
books about Colombia 370
border crossings
  Brazil 26
  Ecuador 26, 297
  general 26
  Panama 26, 135, 148, 304
  Peru 26
  Venezuela 26, 123, 179
Bordones 287
Boroboro 305
Botero, Fernando 213
  Museo Botero (Bogotá) 62
  sculpture in Cartagena 132
  works in Bogotá museums 62, 69, 70
  works in Medellín 211, 212, 215
Boyacá, Battle of 94
Bucaramanga 113
Buenaventura 310
Buga 267
bullfighting 38
burundanga 43
buses 28
business hours 50

C

Cabo Corrientes 308
Cabo de la Vela 180
cabs 30
Cali 252
  accommodation 261
  airport 260
  arrival 260
  art markets 260
  baggage deposit 264
  banks 264
  bars 263
  buses (intercity) 260
  buses (local) 260
  cabs 260
  Catedral Metropolitana 254
  Cerro de Las Tres Cruces 259
  courier companies 264
  Cristo Rey 259
  dance schools 257
  drinking 263
  eating out 261
  entertainment 257, 264
  festivals 264
  football 264
  Gatos del Rio 259
  Gold Museum 258
  health 264
  history 252
  hospital 264
  hotels 261
  Iglesia de la Merced 257
  Iglesia de San Antonio 259
  Iglesia de San Francisco 255
  Iglesia La Ermita 255
  immigration office 264
  internet 264
  La Ermita church 255
  La Merced 255
  La Tertulia Modern Art Museum 259
  laundry 264
  left luggage 264
  markets 260
  Merced 255
  miradores 259
  Museo Arqueológico La Merced 258
  Museo de Arte Moderno La Tertulia 259
  Museo del Oro 258
  nightlife 263
  Plaza de Caycedo 254
  police 264
  post office 264
  restaurants 261
  salsa music 257
  San Antonio church 259
  San Francisco church 255
  shopping 260, 264
  soccer 264
  taxis 260
  Tejada's cats 259
  Terminal de Cali 260
  theatres 264
  tourist information 261
  tours 261
  transport 260
  visa extensions 264
  weather 255
Cali Cartel 258, 351
camping 32
Caño Cristales 322
Cañón del Juanambú 292
Capurganá 147
car rental 29
Cartagena 126
  accommodation 135
  airport 134
  arrival 134
  banks 139
  bars 138
  Bazurto market 136
  bicycles 135
  boats to Panama 135
  Bocachica 140
  Bocagrande 134
  Bóvedas 133
  buses (intercity) 135
  buses (local) 135
  cabs 135
  Casa Museo Rafael Núñez 133
  Castillo San Felipe de Barajas 134
  Catedral Santa Catalina de Alejandría 132
  Centro Histórico 129
  Convento de la Popa 134
  cycling 135
  diving 135
  drinking 138
  eating out 137
  festivals 139
  Getsemaní 133
  health 139
  history 129
  hospital 139
  hotels 135
  Iglesia de Santo Domingo 132
  immigration office 139
  Isla Barú 140
  La Matuna 129
  Las Bóvedas 133
  laundry 139
  Matuna 129
  Mausoleo de Gabo 133
  Mercado Bazurto 136
  Modern Art Museum 131
  moneychangers 139
  Museo de Arte Moderno 131
  Museo de Oro Zenú 132
  Museo Histórico de Cartagena de Indias 132
  Museo Naval del Caribe 131
  Naval Museum 131
  NH Galería 133
  nightlife 138
  old city 129
  Playa Blanca 140
  Plaza de Bolívar 132
  Plaza de la Aduana 131
  Plaza de los Coches 130
  police 139
  post office 139
  Rafael Núñez Museum 133
  restaurants 137
  Santo Domingo church 132
  Santuario de San Pedro Claver 131
  shopping 139
  taxis 135
  Teatro Adolfo Mejía 133
  Terminal de Transportes 135
  tourist information 135
  tours 135
  transport 134, 135
  visa extensions 139
Cartagena, Battle of 340
cartels (cocaine) 218, 258, 351
Cascada del Tigre 305
Cerros de Mavecure 323
champeta music 364
Chicamocha National Park 113

chicha 35
chikungunya 40
children (travel with) 52
Chingaza National Park 74
Chiquinquirá 102
chivas 31
Chorrera del Indio 265
Ciénaga 347
Ciudad Mutis (Bahía Solano) 300
Ciudad Perdida 174
climate 10
cocaine 44, 211, 351
coca leaf 35
Coconuco village 278
Coconuko people 277
Cocora Valley 247
Cocuy National Park 103
coffee
  buying 46
  drinking 35
  farm visits 241, 244, 245
  growing region 230
  history 345
  national coffee park 242
  production 8
Colombian Spanish 373
Comuneros Revolt 341
condors 278, 359
consulates and embassies
  Brazilian consulates 117, 224, 332
  Colombian representation abroad 27
  embassies in Bogotá 83
  Panamanian consulates 148, 224
  Peruvian consulates 224, 332
  Venezuelan consulates 117, 123, 179, 224
Coquí 307
Corral, Juan del 227
costs 47
crafts 46
crime 42, 59
Cruce de la Mina 277
Cúcuta 121
cumbia music 360
currency 49
customs allowances 27
cycling 31

D

Darién 269
deforestation 358
dengue fever 40
Desierto de la Tatacoa 289
diving 37
  Bahía Solano 303
  Cartagena 135
  Isla Gorgona 317
  Providencia (Old Providence) 202
  San Andrés 195
dolphins 328, 357
Doña Juana-Cascabel National Park 292
driving 29
drugs 44, 211
Duque Márquez, Iván 354
duty-free allowances 27

E

ecology 358
Ecoparque Río Pance 23, 265
Eje Cafetera 230
El Cocuy 103
El Dorado 91, 338
electricity 47
ELN 350, 351
El Paraíso Hacienda 266
El Rodadero 163
El Totumo Volcano 143
El Valle 304
embassies. *See also* Consulates and embassies
  Colombian abroad 27
  foreign in Bogotá 83
Emberá people 305
emeralds 46, 68, 82
emergency phone numbers 51
environment 358
Escobar, Pablo 218, 352
Estación Septiembre Reserve 305
ethnic groups 338
exit tax 27

F

Farallones National Park 264, 265
FARC 350, 351, 352, 353, 354
festivals 35
Filandia 247
flamingo sanctuary (La Guajira) 178
flights
  domestic 28
  from Australia and New Zealand 25
  from South Africa 25
  from UK and Ireland 25
  from US and Canada 25
food 32
food glossary 375
football 37
  Bogotá 83
  Cali 264
  Manizales 234
  Medellín 224

G

Gaitán, Jorge Eliécer 67, 71, 349
Galán, José Antonio 70, 341
García Márquez, Gabriel
  and Aracataca 169
  and Barranquilla 155, 157
  books 370, 371, 372
  life 170
  mausoleum 133
  Mompox 149
  tour 129
gender issues 45
Girón 117
Gorgona Island 315
Guachalito 307, 308
Guadalupe 105
guadua bamboo 246
Guajira peninsula 177
Guajira rebellion 341
Guambía 276
Guambiano people 277
Guane 110
Guatapé 224
Guatavita 91
guerrillas 42
Güicán 103
Gustavo Petro 22

H

Hacienda El Paraíso 266
Hacienda Nápoles 218
Hacienda Piédechinche 266
Hato La Aurora 323
health 38
hiking 37
history of Colombia 337
holidays 50
hospedajes 31
hospitals 42
hostels 32
hotels 31

I

Iguaque 100
independence struggle 342
Indigenous peoples
  Arhuaco 182
  Coconuco 277
  Emberá 305
  Guambiano 277
  Kankuamo 182
  Kogi (Kogui) 175
  Kokonuco 277
  Maguta 326
  Muisca 99, 337

INDEX

Nasa 282
Páez 282
Ticuna 326
Wayuu 177, 341
Winkitukas 182
Wiwa 182
Wounaan 305
Yanacona 283
Zenú 132
Inírida 323
insurance 48
internet 48
Ipiales 296
Isla Fuerte (San Bernardo) 146
Isla Gorgona 315
Isla Grande (Rosario Islands) 142
Isla La Corota 296
Isla Malpelo 316
Isla Múcura (San Bernardo) 145
Isla Palma (San Bernardo) 145
Isla Pirata (Rosario Islands) 142
Isla Santa Rosa (Peru) 333
Islas del Rosario 142
Islas de San Bernardo 145
Isla Tintipán (San Bernardo) 145
Isnos 287
Istmo de Malaguita 311
itineraries 20

J

jaguars 358
Jardín 229
Javarí River 328
Johnny Cay 194
Jovi 308
Juanambú Gorge 292
Juanchaco 311
Jurubirá 309

K

Kankuamo Indigenous Reserve 183
Kankuamo people 182
Kasaguadua Natural Reserve 23, 244
kayaking 37, 108, 287
Kitesurfing 269
Kogi (Kogui) people 175
Kokonuko people 277

L

La Barra 312
La Bocana 311

La Chorrera del Indio 265
La Corota Island 296
Ladrilleros 311
Lago Calima 268
Lago Tarapoto 335
La Guajira 177
Laguna de Guatavita 91
Laguna de la Cocha 296
La Loma 309
La Macarena (Bogotá) 69
La Macarena (Meta) 323
La Mina spa 183
land entry 26
La Piedra del Peñol 225
Las Lajas Sanctuary 297
laundry 48
La Vorágine 265
Leticia 324
Leyva 95
LGBTQ+ travellers 45
living in Colombia 48
Llanos region 320, 356
Los Llanos 320, 356
Los Nevados National Park 234

M

M-19 59, 350, 351
Macarena (Bogotá) 69
Macarena (Meta) 323
Maguta people 326
mail 51
Malaguita Isthmus 311
malaria 40
Malpelo Island 316
Manizales 230
maps 49
  Around Cartagena 141
  Barichara 111
  Barranquilla 156
  Bogotá 58
  Bogotá: City Centre 66
  Bucaramanga 114
  Cali 256
  Cali and the southwest 254
  Cartagena 130
  Centre Medellín 212
  Chapinero 71
  Colombia 6
  El Poblado 217
  Itineraries 21
  La Candelaria 60
  Leticia and Tabatinga 325
  Los Llanos and the Amazon 322
  Manizales 231
  Medellín 210
  Medellín and the Zona Cafetera 208
  Mompox 151
  North of Bogotá 88

Pamplona 118
Parque Nacional Natural Los Nevados 235
Parque Nacional Natural Tayrona National 173
Pasto 293
Pereira 237
Popayán 271
Providencia 200
Salento 244
San Agustín 284
San Andrés 188
San Andrés Island 190
San Andrés Town 192
San Gil 107
Santa Marta 160
Sante Fe de Antioquia 227
The Caribbean Coast 128
The Pacific coast 302
Tierradentro 280
Tunja 92
Villa de Leyva 97
Zona Rosa 72
marijuana 44
Masacre de las Bananeras 347
Mavecure Hills 323
Medellín 206
  accommodation 220
  airports 219
  Alpujarra 215
  arrival 219
  banks 224
  Barefoot Park 216
  bars 222
  Basílica de Nuestra Señora de la Candelaria 215
  botanical garden 217
  Botero artworks 211, 212, 215
  buses (intercity) 219
  buses (local) 220
  cable cars 219, 220
  cabs 220
  Candelaria Basilica 215
  car rental 224
  Casa Museo Pedro Nel Gómez 219
  Catedral Metropolitana 214
  Cerro Nutibara 216
  cinemas 224
  city centre 211
  Comuna 13 escalators 219
  consulates 224
  downtown area 211
  drinking 222
  driving 220
  eating out 221
  El Poblado 216
  Ermita de la Veracruz 213
  Escobar tours 218
  festivals 224
  football 224

INDEX

health 224
history 209
hospitals 224
hotels 220
immigration office 224
internet 224
Jardín Botánico 217
La Alpujarra 215
La Gorda 215
laundry 224
Laureles 219
LGBTQ+ Medellín 223
MAMM 216
metro 220
Modern Art Museum 216
moneychangers 224
Museo de Antioquia 211
Museo de Arte Moderno de Medellín 216
Nel Gómez Museum 219
nightlife 223
online information 220
Palacio de la Cultura Rafael Uribe Uribe 213
Parque Arví 216
Parque Berrío 214
Parque de las Luces 216
Parque de los Pies Descalzos 216
Parque Explora 217
Parque San Antonio 215
pharmacies (24hr) 224
pico y placa 220
planetarium 218
Plaza Botero 211
Poblado 216
post office 224
Pueblito Paisa 216
restaurants 221
shopping 223
site of Escobar's death 218
soccer 224
Spanish classes 224
swimming pools 224
taxis 220
Terminal del Norte 219
Terminal del Sur 220
tourist information 220
tours 220
transport 219, 220
visa extensions 224
Medellín Cartel 218, 351
media 49
Meta *departamento* 322
Minca 168
Mocagua 330
Mocoa 292
Mompox 149
money 49
Morromico 309
Molas 46

Mosquera, Tomás Cipriano de 272, 345, 346
motels 32
Muisca people 99, 337
Museo de la Caña de Azúcar 266
music 360

N

Nabusimake 183
Nariño 334
Nariño, Antonio 96, 342
Nariño departamento 291
Nasa people 282
Nevados National Park 234
newspapers 49
Núñez, Rafael 133, 346
Nuquí 307

O

Obando 286
Obando, José María 345, 346
Old Providence (Providencia) 199
O'Leary, Daniel Florence 115, 343
opening hours 50
Orinoquía (Llanos) region 320, 356
Ospina Rodríguez, Mariano 345, 346

P

Páez people 282
Palomino 176
Pamplona 118
Panama, secession of 347
Pance valley 264
Pance village 265
Panguí 307
Parque Cañón del Juanambú 292
Parque Nacional del Café 242
Parque Nacional del Chicamocha 113
Parque Nacional Natural Amacayacu 330
Parque Nacional Natural Complejo Volcánico Doña Juana-Cascabel 292
Parque Nacional Natural Corales del Rosario y San Bernardo 142
Parque Nacional Natural El Cocuy 103
Parque Nacional Natural Farallones 264, 265
Parque Nacional Natural Los Nevados 234

Parque Nacional Natural Puracé 277
Parque Nacional Natural Sumapaz 74
Parque Nacional Natural Tayrona 171
Parque Nacional Natural Utría 306
Pasto 291
Pereira 236
pharmacies 42
phones 50
Piangüita 311
pico y placa 30
Piédechinche Hacienda 266
Piedra del Peñol 225
Pilimbalá (Puente Tierra) 277
Pilón de Azúcar 180
Playa Blanca (near Cartagena) 140
Playa Blanca (Santa Marta) 163
police 44, 224
Popayán 270
population 5
posadas 31
post 51
Pozo Azul 279
prices 47
Providencia (Old Providence) 199
public holidays 50
Pueblito (Tayrona National Park) 172
Puente de Boyacá 94
Puente Tierra 277
Puerto Careño 322
Puerto Gaitán 322
Puerto Indio 309
Puerto Inírida 323
Puerto Jagua 309
Puerto Nariño 334
Punta Gallinas 180
Puracé National Park 277
Puracé Volcano 278

Q

Quesada, Gonzalo Jiménez de 339

R

radio 49
rafting 37, 74, 108, 287
rainfall 10
Raizal culture 189
Ráquira 101
Recinto del Pensamiento 232

reggaeton music 364
religion in Colombia 366
Reserva Estación Septiembre 305
Resguardo Indígena Kankuamo 183
Río Ancho 176
Río Badillo 183
Riohacha 177
Río Negro 74
Río Pance 264
Río Tundó 305
Río Yavarí 328
road distances 29
Rodadero, El 163
Rosario and San Bernardo National Park 142
Rosario Islands 142
rum 35
Rumichaca Bridge 297

S

Sáenz, Manuelita 63, 77, 343
safety (from crime) 42, 59
saints 366
Salento 243
Salinas 279
Salinas de Manaure 179
salsa music 257, 362
Salto de Mortiño 286
San Agustín 283
San Andrés 186
   accommodation 196
   airport 195
   arrival 195
   banks 198
   bars 198
   bicycles 195
   boat trips 196
   botanical garden 194
   car rental 196
   carritos 196
   Casa Museo Isleña 193
   Cayo Bolívar 194
   Cayo Rocoso 191
   Centro 189
   Centro Cultural 191
   church services 198
   Cueva de Morgan 192
   cycling 195
   diving 195
   drinking 198
   driving 196
   eating out 197
   ecology 193
   El Acuario 194
   ferry 195
   First Baptist Church 193, 198
   golf carts 196
   Haynes Cay 194
   health 198
   history 186
   hospital 198
   hotels 196
   Hoyo Soplador 191
   Jardín Botánico 194
   Johnny Cay Regional Park 194
   La Loma 193, 198
   La Piscinita 192
   local buses 195
   Morgan's Cave 192
   music 198
   Nicaraguan claim 189
   nightlife 198
   police 199
   Pueblito Isleño 193
   restaurants 197
   Rocky Cay Beach 191
   San Andrés Town 189
   San Luis 191
   scooter rental 196
   tarjeta de turismo 191
   tourist card 191
   tourist information 196
   tours 196
   transport 195
   West View 192
San Andrés de Pisimbalá 281
San Bernardo Islands 145
San Cipriano 314
San Francisco village 265
San Gil 106
San José de Isnos 286
San Juan hot springs 278
San Martín 330
Santa Catalina Island 199
Santa Cruz del Islote (San Bernardo) 145
Santa Fe de Antioquia 226
Santa Marta 159
   accommodation 164
   airport 164
   arrival 164
   Art Museum 162
   bars 165
   buses (intercity) 164
   cabs 164
   Casa de la Aduana 161
   car rental 164
   cathedral 161
   Centro Histórico 161
   crime 159
   Customs House 161
   drinking 165
   eating out 165
   El Rodadero 163
   festivals 166
   history 159
   hotels 164
   immigration office 166
   Malecón 161
   Museo Bolivariano de Arte Contemporaneo 163
   Museo de Arte 162
   Museo del Oro Tairona 161
   nightlife 165
   old town 161
   Parque de los Novios 162
   Playa Blanca 163
   Playaca 166
   Plaza de Bolívar 161
   Plaza de San Francisco 161
   post office 166
   Quinta de San Pedro Alejandrino 162
   restaurants 165
   Rodadero 163
   safety (from crime) 159
   Taganga 166
   Tairona Gold Museum 161
   taxis 164
   Terminal de Transportes 164
   tourist information 164
   tours 164
   transport 164
   visa extensions 166
Santander, Francisco de Paula 70, 122, 344
Santa Rosa hot springs 240
Santa Rosa Island (Peru) 333
Santos, Juan Manuel 353
Santuario de Fauna y Flora los Flamencos 178
Santuario de Iguaque 100
Santuario de Las Lajas 297
San Vicente hot springs 240
Sapzurro 147
scuba diving 37. *See also* diving
Serranía de la Macarena 322
sexual harassment 45
Shakira 364
shopping 46
Silvia 276
slavery 339, 345
snakes 41
soccer 37. *See also* football
Solano 300
souvenirs 46
Spanish classes 48
   Bogotá 83
   Medellín 224
   San Gil 110
Spanish language 373
spiking 43
sports 36, 108, 115
Suesca 90
Sugar Cane Museum 266
Sumapaz National Park 74
surfing 307
sustainable travel 22

T

Tabatinga (Brazil) 332
Taganga 166
Tatacoa Desert 289
taxis 30
Tayrona National Park 171
tejo 38
telephones 50
television 49
temperatures 10
Termales Agua Tibias 278
Termales de San Juan 278
Termales Santa Rosa 240
Termales San Vicente 240
Ticuna people 326
Tierradentro 279
Tiger Falls 305
time zone 51
tipping 45
Tolú 143
Totumo Volcano 143
tourist information 51
tour operators (abroad) 26
traffic regulations 30
trains 29
transport 28
travel agencies (abroad) 26
travel insurance 48
trekking 37
Tulcán (Ecuador) 297
Tumaco 317
Tundó River 305
Tunja 91
Tuparro 323
TV 49

U

Uribe Uribe, Rafael 70, 214
Uribe Vélez, Álvaro 352
Uribía 179
Utría National Park 306

V

vaccinations 39
Valle de Cocora 247
Valledupar 181
vallenato music 361
vampire bats 328, 358
vegetarian food 34
Vélez 100
Villa de Leyva 95
Villa del Rosario 122
Villavicencio 320
Villavieja 289
visas 27
Volcán de Lodo El Totumo 143
Volcán Puracé 278
volunteering 49
Vorágine 265

W

Wayuu people 177, 341
weather 10
websites on Colombia 52
whale-watching 304, 307, 312, 316, 358
whitewater rafting 37, 74, 108, 287
wildlife 355
Willys jeeps 31, 239
wine 35
Wintukua people 182
Wiwa people 182
women travellers 45
working in Colombia 48
Wounaan people 305

Y

yagé 39
Yanacona people 283
Yavarí River 328
yellow fever 40

Z

Zenú people 132
zika virus 40
Zipaquirá 86
Zona Cafetera 230

Map symbols

The symbols below are used on maps throughout the book

International border	Funicular	Museum	Waterfall
State boundary	International airport	Monument	Gardens
Main road	Domestic airport	Statue	Gate/entrance
Minor road	Transport stop	Mountain peak	Border crossing
Pedestrian road	TransMilenio stop	Rock structure	Boat
Unpaved road	Point of interest	Ruins	Church
Track	National Park	House	Building
Steps	Post office	Church	Stadium
Footpath	Information office	Volcano	Park
Ferry	Internet access	Cave	Cemetery
Wall	Hospital	Wildlife reserve	Beach
Cable car			

Listings key

- Accommodation
- Eating
- Drinking/Nightlife
- Shopping

YOUR TAILOR-MADE TRIP
STARTS HERE

Tailor-made trips and unique adventures crafted by local experts

Rough Guides has been inspiring travellers with lively and thought-provoking guidebooks for more than 35 years. Now we're linking you up with selected local experts to craft your dream trip. They will put together your perfect itinerary and book it at local rates.

Don't follow the crowd – find your own path.

HOW ROUGHGUIDES.COM/TRIPS WORKS

STEP 1

Pick your dream destination, tell us what you want and submit an enquiry.

STEP 2

Fill in a short form to tell your local expert about your dream trip and preferences.

STEP 3

Our local expert will craft your tailor-made itinerary. You'll be able to tweak and refine it until you're completely satisfied.

STEP 4

Book online with ease, pack your bags and enjoy the trip! Our local expert will be on hand 24/7 while you're on the road.

BENEFITS OF PLANNING AND BOOKING AT ROUGHGUIDES.COM/TRIPS

PLAN YOUR ADVENTURE WITH LOCAL EXPERTS
Rough Guides' English-speaking local experts are hand-picked, based on their experience in the travel industry and their impeccable standards of customer service.

SAVE TIME AND GET ACCESS TO LOCAL KNOWLEDGE
When a local expert plans your trip, you save time and money when you book, even during high season. You won't be charged for using a credit card either.

MAKE TRAVEL A BREEZE: BOOK WITH PEACE OF MIND
Enjoy stress-free travel when you use Rough Guides' secure online booking platform. All bookings come with a money-back guarantee.

WHAT DO OTHER TRAVELLERS THINK ABOUT ROUGH GUIDES TRIPS?

Trip to Spain

This Spain tour company did a fantastic job to make our dream trip perfect. We gave them our travel budget, told them where we would like to go, and they did all of the planning. Our drivers and tour guides were always on time and very knowledgable. The hotel accommodations were better than we would have found on our own. Only one time did we end up in a location that we had not intended to be in. We called the 24 hour phone number, and they immediately fixed the situation.

Don A, USA

Trip to Morocco

Our trip was fantastic! Transportation, accommodations, guides – all were well chosen! The hotels were well situated, well appointed and had helpful, friendly staff. All of the guides we had were very knowledgeable, patient, and flexible with our varied interests in the different sites. We particularly enjoyed the side trip to Tangier! Well done! The itinerary you arranged for us allowed maximum coverage of the country with time in each city for seeing the important places.

Sharon, USA

PLAN AND BOOK YOUR TRIP AT ROUGHGUIDES.COM/TRIPS